UNIVERSITY
OF
MARY
HARDIN-BAYLOR

NOTES

ON THE

NEW TESTAMENT

EXPLANATORY AND PRACTICAL

BY

ALBERT BARNES

ENLARGED TYPE EDITION

EDITED BY
ROBERT FREW, D.D.

HEBREWS

BAKER BOOK HOUSE
Grand Rapids, Michigan

Library of Congress Catalog Card Number: 50-7190

ISBN: 0-8010-0541-8

First Printing, September 1949
Second Printing, January 1951
Third Printing, January 1955
Fourth Printing, October 1958
Fifth Printing, January 1961
Sixth Printing, May 1963
Seventh Printing, February 1966
Eighth Printing, December 1968
Ninth Printing, May 1971
Tenth Printing, September 1972
Eleventh Printing, June 1974
Twelfth Printing, February 1976
Thirteenth Printing, January 1977
Fourteenth Printing, February 1978
Fifteenth Printing, February 1979
Sixteenth Printing, May 1980
Seventeenth Printing, August 1981

PRINTED IN THE UNITED STATES OF AMERICA

PUBLISHERS' PREFACE.

THE Epistle to the Hebrews forms a most important part of the New Testament. It exhibits the connection between the Old and New Dispensations of Religion, throws a flood of light on the Old Testament Scripture, and illustrates the Harmony of the Scheme of Redemption, in the midst of changing ages and economies. It contains the most sublime descriptions of the dignity and glory of Christ's person, the excellence of his sacrifice, and the superiority of his gospel; intermingled with hortatory matter, wherever the grand argument can admit of a pause, full of solemnity and pathos.

The Author's Commentary will be regarded by many as even superior, either to that on Romans or Corinthians. Indeed, it may be fairly questioned if there be any English Commentary on the Hebrews which combines, to so great an extent, the advantages both of a critical and practical exposition. Two classes of readers, therefore, seldom both pleased with the same work, will, it is believed, here find equal satisfaction. The critic may have his difficulties resolved, and the Christian his heart improved. In the "Introduction," various important questions, which have long interested the learned, but which in many commentaries are either passed in silence, or dismissed with a word, are here ably handled, if not in every case satisfactorily solved. The points alluded to are those regarding the Pauline origin of the Epistle, the parties to whom it was addressed, the language in which it was written, with its date, occasion, scope, and character. At the same time the critical and doctrinal difficulties throughout the Epistle are fairly met, and treated with ability, scholarship, and candour. In this department of his labours, the Author is fully up to the modern mark, and never leaves the reader to complain that a judgment has been formed in ignorance of what the more recent authorities have alleged, while his independence is everywhere manifest. His criticisms and doctrinal discussions are frequently relieved by the most beautiful and pertinent illustrations. The poets furnish him

with apposite quotations. The beauties of Spenser and Shakspere occasionally adorn his pages. It would be difficult to find a more beautiful exposition than that on angelic ministry, at chap. i. 14, or that on sympathy with the slave, chap. xiii. 3. On this last subject, the Author scorns to maintain a prudential yet criminal silence, and far as his voice goes—and that is throughout America—vindicates the cause of the oppressed.

The peculiarity of this Edition lies in the careful revision to which the text of the Author has been subjected, and the addition, as in the Volumes already published, of supplementary Notes in smaller type, wherever such were deemed necessary. In a few instances where the importance of the subject demanded it, these have extended to considerable length, and will, it is hoped, enhance the value of the work among Scotch Theologians. The Publishers, therefore, send out this Edition of Barnes' Notes on the Hebrews, in the confident expectation that it will prove extremely useful and popular.

INTRODUCTION.

§ 1. *Preliminary Remarks.*

It need not be said that this epistle has given rise to much discussion among writers on the New Testament. Indeed there is probably no part of the Bible in regard to which so many conflicting views have been entertained. The name of the author; the time and place where the epistle was written; the character of the book; its canonical authority; the language in which it was composed; and the persons to whom it was addressed, all have given rise to great difference of opinion. Among the causes of this are the following:—The name of the author is not mentioned. The church to which it was sent, if sent to any particular church, is not designated. There are no certain marks of time in the epistle, as there often are in the writings of Paul, by which we can determine the time when it was written.

It is not the design of these Notes to go into an extended examination of these questions. Those who are disposed to pursue these inquiries, and to examine the questions which have been started in regard to the epistle, can find ample means in the larger works that have treated of it;—in Lardner; in Michaelis' *Introduction;* in the *Prolegomena* of Kuinoel; in Hug's *Introduction;* and particularly in Professor Stuart's invaluable *Commentary on the Epistle to the Hebrews.* No other work on this portion of the New Testament is so complete as his, and in the Introduction he has left nothing to be desired respecting the literature of the epistle.

Controversies early arose in the church on a great variety of questions pertaining to this epistle, which are not yet fully settled. Most of those questions, however, pertain to the *literature* of the epistle, and however they may be decided, are not such as to affect the respect which a Christian ought to have for it as a part of the word of God. They pertain to the inquiries, to whom it was written; and in what language, and at what time it was composed—questions which, in whatever way they may be settled, do not affect its canonical authority, and should not shake the confidence of Christians in it as a part of divine revelation. The only inquiry on these points which it is proper to institute in these Notes is, whether the claims of the epistle to a place in the canon of Scripture are of such a kind as to allow Christians to read it as a part of the oracles of God? May we sit down to it feeling that we are perusing that which has been given by inspiration of the Holy Ghost as a part of revealed truth? Other questions are interesting in their places, and the solution of them is worth all which it has cost; but they need not embarrass us here, nor claim our attention as preliminary to the exposition of the epistle. All that will be attempted, therefore, in this Introduction, will be such a *condensation* of the evidence collected by others, as shall show that this epistle has of right a place in the volume of revealed truth, and is of authority to regulate the faith and practice of mankind.

§ 2. *To whom was the Epistle written?*

It purports to have been written to the "Hebrews." This is not found, indeed, in the body of the epistle, though it occurs in the subscription at the end. It differs from *all* the other epistles of Paul in this respect, and from most of the others in the New Testament. In all of the other epistles of Paul, the church or person to whom the letter was sent is specified in the commencement. This, however, commences in the form of an essay or homily; nor is there anywhere *in* the epistle any direct intimation to what church it was sent. The subscription at the end is of no authority, as it cannot be supposed that the author himself would affix it to the epistle, and as it is known that many of those subscriptions are false. See the remarks at the close of the Notes on Romans, and 1 Corinthians. Several questions present themselves here which we may briefly investigate.

(I.) *What is the evidence that it was written to the Hebrews?* In reply to this we may observe—(1) That the inscription at the commencement, "The Epistle of Paul the Apostle to the Hebrews," though not affixed by the author, may be allowed to express the current sense of the church in ancient times in reference to a question on which they had the best means of judging. These inscriptions at the commencement of the epistles have hitherto in general escaped the suspicion of spuriousness, to which the subscriptions at the close are justly exposed (Michaelis). They should not in any case be called in question, unless there is good reason for doing it either from the epistle itself, or from some other source. This inscription is found in all our present Greek manuscripts, and in nearly all the ancient versions. It is found in the Peshito, the old Syriac version, which was made in the first or in the early part of the second century. It is the title given to the epistle by the Fathers of the second century, and onward (Stuart). (2) The testimony of the Fathers in regard to the fact that it was written to the Hebrews, is unbroken and uniform. With one accord they declare this, and this should be regarded as proof of great value. Unless there is some good reason to depart from such evidence, it should be considered as decisive. In this case there is no good reason for calling it in question, but every reason to suppose it to be correct; nor, so far as I have found, is there anyone who has doubted it. (3) The internal evidence is of the highest character that it was written to Hebrew converts. It treats of Hebrew institutions. It explains their nature. It makes no allusion to Gentile customs or laws. It all along supposes that those to whom it was sent were familiar with the Jewish history; with the nature of the temple service; with the functions of the priestly office; and with the whole structure of the Jewish religion. No other persons than those who had been Jews are addressed throughout the epistle. There is no attempt to explain the nature or design of any customs except those with which they were familiar. At the same time it is equally clear that they were *Jewish converts*—converts from Judaism to Christianity—who are addressed. The writer addresses them as Christians, not as those who were *to be* converted to Christianity; he explains to them the Jewish customs as one would do to those who had been converted from Judaism; he endeavours to guard them from apostasy, as if there were danger that they would *relapse* again into the system from which they were converted. These considerations seem to be decisive; and in the view of all

who have written on the epistle, as well as of the Christian world at large, they settle the question. It has never been held that the epistle was directed to *Gentiles;* and in all the opinions and questions which have been started on the subject, it has been admitted that, wherever they resided, the persons to whom the epistle was addressed were originally Hebrews who had been converted to the Christian religion.

(II.) *To what particular church of the Hebrews was it written?* Very different opinions have been held on this question. The celebrated Storr held that it was written to the Hebrew part of the churches in Galatia; and that the Epistle to the Galatians was addressed to the Gentile part of those churches. Semler and Noessett maintained that it was written to the churches in Macedonia, and particularly to the church of Thessalonica. Bolten maintains that it was addressed to the Jewish Christians who fled from Palestine in a time of persecution, about the year 60, and who were scattered through Asia Minor. Michael Weber supposed that it was addressed to the church at Corinth. Ludwig conjectured that it was addressed to a church in Spain. Wetstein supposes that it was written to the church at Rome. Most of these opinions are mere conjectures, and all of them depend on circumstances which furnish only slight evidence of probability. Those who are disposed to examine these, and to see them confuted, may consult Stuart's *Commentary on the Hebrews,* Intro. § 5–9. The common, and the almost universally received opinion is, that the epistle was addressed to the Hebrew Christians in Palestine. The reasons for this opinion, briefly, are the following: (1) The testimony of the ancient church was uniform on this point—that the epistle was not only written to Hebrew Christians, but to those who were in Palestine. Lardner affirms this to be the testimony of Clement of Alexandria, Jerome, Euthalius, Chrysostom, Theodoret, and Theophylact; and adds that this was the general opinion of the ancients (*Works,* vol. vi. pp. 80, 81, ed. Lond. 1829). (2) The *inscription* at the commencement of the epistle leads to this supposition. That inscription, though not appended by the hand of the author, was early affixed to it. It is found not only in the Greek manuscripts, but in all the early versions, as the Syriac and the Itala; and was doubtless affixed at a very early period, and by whomsoever it was done, it expressed the current opinion at the time. It is hardly possible that a mistake would be made on this point; and unless there is good evidence to the contrary, this ought to be allowed to determine the question. That inscription is, "The Epistle of Paul the Apostle to the Hebrews." But who are the Hebrews— the Ἑβραῖοι? Professor Stuart has endeavoured to show that this was a term that was employed exclusively to denote the *Jews in Palestine,* in contradistinction from foreign Jews, who were called *Hellenists.* Comp. my Notes on Acts vi. 1. Bertholdt declares that there is not a single example which can be found in early times of Jewish Christians out of Palestine being called Hebrews. See a Dissertation on the Greek Language in Palestine, and on the meaning of the word *Hellenists,* by Hug, in the *Bib. Repository,* vol. i. 547, 548. Comp. also Robinson's *Lex.* on the word Ἑβραῖος. If this be so, and if the inscription be of any authority, then it goes far to settle the question. The word *Hebrews* occurs but three times in the New Testament (Acts vi. 1; 2 Cor. xi. 22; Phil. iii. 5), in the first of which it is certain that it is used in this sense, and in both the others of which it is probable. There can be no doubt, it seems to me, that an ancient writer acquainted with the usual

sense of the word *Hebrew*, would understand an inscription of this kind—
"written to the Hebrews"—as designed for the inhabitants of Palestine, and
not for the Jews of other countries. (3) There are some passages in the
epistle itself which Lardner supposes indicate that this epistle was written to
the Hebrews in Palestine, or to those there who had been converted from
Judaism to Christianity. As those passages are not conclusive, and as their
force has been called in question, and with much propriety, by Professor
Stuart (pp. 32–34), I shall merely refer to them. They can be examined
at leisure by those who are so disposed, and though they do not *prove* that the
epistle was addressed to the Hebrew Christians in Palestine, yet they can be
best interpreted on that supposition, and a peculiar significancy would be
attached to them on this supposition. They are the following: chap. i. 2;
iv. 2; ii. 1–4; v. 12; iv. 4–6; x. 26–29, 32–34; xiii. 13, 14. The argument
of Lardner is, that these would be more applicable to their condition than
to others; a position which I think cannot be doubted. Some of them are
of so general character, indeed, as to be applicable to Christians elsewhere,
and in regard to some of them it cannot be certainly demonstrated that the
state of things referred to existed in Judea; but taken together they would be
more applicable *by far* to them than to the circumstances of any others of
which we have knowledge; and this may be allowed to have *some* weight at
least in determining to whom the epistle was sent. (4) The internal evidence of the epistle corresponds with the supposition that it was written to
the Hebrew Christians in Palestine. The passages referred to in the previous remarks (3) might be adduced here as proof. But there is other proof.
It *might* have been otherwise. There might be such strong internal proof
that an epistle was not addressed to a supposed people, as completely to neu-
tralize all the evidence derived from an inscription like that prefixed to this
epistle, and all the evidence derived from tradition. But it is not so here.
All the circumstances referred to in the epistle; the general strain of remark;
the argument; the allusions, are just such as would be likely to be found in
an epistle addressed to the Hebrew Christians in Palestine, and such as would
not be likely to occur in an epistle addressed to any other place or people.
They are such as the following: (*a*) The familiar acquaintance with the
Jewish institutions supposed by the writer to exist among those to whom it
was sent—a familiarity hardly to be expected even of Jews who lived in other
countries. (*b*) The danger so frequently adverted to of their relapsing into
their former state; of apostatizing from Christianity, and of embracing again
the Jewish rites and ceremonies—a danger that would exist nowhere else in
so great a degree as in Judea. Comp. chap. ii. 1–3; iii. 7–11, 15; iv. 1;
vi. 1–8; x. 26–35. (*c*) The nature of the discussion in the epistle—not
turning upon the obligation of circumcision, and the distinction of meats and
drinks, which occupied so much of the attention of the apostles and early Christians in other places—but a discussion relating to the whole structure of the
Mosaic economy, the pre-eminence of Moses or Christ, the meaning of the
rites of the temple, &c. These great questions would be more likely to arise
in Judea than elsewhere, and it was important to discuss them fully, as it is
done in this epistle. In other places they would be of less interest, and would
excite less difficulty. (*d*) The allusion to local places and events; to facts
in their history; and to the circumstances of public worship, which would be
better understood there than elsewhere. There are no allusions—or if there

are they are very brief and infrequent—to heathen customs, games, races, and philosophical opinions, as there are often in the other epistles of the New Testament. Those to whom the epistle was sent, are presumed to have an intimate and minute knowledge of the Hebrew history, and such a knowledge as could be hardly supposed elsewhere. Comp. chap. xi., particularly ver. 32–39. Thus it is implied that they so well understood the subjects relating to the Jewish rites, that it was not necessary that the writer should specify them particularly. See chap. ix. 5. Of what other persons could this be so appropriately said as of the dwellers in Palestine? (e) The circumstances of trial and persecution so often referred to in the epistle, agree well with the known condition of the church in Palestine. That it was subjected to great trials we know; and though this was extensively true of other churches, yet it is probable that there were more vexations and grievous exactions; that there was more spite and malice; that there were more of the trials arising from the separation of families and the losses of property attending a profession of Christianity in Palestine than anywhere else in the early Christian church. These considerations—though not so conclusive as to furnish absolute demonstration—go far to settle the question. They seem to me so strong as to preclude any reasonable doubt, and are such as the mind can repose on with a great degree of confidence in regard to the original destination of the epistle.

(III.) *Was it addressed to a particular church in Palestine, or to the Hebrew Christians there in general?*

Whether it was addressed to the churches in general in Palestine, or to some particular church there, it is now impossible to determine. Prof. Stuart inclines to the opinion that it was addressed to the church in Cesarea. The ancients in general supposed it was addressed to the church in Jerusalem. There are some *local* references in the epistle which look as though it was directed to some particular church. But the means of determining this question are put beyond our reach, and it is of little importance to settle the question. From the allusions to the temple, the priesthood, the sacrifices, and the whole train of peculiar institutions there, it would seem probable that it was directed to the church in Jerusalem. As that was the capital of the nation, and the centre of religious influence; and as there was a large and flourishing church in that city, this opinion would seem to have great probability; but it is impossible now to determine it. If we suppose that the author sent the epistle, in the first instance, to some local church, near the central seat of the great influence which he intended to reach by it—addressing to that church the particular communications in the last verses—we shall make a supposition which, so far as can now be ascertained, will accord with the truth in the case.

§ 3. *The Author of the Epistle.*

To those who are familiar with the investigations which have taken place in regard to this epistle, it need not be said that the question of its authorship has given rise to much discussion. The design of these Notes does not permit me to go at length into this inquiry. Those who are disposed to see the investigation pursued at length, and to see the objections to the Pauline origin examined in a most satisfactory manner, can find it done in the Introduction to the Epistle to the Hebrews, by Prof. Stuart, pp. 77–260. All that my purpose requires is to state, in a very brief manner, the evidence on which it is ascribed to the apostle Paul. That evidence is, briefly, the following:—

(1) That derived from the church at Alexandria. Clement of Alexandria says, that Paul wrote to the Hebrews, and that this was the opinion of Pantaenus, who was at the head of the celebrated Christian school at Alexandria, and who flourished about A.D. 180. Pantaenus lived near Palestine. He must have been acquainted with the prevailing opinions on the subject, and his testimony must be admitted to be proof that the epistle was regarded as Paul's by the churches in that region. Origen, also of Alexandria, ascribes the epistle to Paul; though he says that the *sentiments* are those of Paul, but that the words and phrases belong to some one relating the apostle's sentiments, and as it were commenting on the words of his master. The testimony of the church at Alexandria was uniform after the time of Origen, that it was the production of Paul. Indeed there seems never to have been any doubt in regard to it there. The testimony of that church and school is particularly valuable, because (*a*) it was near to Palestine where the epistle was probably sent; (*b*) Clement particularly had travelled much, and would be likely to understand the prevailing sentiments of the East; (*c*) Alexandria was the seat of the most celebrated theological school of the early Christian ages, and those who were at the head of this school would be likely to have correct information on a point like this; and (*d*) Origen is admitted to have been the most learned of the Greek Fathers, and his testimony that the "sentiments" were those of Paul may be regarded as of peculiar value.

(2) It was inserted in the translation into the Syriac, made very early in the second century, and in the old Italic version, and was hence believed to be of apostolic origin, and is by the inscription in those versions ascribed to Paul. This may be allowed to express the general sense of the churches at that time, as this would not have been done unless there had been a prevailing impression that the epistle was written by him. The fact that it was *early* regarded as an inspired book is also conclusively shown by the fact that the Second Epistle of Peter, and the Second and Third Epistles of John, are not found in that version. They came later into circulation than the other epistles, and were either not possessed, or were not regarded as genuine, by the author of that version. The Epistle to the Hebrews *is* found in those versions, and was, therefore, regarded as one of the inspired books. In those versions it bears the inscription, "To the Hebrews."

(3) This epistle was received as the production of Paul by the Eastern churches. Justin Martyr, who was born at Samaria, quotes it, about the year 140. It was found, as has been already remarked, in the Peshito—the old Syriac version, made in the early part of the second century. Jacob, bishop of Nisibis, also (about A.D. 325) repeatedly quotes it as the production of an apostle. Ephrem Syrus, or the Syrian, ascribes it to Paul. He was the disciple of Jacob of Nisibis, and no man was better qualified to inform himself on this point than Ephrem. No man stands deservedly higher in the memory of the Eastern churches. After him, all the Syrian churches acknowledged the canonical authority of the Epistle to the Hebrews. But the most important testimony of the Eastern church is that of Eusebius, bishop of Cesarea, in Palestine. He is the well-known historian of the church, and he took pains from all quarters to collect testimony in regard to the Books of Scripture. He says, "There are fourteen epistles of Paul, manifest and well known: but yet there are some who reject that to the Hebrews, alleging in behalf of their opinion, that it was not received

by the church of Rome as a writing of Paul." The testimony of Eusebius is particularly important. He had heard of the objection to its canonical authority. He had weighed that objection. Yet in view of the testimony in the case, he regarded it as the undoubted production of Paul. As such it was received in the churches in the East; and the fact which he mentions, that its genuineness had been disputed by the church of Rome, and that he specifies no other church, proves that it had *not* been called in question in the East. This seems to me to be sufficient testimony to settle this inquiry. The writers here referred to lived in the very country to which the epistle was evidently written, and their testimony is uniform. Justin Martyr was born in Samaria; Ephrem passed his life in Syria; Eusebius lived in Cesarea, and Origen passed the last twenty years of his life in Palestine. The churches there were unanimous in the opinion that this epistle was written by Paul, and their united testimony should be regarded as decisive on the question. Indeed when their testimony is considered, it seems remarkable that the subject should have been regarded as doubtful by critics, or that it should have given rise to so much protracted investigation. I might add to the testimonies above referred to, the fact that the epistle was declared to be Paul's by the following persons: Archelaus, bishop of Mesopotamia, about A.D. 300; Adamantius, about 330; Cyril, of Jerusalem, about 348; the council of Laodicea, about 363; Epiphanius, about 368; Basil, 370; Gregory Nazianzen, 370; Chrysostom, 398, &c. &c. Why should not the testimony of such men and churches be admitted? What more clear or decided evidence could we wish in regard to any fact of ancient history? Would not such testimony be ample in regard to an anonymous oration of Cicero, or a poem of Virgil or of Horace? Are we not constantly acting on far feebler evidence in regard to the authorship of many productions of celebrated English writers?

(4) In regard to the Western churches, it is to be admitted that, like the Second Epistle of Peter, and the Second and Third Epistles of John, the canonical authority was for some time doubted, or was even called in question. But this may be accounted for. The epistle had not the name of the author. All the other epistles of Paul had. As the epistle was addressed to the Hebrews in Palestine, it may not have been soon known to the Western churches. As there were spurious epistles and gospels at an early age, much caution would be used in admitting any anonymous production to a place in the sacred canon. Yet it was not *long* before all these doubts were removed, and the Epistle to the Hebrews was allowed to take its place among the other acknowledged writings of Paul. It was received as the epistle of Paul by Hilary, bishop of Poictiers, about A.D. 354; by Lucifer, bishop of Cagliari, 354; by Victorinus, 360; by Ambrose, bishop of Milan, 360; by Rufinus, 397, &c. &c. Jerome, the well-known Latin Father, uses in regard to it the following language: "This is to be maintained, that this epistle, which is inscribed to the Hebrews, is not only received by the churches at the East as the apostle Paul's, but has been in past times by all ecclesiastical writers in the Greek language; although most [Latins] think that Barnabas or Clement was the author." Still it was not rejected by *all* the Latins. Some received it in the time of Jerome as the production of Paul. See Stuart, pp. 114, 115, for the full testimony of Jerome. Augustine admitted that the epistle was written by Paul. He mentions that Paul wrote fourteen epistles, and specifies particularly the Epistle to the Hebrews. He often cites it as a part of Scrip-

ture, and quotes it as the production of an apostle (Stuart, p. 115). From the time of Augustine it was undisputed. By the council of Hippo, A.D. 393, the third council of Carthage, 397, and the fifth council of Carthage, 419, it was declared to be the epistle of Paul, and was as such commended to the churches.

(5) As another proof that it is the writing of Paul, we may appeal to the internal evidence. (*a*) The author of the epistle was the companion and friend of Timothy. "Know ye that our brother Timothy is set at liberty"— or is sent away—ἀπολελυμένον—"with whom, if he come shortly, I will see you," chap. xiii. 23. Sent away, perhaps, on a journey, to visit some of the churches, and expected soon to return. In Phil. ii. 19, Paul speaks of sending Timothy to them "so soon as he should see how it would go with him," at the same time expressing a hope that he should himself see them shortly. What is more natural than to suppose that he *had* now sent Timothy to Philippi; that during his absence he wrote this epistle; that he was waiting for his return; and that he proposed, if Timothy should return soon, to visit Palestine with him? And who would more naturally say this than the apostle Paul—the companion and friend of Timothy; by whom he had been accompanied in his travels; and by whom he was regarded with special interest as a minister of the gospel? (*b*) In chap. xiii. 18, 19, he asks their prayers that he might be restored to them; and in ver. 23, he expresses a confident expectation of being able soon to come and see them. From this it is evident that he was then imprisoned, but had hope of speedy release—a state of things in exact accordance with what existed at Rome, Phil. ii. 17-24. (*c*) He was in bonds when he wrote this epistle, Heb. x. 34, "Ye had compassion of me *in my bonds;*" an expression that will exactly apply to the case of Paul. He was in "bonds" in Palestine; he was two whole years in Cesarea a prisoner (Acts xxiv. 27); and what was more natural than that the Christians in Palestine should have had compassion on him, and ministered to his wants? To what other person would these circumstances so certainly be applicable? (*d*) The salutation (chap. xiii. 24), "they of Italy salute you," agrees with the supposition that it was written by Paul when a prisoner at Rome. Paul writing from Rome, and acquainted with Christians from other parts of Italy, would be likely to send such a salutation. In regard to the *objections* which may be made to this use of the passage, the reader may consult Stuart's Intro. to the Hebrews, p. 127, seq. (*e*) The *doctrines* of the epistle are the same as those which are taught by Paul in his undisputed writings. It is true that this consideration is not conclusive, but the want of it would be conclusive evidence *against* the position that Paul wrote it. But the resemblance is not *general*. It is not such as would be found in the writings of every one who held to the same general system of truth. It relates to *peculiarities* of doctrine, and is such as would be manifested by a man who had been reared and trained as Paul had. (1) No one can doubt that the author was formerly a Jew—and a Jew who had been familiar to an uncommon degree with the institutions of the Jewish religion. Every rite and ceremony; every form of opinion; every fact in their history, is perfectly familiar to him. And though the other apostles were Jews, yet we can hardly suppose that they had the familiarity with the minute rites and ceremonies so accurately referred to in this epistle, and so fully illustrated. With Paul all this was perfectly natural. He had been brought up at the feet of Gamaliel,

and had spent the early part of his life at Jerusalem in the careful study of the Old Testament, in the examination of the prevalent opinions, and in the attentive observance of the rites of religion. The other apostles had been born and trained, apparently, on the banks of Gennesaret, and certainly with few of the opportunities which Paul had had for becoming acquainted with the institutions of the temple service. This consideration is fatal, in my view, to the claim which has been set up for Clement as the author of the epistle. It is wholly incredible that a foreigner should be so familiar with the Jewish opinions, laws, institutions, and history, as the author of this epistle manifestly was. (2) There is the same preference for Christianity over Judaism in this epistle which is shown by Paul in his other epistles, and exhibited in the same form. Among these points are the following:— *The gospel imparts superior light.* Comp. Gal. iv. 3, 9; 1 Cor. xiv. 20; Eph. iv. 11–13; 2 Cor. iii. 18; with Heb. i. 1, 2; ii. 2–4; viii. 9–11; x. 1; xi. 39, 40. *The gospel holds out superior motives and encouragements to piety.* Comp. Gal. iii. 23; iv. 2, 3; Rom. viii. 15–17; Gal. iv. 4; v. 13; 1 Cor. vii. 19; Gal. vi. 15; with Heb. ix. 9, 14; xii. 18–24, 28; viii. 6–13. *The gospel is superior in promoting the real and permanent happiness of mankind.* Comp. Gal. iii. 10; 2 Cor. iii. 7, 9; Rom. iii. 20; iv. 24, 25; Eph. i. 7; Rom. v. 1, 2; Gal. ii. 16; and the same views in Heb. xii. 18–21; ix. 9; x. 4, 11; vi. 18–20; vii. 25; ix. 24. *The Jewish dispensation was a type and shadow of the Christian.* See Col. ii. 16, 17; 1 Cor. x. 1–6; Rom. v. 14; 1 Cor. xv. 45–47; 2 Cor. iii. 13–18; Gal. iv. 22–31; iv. 1–5; and for the same or similar views, see Heb. ix. 9–14; x. 1; viii. 1–9; ix. 22–24. *The Christian religion was designed to be perpetual, while the Jewish was intended to be abolished.* See 2 Cor. iii. 10, 11, 13, 18; iv. 14–16; Rom. vii. 4–6; Gal. iii. 21–25; iv. 1–7; v. 1; and for similar views compare Heb. viii. 6–8, 13; vii. 17–19; x. 1–14. *The person of the Mediator is presented in the same light by the writer of the Epistle to the Hebrews and by Paul.* See Phil. ii. 6–11; Col. i. 15–20; 2 Cor. viii. 9; Eph. iii. 9; 1 Cor. viii. 6; xv. 25–27; and for the same and similar views, see Heb. i. 2, 3; ii. 9, 14; xii. 2; ii. 8; x. 13. *The death of Christ is the propitiatory sacrifice for sin.* See 1 Tim. i. 15; 1 Cor. xv. 3; Rom. viii. 32; iii. 24; Gal. i. 4; ii. 20; 1 Cor. v. 7; Eph. i. 7; Col. i. 14; 1 Tim. ii. 6; 1 Cor. vi. 20; vii. 23; Rom. v. 12–21; iii. 20, 28; viii. 3; 1 Tim. ii. 5, 6. For similar views see Heb. i. 3; ii. 9; v. 8, 9; vii., viii., ix., x. *The general method and arrangement of this epistle and of the acknowledged epistles of Paul are the same.* It resembles particularly the epistles to the Romans and the Galatians, where we have first a doctrinal and then a practical part. The same is true also to some extent of the epistles to the Ephesians, Colossians, and Philippians. The Epistle to the Hebrews is on the same plan. As far as chap. x. 19, it is principally doctrinal; the remainder is mainly practical. *The manner of appealing to, and applying the Jewish Scriptures, is the same in this epistle as in those of Paul.* The general structure of the epistle, and the slightest comparison between them, will show this with sufficient clearness. The general remark to be made in view of this comparison is, that the Epistle to the Hebrews is just such an one as Paul might be expected to write; that it agrees with what we know to have been his early training, his views, his manner of life, his opinions, and his habit in writing; that it accords

better with his views than with those of any other known writer of antiquity; and that it falls in with the circumstances in which he is known to have been placed, and the general object which he had in view. So satisfactory are these views to my mind, that they seem to have all the force of demonstration which can be had in regard to any anonymous publication, and it is a matter of wonder that so much doubt has been experienced in reference to the question who was the author.

It is difficult to account for the fact that the name of the author was omitted. It is found in every other epistle of Paul, and in general it is appended to the other epistles in the New Testament. It is omitted, however, in the three epistles of John, for reasons which are now unknown. And there may have been similar reasons also unknown for omitting it in this case. The simple *fact* is, that it is anonymous; and whoever was the author, the same difficulty will exist in accounting for it. If this fact will prove that Paul was not the author, it would prove the same thing in regard to any other person, and would thus be ultimately conclusive evidence that it *had* no author. What were the reasons for omitting the name can be only matter of conjecture. The most probable opinion, as it seems to me, is this. The name of Paul was odious to the Jews. He was regarded by the nation as an apostate from their religion, and everywhere they showed peculiar malignity against him. See the Acts of the Apostles. The fact that he was so regarded by them might indirectly influence even those who had been converted from Judaism to Christianity. They lived in Palestine. They were near the temple, and were engaged in its ceremonies and sacrifices—for there is no evidence that they broke off from those observances at once on their conversion to Christianity. Paul was abroad. It might have been reported that he was preaching against the temple and its sacrifices, and even the Jewish Christians in Palestine might have supposed that he was carrying matters too far. In these circumstances it might have been *imprudent* for him to have announced his name at the outset, for it might have aroused prejudices which a wise man would wish to allay. But if he could present an argument, somewhat in the form of an essay, showing that he believed that the Jewish institutions were appointed by God, and that he was not an apostate and an infidel; if he could conduct a demonstration that would accord in the main with the prevailing views of the Christians in Palestine, and which would be adapted to strengthen them in the faith of the gospel, and to explain to them the true nature of the Jewish rites, then the object could be gained without difficulty, and they would be prepared to learn that Paul was the author, without prejudice or alarm. Accordingly he thus conducts the argument; and at the close gives them such *intimations* that they would understand who wrote it without much difficulty. If this was the motive, it was an instance of *tact* such as was certainly characteristic of Paul, and such as was not improper for any man. I have no doubt that this was the true motive. It would be soon known who wrote the epistle; and accordingly we have seen the authorship was never a matter of dispute in the Eastern churches.

§ 4. *The Time when the Epistle was written.*

In regard to the time when this epistle was written, and the place where, critics have been better agreed than on most of the questions which have been started in regard to it. Mill was of opinion that it was written by Paul in

the year 63, in some part of Italy, soon after he had been released from imprisonment at Rome. Wetstein was of the same opinion. Tillemont also places this epistle in the year 63, and supposes that it was written while Paul was at Rome, or at least in Italy, and soon after he was released from imprisonment. Basnage supposes it was written about the year 61, and during the imprisonment of the apostle. Lardner supposes also that it was written in the beginning of the year 63, and soon after the apostle was released from his confinement. This also is the opinion of Calmet. The circumstances in the epistle which will enable us to form an opinion on the question about the time and the place are the following:—

(1) It was written while the temple was still standing, and before Jerusalem was destroyed. This is evident from the whole structure of the epistle. There is no allusion to the destruction of the temple or the city, which there certainly would have been if they had been destroyed. Such an event would have contributed much to the object in view, and would have furnished an irrefragable argument that the institutions of the Jews were intended to be superseded by another and a more perfect system. Moreover, there are allusions *in* the epistle which suppose that the temple service was then performed. See Heb. ix. 9; viii. 4, 5. But the city and temple were destroyed in the year 70, and of course the epistle was written before that year.

(2) It was evidently written before the civil wars and commotions in Judea, which terminated in the destruction of the city and nation. This is clear, because there are no allusions to any such disorders or troubles in Palestine, and there is no intimation that they were suffering the evils incident to a state of war. Comp. chap. xii. 4. But those wars commenced A.D. 66, and evidently the epistle was written before that time.

(3) They were not suffering the evils of violent persecution. They had indeed formerly suffered (comp. chap. x. 32, 34); James and Stephen had been put to death (Acts vii., xii.); but there was no violent and bloody persecution then raging in which they were called to defend their religion at the expense of blood and life, chap. x. 32, 33. But the persecution under Nero began in the year 64, and though it began at Rome, and was confined in a considerable degree to Italy, yet it is not improbable that it extended to other places, and it is to be presumed that if such a persecution were raging at the time when the epistle was written there would have been some allusion to this fact. It may be set down, therefore, that it was written before the year 64.

(4) It is equally true that the epistle was written during the latter part of the apostolic age. The author speaks of the *former* days, in which, after they were illuminated, they endured a great fight of afflictions, and when they were made a gazing-stock, both by reproaches and afflictions, and took joyfully the spoiling of their goods, or were plundered by their oppressors (chap. x. 32–34); he speaks of them as having been so long converted that they ought to have been qualified to teach others (chap. v. 12); and hence it is fairly to be inferred that they were not *recent* converts, but that the church there had been established for a considerable period. It may be added, that it was *after* the writer had been imprisoned—as I suppose in Cesarea (see § 3)—when they had ministered to him, chap. x. 34. But this was as late as the year 60.

(5) At the time when Paul wrote the epistles to the Ephesians, Philippians, and Colossians, he had hopes of deliverance. Timothy was evidently with him. But now he was absent, chap. xiii. 23. In the epistle to

the Philippians (chap. ii. 19–23) he says, "But I trust in the Lord Jesus to send Timotheus shortly unto you, that I may be also of good comfort, when I know your state." He expected, therefore, that Timothy would come back to him at Rome. It is probable that Timothy was sent soon after this. The apostle had a fair prospect of being set at liberty, and sent him to them. *During his absence* at this time, it would seem probable, this epistle was written. Thus the writer says (chap. xiii. 23), "Know ye that our brother Timothy is *set at liberty*"—or rather, SENT AWAY, or SENT ABROAD (see Notes on that place); "with whom, if he come shortly, I will see you." That is, if he returns soon, as I expect him, I will pay you a visit. It is probable that the epistle was written while Timothy was thus absent at Philippi, and when he returned, Paul and he went to Palestine, and thence to Ephesus. If so, it was written somewhere about the year 63, as this was the time when Paul was set at liberty.

(6) The epistle was written evidently in Italy. Thus in chap. xiii. 24, the writer says, "They of Italy salute you." This would be the natural form of salutation on the supposition that it was written there. He mentions none by name, as he does in his other epistles, for it is probable that none of those who were at Rome would be known by name in Palestine. But there was a *general* salutation, showing the interest which they had in the Christians in Judea, and expressive of regard for their welfare. This expression is, to my mind, conclusive evidence that the epistle was written in Italy; and *in* Italy there was no place where this would be so likely to occur as at Rome.

§ 5. *The Language in which the Epistle was written.*

This is a vexed and still unsettled question, and it does not seem to be possible to determine it with any considerable degree of certainty. Critics of the ablest name have been divided on it, and what is remarkable, have appealed to the same arguments to prove exactly opposite opinions—one class arguing that the style of the epistle is such as to prove that it was written in Hebrew, and the other appealing to the same proofs to demonstrate that it was written in Greek. Among those who have supposed that it was written in Hebrew are the following, viz.:—Some of the Fathers—as Clement of Alexandria, Theodoret, John Damascenus, Theophylact; and among the moderns, Michaelis has been the most strenuous defender of this opinion. This opinion was also held by the late Dr. James P. Wilson, who says, "It was probably written in the vulgar language of the Jews;" that is, in that mixture of Hebrew, Syriac, and Chaldee, which was usually spoken in the time of the Saviour, and which was known as the Syro-Chaldaic.

On the other hand, the great body of critics have supposed it was written in the Greek language. This was the opinion of Fabricius, Lightfoot, Whitby, Beausobre, Capellus, Basnage, Mill, and others, and is also the opinion of Lardner, Hug, Stuart, and perhaps of most modern critics. These opinions may be seen examined at length in Michaelis' *Introduction*, Hug, Stuart, and Lardner.

The arguments in support of the opinion that it was written in Hebrew are, briefly, the following: (1) The testimony of the Fathers. Thus Clement of Alexandria says, "Paul wrote to the Hebrews in the Hebrew language, and Luke carefully translated it into Greek." Jerome says, "Paul as a Hebrew wrote to the Hebrews in Hebrew—Scripserat ut Hebræus He-

bræis Hebraice;" and then he adds, "this epistle was translated into Greek, so that the colouring of the style was made diverse in this way from that of Paul's." (2) The fact that it was written for the use of the Hebrews, who spoke the Hebrew, or the *Talmudic* language, is alleged as a reason for supposing that it must have been written in that language. (3) It is alleged by Michaelis, that the style of the Greek, as we now have it, is far more pure and classical than Paul elsewhere employs, and that hence it is to be inferred that it was translated by some one who was master of the Greek language. On this, however, the most eminent critics disagree. (4) It is alleged by Michaelis, that the quotations in the epistle, as we have it, are made from the Septuagint, and that they are foreign to the purpose which the writer had in view as they are now quoted, whereas they are exactly in point as they stand in the Hebrew. Hence he infers that the original Hebrew was quoted by the author, and that the translator used the common version at hand instead of making an exact translation for himself. Of the fact alleged here, however, there may be good ground to raise a question; and if it were so, it would not *prove* that the writer might not have used the common and accredited translation, though *less* to his purpose than the original. Of the fact, moreover, to which Michaelis here refers, Prof. Stuart says, "He has not adduced a single instance of what he calls a *wrong translation* which wears the appearance of any considerable probability." The only instance urged by Michaelis which seems to me to be plausible is Heb. i. 7. These are the principal arguments which have been urged in favour of the opinion that this epistle was written in the Hebrew language. They are evidently not conclusive. The only argument of any considerable weight is the testimony of some of the Fathers, and it may be doubted whether they gave this as a matter of historic fact or only as a matter of opinion. See Hug's *Introduction*, § 144. It is morally certain that in one respect their statement cannot be true. They state that it was translated by Luke; but it is capable of the clearest proof that it was not translated by Luke, the author of the Gospel and the Acts of the Apostles, since there is the most remarkable dissimilarity in the style.

On the other hand there are alleged in favour of the opinion that it was written in Greek the following considerations, viz.:—

(1) The fact that we have no Hebrew original. If it was written in Hebrew, the original was early lost. None of the Fathers say that they had seen it; none quote it. All the copies that we have are in Greek. If it was written in Hebrew, and the original was destroyed, it must have been at a very early period, and it is remarkable that no one should have mentioned the fact or alluded to it. Besides, it is scarcely conceivable that the original should have so soon perished, and that the translation should have altogether taken its place. If it was addressed to the Hebrews in Palestine, the same reason which made it proper that it should have been *written* in Hebrew would have led them to *retain* it in that language, and we might have supposed that Origen, or Eusebius, or Jerome, who lived there, or Ephrem the Syrian, would have adverted to the fact that there was there a Hebrew original. The Jews were remarkable for retaining their sacred books in the language in which they were written, and if this were written in Hebrew it is difficult to account for the fact that it was so soon suffered to perish.

(2) The presumption—a presumption amounting to almost a moral certainty—is, that an apostle writing to the Christians in Palestine would write

in Greek. This presumption is based on the following circumstances: (*a*) The
fact that all the other books of the New Testament were written in Greek,
unless the Gospel by Matthew be an exception. (*b*) This occurred in cases
where it would seem to have been as improbable as it was that one writing
to the Hebrews should use that language. For instance, Paul wrote to the
church in Rome in the Greek language, though the *Latin* language was that
which was in universal use there. (*c*) The Greek was a common language
in the East. It seems to have been familiarly spoken, and to have been commonly understood. (*d*) Like the other books of the New Testament, this
epistle does not appear to have been intended to be confined to the Hebrews
only. The writings of the apostles were regarded as the property of the
church at large. Those writings would be copied and spread abroad. The
Greek was a far better language for such a purpose than the Hebrew. It
was polished and elegant; was adapted to moral subjects; was fitted to express delicate shades of thought, and was the language which was best understood by the world at large. (*e*) It was the language which Paul would
naturally use unless there was a strong reason for his employing the Hebrew.
Though he was able to speak in Hebrew (Acts xxi. 40), yet he had spent his
early days in Tarsus, where the Greek was the vernacular tongue, and it was
probably that which he had first learned. Besides this, when this epistle was
written he had been absent from Palestine about twenty-five years, and in
all that time he had been there but a few days. He had been where the
Greek language was universally spoken. He had been among Jews who
spoke that language. It was the language used in their synagogues, and
Paul had addressed them in it. After thus preaching, conversing, and
writing in that language for twenty-five years, is it any wonder that he
should prefer writing in it; that he should naturally do it; and is it not to
be presumed that he would do it in this case? These presumptions are so
strong that they ought to be allowed to settle a question of this kind unless
there is positive proof to the contrary.

(3) There is *internal* proof that it was written in the Greek language.
The evidence of this kind consists in the fact that the writer bases an *argument* on the meaning and force of Greek words, which could not have occurred had he written in Hebrew. Instances of this nature are such as these.
(*a*) In chap. ii. he applies a passage from Ps. viii. to prove that the Son of God
must have had a human nature, which was to be exalted above the angels,
and placed at the head of the creation. The passage is, "Thou hast made
him a little while inferior to the angels," chap. ii. 7, *margin*. In the Hebrew, in Ps. viii. 5, the word rendered *angels*, is אֱלֹהִים—*Elohim*—*God;* and
the sense of *angels* attached to that word, though it may sometimes occur,
is so unusual, that an argument would not have been built on the Hebrew.
(*b*) In chap. vii. 1, the writer has explained the name *Melchisedec*, and translated it *king of Salem*—telling what it is *in Greek*—a thing which would
not have been done had he written in Hebrew, where the word was well
understood. It is *possible*, indeed, that a translator might have done this,
but the explanation seems to be interwoven with the discourse itself, and to
constitute a part of the argument. (*c*) In chap. ix. 16, 17, there is an argument
on the meaning of the word *covenant*—διαθήκη—which could not have occurred had the epistle been in Hebrew. It is founded on the double meaning

of that word—denoting both *a covenant* and *a testament,* or *will.* The Hebrew word—בְּרִית *berith*—has no such double signification. It means *covenant* only, and is never used in the sense of the word *will,* or testament. The proper translation of that word would be συνθήκη—*synthēkē*—but the translators of the Septuagint uniformly used the former, διαθήκη—*diathēkē*—and on this word the argument of the apostle is based. This could not have been done by a translator; it must have been by the original author, for it is incorporated into the argument. (*d*) In chap. x. 3–9, the author proves that Christ came to make an atonement for sin, and that in order to this it was necessary that he should have a human body. He shows not only that this was necessary, but that it was predicted. In doing this, he appeals to Ps. xl. 6, "A body hast thou prepared for me." But the Hebrew here is, "Mine ears hast thou opened." This passage would have been much less pertinent than the other form—"a body hast thou prepared me;" and indeed it is not easy to see how it would bear at all on the object in view. See ver. 10. But in the Septuagint the phrase stands as he quotes it—"a body hast thou prepared for me;" a fact which demonstrates, whatever difficulties there may be about the *principle* on which he makes the quotation, that the epistle was written in Greek. It may be added, that it has in no respects the appearance of a translation. It is not stiff, forced, or constrained in style, as translations usually are. It is impassioned, free, flowing, full of animation, life, and colouring, and has all the appearance of being an original composition. So clear have these considerations appeared, that the great body of critics now concur in the opinion that the epistle was originally written in Greek.

§ 6. *The Design and general Argument of the Epistle.*

The general purpose of this epistle is, to preserve those to whom it was sent from the danger of apostasy. Their danger on this subject did not arise so much from persecution, as from the circumstances which were fitted to attract them again to the Jewish religion. The temple, it is supposed, and indeed it is evident, was still standing. The morning and evening sacrifice was still offered. The splendid rites of that imposing religion were yet observed. The authority of the law was undisputed. Moses was a lawgiver, sent from God, and no one doubted that the Jewish form of religion had been instituted by their fathers in conformity with the divine direction. Their religion had been founded amidst remarkable manifestations of the Deity—in flames, and smoke, and thunder; it had been communicated by the ministration of angels; it had on its side and in its favour all the venerableness and sanction of a remote antiquity; it commended itself by the pomp of its ritual, and by the splendour of its ceremonies. On the other hand, the new form of religion had little or nothing of this to commend it. It was of recent origin. It was founded by the Man of Nazareth, who had been trained up in their own land, who had been a carpenter, and who had had no extraordinary advantages of education. Its rites were few and simple. It had no splendid temple service; it had none of the pomp and pageantry, the music and the magnificence of the ancient religion. It had no splendid array of priests in gorgeous vestments, and it had not been imparted by the ministry of angels. Fishermen were its ministers; and by the body of the nation it

was regarded as a schism, or heresy, that enlisted in its favour only the most humble and lowly of the people.

In these circumstances, how natural was it for the enemies of the gospel in Judea to contrast the two forms of religion, and how keenly would Christians there feel it! All that was said of the antiquity and the divine origin of the Jewish religion they knew and admitted; all that was said of its splendour and magnificence they saw; and all that was said of the humble origin of their own religion they were constrained to concede also. *Their* danger was not that which arises from persecution. It was that of being affected by considerations like these, of relapsing again into the religion of their fathers, and of apostatizing from the gospel; and it was a danger which beset no other part of the Christian world.

To meet and counteract this danger was the design of this epistle. Accordingly the writer contrasts the two religions in all the great points on which the minds of Christians in Judea would be likely to be affected, and shows the superiority of the Christian religion over the Jewish in every respect, and especially in the points that had so much attracted their attention, and affected their hearts. He begins by showing that the *Author* of the Christian religion was superior in rank to any and all who had ever delivered the word of God to man. He was superior to the prophets, and even to the angels. He was over all things, and all things were subject to him. There was, therefore, a special reason why they should listen to him, and obey his commands, chap. i., ii. He was superior to Moses, the great Jewish lawgiver, whom they venerated so much, and on whom they so much prided themselves, chap. iii. Having shown that the Great Founder of the Christian religion was superior to the prophets, to Moses, and to the angels, the writer proceeds to show that the Christian religion was characterized by having a High-priest superior to that of the Jews, and of whom the Jewish high-priest was but a type and emblem. He shows that all the rites of the ancient religion, splendid as they were, were also but types, and were to vanish away—for they had had their fulfilment in the realities of the Christian faith. He shows that the Christian's High-priest derived his origin and his rank from a more venerable antiquity than the Jewish high-priest did—for he went back to Melchisedec, who lived long before Aaron; and that he had far superior dignity, from the fact that he had entered into the Holy of Holies in heaven. The Jewish high-priest entered once a year into the most holy place in the temple; the Great High-priest of the Christian faith had entered into the Most Holy place—of which that was but the type and emblem—into heaven. In short, whatever there was of dignity and honour in the Jewish faith had more than its counterpart in the Christian religion; and while the Christian religion was permanent, that was fading. The rites of the Jewish system, magnificent as they were, were designed to be temporary. They were mere types and shadows of things to come. They had their fulfilment in Christianity. That had an Author more exalted in rank by far than the author of the Jewish system; it had a High-priest more elevated and enduring; it had rites which brought men nearer to God; it was the substance of what in the temple service was type and shadow. By considerations such as these the author of this epistle endeavours to preserve them from apostasy. Why should they go back? Why should they return to a less perfect system? Why go back from the substance to the shadow? Why turn away from the true sacrifice

to the type and emblem? Why linger around the earthly tabernacle, and contemplate the high-priest there, while they had a more perfect and glorious High-priest, who had entered into the heavens? And why should they turn away from the only perfect sacrifice—the great offering made for transgression—and go back to the bloody rites which were to be renewed every day? And why forsake the perfect system—the system that was to endure for ever —for that which was soon to vanish away? The author of this epistle is very careful to assure them that *if* they thus apostatized, there could be no hope for them. If they now rejected the sacrifice of the Son of God, there was no other sacrifice for sin. That was the last great sacrifice for human guilt. It was designed to close all bloody offerings. It was not to be repeated. If that was rejected, there was no other. The Jewish rites were soon to pass away; and even if they were not, they could not cleanse the conscience from sin. Persecuted, then, though they might be—reviled, ridiculed, opposed—yet they should not abandon their Christian hope, for it was their all; they should not neglect him who spake to them from heaven, for in dignity, rank, and authority he far surpassed all who in former times had made known the will of God to men.

This epistle, therefore, occupies a most important place in the volume of revealed truth, and without it that volume would be incomplete. It is the most full explanation which we have of the meaning of the Jewish institutions. In the Epistle to the Romans we have a system of religious doctrine, and particularly a defence of the great doctrine of justification by faith. Important doctrines are discussed in the other epistles; but there was something wanting that would show the meaning of the Jewish rites and ceremonies, and their connection with the Christian scheme; something which would show us how the one was preparatory to the other; and, I may add, something that would restrain the *imagination* in endeavouring to show how the one was designed to introduce the other. The one was a system of *types* and *shadows*. But on nothing is the human mind more prone to wander than on the subject of emblems and analogies. This has been evinced abundantly in the experience of the Christian church, from the time of Origen to the present. Systems of divinity, commentaries, and sermons have shown everywhere how prone men of ardent imaginations have been to find types in everything pertaining to the ancient economy; to discover hidden meanings in every ceremony; and to regard every pin and hook and instrument of the tabernacle as designed to inculcate some *truth*, and to shadow forth some fact or doctrine of the Christian revelation. It was desirable to have *one* book that should tell how that is; to fetter down the imagination and bind it by severe rules, and to restrain the vagaries of honest but credulous devotion. Such a book we have in the Epistle to the Hebrews. The ancient system is there explained by one who had been brought up in the midst of it, and who understood it thoroughly; by one who had a clear insight into the relation which it bore to the Christian economy; by one who was under the influence of divine inspiration, and who could not err. The Bible would have been incomplete without this book: and when I think of the relation between the Jewish and the Christian systems; when I look on the splendid rites of the ancient economy, and ask their meaning; when I wish a full guide to heaven, and ask for that which gives completeness to the whole, I turn instinctively to the Epistle to the Hebrews. When I wish also that which shall give me the most elevated

view of the Great Author of Christianity and of his work, and the most clear conceptions of the sacrifice which he made for sin, and when I look for considerations that shall be most effectual in restraining the soul from apostasy, and for considerations to enable it to bear trials with patience and with hope, my mind recurs to this book, and I feel that the book of revelation, and the hopes of man, would be incomplete without it.

PAUL THE APOSTLE TO THE HEBREWS.

CHAPTER I.

ANALYSIS OF THE CHAPTER.

The main object of the epistle is to commend the Christian religion to those who were addressed in it in such a way as to prevent defection or apostasy from it. This is done, principally, by showing its superiority to the Mosaic system. The great danger of Christians in Palestine was of relapsing into the Jewish system. The imposing nature of its rites; the public sentiment in its favour; the fact of its antiquity, and its undisputed divine origin, would all tend to that. To counteract this, the writer of this epistle shows that the gospel had higher claims on their attention, and that if that was rejected ruin was inevitable. In doing this, he begins, in this chapter, by showing the superiority of the Author of Christianity to prophets and to the angels—that is, that he had a rank that entitled him to the profoundest regard. The drift of this chapter, therefore, is to show the dignity and exalted nature of the Author of the Christian system—the Son of God. The chapter comprises the following points:—

I. The announcement of the fact that God, who had formerly spoken by the prophets, had in this last dispensation spoken by his Son, ver. 1, 2.

II. The statement respecting his rank and dignity. He was (1) the heir of all things; (2) the Creator of the worlds; (3) the brightness of the divine glory and the proper expression of his nature; (4) he upheld all things, ver. 2, 3.

III. The work and exaltation of the Author of the Christian system. (1) He, by his own unassisted agency, purified us from our sins. (2) He is seated at the right hand of God.

(3) He has a more exalted and valuable inheritance than the angels, in proportion as his *name* is more exalted than theirs, ver. 3, 4.

IV. Proofs that what is here ascribed to him belongs to him, particularly that he is declared to be superior to the angels, ver. 5–14.

(1) The angels have never been addressed with the title of Son, ver. 5.

(2) He is declared to be the object of worship by the angels, while they are employed merely as the messengers of God, ver. 6, 7.

(3) He is addressed as God, and his throne is said to be for ever and ever, ver. 8, 9.

(4) He is immutable. He is declared to have laid the foundations of heaven and earth; and though they would perish, yet he would remain the same, ver. 10–12.

(5) None of the angels had been addressed in this manner, but they were employed in the subordinate work of ministering to the heirs of salvation, ver. 13, 14.

From this train of reasoning the inference is drawn in ch. ii. 1–4, that we ought to give diligent heed to what had been spoken. The Great Author of the Christian scheme had peculiar claims to be heard, and there was peculiar danger in disregarding his message. The *object* of this chapter is, to impress those to whom the epistle was addressed with the high claims of the Founder of Christianity, and to show that it was superior in this respect to any other system.

1. *God, who at sundry times.* The commencement of this epistle differs from all the other epistles of Paul. In every other instance he at first announces his own name, and the name of the church or of the individual to whom he wrote. In regard to the

CHAPTER I.

G OD, *a* who at sundry times and
in divers manners spake in

a Nu.12.6,8.

reason why he here varies from that
custom, see the Introduction, § 3.
This commences with the full acknowledgment of his belief that God
had made important revelations in
past times, but that now he had communicated his will in a manner that
more especially claimed their attention. This announcement was of particular importance here. The apostle
was writing to those who had been
trained up in the full belief of the
truths taught by the prophets. As
his object was to show the superior
claims of the gospel, and to lead them
to put confidence in the sacrifice made
by Jesus Christ rather than in the
rites of the Old Testament, it was of
essential importance that he should
admit that their belief of the inspiration of the prophets was well founded.
He was not an infidel. He was not
disposed to call in question the divine
origin of the books which were regarded as given by inspiration. He
fully admitted all that had been held
by the Hebrews on that subject, and
yet affirmed that the *new* revelation
had more important claims to their
attention. The word rendered "at
sundry times" — πολυμερῶς — means
in many parts. It refers here to
the fact that the former revelation
had been given in various parts. It
had not all been given at once. It
had been communicated from time to
time as the exigencies of the people
required, and as God chose to communicate it. At one time it was by
history, then by prophecy, by poetry,
by proverbs, by some solemn and
special message, &c. The ancient revelation was a *collection* of various
writings, on different subjects, and
given at different times; but *now* God
had addressed men by *his Son*—the one
great Messenger who had come to
finish the divine communications, and
to give a uniform and connected revelation to mankind. The contrast here
is between the numerous separate
parts of the revelation given by the

time past unto the fathers by the
prophets,

2 Hath in these last days *b* spoken

b De.18.15.

prophets, and the *oneness* of that
given by his Son. The word used here
does not elsewhere occur in the New
Testament. ¶ *And in divers manners*
—πολυτρόπως. In many ways. It was
not all in one mode or method. He
had employed various ways in communicating his will. At one time it was
by direct communication, at another
by dreams, at another by visions, &c.
In regard to the various methods
which God employed to communicate
his will, see Introduction to Isaiah,
§ 7. In contradistinction from these,
God had now spoken by his Son. He
had addressed men in one uniform
manner. It was not by dreams or
visions—it was a direct communication from him. The word used here,
also, occurs nowhere else in the New
Testament. ¶ *In time past.* Formerly; in ancient times. The series
of revelations began, as recorded by
Moses, with Adam (Gen. iii.), and
terminated with Malachi—a period
of more than three thousand five hundred years. From Malachi to the
time of the Saviour there were no
recorded divine communications, and
the whole period of *written* revelation,
or during which the divine communications were recorded from Moses to
Malachi, was about a thousand years.
¶ *Unto the fathers.* To our ancestors;
to the people of ancient times. ¶ *By
the prophets.* The word *prophet* in
the Scriptures is used in a wide signification. It means not only those who
predict future events, but those who
communicate the divine will on any
subject. See Notes on Rom. xii. 6;
1 Cor. xiv. 1. It is used here in that
large sense — as denoting all those
by whom God had made communications to the Jews in former times.

2. *Hath in these last days.* In this
the final dispensation; or in this dispensation under which the affairs of
the world will be wound up. Phrases
similar to this occur frequently in the
Scriptures. They do not imply that
the world was soon coming to an end,

unto us by *his* Son, whom he hath appointed *c*heir of all things,

c Ps.2.8.

d by whom also he made the worlds;

d Jn.1.3.

but that that was the *last* dispensation, the *last* period of the world. There had been the patriarchal period, the period under the law, the period under the prophets, &c., and *this* was the period during which God's *last* method of communication would be enjoyed, and under which the world would close. It might be a *very long* period, but it would be the *last* one; and so far as the meaning of the phrase is concerned, it might be the longest period, or longer than all the others put together, but still it would be the *last* one. See Notes on Acts ii. 17; Isa. ii. 2. ¶ *Spoken unto us.* The word "*us*" here does not of necessity imply that the writer of the epistle had actually heard him, or that they had heard him to whom the epistle was written. It means that God had now communicated his will to man by his Son. It may be said with entire propriety that God had spoken to *us* by his Son, though *we* have not personally heard or seen him. We have what he spoke and caused to be recorded for our direction. ¶ *By his Son.* The title commonly given to the Lord Jesus, as denoting his peculiar relation to God. It was understood by the Jews to denote equality with God (see Notes on Jn. v. 18; comp. Jn. x. 33, 36), and is used with such a reference here. See Notes on Rom. i. 4, where the meaning of the phrase "Son of God" is fully considered. It is implied here that the fact that the Son of God has spoken to us imposes the highest obligations to attend to what he has said; that he has an authority superior to all those who have spoken in past times; and that there will be peculiar guilt in refusing to attend to what he has said. See ch. ii. 1–4; comp. ch. xii. 25. The *reasons* for the superior respect which should be shown to the revelations of the Son of God may be such as these: — (1) His rank and dignity. He is the equal with God, and is himself called God, Jn. i. 1; Rom. ix. 5. Compare ver. 8 of this

chapter. He has a right, therefore, to command, and when he speaks men should obey. (2) The clearness of the truths which he communicated to man on a great variety of subjects that are of the highest moment to the world. Revelation has been gradual—like the breaking of the day in the east. At first there is a little light; it increases and expands till objects become more and more visible, and then the sun rises in full-orbed glory. At first we discern only the *existence* of some object—obscure and undefined; then we can trace its outline; then its colour, its size, its proportions, its drapery—till it stands before us fully revealed. So it has been with revelation. There is a great variety of subjects which we now see clearly, which were very imperfectly understood by the teaching of the prophets, and would be now if we had only the Old Testament. Among them are the following : — (*a*) The character of God. Christ came to make him known as a *merciful* being, and to show *how* he could be merciful as well as just. The views given of God by the Lord Jesus are far more clear than any given by the ancient prophets; compared with those entertained by the ancient philosophers, they are like the sun compared with the darkest midnight. (*b*) The way in which man may be reconciled to God. The New Testament—which may be considered as that which God "has spoken to us by his Son"—has told us how the great work of being reconciled to God can be effected. The Lord Jesus told us that he came to "give his life a ransom for many;" that he laid down his life for his friends; that he was about to die for man; that he would draw all men to him. The prophets, indeed — particularly Isaiah—threw much light on these points. But the mass of the people did not understand their revelations. They pertained to future events—always difficult to be understood. But Christ has told us the

way of salvation, and he has made it so plain that he who runs may read. (c) The *moral* precepts of the Redeemer are superior to those of any and all that had gone before him. They are elevated, pure, expansive, benevolent—such as became the Son of God to proclaim. Indeed this is admitted on all hands. Infidels are constrained to acknowledge that all the moral precepts of the Saviour are eminently pure and benignant. If they were obeyed, the world would be filled with peace, justice, truth, purity, and benevolence. Error, fraud, hypocrisy, ambition, wars, licentiousness, and intemperance, would cease; and the opposite virtues would diffuse happiness over the face of the world. Prophets had indeed delivered many moral precepts of great importance, but the purest and most extensive body of just principles of good morals on earth are to be found in the teachings of the Saviour. (d) He has given to us the clearest view which man has had of the future state; and he has disclosed in regard to that future state a class of truths of the deepest interest to mankind, which were before wholly unknown or only partially revealed. 1. He has revealed the certainty of a state of future existence—in opposition to the Sadducees of all ages. This was denied before he came by multitudes, and where it was not, the arguments by which it was supported were often of the feeblest kind. The *truth* was held by some—like Plato and his followers—but the *arguments* on which they relied were feeble, and such as were unfitted to give rest to the soul. The *truth* they had obtained by TRADITION; the *arguments* were THEIR OWN. 2. He revealed the doctrine of the resurrection of the body. This before was doubted or denied by nearly all the world. It was held to be absurd and impossible. The Saviour taught its certainty; he raised up more than one to show that it was possible; he was himself raised, to put the whole matter beyond debate. 3. He revealed the certainty of a future judgment—the judgment of all mankind. 4. He disclosed great and

momentous truths respecting the future state. Before he came, all was dark. The Greeks spoke of Elysian fields, but they were dreams of the imagination; the Hebrews had some faint notion of a future state where all was dark and gloomy, with perhaps an occasional glimpse of the truth that there is a holy and blessed heaven; but to the mass of Jewish minds all was obscure. Christ clearly revealed a heaven, and with equal clearness he revealed a hell. He showed us that the one might be gained and the other avoided. He presented important motives for doing it; and had he done nothing more, his communications were worthy the profound attention of mankind. I may add, (3) That the Son of God has claims on our attention from the MANNER in which he spoke. He spoke as one having "authority," Mat. vii. 29. He spoke as a *witness* of what he saw and knew, Jn. iii. 11. He spoke without doubt or ambiguity of God, heaven, and of hell. His is the language of one who is familiar with all that he describes; who saw all, who knew all. There is no hesitancy or doubt in his mind as to the truth of what he speaks; and he speaks as if his whole soul were impressed with its unspeakable importance. Never were so momentous communications made to men of *hell* as fell from the lips of the Lord Jesus (see Notes on Mat. xxiii. 33); never were announcements made so fitted to awe and appal a sinful world. ¶ *Whom he hath appointed heir of all things.* See Ps. ii. 8; comp. Notes on Rom. viii. 17. This is language taken from the fact that he is "*the* SON of God." If a son, then he is an heir—for so it is usually among men. This is not to be taken *literally*, as if he inherits anything as a man does. An heir is one who inherits anything after the death of its possessor—usually his father. But this cannot be applied in this sense to the Lord Jesus. The language is used to denote his rank and dignity as the Son of God. As his Son all things are his, as the property of a father descends to his son at his death. The

3 Who[e] being the brightness of *his* glory, and the express image of his person, and upholding all things

e Jn.1.14; Col.1.15-17.

word rendered *heir* — κληρονόμος — means properly (1) one who acquires anything by lot; and (2) an *heir* in the sense in which we usually understand the word. It may also denote a *possessor* of anything received as a portion, or of property of any kind; see Rom. iv. 13, 14. It is in every instance rendered *heir* in the New Testament. Applied to Christ, it means that as the Son of God he is possessor or lord of all things, or that all things are his; comp. Acts ii. 36; x. 36; Jn. xvii. 10; xvi. 15, "All things that the Father hath are mine." The sense is, that all things belong to the Son of God. Who is so *rich* then as Christ? Who is so able to endow his friends with enduring and abundant wealth? ¶ *By whom.* By whose agency; or he was the actual agent in the creation. Grotius supposes that this means, "on account of whom;" and that the meaning is, that the universe was formed with reference to the Messiah, in accordance with an ancient Jewish maxim. But the more common and classical usage of the word rendered *by* (διὰ), when it governs a genitive, as here, is to denote the instrumental cause; the agent by which anything is done; see Mat. i. 22; ii. 5, 15, 23; Luke xviii. 31; Jn. i. 17; Acts ii. 22, 43; iv. 16; xii. 9; Rom. ii. 16; v. 5. It *may be true* that the universe was formed with reference to the glory of the Son of God, and that this world was brought into being in order to show his glory; but it would not do to establish that doctrine on a passage like this. Its obvious and proper meaning is, that he was the agent in the creation of the universe—a truth that is elsewhere abundantly taught; see Jn. i. 3, 10; Col. i. 16; Eph. iii. 9; 1 Cor. viii. 6. This sense, also, better agrees with the design of the apostle in this place. His object is to set forth the dignity of the Son of God. This is better shown by the consideration that he was the *Creator* of all things

by the word of his power, [f] when he had by himself purged our sins, [g] sat down on the right hand of the Majesty on high.

f ch.7.27; 9.12-14. g Ps.110.1; Ep.1.20,21.

than that all things were made *for* him. ¶ *The worlds.* The universe, the whole creation. So the word here— αἰών—is undoubtedly used in ch. xi. 3. The word properly means *age* — an indefinitely long period of time; then perpetuity, ever, eternity — *always being.* For an extended investigation of the meaning of the word, the reader may consult an essay by Prof. Stuart, in the *Spirit of the Pilgrims,* for 1829, pp. 406–452. From the sense of *age,* or *duration,* the word comes to denote the present and future age; the present world and the world to come; the present world, with all its cares, anxieties, and evils; the men of this world—a wicked generation, &c. Then it means the world—the material universe—creation as it is. The only perfectly clear use of the word in this latter sense in the New Testament is in Heb. xi. 3, and there there can be no doubt— "Through faith we understand that *the worlds* were made by the word of God, so that things which are seen were not made of things which do appear." The passage before us will bear the same interpretation, and this is the most obvious and intelligible. What would be the meaning of saying that the *ages* or *dispensations* were made by the Son of God? The Hebrews used the word עוֹלָם—'olám—in the same sense. It properly means *age, duration;* and thence it came to be used by them to denote the world—made up of *ages* or generations; and then the world itself. This is the fair, and, as it seems to me, the only intelligible interpretation of this passage—an interpretation amply sustained by the texts referred to above as demonstrating that the universe was made by the agency of the Son of God. Comp. Notes on ver. 10, and on Jn. i. 3.

3. *Who being the brightness of* his *glory.* This verse is designed to state the dignity and exalted rank of the

Son of God, and is exceedingly important with reference to a correct view of the Redeemer. Every word which is employed is of great importance, and should be clearly understood in order to a correct apprehension of the passage. First, in what manner does it refer to the Redeemer? To his divine nature? To the mode of his existence before he was incarnate? Or to him as he appeared on earth? Most of the ancient commentators suppose that it referred to his divine dignity before he became incarnate, and proceed to argue on that supposition on the mode of the divine existence. The true solution seems to me to be, that it refers to him as incarnate, but still has reference to him *as* the incarnate *Son of God*. It refers to him as Mediator, but not simply or mainly as a man. It is rather to him as divine—thus, in his incarnation, being the brightness of the divine glory, and the express image of God. That this is the correct view is apparent, I think, from the whole scope of the passage. The drift of the argument is, to show his dignity *as he has spoken to us* (ver. 1), and not in the period antecedent to his incarnation. It is to state his claims to our reverence as sent from God—the last and greatest of the messengers which God has sent to man. But then it is a description of him *as he actually is*—the incarnate Son of God; the equal of the Father in human flesh; and this leads the writer to dwell on his divine character, and to argue from that, ver. 8, 10–12. I have no doubt, therefore, that this description refers to his divine nature, but it is the divine nature as it appears in human flesh. An examination of the words used will prepare us for a more clear comprehension of the sense. The word *glory*—δόξα—means properly *a seeming, an appearance;* and then (1) praise, applause, honour; (2) dignity, splendour, glory; (3) brightness, dazzling light; and (4) excellence, perfection, such as belongs to God and such as there is in heaven. It is probably used here, as the word כָּבוֹד—*kâbhŏdh*—is often among the Hebrews,

to denote splendour, brightness, and refers to the divine perfections as resembling a bright light, or the sun. The word is applied to the sun and stars, 1 Cor. xv. 40, 41; to the light which Paul saw on the way to Damascus, Acts xxii. 11; to the shining of Moses' face, 2 Cor. iii. 7; to the celestial light which surrounds the angels, Rev. xviii. 1; and the glorified saints, Luke ix. 31, 32; and to the dazzling splendour or majesty in which God is enthroned, 2 Thes. i. 9; 2 Pet. i. 17; Rev. xv. 8; xxi. 11, 23. Here there is a comparison of God with the sun; he is encompassed with splendour and majesty; he is a being of light and of infinite perfection. It refers to *all in God* that is bright, splendid, glorious; and the idea is, that the Son of God is the *brightness* of it all. The word rendered *brightness*—ἀπαύγασμα—occurs nowhere else in the New Testament. It means properly *reflected splendour*, or the light which emanates from a luminous body. The rays or beams of the sun are its "brightness," or that by which the sun is seen and known. The sun itself we do not see; the beams which flow from it we do see. The meaning here is, that if God be represented under the image of a luminous body, as he is in the Scriptures (see Ps. lxxxiv. 11; Mal. iv. 2), then Christ is the radiance of that light, the brightness of that luminary (Stuart). He is that by which we perceive God, or by which God is made known to us in his real perfections. Comp. Jn. i. 18; xiv. 9.—It is by him only that the true character and glory of God become known to men. This is true in regard to the great system of revelation, but it is especially true in regard to the views which men have of God, Mat. xi. 27, "No man knoweth the Son but the Father; neither knoweth any man the Father save the Son, and he to whomsoever the Son will reveal him." The human soul is dark respecting the divine character until it is enlightened by Christ. It sees no beauty, no glory in his nature—nothing that excites wonder, or that wins the affections, until it is disclosed by the Redeemer. *Somehow* it happens, account for it as men may, that there

are no elevating practical views of God in the world; no views that engage and hold the affections of the soul; no views that are transforming and purifying, but those which are derived from the Lord Jesus. A man becomes a Christian, and at once he has elevated, practical views of God. He is to Him the most glorious of all beings. He finds supreme delight in contemplating his perfections. But he may be a philosopher or an infidel, and though he may profess to believe in the existence of God, yet the belief excites no practical influence on him; he sees nothing to admire; nothing which leads him to worship him. Comp. Rom. i. 21. ¶ *And the express image.* The word here used—χαρακτὴρ—likewise occurs nowhere else in the New Testament. It is that from which our word *character* is derived. It properly means *a graving-tool;* and then something engraved, or stamped—*a character*—as a letter, mark, sign. The image stamped on coins, seals, wax, expresses the idea: and the sense here is, that if God be represented under the idea of a substance, or being, then Christ is the exact resemblance of that—as an image is of the stamp or die. The resemblance between a stamp and the figure which is impressed is exact; and so is the resemblance between the Redeemer and God. See Col. i. 15, "Who is the image of the invisible God." ¶ *Of his person.* The word *person* with us denotes an individual being, and is applied to human beings, consisting of body and soul. We do not apply it to anything dead—not using it with reference to the body when the spirit is gone. It is applied to a man—with an individual and separate consciousness and will; with body and soul; with an existence separate from others. It is evident that it cannot be used in this sense when applied to God, and that this word does not express the true idea of the passage here. Tindal renders it, more accurately, *substance.* The word in the original —ὑπόστασις—whence our word *hypostasis,* means, literally, *a foundation,* or *substructure.* Then it means a well-founded trust, firm expectation, confi-

dence, firmness, boldness; and then *reality, substance, essential nature.* In the New Testament, it is rendered *confident, or confidence* (2 Cor. ix. 4; xi. 17; Heb. iii. 14); *substance* (Heb. xi. 1); and *person* in the passage before us. It is not elsewhere used. Here it properly refers to the essential nature of God—that which distinguishes him from all other beings, and which, if I may so say, *constitutes him God;* and the idea is, that the Redeemer is the exact resemblance of *that.* This resemblance consists, probably, in the following things—though perhaps the enumeration does not include all—but in these he certainly resembles God, or is his exact image: (1) In his original mode of being, or before the incarnation. Of this we know little. But he had a "glory with the Father before the world was," Jn. xvii. 5. He was "in the beginning with God, and was God," Jn. i. 1. He was in intimate union with the Father, and was one with Him, in certain respects, though in certain other respects there was a distinction. I do not see any evidence in the Scriptures of the doctrine of "eternal generation," and it is certain that that doctrine militates against the *proper eternity* of the Son of God. The natural and fair meaning of that doctrine would be, that there was a time when he had not an existence, and when he began to be, or was begotten. But the Scripture doctrine is, that he had a strict and proper eternity. I see no evidence that he was in any sense *a derived being*—deriving his existence and his divinity from the Father. The fathers of the Christian church, it is believed, held that the Son of God as to his divine, as well as his human nature, was *derived* from the Father. Hence the Nicene creed speaks of him as "begotten of the Father before all worlds; God of God, Light of Light, very God of very God, begotten not made"—language implying derivation in his divine nature. They held, with one voice, that he was God; but it was in this manner. See Stuart, Excursus iii. on the Epistle to the Hebrews. Compare *History of Christian Doctrine,* by W.

T. G. Shedd, D.D., vol. i. pp. 307–354. But this is incredible and impossible. A *derived* being cannot in any proper sense be God; and if there is any attribute which the Scriptures have ascribed to the Saviour with peculiar clearness, it is that of proper eternity, Rev. i. 11, 18; Jn. i. 1.

[Perhaps the doctrine of Christ's natural or eternal Sonship had been as well understood without the help of the term "generation," which adds nothing to our stock of ideas on the subject, and gives rise, as the above remarks prove, to objections which attach altogether to the *word*, and from which the *doctrine* itself is free. In fairness, however, it should be remembered, that, like many other theological terms, the term in question, when applied to Christ's Sonship, is not to be understood in the ordinary acceptation, as implying derivation or extraction. It is used as making some approach to a proper term only, and in this case, as in others of like nature, it is but just to respect the acknowledged rule, that when human phraseology is employed concerning the divine nature, all that is imperfect, all that belongs to the creature, is to be rejected, and that only retained which comports with the majesty of the Creator. It is on this very principle that Professor Stuart, in his first excursus, and Trinitarians generally, have so successfully defended the use of the word "person" to designate a distinction in the Godhead. Overlooking this principle, our author deduces consequences from the doctrine of eternal generation which do not properly belong to it, and which its advocates distinctly repudiate. That doctrine cannot militate against the proper eternity of the Son, since, while it uses the term generation, not *more humano*, but with everything of human infirmity separated from it, it supplies also the adjunct "eternal." Whatever some indiscreet advocates of the eternal Sonship may have affirmed, it should never be forgotten that the ablest friends, equally with the author, contend that there is NO DERIVATION OR COMMUNICATION OF ESSENCE FROM THE FATHER TO THE SON. "Although the terms Father and Son indicate a relation analogous to that among men, yet, as in the latter case, it is a relation between two material and separate beings, and in the former is a relation in the same spiritual essence, the one can throw no light upon the other; and to attempt to illustrate the one by the other is equally illogical and presumptuous. We can conceive the communication of a material essence by one material being to another, because it takes place in the generation of animals; but the communication of a spiritual, indivisible, immutable essence is altogether inconceivable, especially when we add that the supposed communication does not constitute a different being, but takes place in the essences communicating" (Dick's *Theol.* vol. ii. p. 71). It is readily allowed that the fathers, and many since their times, have written unguardedly on this mysterious subject; but their errors, instead of leading us to reject the doctrine entirely, should lead us only to examine the Scriptures more fully and form our opinions on them alone. The excellent author already quoted has well remarked: "I cannot conceive what object they have in view who admit the Divinity but deny the natural Sonship of our Saviour, unless it be to get rid of the strange notions about communication of essence and subordination which have prevailed so much; and in this case, like too many disputants, in avoiding one extreme they run into the other."]

It *may* have been that it was by him that the perfections of God were made known before the incarnation to the angelic world, but on that point the Scriptures are silent. (2) On earth he was the brightness of the divine glory, and the express image of his person. (*a*) It was by him, eminently, that God was made known to men—as it is by the beams of the sun that that is made known. (*b*) He bore an exact resemblance to God. He was just such a being as we should suppose God to be were he to become incarnate, and to act as a man. He was the embodied representation of the Deity. He was pure—like God. He was benevolent—like God. He spake to the winds and storms—like God. He healed diseases—like God. He raised the dead—like God. He wielded the power which God only can wield, and he manifested a character in all respects like that which we should suppose God would evince if he appeared in human flesh, and dwelt among men. And this is saying much. It is in fact saying that the account in the Gospels is real, and that the Christian religion is true. Uninspired men could never have drawn such a character as that of Jesus Christ, unless that character had actually existed. The attempt has often been made to describe God, or to show how he would speak and act if he came down to earth. Thus the Hindoos

speak of the incarnations of Vishnu; and thus Homer, and Virgil, and most of the ancient poets, speak of the appearance of the gods, and describe them as they were supposed to appear. But how different from the character of the Lord Jesus! Their gods are full of passion, and lust, and anger, and contention, and strife; they come to mingle in battles, and to take part with contending armies; they evince the same spirit as *men*, and are merely *men of greater power, and more gigantic passions;* but Christ is GOD IN HUMAN NATURE. The form is that of man; the spirit is that of God. He walks, and eats, and sleeps as a man; he thinks, and speaks, and acts like God. He was born as a man; but the angels adored him as God. As a man he ate; yet by a word he created food for thousands, as if he were God. Like a man he slept on a pillow while the vessel was tossed by the waves; like God he rose, and rebuked the winds and they were still. As a man he went, with affectionate interest, to the house of Martha and Mary; as a man he sympathized with them in their affliction, and wept at the grave of their brother; like God he spoke, and the dead came forth to the land of the living. As a man he travelled through the land of Judea. He was without a home. Yet everywhere the sick were laid at his feet, and health came from his touch, and strength from the words of his lips —as if he were God. As a man he prayed in the garden of Gethsemane; he bore his cross to Calvary; he was nailed to the tree: yet then the heavens grew dark, and the earth shook, and the dead arose—as if he were God. As a man he slept in the cold tomb—like God he rose, and brought life and immortality to light. He lived on earth as a man—he ascended to heaven like God. And in all the life of the Redeemer, in all the variety of trying situations in which he was placed, there was not a word or action which was inconsistent with the supposition that he was the incarnate God. There was no failure of any effort to heal the sick or to raise the dead; no look, no word, no deed that

was not perfectly consistent with this supposition; but on the contrary, his life is full of events which can be explained on no other supposition than that he was the appropriate shining forth of the divine glory, and the exact resemblance of the essence of God. There are not two Gods—as there are not two suns when the sun shines. It is *the one* God, in a mysterious and incomprehensible manner shining upon the world in the face of Jesus Christ. See Notes on 2 Cor. iv. 6. As the wax bears the perfect image of the seal— perfect not only in the outline but in the filling up—in all the lines, and features, and letters, so is it with the Redeemer. There is not one of the divine perfections which has not the counterpart in him, and if the glory of the divine character is seen at all by men, it will be seen in and through him. ¶ *And upholding all things by the word of his power.* That is, by his powerful word, or command. The phrase "word of his power" is a Hebraism, and means his efficient command. There could not be a more distinct ascription of divinity to the Son of God than this. He upholds or sustains all things —that is, the universe. It is not merely the earth; not only its rocks, mountains, seas, animals, and men, but it is the universe—all distant worlds. How can he do this who is not God? He does it by his "word"—his command. What a conception! That a simple *command* should do all this! So the world was made when God "spake and it was done; he commanded and it stood fast," Ps. xxxiii. 9. So the Lord Jesus *commanded* the waves and the winds, and they were still (Mat. viii. 26, 27); so he spake to diseases and they departed, and to the dead and they arose. Comp. Gen. i. 3. I know not how men can *explain away* this ascription of infinite power to the Redeemer. There can be no higher idea of omnipotence than to say of one that he upholds all things by his word; and assuredly he who can *hold up* this vast universe so that it does not sink into anarchy or into nothing, must be God. This power Jesus claimed for himself. See Mat. xxviii. 18. ¶ *When he had by himself purged our sins.*

4 Being made so much better than the angels, as he hath by in-

"By himself"—not by the blood of bulls and lambs, but by his own blood. This is designed to bring in the grand feature of the Christian scheme, that the purification made for sin was by *his* blood, instead of the blood which was shed in the temple service. The word here rendered "purged" means *purified* or *expiated*. See Notes on Jn. xv. 2. The literal rendering is, "having made purification for our sins." The purification or cleansing which he effected was by his blood. See 1 Jn. i. 7, "The blood of Jesus Christ cleanseth from all sin." This the apostle here states to have been the great object for which Christ came, and having done this, he sat down on the right hand of God. See chap. vii. 27; ix. 12–14. It was not merely to *teach* that he came; it was not merely to be an *example;* it was not merely to be a *martyr;* it was to purify the hearts of men, to remove their sins, and to put an end to sacrifice by the sacrifice of himself. ¶ *Sat down on the right hand of the Majesty on high.* Of God. See Notes on Mark xvi. 19; Eph. i. 20–23.

4. *Being made so much better.* Being exalted so much above the angels. The word "better" here does not refer to moral character, but to exaltation of rank. As Mediator; as the Son of God in our nature, he is exalted far above the angels. ¶ *Than the angels.* Than all angels of every rank. See Notes on Eph. i. 21; comp. 1 Pet. iii. 22, "Angels, and authorities, and powers being made subject unto him." He is exalted to his mediatorial throne, and all things are placed beneath his feet. ¶ *As he hath by inheritance.* Or in virtue of his name—the Son of God; an exaltation such as is implied in that name. As a son has a rank in a family above servants; as he has a control over the property above that which servants have, so it is with the Mediator. He is the *Son* of God; angels are the *servants* of God, and the servants of the church. They occupy a place in the universe compared with that which

heritance obtained a more excellent name than they.

5 For unto which of the angels

he occupies, similar to the place which servants in a family occupy compared with that which a son has. To illustrate and prove this is the design of the remainder of this chapter. The argument which the apostle insists on is, that the title "THE Son of God" is to be given to him alone. It has been conferred on no others. Though the angels, and though saints are called in general "*sons* of God," yet the title "THE *Son of God*" has been given to him only. As the apostle was writing to Hebrews, he makes his appeal to the Hebrew Scriptures alone for the confirmation of this opinion. ¶ *A more excellent name.* To wit, the name *Son.* It is a more honourable and elevated name than has ever been bestowed on them. It involves more exalted privileges, and entitles him on whom it is bestowed to higher respect and honour than any name ever bestowed on them.

5. *For unto which of the angels,* &c. The object of this is, to prove that the Son of God, who has spoken to men in these last days, is superior to the angels. As the apostle was writing to those who had been trained in the Jewish religion, and who admitted the authority of the Old Testament, of course he made his appeal to that, and undoubtedly referred for proof to those places which were generally admitted to relate to the Messiah. Abarbanel says, that it was the common opinion of the Jewish doctors that the Messiah would be exalted above Abraham, Moses, and the angels (Stuart). There is a difficulty, as we shall see, in applying the passages which follow to the Messiah—a difficulty which we may find it not easy to explain. Some remarks will be made on the particular passages as we go along. In general it may be observed here, (1) That it is to be presumed that those passages were in the time of Paul applied to the Messiah. He argues from them as though this was commonly understood, and is at no pains to prove it. (2) It is to be pre-

said he at any time, [h]Thou art my Son, this day have I begotten thee?

h Ps.2.7.

And again,[i] I will be to him a Father, and he shall be to me a Son?

i 2 Sa.7.14.

sumed that those to whom he wrote would at once admit this to be so. If this were not so, we cannot suppose that he would regard this mode of reasoning as at all efficacious, or adapted to convince those to whom he addressed the epistle. (3) He did not apprehend that the application which he made of these texts would be called in question by the countrymen of those to whom he wrote. It is to be presumed, therefore, that the application was made in accordance with the received Jewish opinions, and the common interpretation. (4) Paul had been instructed in early life in the doctrines of the Jewish religion, and had been made fully acquainted with the principles of interpretation common among the Jews. It is to be presumed, therefore, that he made these quotations in accordance with the prevalent belief, and with principles which were well understood and admitted. (5) Every age and people have their own modes of reasoning. They may differ from others, and others may regard them as unsound, and yet to that age and people they are satisfactory and conclusive. The ancient philosophers employed modes of reasoning which would not strike us as the most forcible, and which perhaps we should not regard as tenable. So it is with the Chinese, the Hindoos, the Mohammedans now. So it was with the writers of the dark ages who lived under the influence of the scholastic philosophy. They argue from admitted principles in their country and time—just as *we* do in ours. Their reasoning was as satisfactory to them as ours is to us. (6) In a writer of any particular age we are to expect to find the prevailing mode of reasoning, and appeals to the usual arguments on any subject. We are not to look for methods of argument founded on the inductive philosophy in the writings of the schoolmen, or in the writings of Confucius, or in the Vedas and Shasters of the Hindoos. It would be unreasonable to require this. We are to

Vol. IX.

expect that they will be found to reason in accordance with the customs of their time; to appeal to such arguments as were commonly alleged; and if they are reasoning with an adversary, *to make use of the points which he concedes,* and to urge those points as fitted to convince *him.* And this is not necessarily wrong. It may strike him with more force than it does us; it may be that we can see that is not the most solid mode of reasoning, but still it may not be in itself an improper method, and may be of *sufficient* force to carry conviction to a rational mind. That the writers of the New Testament should have used that mode of reasoning sometimes, is no more surprising than that we find writers in China reasoning from acknowledged principles, and in the usual manner there, or than that men in our own land reason on the principles of the inductive philosophy. These remarks may not explain *all* the difficulties in regard to the proof-texts adduced by Paul in this chapter, but they may remove *some* of them, and may so prepare the way that we may be able to dispose of them all as we advance. In the passage which is quoted in this verse, there is not much difficulty in regard to the propriety of its being thus used. The main difficulty lies in the subsequent quotations in the chapter.

[It is, doubtless, of very great importance in conducting an argument to select such proofs as are likely to weigh most with those whom we wish to convince. To argue from *admitted* principles saves both time and labour, and more readily secures success than any other method. To vindicate the apostle, however, on the ground alleged here, under the fifth and sixth particulars, will by many be regarded as scarcely consistent with that respect which the high *authority of inspiration* claims. Ordinary writers *may* employ arguments in themselves inadmissible, but which pass current in their time and country, and therefore serve the *immediate* design equally well with more solid reasoning. The Chinese, Hindoos, &c., may do all this without any reflection on their honesty, and with little perhaps on their wisdom, it being quite un-

reasonable to look for the inductive philosophy among them. But men will expect something more from an inspired apostle. *He* must use no argument merely because it will pass or is commonly employed. He must be wise enough to understand what is the true mode of reasoning on any point, whatever the prevalent fashion may be, and honest enough to employ that mode alone; otherwise the inductive philosophy should enable us now-a-days to detect flaws in the reasoning of inspiration. Admitting, for a moment, that the apostle may possibly have condescended, when reasoning with his Jewish adversary, "to make use of the points which he conceded, and to urge them as fitted to convince *him*," even while he knew that this was not the most solid mode of reasoning, what is to become of those who in course of time acquire sufficient philosophy to discover the real unsoundness of the argument? What are *we* to do? Dismiss the whole, the infidel might sneeringly tell us, as suited to ignorant "Hebrews or Hindoos." Besides, once admitting this principle, there is room for jealousy in regard to the length to which it might be carried. How much of the reasoning in this epistle might be affected by it! The truth is, that the passages quoted must have been *acknowledged by the Jews* properly to belong to the subject or the apostle would not so confidently have adduced them as proof. At the same time, they must in *reality* have belonged to it or he never could have used them at all. "This was not enough," says Owen, "that those with whom he dealt acknowledged these words to be spoken concerning the Messiah, unless they were so really, that so his arguments might proceed *ex veris* as well as *ex concessis*, from what was true as on what was granted." To the same purpose Mr. Scott remarks, "that the compositions of inspired apostles are of equal authority with the passages they adduce; and if they were sufficient proofs to the persons *immediately* concerned, they must be sufficient for all who consider the writer as fully knowing, by divine *inspiration*, both the doctrine of Christ and the true meaning of the Scriptures." It is this fact—the fact of inspiration—that renders such vindication of the apostle's reasoning as that attempted above not only needless but injurious. Besides, when we come to examine the passages in question, the difficulty regarding their application is, after all, not very great, as our author himself, in his able exposition of them, abundantly shows.]

¶ *Said he at any time.* He never used language respecting the angels like that which he employs respecting his Son. He never applied to any one of them the name *Son*. ¶ *Thou art my Son.* The name "*sons* of God," is applied in the Scriptures to saints, and may have been given to the angels. But the argument here is, that the name, "*my Son*" has never been given to any one of them particularly and by eminence. In a large, general sense, they are the sons of God, or the children of God, but the name is given to the Lord Jesus, the Messiah, in a peculiar sense, implying a peculiar relation to him, and a peculiar dominion over all things. This passage is quoted from Psalm ii.—a Psalm which is usually believed to pertain particularly to the Messiah, and one of the few Psalms that have undisputed reference to him. See Notes on Acts iv. 25; xiii. 33. ¶ *This day.* See Notes on Acts xiii. 33, where this passage is applied to the resurrection of Christ from the dead;—proving that the phrase "this day" does not refer to the doctrine of eternal generation, but to the resurrection of the Redeemer—"the FIRST-BEGOTTEN of the dead," Rev. i. 5. Thus Theodoret says of the phrase "this day," "it does not express his eternal generation, but that which is connected with time." The argument of the apostle here does not turn on the *time* when this was said, but on the fact that it *was* said to him and not to any one of the angels, and this argument will have equal force whether the phrase be understood as referring to the fact of his resurrection, or to his previous existence. The structure and scope of the second Psalm refers to his exaltation *after* the kings of the earth set themselves against him, and endeavoured to cast off his government from them. In spite of that, and subsequent to that, he would set his king, which they had rejected, on his holy hill of Zion. See Ps. ii. 2-6. ¶ *Have I begotten thee.* See this place explained in the Notes on Acts xiii. 33. It *must*, from the necessity of the case, be understood figuratively; and must mean, substantially, "I have *constituted*, or *appointed* thee." If it refers to his resurrection, it means that that resurrection was a kind of *begetting* to life, or a beginning of life. See Rev. i. 5. And yet though Paul (Acts xiii. 33)

has applied it to the resurrection of the Redeemer, and though the name "Son of God" is applied to him on account of his resurrection (see Notes on Rom. i. 4), yet I confess that this does not seem to me to come up to *all* that the writer here intended. The phrase, "THE Son of God," I suppose, properly denotes that the Lord Jesus sustained a relation to God, designated by that name, corresponding to the relations which he sustained to man, designated by the name "THE *Son of man.*" The one implied that he had a peculiar relation to God, as the other implied that he had a peculiar relation to man. This is indisputable. But on what particular account the name was given him, or how he was manifested to be the Son of God, has been the great question. Whether the name refers to the mode of his existence before the incarnation, and to his "being begotten from eternity," or to the incarnation and the resurrection, has long been a point on which men have been divided in opinion. The *natural* idea conveyed by the title "THE Son of God" is, that he sustained a relation to God which implied more than was human or angelic; and this is certainly the drift of the argument of the apostle here. I do not see, however, that he refers to the doctrine of "eternal generation," or that he means to teach that. His point is, that God had declared and treated him as *a Son*—as superior to the angels and to men, and that this was shown in what had been said of him in the Old Testament. This would be equally clear, whether there is reference to the doctrine of eternal generation or not. The sense is, "He is more than human. He is more than angelic. He has been addressed and treated as a Son—which none of the angels have. They are regarded simply as ministering spirits. They sustain subordinate stations, and are treated accordingly. He, on the contrary, is the brightness of the divine glory. He is treated and addressed as a Son. In his original existence this was so. In his incarnation this was so. When on earth this was so; and in his resurrection, ascension, and exaltation to the right hand of God, he was treated

in all respects *as a Son*—as superior to all servants, and to all ministering spirits." The exact reference, then, of the phrase "this day have I begotten thee," in the Psalm, is to the act of *constituting* him in a public manner the Son of God—and refers to God's setting him as king on the "holy hill of Zion"—or making him king over the church and the world as Messiah; and this was done, eminently, as Paul shows (Acts xiii.), by the resurrection. It was *based*, however, on what was fit and proper. It was not arbitrary. There was a reason why *he* should thus be exalted rather than a man or an angel; and the reason was, that he was the God incarnate; that he had a nature that qualified him for universal empire; and that he was therefore *appropriately* called "THE Son of God."

[No doctrine is advanced by pressing into its service such texts as sound criticism declares not strictly to belong to it. Yet, without doubt, many advocates of the eternal Sonship have done violence to this passage with the design of upholding their views. That doctrine, however, happily is not dependent on a single text; and ample ground will remain for its friends, even if we admit, as in candour we must, that our author has fully made out his case against this text as a proof one. It seems clear that neither σήμερον nor its corresponding הַיּוֹם can denote eternity; of such signification there is no example. The sense is uniformly confined to limited duration, Ps. xcv. 7; Heb. iv. 7. The order of the second Psalm, too, certainly does prove that the "begetting" took place *after* the opposition which the kings and rulers made to Christ, and not *prior* to it. Accordingly the text is elsewhere quoted in reference to the resurrection of Christ, Rom. i. 4; Acts xiii. 33. Besides, the chief design of the apostle in this place is not so much to show *why* Christ is called the Son of God, as simply to direct attention to the *fact* that he *has* this name, on the possession of which the whole argument is founded. He inherits a name which is *never* given to angels, and that of itself is proof of his superiority to them, whether we suppose the ground of the title to lie in his previous existence, or, with our author, in his incarnate Deity. But on this question, it must be admitted that the passage determines nothing.

All this is substantially allowed by Owen, than whom a more stanch supporter of the doctrine of eternal Sonship cannot be named. "The apostle in this place," says he, "does

not treat of the eternal generation of the Son, but of his exaltation and pre eminence above angels. The word also, היום, constantly in the Scripture denotes some signal time, one day or more. And that expression, 'This day have I begotten thee,' following immediately upon that other typical one, 'I have set my King upon my holy hill of Zion,' seems to be of the same import, and in like manner to be interpreted." On the general doctrine of the Sonship the author has stated his views both here and elsewhere. That it is eternal, or has its origin in the previous existence of Christ, he will not allow. It is given to the second person of the Trinity because he became "God *incarnate*," so that but for the incarnation and the economy of redemption he would not have had this name. But the eternal Sonship of Christ rests on a body of evidence that will not soon or easily be set aside. See that evidence adduced in a Supplementary Note under Rom. i. 4. Meanwhile we would simply ask the reader, if it do not raise our idea of the love of God, in the mission of Christ, to suppose that he held the *dear* relation of Son *previous* to his coming—that, BEING THE SON, he was sent to prove what a sacrifice the FATHER could make in yielding up one so near and so dear. But this astonishing evidence of love, if not destroyed, is greatly weakened, by the supposition that there was no Sonship until the sending of Christ. See also Supplementary Note under ver. 3.]

¶ *And again, I will be to him a Father.* This passage is evidently quoted from 2 Sam. vii. 14. A *sentiment* similar to this is found in Ps. lxxxix. 20–27. As these words were originally spoken, they referred to Solomon. They occur in a promise made to David that he should not fail to have an heir to sit on his throne, or that his throne should be perpetual. The promise was particularly designed to comfort him in view of the fact that God would not suffer *him* to build the temple, because his hands had been defiled with blood. To console him in reference to that, God promises him far greater honour than that would have been. He promises that the house should be built by one of his own family, and that his family and kingdom should be established for ever. That in this series of promises the *Messiah* was included as a descendant of David, was the common opinion of the Jews, of the early Christians, and has been of the great body of interpreters. It was certainly from such passages as this

that the Jews derived the notion which prevailed so universally in the time of the Saviour, that the Messiah was to be the son or the descendant of David. See Mat. xxii. 42–45; ix. 27; xv. 22; xx. 30, 31; Mark x. 47, 48; Luke xviii. 38, 39; Mat. xii. 23; xxi. 9; Jn. vii. 42; Rom. i. 3; Rev. v. 5; xxii. 16. That opinion was universal. No one doubted it; and it must have been common for the Jews to apply such texts as this to the Messiah. Paul would not have done it in this instance unless it had been usual. Nor was it improper. If the Messiah was to be a descendant of David, then it was natural to apply these promises in regard to his posterity in an eminent and peculiar sense to the Messiah. They were a part of the promises which included him, and which terminated in him. The promise, therefore, which is here made is, that God would be to him, in a peculiar sense, a Father, and he should be a Son. It did not, as I suppose, pertain originally in an exclusive sense to the Messiah, but it *included* him as a descendant of David. To him it would be applicable in an eminent degree; and if applicable to him *at all*, it proved all that the passage here is adduced to prove—that the name *Son* is given to the Messiah—a *name* not given to angels. That is the point on which the argument here turns. What is *implied* in the bestowment of that name is another point on which the apostle discourses in the other parts of the argument. I have no doubt, therefore, that while these words originally might have been applicable to Solomon, or to any of the other descendants of David who succeeded him on the throne, yet they at last terminated, and were designed to terminate, in the Messiah—to whom pre-eminently God would be a Father. Comp. Introduction to Isaiah, § 7, iii. (3), and Notes on Isa. vii. 16.

[The promise, doubtless, had a special reference to the Messiah. Nay, we may safely assert that the *chief* reference was to him, for in the case of typical persons and things that which they adumbrate is principally to be regarded. So here, though the original application of the passage be to Solomon, the type of Christ, yet it finds its great and ultimate application in

the person of the glorious Antitype. However strange this double application may seem to us, it is quite in accordance with the whole system of things under the Jewish dispensation. Almost everything connected with it was constructed on this typical principle. This the apostles understood so well that they were never stumbled by it, and what is remarkable, and of the last importance on this subject, *never for a moment drawn from the ultimate and chief design of a promise or prophecy* by its primary reference to the type. They saw *Christ* in it, and made the application *solely* to him, passing over entirely the literal sense, and seizing at once the ultimate and superior import. The very passage in question (2 Sam. vii. 11–17) is thus *directly* applied not only here, but throughout the New Testament, Luke i. 32, 33; Acts ii. 30, 37; xiii. 22, 23. Now certainly the apostles are the best judges in matters of this kind. Their authority in regard to the sense of passages quoted by them from the Old Testament is just as great as in the case of the original matter of the New Testament. That Christ was indeed principally intended is further evident from the fact, that *when the kingdom had passed from the house of David,* succeeding prophets repeat the promise in 2 Sam. vii. as yet to be fulfilled. See Jer. xxxiii. 14, 26. Now, connecting this fact with the direct assertion of the writer of the New Testament above referred to, every doubt must be removed.

It will be alleged, however, that while the direct application to the Messiah, of this and other prophecies, is obvious and authoritative, it is yet desirable—and they who deny inspiration will insist on it as essential—to prove that there is at least nothing in the original places whence the citations are made inconsistent with such application. Such proof seems to be especially requisite here, for immediately after the words, " I will be his Father, and he shall be my Son," there follows, " If he commit iniquity, I will chasten him with the rod of men, and with the stripes of the children of men," 2 Sam. vii. 14, which last sentence, it is affirmed, cannot in any sense be applicable to the Messiah. It has been said in reply, that though such language cannot be applied to Christ *personally*, it may yet refer to him as the *covenant head* of his people. Though there be no iniquity in him, " such failings and transgressions as disannul not the covenant, often fall out on their part for whom he undertaketh therein." In accordance with this view it has been observed by Mr. Pierce, and others after him, that the Hebrew relative אשר should be translated *whosoever,* in which case the sense is, Whosoever of *his children, i.e.* the Messiah's, shall commit iniquity, &c. And to this effect, indeed, is the alteration of the words in the 89th Psalm, where the original covenant is repeated, " If HIS CHILDREN forsake my law—then will I visit their transgression with the rod, and their iniquity with stripes."

Perhaps. however, the better solution of the difficulty is that which at once admits that the words in question cannot apply to the Antitype, but to the type only. It is a mistake to suppose that in a typical passage everything must necessarily have its antitypical reference. The reader will find some excellent and apposite remarks on this subject in Dr. Owen's commentary on the place. " No type," says that judicious writer, " was in all things a type of Christ, but only in that particular wherein he was designed of God so to be. David was a type of Christ, but not in all things that he was and did. In his conquests of the enemies of the church, in his throne and kingdom, he was so; but in his private actions, whether as a man, or as a king, or captain, he was not so. Nay, not all things spoken of him that was a type, even in those respects wherein he was a type, are spoken of him as a type, or have any respect unto the thing signified, but some of them may belong to him in his personal capacity only. And the reason is, that he who was a type by God's institution might morally fail in the performance of his duty, even then and in those things wherein he was a type. And this wholly removes the difficulty connected with the words 'If he sin against me,' for those words relating to the moral duty of Solomon in that wherein he was a type of Christ, namely, the rule and administration of his kingdom, may not at all belong to Christ, who was prefigured by God's institution of things, and not in any moral deportment in the observance of them." These observations seem to contain the true principles of explication in this and similar cases. The solution of Professor Stuart is not materially different. " Did not God," says he, " engage that David should have successors on his *earthly* throne, and also that he *should* have a son who would sit on a *spiritual* throne, and have a kingdom of which David's own was but a mere type? Admitting this, our difficulty is diminished if not removed. *The iniquity committed is predicated of that part of David's seed who might commit it, i.e.* his successors on the *national* throne, while the more exalted condition predicated of his successor belongs to Him to whom was given a *kingdom over all.*"]

6. *And again.* Margin, *When he bringeth in again.* The proper construction of this sentence probably is, " But when, moreover, he brings in," &c. The word "*again*" refers not to the fact that the Son of God is brought *again* into the world, implying that he

6 ¹ And again, when he bringeth in the first-begotten into the world,

_{1 or, When he bringeth again.}

he saith, ᵏ And let all the angels of God worship him.

_{k Ps.97.7.}

had been introduced before; but it refers to the course of the apostle's argument, or to the declaration which is made about the Messiah in another place. "The name *Son* is not only given to him as above, but *also* in another place, or on another occasion, when he brings in the first-begotten into the world." ¶ *When he bringeth in.* When he introduces. So far as the *language* here is concerned this might refer to the *birth* of the Messiah, but it is evident from the whole connection that the writer means to refer to something that is *said* in the Old Testament. This is plain because the passage occurs among quotations designed to prove a specific point—that the Son of God, the Author of the Christian system, was superior to the angels. A *declaration of the writer* here, however true and solemn, would not have answered the purpose. A *proof-text* was wanting—a text which would be admitted by those to whom he wrote to bear on the point under consideration. The meaning then is, "that on another occasion different from those to which he had referred, God, when speaking of the Messiah, or when introducing him to mankind, had used language showing that he was superior to the angels." The meaning of the phrase, "when he bringeth in," therefore, I take to be, when he *introduces* him to men; when he makes him known to the world—to wit, by the declaration which he proceeds immediately to quote. ¶ *The first-begotten.* Christ is called the "*first-begotten*," with reference to his resurrection from the dead, in Rev. i. 5, and Col. i. 18. It is probable here, however, that the word is used, like the word *first-born*, or *first-begotten* among the Hebrews, by way of eminence. As the first-born was the principal heir, and had peculiar privileges, so the Lord Jesus Christ sustains a similar rank in the universe of which God is the Head and Father. See Notes on Jn. i. 14, where the word "only begotten" is used to denote the dignity

and honour of the Lord Jesus. ¶ *Into the world.* When he introduces him to mankind, or declares what he is to be. ¶ *He saith, And let all the angels of God worship him.* Much difficulty has been experienced in regard to this quotation, for it cannot be denied that it is intended to be a quotation. In the Septuagint these very words occur in Deut. xxxii. 43, where they are inserted at the close of the Song of Moses. But they are not in the Hebrew, nor are they in all the copies of the Septuagint. The Hebrew is, "Rejoice, O ye nations, with his people; for he will avenge the blood of his servants, and will render vengeance to his adversaries." The Septuagint is, "Rejoice, ye heavens, with him; and let all the angels of God worship him. Let the nations rejoice with his people, and let all the sons of God be strong in him, for he has avenged the blood of his sons." But there are objections to our supposing that the apostle had this place in his view, which seem to me to settle the matter. (1) One is, that the passage is not in the Hebrew; and it seems hardly credible that in writing to Hebrews, and to those who resided in the very country where the Hebrew Scriptures were constantly used, he should adduce as a proof-text on an important doctrine what was not in their Scriptures. (2) A second is, that it is omitted in all the ancient versions except the Septuagint. (3) A third is, that it is impossible to believe that the passage in question in Deuteronomy had any reference to the Messiah. It does not relate to his "introduction" to the world. It would not occur to any reader to suppose that it had any such reference. The context celebrates the victory over the enemies of Israel which God would achieve. After saying that "his arrows would be drunk with blood, and that his sword would devour flesh with the blood of the slain and of captives, from the time when he began to take vengeance on an enemy," the Septuagint (not the Hebrew) immediately calls on "the heavens to

rejoice at the same time with him, and all the angels of God to worship him." That is, "Let the inhabitants of the heavenly world rejoice in the victory of God over the enemies of his people, and let them pay their adoration to him." But the Messiah does not appear to be alluded to anywhere in the context; much less described as "*introduced into the world.*" There is, moreover, not the slightest evidence that the passage was ever supposed by the Jews to have any such reference; and though it might be said that the apostle merely quoted *language* that expressed his meaning—as we often do when we are familiar with any well-known phrase that will exactly suit our purpose and convey our idea —yet it should be remarked that this is not the way in which this passage is quoted. It is *a proof-text*, and Paul evidently meant to be understood as saying that that passage had a *fair* reference to the Messiah. It is evident, moreover, that it would be admitted to have such a reference by those to whom he wrote. It is morally certain, therefore, that this was *not* the passage which the writer intended to quote. The probability is, that he here referred to Psalm xcvii. 7 (in the Sept. Ps. xcvi. 7). In that place the Hebrew is, "Worship him, all *ye* gods"—כָּל־אֱלֹהִים—*all ye Elohim.* In the Septuagint it is, "Let all his angels worship him;" where the translation is literal, except that the word *God*—"angels *of God*" —is used by the apostle instead of *his* —"all *his* angels"—as it is in the Septuagint. The word "gods"—*Elohim*—is rendered by the word *angels* —but the word may have that sense. Thus it is rendered by the LXX. in Job xx. 15; and in Ps. viii. 6; cxxxvii. 1. It is well known that the word *Elohim* may denote kings and magistrates, because of their rank and dignity; and is there anything improbable in the supposition that, for a similar reason, it may be given also to angels? The fair interpretation of the passage then would be, to refer it to *angelic beings*—and the command in Ps. xcvii. is for them to do homage to the being there referred to. The only question then is, whether the Psalm can be regarded properly as having any reference to the Messiah. Did the apostle fairly and properly use this language as referring to him? On this we may remark, (1) That the *fact* that he uses it thus may be regarded as proof that it would be admitted to be proper by the Jews in his time, and renders it probable that it was in fact so used. (2) Two Jewish Rabbins of distinction —Raschi and Kimchi—affirm that all the Psalms from xciii. to ci. are to be regarded as referring to the Messiah. Such was, and is, the opinion of the Jews. (3) There is nothing *in* the Psalm which forbids such a reference, or which can be shown to be inconsistent with it. Indeed the whole Psalm *might* be taken as beautifully descriptive of the "*introduction*"of the Son of God into the world, or as a sublime and glorious description of his advent. Thus in ver. 1, the earth is called on to rejoice that the Lord reigns. In ver. 2–5, he is introduced or described as coming in the most magnificent manner—clouds and darkness attend him; a fire goes before him; the lightnings play; the hills melt like wax —a sublime description of his coming, with appropriate symbols, to reign, or to judge the world. In ver. 6, it is said that all people shall see his glory; in ver. 7, that all who worship graven images shall be confounded, and *all the angels are required to do him homage;* and in ver. 8–12, the effect of his advent is described as filling Zion with rejoicing, and the hearts of the people of God with gladness. It cannot be *proved*, therefore, that this Psalm had no reference to the Messiah; but the presumption is that it had, and that the apostle has quoted it not only as it was *usually* regarded in his time, but as it was designed by the Holy Ghost. If so, then it *proves*, what the writer intended, that the Son of God should be adored by the angels; and of course that he was superior to them. It proves also more. Whom would God require the angels to adore? A creature? A man? A fellow-angel? To ask these questions is to answer

7 And ²of the angels he saith, | and his ministers a flame of fire.
Who¹ maketh his angels spirits, | 8 But unto the Son *he saith,*

² *unto.*   *l* Ps.104.4.

Psalms cannot mean "who makes the
them. He could require them to wor-
winds his messengers," but that the
ship none but God, and the passage
intention of the Psalmist is to describe
proves that the Son of God is divine.
the *invisible* as well as the *visible*
7. *And of the angels he saith, Who*
majesty of God, and that he refers to
maketh his angels spirits. He gives
the angels as a part of the retinue
to them an inferior name, and assigns
which goes to make up his glory.
to them a more humble office. They
This does not seem to me to be per-
are mere ministers, and have not
fectly certain; but still it cannot be
ascribed to them the name of *Son.*
demonstrated that Paul has made an
They have a name which implies a
improper use of the passage. It is to
more humble rank and office—the
be presumed that *he,* who had been
name "spirit," and the appellation
trained in the knowledge of the He-
"a flame of fire." They obey his
brew language, would have had a bet-
will as the winds and the lightnings
ter opportunity of knowing its fair
do. The *object* of the apostle in this
construction than we can; and it is
passage is to show that the angels
morally certain that he would employ
serve God in a ministerial capacity—
the passage *in an argument* as it was
as the winds do; while the Son is
commonly understood by those to
Lord of all. The one serves him pas-
whom he wrote—that is, to those who
sively, as being wholly under his con-
were familiar with the Hebrew lan-
trol; the other acts as a Sovereign, or
guage and literature. If he has so
as Lord over all, and is addressed and
used the passage; if he has—as no
regarded as the equal with God. This
one can disprove—put the fair con-
quotation is made from Ps. civ. 4.
struction on it, then it is just in point.
The passage *might* be translated,
It proves that the angels are the *at-*
"Who maketh his angels *winds,* and
tendant servants of God; employed
his ministers a flame of fire;" that is,
to grace his train, to do his will, to
"Who makes his angels *like* the winds,
accompany him as the clouds and
or as swift as the winds, and his minis-
winds and lightnings do, and to oc-
ters as rapid, as terrible, and as re-
cupy a subordinate rank in his crea-
sistless as the lightning." So Dod-
tion. ¶ *Flame of fire.* This probably
dridge renders it; and so did the late
refers to lightning—which is often the
Rev. Dr. J. P. Wilson (*MS. Notes*).
meaning of the phrase. The word
The passage in the Psalm is suscepti-
"*ministers*" here means the same as
ble, I think, of another interpretation,
angels, and the sense of the whole is,
and *might* be regarded as meaning,
that the attending retinue of God,
"Who makes the winds his messengers,
when he manifests himself with great
and the flaming fire his ministers;"
power and glory, is like the winds and
and perhaps this is the sense which
the lightning. His angels are like
would most naturally occur to a reader
them. They are prompt to do his
of the Hebrew. The Hebrew, how-
will—rapid, quick, obedient in his
ever, will admit of the construction
service; they are in all respects sub-
here put upon it, and it cannot be
ordinate to him, and occupy, as the
proved that it was not the original in-
winds and the lightnings do, the place
tention of the passage to show that the
of servants. They are not addressed
angels were the mere servants of God,
in language like that which is applied
rapid, quick, and prompt to do his will
to the Son of God, and they must all
—like the winds. The Chaldee Pa-
be far inferior to him.
raphrase renders the passage in the
8. *But unto the Son* he saith. In
Psalm, "Who makes his messengers
Psalm xlv. 6, 7. The fact that the
swift as the wind; his ministers strong
writer of this epistle makes this ap-
like a flame of fire." Prof. Stuart
plication of the Psalm to the Messiah,
maintains that the passage in the
proves that it was so applied in his

Thy^m throne, O God, *is* for ever and ever: a sceptre of ³righteous-

m Ps.45.6,7.   *3 rightness, or straitness.*

ness *is* the sceptre of thy kingdom:

---

time, or that it would be readily admitted to be applicable to him. It has been generally admitted, by both Jewish and Christian interpreters, to have such a reference. Even those who have doubted its primary applicability to the Messiah, have regarded it as referring to him in a secondary sense. Many have supposed that it referred to Solomon in the primary sense, and that it has a secondary reference to the Messiah. To me it seems most probable that it had an original and exclusive reference to the Messiah. It is to be remembered that the hope of the Messiah was the peculiar hope of the Jewish people. The coming of the future king, so early promised, was the great event to which they all looked forward with the deepest interest. That hope inspired their prophets and their bards, and cheered the hearts of the nation in the time of despondency. The Messiah, if I may so express it, was the *hero* of the Old Testament—more so than Achilles is of the *Iliad*, and Æneas of the *Æneid*. The sacred poets were accustomed to employ all their most magnificent imagery in describing him, and to present him in every form that was beautiful in their conception, and that would be gratifying to the pride and hopes of the nation. Everything that is gorgeous and splendid in description is lavished on him, and they were never under any apprehension of attributing to him too great magnificence in his reign; too great beauty of personal character; or too great an extent of dominion. That which would be regarded by them as a magnificent description of a monarch, they freely applied to him; and this is evidently the case in this Psalm. That the description may have been in part derived from the view of Solomon in the magnificence of his court, is possible, but no more probable than that it was derived from the general view of the splendour of any Oriental

monarch, or than that it might have been the description of a monarch which was the pure creation of inspired poetry. Indeed, I see not why this Psalm should ever have been supposed to be applicable to Solomon. His *name* is not mentioned. It has no *peculiar* applicability to him. There is nothing that would apply to him which would not also apply to many an Oriental prince. There are some things in it which are much less applicable to him than to many others. The king here described is *a conqueror.* He "girds his sword on his thigh," and "his arrows are sharp in the hearts of his foes," and "the people are subdued under him." This was not true of Solomon. His was a reign of peace and tranquillity, nor was he ever distinguished for war. On the whole, it seems clear to me, that this Psalm was designed to be a beautiful poetic description of the Messiah *as king.* The images are drawn from the usual characteristics of an Oriental prince, and there are many things in the poem—as there are in parables—for the sake of *keeping*, or *verisimilitude*, and which are not, in the interpretation, to be *cut to the quick.* The writer imagined to himself a magnificent and beautiful prince;—a prince riding prosperously in his conquests; swaying a permanent and wide dominion; clothed in rich and splendid vestments; eminently upright and pure; and scattering blessings everywhere—and that prince was the Messiah. The Psalm, therefore, I regard as relating originally and exclusively to Christ; and though in the interpretation, the *circumstances* should not be unduly pressed, nor an attempt be made to *spiritualize* them, yet the *whole* is a glowing and most beautiful description of Christ as a King. The same principles of interpretation should be applied to it which are applied to parables, and the same allowance should be made for the introduction of circumstances for the sake of *keeping*, or for finishing the story. If this be

the correct view, then Paul has quoted the Psalm in conformity exactly with its original intention, as he undoubtedly quoted it as it was understood in his time. ¶ *Thy throne.* A throne is the seat on which a monarch sits, and is here the symbol of dominion, because kings when acting as rulers sit on thrones. Thus a throne becomes the emblem of authority or empire. Here it means, that his *rule* or *dominion* would be perpetual—*"for ever and ever"*—which assuredly could not be applied to Solomon. ¶ *O God.* This certainly could not be applied to Solomon; but applied to the Messiah it proves what the apostle is aiming to prove—that he is above the angels. The argument is, that a name is given to *him* which is never given to *them.* They are not called *God* in any strict and proper sense. The *argument* here requires us to understand this word as used in a sense more exalted than any name which is ever given to angels, and though it may be maintained that the name here used, אֱלֹהִים—*Elohim*, is given to magistrates or to angels, yet *here* the connection requires us to understand it as used in a sense *superior* to what it ever is when applied to an angel—or of course to any creature, since it was the express design of the argument to prove that the Messiah was superior to the angels. The word *God* should be taken in its natural and obvious sense, unless there is some necessary reason for limiting it. If applied to magistrates (Ps. lxxxii. 6), it *must* be so limited. If applied to the Messiah, there is no such necessity (Jn. i. 1; Isa. ix. 6; 1 Jn. v. 20; Phil. ii. 6), and it should be taken in its natural and proper sense. The *form* here—ὁ Θεὸς—is in the vocative case and not the nominative. It is the usual form of the vocative in the Septuagint, and nearly the only form of it (Stuart). This, then, is a direct address to the Messiah, calling him God; and I see not why it is not to be used in the usual and proper sense of the word. Unitarians propose to translate this, "God is thy throne;" but how can God be *a throne*

of a creature? What is the meaning of such an expression? And what must be the nature of that cause which renders such an argument necessary? —This refers, as it seems to me, to the Messiah *as king.* It does not relate to his mode of existence *before* the incarnation, but to him as the magnificent monarch of his people. Still, the ground or reason why this name is given to him is that he is *divine.* It is language which properly expresses his nature. He must have a divine nature, or such language would be improper. I regard this passage, therefore, as full proof that the Lord Jesus is divine; nor is it possible to evade this conclusion by any fair interpretation of it. It cannot be wrong, then, to address Christ as God; nor, addressing him as such, can it be wrong to regard him as divine. ¶ *Is for ever and ever.* This could not in any proper sense apply to Solomon. As applied to the Messiah, it means that his essential kingdom will be perpetual, Luke i. 33. As Mediator his kingdom will be given up to the Father, or to God without reference to a mediatorial work (1 Cor. xv. 24–28—see Notes on these verses), but his reign over his people will be perpetual. There never will come a time when his people will not obey and serve him, though the peculiar form of his kingdom, as connected with the work of *mediation,* will be changed. The form of the organized church, for example, will be changed, for there shall be no necessity for it in heaven, but the essential dominion and power of the Son of God will not cease. He will have the same dominion which he had before he entered on the work of mediation; and that will be eternal. It is also true that, compared with earthly monarchs, his kingdom will be perpetual. They soon die. Dynasties pass away. But *his* empire extends from age to age, and is properly a *perpetual* dominion. The fair and obvious interpretation of this passage would satisfy me, were there nothing else, that this Psalm had no reference to Solomon, but was designed originally as a description of the Messiah as

9 Thou hast loved righteousness, and hated iniquity; therefore God,

even thy God, hath anointed thee with the oil of gladness above thy fellows.

---

the expected King and Prince of his people. ¶ *A sceptre of righteousness.* That is, a right or just sceptre. The phrase is a Hebraism. The former expression described the *perpetuity* of his kingdom; this describes its *equable nature.* It would be just and equal. See Notes on Isa. xi. 5. A *sceptre* is a staff or wand usually made of wood, five or six feet long, and commonly overlaid with gold, or ornamented with golden rings. Sometimes, however, the sceptre was made of ivory, or wholly of gold. It was borne in the hands of kings as an emblem of authority and power. Probably it had its origin in the staff or crook of the shepherd—as kings were at first regarded as the *shepherds* of their people. Thus Agamemnon is commonly called by Homer the *shepherd* of the people. The *sceptre* thus becomes the emblem of kingly office and power—as when we speak of *swaying a sceptre;* — and the idea here is, that the Messiah would be a *king,* and that the authority which he would wield would be equitable and just. He would not be governed, as monarchs often are, by caprice, or by the wishes of courtiers and flatterers; he would not be controlled by mere *will* and the love of arbitrary power; but the execution of his laws would be in accordance with the principles of equity and justice.—How well this accords with the character of the Lord Jesus we need not pause to show. Comp. Notes on Isa. xi. 2–5.

9. *Thou hast loved righteousness.* Thou hast been obedient to the law of God, or holy and upright. Nothing can be more truly adapted to express the character of anyone than this is to describe the Lord Jesus, who was "holy, harmless, undefiled," who "did no sin, and in whose mouth no guile was found;" but it is with difficulty that this can be applied to Solomon. Assuredly, for a considerable part of his life, this declaration could not be appropriate to him; and it seems to me that it is not to be regarded as

descriptive of him at all. It is language prompted by the warm and pious imagination of the Psalmist describing the future Messiah—and, as applied to him, is true to the letter. ¶ *Therefore God, even* thy *God.* The word *even* inserted here by the translators, weakens the force of the expression. This *might* be translated, "O God, thy God hath anointed thee." So it is rendered by Doddridge, Clarke, Stuart, and others. The Greek will bear this construction, as well the Hebrew in Ps. xlv. 7. In the *margin* in the Psalm it is rendered "O God." This is the most natural construction, as it accords with what is just said before. "Thy throne, O God, is for ever. Thou art just and holy, therefore, O God, thy God hath anointed thee," &c. It is not material, however, which construction is adopted. ¶ *Hath anointed thee.* Anciently kings and priests were consecrated to their office by pouring oil on their heads. See Lev. viii. 12; Num. iii. 3; 1 Sam. x. 1; 2 Sam. ii. 7; Ps. ii. 6; Isa. lxi. 1; Acts iv. 27; x. 38; comp. Notes on Mat. i. 1. The expression *"to anoint,"* therefore, comes to mean to consecrate to office, or to set apart to some public work. This is evidently the meaning in the Psalm, where the whole language refers to the appointment of the personage there referred to to the kingly office. ¶ *The oil of gladness.* This probably means the perfumed oil that was poured on the head, attended with expressions of joy and rejoicing. The inauguration of the Messiah as king would be an occasion of rejoicing and triumph. Thousands would exult at it—as in the coronation of a king; and thousands would be made glad by such a consecration to the office of Messiah. ¶ *Above thy fellows.* Above thine associates; that is, above all who sustain the kingly office. He would be more exalted than all other kings. Doddridge supposes that it refers to angels, who might have been

10 And, *Thou, Lord, in the beginning hast laid the foundation of

n Ps. 102. 25.

the earth; and the heavens are the works of thine hands;

---

associated with the Messiah in the government of the world. But the more natural construction is to suppose that it refers to kings, and to mean that he was the most exalted of all.

10. *And.* That is, "To add another instance;" or, "to the Son he saith in another place, or in the following language." This is connected with ver. 8. "Unto the Son he saith (ver. 8), Thy throne, &c.—*and* (ver. 10) he *also* saith, Thou Lord," &c. That this is the meaning is apparent, because (1) the *object* of the whole quotation is to show the exalted character of the Son of God, and (2) an address here to JEHOVAH would be wholly irrelevant. Why, in the argument designed to prove that the Son of God is superior to the angels, should the writer break out in an address to JEHOVAH in view of the fact that he had laid the foundations of the world, and that he himself would continue to live when the heavens should be rolled up and pass away? Such is not the manner of Paul or of any other good writer, and it is clear that the writer here designed to adduce this as applicable to the Messiah. Whatever difficulties there may be about the principles on which it is done, and the reason why *this* passage was selected for the purpose, there can be no doubt about the *design* of the writer. He *meant* to be understood as applying it to the Messiah beyond all question, or the quotation is wholly irrelevant, and it is inconceivable why it should have been made. ¶ *Thou, Lord.* This is taken from Ps. cii. 25-27. The quotation is made from the Septuagint with only a slight variation, and is an accurate translation of the Hebrew. In the Psalm, there can be no doubt that JEHOVAH is intended. This is apparent on the face of the Psalm, and particularly because the *name* JEHOVAH is introduced in ver. 1, 12, and because he is addressed as the Creator of all things, and as immutable. No one, on reading the Psalm, ever would doubt that it refers to God, and if the apostle meant to apply it to the Lord Jesus, it proves most conclusively that he is divine. In regard to the difficult inquiry *why* he applied this to the Messiah, or on what principle such an application can be vindicated, we may perhaps throw some light by the following remarks. It must be admitted, indeed, that probably few persons, if any, on reading the *Psalm*, would suppose that it referred to the Messiah; but (1) the *fact* that the apostle thus employs it, proves that it was understood in his time to have such a reference, or at least that those to whom he wrote would admit that it had such a reference. On no other principle would he have used it in an argument. This is at least of some consequence in showing what the prevailing interpretation was. (2) It cannot be demonstrated that it had no such reference, for such was the habit of the sacred writers in making the future Messiah the theme of their poetry, that no one can *prove* that the writer of this Psalm did not design that the Messiah should be the subject of his praise. (3) There is nothing in the Psalm which *may* not be applied to the Messiah; but there is much in it that is peculiarly applicable to him. Suppose, for example, that the Psalmist (ver. 1-11), in his complaints, represents the people of God before the Redeemer appeared—as lowly, sad, dejected, and afflicted—speaking of himself as *one* of them, and as a *fair representative* of that people, the remainder of the Psalm will well agree with the promised redemption. Thus having described the sadness and sorrow of the people of God, he speaks of the fact that God would arise and have mercy upon Zion (ver. 13, 14), that the heathen would fear the name of the Lord, and all the kings of the earth would see his glory (ver. 15), and that when the Lord should build up Zion, he would appear in his glory,

11 They shall perish, but thou remainest: and they all shall wax old as doth a garment;

---

ver. 16. To whom else could this be so well applied as to the Messiah? To what time so well as to his time? Thus, too, in ver. 20, it is said that the Lord would look down from heaven "to hear the groaning of the prisoner, and to loose them that are appointed to death"—language remarkably resembling that used by Isaiah, ch. lxi. 1, which the Saviour applies to himself, in Luke iv. 17-21. The passage, then, quoted by the apostle (ver. 25-27 of the Psalm) is designed to denote the *immutability* of the Messiah, and the fact that in him all the interests of the church are safe. He will not change. He has formed all things, and he will remain the same. His kingdom will be permanent amidst all the changes occurring on earth, and his people have no cause of apprehension or alarm, ver. 28. (4) Paul applies this language to the Messiah in accordance with the doctrine which he had stated (ver. 2), that it was by him that God "made the worlds." Having stated that, he seems to have felt that it was not improper to apply to him any of the passages occurring in the Old Testament which speak of the work of creation. The argument is this, "Christ was in fact the creator of all things. But to the Creator there is applied language in the Scriptures which shows that he is far exalted above the angels. He will remain the same, while the heavens and the earth fade away. His years are enduring and eternal. *Such* a being MUST be superior to the angels; such a being must be divine." The words "Thou, Lord"—σὺ Κύριε—are not in the Hebrew of the Psalm, though they are in the Septuagint. In the Hebrew, in the Psalm (ver. 24), it is an address to God—"I said, O my God"—אֵלִי— but there can be no doubt that the Psalmist meant to address JEHOVAH, and that the word *God* is used in its proper sense, denoting divinity. See ver. 1, 12, of the Psalm. ¶ *In the beginning.* See Gen. i. 1. When the world was made. Comp. Notes on Jn. i. 1, where the same phrase is applied to the Messiah—"In the beginning was the Word." ¶ *Hast laid the foundation of the earth.* Hast made the earth. This language is such as is common in the Scriptures, where the earth is represented as laid on a foundation, or as supported as a building is. It is figurative language, derived from the act of rearing an edifice. The meaning here is, that the Son of God was the *original* creator or founder of the universe. He did not merely arrange it out of pre-existing materials, but he brought it into existence by his own word and power. ¶ *And the heavens are the works of thine hands.* This *must* demonstrate that the Lord Jesus demonstrate that the Lord Jesus divine. He that made the heavens must be God. No creature could perform a work like that; nor can we conceive that power to create the vast array of distant worlds could possibly be delegated. If that power could be delegated, there is not an attribute of Deity which may not be, and thus all our notions of what constitutes divinity would be utterly confounded. The word "heavens" here, must mean all parts of the universe except the earth. See Gen. i. 1. The word *hands* is used, because it is by the hands that we usually perform any work.

11. *They shall perish.* That is, the heavens and the earth. They will pass away; or they will be destroyed. Probably no more is meant by the phrase here, than that important changes will take place in them, or that they will change their form. Still it is not possible to foresee what revolutions may yet take place in the heavenly bodies, or to say that the present universe may not at some period be destroyed, and be succeeded by another creation still more magnificent. He that created the universe by a word, can destroy it by the same word; and he that formed the present frame of nature can cause it to be succeeded by another not less wonderful and glorious. The Scriptures seem to hold out the idea that the present

12 And as a vesture shalt thou fold them up, and they shall be changed: but thou art the same, and thy years shall not fail.

13 But to which of the angels said he at any time, *o* Sit on my right hand, until I make thine enemies thy footstool?

o Ps.110.1.

---

frame of the universe will be destroyed. See 2 Pet. iii. 10–13; Mat. xxiv. 35. ¶ *But thou remainest.* Thou shalt not die or cease to be. What a sublime thought! The idea is, that though the heavens and earth should suddenly disappear, or though they should gradually wear out and become extinct, yet there is one infinite Being who remains unaffected and unchanged. Nothing can reach or disturb him. All these changes will take place under his direction, and by his command. See Rev. xx. 11. Let us not be alarmed, then, at any revolution or change which may occur. Let us not fear though we should see the heavens rolled up as a scroll, and the stars falling from their places. God, the Creator and Redeemer, presides over all. He is unchanged. He ever lives; and though the universe should pass away, it will be only at his bidding, and under his direction. ¶ *And they all shall wax old.* Shall *grow* or become old. The word *wax* is an old Saxon word, meaning to grow, to increase, or to become. The heavens here are compared with a garment, meaning that as that grows old and decays, so it will be with the heavens and the earth. The language is evidently figurative; and yet who can tell how much literal truth there may be couched under it? Is it absurd to suppose that that sun, which daily sends forth so many countless millions of beams of light over the universe, may in a course of ages become diminished in its splendour, and shine with feeble lustre? Can there be constant exhaustion, a constant burning like that, and yet no tendency to decay at some far distant period? Not unless the material for its splendour shall be supplied from the boundless resources of the Great Source of Light—God; and when he shall choose to withhold it, even that glorious sun must be dimmed of its splendour, and shine with enfeebled beams, or go out altogether.

12. *And as a vesture.* A garment; —literally something thrown around —περιβόλαιον—and denoting properly the outer garment, the cloak or mantle. See Notes on Mat. v. 40. ¶ *Shalt thou fold them up.* That is, the heavens. They are represented in the Scriptures as *an expanse*, or something spread out (Heb. in Gen. i. 7); as a *curtain*, or *tent* (Isa. xl. 22); and as a *scroll* that might be spread out or rolled up like a book or volume, Isa. xxxiv. 4; Rev. vi. 14. Here they are represented as a garment or mantle that might be folded up—language borrowed from folding up and laying aside garments that are no longer fit for use. ¶ *And they shall be changed.* That is, they will be exchanged for others, or will give place to the new heavens and the new earth, 2 Pet. iii. 13. The meaning is, that the present form of the heavens and the earth is not to be permanent, but is to be succeeded by others, or to pass away, but that the Creator is to remain the same. ¶ *Thou art the same.* Thou wilt not change. ¶ *And thy years shall not fail.* Thou wilt exist for ever unchanged. What could more clearly prove that he of whom this is spoken is immutable? Yet it is indubitably spoken of the Messiah, and must demonstrate that he is divine. These attributes cannot be conferred on a creature; and nothing can be clearer than that he who penned the epistle believed that the Son of God was divine.

13. *But to which of the angels.* The apostle adduces one other proof of the exaltation of the Son of God above the angels. He asks where there is an instance in which God has addressed any one of the angels, and asked him to sit at his right hand until he should subdue his enemies under him? Yet that high honour had been conferred on the Son

14 Are they not all *p* ministering spirits, *q* sent forth to minister for them who shall be *r* heirs of salvation?

p Ps.103.21; Da.7.10.　　*q* Ge.19.15,16; Ps.34.7.

r Ro.8.17.

of God; and he was therefore far exalted above them. ¶ *Sit on my right hand.* See Notes on ver. 3. This passage is taken from Ps. cx. 1—a Psalm that is repeatedly quoted in this epistle as referring to the Messiah, and this very passage is applied by the Saviour to himself, in Mat. xxii. 43, 44, and by Peter it is applied to him in Acts ii. 34, 35. There can be no doubt, therefore, of its applicability to the Messiah. ¶ *Until I make thine enemies thy footstool.* Until I reduce them to entire subjection. A footstool is what is placed under the feet when we sit on a chair, and the phrase here means that an enemy is entirely subdued. Comp. Notes on 1 Cor. xv. 25. The phrase *to make an enemy a footstool,* is borrowed from the custom of ancient warriors, who stood on the necks of vanquished kings on the occasion of celebrating a triumph over them as a token of their complete prostration and subjection. See Notes on Is. x. 6. The enemies here referred to are the foes of God and of his religion, and the meaning is, that the Messiah is to be exalted *until* all those foes are subdued. Then he will give up the kingdom to the Father. See Notes on 1 Cor. xv. 24–28. The exaltation of the Redeemer, to which the apostle refers here, is to the *mediatorial* throne. In this he is exalted far above the angels. His foes are to be subdued to him, but angels are to be employed as mere instruments in that great work.

14. *Are they not all.* There is not one of them that is elevated to the high rank of the Redeemer. Even the most exalted angel is employed in the comparatively humble office of a ministering spirit appointed to assist the heirs of salvation. ¶ *Ministering spirits.* A *ministering spirit* is one that is employed to execute the will of God. The proper meaning of the word here—λειτουργικὰ (whence our word *liturgy*)—is, *pertaining to public service,* or *the service of the people*

(λαός); and is applied particularly to those who were engaged in the public service of the temple. They were those who rendered aid to others; who were helpers, or servants. Such is the meaning as used here. They are employed to render *aid* or *assistance* to others—to wit, to Christians. ¶ *Sent forth.* Appointed by God for this. They are *sent;* are under his control; are in a subordinate capacity. Thus Gabriel was *sent* forth to convey an important message to Daniel, Dan. ix. 21–23. ¶ *To minister.* For the aid or succour of such. They come to render them assistance —and, if employed in this humble office, how much inferior to the dignity of the Son of God—the Creator and Ruler of the worlds! ¶ *Who shall be heirs of salvation.* To the saints; to Christians. They are called " *heirs* of salvation" because they are adopted into the family of God, and are treated as his sons. See Notes on Rom. viii. 14–17. The main point here is, that the angels are employed in a much more humble capacity than the Son of God; and, therefore, that he himself sustains a far more elevated rank. But while the apostle has proved that, he has incidentally stated an exceedingly interesting and important doctrine, that the angels are employed to further the salvation of the people of God, and to assist them in their journey to heaven. In this doctrine there is nothing absurd. It is no more improbable that angels should be employed to aid man, than that one man should aid another; certainly not as improbable as that the Son of God should come down "not to be ministered unto but to minister " (Mat. xx. 28), and that he performed on earth the office of a servant, Jn. xiii. 1–15. Indeed, it is a great principle of the divine administration that one class of God's creatures are to minister to others; that one is to aid another—to assist him in trouble, to provide for him when poor, and to counsel him in perplexity. We

are constantly deriving benefit from others, and are dependent on their counsel and help. Thus God has appointed parents to aid their children; neighbours to aid their neighbours; the rich to aid the poor; and all over the world the principle is seen, that one is to derive benefit from the assistance rendered by others. Why may not the angels be employed in such a service? They are pure, benevolent, powerful; and as man was ruined in the fall by the temptation offered by one of an angelic, though fallen nature, why should not others of angelic, unfallen holiness come to assist in repairing the evils which their fallen, guilty brethren have inflicted on the race? There seems to be a beautiful propriety in bringing *aid* from another race, as *ruin* came from another race; and that as those endowed with angelic might, though with fiendish malignity, ruined man, those with angelic might, but heavenly benevolence, should assist in his recovery and salvation. Farther, it is, from the necessity of the case, a great principle, that the weak shall be aided by the strong; the ignorant by the enlightened; the impure by the pure; the tempted by those who have not fallen by temptation. All over the world we see this principle in operation; it constitutes the beauty of the moral arrangements on the earth; and why shall not this be extended to the inhabitants of other abodes? Why shall not angels, with their superior intelligence, benevolence, and power, come in to perfect this system, and show how much it is adapted to glorify God?—In regard to the *ways* in which angels become ministering spirits to the heirs of salvation, the Scriptures have not fully informed us, but facts are mentioned which will furnish some light on the inquiry. What they do *now* may be learned from the Scripture account of what they *have* done—as it seems to be a fair principle of interpretation that they are engaged in substantially the same employment in which they have ever been. The following methods of angelic interposition in behalf of man are noted in the Scrip-

tures: (1) They feel a deep interest in man. Thus the Saviour says, "There is joy in the presence of the angels of God over one sinner that repenteth," Luke xv. 10. Thus also he says, when speaking of the "little ones" that compose his church, "in heaven their angels do always behold the face of my Father which is in heaven," Mat. xviii. 10. (2) They feel a special interest in all that relates to the redemption of man. Thus Peter says of the things pertaining to redemption, "which things the angels desire to look into," 1 Pet. i. 12. In accordance with this they are represented as praising God over the fields of Bethlehem, where the shepherds were to whom it was announced that a Saviour was born (Luke ii. 13); an angel announced to Mary that she would be the mother of the Messiah (Luke i. 26); an angel declared to the shepherds that he was born (Luke ii. 10); the angels came and ministered to him in his temptation (Mat. iv. 11); an angel strengthened him in the garden of Gethsemane (Luke xxii. 43); angels were present in the sepulchre where the Lord Jesus had been laid, to announce his resurrection to his disciples (Jn. xx. 12); and they reappeared to his disciples on Mount Olivet to assure them that he would return and receive his people to himself, Acts i. 10. (3) They appear for the defence and protection of the people of God. Thus it is said (Ps. xxxiv. 7), "The angel of the Lord encampeth round about them that fear him, and delivereth them." Thus two angels came to hasten Lot from the cities of the plain, and to rescue him from the impending destruction, Gen. xix. 1, 15. Thus an angel opened the prison doors of the apostles, and delivered them when they had been confined by the Jews, Acts v. 19. Thus the angel of the Lord delivered Peter from prison when he had been confined by Herod, Acts xii. 7, 8. (4) Angels are sent to give us strength to resist temptation. Aid was thus furnished to the Redeemer in the garden of Gethsemane, when there "appeared an angel from heaven strengthening him," Luke xxii.

43. The great trial there seems to have been somehow connected with temptation; some influence of the power of darkness, or of the prince of evil, Luke xxii. 53; comp. Jn. xiv. 30. In the aid which they thus rendered to the tempted Redeemer, and in the assistance which they render to us when tempted, there is a special fitness and propriety. Man was at first tempted by a fallen angel. No small part—if not all the temptations in the world—are under the direction now of fallen angels. They roam at large "seeking whom they may devour," 1 Pet. v. 8. The temptations which occur in life, the numerous allurements which beset our path, all have the marks of being under the control of dark and malignant spirits. What, therefore, can be more appropriate than that for the pure angels of God to interpose and aid man against the skill and wiles of these fallen and malignant spirits? Fallen angelic power and skill—power and skill far above the capability and the strength of man—are employed to ruin us, and how desirable is it that like power and skill, under the guidance of benevolence, should come to aid us! (5) They support us in affliction. Thus an angel brought a cheering message to Daniel (Dan. ix.); the angels were present to give comfort to the disciples of the Saviour when he had been taken from them by death, and when he ascended to heaven (Acts i. 10, 11). Why may it not be so now, that important consolations, in some way, are imparted to us by angelic influence? And (6) they attend dying saints, and conduct them to glory. Thus the Saviour says of Lazarus that when he died he was "carried by the angels into Abraham's bosom," Luke xvi. 22. Is there any impropriety in supposing that the same thing may be done still? Assuredly if anywhere heavenly aid is needed, it is when the spirit leaves the body. If anywhere a guide is needed, it is when the ransomed soul goes up the unknown path to God. And if angels are employed on any messages of mercy to mankind, it is proper that it should be when life is closing, and

when the spirit is about to ascend to heaven. Should it be said that they are invisible, and that it is difficult to conceive how we can be aided by beings whom we never see, I answer, I know that they are unseen. They no longer *appear* as they once did to be the *visible* protectors and defenders of the people of God. But no small part of the assistance which we receive from others comes from sources unseen by us. We owe more to *unseen* benefactors than to those whom we see, and the most grateful of all aid, perhaps, is that which is furnished by a hand which we do not see, and in quarters which we cannot trace. How many an orphan is benefited by some unseen and unknown benefactor! So it may be a part of the great arrangements of divine Providence that many of the most needed and acceptable interpositions for our welfare should come to us from invisible sources, and be conveyed to us from God by unseen hands.

REMARKS.

(1) The Christian religion has a claim on the attention of man. God has spoken to us in the gospel by his Son, ver. 1, 2. This fact constitutes a *claim* on us to attend to what is spoken in the New Testament. When God sent prophets to address men, endowing them with more than human wisdom and eloquence, and commanding them to deliver solemn messages to mankind, *that* was a reason why men should hear. But how much more important is the message which is brought by his own Son! How much more exalted the Messenger! How much higher his claim to our attention and regard! Comp. Mat. xxi. 37. Yet it is lamentable to reflect how few attended to him when he lived on the earth, and how few comparatively regard him now. The great mass of men feel no interest in the fact that the Son of God has come and spoken to the human race. Few take the pains to *read* what he said, though all the records of the discourses of the Saviour could be read in a few hours. A newspaper is read; a poem; a novel; a play; a history

of battles and sieges; but the New Testament is neglected, and there are thousands even in Christian lands who have not even read through the Sermon on the Mount! Few also listen to the truths which the Redeemer taught when they are proclaimed in the sanctuary. Multitudes never go to the place where the gospel is preached; multitudes when there are engaged in thinking of other things, or are wholly inattentive to the truths which are proclaimed. Such a reception has the Son of God met with in our world! The most wonderful of all events is, that he should have come from heaven to be the teacher of mankind; next to that, the most wonderful event is that, when he has come, men feel no interest in the fact, and refuse to listen to what he says of the unseen and eternal world. What a man will say about the *possibility* of making a fortune by some wild speculation will be listened to with the deepest interest; but what the Redeemer says about the *certainty* of heaven, and eternal riches there, excites no emotion : what one from the dead might say about the unseen world would excite the profoundest attention; what he has said who has always dwelt in the unseen world, and who knows all that has occurred there, and all that is yet to occur, awakens no interest, and excites no inquiry. Such is man. The visit, too, of an illustrious stranger — like Lafayette to America—will rouse a nation, and spread enthusiasm everywhere; the visit of the Son of God to the earth on a great errand of mercy is regarded as an event of no importance, and excites no interest in the great mass of human hearts.

(2) Christ is divine. In the view of the writer of this epistle he was undoubtedly regarded as equal with God. This is so clear that it seems wonderful that it should ever have been called in question. He who made the worlds; who is to be worshipped by the angels; who is addressed as God; who is said to have laid the foundation of the earth, and to have made the heavens, and to be unchanged when all these things shall pass away, must be divine. These are the attributes of God, and belong to him alone. They *could not* be spoken of a man, an angel, an archangel. It is impossible to conceive that attributes like these could belong to a creature. If they could, then all our notions of what constitutes the distinction between God and his creatures are confounded, and we can have no intelligible idea of God.

(3) It is not improbable that Christ is the medium of communicating the knowledge of the divine essence and perfections to all worlds. He is the brightness of the divine glory—the showing forth—the manifestation of God, ver. 3. The body of the sun is not seen — certainly not by the naked eye. We cannot look upon it. But there is a shining, a brightness, a glory, a manifestation which *is* seen. It is in the sunbeams, the manifestation of the glory and the existence of the sun. By his shining the sun is known. So the Son of God —incarnate or not—may be the manifestation of the divine essence. And from this illustration, may we not without irreverence derive an illustration of the doctrine of the glorious Trinity? There is the body of the sun—to us invisible—yet great and glorious, the source of all light, and heat, and life; the fountain of all that warms and enlivens. Should he be extinct all would die. Thus may it not be with God the Father; God the eternal and unchanging essence—the fountain of all light and life in the universe? In the sun there is also the *manifestation*—the shining — the glorious light. The brightness which we see emanates from that—emanates at once, continually, always. While the sun exists, that exists, and cannot be separated from it. By that brightness the sun is seen; by that the world is enlightened. Without those beams there would be no light, but all would be involved in darkness. What a beautiful representation of the Son of God—the brightness of the divine glory; the medium by which God is made known; the source of light to man, and, for aught we know, to the universe!

When he shines on men, there is light; when he does not shine, there is as certain moral darkness as there is night when the sun sinks in the west. And, for aught we can see, the manifestation which the Son of God makes may be as necessary in all worlds to a proper contemplation of the divine essence, as the beams of the sun are to understand its nature. Then there are the warmth, the heat, and the vivifying influences of the sun —an influence which is the source of life and beauty to the material world. It is not the mere shining—it is the attendant warmth and vivifying power. All nature is dependent on it. Each seed, and bud, and leaf, and flower; each spire of grass, and each animal on earth, and each bird on the wing, is dependent on it. Without that, vegetation would decay at once, and animal life would be extinct, and universal death would reign. What a beautiful illustration of the Holy Spirit, and of his influences on the moral world! "The LORD God is *a Sun*" (Ps. lxxxiv. 11); and I do not see that it is improper thus to derive from the sun an illustration of the doctrine of the Trinity. I am certain we should know nothing of the sun but for the beams that reveal him, and that enlighten the world; and I am certain that all animal and vegetable life would die if it were not for his vivifying and quickening rays. I do not see that it may not be equally probable that the nature, the essence of God would be unknown were it not manifested by the Son of God; and I am certain that all moral and spiritual life would die were it not for the quickening and vivifying influences of the Holy Spirit on the human soul.

(4) Christ has made an atonement for sin, ver. 3. He has done it by "*himself.*" It was not by the blood of bulls and of goats; it was by his own blood. Let us rejoice that we have not now to come before God with a bloody offering; that we need not come leading up a lamb to be slain, but that we may come confiding in that blood which has been shed for the sins of mankind. The great sacrifice has been made. The victim is slain. The blood has been offered which expiates the sin of the world. We may now come at once to the throne of grace, and plead the merits of that blood. How different is our condition from that of the ancient Jewish worshippers! They were required to come leading the victim that was to be slain for sin, and to do this every year and every day. We may come with the feeling that the one great sacrifice has been made for us; that it is never to be repeated, and that in that sacrifice there is merit sufficient to cancel all our sins. How different our condition from that of the heathen! They, too, lead up sacrifices to be slain on bloody altars. They offer lambs, and goats, and bullocks, and captives taken in war, and slaves, and even their own children! But amidst these horrid offerings, while they show their deep conviction that *some* sacrifice is necessary, they have no promise—no evidence whatever, that the sacrifice will be accepted. They go away unpardoned. They repeat the offering with no evidence that their sins are forgiven, and at last they die in despair! We come assured that the "blood of Jesus Christ cleanseth from all sin,"—and the soul rejoices in the evidence that all past sins are forgiven, and is at peace with God.

(5) Let us rejoice that the Lord Jesus is thus exalted to the right hand of God, ver. 3, 4. He has gone into heaven. He is seated on the throne of glory. He has suffered the last pang, and shed the last drop of blood that will ever be necessary to be shed for the sins of the world. No spear of a soldier is again to enter his side, and no cold tomb is again to receive him. He is now happy and glorious in heaven. The angels there render him homage (ver. 6), and the universe is placed under his control.

(6) It is right to *worship* the Lord Jesus. When he came into the world the *angels* were required to do it (ver. 6), and it cannot be wrong for *us* to do it now. If the angels in heaven might properly adore him, we may. If

they offered him adoration, he is divine. Assuredly God would not require them to worship a fellow-angel or a man! I feel safe in adoring where angels adore; I do not feel that I have a right to withhold my homage where they have been required to render theirs.

(7) It is right to address the Lord Jesus as God, ver. 8. If he is so addressed in the language of inspiration, it is not improper for us so to address him. We do not err when we adhere closely to the language of the Bible; nor can we have a stronger evidence that we are right than when we express our sentiments and our devotions in the very language of the sacred Scriptures.

(8) The kingdom of the Redeemer is a righteous kingdom. It is founded in equity, ver. 8, 9. Other kingdoms have been kingdoms of cruelty, oppression, and blood. Tyrants have swayed an iron sceptre over men. But not thus with the Redeemer in his kingdom. There is not a law there which is not equal and mild; not a statute which it would not promote the temporal and eternal welfare of man to obey. Happy is the man that is wholly under his sceptre; happy the kingdom that yields entire obedience to his laws!

(9) The heavens will perish; the earth will decay, ver. 10, 11. Great changes have already taken place in the earth—as the researches of geologists show; and we have no reason to doubt that similar changes may have occurred in distant worlds. Still greater changes may be expected to occur in future times, and some of them we may be called to witness. Our souls are to exist for ever; and far on in future ages—far beyond the utmost period which we can now compute—we may witness most important changes in these heavens and this earth. God may display his power in a manner which has never been seen yet; and safe near his throne his people may be permitted to behold the exhibition of power of which the mind has never yet had the remotest conception.

(10) Yet amidst these changes, the Saviour will be the same, ver. 12. He changes not. In all past revolutions he has been the same. In all the changes which *have* occurred in the physical world, he has been unchanged; in all the revolutions which have occurred among kingdoms, he has been unmoved. One change succeeds another; kingdoms rise and fall and empires waste away; one generation goes off to be succeeded by another, but he remains the same. No matter what tempests howl, how wars rage, how the pestilence spreads abroad, or how the earth is shaken by earthquakes, still the Redeemer is the same. And no matter what are *our* external changes, he is the same. We change from childhood to youth, to manhood, to old age, but he changes not. We are in prosperity or adversity; we may pass from affluence to poverty, from honour to dishonour, from health to sickness, but he is the same. We shall go and lie down in the cold tomb, and our mortal frames will decay, but he will be the same during our long sleep, and he will remain the same till he shall return and summon us to renovated life. I rejoice that in all the circumstances of life I have the same Saviour. I know what he is. I know, if the expression may be allowed, "where he may be found." Man may change by caprice, or whim, or by some new suggestion of interest, of passion, or ambition. I go to my friend to-day, and find him kind and true—but I have no absolute certainty that I shall find him such to-morrow. His feelings, from some unknown cause, may have become cold toward me. Some enemy may have breathed suspicion into his ear about me, or he may have formed some stronger attachment, or he may be sick, or dead. But nothing like this can happen in regard to the Redeemer. He changes not. I am sure that he is always the same. No one can influence him by slander; no new friendship can weaken the old; no sickness or death can occur to him to change him; and though the heavens be on fire, and the earth be convulsed, he is THE SAME. In such a Saviour I may confide; in such a

friend why should not all confide? Of earthly attachments it has been too truly said,

> " And what is friendship but a name,
>   A charm that lulls to sleep;
> A shade that follows wealth or fame,
>   But leaves the wretch to weep?"

But this can never be said of the attachment formed between the Christian and the Redeemer. That is unaffected by external changes; that will live in all the revolutions of material things; and when all earthly ties shall be severed, that will survive the dissolution of all things.

(11) We see the dignity of man, ver. 13, 14. Angels are sent to be his attendants. They come to minister to him here, and to conduct him home "to glory." Kings and princes are surrounded by armed men, or by sages called to be their counsellors; but the most humble saint *may be* encompassed by a retinue of beings of far greater power and of more elevated rank. The angels of light and glory feel a deep interest in the salvation of men. They come to attend the redeemed; they wait on their steps; they sustain them in trial; they accompany them when departing to heaven. It is a higher honour to be attended by one of those pure intelligences than by the most elevated monarch that ever swayed a sceptre or wore a crown; and the obscurest Christian will soon be himself conducted to a throne in heaven, compared with which the most splendid seat of royalty on earth loses its lustre and fades away.

> " And is there care in heaven? and is there love
>   In heavenly spirits to these creatures base,
> That may compassion of their evils move?
>   There is:—else much more wretched were the case
> Of men than beasts; But O! th' exceeding grace
>   Of Highest God that loves his creatures so,
> And all his works of mercy doth embrace,
>   That blessed angels he sends to and fro,
> To serve to wicked man, to serve his wicked foe!
>
> " How oft do they their silver bowers leave,
>   To come to succour us that succour want!
> How do they with golden pinions cleave
>   The yielding skies, like flying pursuivant
> Against foul fiends to aid us militant!
>   They for us fight, they watch and duly ward,
> And their bright squadrons round about us plant;
>   And all for love and nothing for reward;
> O why should Heavenly God to men have such
>   regard!"
>   Spenser's *Faery Queen*, b. ii. canto viii. 1, 2.

(12) How much has God done for the salvation of man! He formed an eternal plan. He has sent his prophets to communicate his will. He has sent his Son to bear a message of mercy, and to die the just for the unjust. He has exalted him to heaven, and placed the universe under his control that man may be saved. He has sent his Holy Spirit, his ministers and messengers, for this. And last, to complete the work, he sends his angels to be ministering spirits; to sustain his people; to comfort them in dying; to attend them to the realms of glory. What an interest is felt in the salvation of a single Christian! What a value he has in the universe! How important it is, therefore, that he should be holy! A man who has been redeemed by the blood of the Son of God should be pure. He who is an heir of life should be dead to the world. He who is attended by celestial beings, and who is soon—he knows not *how* soon—to be translated to heaven, should be holy. Are angels my attendants? Then I should walk worthy of my companionship. Am I soon to go and dwell with angels? Then I should be pure. Are these feet soon to tread the courts of heaven? Is this tongue soon to unite with heavenly beings in praising God? Are these eyes soon to look on the throne of eternal glory, and on the ascended Redeemer? Then these feet, and eyes, and lips should be pure and holy; then I should be dead to the world; then I should live only for heaven.

CHAPTER II.

ANALYSIS OF THE CHAPTER.

The main object of this chapter is, to show that we should attend diligently to the things which were spoken by the Lord Jesus, and not suffer them to glide away from us. The apostle seems to have supposed that some might be inclined to disregard what was spoken by one of so humble appearance as Jesus of Nazareth; and that they would allege that the Old Testament had been given by the interposition of angels, and was therefore more worthy of atten-

CHAPTER II.

THEREFORE we ought to give the more earnest heed to the things which we have heard, lest at any time we should ¹let *them* slip.

---

¹ *run out, as leaking vessels.*

tion. To meet this, he shows that important objects were accomplished by his becoming a man; and that even as a man, power and dignity had been conferred on him superior to that of the angels. In illustration of these points, the chapter contains the following subjects:—(1) An exhortation not to suffer the things which had been spoken to slip from the mind—or in other words, to attend to them diligently and carefully. The *argument* is, that if what was spoken by the angels under the old dispensation claimed attention, much more should that be regarded which was spoken by the Son of God, ver. 1–4. (2) Jesus had been honoured, as incarnate, in such a way as to show that he had a right to be heard, and that what he said should receive the profound attention of men, ver. 5–9. The world to come had not been put under the angels as it had been under him (ver. 5); the general principle had been stated in the Scriptures that all things were put under man (ver. 6, 7), but this was fulfilled only in the Lord Jesus, who had been made a little lower than the angels, and when so made had been crowned with glory and honour, ver. 9. His appearance as a man, therefore, was in no way inconsistent with what had been said of his dignity, or his claim to be heard. (3) The apostle then proceeds to show why he became a man, and why, though he was so exalted, he was subjected to such severe sufferings; and with this the chapter closes, ver. 10–18. It was because this was *proper* from the relation which he sustained to man. The argument is, that the Redeemer and his people were identified; that he did not come to save *angels*, and that, therefore, there was a propriety in his assuming the nature of man, and being subjected to trials like those whom he came to save. In all things it behoved him to be made like his brethren, in order to redeem them, and in order

to set them an example, and to show them how to suffer. The humiliation, therefore, of the Redeemer; the fact that he appeared as a man, and that he was a sufferer, so far from being a reason why he should not be *heard*, is rather an additional reason why we should attend to what he said. He has a claim to the right of being heard not only from his original dignity, but from the friendship which he has evinced for us in taking upon himself our nature, and suffering in our behalf.

1. *Therefore.* Greek, "On account of this"—Διὰ τοῦτο—that is, on account of the exalted dignity and rank of the Messiah as stated in the previous chapter. The sense is, "Since Christ, the author of the new dispensation, is so far exalted above the prophets, and even the angels, we ought to give the more earnest attention to all that has been spoken." ¶ *We ought.* It is *fit* or *proper* (Greek δεῖ) that we should attend to those things. When the Son of God speaks to men, every consideration makes it appropriate that they should attend to what is spoken. ¶ *To give the more earnest heed.* The more strict attention. ¶ *To the things which we have heard.* Whether directly from the Lord Jesus, or from his apostles. It is possible that some of those to whom the apostle was writing had heard the Lord Jesus himself preach the gospel; others had heard the same truths declared by the apostles. ¶ *Lest at any time.* We ought to attend to those things at all times. We ought never to forget them; never to be indifferent to them. We are sometimes interested in them, and then we feel indifferent to them; sometimes at leisure to attend to them, and then the cares of the world, or the heaviness and dulness of the mind, or a cold and languid state of the affections, renders us indifferent to them, and they are suffered to pass out of the mind without concern. Paul says, that

this ought *never* to be done. At no time should we be indifferent to those things. They are always important to us, and we should never be in a state of mind when they would be uninteresting. At all times; in all places; and in every situation of life, we should feel that the truths of religion are of more importance to us than all other truths, and nothing should be suffered to efface their image from the heart. ¶ *We should let* them *slip.* Margin, *run out, as leaking vessels.* Tindal renders this, "Lest we be spilt." The expression here has given rise to much discussion as to its meaning, and has been very differently translated. Doddridge renders it, "Lest we let them flow out of our minds." Prof. Stuart, "Lest at any time we should slight them." Whitby, "That they may not entirely slip out of our memories." The word here used— παραρρέω—occurs nowhere else in the New Testament. The Septuagint translators have used the word but once: Prov. iii. 21, "Son, do not pass by (μὴ παραρρυῇς), but keep my counsel;" that is, do not pass by my advice by neglect, or suffer it to be disregarded. The word means, according to Passow, to flow by, to flow over; and then to go by, to fall, to go away. It is used to mean to flow near, to flow by—as of a river; to glide away, to escape—as from the mind, that is, to forget; and to glide along—as a thief does by stealth. See Robinson's *Lex.* The Syriac and Arabic translators have rendered it, *that we may not fall.* After all that has been said on the meaning of the word here (comp. Stuart, *in loco*), it seems to me that the true sense of the expression is that of flowing, or gliding by—as a river; and that the meaning here is, that we should be very cautious that the important truths spoken by the Redeemer and his apostles should not be suffered to *glide by* us without attention, or without profit. We should not allow them to be like a stream that, flows on without benefiting us; that is, we should endeavour to secure and retain them as our own. The truth taught is, that there is great danger, now that the true system of

religion has been revealed, that it will not profit us, but that we shall lose all the benefit of it. This danger may arise from many sources—some of which are the following:—(1) We may have no just sense of the *importance* of the truths revealed; and before their importance is felt, they may be beyond our reach. So we are often deceived in regard to the importance of objects; and before we perceive their value they are irrecoverably gone. Thus it is often with time, and with the opportunities of obtaining an education, or of accomplishing any object which is of value. The opportunity is gone before we perceive its importance. So the young allow the most important period of life to glide away before they perceive its value, and the opportunity of making much of their talents is lost because they did not embrace the opportunities for improvement which they enjoyed. (2) By being engrossed in business. We feel that *that* is now the most important thing. That claims all our attention. We have no time to pray, to read the Bible, to think of religion, for the cares of the world engross all the time—and the opportunities of salvation glide insensibly away, until it is too late. (3) By being attracted by the pleasures of life. We attend to them now, and are drawn along from one to another, until religion is suffered to glide away, with all its hopes and consolations, and we perceive, too late, that we have let the opportunity of salvation slip for ever. Allured by those pleasures, the young neglect it; and new pleasures starting up in future life carry on the delusion, until every favourable opportunity for salvation has passed away. (4) We suffer favourable *opportunities* to pass by without improving them. Youth is by far the best time, as it is the most appropriate time, to become a Christian—and yet how easy is it to allow that period to slip away without becoming interested in the Saviour! One day glides on after another, and one week, one month, one year passes away after another— like a gently-flowing stream—until all the precious time of youth has

2 For if the word ^aspoken by angels was stedfast, and ^bevery

a Ac.7.53.   b Nu.15.31.

gone, and we are not Christians. So a revival of religion is a favourable time—and yet many suffer this to pass by without becoming interested in it. Others are converted, and the heavenly influences descend all around us, but we are unaffected, and the season so full of happy and heavenly influences is gone—to return no more. (5) We let the favourable season slip, because we design to attend to it at some future period of life. So youth defers it to manhood—manhood to old age—old age to a death-bed—and then neglects it—until the whole of life has glided away, and the soul is not saved. Paul knew man. He knew how prone he was to let the things of religion slip out of the mind —and hence the earnestness of his caution that we should give heed to the subject now—lest the opportunity of salvation should soon glide away. When once passed, it can never be recalled. Learn hence, (1) That the truths of religion will not benefit us unless we give heed to them. It will not save us that the Lord Jesus has come and spoken to men, unless we are disposed to listen. It will not benefit us that the sun shines, unless we open our eyes. Books will not benefit us, unless we read them; medicine, unless we take it; nor will the fruits of the earth sustains our lives, however rich and abundant they may be, if we disregard and neglect them. So with the truths of religion. There is truth enough to save the world—but the world disregards and despises it. (2) It needs not great sins to destroy the soul. Simple *neglect* will do it as certainly as atrocious crimes. Every man has a sinful heart that will destroy him unless he makes an effort to be saved; and it is not merely the great sinner, therefore, who is in danger. It is the man who *neglects* his soul—whether a moral or an immoral man—the daughter of amiableness, or the daughter of vanity and vice, who is unwilling to attend to the voice of

transgression and disobedience received a just recompense of reward; 3 How^c shall we escape, if we

c ch.4.1,11.

conscience and of God, and to embrace the Saviour.

2. *For if the word spoken by angels.* The revelation in the Old Testament. It was indeed given by *Jehovah*, but it was the common opinion of the Hebrews that it was by the ministry of angels. See Notes on Acts vii. 38, 53, and Gal. iii. 19, where this point is fully considered. As Paul was discoursing here of the superiority of the Redeemer to the angels, it was to the point to refer to the fact that the law had been given by their ministry. ¶ *Was stedfast.* Was *firm*—βέβαιος— settled, established. It was not vacillating and fluctuating. It determined what crime was, and it was firm in its punishment. It did not yield to circumstances; but if not obeyed in all respects, it denounced punishment. See Deut. xvii. 2-13; Heb. x. 28. The idea here is not that everything was *fulfilled*, but it is, that the law so given could not be violated with impunity. It was not *safe* to violate it, but it took notice of the slightest failure to yield perfect obedience to its demands. ¶ *And every transgression.* Literally, *going beyond, passing by.* It means every instance of *disregarding* the law. ¶ *And disobedience.* Every instance of *not hearing* the law —παρακοὴ—and hence every instance of disobeying it. The word here stands opposite to *hearing* it, or attending to it—and the sense of the whole is, that the slightest infraction of the law was sure to be punished. It made no provision for indulgence in sin; it demanded prompt, implicit, universal, and entire obedience. ¶ *Received a just recompense of reward.* Was strictly punished, or subjected to due retribution. This was the character of the law. It threatened punishment for each and every offence, and made no allowance for transgression in any form. Comp. Num. xv. 30, 31.

3. *How shall we escape.* How shall we escape the just recompense due to

neglect so great salvation; ^dwhich
at the first began to be spoken by

the Lord, and was confirmed unto
us by them that heard *him;*

d Mar.1.14.

transgressors? What way is there
of being saved from punishment, if
we suffer the great salvation to be
neglected, and do not embrace its offers? The sense is, that there *is* no
other way of salvation, and that the
neglect of this will be followed by
certain destruction. *Why* it will, the
apostle proceeds to show, by stating
that this plan of salvation was proclaimed first by the Lord himself, and
had been confirmed by the most decided and amazing miracles. ¶ *If
we neglect.* It is not merely, if we commit great sins. Neither is it, if we are
murderers, adulterers, thieves, infidels,
atheists, scoffers. It is, if we merely
neglect this salvation—if we do not
embrace it—if we suffer it to pass
unimproved. *Neglect* is enough to
ruin a man. A man who is in business need not commit forgery or rob-
bery, to ruin himself; he has only to
neglect his business, and his ruin is
certain. A man who is lying on a
bed of sickness need not cut his
throat to destroy himself; he has only
to *neglect* the means of restoration,
and he will be ruined. A man floating in a skiff above Niagara need
not move an oar or make an effort to
destroy himself; he has only to *neglect* using the oar at the proper time,
and he will certainly be carried over
the cataract. Most of the calamities
of life are caused by simple *neglect.*
By neglect of education children grow
up in ignorance; by neglect a farm
grows up to weeds and briars; by
neglect a house goes to decay; by
neglect of sowing, a man will have no
harvest; by neglect of reaping, the
harvest would rot in the fields. No
worldly interest can prosper where
there is neglect; and why may it not
be so in religion? There is nothing
in earthly affairs that is valuable
that will not be ruined if it is not
attended to—and why may it not be
so with the concerns of the soul?
Let no one infer, therefore, because he
is not a drunkard, or an adulterer, or a

murderer, that therefore he will be
saved. Such an inference would be as
irrational as it would be for a man to
infer that *because* he is not a murderer
his farm will produce a harvest, or that
because he is not an adulterer *therefore* his merchandise will take care
of itself. Salvation would be worth
nothing if it cost no effort—and
there will be *no* salvation where no
effort is put forth. ¶ *So great salvation.* Salvation from sin and from
hell. It is called *great* because (1)
its author is great. This is perhaps
the main idea in this passage. It
"began to be spoken by the Lord;" it
had for its author the Son of God,
who is so much superior to the angels; whom the angels were required
to worship (chap. i. 6); who is expressly
called God (chap. i. 8); who made all
things, and who is eternal, chap. i. 10
–12. A system of salvation promulgated by him *must* be of infinite importance, and must have a claim to the
attention of man. (2) It is *great* because it saves from great sins. It is
adapted to deliver from *all* sins, no
matter how aggravated. No one is
saved who feels that his sins are small,
or that they are of no consequence.
Each one who is saved sees his sins to
be black and aggravated, and each one
who enters heaven will go there feeling
and confessing that it is a great salvation which has brought such a sinner
there. Besides, this salvation delivers
from all sin—no matter how gross and
aggravated. The adulterer, the murderer, the blasphemer, may come and
be saved, and the salvation which re-
deems such sinners from eternal ruin
is *great.* (3) It is great because it
saves from great dangers. The danger of an eternal hell besets the path
of each one. All do not see it; and
all will not believe it when told of it.
But this danger hovers over the path
of every mortal. The danger of an
eternal hell! Salvation from everlasting burnings! Deliverance from
unending ruin! Surely that salvation
must be great which will save from

4 God* also bearing *them* witness, both with signs and wonders, and

a Ac.14.3.

with divers miracles, and [2]gifts of the Holy Ghost, according to his own will?

[2] or, *distributions.*

such a doom! If that salvation is neglected, the danger still hangs over each and every man. The gospel did not *create* that danger—it came to deliver from it. Whether the gospel be true or false, each man is by nature exposed to eternal death—just as each one is exposed to temporal death whether the doctrine of the immortality of the soul and of the resurrection be true or false. The gospel comes to provide a remedy for dangers and woes—it does not create them; it comes to deliver men from great dangers—not to plunge them into them. *Back of the gospel,* and before it was preached at all, men were in danger of everlasting punishment, and that system which came to proclaim deliverance from such a danger is great. (4) The salvation itself is great in heaven. It exalts man to infinite honours, and places on his head an eternal crown. Heaven with all its glories is offered to us; and *such* a deliverance, and such an elevation to eternal honours, deserves to be called GREAT. (5) It is great because it was effected by displays of infinite power, wisdom, and love. It was procured by the incarnation and humiliation of the Son of God. It was accomplished amidst great sufferings and self-denials. It was attended with great miracles. The tempest was stilled, and the deaf were made to hear, and the blind were made to see, and the dead were raised, and the sun was darkened, and the rocks were rent. The whole series of wonders connected with the incarnation and death of the Lord Jesus, was such as the world had not elsewhere seen, and such as was fitted to hold the race in mute admiration and astonishment. If this be so, then religion is no trifle. It is not a matter of little importance whether we embrace it or not. It is the most momentous of all the concerns that pertain to man; it has a claim on his attention which nothing else can have. Yet the mass of men live in

the *neglect* of it. It is not that they are professedly Atheists, or Deists, or that they are immoral or profane; it is not that they oppose religion, and ridicule it, and despise it; it is that they simply *neglect* it. They pass it by. They attend to other things. They are busy with their pleasures, or in their counting-houses, in their workshops, or on their farms; they are engaged in politics, or in bookmaking, and they *neglect* religion at present as a thing of small importance—proposing to attend to it hereafter, as if they acted on the principle that everything else was to be attended to *before* religion. ¶ *Which at the first.* Greek, *which received the beginning of being spoken.* The meaning is correctly expressed in our translation. Christ *began* to preach the gospel; the apostles followed him. John the Baptist prepared the way; but the Saviour was properly the first preacher of the gospel. ¶ *By the Lord.* By the Lord Jesus. See Notes on Acts i. 24. ¶ *And was confirmed unto us,* &c. They who heard him preach, that is, the apostles, were witnesses of what he said, and certified us of its truth. When the apostle here says "*us,*" he means the church at large. Christians were assured of the truth of what the Lord Jesus spake by the testimony of the apostles; or the apostles communicated it to those who had not heard him in such a manner as to leave no room for doubt.

4. *God also bearing* them *witness.* By miracles. Giving them the sanction of his authority, or showing that they were sent by him. No man can work a miracle by his own power. When the dead are raised, the deaf are made to hear, and the blind are made to see by a word, it is the power of God alone that does it. He thus becomes a *witness* to the divine appointment of him by whose instrumentality the miracle is wrought; or furnishes an attestation that what he *says* is true.

5 For unto the angels hath he not put in subjection the world to come, whereof we speak.

See Notes on Acts xiv. 3. ¶ *With signs and wonders.* These words are usually connected in the New Testament. The word rendered *signs*— σημεῖον—means any miraculous event that is fitted to show that what had been predicted by a prophet would certainly take place. See Mat. xii. 38. Comp. Notes on Isa. vii. 11. A *wonder* — τέρας — denotes a portent, or prodigy—something that is fitted to excite wonder or amazement—and hence a miracle. The words together refer to the various miracles which were performed by the Lord Jesus and his apostles, designed to confirm the truth of the Christian religion. ¶ *And with divers miracles.* Various miracles, such as healing the sick, raising the dead, &c. The miracles were not of one class merely, but were various, so that all pretence of deception should be taken away. ¶ *And gifts of the Holy Ghost.* Margin, *distributions.* The various influences of the Holy Spirit enabling them to speak different languages, and to perform works beyond the power of man. See Notes on 1 Cor. xii. 4–11. ¶ *According to his will.* As he chose. He acted as a sovereign in this. He gave them where he pleased, and imparted them in such measure as he chose. The sense of this whole passage is, "The gospel has been promulgated to man in a solemn manner. It was first published by the Lord of glory himself. It was confirmed by the most impressive and solemn miracles. It is undoubtedly a revelation from heaven, and was given in more solemn circumstances than the law of Moses, and its threatenings are more to be dreaded than those of the law. Beware, therefore, how you trifle with it, or disregard it. It cannot be neglected with safety; its neglect or rejection *must* be attended with condemnation."

5. *For unto the angels hath he not put in subjection.* In this verse the apostle returns to the subject which he had been discussing in chap. i.— the superiority of the Messiah to the angels. From that subject he had been diverted (chap. ii. 1–4), by showing them what must be the consequences of defection from Christianity, and the danger of neglecting it. Having shown that, he now proceeds with the discussion, and shows that an honour had been conferred on the Lord Jesus which had never been bestowed on the angels—to wit, *the supremacy over this world.* This he does by proving from the Old Testament that such a dominion was given to *man* (ver. 6–8), and then that this dominion was *in fact* exercised by the Lord Jesus, ver. 9. At the same time, he meets an objection which a Jew would be likely to make. It is, that Jesus appeared to be far inferior to the angels. He was a man of a humble condition. He was poor, and despised. He had none of the external honour which was shown to Moses —the founder of the Jewish economy; none of the apparent honour which belongs to angelic beings. This implied objection the apostle removes by showing the reason why he became so. It was proper, since he came to redeem man, that he should be a man, and not take on himself the nature of angels; and for the same reason it was proper that he should be subjected to sufferings, and be made a man of sorrows, ver. 10–17. The remark of the apostle in the verse before us is, that God had never put the world in subjection to the angels as he had to the Lord Jesus. They had no jurisdiction over it; they were mere ministering spirits; but the world had been put under the dominion of the Lord Jesus. ¶ *The world to come.* The word here rendered *world*—οἰκουμένη—means properly *the inhabited* or *inhabitable* world. See Mat. xxiv. 14; Luke ii. 1; iv. 5; xxi. 26 (Greek); Acts xi. 28; xvii. 6, 31; xix. 27; xxiv. 5; Rom. x. 18; Heb. i. 6; Rev. iii. 10; xii. 9; xvi. 14 — in all which places, but one, it is rendered *world.* It occurs nowhere else in the New Testament. The proper meaning is the

6 But one in a certain place testified, saying, *What is man, that

f Ps.8.4,&c.

that thou art mindful of him? or
the son of man, that thou visitest
him?

world or *earth* considered as inhabitable—and here the jurisdiction refers
to the control over man, or the dwellers on the earth. The phrase "the
world *to come*," occurs not unfrequently in the New Testament. Comp.
Eph. ii. 7; 1 Cor. x. 11; Heb. vi. 5.
The same phrase "the world to come"
—עוֹלָם הַבָּא—occurs often in the Jewish writings. According to Buxtorf
(*Lex. Ch. Talm. Rab.*) it means, as
some suppose, "the world which is to
exist after this world is destroyed,
and after the resurrection of the
dead, when souls shall be again united
to their bodies." By others it is
supposed to mean "the days of the
Messiah, when he shall reign on the
earth." To me it seems to be clear
that the phrase here means, *the world
under the Messiah*—the world, age,
or dispensation which was to succeed
the Jewish, and which was familiarly
known to them as "the world to
come;" and the idea is, that that
world, or age, was placed under the
jurisdiction of the Christ, and not of
the angels. This point the apostle
proceeds to make out. Comp. Notes
on Isa. ii. 2. ¶ *Whereof we speak.* "Of
which I am writing;" that is, of the
Christian religion, or the reign of the
Messiah.

6. *But one in a certain place testified.*
The apostle was writing to those who
were supposed to be familiar with the
Hebrew Scriptures, and where it
would be necessary only to make a
reference in general without mentioning the name of the book where the
quotation was found. The place
which is quoted here is Psa. viii. 4–6.
The *argument* of the apostle is this—
that there existed in the sacred Scriptures a declaration that "all things
were placed under the control and
jurisdiction of MAN," but that that
had not yet been accomplished. It
was not true, in fact (ver. 8), that all
things were subject to man, and the
complete truth of that declaration
would be found only in the jurisdic-

tion conferred on the Messiah—THE
MAN, by way of eminence—the incarnate Son of God. It would not occur to anyone, probably, in reading
the Psalm, that the verse here quoted
had any reference to the Messiah. It
seems to relate to the dominion which
God had given *man* over his works in
this lower world, or to the fact that
he was made lord over all things.
That dominion is apparent, to a considerable extent, everywhere, and is a
standing proof of the truth of what
is recorded in Gen. i. 26, that God
originally gave dominion to man over
the creatures on earth, since it is only
by this supposition that it can be accounted for that the horse, the ele-
phant, the ox, and even the panther
and the lion, are subject to the control of man. The argument of Paul
seems to be this: "Originally this
control was given to man. It was
absolute and entire. All things were
made subject to him, and all obeyed.
Man was made a little lower than the
angels, and was the undisputed lord
of this lower world. He was in a
state of innocence. But he rebelled,
and this dominion has been in some
measure lost. It is found complete
only in the *second man, the lord from
heaven* (1 Cor. xv. 47), the Lord Jesus,
to whom this control is absolutely
given. He comes up to the complete
idea of *man*—man as he was in innocence, and man as he was described
by the Psalmist, as having been made
a little lower than the angels, and
as having entire dominion over the
world." Much difficulty has been
felt by commentators in regard to
this passage, and to the principle on
which it is quoted. The above seems
to me to be that which is most probably true. There are two other methods by which an attempt has been
made to explain it. One is, that Paul
uses the words here by way of *allusion*, or *accommodation* (Doddridge),
as words that will express his meaning, without designing to say that the

Psalm originally had any reference to the Messiah. Most of the later commentators accord with this opinion. The other opinion is, that David originally referred to the Messiah; that he was deeply and gratefully affected in view of the honour that God had conferred on him; and that in looking down by faith on the posterity that God had promised him (see 2 Sam. vii. 14), he saw one among his own descendants to whom God would give this wide dominion, and expresses himself in the elevated language of praise. This opinion is defended by Professor Stuart. See his *Com. on the Hebrews*, Excursus ix.

[That the grand and ultimate reference in the eighth Psalm is to the person of the Messiah none can reasonably doubt. Both our Lord and his apostles have affirmed it, Mat. xxi. 15, 16; 1 Cor. xv. 27; Eph. i. 22. Add to these the place before us, where, as the quotation is introduced *in the midst of an argument, and by way of proof*, the idea of *accommodation* is inconsistent with the wisdom and honesty of the apostles, and therefore inadmissible. The opposite extreme, however, of *sole and original* reference to the Messiah is not so certain. There is a more obvious and primary reference, which at once strikes the reader of the Psalm, and which, therefore, should not be rejected till disproved. The conjecture which a learned author mentioned above has made regarding the course of thought in the Psalmist's mind—supposing him to have been occupied with the contemplation of the covenant, as recorded in 2 Sam. vii., and of that illustrious descendant, who should be the Son of God, and on whom should be conferred universal empire, at the very time in which he composed the Psalm—is ingenious, but not satisfactory. The least objectionable view is that of *primary* and *secondary*, or *prophetic* reference. This relieves us from the necessity of setting aside the obvious sense of the original place, and at the same time preserves the more exalted sense which our Lord and his apostles have attached to it, and the Spirit of course intended to convey. And in order to preserve this last sense it is not necessary to ascertain what was the course of feeling in the Psalmist's mind, or whether *he* really had the Messiah in view, since the prophets, on many occasions, might be ignorant of the full import of the words which the Holy Ghost dictated to them. This view, moreover, is all that the necessity of the case demands. It suits the apostle's argument, since the great and pro-

phetic reference is to the Messiah. It presents, also, a complete πληρωσις of the eighth Psalm, which it is allowed on all hands the primary reference alone could not do. It is sufficiently clear that such universal dominion belongs not to man in his present fallen state. Even if it be allowed that the contemplation of David regarded *man as innocent, as he was when created*, yet absolutely universal dominion did not belong to Adam. Christ alone is Lord of all. Creation, animate and inanimate, is subject to him.

Here, then, we have what has been well styled "the safe middle point, the μέτρον ἄριστον, between the two extremes of supposing this and such like passages to belong only to the Messiah, or only to him concerning whom they were first spoken." This middle point has been ably defended by Bishop Middleton. "Indeed," says he, "on no other hypothesis can we avoid one of two great difficulties, for else we must assert that the multitudes of applications made by Christ and his apostles are fanciful and unauthorized, and wholly inadequate to prove the points for which they are cited; or, on the other hand, we must believe that the obvious and natural sense of such passages was never intended, and that it is a mere illusion. Of the eighth Psalm the primary import is so certain that it could not be mistaken." The only objection to this double reference worthy of being noticed is connected with the clause, 'Ηλαττωσας αὐτον βραχύ τι παρ' ἀγγελους, which, it is affirmed, must possess two senses, not only different, but opposite and contradictory. In its primary application to *man* the idea is plainly that of exaltation and honour. Such was the dignity of man that he was made *but a little* lower than the angels; on the other hand, the secondary, or prophetic application, gives to the language the sense of humiliation or depression. For, considering the original dignity of Christ, the being made lower than the angels cannot otherwise be regarded. But may not the clause in both applications have the idea of exaltation attached to it? If so, the objection is at once met. And that this is the case has, we think, been satisfactorily made out. "What," asks Prof. Stuart, "is his (Paul's) design? To prove that Christ in his human nature is exalted above angels. How does he undertake to prove this? First by showing that this nature is made but little inferior to that of the angels, and next that it has been exalted to the empire of the world." This note has been extended to such length, because it involves a *principle* applicable to a multitude of passages. On the whole, it may be observed in reference to all these cases of quotation, that the mind of the pious and humble reader will not be greatly distressed by any difficulties connected with their ap-

plication, but will ever rest satisfied with the assertion and authority of men who spake as they were moved by the Holy Ghost.]

¶ *What is man*, &c. What is there in man that entitles him to so much notice? Why has God conferred on him so signal honours? Why has he placed him over the works of his hands? He seems so insignificant; his life is so much like a vapour; he so soon disappears, that the question may well be asked why this extraordinary dominion is given him?—He is so sinful also, and so unworthy; he is so much unlike God, and so passionate and revengeful; he is so prone to *abuse* his dominion, that it may well be asked why God has given it to him? Who would suppose that God would give such a dominion over his creatures to one who was so prone to abuse it as man has shown himself to be?— He is so *feeble*, also, compared with other creatures—even of those which are made subject to him—that the question may well be asked why God has conceded it to him? Such questions may be asked when we contemplate man *as he is*. But similar questions may be asked if, as was probably the case, the Psalm here be supposed to have had reference to man *as he was created*. Why was one so feeble, and so comparatively without strength, placed over this lower world, and the earth made subject to his control? Why is it that, when the heavens are so vast and glorious (Ps. viii. 3), God has taken such notice of man? Of what consequence can *he* be amidst works so wonderful? "When I look on the heavens, and survey their greatness and their glory," is the sentiment of David, "why is it that *man* has attracted so much notice, and that he has not been wholly overlooked in the vastness of the works of the Almighty? Why is it that instead of this he has been exalted to so much dignity and honour?" This question, thus considered, strikes us with more force now than it could have struck David. Let anyone sit down and contemplate the heavens as they are disclosed by the discoveries of modern astronomy, and he may well ask the question, "What is *man* that he should have attracted the attention of God, and been the object of so much care?" The same question would not have been inappropriate to David if the Psalm be supposed to have had reference originally to the Messiah, and if he was speaking of himself particularly as the ancestor of the Messiah. "What is man; what am I; what can any of my descendants be, who must be of mortal frame, that this dominion should be given him? Why should anyone of a race so feeble, so ignorant, so imperfect, be exalted to such honour?" *We* may ask the question here, and it may be asked in heaven with pertinency and with power, "Why was *man* so honoured as to be united to the Godhead? Why did the Deity appear in the human form? What was there *in man* that should entitle him to this honour of being united to the Divinity, and of being thus exalted above the angels?" The wonder is not yet solved; and we may well suppose that the angelic ranks look with amazement—but without envy—on the fact that *man*, by his union with the Deity in the person of the Lord Jesus, has been raised above them in rank and in glory. ¶ *Or the son of man*. This phrase means the same as *man*, and is used merely to give *variety* to the mode of expression. Such a change in words and phrases, when the same thing is intended, occurs constantly in Hebrew poetry. The name "son of man" is often given to Christ to denote his intimate connection with our race, and the interest which he felt in us, and is the *common* term which the Saviour uses when speaking of himself. Here it means *man*, and may be applied to human nature everywhere—and therefore to human nature in the person of the Messiah. ¶ *That thou visitest him*. That thou shouldst regard him, or treat him with so much honour. Why is he the object of so much interest to the divine mind?

7. *Thou madest him a little lower than the angels*. Margin, *a little while inferior to*. The Greek may here mean a little inferior in rank, or inferior for a little time. But the probable meaning is, that it refers to inferiority of

7 Thou madest him [3] a little lower than the angels; thou crownedst him with glory and honour, and didst set him over the works of thy hands:

[3] or, *a little while inferior to.*

8 Thou hast put all things in subjection under his feet. For in that he put all in subjection under him, he left nothing *that is* not put under him. But[g] now we see not yet all things put under him.

g 1 Co.15.24.

rank. Such is its obvious sense in Ps. viii., from which this is quoted. The meaning is, that God had made man but little inferior to the angels in rank. He *was* inferior, but still God had exalted him almost to their rank. Feeble and weak and dying as he was, God had given him a dominion and a rank almost like that of the angels. The wonder of the Psalmist is, that God had given to human nature so much honour—a wonder that is not at all diminished when we think of the honour done to man by his connection with the divine nature in the person of the Lord Jesus. If, in contemplating the race as it appears; if, when we look at the dominion of man over the lower world, we are amazed that God has bestowed so much honour on our nature, how much more should we wonder that he has honoured man by his connection with the Divinity. Paul applies this to the Lord Jesus. His object is to show that he is superior to the angels. In doing this he shows that he had a nature given him in itself but little inferior to the angels, and then that that had been exalted to a rank and dominion far above theirs. That such honour should be put on *man* is what is fitted to excite amazement, and well may one continue to ask *why* it has been done? When we survey the heavens, and contemplate their glories, and think of the exalted rank of other beings, we may well inquire why has such honour been conferred on man? ¶ *Thou crownedst him with glory and honour.* That is, with exalted honour. Glory and honour here are nearly synonymous. The meaning is, that elevated honour had been conferred on human nature. A most exalted and extended dominion had been given to *man*, which showed that God had greatly honoured him. This appeared eminently in the person of

the Lord Jesus, "the exalted Man," to whom this dominion was given in the widest extent. ¶ *And didst set him over,* &c. *Man* has been placed over the other works of God (1) by the original appointment (Gen. i. 26); (2) man at large—though fallen, sinful, feeble, dying; (3) man, eminently in the person of the Lord Jesus, in whom human nature has received its chief exaltation. This is what is particularly in the eye of the apostle—and the language of the Psalm will accurately express this exaltation.

8. *Thou hast put all things in subjection,* &c. Ps. viii. 6. That is, all things are put under the control of man, or thou hast given him dominion over all things. ¶ *For in that he put all in subjection.* The meaning of this is, that "the *fair interpretation* of the passage in the Psalm is, that the dominion of *man*, or of human nature over the earth, was to be absolute and total. Nothing was to be excepted. But this is not now the fact in regard to man in general, and can be true only of human nature in the person of the Lord Jesus. There the dominion is absolute and universal." The point of the argument of the apostle may be thus expressed : "It was the original appointment (Gen. i. 26) that man should have dominion over this lower world, and be its absolute lord and sovereign. Had he continued in innocence, this dominion would have been entire and perpetual. But he fell, and we do not now see him exerting this dominion. What is said of the dominion of *man* can be true only of human nature in the person of the Lord Jesus, and there it *is* completely fulfilled." ¶ *But now we see not yet all things put under him.* That is, "It is not now true that all things are subject to the control of man. There is indeed a *general* dominion

9 But we see Jesus, [h] who was made a little lower than the angels, for[4] the suffering of death, [i] crowned with glory and honour; that [k] he by the grace of God should taste death for every man.

h Phi.2.8,9.   4 or, *by*.   i Ac.2.23.   k Jn.3.16.

over the works of God, and over the inferior creation. But the control is not universal. A large part of the animal creation rebels, and is brought into subjection only with difficulty. The elements are not entirely under his control; the tempest and the ocean rage; the pestilence conveys death through city and hamlet. The dominion of man is a broken dominion. His government is an imperfect government. The world is not *yet* put wholly under his control, but enough has been done to constitute a pledge that it will yet be done. It will be fully accomplished only in him who sustains our nature, and to whom dominion is given over all worlds."

9. *But we see Jesus.* "We do not see that man elsewhere has the extended dominion of which the Psalmist speaks. But we see the fulfilment of it in Jesus, who was crowned with glory and honour, and who has received a dominion that is superior to that of the angels." The *point* of this is, not that he suffered, and not that he tasted death for every man; but that *on account of this*, or as a *reward* for thus suffering, he was crowned with glory and honour, and that he thus fulfilled all that David (Ps. viii.) had said of the dignity and honour of man. The object of the apostle is, to show that he was *exalted*, and in order to this he shows *why* it was—to wit, because he had suffered death to redeem man. Comp. Phil. ii. 8, 9. ¶ *Who was made a little lower than the angels.* That is, as a man, or when on earth. His assumed rank was inferior to that of the angels. He took upon himself not the nature of angels (ver. 16), but the nature of man. The apostle is probably here answering some implied objections to the rank which it was claimed that the Lord Jesus had, or which *might* be urged to the views which he was defending. Those objections were mainly two. First,

that Jesus was a man; and second, that he suffered and died. If that was the fact, it was natural to ask *how* he could be superior to the angels? How could he have had the rank which was claimed for him? This he answers by showing first, that his condition as a man was *voluntarily* assumed—"he was *made* lower than the angels;" and second, by showing that, as a consequence of his sufferings and death, he was immediately crowned with glory and honour. This state of humiliation became him in the great work which he had undertaken, and he was immediately exalted to universal dominion, and as Mediator was raised to a rank far above the angels. ¶ *For the suffering of death.* Margin, *by*. The meaning of the preposition here rendered "for" (διὰ, here governing the accusative) is, "on account of;" that is, Jesus, on account of the sufferings of death, or in virtue of that, was crowned with glory and honour. His crowning was the result of his condescension and sufferings. See Notes on Phil. ii. 8, 9. It does not here mean, as our translation would seem to imply, that he was made a little lower than the angels *in order* to suffer death, but that *as a reward* for having suffered death he was raised up to the right hand of God. ¶ *Crowned with glory and honour.* That is, at the right hand of God. He was raised up to heaven, Acts ii. 33; Mark xvi. 19. The meaning is, that he was crowned with the highest honour on account of his sufferings. Comp. Phil. ii. 8, 9; Heb. xii. 2; v. 7–9; Eph. i. 20–23. ¶ *That he.* Or rather, "*since* he by the grace of God tasted death for every man." The sense is, that *after* he had thus tasted death, and as a consequence of it, he was thus exalted. The word here rendered "*that*"—ὅπως—means usually and properly *that, so that, in order that, to the end that, &c.* But it *may* also mean *when, after that, after.* See Notes

on Acts iii. 19. This is the interpretation which is given by Professor Stuart (*in loco*), and this interpretation seems to be demanded by the connection. The general interpretation of the passage has been different. According to the explanation commonly adopted, the sense is, "We see Jesus, for the suffering of death, crowned with glory and honour, so as that, by the grace of God, he might taste of death for every man." See Robinson's *Lex.* on the word ὅπως, and Doddridge on the place. But it is natural to ask *when* Jesus was thus crowned with glory and honour? It was not *before* the crucifixion—for he was then poor and despised. The connection seems to require us to understand this of the glory to which he was exalted in heaven, and this was *after* his death, and could not be in *order* that he might taste of death. I am disposed, therefore, to regard this as teaching that the Lord Jesus was exalted to heaven in virtue of the atonement which he had made, and this accords with Phil. ii. 8, 9, and Heb. xii. 2. It accords both with *the fact* in the case, and with the design of the apostle in the argument before us. ¶ *By the grace of God.* By the favour of God, or by his benevolent purpose toward men. It was not by any *claim* which man had, but was by his special favour. ¶ *Should taste death.* Should die; or should experience death. See Mat. xvi. 28. Death is here represented as something bitter and unpalatable—something unpleasant—as an object may be to the taste. Or the language may be taken from *a cup* —since to experience calamity and sorrow is often represented as drinking a cup of woes, Ps. xi. 6; lxxiii. 10; lxxv. 8; Isa. li. 17; Mat. xx. 22; xxvi. 39. ¶ *For every man.* For all—ὑπὲρ παντὸς—for each and all—whether Jew or Gentile; bond or free; high or low; elect or non-elect. How could words affirm more clearly that the atonement made by the Lord Jesus was unlimited in its nature and design? How can we now express that idea in more clear or intelligible language? That this refers to the atonement is evident, for it says that

he "tasted death" for them. The friends of the doctrine of general atonement do not desire any other than Scripture language in which to express their belief. It expresses the doctrine exactly—without any need of modification or explanation. The advocates of the doctrine of limited atonement *cannot* thus use Scripture language to express their belief. They cannot incorporate it into their creeds that the Lord Jesus "tasted death FOR EVERY MAN." They are compelled to modify it, to limit it, to explain it, in order to prevent error and misconception. But that system *cannot* be true which requires men to shape and modify the plain language of the Bible in order to keep men from error! Comp. Notes on 2 Cor. v. 14, where this point is considered at length.

[With the author's views on the doctrine of atonement we accord in the main, yet are here tempted to ask if the advocates of universal atonement would not be under the like necessity of explaining, modifying,or *extending* such passages as limit or seem to limit the atonement of Christ, and if in framing a creed the advantage would not lie about equal on either side? Neither party would be contented to set down in it those Scriptures which seemed least favourable to themselves without note or explanation. If this remark appear unjust, inasmuch as the universalist could admit into his creed that "Christ laid down his life for the sheep," though at the same time he believed farther, that he laid it down not for them only, nay, not for them in any special sense *more than for others*, let it be observed that the limitarian could just as well admit into his that "Christ tasted death for every man," or for all men (ὑπὲρ παντος), though he might believe farther, not for all specially, not for all efficaciously, or with Prof Stuart on the place, not for all universally, but "for all without distinction, that is, both Jew and Gentile." It is indeed difficult to say on which side explanation would be most needed. In the case of the limited passage it would require to be observed first, that the atonement extended farther than *it* intimated, and besides, that there was no special reference to the parties specified—the sheep, namely. There would be required, in truth, both extension and limitation, that is, if a creed were to be made or a full view of opinion given. They seem to come nearest the truth on this subject who deny neither the general nor special aspect of the atonement. On the one hand there is a large class of *universal passages* which

cannot be satisfactorily explained on any other principle than that which regards the atonement as a great remedial plan that rendered it consistent with the divine honour to extend mercy to guilty men at large, and which would have been equally requisite had there been an intention to save one or millions, numbers, indeed, not forming any part of the question. On the other hand, there is a large class of *special* texts which cannot be explained without admitting, that while this atonement has reference to all, *yet God in providing it had a special design to save his people by it.* See the whole subject fully discussed on the Author's Note referred to above, and in the Supplementary Note on the same passages, which contains a digest of the more recent controversies on the point.]

Learn hence (ver. 6–9), from the incarnation of the Son of God, and his exaltation to heaven, what an honour has been conferred on human nature. When we look on the weakness and sinfulness of our race we may well ask, What is man that God should honour him or regard him? He is the creature of a day. He is feeble and dying. He is lost and degraded. Compared with the universe at large, he is a speck, an atom. He has done nothing to deserve the divine favour or notice, and when we look at the race at large we can do it only with sentiments of the deepest humiliation and mortification. But when we look at human nature in the person of the Lord Jesus we see it honoured there to a degree that is commensurate with all our desires, and that fills us with wonder. We feel that it is an honour to human nature—that it has done much to elevate man—that the world has produced such a man as Howard or Washington. But how much more has that nature been honoured in the person of the Lord Jesus! (1) What an honour to us it was that he should take our nature into intimate union with himself — passing by the angelic hosts and becoming a man! (2) What an honour it was that human nature in that union was so pure and holy; that *man*—everywhere else so degraded and vile—*could* be seen to be noble and pure and godlike! (3) What an honour it was that the divinity should speak to men in connection with human nature and perform such wonder-

ful works; that the pure precepts of religion should come forth from human lips; that the great doctrines of eternal life should be uttered by *a man;* and that from human hands should go forth power to heal the sick and to raise the dead! (4) What an honour to man it was that the atonement for sin should be made in his own nature, and that the universe should be attracted to that scene where one in our form, and with flesh and blood like our own, should perform that great work! (5) What an honour it is to man that his own nature is exalted far above all heavens! That one in our form sits on the throne of the universe! That adoring angels fall prostrate before him! That to him is intrusted all power in heaven and on earth! (6) What an honour to man that one in his nature should be appointed to judge the worlds! That one in our own form, and with a nature like ours, shall sit on the throne of judgment and pronounce the final doom on angels and men! That assembled millions shall be constrained to bow before him and receive their eternal doom from his hands! That prince and potentate—the illustrious dead of all past times and the mighty men who are yet to live—shall all appear before him, and all receive from him the sentence of their final destiny! I see, therefore, the highest honour done to my nature as a man—not in the deeds of proud conquerors, not in the lives of sages and philanthropists, not in those who have carried their investigations farthest into the obscurities of matter and of mind, not in the splendid orators, poets, and historians of other times or that now live—much as I may admire them or feel it an honour to belong to a race which has produced such illustrious men—but in the fact that the Son of God has chosen a body like my own in which to dwell; in the inexpressible loveliness evinced in his pure morals, his benevolence, his blameless life; in the great deeds that he performed on earth; in the fact that it was this form that was chosen in which to make atonement for sin; in the honours that now cluster around him in heaven, and the

10 For it ¹became him, ᵐfor whom *are* all things, and by whom *are* all things, in bringing many

l Lu.24.26,46.   *m* Ro.11.36.

glories that shall attend him when he shall come to judge the world.

> " Princes to his imperial name
> Bend their bright sceptres down;
> Dominions, thrones, and powers rejoice
> To see him wear the crown.

> " Archangels sound his lofty praise
> Through every heavenly street,
> And lay their highest honours down,
> Submissive at his feet.

> " Those soft, those blessed feet of his,
> That once rude iron tore—
> High on a throne of light they stand,
> And all the saints adore.

> " His head, the dear, majestic head,
> That cruel thorns did wound—
> See—what immortal glories shine,
> And circle it around !

> " This is the man, th' exalted Man,
> Whom we, unseen, adore;
> But when our eyes behold his face,
> Our hearts shall love him more."

10. *For it became him.* There was a fitness or propriety in it; it was such an arrangement as became God to make in redeeming many that the great agent by whom it was accomplished should be made complete in all respects by sufferings. The apostle evidently means by this to meet an objection that might be offered by a Jew to the doctrine which he had been stating—an objection drawn from the fact that Jesus was a man of sorrows, and that his life was a life of affliction. This objection he meets by stating that there was a *fitness* and *propriety* in that fact, or that there was a reason for it—a reason drawn from the plan and character of God. It was fit, in the nature of the case, that he should become qualified to be a *complete* or *perfect Saviour*—a Saviour just adapted to the purpose undertaken —by sufferings. The *reason* why this is so the apostle does not state. The amount of it probably was, that it became him as a Being of infinite benevolence; it was fit that He who wished to provide a perfect system of redemption *should* subject his Son to such sufferings as would completely qualify him to be a Saviour for all mankind. This subjection to his humble condi-

sons unto glory, to make the ⁿcaptain of their salvation ᵒperfect through sufferings.

n Is.55.4.   *o* Lu.13.32.

tion and to his many woes made him such a Saviour as man needed, and qualified him fully for his work. There was a propriety that he who should redeem the suffering and the lost should partake of their nature; that he should in all respects identify himself with them; that he should share their woes, and receive in himself the consequences of their sins. ¶ *For whom* are *all things.* With respect to whose glory the whole universe was made, and with respect to whom the entire arrangement for salvation has been formed. The phrase is synonymous with " the Supreme Ruler ; " and the idea is, that it became the Sovereign of the universe to provide a *perfect* scheme of salvation, even though it involved the humiliation and death of his own Son. ¶ *And by whom* are *all things.* By whose agency everything is made. As it was by his agency, therefore, that the plan of salvation was entered into, there was a *fitness* that it should be perfect. It was not the work of fate or chance, and there was a propriety that the whole plan should bear the mark of the infinite wisdom of its Author. ¶ *In bringing many sons unto glory.* To heaven. This was the plan. It was to bring many to heaven who should be regarded and treated as his *sons.* It was not a plan to save a *few*, but to save *many.* Learn hence, (1) That the plan was full of benevolence. (2) No representation of the gospel should ever be made which will leave the impression that a few only, or a small part of the whole race, will be saved. There is no such representation in the Bible, and it should not be made. God intends, taking the whole race together, to save a large portion of the human family. Few in ages that are past, it is true, may have been saved; few now are his friends and are travelling to heaven; but there are to be brighter days on earth. The period is to arrive when the gospel will spread over all lands, and during that

11 For both he that sanctifieth
and they who are sanctified *are* *p*all

p Jn.17.21.

of one: for which cause he is not
ashamed to call them brethren;

---

long period of the millennium, innumerable millions will be brought
under its saving power, and be admitted to heaven. All exhibitions of the
gospel are wrong which represent it
as narrow in its design, narrow in its
offer, and narrow in its result. ¶ *To
make the captain of their salvation.* The
Lord Jesus, who is represented as the
leader or commander of the army of
the redeemed—"the sacramental host
of God's elect." The word "captain"
we apply now to an inferior officer—
the commander of a "company" of
soldiers. The Greek word—ἀρχηγὸς
—is a more general term, and denotes,
properly, the author or source of anything; then a leader, chief, prince.
In Acts iii. 15, it is rendered *prince:*
"and killed *the Prince* of life." So in
Acts v. 31, "Him hath God exalted
to be *a Prince* and a Saviour."ʼ In
Heb. xii. 2, it is rendered *author:*
"Jesus, *the author* and finisher of our
faith." Comp. Notes on that place.
¶ *Perfect through sufferings.* Complete by means of sufferings; that is,
to render him wholly qualified for his
work, so that he should be a Saviour
just adapted to redeem man. This
does not mean that he was *sinful* before, and was made *holy* by his sufferings; nor that he was not in all respects
a perfect man before; but it means,
that by his sufferings he was made
wholly fitted to be a Saviour of men;
and that, therefore, the fact of his
being a suffering man was no evidence,
as a Jew might have urged, that he
was not the Son of God. There was
a *completeness, a filling up,* of all which
was necessary to his character as a
Saviour, by the sufferings which he
endured. We are made morally *better*
by afflictions, if we receive them in a
right manner—for we are sinful, and
need to be purified in the furnace of
affliction; Christ was not made *better,*
for he was before perfectly holy, but
he was completely endowed for the
work which he came to do, by his
sorrows. Nor does this mean here

precisely that he was exalted to heaven
as a reward for his sufferings, or that
he was raised up to glory as a consequence of them—which was true in
itself—but that he was rendered complete, or fully qualified to be a Saviour,
by his sorrows. He was rendered thus
complete, (1) Because his suffering in
all the forms that flesh is liable to,
made him an example to all his people
who shall pass through trials. They
have before them a perfect model to
show them how to bear afflictions.
Had this not occurred, he could not
have been regarded as a *complete* or
perfect Saviour—that is, such a Saviour
as we need. (2) He is able to sympathize with them, and to succour
them in their temptations, ver. 18.
(3) By his sufferings an atonement
was made for all sin. He would have
been an *imperfect* Saviour—if the name
Saviour could have been given to him
at all—if he had not died to make an
atonement for all forms of transgression. To render him *complete* as a
Saviour, it was necessary that he
should suffer and die; and when he
hung on the cross, in the agonies of
death, he could appropriately say, "It
is *finished.* The work is complete.
All has been done that could be required to be done; and man may now
have the assurance that he has a perfect Saviour—perfect not only in moral
character, but perfect in his work, and
in his adaptedness to the condition of
men." See chap. v. 8, 9. Comp.
Notes on Luke xiii. 32.

11. *For both he that sanctifieth.* This
refers, evidently, to the Lord Jesus.
The *object* is to show that there was
such a union between him and those
for whom he died, as to make it necessary that he should partake of the
same nature, or that he should be a
suffering man, ver. 14. He undertook to redeem and sanctify them.
He called them brethren. He identified himself with them. There was,
in the great work of redemption, a
oneness between him and them, and
hence it was necessary that he should

12 Saying, ^qI will declare thy name unto my brethren; in the midst of the church will I sing praise unto thee.

q Ps. 22. 22.

---

assume their nature; and the fact, therefore, that he appeared as a suffering *man* does not at all militate with the doctrine that he had a more exalted nature, and was even above the angels. Professor Stuart endeavours to prove that the word *sanctify* here is used in the sense of, *to make expiation* or *atonement*, and that the meaning is, "he who maketh expiation, and they for whom expiation is made." Bloomfield gives the same sense to the word, and so also does Rosenmüller. That the word *may* have such a signification it would be presumptuous in any one to doubt, after the view which such men have taken of it; but it may be doubted whether this idea is necessary here. The word *sanctify* is a general term, meaning to make holy or pure; to consecrate, set apart, devote to God; to regard as holy, or to hallow. Applied to the Saviour here, it may be used in this general sense—that he consecrated, or devoted himself to God—as eminently *the consecrated* or *holy one*—the Messiah. Comp. Notes on Jn. xvii. 19. As applied to his people, it may mean that *they*, in like manner, were *the* consecrated, the holy, the pure, on earth. There is a richness and fulness in the word when so understood, which there is not when it is limited to the idea of expiation; and it seems to me that it is to be taken in its richest and fullest sense, and that the meaning is, "the great consecrated Messiah—the Holy One of God—and his consecrated and holy followers, are all of one." ¶ *All of one.* Of one family; spirit; Father; nature. Either of these significations will suit the connection, and some such word must be understood. The meaning is, that they were united, or partook of *something* in common, so as to constitute a *oneness*, or a brotherhood; and that since this was the case, there was a propriety in his taking their nature. It does not mean that they were *originally* of one nature or family; but

that it was understood in the writings of the prophets that the Messiah would partake of the nature of his people, and that *therefore*, though he was more exalted than the angels, there was a propriety that he should appear in the human form. Comp. Jn. xvii. 21. ¶ *For which cause.* That is, because he is thus united with them, or has undertaken their redemption. ¶ *He is not ashamed.* As it might be supposed that one so exalted and pure would be. It might have been anticipated that the Son of God would refuse to give the name *brethren* to those who were so humble, so sunken, and so degraded as those whom he came to redeem. But he is willing to be ranked with them, and to be regarded as one of their family. ¶ *To call them brethren.* To acknowledge himself as of the same family, and to speak of them as his brothers. That is, *he is represented as speaking of them in this manner in the prophecies respecting the Messiah*—for this interpretation the argument of the apostle demands. It was material for him to show that he was so represented in the Old Testament. This he does in the following verses.

12. *Saying.* This passage is found in Ps. xxii. 22. The whole of that Psalm has been commonly referred to the Messiah; and in regard to such a reference there is less difficulty than attends most of the other portions of the Old Testament that are usually supposed to relate to him. The following verses of the Psalm are applied to him, or to transactions connected with him in the New Testament, ver. 1, 8, 18; and the whole Psalm is so strikingly descriptive of his condition and sufferings, that there can be no reasonable doubt that it had an original reference to him. There is much in the Psalm that cannot be well applied to David; there is nothing which cannot be applied to the Messiah; and the proof seems to be clear that Paul quoted this passage in accordance with the original

13 And again, *r*I will put my trust in him.　And again, *s*Be-

hold I and the children *t*which God hath given me.

r Ps.18.2.　　　s Is.8.18.

t Jn.17.6–12.

sense of the Psalm.　The *point* of the quotation here is not that he would "declare the name" of God, but that he gave the name *brethren* to those whom he addressed.　¶ *I will declare thy name.* I will make thee known. The word "name" is used, as it often is, to denote God himself.　The meaning is, that it would be a part of the Messiah's work to make known to his disciples the character and perfections of God, or to make them acquainted with God.　He performed this.　In his parting prayer (Jn. xvii. 6), he says, "I have manifested thy name unto the men whom thou gavest me out of the world."　And again, ver. 26, "And I have declared unto them thy name, and will declare it."　¶ *Unto my brethren.* The point of the quotation is in these words.　He spoke of them as *brethren.* Paul is showing that he was not ashamed to call them such.　As he was reasoning with those who had been *Jews*, and as it was necessary as a part of his argument to show that what he maintained respecting the Messiah was found in the Old Testament, he makes his appeal to that, and shows that the Redeemer is represented as addressing his people as *brethren.* It would have been easy to appeal to *facts*, and to have shown that the Redeemer used that term familiarly in addressing his disciples (comp. Mat. xii. 48, 49; xxv. 40; xxviii. 10; Luke viii. 21; Jn. xx. 17), but that would not have been pertinent to his object.　Those passages, however, are full proof to *us* that the prediction in the Psalm was literally fulfilled.　¶ *In the midst of the church.* That is, in the assembly of my brethren.　The *point* of the proof urged by the apostle lies in the first part of the quotation.　This latter part seems to have been adduced because it might assist their memory to have the whole verse quoted; or because it contained an interesting truth respecting the Redeemer, though not precisely a *proof* of what he was urging; or be-

cause it *implied* substantially the same truth as the former member. It shows that he was *united* with his church; that he was one of them; that he mingled with them as among brethren.　¶ *Will I sing praise.* That the Redeemer united with his disciples in singing praise, we may suppose to have been in the highest degree probable—though, I believe, but a single case is mentioned—that at the close of the supper which he instituted to commemorate his death, Mat. xxvi. 30. This, therefore, proves what the apostle intended—that the Messiah was among them as his brethren; that he spoke to them as such; and that he mingled in their devotions as one of their number.

13. *And again.* That is, it is said in another place, or language is used of the Messiah in another place, indicating the confidence which he put in God, and showing that he partook of the feelings of the children of God, and regarded himself as identified with them.　¶ *I will put my trust in him.* I will confide in God; implying (1) a sense of dependence on God; and (2) confidence in him.　It is with reference to the former idea that the apostle seems to use it here—as denoting a condition where there was felt to be need of divine aid.　His object is to prove that he took part with his people, and regarded them as brethren; and the purpose of this quotation seems to be to show that he was in such a situation as to make an expression of *dependence* proper. He used language which showed that he was one with his people, sharing their dependence and their piety, and that he could mingle with the tenderest sympathy in all their feelings.　It is not certain from what place this passage is quoted.　In Ps. xviii. 3, and the corresponding passage in 2 Sam. xxii. 3, the Hebrew is אֶחֱסֶה־בּוֹ —"I will trust in him;" but this Psalm has never been regarded as having any reference to the Messiah,

even by the Jews, and it is difficult
to see how it could be considered as
having any relation to him.   Most
critics, therefore, as Rosenmüller, Calvin, Koppe, Bloomfield, Stuart, &c.,
regard the passage as taken from Is.
viii. 17.   The reasons for this are,
(1) that the words are the same in
the Septuagint as in the epistle to
the Hebrews; (2) that the apostle
immediately quotes the next verse as
applicable to the Messiah; (3) that
no other place occurs where the same
expression is found.   The Hebrew
in Is. viii. 17, is וְקִוֵּיתִי לוֹ — "I will
wait for him," or I will trust in him
—rendered by the Septuagint πεποι-
θὼς ἔσομαι ἐπ' αὐτῷ—the same phrase
precisely as is used by Paul — and
there can be no doubt that he meant
to quote it here.   The *sense* in Isaiah
is, that he as a prophet had closed his
message to the people; he had been
directed to seal up the testimony; he
had exhorted the nation to repent,
but he had done it in vain; and he
had now nothing to do but to put
his trust in the Lord, and commit the
whole cause to him.   His only hope
was in God; and he calmly and confidently committed his cause to him.
Paul evidently designs to refer this to
the Messiah; and the sense as applied
to him is, "The Messiah in using this
language expresses himself *as a man.*
It is *men* who exercise dependence on
God; and by the use of this language
he speaks as one who had the nature
of man; who expressed the feelings
of the pious; and who showed that
he was one of them, and that he regarded them as brethren."   There is
not much difficulty in the *argument*
of the passage, for it is seen that in
such language he must speak as *a
man,* or as one having human nature;
but the main difficulty is on the question how this and the verse following
can be applied to the Messiah? In the
prophecy they seem to refer solely to
Isaiah, and to be expressive of his
feelings alone—the feelings of a man
who saw little encouragement in his
work, and who, having done all that
he could do, at last put his sole trust
in God.   In regard to this difficult and

yet unsettled question, the reader may
consult my Introduction to Isaiah, § 7.
The following remarks may serve in
part to remove the difficulty: (1) The
passage in Isaiah (viii. 17, 18) occurs
in the midst of a number of predic-
tions relating to the Messiah — preceded and followed by passages that
had an ultimate reference undoubtedly to him.   See Isa. vii. 14; viii. 8;
ix. 1–7, and Notes on those passages.
(2) The language, if used of Isaiah,
would as accurately and fitly express
the feelings and the condition of the
Redeemer. There was such a remarkable similarity in the circumstances,
that the same language would express
the condition of both.   Both had delivered a solemn message to men; both
had come to exhort them to turn to
God, and to put their trust in him,
and both with the same result. The
nation had disregarded them alike,
and now their only hope was to confide in God, and the language here
used would express the feelings of
both—"I will *trust in God.   I will
put confidence in him, and look to
him."   (3) There can be little doubt
that in the time of Paul this passage
was regarded by the Jews as applicable to the Messiah.   This is evident,
because (*a*) Paul would not have so
quoted it as a *proof-text* unless it
would be admitted to have such a
reference by those to whom he wrote;
and (*b*) because in Rom. ix. 32, 33, it is
evident that the passage in Isa. viii. 14
is regarded as having reference to the
Messiah, and as being so admitted by
the Jews.   It is true that this may be
considered merely as an argument *ad
hominem*—or an argument from what
was admitted by those with whom he
was reasoning, without vouching for
the precise accuracy of the manner in
which the passage was applied; but
that method of argument is admitted
elsewhere, and why should we not
expect to find the sacred writers
reasoning as other men do, and especially as was common in their own
times?

[Yet the integrity of the apostle would seem
to demand that he argue, not only *ex concessis,*
but *ex veris.* We cannot suppose for a moment
that the sacred writers (whatever others might

14 Forasmuch then as the children are partakers of flesh and

blood, ^u he also himself likewise took

u Jn.1.14.

do) would take advantage of erroneous admis-
sions.   We would rather expect them to correct these.   Proceed upon them they could not.
See the Supplementary Note on chap. i. 5.
Without the help of this defence, what the
author has otherwise alleged here is enough to
vindicate the use the apostle has made of the
passage.   See also the Note on chap. ii. 6.]

The apostle is showing them that according to *their own Scriptures,* and
in accordance with principles which
they themselves admitted, it was necessary that the Messiah should be
a man and a sufferer; that he should
be identified with his people, and be
able to use language which would
express that condition.   In doing this,
it is not remarkable that he should
apply to him language which *they*
admitted to belong to him, and which
would accurately describe his condition.   (4) It is not necessary to suppose that the passage in Isaiah had
an *original* and *primary* reference to
the Messiah.   It is evident from the
connection that it had not.   There
was a *primary* reference to Isaiah
himself, and to his children as being
emblems of certain truths.   But still
there was a strong *resemblance,* in
certain respects, between his feelings
and condition and those of the Messiah — such a resemblance that the
one would not unaptly symbolize the
other.   There was such a resemblance
that the mind, probably of the prophet himself, and of the people, would
look forward to the more remote but
similar event—the coming, and the circumstances, of the Messiah.   So strong
was this resemblance, and so much did
the expressions of the prophet on that
occasion accord with his declarations
elsewhere pertaining to the Messiah,
that in the course of time they came
to be regarded as relating to him in
a very important sense, and as destined to have their complete fulfilment when he should come.   As such
they seem to have been used in the
time of Paul; and no one can PROVE
that the application was improper.
Who can demonstrate that God did

not *intend* that those transactions referred to by Isaiah should be designed as symbols of what would occur
in the time of the Redeemer?   They
were certainly symbolical actions—
for they are expressly so said to have
been by Isaiah himself (Isa. viii. 18),
and none can demonstrate that they
might not have had an ultimate reference to the Redeemer.   ¶ *And again.*
In another verse, or in another declaration; to wit, Isa. vii. 18.   ¶ *Behold I
and the children which God hath given
me.*   This is only a part of the passage in Isaiah, and seems to have been
partially quoted because the *point* of
the quotation consisted in the fact
that he sustained to them somewhat
of the relation of a parent toward his
children—as having the same *nature,*
and as being identified with them in
interest and feeling.   As it is used by
Isaiah, it means that he and his children were "for signs and emblems"
to the people of his time—to communicate and confirm the will of God,
and to be pledges of the divine favour
and protection.   See Notes on the
passage in Isaiah.   As applied to the
Messiah, it means that he sustained
to his people a relation so intimate
that they could be addressed and regarded as his children.   They were of
one family, one nature.   He became
one of them, and he had in them all
the interest which a father has in his
sons.   He had, therefore, a nature like
ours; and though he was exalted
above the angels, yet his relation to
man was like the most tender and
intimate earthly connections, showing
that he took part in the same nature
with us.   The *point* is, that he was a
man; that since those who were to
be redeemed partook of flesh and
blood, *he* also took part of the same
(ver. 14), and thus identified himself
with them.

14. *Forasmuch then.*   Since; or because.   ¶ *As the children.*   Those who
were to become the adopted children
of God; or who were to sustain that
relation to him.   ¶ *Are partakers of*

part of the same; that *through death he might destroy him that

v 1 Co.15.54.

flesh and blood. Have a human, and not an angelic nature. Since they are men, he became a man. There was a fitness or propriety that he should partake of their nature. See Notes on 1 Cor. xv. 50; Mat. xvi. 17. ¶ *He also himself*, &c. He also became a man, or partook of the same nature with them. See Notes on Jn. i. 14. ¶ *That through death.* By dying. It is implied here (1) that the work which he undertook of destroying him that had the power of death, was to be accomplished by *his own dying;* and (2) that in order to this, it was necessary that he should be a man. An angel does not die, and therefore he did not take on him the nature of angels; the Son of God in his divine nature could not die, and therefore he assumed a form in which he *could* die—that of a man. In that nature the Son of God could taste of death; and thus he could destroy him that had the power of death. ¶ *He might destroy.* That he might *subdue*, or that he might overcome him, and destroy his dominion. The word *destroy* here is not used in the sense of *closing life*, or of *killing*, but in the sense of bringing into subjection, or crushing his power. This is the work which the Lord Jesus came to perform—to destroy the kingdom of Satan in the world, and to set up another kingdom in its place. This was understood by Satan to be his object. See Notes on Mat. viii. 29; Mark i. 24. ¶ *That had the power of death.* I understand this as meaning that the devil was the *cause* of death in this world. He was the means of its introduction, and of its long and melancholy reign. This does not *affirm* anything of his power of inflicting death in particular instances—whatever may be true on that point—but that *death* was a part of his dominion; that he introduced it; that he seduced man from God, and led on the train of woes which result in death. He also made it terrible. Instead of being regarded as

had the power of death, that is, the devil;

falling asleep, or being looked on without alarm, it becomes under him the means of terror and distress. What *power* Satan may have in inflicting death in particular instances no one can tell. The Jewish Rabbins speak much of Sammael, "the angel of death"—מַלְאַךְ הַמָּוֶת—*malach-hammaveth*, who they supposed had the control of life, and who was the great messenger employed in closing it. The Scriptures, it is believed, are silent on that point. But that Satan was the means of introducing "death into the world, and all our woe," no one can doubt; and over the whole subject, therefore, he may be said to have had *power.* To *destroy* that dominion; to rescue man; to restore him to life; to place him in a world where death is unknown; to introduce a state of things where *not another one would ever die*, was the great purpose for which the Redeemer came. What a noble object! What enterprise in the universe has been so grand as this? Surely an undertaking that contemplates the annihilation of DEATH; that designs to bring this dark dominion to an end, is full of benevolence, and should commend itself to every man as worthy of his profound attention and gratitude. What woes are caused by death in this world! They are seen everywhere. The earth is "arched with graves." It is a "vast revolving grave." In almost every dwelling death has been doing his work of misery. The palace cannot exclude him; and he comes unbidden into the cottage. He finds his way to the dwelling of ice in which the Esquimaux and the Greenlander live; to the tent of the Bedouin Arab, and the wandering Tartar; to the wigwam of the Indian, and to the harem of the Turk; to the splendid mansion of the rich, and to the abode of the poor. That reign of death has now extended near six thousand years, and will travel on to future times—meeting each genera-tion, and consigning the young, the

15 And deliver them who through | *fear of death were all their life-time subject to bondage.

w Lu.1.74.

vigorous, the lovely, and the pure, to dust. Shall that gloomy reign continue for ever? Is there no way to arrest it? Is there no place where death can be excluded? Yes; *heaven* —and the object of the Redeemer is to bring us there.

15. *And deliver them.* Not all of them *in fact,* though the way is open for all. This deliverance relates (1) to the *dread* of death. He came to free men from that. (2) From death itself—that is, ultimately to bring them to a world where death will be unknown. The *dread* of death may be removed by the work of Christ, and they who had been subject to constant alarms on account of it may be brought to look on it with calmness and peace; and ultimately they will be brought to a world where it will be wholly unknown. The *dread* of death is taken away, or they are delivered from that, because (*a*) the *cause* of that dread—to wit, sin—is removed. See Notes on 1 Cor. xv. 54, 55. (*b*) Because they are enabled to look to the world beyond with triumphant joy. Death conducts them to heaven. A Christian has nothing to fear in death; nothing beyond the grave. In no part of the universe has he anything to dread, for God is his friend, and he will be his Protector everywhere. On the dying bed; in the grave; on the way up to the judgment; at the solemn tribunal; in the eternal world, he is equally under the eye and the protection of his Saviour —and of what should he be afraid? ¶ *Who through fear of death.* From the dread of dying; that is, whenever they think of it, and they think of it *so often* as to make them slaves of that fear. This obviously means the natural dread of dying, and not particularly the fear of punishment beyond. It is *that* indeed which often gives its principal terror to the dread of death, but still the apostle refers here evidently to natural death, as an object which men fear. All men have, by nature, this dread of dying, and perhaps some of the inferior creation

have it also. It is certain that it exists in the heart of every *man,* and that God has implanted it there for some wise purpose. There is the dread (1) of the dying pang. (2) Of the darkness and gloom of mind that attends it. (3) Of the unknown world beyond—the "evil that we know not of." (4) Of the chilliness, the loneliness, and the darkness of the tomb. (5) Of the solemn trial at the bar of God. (6) Of the condemnation which awaits the guilty—the apprehension of future woe. There is no other evil that we fear so much as we do DEATH, and there is nothing more clear than that God *intended* that we should have a dread of dying. The REASONS why he designed this are equally clear. (1) One may have been to lead men to *prepare* for it— which otherwise they would neglect. (2) Another, to *deter them from committing self-murder* —where nothing else would deter them. Facts have shown that it was necessary that there should be some strong principle in the human bosom to prevent this crime. So sick do men become of the life that God gave them; so weary of the world; so overwhelmed with calamity; so oppressed with disappointment and cares, that they lay violent hands on themselves, and rush unbidden into the awful presence of their Creator. This would occur more frequently by far than it now does, if it were not for the salutary fear of death which God has implanted in every bosom. The feelings of the human heart on this subject were never more accurately or graphically drawn than in the celebrated soliloquy of Hamlet—

> "To die;—to sleep—
> No more;—and by a sleep, to say we end
> The heart-ache, and the thousand natural shocks
> That flesh is heir to,—'tis a consummation
> Devoutly to be wished. To die—to sleep—
> To sleep!—perchance to dream;—ay, there's the rub;
> For in that sleep of death what dreams may come,
> When we have shuffled off this mortal coil,
> Must give us pause:—there's the respect
> That makes calamity of so long a life·

16 For verily [5] he took not on *him*　　| *the nature of* angels; but he took on

[5] *he taketh not hold of angels, but of the seed of Abraham he taketh hold.*　　| *him* the seed of Abraham.

For who would bear the whips and scorns of time,
The oppressor's wrong, the proud man's contumely,
The pangs of despised love, the law's delay,
The insolence of office, and the spurns
That patient merit of the unworthy takes,
When he himself might his quietus make
With a bare bodkin? Who would fardels bear,
To grunt and sweat under a weary life,
But that the dread of something after death,—
The undiscovered country from whose bourne
No traveller returns,—puzzles the will,
And makes us rather bear those ills we have,
Than fly to others that we know not of?
Thus conscience does make cowards of us all,
And thus the native hue of resolution
Is sicklied o'er with the pale cast of thought;
And enterprises of great pith and moment
With this regard their currents turn awry,
And lose the name of action."

God *designed* that man should be deterred from rushing uncalled into his awful presence by this salutary dread of death, and his implanting this feeling in the human heart is one of the most striking and conclusive proofs of a moral government over the world. This instinctive dread of death can be overcome *only* by religion—and *then* man does not NEED it to reconcile him to life. He becomes submissive to trials. He is willing to bear all that is laid on him. He resigns himself to the dispensations of Providence, and feels that life, even in affliction, is the gift of God, and is a valuable endowment. He now dreads *self-murder* as a crime of deep dye, and religion restrains him and keeps him by a more gentle and a more effectual restraint than the dread of death. The man who has true religion is willing to live or to die; he feels that life is the gift of God, and that he will take it away in the best time and manner; and feeling this, he is willing to leave all in his hands. We may remark, (1) How much do we owe to religion! It is the only thing that will effectually take away the dread of death, and yet secure this point—to make man willing to live in all the circumstances where God may place him. It is *possible* that philosophy or stoicism may remove to a great extent the dread of death, but then it will be likely to make a man *willing* to take his life if he is

placed in trying circumstances. Such an effect it had on Cato in Utica; and such an effect it had on Hume, who maintained that suicide was lawful, and that to turn a current of blood from its accustomed channel was of no more consequence than to change the course of any other fluid! (2) In what a sad condition is the sinner! Thousands there are who never think of death with composure, and who all their life long are subject to bondage through the fear of it. They never think of it if they can avoid it; and when it is forced upon them, it fills them with alarm. They attempt to drive the thought away. They travel to other lands; they plunge into business; they occupy the mind with trifles; they read works of fiction; they seek the society of the gay; they visit the assembly room, the theatre, the opera; they attempt to drown their fears in the intoxicating bowl: but all this tends only to make death more terrific and awful when the reality comes. If man were wise, he would seek an interest in that religion which, if it did nothing else, would deliver him from the dread of death; and the influence of the gospel in this respect, if it exerted no other, is worth to a man all the sacrifices and self-denials which it would ever require. ¶ *All their lifetime subject to bondage.* Slaves of fear; in a depressed and miserable condition, like slaves under a master. They have no freedom; no comfort; no peace. From this miserable state Christ comes to deliver man. Religion enables him to look calmly on death and the judgment, and to feel that all will be well.

16. *For verily.* Truly. ¶ *He took not on* him the nature of *angels*. Margin, *he taketh not hold of angels, but of the seed of Abraham he taketh hold.* The word here used—ἐπιλαμβάνεται—means, to take hold upon; to seize; to surprise; to take hold with a view to detain for one's self (Robinson). Then it means to take hold of one as by the hand—with a view to aid, con-

17 Wherefore in all things it behoved him to be made like unto *his*

duct, or succour, Mark viii. 23; Acts xxiii. 19. It is rendered *took*, Mark viii. 23; Luke ix. 47; xiv. 4; Acts ix. 27; xvii. 19; xviii. 17; xxi. 30, 33; xxiii. 19; Heb. viii. 9; *caught*, Mat. xiv. 31; Acts xvi. 19; *take hold*, Luke xx. 20, 26; *lay hold*, and *laid hold*, Luke xxiii. 26; 1 Tim. vi. 12. The general idea is that of seizing upon, or laying hold of anyone—no matter what the object is—whether to aid, to drag to punishment, or simply to conduct. Here it means to lay hold with reference to *aid*, or *help;* and the meaning is, that he did not seize the nature of angels, or take it to himself with reference to rendering *them* aid, but he assumed the nature of man— in order to aid *him.* He undertook the work of human redemption, and consequently it was necessary for him to be a man. ¶ *But he took on* him *the seed of Abraham.* He came to help the descendants of Abraham, and consequently, as they were men, he became a man. Writing to Jews, it was not unnatural for the apostle to refer particularly to them as the descendants of Abraham, though this does not exclude the idea that he died for the whole human race. It was true that he came to render aid to the descendants of Abraham, but it was also true that he died for all. The fact that I love one of my children, and that I make provision for his education, and *tell* him so, does not exclude the idea that I love the others also, or make it improper for me to make to them a similar appeal.

17. *Wherefore in all things.* In respect to his body; his soul; his rank and character. There was a propriety that he should be like them, and partake of their nature. The meaning is, that there was a fitness that nothing should be wanting in him in reference to the innocent propensities and sympathies of humanity. ¶ *It behoved him.* It became him; or there was a fitness and propriety in it. The reason why it was proper, the apostle proceeds to state. ¶ *Like*

brethren, that he might be *x*a merciful and faithful high priest in

x Ge.19.15,16.

unto his *brethren.* Like unto those who sustained to him the relation of brethren; particularly as he undertook to redeem the descendants of Abraham, and as he was a descendant of Abraham himself, there was a propriety that he should be like them. He calls them brethren; and it was proper that he should show that he regarded them as such by assuming their nature. ¶ *That he might be a merciful and faithful high priest.* (1) That he might be *merciful;* that is, compassionate. That he might know how to pity us in our infirmities and trials, by having a nature like our own. (2) That he might be *faithful;* that is, perform with fidelity all the functions pertaining to the office of high-priest. The idea is, that it was needful that he should become a man; that he should experience, as we do, the infirmities and trials of life; and that, by being a man, and partaking of all that pertained to man except his sins, he might feel how necessary it was that there should be *fidelity* in the office of high-priest. Here was a race of sinners and sufferers. They were exposed to the wrath of God. They were liable to everlasting punishment. The judgment impended over the race, and the day of vengeance hastened on. *All now depended on the Great High-priest.* All their hope was in his *fidelity* to the great office which he had undertaken. If he was faithful, all would be safe; if unfaithful, all would be lost. Hence the necessity that he should enter fully into the feelings, the fears, and the dangers of man; that he should become one of the race and be identified with them, so that he might be qualified to perform with faithfulness the great trust committed to him. ¶ *High priest.* The Jewish high-priest was the successor of Aaron, and was at the head of the ministers of religion among the Jews. He was set apart with solemn ceremonies—clad in his sacred vestments—and anointed with

things *pertaining* to God, to make reconciliation for the sins of the people.

18 For in that he himself hath suffered, being tempted, he is able to succour them that are tempted.

---

oil, Ex. xxix. 5–9; Lev. viii. 2. He was by his office the general judge of all that pertained to religion, and even of the judicial affairs of the Jewish nation, Deut. xvii. 8–12; xix. 17; xxi. 5; xxxiii. 9,10. He only had the privilege of entering the most holy place once a year, on the great day of expiation, to make atonement for the sins of the people, Lev. xvi. 2, &c. He was the oracle of truth—so that, when clothed in his proper vestments, and having on the Urim and Thummim, he made known the will of God in regard to future events. The Lord Jesus became in the Christian dispensation what the Jewish high-priest was in the old; and an important object of this epistle is to show that he far surpassed the Jewish high-priest, and in what respects the Jewish high-priest was designed to typify the Redeemer. Paul, therefore, early introduces the subject, and shows that the Lord Jesus came to perform the functions of that sacred office, and that he was eminently qualified for it. ¶ *In things* pertaining *to God.* In offering sacrifice; or in services of a religious nature. The *great* purpose was to offer sacrifice, and to make intercession; and the idea is, that Jesus took on himself our nature that he might sympathize with us; that thus he might be faithful to the great trust committed to him—the redemption of the world. Had *he* been unfaithful, all would have been lost, and the world would have sunk down to woe. ¶ *To make reconciliation.* By his death as a sacrifice. The word here used—ἱλάσκομαι—occurs but in one other place in the New Testament (Luke xviii. 13), where it is rendered "God *be merciful* to me a sinner;" that is, be reconciled to me. The *noun* (ἱλασμός, *propitiation*) is used in 1 Jn. ii. 2; iv. 10. The word here means properly to *appease,* to reconcile, to conciliate; and hence to *propitiate* AS TO *sins;* that is, to propitiate God in reference to sins, or to render him propitious.

The Son of God became a man that he might so fully enter into the feelings of the people as to be faithful, and that he might be qualified as a high-priest to perform the great work of rendering God propitious in regard to sins. How he did this is fully shown in the subsequent parts of the epistle.

18. *For in that he himself hath suffered.* Because he has suffered, he is able to sympathize with sufferers. ¶ *Being tempted.* Or, being *tried.* The Greek word here used is more general in its meaning than the English word *tempted.* It means to *put to the proof;* to try the nature or character of; and this may be done either (1) by subjecting a person to *afflictions* or *sufferings* that his true character may be tried—that it may be seen whether he has sincere piety and love to God; or (2) by allowing one to fall into *temptation,* properly so called—where some strong inducement to evil is presented to the mind, and where it becomes thus a *trial* of virtue. The Saviour was subjected to both these in as severe a form as men have been ever called to endure. His sufferings surpassed all others; and the temptations of Satan (see Mat. iv.) were presented in the most alluring form in which he could exhibit them. Being *proved* or *tried* in both these respects, he showed that he had a strength of virtue which could bear all that could ever occur to seduce him from attachment to God; and at the same time to make him a perfect model for those who should be tried in the same manner. ¶ *He is able to succour,* &c. This does not mean that he would not have had *power* to assist others if he had not gone through these sufferings himself, but that he is now qualified to sympathize with them from the fact that he has endured like trials.

"He knows what sore temptations mean,
    For he has felt the same."

The idea is, that one who has himself been called to suffer, is able to sympa-

thize with those who suffer; that one who has been tempted, is able to sympathize with those who are tempted in like manner; that one who has been sick, is qualified to sympathize with the sick; that one who has lost a child, can sympathize with him who follows his beloved son or daughter to the grave; that one who has had some strong temptation to sin urged upon himself, can sympathize with those who are now tempted; that one who has never been sick, or who has never buried a friend, or been tempted, is poorly qualified to impart consolation in such scenes. Hence it is that ministers of the gospel are often—like their Master—much persecuted and afflicted, that they may be able to assist others. Comp. 2 Cor. i. 4. Hence they are called to part with the children of their love, or to endure long and painful sicknesses, or to pass through scenes of poverty and want, that they may sympathize with the most humble and afflicted of their flock. And they should be willing to endure all this; for (1) thus they are like their Master (comp. Col. i. 24; Phil. iii. 10); and (2) they are thus enabled to be far more extensively useful. Many a minister owes a large part of his usefulness to the fact that he has been much afflicted; and for those afflictions, therefore, he should unfeignedly thank God. The idea which is here expressed by the apostle—that one is enabled to sympathize with others from having himself suffered—was long since beautifully expressed by Virgil :

Me quoque per multos similis fortuna labores,
Jactatam, hac demum voluit consistere terra.
Non ignara mali, miseris succurrere disco.
              Æn. i. 628.

For I myself, like you, have been distressed,
Till heaven afforded me this place of rest;
Like you, an alien in a land unknown,
I learn to pity woes so like my own.
              DRYDEN.

Jesus is thus able to alleviate the sufferer. In all our temptations and trials let us remember (1) that he suffered more—infinitely more—than we can do, and that in all our sorrows we shall never reach what he endured. We enter no region of trial where he has not gone before us; we tread no dark and gloomy way where he has not gone before us. (2) Let us remember that he is to us *a brother,* for he " is not ashamed to call us brethren." He had a nature like ours; he condescended to appear as one of our race, with all the innocent propensities and passions of a man. What matchless condescension! And what an honour for *us* to be permitted to address him as an " elder brother," and to know that he feels a deep sympathy in our woes! (3) Let us then, in all times of affliction, look to him. Go not, suffering Christian, to philosophy; attempt not to deaden your feelings by the art of the Stoic; but go at once to the Saviour—the great sympathizing Highpriest, who is able to succour you and cast your burdens on him.

" His heart is made of tenderness,
   His soul is filled with love.

" Touch'd with a sympathy within,
   He knows our feeble frame;
He knows what sore temptations mean,
   For he has felt the same.

" Then let our humble faith address
   His mercy and his power;
We shall obtain delivering grace
   In every trying hour."

CHAPTER III.

ANALYSIS OF THE CHAPTER.

The Jews valued their religion on many accounts. One was, that it had been given by the instrumentality of distinguished prophets sent from God, and by the medium of angels. The apostle, in the previous chapters, had shown that in these respects the Christian religion had the advantage over theirs, for it had been communicated by one who was superior to any of the prophets, and who had a rank above the angels. Next to this, they valued their religion because it had been imparted by a lawgiver so eminent as Moses—a man more distinguished than any other one on earth as a legislator. To him they looked with pride as the founder of their economy, and the medium through whom God had given them their peculiar laws. Next to him,

CHAPTER III.

WHEREFORE, holy brethren, partakers of the heavenly

calling, consider the Apostle and [a] High Priest of our profession, Christ Jesus;

a ch. 4. 14.

---

their high-priest was the most important functionary in the nation. He was at the head of their religion, and served to distinguish it from all others, for they had no conception of any form of true religion unless the office of high-priest was recognized. The apostle, therefore, proceeds to show that in these respects the Christian religion had lost nothing, but had the advantage over the Jewish altogether; that it was founded by one superior to Moses; and that Christ, as high-priest, was superior by far to the high-priest of the Jews.

This chapter, and to ver. 13 of chap. iv., relates to the first of these points, and is occupied with showing the superiority of the Redeemer to Moses, and the consequences which result from the admission of that fact. It consists, therefore, of two parts.

I. The first is employed in showing, that if the author of the Christian religion is compared with Moses, he has the preference, ver. 1–6. Moses was indeed faithful, but it was *as a servant.* Christ was faithful *as a son.* He had a rank as much above that of Moses as one who builds a house has over the house itself.

II. The consequences that resulted from that, chap. iii. 7–19, and chap. iv. 1–13. The general doctrine here is, that there would be special danger in apostatizing from the Christian religion—danger far superior to that which was threatened to the Israelites if they were disobedient to Moses. In illustrating this, the apostle is naturally led to a statement of the warnings against defection under Moses, and of the consequences of unbelief and rebellion there. He entreats them, therefore, (1) Not to harden their hearts against God, as the Israelites did who were excluded from Canaan, ver. 7–11. (2) To be on their guard against unbelief, ver. 12. (3) To exhort one another constantly, and to stimulate one another, that they might not fall away, ver. 13.

(4) To hold the beginning of their confidence steadfast unto the end, and not to provoke God as they did who came out of Egypt, ver. 14–19. In the following chapter (ver. 1–13) he completes the exhortation, by showing them that many who came out of Egypt were excluded from the Promised Land, and that there was equal danger now; and he then proceeds with the comparison of Christ with the Jewish high-priest, and extends that comparison through the remainder of the doctrinal part of the epistle.

1. *Wherefore.* That is, since Christ sustains such a character as has been stated in the previous chapter; since he is so able to succour those who need assistance; since he assumed our nature that he might be a merciful and faithful high-priest, his character ought to be attentively considered, and we ought to endeavour fully to understand it. ¶ *Holy brethren.* The name *brethren* is often given to Christians to denote that they are of one family. It is *possible,* also, that the apostle may have used the word here in a double sense—denoting that they were his brethren both as *Christians* and as *Jews.* The word *holy* is applied to them to denote that they were set apart to God, or that they were sanctified. The Jews were often called a "holy people," as being consecrated to God; and Christians are holy, not only as consecrated to God, but as sanctified. ¶ *Partakers of the heavenly calling.* On the meaning of the word *calling,* see Notes on Eph. iv. 1. The "*heavenly* calling" denotes the calling which was given to them from heaven, or which was of a heavenly nature. It pertained to heaven, not to earth; it came from heaven, not from earth; it was a calling to the reward and happiness of heaven, and not to the pleasures and honours of the world. ¶ *Consider.* Attentively ponder all that is said of

2 Who was faithful to him that appointed[1] him, as also [b]Moses *was faithful* in all his house.

1 *made.*   b Nu.12.7.

3 For this *man* was [c]counted worthy of more glory than Moses, inasmuch as [d]he who hath builded

c ch.2.9; Is.22.23,24; Re.5.11-13; Mat.16.18.
d Zec.6.12,13.

the Messiah. Think of his rank; his dignity; his holiness; his sufferings; his death; his resurrection; his ascension; his intercession. Think of him that you may see the claims to a holy life; that you may learn to bear trials; that you may be kept from apostasy. The character and work of the Son of God are worthy of the profound and prayerful consideration of every man; and especially every Christian should reflect much on him. Of the friend that we love we think much; but what friend have we like the Lord Jesus? ¶ *The Apostle.* The word *apostle* is nowhere else applied to the Lord Jesus. The word means one who *is sent;* and in this sense it might be applied to the Redeemer as one *sent* by God, or as, by way of eminence, THE one sent by him. But the connection seems to demand that there should be some allusion here to one who sustained a similar rank among the Jews; and it is probable that the allusion is to *Moses*, as having been the great apostle of God to the Jewish people, and that Paul here means to say, that the Lord Jesus, under the new dispensation, filled the place both of Moses *and* of the high-priest under the old, and that the office of "apostle" and "high-priest," instead of being now separated, as it was between Moses and Aaron under the old dispensation, was now blended in the Messiah. The name *apostle* is not, indeed, given to Moses directly in the Old Testament, but the verb from which the Hebrew word for apostle is derived is frequently given him. Thus in Ex. iii. 10, it is said, "Come now, therefore, and *I will send thee* unto Pharaoh." And in verse 13, "The God of your fathers *hath sent me unto* you." So also in ver. 14, 15 of the same chapter. From the word there used—שָׁלַח, *to send*—the word denoting *apostle*—שָׁלִיחַ—is derived; and it is not improbable that Moses

would be regarded as being, by way of eminence, THE one *sent* by God. Further, the Jews applied the word שָׁלִיחַ—*apostle*, to the minister of the synagogue; to him who presided over its affairs, and who had the general charge of the services there; and in this sense it might be applied, by way of eminence, to Moses as being the general director and controller of the religious affairs of the nation, and as *sent* for that purpose. The object of Paul is to show that the Lord Jesus in the Christian system—as the great apostle sent from God—sustained a rank and office similar to this, but superior in dignity and authority. ¶ *And High Priest.* One great object of this epistle is to compare the Lord Jesus with the high-priest of the Jews, and to show that he was in all respects superior. This was important, because the office of high-priest was that which eminently distinguished the Jewish religion, and because the Christian religion proposed to abolish that. It became necessary, therefore, to show that all that was sacred and valuable in that office was to be found in the Christian system. This was done by showing that in the Lord Jesus all the characteristics of a high-priest were combined; that all the functions which had been performed in the Jewish ritual were performed by him; and that all which had been prefigured by the Jewish high-priest was fulfilled in him. The apostle here merely alludes to him, or names him as the high-priest, and then postpones the consideration of his character in that respect till after he had compared him with Moses. ¶ *Of our profession.* Of our religion; of that religion which we profess. The apostle and high-priest whom we acknowledged as ours when we embraced the Christian religion.

2. *Who was faithful.* See Notes on chap. ii. 17. He performed with fidel-

ity all the offices intrusted to him. ¶ *To him that appointed him.* Margin, *made.* The word *made*, however, is used in the sense of constituted, or appointed. The meaning is, that he was faithful to God. Perhaps Paul urges on them the necessity of considering *his fidelity*, in order to keep *them* from the danger of apostasy. A leading object of this epistle was to preserve those whom he addressed from apostatizing from God amidst the temptations and trials to which they were exposed. In doing this, what could be a more powerful argument than to direct their attention to the unwavering constancy and fidelity of the Lord Jesus? The *importance* of such a virtue in the Saviour is manifest. It is seen everywhere; and all the great interests of the world depend on it. A husband should maintain inviolate fidelity toward a wife, and a wife toward her husband; a child should be faithful to a parent, an apprentice to his employer, a lawyer to his client, a physician to his patient, an ambassador to the government that commissions him. No matter what may be the temptations in the way, in all these, and in all other relations, there should be inviolate fidelity. The welfare of the world depended on the faithfulness of the Lord Jesus. Had *he* failed in that, all would have been lost. His fidelity was worthy of the more attentive consideration from the numerous temptations which beset his path, and the attempts which were made to turn him aside from his devotedness to God. Amidst all the temptations of the adversary, and all the trials through which he passed, he never for a moment swerved from fidelity to the great trust which had been committed to his hands. What better example to preserve them from the temptations' to apostasy could the apostle propose to the Christians whom he addressed? What, in these temptations and trials, could be more appropriate than for them to "*consider*" the example of the great apostle and high-priest of their profession? What more proper for us now in the trials and temptations of *our* lives,

than to keep that great and glorious example continually before our eyes? ¶ *As also Moses* was faithful. Fidelity to God was remarkable in Moses. In all the provocations and rebellions of the Jews, he was firm and unwavering. This is affirmed of him in Num. xii. 7, to which place the apostle here alludes, "My servant Moses is not so, who is faithful in all his house." The word *house*, as applied to Moses, is used probably in the sense of *family*, as it often is, and refers to the *family* over which he presided—that is, the Jewish nation. The whole Jewish people were *a household*, or the family of God, and Moses was appointed to preside over it, and was faithful in the functions of his office there.

3. *For this* man. The Lord Jesus. The word "*man*" is understood, but there can be no doubt that he is referred to. ¶ *Was counted worthy.* Was more worthy; or *is* more worthy. The word here used does not refer to anything that had been *said* of him, or to any estimate which had been made of him. It means simply that he deserved more honour than Moses. *How* he was so, Paul proceeds to show. ¶ *Of more glory*—δόξης. Honour, dignity, regard. He had a higher rank, and he was worthy of more respect. This was saying much for the Messiah, and that it was proper to say this, Paul proceeds to show. He did not attempt in any way to undervalue Moses and his institutions. He gave him all the honour which the Jews were themselves disposed to render him. He admitted that he had been eminently faithful in the station where God had placed him; and he then proceeds to show that the Lord Jesus was entitled to honour superior to that, and that hence the Christian religion had more to attach its friends to it than the Jewish had. ¶ *Inasmuch as he who hath builded the house.* The idea here is, either that he who is the maker of a house—the architect—is worthy of more respect than the house itself; or that he who is the founder of a family is worthy of more honour than the family of which he is the founder. It seems to me that the former is the meaning—for the

the house hath more honour than the house.

4 For every house is builded by some *man;* ^ebut he that built all things *is* God.

e Is.42.5; Ep.2.10; 3.9.

latter is not always true. The founder of a family may be really deserving of much less respect than some of his descendants. But it is *always* true that the architect is worthy of more respect than the house which he makes. He exhibits intellect and skill. The house, however splendid, has neither. The plan of the house was drawn by him; its beauty, its proportions, its ornaments, are what he made them, and but for him they would not have existed. Michael Angelo was worthy of more honour than "St. Peter's" at Rome; and Sir Christopher Wren worthy of more than "St. Paul's" at London. Galileo is worthy of more praise than the telescope, and Fulton more than the steam-engine. All the evidence of skill and adaptedness that there is in an invention had its origin in the inventor; all the beauty of a statue or a temple had its origin in the mind of him that designed it. An author is worthy of more honour than a book; and he that forms a work of art is worthy of more respect than the work itself. This is the idea here. Paul assumes that *all* things owed their origin to the Son of God, chap. i. 2, 8, 10. He was the author of the universe; the source of all wise and well-founded systems; the originator of the Jewish dispensation over which Moses presided. Whatever beauty or excellence there might have been, therefore, in that system, was to be traced to him; and whatever ability even Moses displayed was imparted by him. Christ is really the head of the family over which Moses presided, and has claims, therefore, to higher honour as such.

4. *For every house is builded by some* man. The words in this verse are plain, and the sentiment in it clear. The only difficulty is in seeing the connection, and in understanding how it is intended to bear on what precedes, or on what follows. It is clear that every house must have a builder,

and equally clear that God is the Creator of all things. But what is the meaning of the passage in this connection? What is its bearing on the argument? If the verse was entirely omitted, and the fifth verse read in connection with the third, there would be apparently nothing wanting to complete the sense of the writer, or to finish the comparison which he had commenced. Various ways have been adopted to explain the difficulty. Perhaps the following observations may remove it, and express the true sense: (1) Every family must have a founder; every dispensation an author; every house a builder. There must be some one, therefore, over *all* dispensations—the old and the new—the Jewish and the Christian. (2) Paul *assumes* that the Lord Jesus is divine. He had demonstrated this in chap. i.; and he argues *as if* this were so, without now stopping to prove it, or even to affirm it expressly. (3) God must be over *all things.* He is Creator of all, and he must, therefore, be over all. As the Lord Jesus, therefore, is divine, he must be over the Jewish dispensation as well as the Christian—or he must, as God, have been at the head of that—or over his own family or household. (4) As such, he must have a glory and honour which could not belong to Moses. He, in his divine character, was the author of both the Jewish and the Christian dispensations, and he must, therefore, have a rank far superior to that of Moses—which was the point which the apostle designed to illustrate. The meaning of the whole may be thus expressed: "The Lord Jesus is worthy of more honour than Moses. He is so, as the maker of a house deserves more honour than the house. He is divine. In the beginning he laid the foundation of the earth, and was the agent in the creation of all things, chap. i. 2, 10. He rules, therefore, over all things, and, as supreme, must preside alike over

5 And *f* Moses verily *was* faithful in all his house, *g* as a servant, *h* for a testimony of those things which were to be spoken after;

6 But Christ *i* as a son over his

f Nu.12.7.   *g* Jos.1.2.   *h* De.18.15-19.   *i* Ps.2.7,12.

own house; *k* whose house are we, *l* if we hold fast the confidence and the rejoicing of the hope firm unto the end.

k 1 Pe.2.5.   *l* Mat.10.22; ch.10.38,39.

the Jewish and the Christian dispensations—for there must have been some one over them, or the author of them, as really as it must be true that every house has been built by some person. Being, therefore, over all things, and at the head of all dispensations, he MUST be more exalted than Moses." This seems to me to be the argument—an argument which is based on the supposition that he is at the head of all things, and that he was the agent in the creation of all worlds. This view will make all consistent. The Lord Jesus will be seen to have a claim to far higher honour than Moses, and Moses will be seen to have derived all *his* honour from the Mediator, by whom, and under whose administration, he had been appointed to the office which he held.

5. *Moses* was *faithful—as a servant.* Not as the head of the dispensation; not as having originated it; but as in the employ and under the direction of its great Founder and Author—the Messiah. As such a servant he deserves all the honour for fidelity which has ever been claimed for him, but it cannot be the honour which is due to him who is at the head of the family or house. Paul *assumed* that Moses was a *servant,* and argued on that supposition, without attempting to prove it, because it was so often affirmed in the Old Testament, and must have been conceded by all the Jews. In numerous instances he is spoken of as "THE servant of the Lord." See Josh. i. 1, 2; ix. 24; 1 Chr. vi. 49; 2 Chr. xxiv. 9; Neh. x. 29; Dan. ix. 11; Ex. xiv. 31; 1 Ki. viii. 56; Psa. cv. 26. As this point was undisputed, it was only necessary to show that the Messiah was superior to *a servant,* in order to make the argument clear. ¶ *For a testimony.* To bear witness to those truths which were to be revealed; that is, he was the instrument

of the divine communications to the people, or the medium by which God made his will known. He did not *originate* the truths himself; but he was the mere medium by which God made them known to his people—a servant whom He employed to communicate his will. The word "*after*" here is not necessary in order to a just translation of this passage, and obscures the sense. It does not mean that he was a witness of those truths which were to be spoken *subsequently* to his time under another dispensation, nor of those truths which the apostle proposed to consider in another part of the epistle, as Doddridge supposes; but it means merely that Moses stood forth as a public witness of the truths which God designed to reveal, or which were to be spoken. God did not speak to his people *directly,* face to face, but he spoke through Moses as an organ or medium. The sense is, Moses was a mere *servant* of God to communicate his will to man.

6. *But Christ as a son over his own house.* He is not a servant. To the whole household or family of God he sustains the same relation which a son and heir in a family does to the household. That relation is far different from that of a servant. Moses was the latter; Christ was the former. To God he sustained the relation of a Son, and recognized him as his Father, and sought in all things to do his will; but over the whole family of God—the entire church of all dispensations—he was like a son over the affairs of a family. Compared with the condition of a servant, Christ is as much superior to Moses as a son and heir is to the condition of a servant. A servant owns nothing; is heir to nothing; has no authority; has no right to control anything, and is himself wholly at the will of another. A son is the heir of all; has a prospective right to all; and is looked up to

7 Wherefore, (as the Holy Ghost saith, *m*To-day, if ye will hear his voice,

m Ps.95.7; ver.15.

8 Harden*n* not your hearts, as in the provocation, in the day of temptation in the wilderness;

n 2 Ch.30.8; Eze.18.30,31; ver.12,13.

by all with respect. But the idea here is not merely that Christ is *a son;* it is that *as* a son he is placed over the whole arrangements of the household, and is one to whom all is intrusted as if it were his own. ¶ *Whose house we are.* Of whose family we are a part, or to which we belong. That is, we belong to the family over which Christ is placed, and not to that which was subject to Moses. ¶ *If we hold fast.* A leading object of this epistle is to guard those to whom it was addressed against the danger of apostasy. Hence this is introduced on all suitable occasions, and the apostle here says, that the only evidence which they could have that they belonged to the family of Christ, would be that they held fast the confidence which they had unto the end. If they did not do that, it would demonstrate that they never belonged to his family; for evidence of having belonged to his household was to be furnished only by perseverance to the end. ¶ *The confidence.* The word here used properly means *the liberty of speaking boldly and without restraint;* then it means boldness or confidence in general. ¶ *And the rejoicing.* The word here used means properly *glorying, boasting,* and then *rejoicing.* These words are used here in an adverbial signification, and the meaning is, that the Christian has *a confident and a rejoicing hope.* It is (1) confident; bold; firm. It is not like the timid hope of the Pagan, and the dreams and conjectures of the philosopher; it is not that which gives way at every breath of opposition; it is bold, firm, and manly. It is (2) *rejoicing*—triumphant, exulting. Why should not the hope of heaven fill the soul with joy? Why should not he exult who has the prospect of being happy for ever? ¶ *Unto the end.* To the end of life. Our religion, our hope, our confidence in God must be persevered in to the end of life if we

would have evidence that we are his children. If hope is cherished for a while and then abandoned; if men profess religion and then fall away— no matter what were their raptures and triumphs—it proves that they never had any real piety. No evidence can be strong enough to prove that a man is a Christian, unless it leads him to persevere to the end of life.

7. *Wherefore.* In view of the fact that the Author of the Christian dispensation has a rank superior to that of Moses. Because Christ has claims on us far greater than those which Moses had, let us hearken to his voice, and dread his displeasure. ¶ *As the Holy Ghost saith.* In Psa. xcv. 7-11. This is full proof that, in the estimation of the author of this epistle, the writer of this Psalm was inspired. The Holy Ghost speaks through the word which he has revealed. The apostle quotes this passage, and applies it to those whom he addressed, because the admonition was as pertinent and important under the Christian dispensation as it was under the Jewish. The danger of hardening the heart by neglecting to hear his voice was as great, and the consequences would be as fearful and alarming. We should regard the solemn warnings in the Old Testament, against sin, and against the danger of apostasy, as addressed by the Holy Ghost to *us.* They are as applicable to us as they were to those to whom they were at first addressed; and we need all the influence of such appeals, to keep us from apostasy, as much as they did. ¶ *To-day.* Now; at present. At the very time when the command is addressed to you. It is not to be put off till to-morrow. All God's commands relate to *the present*—to this day—to the passing moment. He gives us no commands *about the future.* He does not require us to repent and to turn to him *to-morrow,* or

ten years hence. The reasons are obvious. (1) Duty pertains to the present. It is our duty to turn from sin, and to love him NOW. (2) We know not that we shall live to another day. A command, therefore, could not extend to that time unless it were accompanied with *a revelation* that we should live till then—and such a revelation God does not choose to give. Every one, therefore, should feel that whatever commands God addresses to him are addressed to him *now*. Whatever guilt he incurs by neglecting those commands is incurred *now*. For the *present* neglect and disobedience each one is to answer, and each one must give account to God for what he does TO-DAY. ¶ *If ye will hear.* If you are willing to hearken to God, listen now, and do not defer it to a future period. There is much in a *willingness* to hear the voice of God. A *willingness* to learn is usually the precursor of great attainments in knowledge. A *willingness* to reform is usually the precursor of reformation. Get a man *willing* to break off his habits of profaneness or intemperance, and usually all the rest is easy. The great difficulty in the mind of a sinner is in his *will*. He is unwilling to hear the voice of God; unwilling that he should reign over him; unwilling now to attend to religion. While this unwillingness lasts he will make no efforts, and he sees, or he creates, a thousand difficulties in the way of his becoming a Christian. But when that unwillingness is overcome, and he is disposed to engage in the work of religion, difficulties vanish, and the work of salvation becomes easy. ¶ *His voice.* The voice of God speaking to us (1) in his written word; (2) in the preached gospel; (3) in our own consciences; (4) in the events of his providence; (5) in the admonitions of relatives and friends. Whatever conveys to us the truth of God, or is adapted to impress that on us, may be regarded as *his voice* speaking to us. He thus speaks to us *every day* in some of these ways; and every day, therefore, he entreats us not to harden our hearts.

8. *Harden not your hearts.* Do not render the heart insensible to the divine voice and admonition. A hard heart is that where the conscience is seared and insensible; where truth makes no impression; where no religious effect is produced by afflictions; where preaching is listened to without interest; and where the mind is unaffected by the appeals of friends. The idea here is, that a refusal to listen to the voice of God is connected with a hardening 'of the heart. This occurs in two ways. (1) The very refusal to do this tends to harden it. (2) In order to resist the appeals of God, men must resort to the means of *voluntarily* hardening the heart. This they do by setting themselves against the truth; by the excuses which they offer for not becoming Christians; by plunging into sin in order to avoid serious impressions; and by direct resistance of the Holy Ghost. No inconsiderable part of the efforts of sinners consists in endeavouring to produce insensibility in their minds to the truth and the appeals of God. ¶ *As in the provocation.* Literally, *in the embittering—* ἐν τῷ παραπικρασμῷ. Then it means that which embitters or provokes the mind—as disobedience. Here it refers to what they did to *embitter* the mind of God against them; that is, to the course of conduct which was adopted to provoke him to wrath. ¶ *In the day of temptation.* In the *time* of temptation—the word *day* being used here, as it is often, to denote an indefinite period, or *time* in general. The word *temptation* here refers to the various provocations by which they *tried* the patience of God. They rebelled against him; they did that which put the divine patience and forbearance to a trial. It does not mean that they tempted God to do evil, but that his long-suffering was put to the test by their sins. ¶ *In the wilderness.* The desert through which they passed. The word *wilderness* in the Scriptures commonly means *a desert.* See Notes on Mat. iii. 1. "One provocation was in demanding bread at Sin; a second, for want of water at Massah or Meribah; a third time, at Sinai with the golden calf; a fourth time, at Tab-

9 When your fathers tempted me, proved me, and saw my works forty years.

10 Wherefore I was grieved with that generation, and said, They do

alway err in *their* heart; and they have not known my ways.

11 So I sware in my wrath, [2] They shall not enter into my rest.)

[2] *If they shall enter.*

---

erah for want of flesh; a fifth time, at Kadesh when they refused to go up into Canaan, and the oath came that they should die in the wilderness. A like refusal may prevent us from entering into rest" (Dr. J. P. Wilson, *MS. Notes*).

9. *Proved me.* "As if they would have made an experiment how much it was possible for me to bear" (Doddridge). The meaning is, they put my patience to a thorough trial. ¶ *And saw my works.* That is, my miracles, or my interpositions in their behalf. They saw the wonders at the Red Sea, the descent on Mount Sinai, the supply of manna, &c., and yet while seeing those works they rebelled. Even while sinners look on the doings of God, and are surrounded by the proofs of his power and goodness, they rebel, and provoke him to anger. Men sin when God is filling their houses with plenty; when he opens his hand daily to supply their wants; when they behold the manifestations of his goodness on the sea and on the land; and even in the midst of all the blessings of redemption, they provoke him to wrath. ¶ *Forty years.* The whole time during which they were passing from Egypt to the Promised Land. This may mean either that they saw his works forty years, or that they tempted him forty years. The sense is not materially affected, whichever interpretation is preferred.

10. *Wherefore I was grieved.* On the word *grieved*, see Notes on Eph. iv. 30. The word here means that he was offended with, or that he was indignant at, them. ¶ *They do alway err in* their *heart.* Their long trial of forty years had been sufficient to show that it was a characteristic of the people that they were disposed to wander from God. Forty years are enough to show what the character is. They had seen his works; they had been under his guidance; they

had received his law; and yet their conduct during that time had shown that they were not disposed to obey him. So of an individual. A man who has lived in sin forty years; who during all that time has rebelled against God, and disregarded all his appeals; who has lived for himself and not for his Maker, has shown what his character is. Longer time is unnecessary; and if God should then cut him down and consign him to hell, he could not be blamed for doing it. A man who during forty years will live in sin, and resist all the appeals of God, shows what is in his heart, and no injustice is done if *then* he is summoned before God, and if he swears that he shall not enter into his rest. ¶ *And they have not known my ways.* They have been rebellious. They have not been acquainted with the true God; or they have not *approved* my doings. The word *know* is often used in the Scriptures in the sense of *approving*, or *loving.* See Notes on Mat. vii. 23.

11. *So I sware in my wrath.* God is often represented in the Scriptures as *swearing*—and usually as swearing by himself, or by his own existence. Comp. chap. vii. 16–18. Of course this is figurative, and denotes a strong affirmation, or a settled and determined purpose. An oath with us implies the strongest affirmation, or the expression of the most settled and determined purpose of mind. The meaning here is, that so refractory and perverse had they showed themselves, that he solemnly resolved that they should never enter into the land of Canaan. ¶ *They shall not enter into my rest.* Margin, as in the original, *If they shall enter.* That is, they shall not enter. The word (אִם) *if* has this negative meaning in Hebrew, and this meaning is transferred to the Greek word *if*. Compare 1 Sam. iii. 17; 2 Sam. iii. 35; 2 Ki. vi. 31. It is called

12 Take heed, brethren, lest there be in any of °you an evil heart of

o Mar.7.21-23.

unbelief, in ᵖdeparting from the living God.

p Je.2.13.

"my rest" here, meaning that it was such rest as God had provided, or such as he enjoyed. The particular *rest* referred to here was that of the land of Canaan, but which was undoubtedly regarded as emblematic of the "*rest*" in heaven. Into that rest God solemnly said they should never enter. They had been rebellious. All the means of reclaiming them had failed. God had warned and entreated them; he had caused his mercies to pass before them, and had visited them with judgments in vain; and he now declares that for all their rebellion they should be excluded from the Promised Land. He speaks here in the manner of men. Men are affected with feelings of indignation in such circumstances, and God makes use of language which expresses such feelings. But we are to understand it in a manner consistent with his character, and we are not to suppose that he is affected with the same emotions as those which agitate the bosoms of men. The meaning is, that he formed and expressed a deliberate and solemn purpose that they should never enter into the Promised Land. Whether this *rest* refers here to heaven, and whether the meaning is that God would exclude them from that blessed world, will be more appropriately considered in the next chapter. The particular idea is, that they were to be excluded from the Promised Land, and that they should fall in the wilderness. No one can doubt, also, that their conduct had been such as to show that the great body of them were unfit to enter into heaven.

12. *Take heed, brethren.* In view of the conduct of the rebellious Jews, and of their fearful doom, be on your guard lest you also be found to have had the same feelings of rebellion and unbelief. See to it, that under the new dispensation, and in the enjoyment of the privileges of the gospel, you be not found to manifest such feelings as will exclude you from the

heavenly world. The *principle* has been settled by their unbelief that they who oppose God will be excluded from his rest. That may be shown under all dispensations, and in all circumstances, and there is not less danger of it under the gospel than there was when the fathers were conducted to the Promised Land. You are travelling through a wilderness—the barren wilderness of this world. You are exposed to trials and temptations. You meet with many a deadly and mighty foe. You have hearts prone to apostasy and sin. You are seeking a land of promise—a land of rest. You are surrounded by the wonders of almighty power, and by the proofs of infinite beneficence. Disobedience and rebellion in you will as certainly exclude you from heaven, as their rebellion did them from the Promised Land; and as their great sin was unbelief, be on your guard lest *you* manifest the same. ¶ *An evil heart of unbelief.* An evil, unbelieving heart. The word *unbelief* is used to qualify the word *heart*, by a Hebraism—a mode of speech that is common in the New Testament. An unbelieving heart was the cause of their apostasy, and that which worked *their* ruin will produce ours. The root of their evil was *a want of confidence in God;* for this is what is meant here by a heart of unbelief. The great difficulty on earth everywhere is *a want of confidence in God;* and this has produced all the ills that man has ever suffered. It led to the first apostasy; and it has led to every other apostasy —and will continue to produce the same effects to the end of the world. The apostle says that this heart of unbelief is "*evil.*" Men often maintain that it is a matter of little consequence whether they have faith or not, provided their *conduct* is right; and hence they do not see or admit the propriety of what is said about the consequences of unbelief in the Scriptures. But what do they say

13 But *q*exhort one another daily, while it is called To-day; lest any

q ch.10.24.

about a want of confidence between a husband and wife? Are there no evils in that? What husband can sleep with quietness on his pillow if he has no confidence in the virtue of his wife? What child can have peace who has no confidence in a parent? How can there be prosperity in a community where there is no confidence in a bank, or an insurance office, or where one merchant has no confidence in another; where a neighbour has no confidence in his neighbour; where the sick have no confidence in a physician, and where, in general, all confidence is broken up between man and man? If I wished to produce the deepest distress in any community, and had the power, I would produce the same want of confidence between man and man which there is now between man and his Maker. I would thus take away sleep from the pillow of every husband and wife, and every parent and child; I would make every man wretched with the feeling that all the property which he had was insecure. Among men nothing is seen to be productive of greater evil than a want of confidence or faith, and why should not the same evil exist in the divine administration? And if want of confidence produces such results between man and man, why should it not produce similar, or greater, miseries where it occurs in relation to God? There is not an evil that man endures which might not be alleviated or removed by *confidence* in God; and hence the great object of the Christian religion is, to restore to man his lost confidence in the God that made him. Hence *faith* is everywhere made an essential condition of salvation. ¶ *In departing from the living God.* Manifested in departing from him; or leading to a departure from him. The idea is, that such a heart of unbelief would be connected with apostasy from God. All apostasy first exists in the heart, and is then manifested

of you be hardened through the deceitfulness of sin.

in the life. They who indulge in unbelief in any form, or in regard to any subject, should remember that this is the great source of all alienation from God, and that, if indulged, it will lead to complete apostasy. They who wish to live a life of piety should keep *the heart* right. He that lives "by the faith of the Son of God" is safe; and none is safe but he.

13. *But exhort one another daily.* This is addressed to the members of the churches; and it follows, therefore, (1) that it is their duty to exhort their brethren; and (2) that it is their duty to do it *daily*—that is, constantly. See chap. x. 24; 1 Thes. iv. 18; v. 11. Comp. Notes on Rom. xii. 8. While this is the special duty of the ministers of the gospel (1 Tim. vi. 2; 2 Tim. iv. 2; Tit. ii. 6, 15), it is also the duty of all the members of the churches, and a most important but much-neglected duty. This does not refer to *public* exhortation, which more appropriately pertains to the ministers of the gospel, but to that private watch and care which the individual members of the church should have over one another. But in what cases is such exhortation proper? What rules should regulate it? I answer, it may be regarded as a duty, or is to be performed in such cases as the following: (1) Intimate friends in the church should exhort and counsel each other; should admonish each other of their faults; should aid each other in the divine life. (2) Parents should do the same thing to their children. They are placed particularly under their watch and care. A pastor cannot often see the members of his flock in private, and a parent may greatly assist him in his work by watching over the members of their families who are connected with the church. (3) Sabbath-school teachers may aid much in this duty. They are to be assistants to parents and to pastors. They often have under their care youthful members of the churches. They have an oppor-

tunity of knowing their state of mind, their temptations, and their dangers, better than the pastor can have. It should be theirs, therefore, to exhort them to a holy life. (4) The aged should exhort the young. Every aged Christian may thus do much for the promotion of religion. His experience is the property of the church; and he is bound so to employ it as to be useful in aiding the feeble, reclaiming the wandering, recovering the backslider, and directing the inquiring. There is a vast amount of *spiritual capital* of this kind in the church that is unemployed, and that might be made eminently useful in helping others to heaven. (5) Church members should exhort one another. There may not be the intimacy of personal friendship among all the members of a large church, but still the connection between them should be regarded as sufficiently tender and confidential to make it proper for anyone to admonish a brother who goes astray. They belong to the same communion. They sit down at the same supper of the Lord. They express their assent to the same articles of faith. They are regarded by the community as united. Each member sustains a portion of the honour and the responsibility of the whole; and each member should feel, therefore, that he has a right, and that it is his duty, to admonish a brother if he goes astray. Yet this duty is greatly neglected. In what church is it performed? How often do church members see a fellow-member go astray without any exhortation or admonition! How often do they hear reports of the inconsistent lives of other members, and perhaps contribute to the circulation of those reports themselves, without any pains taken to inquire whether they are true! How often do the poor fear the rich members of the church, or the rich despise the poor, and see one another live in sin, without any attempt to entreat or save them! I would not have the courtesies of life violated. I would not have any assume a dogmatical or dictatorial air. I would have no one step out of his proper

sphere of life. But the principle which I would lay down is, that the fact of church membership should inspire such confidence as to make it proper for one member to exhort another whom he sees going astray. Belonging to the same family; having the same interest in religion; all suffering when one suffers, why should they not be allowed tenderly and kindly to exhort one another to a holy life? ¶ *While it is called To-day.* While life lasts; or while you may be permitted to use the language "To-day hear the voice of God." The idea is, that the exhortation is not to be intermitted. It is to be our daily business to admonish and exhort one another. Christians are liable every day to go astray; every day they need help in the divine life; and they who are fellow-heirs with them of salvation should be ready every day to counsel and advise them. ¶ *Lest any of you be hardened.* See Notes on ver. 8. It is *possible* for Christians to become in a sense *hardened.* Their minds become less sensitive than they were to the claims of duty, and their consciences become less tender. Hence the propriety of mutual exhortation, that they may always have the right feeling, and may always listen to the commands of God. ¶ *The deceitfulness of sin.* See Notes on Eph. iv. 22. Sin is always deceitful. It promises more than it performs. It assures us of pleasure which it never imparts. It leads us on beyond what was anticipated when we began to indulge in it. The man who commits sin is always under a delusion; and sin, if he indulges it, will lead him on from one step to another until his heart becomes entirely hardened. Sin puts on plausible appearances and pretences; it assumes the name of virtue; it offers excuses and palliations until the victim is ensnared, and then, spellbound, he is hurried on to every excess. If sin was always seen in its true aspect when man is tempted to commit it, it would be so hateful that he would flee from it with the utmost abhorrence. What young man would become a drunkard, if he saw, when he began, exactly the career which he

14 For we are made partakers of
Christ, *if we hold the beginning

r ver.6.

of our confidence stedfast unto the
end;

would run? Who that is now vigorous
and healthful, with fair prospects of
usefulness and happiness, would ever
touch the intoxicating bowl, if he saw
what he *would be* when he became a
sot? Who would ever enter the room
of the gambler if he saw just where
indulgence would soon lead him, and
if at the commencement he saw exactly
the woe and despair which would inevitably ensue? Who would become
a voluptuary and a sensualist, if he
saw exactly the close of such a career?
Sin deceives, deludes, blinds. Men
do not, or will not, see the fearful results of indulgence. They are deluded
by the hope of happiness or of gain;
they are drawn along by the fascina-
tions and allurements of pleasure, until the heart becomes hard and the
conscience seared, and then they give
way without remorse. From such a
course the apostle would have Christians guarded by kind and affectionate
exhortation. Each one should feel that
he has an interest in keeping his
brother from such a doom; and each
Christian thus in danger should be
willing to listen to the kind exhortation of a Christian brother.

14. *For we are made partakers of
Christ.* We are spiritually united to
the Saviour. We become one with
him. We partake of his spirit and
his allotments. The sacred writers
are accustomed to describe the Christian as being closely united to the
Saviour, and as being *one* with him.
See Notes on Jn. xv. 1-7. Comp.
Jn. xvii. 21, 23; Eph. v. 30; 1 Cor.
xii. 27. The idea is, that we participate in all that pertains to him. It
is a union of feeling and affection; a
union of principle and of congeniality;
a union of dependence as well as love;
a union where nothing is to be imparted by us, but everything gained;
and a union, therefore, on the part of
the Redeemer of great condescension.
It is the union of the branch and the
vine, where the branch is supported
and nourished *by* the vine, and not

the union of the ivy and the oak,
where the ivy has its own roots, and
merely clings around the oak and
climbs up upon it. What else can be
said so honourable of man as that he
is "a partaker of Christ;" that he
shares his feelings here, and that he
is to share his honours in a brighter
world? Compared with this, what is
it to participate with the rich and the
gay in their pleasures; what would it
be to share in the honours of conquerors and kings?

[Μετοχοι του Χριστου cannot signify, as some
explain, participation *merely* in the blessings
of Christ's death, but must be referred, as
our author here affirms, to the spiritual union
which subsists between Christ and his people.
That union doubtless involves, as necessary
consequents, "a union of feeling and affection,
a union of principle and congeniality, a union
of dependence and love." Yet, we think, it is
something more. It is a *real* and *vital* union,
formed by the one Spirit of Christ, pervading
the head and the members of the mystical
body. And *this* is the *foundation* of all union
of affection, &c. For a condensed view of the
subject see the Supplementary Note on Rom.
viii. 10.]

¶ *If we hold the beginning of our confidence stedfast.* See Notes on ver. 6.
If we continue to maintain the same
confidence which we had in the beginning, or which we showed at the
commencement of our Christian life.
At first, they had been firm in the
Christian hope. They evinced true and
strong attachment to the Redeemer.
They were ardent and devoted to his
cause. If they continued to maintain
that to the end—that is, the end of life;
if in the midst of all temptations
and trials they adhered inflexibly to
the cause of the Saviour, they would
show that they were true Christians,
and would partake of the blessedness
of the heavenly world with the Redeemer. The idea is, that it is only
perseverance in the ways of religion
that constitutes certain evidence of
piety. Where piety is manifested
through life, or where there is an
untiring devotion to the cause of God,

15 While it is said, ⁸To-day if | ye will hear his voice, harden not
⁸ ver.7. | your hearts, as in the provocation.

there the evidence is clear and undoubted. But where there is at first great ardour, zeal and confidence, which soon dies away, then it is clear that there never was any real attachment to him and his cause. It may be remarked here, that the "beginning of the confidence" of those who are deceived, and who know nothing about religion at heart, is often bolder than where there is true piety. The hypocrite makes up in ardour what he lacks in sincerity; and he who is really deceived, is usually deceived under the influence of some strong and vivid emotion which he mistakes for true religion. Often the sincere convert is calm, though decided, and sometimes is even timorous and doubting; while the self-deceiver is noisy in profession, clamorous in his zeal, and much disposed to blame the lukewarmness of others. Evidence of true piety, therefore, should not be built on that early zeal; nor should it be concluded that because there is ardour, there is of necessity genuine religion. Ardour is valuable, and true religion is ardent; but there *is* other ardour than that which the gospel inspires. The evidence of genuine piety is to be found in that which will bear us up under trials; which will endure amidst persecution and opposition; and which will accompany us with a sanctifying influence to the end of life. The doctrine here is, that it is necessary to persevere if we would have evidence of true piety. This doctrine is taught everywhere in the Scriptures. Persevere in what? I answer, (1) Not merely in a profession of religion. A man may do that and have no piety. (2) Not in zeal for party or sect. The Pharisees had that to the end of their lives. (3) Not in mere honesty and correctness of external deportment. A man may do that *in* the church as well as *out* of it, and yet have no religion. But we should persevere—(1) In the love of God and of Christ—in conscious, ardent, steady attachment to Him to

whom our lives are professedly devoted. (2) In the secret duties of religion. In that watchfulness over the heart; that communion with God; that careful study of the Bible; that guardianship over the temper; that habitual intercourse with God in secret prayer which is appropriate to a Christian, and which marks the Christian character. (3) In the performance of the public duties of religion; in leading a *Christian* life—as distinguished from a life of worldliness and vanity; a life of mere morality and honesty; a life such as thousands lead who are out of the church. There is something which distinguishes a Christian from one who is not a Christian—a religious from an irreligious man. There is *something* in religion; *something* which serves to characterize a Christian, and unless that something is manifested, there can be no evidence of true piety. The Christian is to be distinguished in temper, feeling, deportment, aims, plans, from the men of this world—and unless those characteristics are shown in the life and deportment, there can be no well-founded evidence of religion. Learn, (1) That it is not mere *feeling* that furnishes evidence of religion. (2) That it is not mere *excitement* that constitutes religion. (3) That it is not mere ardour. (4) That it is not mere zeal. All these may be temporary. Religion is something that lasts through life. It goes with a man everywhere. It is with him in trial. It forms his plans; regulates his temper; suggests his words; prompts to right actions. It lives with him in all his external changes; goes with him through the dark valley of death; accompanies him up to the bar of God, and is with him for ever.

15. *While it is said, To-day, &c.* That is, persevere as long as life lasts, or as long as it can be said "to-day;" for it is only by persevering in this manner that you will have evidence that you are the friends of the Redeemer. This is a quotation from

16 For*t* some, when they had heard, did provoke: howbeit not

t Nu.14.2,&c.

all that came out of Egypt by Moses.

Ps. xcv. 7. Paul means, undoubtedly, to make use of this language himself as a direct exhortation to the Christians to whom he was writing. He entreats them, therefore, as long as it could be said "to-day," or as long as life lasted, to take care lest they should harden their hearts as had been done in the temptation in the wilderness.

16. *For some.* Some of the Hebrews who came out of Egypt. The truth was, that a large proportion of them rebelled against God, and provoked him to indignation. It is somewhat remarkable that though *all* the Hebrews seem to have joined in the provocation — except a very small number—Paul, in the word "*some,*" should have used language which would seem to imply that the number which rebelled was comparatively small. Another version, therefore, has been given to this passage by some of the most eminent critics, consisting merely in a change in the punctuation, by which a different view is given of the entire sentence. According to this it would be a question, and would mean, "But who were they who when they had heard did provoke? Were they not all, indeed, who came out of Egypt under Moses? And with whom was he angry forty years? Was it not with those who sinned, whose carcasses fell in the wilderness?" This version was adopted by Chrysostom, Theodoret, and others of the Fathers; and is adopted by Rosenmüller, Clarke, Stuart, Pyle, and some others. In favour of it, it may be alleged (1) that the Greek will bear it, all the change required being in the punctuation; (2) that it avoids the difficulty which exists in the other interpretation, of supposing the apostle to imply that but few of them rebelled, when the truth was that it was nearly all; (3) that it thus accords with the remainder of the exhortation, which consists in a series of questions; and (4) that it agrees with the scope and design

of the whole. The object was not to state that it was not *all* who came out of Egypt that rebelled, or that the number was small, but that the great body of them rebelled and fell in the wilderness, and that Christians should be admonished by their example. These reasons seem to be so strong as to make it probable that this is the true construction, and the sense then will be, "For who were they that, having heard, did provoke? Were they not all who came out of Egypt under Moses?" ¶ *When they had heard.* Had heard God speaking to them, and giving them his commands. ¶ *Did provoke.* Provoked him to anger; or their conduct was such as was fitted to produce indignation. See Notes on ver. 8. ¶ *Howbeit—* ἀλλ'. *But.* This particle "in a series of questions, and standing at the head of a question, means *but, further.* It serves to connect, and give intensity to the interrogation" (Stuart). Paul means to ask with emphasis whether the great mass of those who came out of Egypt did not apostatize? At the same time he means to intimate that there is no security that they who have witnessed remarkable manifestations of the greatness of God, and who have partaken of extraordinary mercies, will not apostatize and perish. As the Hebrews, who heard God speak from Mount Sinai, revolted and perished, so it is possible that they who witness the mercies of God in redemption may be in danger of abusing all those mercies, and of perishing. By the example, therefore, of the disobedient Israelites, he would admonish professed Christians of their danger. ¶ *Not all,* &c. According to the interpretation proposed above, "Were they not all who came out of Egypt?" Or, "Did not all who came out of Egypt?" The word *all* here is not to be taken in the strict sense. It is often used to denote the great body; a large proportion; or vast multitudes. Thus it is used in Mat. iii. 5, "Then went out to him Jerusalem,

17 But with whom was he grieved forty years? *was it* not with them that had sinned, *u* whose carcases fell in the wilderness?

18 And to whom *v* sware he that

u Nu.26.64,65; Jude 5.　　*v* De.1.34,35.

they should not enter into his rest, but to them that believed not?

19 So *w* we see that they could not enter in because of unbelief.

w ch.4.6.

and *all* Judea, and *all* the region round about Jordan." So in John iii. 26, "The same baptizeth, and *all* men come to him." So Phil. ii. 21, "For *all* seek their own;" 2 Cor. iii. 2, " Ye are our epistle, known and read of *all* men." *In fact*, there were two exceptions — and but two — of the adults who came out of Egypt—Caleb and Joshua, Num. xiv. 30. All the others murmured against the Lord, and were prohibited from entering the Promised Land. Of the great multitudes who came out of Egypt, and who murmured, the exception was so small that the apostle had no scruple in saying in general that they were *all* rebellious.

17. *But with whom was he grieved forty years?* With whom was he *angry*. See Notes on ver. 10. ¶ *Was it not with them that had sinned.* That had sinned in various ways—by rebellion, murmuring, unbelief. As God was angry with them for their sins, we have the same reason to apprehend that he will be angry with *us* if we sin; and we should, therefore, be on our guard against that unbelief which would lead us to depart from him, ver. 12. ¶ *Whose carcases fell*, &c. Num. xiv. 29. That is, they all died, and were left on the sands of the desert. The whole generation was strewed along in the way to Canaan. All those who had seen the wonders that God had done "in the land of Ham," and who had been rescued in so remarkable a manner from oppression, were thus cut down, and died in the deserts through which they were passing, Num. xxvi. 64, 65. Such an example of the effects of revolt against God, and of unbelief, was well fitted to admonish Christians in the time of the apostle, and is equally well fitted to admonish us now, of the danger of the sin of unbelief. We are not to suppose, however, that all

those who thus died were excluded from heaven. Moses and Aaron were among the number of those who were not permitted to enter the Promised Land, but of their piety there can be no doubt. Beyond all question, also, there were many others of that generation who were truly pious. But at different times they seem all to have partaken of the prevalent feelings of discontent, and were all involved in the sweeping condemnation that they should die in the wilderness.

18. *And to whom sware he.* See Notes on ver. 11. ¶ *But to them that believed not?* That did not confide in God. Deut. i. 32, "Yet in this thing *ye did not believe* the Lord your God." In consequence of this want of faith, God solemnly sware unto them that they should not enter into the Promised Land, Deut. i. 34, 35, "And the Lord heard the voice of your words, and was wroth, and sware, saying, Surely there shall not one of these men of this evil generation see that good land which I sware to give unto your fathers, save Caleb," &c. The distinct reason, therefore, assigned by Moses why they did not enter the Promised Land, was a want of faith, and this accords directly with the design of the apostle here. He is exhorting those whom he addressed to beware of an evil heart of unbelief, ver. 12. He says that it was such a heart that excluded the Hebrews from the Promised Land. The same thing, says he, must exclude you from heaven—the promised home of the believer; and if that firm confidence in God and his promises which he requires is wanting, you will be excluded from the world of eternal rest.

19. *So we see*, &c. We see, from the direct testimony of the Old Testament, that unbelief was the reason why they were excluded from the Promised Land. Let us learn, in view of the reasoning and exhortations here:

(1) The evil of unbelief. It excluded that whole generation, consisting of many hundred thousand souls, from the land of promise—the land to which they had looked with ardent hopes, and with warm desires. It will exclude countless millions from heaven. A *want of confidence in God* is the great source of evil in this world, and will be the cause of wretchedness to all eternity of unnumbered hosts. But surely that was not a small or unimportant thing which strewed the desert with the bones of that whole generation whom God had in so remarkable a manner rescued from Egyptian servitude. And that cannot be a small matter which will cause multitudes to sink down to infinite wretchedness and despair.

(2) Let us, who are professed Christians, be cautious against indulging unbelief in our hearts. Our difficulties all begin there. We lose confidence in God. We doubt his promises, his oaths, his threatenings. In dark and trying times we begin to have doubts about the wisdom of his dealings and about his goodness. Unbelief once admitted into the heart is the beginning of many woes. When a man loses confidence in God, he is on a shoreless ocean that is full of whirlpools, and rocks, and quicksands, and where it is *impossible* to find a secure anchorage. There is nothing to which he may moor his driven bark; and he will never find safety or peace till he comes back to God.

(3) Let us live a life of faith—so live that we may say with Paul, "The life that I now live in the flesh, I live by the faith of the Son of God, who loved me, and gave himself for me," Gal. ii. 20. So living, we shall have peace. The mind will be at rest. Storms and tempests may blow, but we shall be secure. Others may be troubled in the vicissitudes of life, but *our* minds will be calm.

(4) Let us live expecting the future "*rest*" that remains for us. Let us keep our eye fixed upon it. To us there is a rest promised, as there was to the Hebrews whom God had delivered from the land of oppression; and we may by faith attain to that "rest" as they might have reached the land of Canaan.

(5) Let us persevere to the end. He that draws back must be lost. He that does not endure to the end of life in the ways of religion, can never have been a Christian. There is nothing which will furnish certain evidence of religion unless our piety is such as to lead us to persevere till death. The man who enters on the professed Christian life expecting to fall away, or who can look upon the possibility of falling away without concern, has never known anything of the nature of true religion. He cannot be a Christian. He may have had raptures and visions; he may be a loud professor and a noisy and zealous partisan, but he has no evidence that he has ever known anything about religion. That religion which is not connected with a firm and determined purpose, by the grace of God, to persevere to the end of life, is no true religion; and a man who *expects* to fall away and go back again to the world, or who can look at such an idea without alarm, should regard it as a settled matter that he has no true knowledge of God.

(6) No man should delay the work of salvation to a future time. *To-day* is the accepted time; to-day the only time of which we have any security. God speaks *to-day*, and to-day his voice should be heard. No man, on any subject, should defer till to-morrow what ought to be done to-day. He who puts off religion till a future time neglects his own best interest; violates most solemn obligations; and endangers his immortal soul. What security *can* anyone have that he will live to see another day? What evidence has he that he will be any more disposed to attend to his salvation then than he is now? What evidence can he have that he will not provoke God by this course, and bring condemnation on his soul? Of all delusions, that is the most wonderful by which dying men are led to defer attention to the concerns of the soul to a future period of life. Nowhere has Satan such advantage as in keeping this delusion before the

mind; and if in respect to anything the voice of warning and alarm should be lifted loud and long, it is in reference to this. Oh, why will not men be wise *to-day?* Why will they not embrace the offer of salvation *now?* Why will they not *at once* make sure of eternal happiness? And why, amidst the changes and trials of this life, will they not so secure the everlasting inheritance as to feel that *that* is safe—that there is one thing at least that cannot be shaken and disturbed by commercial embarrassment and distress; one thing secure, though friends and kindred are torn away from them; one thing safe when their own health fails, and they lie down on the bed where they will bid adieu to all earthly comforts, and from which they will never rise?

CHAPTER IV.

ANALYSIS OF THE CHAPTER.

This chapter comprises two parts. In the first (ver.1–13) the apostle pursues and completes the exhortation which he had commenced in the previous chapter, drawn from the comparison of the Saviour with Moses (see the Analysis of chap. iii.); and in the second part (ver. 14–16) he enters on the consideration of the character of Christ as a high-priest, which is pursued to the end of the doctrinal part of the epistle.

In the first part (ver. 1–13) he describes more at length the character of the "*rest*" to which he had referred in the previous chapter. He shows (ver. 1) that the promise of a "*rest*" yet remains, and that there is still danger, as there was formerly, of coming short of it, or of losing it. He affirms that such was the nature of that promise, that it is applicable to us as well as to those to whom it was first made, and that the promise of rest as really pertains to Christians now as it did to the Hebrews of old, ver. 2. The reason, he adds (ver. 2), why *they* did not enter into that rest was, that they had not faith. This he had established in the previous chapter, ver. 18. In ver. 3–6 he proceeds to demonstrate more at length that there is a "rest" remaining for those

who believe. The great object, in this part of the chapter, is to prove that a "rest" remains for believers now; a rest of a spiritual character, and much more desirable than that of the land of Canaan; a rest to which Christians may look forward, and which there may be danger of losing. Addressing Hebrew Christians, he, of course, appeals to the Old Testament, and refers to several places where the word "*rest*" occurs, and argues that those expressions are of such a character as to show that there remains a "rest" for Christians yet. It would have been easy to have *affirmed* this as a part of the Christian revelation, but throughout the epistle he is bringing his illustrations from the Old Testament, and showing to the Hebrew Christians, to whom he wrote, that there were abundant considerations *in the Old Testament itself* to constitute an argument why they should adhere inviolably to the Christian religion. He says, therefore (ver. 4), that God himself had spoken of *his own rest* from his works; that when he had finished the work of creation he had instituted a *rest* which was characterized by the peace, the beauty, and the order of the first Sabbath after the work of creation, when all was new, lovely, and pure. That might be called the *rest of God* —a beautiful emblem of that which dwells around his throne in heaven. The meaning of this verse (ver. 4) is, that the Bible spoke early of a *rest* which appertained to God himself. In ver. 5 he goes on to say that the prospect of entering into *his* rest was spoken of as a possible thing; that some were excluded, but that there was a place deserved to be called "the rest of God"—"My rest"—to which all may come. Of course that "rest" must be of a spiritual nature, and must be different from that of the Promised Land. That "*rest*" the apostle *implies* it was possible to attain. He does not argue this point at length, but he assumes that God would not create a place of "rest" in vain; that it was made to be enjoyed; and that since those to whom it was at first offered were excluded, it must follow that it remained still; and as they

CHAPTER IV.

LET*ᵃ* us therefore fear, lest, a promise being left *us* of en-

a ch.12.15.

---

were excluded by the want of *faith*, it would follow, also, that it was reserved for those who *had* faith. Of course, therefore, it is offered to Christians now, ver. 6.

This view he proceeds to confirm by another consideration, ver. 7, 8. It is, that David, who lived nearly five hundred years after the land of promise had been occupied by the Israelites, spoke *then* of the possibility of entering into such a "rest." He says (Ps. xcv. 7) that, in his time, the people were called to hear the voice of God; that God warned them against the guilt and danger of hardening their hearts; that he reminded them that it was by that that the Israelites were excluded from the Promised Land, and that he said that the same thing would occur if those in his own time should harden their hearts. It followed, therefore, that even in the time of David there was a hope and promise of "rest;" and that there was something more intended for the true people of God than merely entering into the Promised Land. There must be something in advance of that; something that existed to the time of David—and it must be, therefore, a spiritual rest. This, the apostle adds, ver. 8, is conclusive; for if Joshua had given them all the "rest" that was contemplated, then David would not have spoken as he did of the danger of being excluded from it in his time. He, therefore (ver. 9), comes to the conclusion that there must *still* remain a "rest" for the people of God, a "*rest*" to which those to whom he wrote were invited, and which they were in danger of losing by unbelief. He adds (ver. 10), that he who enters into that "rest" ceases from toil, as God did from his when he had finished the work of creation. Since, therefore, there is such a "rest," and since there is danger of coming short of it, the apostle urges them (ver. 11) to make every effort to enter into it.

tering into his rest, any of you should seem to come short of it.

He adds (ver. 12, 13), as a consideration to quicken them to earnest effort, and to anxious care lest they should be deceived, and should fail of it, the fact that God cannot be deceived; that his word penetrates the heart, and that everything is naked and open before him. There should, therefore, be the most faithful investigation of the heart, lest they should fail of the grace of God, and lose the hoped-for rest.

In the second portion of the chapter (ver. 14–16), he enters on the consideration of the character of Christ as High-priest, and says that since we have such an High-priest as he is, we should be encouraged to come boldly to the throne of grace, and in all our conscious weakness and helplessness should look to him for aid.

1. *Let us therefore fear.* Let us be apprehensive that we may possibly fail of that rest. The kind of *fear* which is recommended here is that which leads to caution and care. A man who is in danger of losing his life or health should be watchful; a seaman that is in danger of running on a lee-shore should be on his guard. So we who have the offer of heaven, and who yet are in danger of losing it, should take all possible precautions lest we fail of it. ¶ *Lest a promise being left* us. Paul assumes here that there *is* such a promise. In the subsequent part of the chapter, he goes more into the subject, and proves from the Old Testament that there is such a promise made to us. It is to be remembered that Paul had not the New Testament then to appeal to, as we have, which is perfectly clear on the subject, but that he was obliged to appeal to the Old Testament. This he did, not only because the New Testament was not then written, but because he was reasoning with those who had been Hebrews, and who regarded the authority of the Old Testament as decisive. If his reasoning to us appears somewhat obscure, we should put ourselves in his place, and

2 For unto us was the gospel preached, as well as unto them: but the word ¹preached did not profit

1 *of hearing.*

should remember that those whom he addressed had not the full light which we have now in the New Testament. ¶ *Of entering into his rest.* The "rest" of God—the "rest" belonging to that world where he dwells. It is called *his* "rest" because it is that which he enjoys, and which he alone can confer. There can be no doubt that Paul refers here to heaven, and means to say that there is a promise left to Christians of being admitted to the enjoyment of that blessed world where God dwells. ¶ *Any of you should seem to come short of it.* The word *"seem"* here is used as a form of gentle and mild address, implying the possibility of thus coming short. The word here—δοκέω—is often so used as to appear to give no essential addition to the sense of a passage, though it is probable that it always gave a different shade to the meaning. Thus the phrase *esse videatur* is often used by Cicero at the end of a period, to denote merely that a thing *was*—though he expressed it as though it merely *seemed* to be. Such language is often used in argument or in conversation as a *modest* expression, as when we say a thing *seems* to be so and so, instead of saying "it *is.*" In some such sense Paul probably used the phrase here—perhaps as expressing what we would by this language —"lest it should *appear* at last that any of you had come short of it." The phrase "come short of it" is probably used with reference to the journey to the Promised Land, where they who came out of Egypt *came short* of that land, and fell in the wilderness. They did not reach it. This verse teaches the important truth that, though heaven is offered to us, and though a "rest" is promised to us if we seek it, yet that there is reason to think that many will fail of reaching it who had expected to obtain it. Among those will be the following classes: (1) Those who are

them, ²not being mixed with faith in them that heard *it.*

2 or, *because they were not united by faith to.*

professors of religion, but who have never known anything of true piety. (2) Those who are expecting to be saved by their own works, and are looking forward to a world of rest on the ground of what their own hands can do. (3) Those who defer attention to the subject from time to time, until it becomes too late. They expect to reach heaven, but they are not ready to give their hearts to God *now,* and the subject is postponed from one period to another, until death arrests them unprepared. (4) Those who have been awakened to see their guilt and danger, and who have been almost but not quite ready to give up their hearts to God. Such were Agrippa, Felix, the young ruler (Mark x. 21); and such are all those who are *almost* but not *quite* prepared to forsake the world, and to devote themselves to the Redeemer. To all these the promise of "rest" is made, if they will accept of salvation as it is offered in the gospel; all of them cherish a hope that they will be saved; and all of them are destined alike to be disappointed. With what earnestness, therefore, should we strive that we may not fail of the grace of God!

2. *For unto us was the gospel preached, as well as unto them.* This translation by no means conveys the sense of the original. According to this, it would seem that the *gospel,* as we understand it, or the whole plan of salvation, was communicated to *them,* as well as to *us.* But this is by no means the idea. The discussion has reference only to *the promise of rest,* and the assertion of the apostle is, that this *good news* of a promise of rest is made to *us* as really as it was made to *them.* "Rest" was promised to them in the land of Canaan—an emblem of the eternal rest of the people of God. That was unquestioned, and Paul took it for granted. His object now is, to show that a promise of "rest" is as really made to us as

it was to them, and that there is the same danger of failing to secure it as there was then. It was important for him to show that there was such a promise made to the people of God in his time, and as he was discoursing of those who were Hebrews, he of course made his appeal to the Old Testament. The literal translation would be, "For we are *evangelized*—ἐσμεν εὐηγγελισμένοι—as well as they." The word *evangelize* means, to communicate good news, or glad tidings; and the idea here is, that the good news, or glad tidings of "rest," is announced to us as really as it was to them. This the apostle proves in the following verses. ¶ *But the word preached.* Margin, *of hearing.* The word *preach* we also use now, in a technical sense, as denoting a formal proclamation of the gospel by the ministers of religion. But this is not the idea here. The language means, simply, the word *which they heard;* and refers particularly to the promise of "rest" which was made to them. That message was communicated to them by Moses. ¶ *Did not profit them.* They derived no advantage from it. They rejected and despised it, and were, therefore, excluded from the Promised Land. It exerted no influence over their hearts and lives, and they lived and died as though no such promise had been made. Thus many persons live and die now. The offer of salvation is made to them. They are invited to come and be saved. They are assured that God is willing to save them, and that the Redeemer stands with open arms to welcome them to heaven. They are trained up under the gospel; are led early in life to the sanctuary; are in the habit of attending on the preaching of the gospel all their days, but still what they hear exerts no saving influence on their hearts. At the close of life, all that could be truly said of them is, that they have not been *profited;* it has been no real advantage to them, in regard to their final destiny, that they have enjoyed so many privileges. ¶ *Not being mixed with faith in them that heard it.* Margin, "or, *because they were not united by faith to.*"

There are some various readings on this text, and one of these has given occasion to the version in the margin. Many MSS., instead of the common reading — συγκεκραμένος — by which the word *mixed* would be united to ὁ λόγος—"*the word,*" have another reading — συγκεκραμένους — according to which the word *mixed* would refer to "*them,*" and would mean that they who heard the word and rejected it were not *mixed,* or united with those who believed it. The former reading makes the best sense, and is the best sustained; and the idea is, that the message which was preached was not received into the heart by faith. They were destitute of faith, and the message did not profit them. The word *mixed* is supposed by many of the best critics to refer to the process by which *food* is made nutritive, by being properly *mixed* with the saliva and the gastric juice, and thus converted into chyme and chyle, and then changed into blood. If suitably *mixed* in this manner, it contributes to the life and health of the bodily frame; if not, it is the means of disease and death. So, it is supposed, the apostle meant to say of the message which God sends to man. If properly received, if mixed or united with faith, it becomes the means of spiritual support and life. If not, it furnishes no aliment to the soul, and will be of no advantage. As food, when properly digested, incorporates itself with the body, and gives it support, so those critics suppose it to be of the word of God, that it incorporates itself with the internal and spiritual man, and gives it support and life. It may be doubted, however, whether the apostle had any such allusion as this, and whether it is not rather a refinement of the critics than a sentiment of Paul. The *word* used here properly denotes a mixing or mingling together, like water and wine, 2 Mac. xv. 39; a uniting together in proper proportions and order, as of the body, 1 Cor. xii. 24; and it may refer here merely to a proper *union* of faith with the word, in order that it might be profitable. The idea is, that merely to *hear* the

3 For we which have believed do enter into rest; as he said, *b* As I have sworn in my wrath, if they

b Ps.95.11.

shall enter into my rest; although the works were finished from the foundation of the world.

---

message of life with the outward ear will be of no advantage. It must be *believed,* or it will be of no benefit. The message is sent to mankind at large. But this message is of no advantage to multitudes, for such reasons as these: (1) Many do not attend to it at all. They do not even *listen* respectfully to it. Multitudes never go near the place where the gospel is proclaimed; and many, when there, and when they *seem* to attend, have their minds and hearts on other things. (2) Many do not *believe* it. They have doubts about the whole subject of religion, or about the particular doctrines of the gospel; and while they do not believe it, how can they be benefited by it? How can a man be profited by the records of *history* if he does not believe them? How can one be benefited by the truths of *science* if he does not believe them? If a man was assured that by going to a certain place he might close a bargain that would be a great advantage to him, of what use would this information be to him if he did not believe a word of it? So of the knowledge of salvation; the facts of the history recorded in the Bible; the offer of eternal life. (3) Men do not allow the message of life to influence their conduct, and of course it is of no advantage to them. Of what use can it be if they steadily resist all the influence which it would have, and ought to have, on their lives? They live as though it were ascertained that there is no truth in the Bible; that there is no reason for being influenced by the offered hope of eternal life; that there is no occasion for being alarmed by the threatened danger of eternal death. Resolved to pursue a course of life that is at variance with the commands of God, they cannot be profited by the message of salvation. Having no faith which influences and controls the heart, they are not in the least benefited by the offer

of heaven. When they die their condition is in no wise made better by the fact that they were trained up in a pious family; that they were instructed in the Sabbath-school; that they had the Bible in their dwellings, and that they sat regularly under a preached gospel. For any *advantage* to be derived from all this in the future world, they might as well have been born in a heathen land. Nay, it would have been better for them. The only effect of these privileges is to harden them in guilt, and to sink them deeper in hell. See Notes on 2 Cor. ii. 16.

3. *For we which have believed do enter into rest.* That is, it is a certain fact that believers *will* enter into rest. That promise is made to "believers;" and as we have evidence that *we* come under the denomination of believers, it will follow that *we* have the offer of rest as well as they. That this is so, the apostle proceeds to prove; that is, he proceeds to show, from the Old Testament, that there was a promise to "believers" that they would enter into rest. Since there was such a promise, and since there was danger that by unbelief that "rest" might be lost, he proceeds to show them the danger, and to warn them of it. ¶ *As he said,* &c. See chap. iii. 11. The meaning of this passage is this:— "God made a promise of rest to those who believe. They to whom the offer was first made failed, and did not enter in. It must follow, therefore, that the offer extended to others, since God designed that *some* should enter in, or that it should not be provided in vain. To them it was a solemn declaration that *unbelievers* should not enter in, and this implied that *believers* would. As we now," says he, "sustain the character of *believers,* it follows that to *us* the promise of rest is now made, and we may partake of it." ¶ *If they shall enter,* &c. That is, they shall *not* enter in. See chap. iii. 11. The "rest" here

spoken of, as reserved for Christians, must be different from that of the Promised Land. It is something that pertains to Christians now, and it must, therefore, refer to the "rest" that remains in heaven. ¶ *Although the works were finished*, &c. This is a difficult expression. It may be asked, what works are referred to? How does this bear on the subject under discussion? How can it be a proof that there remains a "rest" to those who believe now? For this was the point to be demonstrated; and this passage was designed clearly to bear on that point. As it is in our translation, the passage seems to make no sense whatever. Tindal renders it, "And that spake he verily long after that the works were made from the foundation of the world laid;" which makes much better sense than our translation. Doddridge explains it as meaning, "And this may lead us further to reflect on what is elsewhere said concerning his works as they were finished from the foundation of the world." But it is difficult to see why they should reflect on his works just then, and how this would bear on the case in hand. Professor Stuart supposes that the word "rest" must be understood here before "*works*," and translates it, "Shall not enter into my rest—to wit, rest from the works which were performed when the world was founded." Professor Robinson (*Lex.*) explains it as meaning, "The rest here spoken of, 'MY rest,' could not have been God's resting from his works (Gen. ii. 2), for this rest, the Sabbath, had already existed from the creation of the world." Dr. J. P. Wilson (*MS. Notes*) renders it, "For we who have believed, do enter into rest (or a cessation) indeed (καίτοι) of the works done (among men) from the beginning of the world." Amidst this variety of interpretation it is difficult to determine the true sense. But perhaps the main thought may be collected from the following remarks: (1) The Jews, as the people of God, had a rest promised them in the land of Canaan. Of that they failed by their unbelief. (2) The purpose of

the apostle was to prove that there was a similar promise made to the people of God long subsequent to that, and to which *all* his people were invited. (3) *That* rest was not that of the Promised Land, it was such as *God had himself* when he had finished the work of creation. That was peculiarly *his rest* — the rest of God, without toil, or weariness, and after his whole *work* was finished. (4) His people were invited to the same *rest* —the rest of God; to partake of his felicity; to enter into that bliss which *he* enjoyed when he had finished the work of creation. The happiness of the saints was to be *like* that. It was to be *in their case* also a rest from toil, to be enjoyed at the end of all that *they* had to do. To prove that Christians were to attain to *such* a rest, was the purpose which the apostle had in view—showing that it was a general doctrine pertaining to believers in every age, that there was a promise of rest for them. I would then regard the middle clause of this verse as a parenthesis, and render the whole, "For we who are believers shall enter into rest — [the rest] indeed which occurred when the works were finished at the foundation of the world—as he said [in one place], as I have sworn in my wrath they shall not enter into *my* rest." That was the true rest—such rest or repose as *God* had when he finished the work of creation—such as he has now in heaven. This gives the highest possible idea of the dignity and desirableness of that "rest" to which we look forward—for it is to be such as God enjoys, and is to elevate us more and more to him. What more exalted idea can there be of happiness than to participate in the calmness, the peace, the repose—the freedom from raging passions, from wearisome toil, and from agitating cares—which God enjoys? Who, torn with conflicting passions here, wearied with toil and distracted with care, ought not to feel it a privilege to look forward to that rest? Of this rest the Sabbath and the Promised Land were emblems. They to whom the promise was made did not enter in, but some *shall* enter

4 For he spake in a certain place of the seventh *day* on this wise, And *c* God did rest the seventh day from all his works.

c Ge.2.2.

in, and the promise, therefore, pertains to us.

4. *For he spake.* Gen. ii. 2. ¶ *And God did rest.* At the close of the work of creation he rested. The work was done. *That* was the rest of God. He was happy in the contemplation of his own works; and he instituted that day to be observed as a memorial of *his* resting from his works, and as a *type* of the eternal rest which remains for man. The idea is this—that the notion of *rest* of some kind runs through all dispensations. It was seen in the finishing of the work of creation, it was seen in the appointment of the Sabbath; was seen in the offer of the Promised Land, and it is seen now in the promise of heaven. All dispensations contemplate *rest*, and there must be such a prospect before man now. When it is said that "God did *rest*," of course it does not mean that he was wearied with his toil, but merely that he *ceased* from the stupendous work of creation. He no more put forth creative energy, but calmly contemplated his own works in their beauty and grandeur, Gen. i. 31. In carrying forward the great affairs of the universe, he always has been actively employed (Jn. v. 17), but he is not employed in the work of *creation* properly so called. That is done; and the sublime cessation from that constitutes the "rest of God."

5. *And in this* place *again.* Ps. xcv. 11. ¶ *If they shall enter.* That is, they shall *not* enter. See Notes on chap. iii. 11. The object of quoting this here seems to be twofold: (1) To show that even in this Psalm God spoke of *his* rest, and said that they should not enter into it; and (2) it is connected with ver. 6, and is designed to show that it was implied that a rest yet remained. "That which deserves to be called *the divine rest* is spoken of in the Scriptures, and

5 And in this *place* again, If they shall enter into my rest.

6 Seeing therefore it remaineth that some must enter therein, and

as *they* did not enter into it, it follows that it must be in reserve for some others, and that the promise must still remain."

6. *Seeing therefore it remaineth that some must enter therein.* That is, "Since there is a rest spoken of in the Scriptures, implying that it is to be enjoyed by some, and since they to whom it was first promised did not inherit it, it follows that it must still be in reserve." This is the conclusion which the apostle draws from the argument in the previous verses, and is connected with ver. 9, where he says that "there remaineth a rest to the people of God"—the point to which the whole argument tended. The statement in ver. 7, 8 is to be regarded as an *interruption* in the progress of the argument, or as the suggestion of a new thought, or a new argument, bearing on the subject, which he sets down even while stating the conclusion from his argument. It has the appearance of being *suggested* to him as a new thought of importance, and which he preferred to place even in the midst of the summing up of the argument rather than omit it altogether. It denotes a state of mind full of the subject, and where one idea came hastening after another, and which it was deemed important to notice, even though it should seem to be out of place. The thing affirmed in this verse (6) is, that it was a settled or indisputable matter that some would enter into rest. The implied *argument* to prove this is, (1) that there was a "rest" spoken of which deserved to be called *a divine rest*, or the "rest of God;" (2) it could not be supposed that God would prepare such a rest in vain, for it would follow that if he had fitted up a world of rest, he designed that it should be occupied. As he knew, therefore, that they to whom it was first offered would not enter in, it must be that he designed it for some others,

they*d* to whom ³it was first preached entered not in because of unbelief.

7 Again, he limiteth a certain day, saying in David, To-day,

d ch.3.19.   ³ or, *the gospel.*

after so long a time; as it is said, *e*To-day, if ye will hear his voice, harden not your hearts.

8 For if ⁴Jesus had given them

e Ps.95.7.   ⁴ That is, *Joshua.*

---

and that it *remained* to be occupied by us now. ¶ *And they to whom it was first preached.* Margin, *the gospel.* Greek, *evangelized;* that is, to whom the good news of the rest was first announced—the Israelites. ¶ *Entered not in because of unbelief.* See Notes on chap. iii. 19.

7. *Again, he limiteth.* He designates, or definitely mentions. The word rendered *limiteth*—ὁρίζει—means to *bound,* to set a boundary—as of a field or farm; and then to determine or fix definitely, to designate, appoint. Here it means, that he specifies particularly, or mentions expressly. ¶ *A certain day.* A particular time; he mentions TO-DAY particularly. That is, in the time of David, he uses the word "*to-day*," as if there was *then* an offer of rest, and as if it were then possible to enter into it. The object of the additional thought was to show that the offer of rest was not confined to the Israelites, to whom it was first made; that David regarded it as existing in his day; and that man might even then be invited to come and partake of the rest that was promised. "Nearly five hundred years after the time when the Israelites were going to the Promised Land, and when the offer of rest was made to them, we hear David speaking of *rest* still; rest which was offered in his time, and which might then be lost by hardening the heart. It could not be, therefore, that the offer of rest pertained *merely* to the Promised Land. It must be something 'in advance of that. It must be something existing in the time of David. It must be an offer of heaven." A Jew might feel the force of this argument more than we do; still it is conclusive to prove the point under consideration, that there was a rest spoken of long after the offer of the Promised Land, and that all the promises could not have pertained to that. ¶ *Saying in Da-*

vid. In a Psalm composed by David, or rather, perhaps, saying *by* David; that is, God spake by him. ¶ *To-day.* Now:—that is, even in the time of David. ¶ *After so long a time.* So long after the first promise was made—to wit, about five hundred years. These are the words of Paul calling attention to the fact that so long a time after the entrance into the Promised Land there was still a speaking of "*to-day,*" as if even then they were called to partake of the rest. ¶ *As it is said.* To quote it exactly; or to bring the express authority of the Scriptures. It is expressly said even after that long time, "to-day—or NOW, if you will hear his voice." All this is to prove that even in that time there was an offer of rest.

8. *For if Jesus.* Margin, "That is, *Joshua.*" The Syriac renders it, "Joshua the son of Nun." *Jesus* is the Greek mode of writing *Joshua,* and there can be no doubt that Joshua is here intended. The object is to prove that Joshua did *not* give the people of God such a rest as to make it improper to speak of a "rest" after that time. "If Joshua had given them a complete and final rest; if by his conducting them to the Promised Land all had been done which had been contemplated by the promise, then it would not have been alluded to again, as it was in the time of David." Joshua did give them a *rest* in the Promised Land; but it was not all which was intended, and it did not exclude the promise of another and more important rest. ¶ *Then would he not.* Then *God* would not have spoken of another time when that rest could be obtained. That other time, referred to by the phrase "another day," is that which is mentioned before by the phrase "*to-day,*" and refers to the time in which it is spoken of long after Joshua—to wit, in the time of David.

rest, then would he not afterward have spoken of another day.

9 There remaineth therefore a ⁵rest to the people of God.

⁵ or, *keeping of a Sabbath.*

---

9. *There remaineth therefore a rest.* This is the conclusion to which the apostle comes. The meaning is this, that according to the Scriptures there is *now* a promise of rest made to the people of God. It did not pertain merely to those who were called to go to the Promised Land, nor to those who lived in the time of David, but it is *still* true that the promise of rest pertains to *all* the people of God of every generation. The *reasoning* by which the apostle comes to this conclusion is briefly this. (1) That there was a *rest*—called "the rest of God"—spoken of in the earliest period of the world—implying that God meant that it should be enjoyed. (2) That the Israelites, to whom the promise was made, failed of obtaining that which was promised, by their unbelief. (3) That God intended that *some* should enter into his rest—since it would not be provided in vain. (4) That long after the Israelites had fallen in the wilderness, we find the same reference to a *rest* which David in his time exhorts those whom he addressed to endeavour to obtain. (5) That if all that had been meant by the word *rest*, and by the promise, had been accomplished when Joshua conducted the Israelites to the land of Canaan, we should not have heard another day spoken of when it was possible to forfeit that rest by unbelief. It followed, therefore, that there was something besides that; something that pertained to all the people of God to which the name *rest* might still be given, and which they were exhorted still to obtain. The word *rest* in this verse—σαββατισμὸς, *Sabbatism*—in the margin is rendered *keeping of a Sabbath.* It is a different word from σάββατον, *the Sabbath;* and it occurs nowhere else in the New Testament, and is not found in the Septuagint. It properly means *a keeping Sabbath*—from σαββατίζω, *to keep Sabbath.* This verb, not used in the New Testament, occurs frequently in the Septuagint, Ex. xvi. 30; Lev. xxiii.

32; xxvi. 35; 2 Chr. xxxvi. 21; and in 3 Esdr. i. 58; 2 Macca. vi. 6. It differs from the word *Sabbath.* That denotes *the time*—*the day;* this, *the keeping*, or *observance* of it; *the festival.* It means here *a resting*, or an observance of sacred repose, and refers undoubtedly to heaven, as a place of eternal rest with God. It cannot mean the rest in the land of Canaan—for the drift of the writer is to prove that that is *not* intended. It cannot mean the *Sabbath*, properly so called—for then the writer would have employed the usual word σάββατον, *Sabbath.* It cannot mean the Christian Sabbath—for the object is not to prove that there is such a day to be observed, and his reasoning about being excluded from it by unbelief and by hardening the heart would be irrelevant. It must mean, therefore, *heaven*—the world of spiritual and eternal rest; and the assertion is, that there *is* such a *resting*, or *keeping of a Sabbath* in heaven for the people of God. Learn hence, (1) That heaven is a place of cessation from wearisome toil. It is to be like the "rest" which God had after the work of creation (see Notes on verse 4), and of which that was the type and emblem. There will be *employment* there, but it will be without fatigue; there will be the occupation of the mind, and of whatever powers we may possess, but without weariness. Here we are often worn down and exhausted. The body sinks under continued toil, and falls into the grave. There the slave will rest from his task; the man here oppressed and broken down by anxious care will cease from his labours. We know but little of heaven; but we know that a large part of what now oppresses and crushes the frame will not exist there. Slavery will be unknown; the anxious care for support will be unknown, and all the exhaustion which proceeds from the love of gain, and from ambition, will be unknown. In the wearisome toils

10 For he that is entered into his rest, he also hath ceased from his own works, as God *did* from his.

11 Let*ͧ* us labour therefore to

f 2 Pe.1.10.

enter into that rest, lest any man fall after the same example of [6]unbelief.

[6] or, *disobedience.*

---

of life, then, let us look forward to the *rest* that remains in heaven, and as the labourer looks to the shades of the evening or to the Sabbath as a period of rest, so let us look to heaven as the place of eternal repose. (2) Heaven will be like a Sabbath. The best description of it is to say it is *an eternal Sabbath.* Take the Sabbath on earth when best observed, and extend the idea to eternity, and let there be separated all idea of imperfection from its observance, and that would be heaven. The Sabbath is holy; so is heaven. It is intended for worship; so is heaven. It is for praise and for the contemplation of heavenly truth; so is heaven. The one is appointed that we may lay aside worldly cares and anxieties for a little season here; the other that we may lay them aside for ever. (3) The Sabbath here should be like heaven. It is designed to be its type and emblem. So far as the circumstances of the case will allow, it should be just like heaven. There should be the same employments; the same joys; the same communion with God. One of the best rules for employing the Sabbath aright is, to think what heaven will be, and then to endeavour to spend it in the same way. One day in seven at least should remind us of what heaven is to be; and that day may be, and should be, the most happy of the seven. (4) They who do not love the Sabbath on earth are not prepared for heaven. If it is to them a day of tediousness; if its hours move heavily; if they have no delight in its sacred employments, what would an eternity of such days be? How would *they* be passed? Nothing can be clearer than that if we have no such happiness in a season of holy rest, and in holy employments here, we are wholly unprepared for heaven. To the Christian it is the subject of the highest joy in anticipation, that

heaven is to be *one long unbroken* SABBATH—an eternity of successive Sabbath hours. But what, to a sinner, could be a more repulsive and gloomy prospect than such an eternal Sabbath? (5) If this be so, then what a melancholy view is furnished as to the actual preparation of the great mass of men for heaven! How is the Sabbath now spent? In idleness; in worldly business; in travelling; in hunting and fishing; in light reading and conversation; in sleep; in visiting; in riding, walking, lounging, *ennui;* in revelry and dissipation;—in any and every way *except the right way;* in every way except in holy communion with God. What would the race be if once translated to heaven as they are! What a prospect would it be to this multitude to have to spend *an eternity* which would be but a prolongation of the Sabbath of holiness! (6) Let those who love the Sabbath rejoice in the prospect of eternal rest in heaven. In our labour let us look to that world where wearisome toil is unknown; in our afflictions, let us look to that world where tears never fall; when our hearts are pained by the violation of the Sabbath all around us, let us look to that blessed world where such violation will cease for ever. It is not far distant. A few steps will bring us there. Of any Christian it may be said that perhaps his next Sabbath will be spent in heaven—near the throne of God.

10. *For he that is entered into rest.* That is, the man who is so happy as to reach heaven, will enjoy a rest similar to that which God had when he finished the work of creation. It will be (1) a cessation from toil; and (2) it will be a rest similar to that of God—the same kind of enjoyment, the same freedom from care, anxiety, and labour. How happy, then, are they who have entered into heaven! Their toils are over. Their labours are ended. Never again will they know fatigue.

12 For the *g* word of God *is* quick, and powerful, and sharper than any two-edged *h* sword, piercing even to the dividing asunder of soul and

g Is.49.2.   *h* Re.1.16.

spirit, and of the joints and marrow, and *is* a *i* discerner of the thoughts and intents of the heart.

i Ps.139.2; Je.17.10; Re.2.23.

Never more will they feel anxious care. Let us learn, then, (1) not to mourn improperly for those who have left us, and gone to heaven. Happy in the rest of God, why should not we rejoice? Why wish them back again in a world of toil? (2) Let us, in our toils, look forward to the world of rest. Our labours will be over. The weary man will lay down his burden; the exhausted frame will know fatigue no more. Rest is sweet at night after the toils of day; how much more sweet will it be in heaven after the toils of life! Let us (3) labour while it is called to-day. All that we have to do is to be done soon. We shall soon cease from *our* work as God did from his. What we have to do for the salvation of children, brothers, sisters, friends, and for the world, is to be done soon. From the abodes of bliss we shall not be sent forth to speak to our kindred of the blessedness of that world, or to admonish our friends to escape from the place of despair. The pastor will not come again to warn and invite his people; the parent will not come again to tell his children of the Saviour and of heaven; the neighbour will not come to admonish his neighbour. Comp. Luke xvi. 24–29. We shall ALL have ceased from *our* work as God did from *his;* and never again shall we speak to a living friend to invite him to heaven.

11. *Let us therefore labour.* Let us earnestly strive. Since there *is* a rest whose attainment is worth all our efforts; since so many have failed of reaching it by their unbelief; and since there is so much danger that we may fail of it also, let us give all diligence that we may enter into it. Heaven is never obtained but by diligence. No one enters there who does not earnestly desire it, and who does not make a sincere effort to reach it. ¶ *Of unbelief.* Margin, *disobedience.*

The word *unbelief* best expresses the sense, as the apostle was showing that this was the principal thing that prevented men from entering into heaven. See Notes on chap. iii. 12.

12. *For the word of God.* The design of this and the following verse is obvious. It is to show that we cannot escape the notice of God; that all insincerity, unbelief, hypocrisy, will be detected by him; and that, since our hearts are perfectly open before him, we should be sincere, and should not attempt to deceive him. The sense is, that the truth of God is all-penetrating and searching; that the real thoughts and intents of the heart will be brought to light, and that if there is insincerity and self-deception, there can be no hope of escape. There has been a great variety of opinion here about the meaning of the phrase "the word of God." Some have supposed that it means the Lord Jesus; others, the whole of the divine revelation; others, the gospel; others, the particular threatening referred to here. The "word of God" is *that which God speaks*—whether it be a promise or a threatening; whether it be law or gospel; whether it be a simple declaration or a statement of a doctrine. The idea here is, that what *God has said* is fitted to detect hypocrisy, and to lay open the true nature of the feelings of the soul, so that there can be no escape for the guilty. His *truth* is adapted to bring out the real feelings, and to show man exactly what he is. Truth always has this power —whether preached, or read, or communicated by conversation, or impressed upon the memory and conscience by the Holy Spirit. There can be no escape from the penetrating, searching application of the truth of God. That truth has power to show what man is, and is like a penetrating sword that lays open the whole soul. Comp. Isa. xlix. 2.

The phrase "the word of God" here may be applied, therefore, to the *truth* of God, however made known to the mind. In some way it will bring out the real feelings, and show what man is. ¶ *Is quick.* Greek ζῶν, *living.* It is not dead, inert, and powerless. It has a *living* power, and is energetic and active. It is *adapted* to produce this effect. ¶ *And powerful.* Mighty. Its power is seen in awakening the conscience; alarming the fears; laying bare the secret feelings of the heart; and causing the sinner to tremble with the apprehension of the coming judgment. All the great changes in the moral world for the better have been caused by the power of truth. They are such as the truth in its own nature is fitted to effect, and if we may judge of its power by the greatness of the revolutions produced, no words can overestimate the might of the truth which God has revealed. ¶ *Sharper than any two-edged sword.* Literally, *two-mouthed* sword—δίστο-μον. The word *mouth* was given to the sword because it seemed to *devour* all before it. It consumed or destroyed, as a wild beast does. The comparison of the word of God to a sword or to an arrow, is designed to show its power of penetrating the heart, Eccl. xii. 11, "The words of the wise are as goads, and as nails fastened by the masters of assemblies;" Isa. xlix. 2, "And he hath made my mouth like a sharp sword;" Rev. i. 16, "And out of his mouth went a sharp two-edged sword." Comp. Rev. ii. 12, 16; xix. 15. The comparison is common in the classics, and in Arabic poetry. See Gesenius, on Isa. xlix. 2. The idea is that of piercing, or penetrating; and the meaning here is, that the word of God reaches the *heart*— the very centre of action, and lays open the motives and feelings of the man. It was common among the ancients to have a sword with two edges. The Roman sword was usually made in this manner. The fact that it had two edges made it more easy to penetrate, as well as to cut with every way. ¶ *Piercing even to the dividing asunder.* Penetrating so as to divide. ¶ *Soul and spirit.* The animal life from the

immortal soul. The former word here—ψυχή, *soul*—is evidently used to denote the *animal life*, as distinguished from the mind or soul. The latter word—πνεῦμα, *spirit*—means the soul; the immaterial and immortal part; that which lives when the animal life is extinct. This distinction occurs in 1 Thes. v. 23, "Your whole spirit, and soul, and body;" and it is a distinction which we are constantly in the habit of making. There is the body in man—the animal life—and the immortal part that leaves the body when life is extinct. Mysteriously united, they constitute one man. When the animal life is separated from the soul, or when the soul leaves the animated body, the body dies, and life is extinct. To separate the one from the other is, therefore, the same as to take life— and this is the idea here, that the word of God is like a sharp sword that inflicts deadly wounds. The sinner "*dies;*"—that is, he becomes dead to his former hopes, or is "slain" by the law, Rom. vii. 9, "I was alive without the law once; but when the commandment came, sin revived, and I died." This is the power referred to here—the power of destroying the hope of the sinner; cutting him down under conviction; prostrating him as if a sword had pierced his heart. ¶ *And of the joints and marrow.* The figure is still continued of the sword that takes life. Such a sword would seem to penetrate even the joints and marrow of the body. It would separate the joints, and pierce through the very bones to the marrow. A similar effect, Paul says, is produced by truth. It seems to penetrate the very essence of the soul, and lay it all open to the view. ¶ *And is a discerner of the thoughts.* It shows what the thoughts and intentions are. Professor Stuart, Bloomfield, and some others, suppose that the reference here is to *God* speaking by his word. But the more natural construction certainly is, to refer it to the word or truth of God. It is true that God searches the heart, and knows the thoughts, but that is not the truth which is prominent here. It is, that

the thoughts and intents of the heart are brought out to view by the word of God. And can anyone doubt this? See Rom. vii. 7. Is it not true that men are made to see their real character under the exhibition of the truth of God? That in the light of the law they see their past lives to be sinful? That the exhibition of truth calls to their recollection many long-forgotten sins? And that their real feelings are disclosed when the truth of God is proclaimed? Men then are made to look upon their motives as they had never done before, and to see in their hearts feelings whose existence they would not have suspected if it had not been for the exhibition of the truth. The exhibition of the truth is like pouring down the beams of the sun at midnight on a dark world; and the truth lays open the real feelings of the sinner as that sun would disclose the deeds of wickedness that are now performed under cover of the night. Many a man has a deep and fixed hostility to God and to his gospel, who might never be sensible of it if the truth was not faithfully proclaimed. The particular idea here is, that the truth of God will detect the feelings of the hypocrite and self-deceiver. They cannot always conceal their emotions, and the time will come when truth, like light poured into the soul, will reveal their unbelief and their secret sins. They who are cherishing a hope of salvation, therefore, should be on their guard lest they mistake the name for the reality. Let us learn from this verse (1) the power of truth. It is *fitted* to lay open the secret feelings of the soul. There is not an effect produced in awakening a sinner, or in his conviction, his conversion, and his sanctification, which the truth is not *adapted* to produce. The truth of God is not dead; nor fitted to make men *worse;* nor designed merely to show its own *weakness,* and to be a mere *occasion* on which the Holy Spirit acts on the mind;—it is in its own nature FITTED to produce just the effects which are produced when it awakens, convicts, converts, and sanctifies the soul. (2) The truth should be preached

with the feeling that it is adapted to this end. Men who preach should endeavour to understand the nature of the mind and of the moral feelings, as really as he who would inflict a deadly wound should endeavour to understand enough about anatomy to know where the heart is, or he who administers medicine should endeavour to know what is adapted to remove certain diseases. And he who has no belief in the efficacy of truth to produce any effect, resembles one who should suppose that all knowledge of the human system was needless to him who wished to perform a surgical operation, and who should cut at random—piously leaving it with God to direct the knife; or he who should go into a hospital of patients and administer medicines indiscriminately—devoutly saying that all healing must come from God, and that the use of medicine was only to show its own weakness! Thus many men seem to preach. Yet for aught that appears truth is just as wisely adapted to save the soul as medicine is to heal the sick; and why then should not a preacher be as careful to study the nature of truth, and its adaptedness to a particular end, as a student of the healing art is to understand the adaptedness of medicine to cure disease? The true way of preaching is, to feel that truth is adapted to the end in view; to select that which is best fitted for that end; to preach as if the whole result depended on getting that truth before the mind and into the heart—and *then* to leave the whole result with God—as a physician with right feelings will exert all his skill to save his patient, and then commit the whole question of life and health to God. He will be more likely to praise God intelligently who believes that he has wisely adapted a plan to the end in view, than he who believes that he works only at random.

13. *Neither is there any creature that is not manifest in his sight.* There is no being who is not wholly known to God. All his thoughts, his feelings, his plans, are distinctly understood. Of the truth of this there can be no

13 Neither is there any creature that is not manifest in his sight : but all things *are* [k]naked and opened unto the eyes of him with whom we have to do.

k Pr.15.11.

doubt. The *design* of the remark here is, to guard those to whom the apostle was writing from self-deception—since they could conceal nothing from God. ¶ *All things* are *naked.* Exposed; uncovered. There is nothing that can be concealed from God. Ps. cxxxix. 11, 12.

> " The veil of night is no disguise,
> No screen from thy all-searching eyes;
> Thy hands can seize thy foes as soon
> Through midnight shades as blazing noon."

¶ *And opened*—τετραχηλισμένα. The word here used — τραχηλίζω — properly means, (1) to lay bare the neck, or to bend it back, so as to expose the throat to being cut. (2) To expose; to lay open in any way. *Why* the word is used here has been a matter of inquiry. Some have supposed that the phrase is derived from offering sacrifice, from the fact that the priest carefully examined the victim to see whether it was sound, before it was offered. But this is manifestly a forced exposition. Others have supposed that it is derived from the custom of bending back the head of a criminal so as to look full in his face, and recognize him, so as not to be mistaken; but this is equally forced and unnatural. This opinion was first proposed by Erasmus, and has been adopted by Clarke and others. Bloomfield, following, as he says, the interpretation of Chrysostom, Grotius (though this is not the sentiment of Grotius), Beza, Atling, Hammond, and others, supposes the allusion to be to the custom of cutting the animal down the backbone through the spinal marrow, and thus of laying it open entirely. This sense would well suit the connection. Grotius supposes that it means to strip off the skin by dividing it at the neck and then removing it. This view is also adopted substantially by Doddridge. These explanations are forced, and imply a departure more or less from the proper meaning of the Greek word. The most simple and obvious meaning is usually the best in explaining the Bible. The word which the apostle employs relates to *the neck*—τράχηλος—and not to the spinal marrow or the skin. The proper meaning of the verb is *to bend the neck back,* so as to expose it in front, when an animal is slain (Passow). Then it means to make bare; to remove everything like covering; to expose a thing entirely—as the naked neck is for the knife. The allusion here is undoubtedly to the *sword* which Paul had referred to in the previous verse, as dividing the soul and spirit, and the joints and marrow; and the meaning is, that to God, in whose hands that sword was held, everything was exposed. We are in relation to that like an animal whose neck is bent back, and laid bare, and ready for the slaughter. Nothing *hinders* God from striking; there is nothing that can prevent that sword from penetrating the heart—any more than, when the neck of the animal is bent back and laid bare, there is anything that can hinder the sacrificing priest from thrusting the knife into the throat of the victim. If this is the true interpretation, then what an affecting view does it give of the power of God, and of the exposedness of man to destruction! All is bare, naked, open. There is no concealment; no hindrance; no power of resistance. In a moment God can strike, and his dreadful sentence falls on the sinner like the knife on the exposed throat of the victim. What emotions should the sinner have who feels that he is exposed each moment to the sentence of eternal justice— to the sword of God—as the animal with bent-back neck is exposed to the knife! And what solemn feelings should be awakened in the mind when it is remembered that everything is naked and open before God! Were we *transparent,* so that the world could see all that we are, who would dare go abroad? Who would wish the world to read his thoughts and

14 Seeing then that we have a great high priest, that is *passed

l ch.9.12,24.

into the heavens, Jesus the Son of God, let us *m*hold fast *our* profession.

m ch.10.23.

feelings for a single day? Who would wish his best friends to look in upon his naked soul, as we can look into a room through a window? Oh what blushes and confusion; what a hanging down of the head, and what an effort to escape from the gaze of men would there be, if every one knew that his secret feelings were seen by every person whom he met! Social enjoyment would end; and the now gay and blithe multitudes in the streets would become processions of downcast and blushing convicts. And yet all these are known to God. He reads every thought; sees every feeling; looks through the whole soul. How careful should we be to keep our hearts pure; how anxious that there should be nothing there that we are not *willing* to have known! ¶ *With whom we have to do.* Literally, *with whom is our account.* Our account; our reckoning is to be with him before whom all is naked and open. We cannot, therefore, impose on him. We cannot pass off hypocrisy for sincerity. He will judge us according to truth, not according to appearances; and his sentence, therefore, will be just. A man who is to be tried by one who *knows all about him* should be a pure and holy man.

14. *Seeing then that we have a great high priest.* The apostle here resumes the subject which had been slightly hinted at in chap. ii. 17; iii. 1, and pursues it to the end of chap. x. The *object* is to show that Christians have a great High-priest as really as the Jews had; to show wherein he surpassed the Levitical priesthood; to show how all that was said of the Aaronic priesthood, and all the types pertaining to that priesthood, were fulfilled in the Lord Jesus; and to state and illustrate the nature of the consolations which Christians may derive from the fact that they have such an high-priest. One of the things on which the Jews most valued their religion, was the fact that it had such

a minister of religion as their highpriest—the most elevated functionary of that dispensation. It came, therefore, to be of the utmost importance to show that Christianity was not inferior to the Jewish religion in this respect, and that the High-priest of the Christian profession would not suffer in point of dignity, in the value of the blood with which he would approach God, and in the efficacy of his intercession, when compared with the Jewish high-priest. Moreover, it was a doctrine of Christianity that the Jewish ritual was to pass away; that its temple services were to cease. It was, therefore, of vast importance to show *why* they passed away, and how they were superseded. To do this, the apostle is led into this long discussion respecting their nature. He shows that they were designed to be typical. He demonstrates that they could not purify the heart, and give peace to the conscience. He proves that they were all intended to point to something future, and to introduce the Messiah to the world; and that, when this object was accomplished, their great end was secured, and they were thus all fulfilled. In no part of the Bible can there be found so full an account of the design of the Mosaic institutions as in chap. v.–x. of this epistle; and were it not for this the volume of inspiration would be incomplete. We should be left in the dark on some of the most important subjects in revelation; we should ask questions for which we could find no certain answer. The phrase "*great high priest*" here is used with reference to a known usage among the Jews. In the time of the apostle the name high-priest pertained not only to him who actually held the office, and who had the right to enter into the holy of holies, but to his deputy, and to those who had held the office but who had retired from it, and perhaps also the name was given to the head of each one of the twenty-four courses

15 For we have not an high priest which cannot be [n]touched.

n Ho.11.8.

with the feeling of our infirmities; but was in all points tempted like as *we are, yet* [o]without sin.

o 1 Pe.2.22; 1 Jn.3.5.

or classes into which the priests were divided. Comp. Notes on Luke i. 5; Mat. xxvi. 3. The name "great high priest" would designate him who actually held the office, and was at the head of all the other priests; and the idea here is, not merely that the Lord Jesus was *a priest,* but that he was at the head of all. In the Christian economy he sustained a rank that corresponded with that of the great high-priest in the Jewish. ¶ *That is passed into the heavens.* Chap. ix. 12, 24. The Jewish high-priest went once a year into the most holy place in the temple, to offer the blood of the atonement. See Notes on chap. ix. 7. Paul says that the Christian High-priest has gone, in like manner, into heaven. He has gone there also to make intercession, and to sprinkle the blood of the atonement on the mercy-seat. See Notes on chap. ix. 24, 25. ¶ *Jesus the Son of God.* Not a descendant of Aaron, but one much greater—the Son of God. See Notes on chap. i. 2. ¶ *Let us hold fast our profession.* See Notes on chap. iii. 1; x. 22, 23. This is the drift and scope of the epistle—to show that Christians should hold fast their profession, and not apostatize. The object of the apostle now is, to show why the fact that we have such a high-priest, is a reason why we should hold fast our professed attachment to him. These reasons—which are drawn out in the succeeding chapters—are such as the following:—(1) We may look to him for assistance—since he can be touched with the feeling of our infirmities, chap. iv. 15, 16. (2) The impossibility of being renewed again if we should fall away from him, since there is but *one* such High-priest, and since the sacrifice for sin can never be repeated, chap. vi. (3) The fact that all the ancient types were fulfilled in him, and that everything which there was in the Jewish dispensation to keep men from apostasy exists much more powerfully in the

Christian scheme. (4) The fact that they who rejected the laws of Moses died without mercy, and much more must anyone who should reject the Son of God expect certain and fearful severity, chap. x. 27–30. By considerations such as these, the apostle aims to show them the danger of apostasy, and to urge them to a faithful adherence to their Christian profession.

15. *For we have not an high priest which cannot be touched.* Our High-priest is not cold and unfeeling. That is, we have one who is abundantly qualified to sympathize with us in our afflictions, and to whom, therefore, we may look for aid and support in trials. Had we a high-priest who was cold and heartless, who simply performed the external duties of his office without entering into the sympathies of those who came to seek for pardon, who had never experienced any trials, and who felt himself above those who sought his aid, we should necessarily feel disheartened in attempting to overcome our sins, and to live to God. His coldness would repel us; his stateliness would awe us; his distance and reserve would keep us away, and perhaps render us indifferent to all desire to be saved. But tenderness and sympathy attract those who are feeble, and kindness does more than anything else to encourage those who have to encounter difficulties and dangers. See Notes on chap. ii. 16–18. Such tenderness and sympathy has *our* great High-priest. ¶ *But was in all points tempted like as* we are. *Tried* as we are. See Notes on chap. ii. 18. He was subjected to all the kinds of trial to which we can be, and he is, therefore, able to sympathize with us and to aid us. He was tempted—in the literal sense; he was persecuted; he was poor; he was despised; he suffered bodily pain; he endured the sorrows of a lingering and most cruel death. ¶ Yet *without*

16 Let us therefore *p* come boldly unto the throne of grace, that we may obtain mercy, and find grace to help in time of need.

p Ep.3.12; ch.10.19-22.

---

sin. 1 Pet. ii. 22, "Who did no sin;" Isa. liii. 9, "He had done no violence, neither was any deceit in his mouth;" Heb. vii. 26, "Who is holy, harmless, undefiled, separate from sinners." The importance of this fact—that the great High-priest of the Christian profession was "without sin"—the apostle illustrates at length in chap. vii., viii., ix. He here merely alludes to it, and says that one who was "without sin" was able to assist those who were sinners, and who put their trust in him.

16. *Let us therefore come boldly unto the throne of grace.* "The throne of grace!" What a beautiful expression. A throne is the seat of a sovereign; a throne of grace is designed to represent a sovereign seated to dispense mercy and pardon. The illustration or comparison here may have been derived from the temple service. In that service God is represented as seated in the most holy place on the mercy-seat. The Jewish high-priest approached that seat or throne of the divine majesty with the blood of the atonement to make intercession for the people, and to plead for pardon. See Notes on chap. ix. 7, 8. That scene was emblematic of heaven. God is seated on a throne of mercy. The great High-priest of the Christian calling, having shed his own blood to make expiation, is represented as approaching God, and pleading for the pardon of men. To a God willing to show mercy he comes with the merits of a sacrifice sufficient for all, and pleads for their salvation. We may, therefore, come with boldness and look for pardon. We come not depending on our own merits, but we come where a sufficient sacrifice has been offered for human guilt; and where we are assured that God is merciful. We may, therefore, come without hesitancy, or trembling, and ask for all the mercy that we need. ¶ *That we may obtain mercy.* This is what we want *first.* We need pardon —as the first thing when we come

to God. We are guilty and self-condemned—and our first cry should be for *mercy—mercy.* A man who comes to God not feeling his need of mercy, must fail of obtaining the divine favour; and he will be best prepared to obtain that favour who has the deepest sense of his need of forgiveness. ¶ *And find grace.* Favour—strength, help, counsel, direction, support, for the various duties and trials of life. This is what we *next* need—we all need—we always need. Even when pardoned, we need grace to keep us from sin; to aid us in duty; to preserve us in the day of temptation. And feeling our need of this, we may come and ask of God *all* that we want for this purpose. Such is the assurance given us; and to this bold approach to the throne of grace all are freely invited. In view of it, let us (1) rejoice that there *is* a throne of grace. What a world would this be if God sat on a throne of *justice* only, and if no mercy were ever to be shown to men! Who is there who would not be overwhelmed with despair? But it is not so. He is on A THRONE OF GRACE. By day and by night, from year to year, from generation to generation, he is on such a throne. In every land he may be approached, and in as many different languages as men speak, may they plead for mercy. In all times of our trial and temptation we may be assured that he is seated on that throne, and that, wherever we are, we may approach him with acceptance. (2) We *need* the privilege of coming before such a throne. We are sinful, and need mercy; we are feeble, and need grace to help us. There is not a day of our lives in which we do not need pardon; not an hour in which we do not need grace. (3) How obvious are the propriety and necessity of prayer! Every man is a sinner, and should pray for pardon; every man is weak, feeble, dependent, and should pray for grace. Not till a man can prove that he has never committed

any sin, should he maintain that he has no need of pardon; not till he can show that he is able alone to meet the storms and temptations of life, should he feel that he has no need to ask for grace. Yet who can feel this? And how strange it is that all men do not pray! (4) It is easy to be forgiven. All that needs to be done is to plead the merits of our great High-priest, and God is ready to pardon. Who would not be glad to be able to pay a debt in a manner so easy? Yet how few there are who are willing to remove the debt incurred by sin by so simple an act as that of pleading what the great High-priest, the Son of God, has done to cancel it! (5) It is easy to obtain all the grace that we need. We have only to *ask for it*—and it is done. How easy, then, to meet temptation, if we would! How strange that any should rely on their own strength, when they may lean on the arm of God! (6) If men are not pardoned, and if they fall into sin and ruin, they alone are to blame. There IS A THRONE OF GRACE. It is always accessible. There IS A GOD. He is always ready to pardon. There IS A REDEEMER. He is the great High-priest of men. He is always interceding. His merits may *always* be pleaded as the ground of our salvation. Why, then, oh why, should any remain unforgiven and perish? On them alone the blame must lie. In their own bosoms is the reason why they are not saved.

CHAPTER V.

ANALYSIS OF THE CHAPTER.

In this chapter the subject of the priestly office of Christ is continued and further illustrated. It had been introduced chap. ii. 17, 18; chap. iii. 1; chap. iv. 14–17. The Jews regarded the office of high-priest as an essential feature in the true religion; and it became, therefore, of the highest importance to show that in the Christian system there was a high-priest every way equal to that of the Jews. In his rank, in his character, and in the sacrifice which he offered, he was more than equal to the Jewish high-priest; and they who had for-

saken Judaism, and embraced Christianity, had lost nothing in this respect by the change, and had gained much. It became necessary, therefore, in making out this point, to institute a comparison between the Jewish high-priest and the Great Author of the Christian religion, and this comparison is pursued in this and the following chapters. The comparison, in this chapter, turns mainly on the *qualifications* for the office, and the question whether the Lord Jesus had those qualifications. The chapter embraces the following points:—

I. The qualifications of a Jewish high-priest, ver. 1–4. They are these: (1) He must have been ordained or appointed by God for the purpose of offering gifts and sacrifices for sins, ver. 1. (2) He must be tender and compassionate in his feelings, so that he can *sympathize* with those for whom he ministers, ver. 2. (3) He must have an offering to bring to God, and be able to present a sacrifice alike for himself and for the people, ver. 3. (4) He could not take this honour on himself, but must have evidence that he was called of God, as was Aaron, ver. 4.

II. An inquiry whether these qualifications were found in the Lord Jesus, the great High-priest of the Christian dispensation, ver. 5–10. In considering this, the apostle specifies the following qualifications in him, corresponding to those which he had said were required in the Jewish high-priest: (1) He did not take this honour on himself, but was called directly by God, and after an order superior to the Aaronic priesthood—the order of Melchisedec, ver. 5, 6, 9, 10. (2) He was kind, tender, and compassionate, and showed that he was able to sympathize with those for whom he had undertaken the office. When on earth, he had evinced all the tenderness which could be desired in one who had come to pity and save mankind. He had a tender, sensitive, sympathizing nature. He felt deeply as a man, under the pressure of the great sufferings which he endured, and thus showed that he was abundantly quali-

CHAPTER V.

FOR every high priest taken from among men is *a*ordained

a ch.8.3.

fied to sympathize with his people, ver. 7, 8.

III. In ver. 10 the apostle had introduced, incidentally, a topic of great difficulty; and he adds (ver. 11–14), that he had much to say on that subject, but that those whom he addressed were not qualified then to understand it. They ought to have been so far advanced in knowledge as to have been able to embrace the more abstruse and difficult points connected with the doctrines of Christianity. But they needed, he says, instruction even yet in the more simple elements of religion, and he feared that what he had to say of Melchisedec would be far above their comprehension. This point, therefore, he drops for the present, and in chap. vi. states again, and at greater length, the danger of apostasy, and the importance of perseverance in endeavouring to comprehend the sublime mysteries of the Christian religion; and then (chap. vii.) he resumes the subject of the comparison between Christ and Melchisedec.

1. *For every high priest.* That is, among the Jews, for the remarks relate to the Jewish system. The Jews had one high-priest who was regarded as the successor of Aaron. The word "*high*-priest" means *chief priest*—that is, a priest of higher rank and office than others. By the original regulation the Jewish high-priest was to be of the family of Aaron (Ex. xxix. 9), though in later times the office was frequently conferred on others. In the time of the Romans it had become venal, and the Mosaic regulation was disregarded, 2 Mac. iv. 7; Jos. *Antiq.* xv. 3. 1. It was no longer held for life, so that there were several persons at one time to whom was given the title of high-priest. The high-priest was at the head of religious affairs, and was the ordinary judge of all that pertained to religion, and even a minister of justice or a judge, Deut.

for men in things *pertaining* to God, that he may offer both gifts and sacrifices for sins:

xvii. 8–12; xix. 17; xxi. 5; xxiii. 9, 10. He only had the privilege of entering the most holy place once a year, on the great day of atonement, to make expiation for the sins of the people, Lev. xvi. He was to be the son of one who had married a virgin, and was to be free from any corporeal defect, Lev. xxi. 13. The *dress* of the high-priest was much more costly and magnificent than that of the inferior order of priests, Ex. xxxix. 1–9. He wore a mantle or robe—*meil* מְעִיל—of blue, with the borders embroidered with pomegranates in purple and scarlet; an *ephod*—אֵפוֹד—made of cotton, with crimson, purple, and blue, and ornamented with gold, worn over the robe or mantle, without sleeves, and divided below the arm-pits into two parts or halves, of which one was in front, covering the breast, and the other behind, covering the back. In the ephod was a breastplate of curious workmanship, and on the head a mitre. The breastplate was a piece of broidered work about ten inches square, and was made double, so as to answer the purpose of a pouch or bag. It was adorned with twelve precious stones, each one having the name of one of the tribes of Israel. The two upper corners of the breast-plate were fastened to the ephod, and the two lower to the girdle. ¶ *Taken from among men.* There may be an allusion here to the fact that the great High-priest of the Christian dispensation had a higher than human origin, and was selected from a rank far above men. Or it may be that the meaning is, that every high-priest on earth—including all under the old dispensation and the great High-priest of the new—is ordained with reference to the welfare of men, and to bring some valuable offering for man to God. ¶ *Is ordained for men.* Is set apart or consecrated for the welfare of men. The Jewish high-priest was set apart to his office with great solemnity. See

2 Who can [1] have compassion on the ignorant, and on them that are out of the way; for that [b] he himself also is compassed with infirmity.

[1] or, *reasonably bear with.*   [b] ch.7 28.

3 And by reason hereof he ought, as for the people, [c] so also for himself, to offer for sins.

[c] Le.9.7.

Ex. xxix. ¶ *In things* pertaining *to God.* In religious matters, or with reference to the worship and service of God. He was not to be a civil ruler, nor a teacher of science, nor a military leader, but his business was to superintend the affairs of religion. ¶ *That he may offer both gifts.* That is, thank-offerings, or oblations which would be the expressions of gratitude. Many such offerings were made by the Jews under the laws of Moses, and the high-priest was the medium by whom they were to be presented to God. ¶ *And sacrifices for sins.* Bloody offerings; offerings made of slain beasts. The blood of expiation was sprinkled by him on the mercy-seat, and he was the appointed medium by which such sacrifices were to be presented to God. See Notes on chap. ix. 6–10. We may remark here, (1) That the proper office of a priest is to present a *sacrifice* for sin. (2) It is improper to give the name *priest* to a minister of the gospel. The reason is, that he offers no sacrifice; he sprinkles no blood. He is appointed to "preach the word," and to lead the devotions of the church, but not to offer sacrifice. Accordingly, the New Testament maintains entire consistency on this point, for the name *priest* is in no instance given to the apostles, or to any other minister of the gospel. Among the Papists there is *consistency*—though founded on a gross and dangerous error—in the use of the word *priest.* They believe that the minister of religion offers up "the real body and blood of our Lord;" that the bread and wine are changed by the words of consecration into the "body and blood, the soul and divinity, of the Lord Jesus" (*Decrees of the Council of Trent*), and that *this* is really offered by him as a sacrifice. Accordingly, they "elevate the host;" that is, they lift up, or offer, the sacrifice, and require all to

bow before it and worship, and with this view they are *consistent* in retaining the word *priest.* But why should this name be applied to a *Protestant* minister, who believes that all this is blasphemy, and who claims to have no *sacrifice* to offer when he comes to minister before God? The great sacrifice—the one sufficient atonement—has been offered, and the ministers of the gospel are appointed to proclaim that truth to men, not to offer sacrifices for sin.

2. *Who can have compassion.* Margin, *reasonably bear with.* The idea is that of *sympathizing with.* The high-priest is taken from among men, in order that he may have a fellow-feeling for those on whose behalf he officiates. Sensible of his own ignorance, he is able to sympathize with those who are ignorant; and compassed about with infirmity, he is able to succour those who have like infirmities. ¶ *And on them that are out of the way.* The erring and the guilty. If he were taken from an order of beings superior to men, he would be less qualified to sympathize with those who feel that they are sinners, and that they need forgiveness. ¶ *For that he himself also is compassed with infirmity.* See chap. vii. 28. He is liable to err; is subject to temptation; he must die, and appear before God;—and encompassed with these infirmities, he is better qualified to minister in behalf of guilty and dying men. For the same reason it is that the ministers of the gospel are chosen from among men. They are of like passions with others. They are sinners; they are dying men. They can enter into the feelings of those who are conscious of guilt; they can sympathize with those who tremble in dread of death; they can partake of the emotions of those who expect soon to appear before God.

3. *And by reason hereof.* Because he is a sinner; an imperfect man. ¶ *As for the people, so also for himself, to*

4 And *d*no man taketh this honour unto himself, but he that is called of God, *e*as *was* Aaron.

5 So also *f*Christ glorified not

d 2 Ch.26.18. *e* Ex.28.1; Nu.16.40. *f* Jn.8.54.

himself to be made an high priest; but he that said unto him, *g*Thou art my Son, to-day have I begotten thee.

g Ps.2.7.

offer for sins. To make an expiation for sins. He needs the same atonement; he offers the sacrifice for himself which he does for others, Lev. ix. 7. The same thing is true of the ministers of religion now. They come before God feeling that they have need of the benefit of the same atonement which they preach to others; they plead the merits of the same blood for their own salvation which they show to be indispensable for the salvation of others.

4. *And no man taketh this honour to himself.* No one has a right to enter on this office unless he has the qualifications which God has prescribed. There were fixed and definite laws in regard to the succession in the office of the high-priest, and to the qualifications of him who should hold the office. ¶ *But he that is called of God, as was Aaron.* Aaron was designated by name. It was necessary that his successors should have as clear evidence that they were called of God to the office, as though they had been mentioned by name. The manner in which the high-priest was to succeed to the office was designated in the law of Moses, but in the time of Paul these rules were little regarded. The office had become venal, and was conferred at pleasure by the Roman rulers. Still it was true that, according to the law, to which alone Paul here refers, no one might hold this office but he who had the qualifications which Moses prescribed, and which showed that he was called of God. We may remark here, (1) That this does not refer so much to an *internal* as to an *external* call. He was to have the qualifications prescribed in the law—but it is not specified that he should be conscious of an internal call to the office, or be influenced by the Holy Spirit to it. Such a call was, doubtless, in the highest degree desirable, but it was not prescribed

as an essential qualification. (2) This has no reference to the call to the work of the Christian ministry, and should not be applied to it. It should not be urged as a proof-text to show that a minister of the gospel should have a "call" directly from God, or that he should be called according to a certain order of succession. The object of Paul is not to state this— whatever may be the truth on this point. His object is, to show that the Jewish high-priest was called of God to *his* office in a certain way, showing that he held the appointment from God, and that *therefore* it was necessary that the great High-priest of the Christian profession should be called in a similar manner. To this alone the comparison should be understood as applicable.

5. *So also Christ glorified not himself.* See Notes on Jn. viii. 54. The meaning is, that Jesus was not ambitious; that he did not obtrude himself into the great office of high-priest; that he did not enter upon its duties without being regularly called to it. Paul claimed that Christ held that office; but, as he was not descended from Aaron, and as no one might perform its duties without being regularly called to it, it was incumbent on him to show that Jesus was not an intruder, but had a regular vocation to that work. This he shows by a reference to two passages of the Old Testament. ¶ *But he that said unto him.* That is, he who said to him, "Thou art my Son," exalted him to that office. He received his appointment from him. This was decisive in the case, and this was sufficient, if it could be made out; for the only claim which Aaron and his successors could have to the office, was the fact that they had received their appointment from God. ¶ *Thou art my Son.* Ps. ii. 7. See this passage explained in the Notes on Acts xiii. 33. It is

6 As he saith also in another *place*, ^hThou *art* a priest for ever after the order of Melchisedec.

7 Who in the days of his flesh, when he had ⁱoffered up prayers

here used with reference to the designation to the priestly office, though in the Psalm it is applied more particularly to the anointing to the office of king. The propriety of this application is founded on the fact that the language in the Psalm is of so general a character, that it may be applied to *any* exaltation of the Redeemer, or to any honour conferred on him. It is here used with strict propriety, for Paul is saying that Jesus did not exalt *himself*, and in proof of that he refers to the fact that *God* had exalted him by calling him his "Son."

6. *As he saith also in another* place. Ps. cx. 4. ¶ *Thou* art *a priest for ever.* It is evident here that the apostle means to be understood as saying that the Psalm referred to Christ, and this is one of the instances of quotation from the Old Testament respecting which there can be no doubt. Paul makes much of this argument in a subsequent part of this epistle (chap. vii.), and reasons as if no one would deny that the Psalm had a reference to the Messiah. It is clear from this that the Psalm was understood by the Jews at that time to have such a reference, and that this was so universally admitted that no one would call it in question. That the Psalm refers to the Messiah has been the opinion of nearly all Christian commentators, and has been admitted by the Jewish Rabbins in general also. The *evidence* that it refers to the Messiah is such as the following: (1) It is a Psalm of David, and yet is spoken of one who was superior to him, and whom he calls his "Lord," ver. 1. (2) It cannot be referred to JEHOVAH himself, for he is expressly (ver. 1) distinguished from him who is here addressed. (3) It cannot be referred to anyone in the time of David, for there was no one to whom he would attribute this character of superiority but God. (4) For the same reason there was no one among his posterity, except the Messiah, to whom

he would apply this language. (5) It is expressly ascribed by the Lord Jesus to himself, Mat. xxii. 43, 44. (6) The scope of the Psalm is such as to be applicable to the Messiah, and there is no part of it which would be inconsistent with such a reference. Indeed, there is no passage of the Old Testament of which it would be more universally conceded that there was a reference to the Messiah than this Psalm. ¶ *Thou* art *a priest.* He is not here called a *high-priest*, for Melchisedec did not bear that title, nor was the Lord Jesus to be a high-priest exactly in the sense in which the name was given to Aaron and his successors. A word is used, therefore, to denote that he would be a *priest* simply, or would sustain the priestly office. This was all that was needful to the present argument, which was, that he was *designated by God* to the priestly office, and that he had not intruded himself into it. ¶ *For ever.* This was an important circumstance, of which the apostle makes much use in another part of the epistle. See Notes on chap. vii. 8, 23, 24. The priesthood of the Messiah was not to change from hand to hand; it was not to be laid down at death; it was to remain unchangeably the same. ¶ *After the order.* The word rendered *order*—τάξις—means "a setting in order"—hence arrangement or disposition. It may be applied to ranks of soldiers, to gradations of office, or to any rank which men sustain in society. To say that he was of the same *order* with Melchisedec was to say that he was of the same *rank* or *station.* He was like him in his designation to the office. In what respects he was like him the apostle shows more fully in chap. vii. *One* particular in which there was a striking resemblance, which did not exist between Christ and any other high-priest, was, that Melchisedec was both a *priest* and a *king.* None of the kings of the Jews were priests, nor were any of the priests

and supplications, with strong crying and tears, unto *him that was

ever elevated to the office of king.
But in Melchisedec these offices were
united, and this fact constituted a
striking resemblance between him and
the Lord Jesus. It was on this principle that there was such pertinency
in quoting here the passage from the
second Psalm. See ver. 5. The meaning is, that Melchisedec was of a peculiar rank or order, that he was not
numbered with the Levitical priests,
and that there were important features in his office which differed from
theirs. In those features it was distinctly predicted that the Messiah
would resemble him. ¶ *Melchisedec.*
See Notes on chap. vii. 1, seq.

7. *Who.* That is, the Lord Jesus,
for so the connection demands. The
object of this verse and the two following is to show that the Lord Jesus had
that qualification for the office of priest
to which the apostle had referred in
ver. 2. It was one important qualification for that office that he who sustained it should be able to show compassion, to aid those that were out of
the way, and to sympathize with sufferers; in other words, they were
themselves encompassed with infirmity, and thus were able to succour
those who were subjected to trials.
The apostle shows now that the Lord
Jesus had those qualifications, as far
as it was possible for one to have them
who had no sin. In the days of his
flesh he suffered intensely; he prayed
with fervour; he placed himself in a
situation where he learned subjection
and obedience by his trials; and in
all this he went far beyond what had
been evinced by the priests under the
ancient dispensation. ¶ *In the days
of his flesh.* When he appeared on
earth as a man. Flesh is here used
to denote human nature, and especially
human nature as susceptible of suffering. The Son of God still is united
to human nature, but it is human nature glorified, for in his case, as in all
others, "flesh and blood cannot inherit
the kingdom of God," 1 Cor. xv. 50.

able to save him from death, and
was heard ²in that he feared;

He has now a glorified body (Phil. iii.
21), such as the redeemed will have in
the future world. Comp. Rev. i. 13-17.
The phrase "*days* of his flesh" means
the *time* when he was incarnate or
when he lived on earth in human form.
The particular time here referred to
evidently was the agony in the garden
of Gethsemane. ¶ *Prayers and supplications.* These words are often used
to denote the same thing. If there
is a difference, the former—δεήσεις—
means petitions which arise *from a
sense of need*—from δέομαι, *to want, to
need;* the latter refers usually to supplication *for protection,* and is applicable to one who, under a sense of
guilt, flees to an altar with the symbols of supplication in his hand. Suppliants in such cases often carried an
olive-branch as an emblem of the
peace which they sought. A fact is
mentioned by Livy respecting the
Locrians that may illustrate this passage: "Ten delegates from the Locrians, squalid and covered with rags,
came into the hall where the consuls
were sitting, extending the badges of
suppliants—olive-branches—according to the custom of the Greeks, and
prostrated themselves on the ground
before the tribunal, with a lamentable
cry" (lib. xxix. c. 16). The particular
idea in the word here used—ἱκετηρία—
is petition for *protection, help,* or *shelter*
(Passow), and this idea accords well
with the design of the passage. The
Lord Jesus prayed as one who had
need, and as one who desired *protection, shelter,* or *help.* The words here,
therefore, do not mean the same thing,
and are not merely intensive, but they
refer to distinct purposes which the
Redeemer had in his prayers. He was
about to die, and, as a man, he needed
divine *help;* he was, probably, tempted
in that dark hour (see Notes on Jn. xii.
30), and he fled to God for *protection.*
¶ *With strong crying.* This word
does not mean *weeping* as the word
"crying" does familiarly with us. It
rather means an outcry, the voice of

wailing and lamentation. It is the cry for help of one who is deeply distressed or in danger; and it refers here to the *earnest petition* of the Saviour when in the agony of Gethsemane or when on the cross. It is the *intensity of the voice* which is referred to when it is raised by an agony of suffering, Luke xxii. 44, "He prayed more earnestly;" Mat. xxvii. 46, "And about the ninth hour Jesus cried with a loud voice, My God, my God, why hast thou forsaken me?" See also Mat. xxvi. 38, 39; xxvii. 50. ¶ *And tears.* Jesus wept at the grave of Lazarus (Jn. xi. 35), and over Jerusalem, Luke xix. 41. It is not expressly stated by the evangelists that he *wept* in the garden of Gethsemane, but there is no reason to doubt that he did. In an agony so intense as to cause a bloody sweat, there is every probability that it would be accompanied with tears. We may remark, then, (1) That there is nothing *dishonourable* in tears, and that no man should be ashamed on proper occasions to weep. The fact that the Son of God wept is a full demonstration that it is not disgraceful to shed tears. God has so made us as to express sympathy for others by weeping. Comp. Rom. xii. 15. Religion does not make the heart insensible and hard as stoical philosophy does; it makes it tender and susceptible to impression. (2) It is not *improper* to weep. The Son of God wept; and if he poured forth tears, it cannot be wrong for us. Besides, it is a great law of our nature that in suffering we should find relief by tears. God would not have so made us if it had been wrong. (3) The fact that the Son of God thus wept should be allowed deeply to affect our hearts.

"He wept that we might weep;
Each sin demands a tear."

He wept that he might redeem us; we should weep that our sins were so great as to demand these bitter woes for our salvation. That we had sinned; that our sins caused him such anguish; that he endured for us this bitter conflict, should make us weep. Tear should answer to tear, and sigh respond to sigh, and groan to groan, when we contemplate the sorrows of the Son of God in accomplishing our redemption. That man must have a hard heart who has never felt an emotion of sorrow when he has reflected that the Son of God wept, and bled, and died for him. ¶ *Unto him that was able.* To God. He alone was able to save. In such a conflict man could not aid, and the help of angels, ready as they were to assist him, could not sustain him. We may derive aid from man in trial; we may be comforted by sympathy and counsel; but there are sorrows where God only can uphold the sufferer. That God was *able* to uphold him in his severe conflict, the Redeemer could not doubt; nor need *we* doubt it in reference to ourselves when deep sorrows come over our souls. ¶ *To save him from death.* It would seem from this, that what constituted the agony of the Redeemer was the dread of death, and that he prayed that he might be saved from that. This might be, so far as the language is concerned, either the dread of death on the spot by the intensity of his sufferings and by the power of the tempter, or it might be the dread of the approaching death on the cross. As the Redeemer, however, knew that he was to die on the cross, it can hardly be supposed that he apprehended death in the garden of Gethsemane. What he prayed for was, that, if it were possible, he might be spared from a death so painful as he apprehended, Mat. xxvi. 39. Feeling that God had *power* to save him from that mode of dying, the burden of his petition was, that, if human redemption could be accomplished without such sufferings, it might please his Father to remove that cup from him. ¶ *And was heard.* In Jn. xi. 42, the Saviour says, "I knew that thou hearest me always." In the garden of Gethsemane, he was heard. His prayer was not disregarded, though it was not *literally* answered. The cup of death was not taken away; but his prayer was not disregarded. What answer was given; what assurance or support was imparted to his soul, we are not informed. The case, however, shows us, (1) That prayer may be

heard even when the sufferings which are dreaded, and from which we prayed to be delivered, may come upon us. They may come with such assurances of divine favour, and such supports, as will be full proof that the prayer was not disregarded. (2) That prayer offered in faith may not be always *literally* answered. No one can doubt that Jesus offered the prayer of faith; and it is as little to be doubted, if he referred in the prayer to the death on the cross, that it was not *literally* answered. Comp. Mat. xxvi. 39. In like manner, it may occur now, that prayer shall be offered with right feeling, and with an earnest desire for the object, which may not be literally answered. Christians, even in the highest exercise of faith, are not inspired to know what is best for them; and as long as this is the case, it is possible that they may ask for things which it would not be for their own good to have granted. They who maintain that the prayer of faith is always literally answered, must hold that the Christian is under such a guidance of the Spirit of God that he cannot ask anything amiss. See Notes on 2 Cor. xii. 8, 9. ¶ *In that he feared.* Margin, *for his piety.* Coverdale, "Because he had God in honour." Tindal, "Because he had God in reverence." Professor Stuart renders it, "And was delivered from that which he feared." So also Doddridge. Whitby, "Was delivered from his fear." Luther renders it, "And was heard for that he had God in reverence"— *dass er Gott in Ehren hatte.* Beza renders it, "His prayers being heard, he was delivered from fear." From this variety in translating the passage, it will be seen at once that it is attended with difficulty. The Greek is literally "from fear, or reverence" —ἀπὸ της εὐλαβείας. The word occurs in the New Testament only in one other place (Heb. xii. 28), where it is rendered *"fear"*—"Let us serve him with reverence and godly *fear.*" The word properly means *caution, circumspection;* then timidity, fear; then the fear of God, reverence, piety. Where the most distinguished scholars have differed as to the meaning

of a Greek phrase, it would be presumption in me to attempt to determine its sense. The most natural and obvious interpretation, however, is, that it means that he was heard on account of his reverence for God; his profound veneration; his submission. Such was his piety that the prayer was *heard*, though it was not literally *answered.* A prayer may be heard and yet not literally answered; it may be acceptable to God, though it may not consist with his arrangements to bestow the very blessing that is sought. The posture of the mind of the Redeemer, perhaps, was something like this: He knew that he was about to be put to death in a most cruel manner. His tender and sensitive nature, as a man, shrank from such a death. As a man he went, under the pressure of his great sorrows, and pleaded that the cup might be removed, and that the race might be redeemed by a less fearful kind of suffering. That arrangement, however, could not be made. Yet the spirit which he evinced; his desire to do the will of God; his resignation and the confidence in his Father, were such as were acceptable in his sight. They showed that he had unconquerable virtue; that no power of temptation, and no prospect of the intensest woes which human nature could endure, could alienate him from piety. To show this was an object of inestimable value, and, much as it cost the Saviour, was worth it all. So now it is worth much to see what Christian piety can endure; what strong temptations it can resist; and what strength it has to bear up under accumulated woes;—and even though the prayer of the pious sufferer is not directly answered, yet that prayer is acceptable to God, and the result of such a trial is worth all that it costs.

8. *Though he were a Son.* Though the Son of God. Though he sustained this exalted rank, and was conscious of it, yet he was willing to learn experimentally what is meant by obedience in the midst of sufferings. ¶ *Yet learned he obedience.* That is, he learned experimentally and practically. It cannot be supposed that

8 Though he were a Son, yet learned he [l] obedience by the things which he suffered;

9 And being [m] made perfect, he became the author of eternal salvation unto all them that obey him;

[l] Phi.2.8.　　[m] ch.2.10.

10 Called of God [n] an high priest after the order of Melchisedec.

11 Of whom we have many things to say, and hard to be uttered, seeing ye are dull of hearing.

[n] ver.6.

he did not *know* what obedience was; or that he was *indisposed* to obey God before he suffered; or that he had, as we have, perversities of nature leading to rebellion which required to be subdued by suffering;—but that he was willing to *test* the power of obedience in sufferings; to become personally and practically acquainted with the nature of such obedience in the midst of protracted woes. Comp. Notes on Phil. ii. 8. The *object* here is, to show how well fitted the Lord Jesus was to be a Saviour for mankind; and the argument is, that he has set us an example, and has shown that the most perfect obedience may be manifested in the deepest sorrows of the body and the soul. Learn hence, that one of the objects of affliction is to lead us *to obey God.* In prosperity we forget it. We become self-confident and rebellious. *Then* God lays his hand upon us; breaks up our plans; crushes our hopes; takes away our health, and teaches us that we *must* be submissive to his will. Some of the most valuable lessons of obedience are learned in the furnace of affliction; and many of the most submissive children of the Almighty have been made so as the result of protracted woes.

9. *And being made perfect.* That is, being made a *complete* Saviour—a Saviour fitted in all respects to redeem men. Sufferings were necessary to the *completeness* or the *finish* of his character as a Saviour, not to his moral perfection, for he was always without sin. See this explained in the Notes on chap. ii. 10. ¶ *He became the author.* That is, he was the procuring cause (αἴτιος) of salvation. It is to be traced wholly to his sufferings and death. See Notes on chap. ii. 10. ¶ *Unto all them that obey him.* It is not to save those who live in sin.

Only those who *obey* him have any evidence that they will be saved. See Notes on Jn. xiv. 15.

10. *Called of God.* Addressed by him, or greeted by him. The word here used does not mean that he was *appointed* by God, or "*called*" to the office, in the sense in which we often use the word, but simply that he was *addressed* as such, to wit, in Ps. cx. ¶ *An high priest.* In the Septuagint (Ps. cx. 4), and in ver. 6, above, it is rendered *priest—ἱερεὺς*; but the Hebrew word—כֹּהֵן *kohhēn*—is often used to denote the high-priest, and may mean either. See Septuagint in Lev. iv. 3. Whether the word *priest*, or *high priest*, be used here, does not affect the argument of the apostle. ¶ *After the order of Melchisedec.* See Notes on ver. 6.

11. *Of whom we have many things to say.* There are many things which seem strange in regard to him; many things which are hard to be understood. Paul knew that what he had to say of this man as a type of the Redeemer would excite surprise, and that many might be disposed to call it in question. He knew that, in order to be understood, what he was about to say required a familiar acquaintance with the Scriptures, and a strong and elevated faith. A young convert, one who had just commenced the Christian life, could hardly expect to be able to understand it. The same thing is true now. One of the first questions which a young convert often asks, is, Who was Melchisedec? And one of the things which most uniformly perplex those who begin to study the Bible, is, the statement which is made about this remarkable man. ¶ *Hard to be uttered.* Rather, hard to be *interpreted*, or *explained*. So the Greek word means. ¶ *Seeing ye are dull of hearing.* That is, when they ought to have been ac-

12 For when for the time ye ought to be teachers, ye have need that one teach you again which *be* the first principles of the oracles of God; and are become °such as have need of milk, and not of strong meat.

o 1 Co.3.1–3.

quainted with the higher truths of religion, they had shown that they received them slowly, and were dull of apprehension. On what particular *fact* Paul grounded this charge respecting them is unknown; nor could we know, unless we were better acquainted with the persons to whom he wrote, and their circumstances, than we now are. But he had doubtless in his eye some fact which showed that they were slow to understand the great principles of the gospel.

12. *For when for the time.* Considering the time which has elapsed since you were converted. You have been Christians long enough to be expected to understand such doctrines. This verse proves that those to whom he wrote were not recent converts. ¶ *Ye ought to be teachers.* You ought to be able to instruct others. He does not mean to say, evidently, that they ought all to become public teachers, or preachers of the gospel, but that they ought to be able to explain to others the truths of the Christian religion. As parents, they ought to be able to explain them to their children; as neighbours, to their neighbours; as friends, to those who were inquiring the way to life. ¶ *Ye have need.* That is, probably, the mass of them had need. As a people, or a church, they had shown that they were ignorant of some of the very elements of the gospel. ¶ *Again.* This shows that they *had been* taught on some former occasion what were the first principles of religion, but they had not followed up the teaching as they ought to have done. ¶ *The first principles.* The very elements; the rudiments; the first lessons—such as children learn before they advance to higher studies. See the word here used explained in the Notes on Gal. iv. 3, under the word "*elements.*" The Greek word is the same. ¶ *Of the oracles of God.* Of the Scriptures, or what God has spoken. See Notes on Rom. iii.

2. The phrase here may refer to the writings of the Old Testament, and particularly to those parts which relate to the Messiah; or it may include all that God had at that time revealed, in whatever way it was preserved. In 1 Pet. iv. 11, it is used with reference to the Christian religion, and to the doctrines which God had revealed in the gospel. In the passage before us, it may mean *the divine oracles or communications,* in whatever way they had been made known. They had shown that they were ignorant of the very rudiments of the divine teaching. ¶ *And are become such.* There is more meant in this phrase than that they simply *were* such persons. The word rendered "are become"—γίνομαι— sometimes implies *a change of state,* or a passing from one state to another —well expressed by the phrase "are become." See Mat. v. 45; iv. 3; xiii. 32; vi. 16; x. 25; Mark i. 17; Rom. vii. 3, 4. The idea here is, that they had passed from the hopeful condition in which they were when they showed that they had an acquaintance with the great principles of the gospel, and that they had become such as to need again the most simple form of instruction. This agrees well with the general strain of the epistle, which is to preserve them from the danger of apostasy. They were verging toward it, and had come to that state where, if they were recovered, it must be by being again taught the elements of religion. ¶ *Have need of milk.* Like little children. You can bear only the most simple nourishment. The meaning is, that they were incapable of receiving the higher doctrines of the gospel, as much as little children are incapable of digesting solid food. They were, in fact, in a state of spiritual infancy. ¶ *And not of strong meat.* Greek, "strong food." The word *meat* with us is used now to denote only animal food. Formerly it meant food in general. The Greek word here means *nourishment.*

13 For every one that useth milk ³*is* unskilful in the word of righteousness: for he is a babe.

14 But strong meat belongeth to them that are ⁴of full age, *even* those who by reason of ⁵use have their senses exercised to discern both good and evil.

³ *hath no experience.*

⁴ or, *perfect.*   ⁵ or, *an habit;* or, *perfection.*

13. *For every one that useth milk.* Referring to the food of children. The apostle has here in view those Christians who resemble children in this respect, that they are not capable of receiving the stronger food adapted to those of mature age. ¶ *Is unskilful.* Inexperienced; who has not acquired skill by practising an art. The word is properly applied to one who has not experience. Here it does not mean that they were not true Christians—but that they had not the experience or knowledge requisite to enable them to understand the higher mysteries of the Christian religion. ¶ *In the word of righteousness.* The doctrine respecting the way in which men become righteous, or the way of salvation by the Redeemer. See Notes on Rom. i. 17. ¶ *For he is a babe.* That is, in religious matters. He understands the great system only as a child understands things. It is common to speak of "babes in knowledge," as denoting a state of ignorance.

14. *Strong meat.* Solid food pertains to those of maturer years. So it is with the higher doctrines of Christianity. They can be understood and appreciated only by those who are advanced in Christian experience. ¶ *Of full age.* Margin, *perfect.* The expression refers to those who are grown up. ¶ *Who by reason of use.* Margin, or, *an habit;* or, *perfection.* Coverdale and Tindal render it, "through custom." The Greek word means *habit, practice.* The meaning is, that by long experience they had arrived to that state in which they could appreciate the more elevated doctrines of Christianity. The reference in the use of this word is not to those who *eat food*—meaning that by long use they are able to distinguish good from bad—but it is to experienced Christians, who by long experience are able to distinguish

that which is useful, in pretended religious instruction, from that which is injurious. It refers to the delicate taste which an experienced Christian has in regard to those doctrines which impart most light and consolation. Experience will thus enable one to discern what is fitted to the soul of man; what elevates and purifies the affections; and what tends to draw the heart near to God. ¶ *Have their senses.* The word here used means properly *the senses* — as we use the term; the seat of sensation, the smell, the taste, &c. Then it means *the internal sense,* the faculty of perceiving truth; and this is the idea here. The meaning is, that by long experience Christians come to be able to understand the more elevated doctrines of Christianity; they see their beauty and value, and they are able carefully and accurately to distinguish them from error. Compare Notes on Jn. vii. 17. ¶ *To discern both good and evil.* That is, in doctrine. They will appreciate and understand that which is true; they will reject that which is false.

REMARKS.

1. Let us rejoice that we have a High-priest who is duly called to take upon himself the functions of that great office, and who lives for ever, ver. 1–6. True, he was not of the tribe of Levi; he was not a descendant of Aaron; but he had a more noble elevation, and a more exalted rank. He was the Son of God, and was called to his office by special divine designation. He did not obtrude himself into the work; he did not unduly exalt himself, but he was directly called to it by the appointment of God. When, moreover, the Jewish high-priests could look back on the long line of their ancestors, and trace the succession up to Aaron, it was in the power of the great High-priest of the Christian faith to look farther back

still, and to be associated in the office with one of higher antiquity than Aaron, and of higher rank—one of the most remarkable men of all ancient times—he whom Abraham acknowledged as his superior, and from whom Abraham received the benediction.

2. It is not unmanly to weep, ver. 7. The Son of God poured out prayers and supplications with strong crying and tears. He wept at the grave of Lazarus, and he wept over Jerusalem. If the Redeemer wept, it is not unmanly to weep; and we should not be ashamed if tears are seen streaming down our cheeks. Tears are appointed by God to be the natural expression of sorrow, and often to furnish a relief to a burdened soul. We instinctively honour the man whom we see weeping when there is occasion for grief. We sympathize with him in his sorrow, and we love him the more. When we see a father who could face the cannon's mouth without shrinking, weeping over the open grave of a daughter, we honour him more than we could otherwise do. He shows that he has a heart that can love and feel, as well as courage that can meet danger without alarm. Washington wept when he signed the death-warrant of Major André; and who ever read that affecting account without feeling that his character was the more worthy of our love? There is enough in the world to make us weep. Sickness, calamity, death, are around us. They come into our dwellings, and our dearest objects of affection are taken away, and *God intends* that we shall deeply feel. Tears here will make heaven more sweet; and our sorrows on earth are intended to prepare us for the joy of that day when it shall be announced to us that "all tears shall be wiped away from every face."

3. We see the propriety of prayer in view of approaching death, ver. 7. The Redeemer prayed when he felt that he must die. We know, also, that we must die. True, we shall not suffer as he did. He had pangs on the cross which no other dying man ever bore. But death to us is an object of dread. The hour of death is a fearful hour. The scene when a man dies is a gloomy scene. The sunken eye, the pallid cheek, the clammy sweat, the stiffened corpse, the coffin, the shroud, the grave, are all sad and gloomy things. We know not, too, what severe pangs we may have when we die. Death may come to us in some peculiarly fearful form; and in view of its approach in *any way* we should pray. Pray, dying man, that you may be prepared for that sad hour; pray that you may not be left to complain, and rebel, and murmur then; pray that you may lie down in calmness and peace; pray that you may be enabled *to honour God even in death*.

4. It is not sinful to dread death, ver. 7. The Redeemer dreaded it. His human nature, though perfectly holy, shrank back from the fearful agonies of dying. The fear of death, therefore, in itself is not sinful. Christians are often troubled because they have not that calmness in the prospect of death which they suppose they ought to have, and because their nature shrinks back from the dying pang. They suppose that such feelings are inconsistent with religion, and that they who have them cannot be true Christians. But they forget their Redeemer and his sorrows; they forget the earnestness with which he pleaded that the cup might be removed. Death is in itself fearful, and it is a part of our nature to dread it, and even in the best of minds sometimes the fear of it is not wholly taken away until the hour comes, and God gives "*dying grace*." There are probably two reasons why God made death so fearful to man. (1) One is, to impress him with the importance of being prepared for it. Death is to him the entrance on an endless being, and it is an object of God to keep the attention fixed on that as a most momentous and solemn event. The ox, the lamb, the robin, the dove, have no immortal nature, no conscience, no responsibility, and no need of making preparation for death—and hence —except in a very slight degree—they seem to have no dread of dying. But not so with man. He has an undy-

ing soul. His main business here is
to prepare for death and for the world
beyond; and hence, by all the fear of
the dying pang, and by all the horror
of the grave, God would fix the attention of man on his own death as
a most momentous event, and lead
him to seek that hope of immortality
which alone can lay the foundation
for any proper removal of the fear of
dying. (2) The other reason is, to
deter man from taking his own life.
To keep him from this, he is made so
as to start back from death. He fears
it; it is to him an object of deepest
dread; and even when pressed down
by calamity and sadness, as a general
law, he "had rather bear the ills he
has, than fly to others that he knows
not of." Man is the only creature in
reference to whom this danger exists.
There is no one of the brute creation,
unless it be the scorpion, that will
take its own life, and hence they have
not such a dread of dying. But we
know how it is with man. Weary of
life; goaded by a guilty conscience;
disappointed and heart-broken, he is
under strong temptation to commit
the enormous crime of self-murder,
and to rush uncalled to the bar of
God. As one of the means of deter-
ring from this, God has so made us
that we fear to die; and thousands
are kept from this enormous crime by
this fear, when nothing else would
save them. It is benevolence, therefore, to the world, that man is afraid
to die; and, in every pang of the
dying struggle, in everything about
death that makes us turn pale and
tremble at its approach, there is in
some way the manifestation of goodness to mankind.

5. We may be comforted in the
prospect of death by looking at the
example of the Redeemer, ver. 7.
Much as we may fear to die, and much
as we may be left to suffer then, of
one thing we may be sure; it is, that
he has gone beyond us in suffering.
The sorrows of *our* dying will never
equal his. We shall never go through
such scenes as occurred in the garden of Gethsemane and on the cross.
It may be some consolation that human nature has endured greater pangs

than we shall, and that there is one
who has surpassed us even in our
keenest sufferings. It *should* be to
us a source of consolation, also, of the
highest kind, that he did it that he
might alleviate our sorrows, and that
he might drive away the horrors of
death from us by "bringing life and
immortality to light," and that as the
result of *his* sufferings our dying moments may be calm and peaceful.

6. It often occurs that men are true
Christians, and yet are ignorant of
some of the elementary principles of
religion, ver. 12. This is owing to
such things as the following:—a want
of early religious instruction; the
faults of preachers who fail to teach
their people; a want of proper interest
in the subject of religion, and the
interest which they feel in other
things above that which they feel in
religion. It is often surprising what
vague and unsettled opinions many
professed Christians have on some of
the most important points of Christianity, and how little qualified they
are to defend their opinions when
they are attacked. Of multitudes in
the church even now it might be said,
that they "need some one to teach
them what are the very first principles of true religion." To some
of the *elementary* doctrines of Christianity, about deadness to the world,
about self-denial, about prayer, about
doing good, and about spirituality,
they are utter strangers. So of forgiveness of injuries, and charity, and
love for a dying world. These are the
elements of Christianity—rudiments
which children in righteousness should
learn; and yet they are *not* learned
by multitudes who bear the Christian
name.

7. All Christians ought to be *teachers*,
ver. 12. I do not mean that they
should all be *preachers*; but they
should all so live as to *teach* others
the true nature of religion. This they
should do by their example; by their
daily conversation, and by all the ability which they have to impart knowledge to the ignorant and the young.
Any Christian is qualified to impart
useful instruction to others. The
servant of lowest rank may teach his

master how a Christian should live. A child may thus teach a parent how he should live, and his daily walk may furnish to the parent lessons of inestimable value. Neighbours may thus teach neighbours, and strangers may learn of strangers. Every Christian has a knowledge of the way to be saved which it would be of the highest value to others to possess, and is qualified to tell the rich, the proud, and the learned sinner, that about himself, and the final destiny of man, of which he is now wholly ignorant. Let it be remembered, also, that the world derives its views of the nature of religion from the lives and conduct of its professed friends. It is not from the Bible, or from the pulpit, or from books, that men learn what Christianity is; it is from the daily walk of those who profess to be its friends; and every day we live, a wife, a child, a neighbour, or a stranger, is forming *some* view of the nature of religion from what they see in us. How important, therefore, it is that we so live as to communicate to them just views of what constitutes religion!

CHAPTER VI.

ANALYSIS OF THE CHAPTER.

In chap. v. 10, 11, the apostle had said that the Lord Jesus was called to the office of high-priest after the order of Melchisedec, and that there were many things to be said of him which were not easy to be understood. They had not, he says, advanced as far in the knowledge of the true religion as might have been reasonably expected, but had rather gone back, chap. v. 12-14. The design of this chapter seems to be to warn them against the danger of going back *entirely*, and to encourage them to make the highest attainments possible in the knowledge of Christianity, and in the divine life. The apostle would not only keep them from total apostasy, but would stimulate them to make all the advances which they possibly could make, and particularly he designs to prepare them to receive what he had yet to say about the higher doctrines of the Christian re-

ligion. In doing this he presents the following considerations:—

(1) An exhortation to leave the elements or rudiments of the Christian religion, and to go on to the contemplation of the higher doctrines. The elements or rudiments were the doctrines of repentance, of faith, of the laying on of hands, of the resurrection of the dead, and of eternal judgment. These entered into the very nature of Christianity. They were its first principles, and were indispensable. The higher doctrines related to other matters, which the apostle called them now to contemplate, ver. 1-3.

(2) He warns them, in the most solemn manner, against apostasy. He assures them that *if* they should apostatize, it would be impossible to renew them again. They could not fall away from grace, and again be renewed; they could not, after having been Christians and then apostatizing, be recovered. Their fall in that case would be final and irrecoverable, for there was no other way by which they could be saved; and by rejecting the Christian scheme, they would reject the only plan by which they could ever be brought to heaven. By this solemn consideration, therefore, he warns them of the danger of going back from their exalted hopes, or of neglecting the opportunities which they had to advance to the knowledge of the higher truths of religion, ver. 4-6.

(3) This sentiment is illustrated (ver. 7, 8) by a striking and beautiful figure drawn from agriculture. The sentiment was, that they who did not improve their advantage, and grow in the knowledge of the gospel, but who should go back and apostatize, would inevitably be destroyed. They *could not* be renewed and saved. It will be, says the apostle, as it is with the earth. That which receives the rain that falls, and that bears its proper increase for the use of man, partakes of the divine blessing. That which does not—which bears only thorns and briers—is rejected, and is nigh to cursing, and will be burned with fire.

(4) Yet the apostle says, he hoped better things of them. They had,

CHAPTER VI.

THEREFORE,[a] leaving [1]the principles of the doctrine of

a Phi.3.12–14.
1 or, *the word of the beginning of Christ.*

Christ, let us go on unto perfection; not laying again the foundation of repentance from [b]dead works, and of [c]faith toward God,

b ch.9.14.   c ch.11.6.

indeed, receded from what they had been. They had not made the advances which he says they might have done. But still, there was reason to hope that they would not wholly apostatize, and be cast off by God. They *had* shown that they had true religion, and he believed that God would not forget the evidence which they had furnished that they loved him, ver. 9, 10.

(5) He expresses his earnest wish that they *all* would show the same diligence until they attained the full assurance of hope, ver. 11, 12.

(6) To encourage them in this, he refers them to the solemn oath which God had taken, and to his sacred covenant with them confirmed by an oath, in order that they might have true consolation, and be sustained in the temptations and trials of life. That hope was theirs. It was sure and steadfast. It entered into that within the veil; it had been confirmed by him who had entered heaven as the great High-priest after the order of Melchisedec, ver. 13–20. By such considerations he would guard them from the danger of apostasy; he would encourage them to diligence in the divine life; and he would seek to prepare them to welcome the more high and difficult doctrines of the Christian religion.

1. *Therefore.* "Since, as was stated in the previous chapter, you *ought* to be capable of comprehending the higher doctrines of religion; since those doctrines are adapted to those who have been for a considerable time professors of Christianity, and have had opportunities of growing in knowledge and grace—as much as strong meat is for those of mature years— leave now the elements or rudiments of Christian doctrine, and go on to understand its higher mysteries." The idea is, that the elements of Christianity were no more adapted to those

who had so long been acquainted with the way of salvation, than milk was for grown persons. ¶ *Leaving.* Dismissing; intermitting; passing by the consideration of, with a view to advance to something higher. The apostle refers to his discussion of the subject, and also to their condition. He wished to go on to the contemplation of higher doctrines, and he desired that they would no longer linger around the mere elements. "Let us advance to a higher state of knowledge than the mere elements of the subject." On the sense of the word "leaving," or quitting with a view to engage in something else, see Mat. iv. 20, 22; v. 24. ¶ *The principles.* Margin, *the word of the beginning of Christ.* Tindal renders it, "Let us leave the doctrine pertaining to the beginning of a Christian man." Coverdale, "Let us leave the doctrine pertaining to the beginning of a Christian life." On the word "principles" see Notes on chap. v. 12. The Greek there, indeed, is not the same as in this place, but the idea is evidently the same. The reference is to what he regarded as the very elements of the Christian doctrine; and the meaning is, "Let us no longer linger here. We should go on to higher attainments. We should wholly understand the system. We should discuss and receive its great principles. You have been Christians long enough to have understood these; but you linger among the very elementary truths of religion. But you cannot remain here. You must either advance or recede; and if you do not go forward you will go back into entire apostasy, when it will be *impossible* to be renewed." The apostle here, therefore, does not refer to his *discussion* of the points under consideration as the main thing, but to *their state* as one of danger; and, in writing to them, he was not content to discuss the elements of religion as

being alone fitted to their condition, but would have them make higher attainments, and advance to the more elevated principles of the gospel. ¶ *Of the doctrine.* Literally, "*the word*"—λόγον—of the beginning of Christ. That is, what is *spoken* as pertaining to Christ, the *instruction* which has been given in regard to him and his system. ¶ *Of Christ.* Which pertain to the Messiah. Either that which he taught or that which is taught of him and his religion. Most probably it is the latter—that which pertains to the Messiah or to the Christian revelation. The idea is, that there is a set of truths which may be regarded as lying at the foundation of Christian doctrine, and those truths they had embraced, but had not advanced beyond them. ¶ *Let us go on.* Let us advance to a higher state of knowledge and holiness. The reference is alike to his discussion of the subject and to their advancement in piety and in knowledge. He would not linger around these elements in the discussion, nor would he have them linger at the threshold of the Christian doctrines. ¶ *Unto perfection.* Comp. Notes on chap. ii. 10. The word is used here evidently to denote an advanced state of Christian knowledge and piety; or the more elevated Christian doctrines, and the holier living to which it was their duty to attain. It does not refer solely to the intention of the apostle to *discuss* the more elevated doctrines of Christianity, but *to such an advance as would secure them from the danger of apostasy.* If it should be said, however, that the word "*perfection*" is to be understood in the most absolute and unqualified sense, as denoting entire freedom from sin, it may be remarked, (1) That this does not prove that they ever in fact attained to it, nor should this be adduced as a text to show that such an attainment is ever made. To exhort a man to do a thing, however reasonable, is no proof in itself that it is ever done. (2) It *is* proper to exhort Christians to aim at entire perfection. Even if none have ever reached that point on earth, that fact does not make it any the less desirable or proper to aim at it. (3) There is much in making an honest attempt to be perfectly holy, even though we should not attain to it in this life. No man accomplishes much who does not aim high. ¶ *Not laying again the foundation.* Not laying down, as one does a foundation for an edifice. The idea is, that they were not to begin and build all this over again. They were not to make it necessary to lay down again the very corner-stones and the foundations of the edifice, but since these *were* laid already they were to go on and build the superstructure and complete the edifice. ¶ *Of repentance from dead works.* From works that *cause* death or condemnation, or that have no vitality or life. The reference may be either to those actions which were sinful in their nature, or to those which related to the *forms* of religion, where there was no spiritual life. This was the character of much of the religion of the Jews; and conversion to the true religion consisted greatly in repentance for having relied on those heartless and hollow forms. It is possible that the apostle referred mainly to these, as he was writing to those who had been Hebrews. When formalists are converted, one of the first and the main exercises of their minds in conversion consists in deep and genuine sorrow for their dependence on those forms. Religion is life; and irreligion is a state of spiritual death (comp. Notes on Eph. ii. 1), whether it be in open transgression or in false and hollow forms of religion. The apostle has here stated what is the first element of the Christian religion. It consists in genuine sorrow for sin, and a purpose to turn from it. See Notes on Mat. iii. 2. ¶ *And of faith toward God.* See Notes on Mark xvi. 16. This is the *second* element in the Christian system. Faith is everywhere required in order to salvation, but it is usually faith *in the Lord Jesus* that is spoken of. See Acts xx. 21. Here, however, faith *in God* is particularly referred to. But there is no essential difference. It is faith in God in regard to his existence and perfections, and to his plan of saving men. It includes, therefore, faith in his message

2 Of the doctrine of *baptisms, and of *laying on of hands, and of *resurrection of the dead, and of eternal judgment.

d Ac.19.4,5.　　　e Ac.8.17.　　　　f Ac.17.31; 26.8.

and messenger, and thus embraces the plan of salvation by the Redeemer. There is but one God—"the God and Father of our Lord Jesus Christ;" and he who believes in the true God believes in him as Father, Son, and Holy Ghost—the Author of the plan of redemption and the Saviour of lost men. No one can believe *in the true God* who does not believe in the Saviour. Comp. Jn. v. 23; xvii. 3. He who supposes that he confides *in any other* God than the Author of the Christian religion worships a being of the imagination as really as though he bowed down to a block of wood or stone. If Christianity is true there is no such God as the infidel professes to believe in, any more than the God of the Brahmin has an existence. To believe *in God*, therefore, is to believe in him as he *actually exists*—as the true God—the Author of the great plan of salvation by the Redeemer. It is needless to attempt to show that faith in the true God is essential to salvation. How can he be saved who has no *confidence* in the God that made him?

2. *Of the doctrine of baptisms.* This is mentioned as the *third* element or principle of the Christian religion. The Jews made much of various kinds of *washings*, which were called *baptisms.* See Notes on Mark vii. 4. It is supposed, also, that they were in the practice of baptizing proselytes to their religion. See Notes on Mat. iii. 6. Since they made so much of various kinds of ablution, it was important that the true doctrine on the subject should be stated as one of the elements of the Christian religion, that the converted Hebrews, to whom the epistle was written, might be recalled from superstition, and that they might enjoy the benefits of what was designed to be an important aid to piety—the true doctrine of baptisms. It will be observed that the plural form is used here—*baptisms.* There are two baptisms whose necessity is taught by the Christian religion—baptism by water and baptism by the Holy Ghost—the first of which is an emblem of the second. These are stated to be among the *elements* of Christianity, or the things which Christian converts would naturally first learn. The necessity of both is taught. "He that believeth and is *baptized* shall be saved," Mark xvi. 16. "Except a man be born of water and of the Spirit, he cannot enter into the kingdom of God," Jn. iii. 5. On the baptism of the Holy Ghost see Notes on Mat. iii. 11; Acts i. 5; comp. Acts xix. 1–6. To understand the true doctrine respecting baptism was one of the first principles to be learned then, as it is now, as baptism is the rite by which we are *initiated* into the church. This was supposed to be so simple that young converts could understand it as one of the elements of the true religion, and the teaching on that subject now should be made so plain that the humblest disciple may comprehend it. If it was an element or first principle of religion, if it was presumed that anyone who entered the church could understand it, can it be believed that it was then so perplexing and embarrassing as it is often made now? Can it be believed that a vast array of learning, and a knowledge of languages, and a careful inquiry into the customs of ancient times, was needful in order that a candidate for baptism should understand its nature? The truth is, that it was probably regarded as among the most simple and plain matters of religion; and every convert was supposed to understand that the application of water to the body in this ordinance, in any mode, was designed to be merely emblematic of the influences of the Holy Ghost. ¶ *And of laying on of hands.* This is the *fourth* element or principle of religion. The Jews practised the laying on of hands on a great variety of occasions. It was done when a blessing was imparted to anyone; when prayer was made

for one; and, when they offered sacrifice, they laid their hands on the head of the victim, confessing their sins, Lev. xvi. 21; xxiv. 14; Num. viii. 12. It was done on occasions of solemn consecration to office, and when one friend supplicated the divine favour on another. In like manner, it was often done by the Saviour and the apostles. The Redeemer laid his hands on children to bless them, and on the sick when he healed them, Mat. xix. 13; Mark v. 23; Mat. ix. 18. The apostles, also, laid hands on others in the following circumstances: (1) In healing the sick, Acts xxviii. 8. (2) In ordination to office, 1 Tim. v. 22; Acts vi. 6. (3) In imparting the miraculous influences of the Holy Spirit, Acts viii. 17, 19; xix. 6. The true doctrine respecting the design of laying on the hands, as connected with religious rites, is said here to be one of the very elements of the Christian religion which was easily understood. That the custom of laying on the hands, as symbolical of imparting spiritual gifts, prevailed in the church in the time of the apostles, no one can doubt. But on the question whether it is to be regarded as of perpetual obligation in the church, we are to remember, (1) That the apostles were endowed with the power of imparting the influences of the Holy Ghost in a miraculous or extraordinary manner. It was with reference to such an imparting of the Holy Spirit that the expression is used in each of the cases where it occurs in the New Testament. (2) The Saviour did not appoint the imposition of the hands of a "bishop" to be one of the rites or ceremonies to be observed perpetually in the church. The injunction to be baptized and to observe his supper is positive, and is universal in its obligation. But there is no such command respecting the imposition of hands. (3) No one now is intrusted with the power of imparting the Holy Spirit in that manner. There is no class of officers in the church that can make good their claim to any such power. What evidence is there that the Holy Spirit is imparted at the rite of "confirma-

tion?" (4) It is liable to be abused; to lead persons to substitute the form for the thing; or to think that because they have been "confirmed," that therefore they are sure of the mercy and favour of God. Still, if it be regarded as a *simple form of admission to a church*, without claiming that it is enjoined by God, or that it is connected with any authority to impart the Holy Spirit, no objection can be made to this, any more than to any other form of recognizing church membership. Every pastor has a right, if he chooses, to lay his hands on the members of his flock, and to implore a blessing on them, on their admission to the church; and such an act, on making a profession of religion, would have much in it that would be appropriate and solemn. ¶ *And of resurrection of the dead.* This is mentioned as the *fifth* element or principle of the Christian religion. This doctrine was denied by the Sadducees (Mark xii. 18; Acts xxiii. 8), and was ridiculed by philosophers, Acts xvii. 32. It was, however, clearly taught by the Saviour (Jn. v. 28, 29), and became one of the cardinal doctrines of his religion. By the resurrection of the dead, however, in the New Testament, there is more intended than the resurrection of the *body*. The question about the resurrection included the whole inquiry about the future state, or whether man would *live at all* in the future world. Compare Notes on Mat. xxii. 23; Acts xxiii. 6. This is one of the most important subjects that can come before the human mind, and one on which man has felt more perplexity than on any other. The belief of the resurrection of the dead is an elementary article in the system of Christianity. It lies at the foundation of all our hopes. Christianity is designed to prepare us for a future state; and one of the first things, therefore, in the preparation, is to assure us there *is* a future state, and to tell us what it is. It is, moreover, a *peculiar* doctrine of Christianity. The belief of the resurrection is found in no other system of religion, nor is there a ray of light shed upon the fu-

3 And this will we do, *g*if God permit.

4 For *it is* *h*impossible for those

g Ja.4.15.
h Mat.5.13; 12.31,32; Jn.15.6; ch.10.26; 2 Pe.2.20, 21; 1 Jn.5.16.

who were once enlightened, and have tasted of the heavenly gift, and were made partakers of the Holy Ghost,

---

ture condition of man by any scheme of human philosophy or religion. ¶ *And of eternal judgment.* This is the *sixth* element or principle of religion. It is, that there will be a judgment whose consequences will be eternal. It does not mean, of course, that the *process* of the judgment will be eternal, or that the judgment-day will continue for ever; but that the *results* or *consequences* of the decision of that day will continue for ever. There will be no appeal from the sentence, nor will there be any reversal of the judgment then pronounced. What is decided then will be determined for ever. The approval of the righteous will fix their state eternally in heaven, and, in like manner, the condemnation of the wicked will fix their doom for ever in hell. This doctrine was one of the earliest that was taught by the Saviour and his apostles, and is inculcated in the New Testament perhaps with more frequency than any other. That the consequences or results of the judgment will be *eternal*, is abundantly affirmed. See Mat. xxv. 46; Jn. v. 29; 2 Thes. i. 9; Mark ix. 45, 48.

3. *And this will we do.* We will make these advances toward a higher state of knowledge and piety. Paul had confidence that they would do it (see ver. 9, 10), and though they had lingered long around the elements of Christian knowledge, he believed that they would yet go on to make higher attainments. ¶ *If God permit.* This is not to be interpreted as if God was *unwilling* that they should make such advances, or as if it were *doubtful* whether he would allow it if they made an honest effort, and their lives were spared; but it is a phrase used to denote their *dependence* on him. It is equivalent to saying, "If he would spare their lives, their health, and their reason; if he would continue the means of grace, and would

impart his Holy Spirit; if he would favour their efforts and crown them with success, they would make these advances." In reference to *anything* that we undertake, however pleasing to God in itself, it is proper to recognize our entire dependence on God. See Jam. iv. 13–15. Compare Notes on Jn. xv. 5.

4. *For* it is *impossible.* It is needless to say that the passage here (ver. 4–6) has given occasion to much controversy, and that the opinions of commentators and of the Christian world are yet greatly divided in regard to its meaning. On the one hand, it is held that the passage is not intended to describe those who are true Christians, but only those who have been awakened and enlightened, and who then fall back; and on the other, it is maintained that it refers to those who *are* true Christians, and who then apostatize. The contending parties have been Calvinists and Arminians; each party, in general, interpreting it according to the views which are held on the question about falling from grace. I shall endeavour, as well as I may be able, to state the true meaning of the passage by an examination of the words and phrases in detail, observing here, in general, that it seems to me that it refers to true Christians, and that the object is to keep them from apostasy; and that it teaches that, if they should apostatize, it would be impossible to renew them again, or to save them. That it refers to true Christians will be apparent from these considerations: (1) Such is the sense which would strike the great mass of readers. Unless there were some theory to defend, the great body of readers of the New Testament would consider the expression here used as describing true Christians. (2) The connection demands such an interpretation. The apostle was addressing Christians. He was endeavouring to keep them

from apostasy. The object was not to keep those who were awakened and enlightened from apostasy, but it was to preserve those who were already in the church of Christ from going back to perdition. The kind of exhortation appropriate to those who were awakened and convicted, but who were not truly converted, would be *to become converted;* not to warn them of the danger of *falling away.* Besides, the apostle would not have said of such persons that they *could not* be converted and saved. But of sincere Christians it might be said, with the utmost propriety, that they *could not* be renewed again and be saved if they should fall away—because they rejected the only plan of salvation after they had tried it, and renounced the only scheme of redemption after they had tasted its benefits. If that plan could not save them, what could? If they neglected that, by what other means could they be brought to God? (3) This interpretation accords, as I suppose, with the exact meaning of the phrases which the apostle uses. An examination of those phrases will show that he refers to those who are sincere believers. The phrase "it is impossible" obviously and properly denotes absolute impossibility. It has been contended, by Storr and others, that it denotes only great difficulty. But the meaning which would at first strike all readers would be that *the thing could not be done;* that it was not merely very difficult, but absolutely impracticable. The word 'αδύνατον occurs in the New Testament only in the following places, in all which it denotes that the thing could not be done: Mat. xix. 26; Mark x. 27, "With men this is impossible;" that is, men could not save one who was rich, implying that the thing was wholly beyond human power. Luke xviii. 27, "The things which are impossible with men are possible with God"—referring to the same case. Acts xiv. 8, "A man of Lystra, *impotent* in his feet;" that is, who was wholly *unable* to walk. Rom. viii. 3, "For what the law could not do;" what was absolutely *impossible* for the law to accomplish; that is, to save men. Heb. vi. 18, "In which it was *impossible* for God to lie." Heb. x. 4, "It is not *possible* for the blood of bulls and of goats to take away sin." Heb. xi. 6, "Without faith it is *impossible* to please God." In all these instances the word denotes absolute impossibility, and these passages show that it is not merely a great difficulty to which the apostle refers, but that he meant to say that the thing was wholly impracticable; that it could not be done. And if this be the meaning, then it proves that *if* those referred to should fall away, they could never be renewed. Their case was hopeless, and they must perish:—that is, if a true Christian should apostatize, or fall from grace, *he never could be renewed again,* and could not be saved. Paul did not teach that he might fall away and be renewed again as often as he pleased. He had other views of the grace of God than this; and he meant to teach that, if a man should once cast off true religion, his case was hopeless, and he must perish; and by this solemn consideration — the only one that would be effectual in such a case — he meant to guard them against the danger of apostasy. ¶ *For those who were once enlightened.* The phrase "to be enlightened" is one that is often used in the Scriptures, and may be applied either to one whose understanding has been enlightened to discern his duty, though he is not converted (comp. Notes on Jn. i. 9); or more commonly to one who is truly converted. See Notes on Eph. i. 18. It does not of necessity refer to true Christians, though it cannot be denied that it obviously suggests the idea that the heart is truly changed, and that it is most commonly used in that sense. Comp. Ps. xix. 8. Light, in the Scriptures, is the emblem of knowledge, holiness, and happiness; and there is no impropriety here in understanding it, in accordance with the more decisive phrases which follow, as referring to true Christians. ¶ *And have tasted.* To *taste* of a thing means, according to the usage in the Scriptures, to *experience,* or to *understand* it. The expression is derived from the fact that

5 And have tasted the good word of God, and the powers of the world to come,

6 If *they shall fall away, to re-

i Is.1.28.

new them again unto repentance; seeing they crucify to themselves the Son of God afresh, and put *him* to an open shame.

the *taste* is one of the means by which we ascertain the nature or quality of an object. Comp. Mat. xvi. 28; Jn. viii. 51; Heb. ii. 9. The proper idea here is, that they had *experienced* the heavenly gift, or had learned its nature. ¶ *The heavenly gift.* The gift from heaven, or which pertains to heaven. Comp. Notes on Jn. iv. 10. The expression properly means some favour or gift which has descended from heaven, and may refer to any of the benefits which God has conferred on man in the work of redemption. It might include the plan of salvation; the forgiveness of sins; the enlightening, renewing, and sanctifying influences of the Holy Spirit, or any one of the graces which that Spirit imparts. The use of the article, however—"*the* heavenly gift"—limits it to something special as being conferred directly from heaven, and the connection would seem to demand that we understand it of some *peculiar* favour which could be conferred only on the children of God. It is an expression which *may* be applied to sincere Christians; it is at least doubtful whether it *can* with propriety be applied to any other. ¶ *And were made partakers of the Holy Ghost.* Partakers of the influences of the Holy Ghost—for it is only in this sense that we can partake of the Holy Spirit. We *partake* of food when we share it with others; we *partake* of pleasure when we enjoy it with others; we *partake* of spoils in war when they are divided between us and others. So we partake of the influences of the Holy Spirit when we share these influences conferred on his people. This is not language which can properly be applied to anyone but a true Christian; and although it is true that an unpardoned sinner may be enlightened and awakened by the Holy Spirit, yet the language here used is not such as would be likely to be employed to describe his state.

It is too clearly expressive of those influences which renew and sanctify the soul. It is as elevated language as can be used to describe the joy of the Christian, and is undoubtedly employed in that sense here. If it is not, it would be difficult to find any language which would properly express the condition of a renewed heart. Grotius, Bloomfield, and some others understood this of the miraculous gifts of the Holy Spirit. But this is not necessary, and does not accord well with the general description here, which evidently pertains to the mass of those whom the apostle addressed.

5. *And have tasted the good word of God.* That is, either the doctrines which he teaches, and which are good, or pleasant to the soul; or the word of God which is connected with *good*, that is, which promises good. The former seems to me to be the correct meaning—that the word of God, or the truth which he taught, was itself a good. It was that which the soul desired, and in which it found comfort and peace. Comp. Psa. cxix. 103; cxli. 6. The meaning here is, that they had experienced the excellency of the truth of God; they had seen and enjoyed its beauty. This is language which cannot be applied to an impenitent sinner. He has no *relish* for the truth of God; he sees no beauty in it; he derives no comfort from it. It is only the true Christian who has pleasure in its contemplation, and who can be said to "taste" and enjoy it. This language describes a state of mind of which every sincere Christian is conscious. It is that of pleasure in the word of God. He loves the Bible; he loves the truth of God that is preached. He sees an exquisite beauty in that truth. It is not merely in its poetry; in its sublimity; in its argument; but he has now a *taste* or *relish* for the truth itself, which he had not before his con-

version. Then he might have admired the Bible for its beauty of language or for its poetry; he might have been interested in preaching for its eloquence or power of argument; but now his love is for *the truth.* Comp. Ps. xix. 10. There is no book that he so much delights in as the Bible; he has no pleasure so pure as that which he has in contemplating the truth. Comp. Jos. xxi. 45; xxiii. 15. ¶ *And the powers of the world to come.* Or of the "coming age." "The age to come" was a phrase in common use among the Hebrews, to denote the future dispensation, the times of the Messiah. The same idea was expressed by the phrases "the last times," "the end of the world," &c., which are of so frequent occurrence in the Scriptures. They all denoted an age which was to succeed the old dispensation—the time of the Messiah; or the period in which the affairs of the world would be wound up. See Notes on Isa. ii. 2. Here it evidently refers to that period, and the meaning is, that they had participated in the peculiar blessings to be expected in that dispensation—to wit, in the clear views of the way of salvation, and the influences of the Holy Spirit on the soul. The word "powers" here implies that in that time there would be some extraordinary manifestation of the *power* of God. An unusual energy would be put forth to save men, particularly as evinced by the agency of the Holy Spirit on the heart. Of this "power" the apostle here says they of whom he spake had partaken. They had been brought under the awakening and renewing energy which God put forth under the Messiah in saving the soul. They had experienced the promised blessings of the new and last dispensation; and the language here is such as appropriately describes Christians, and such as can be applicable to no other. It may be remarked respecting the various expressions used here (ver. 4, 5), (1) That they are such as properly denote a renewed state. They obviously describe the condition of a Christian; and though it may not be certain that any *one* of them, if taken by itself, would *prove*

that the person to whom it was applied was truly converted, yet, taken together, it is clear that they are designed to describe such a state. If they are not, it would be difficult to find any language which would be properly descriptive of the character of a sincere Christian. I regard the description here, therefore, as that which is clearly designed to denote the state of those who were born again, and who were the true children of God; and it seems plain to me that no other interpretation would have ever been thought of, if this view had not seemed to conflict with the doctrine of the "perseverance of the saints." (2) There is a regular gradation here from the first elements of piety in the soul to its highest developments; and, whether the apostle so designed it or not, the language describes the successive steps by which a true Christian advances to the highest stage of Christian experience. The mind is (*a*) enlightened; then (*b*) *tastes* the gift of heaven, or has some experience of it; then (*c*) it is made to partake of the influences of the Holy Ghost; then (*d*) there is experience of the excellence and loveliness of the Word of God; and (*e*) finally there is a participation of the full "powers" of the new dispensation; of the extraordinary energy which God puts forth in the gospel to sanctify and save the soul.

6. *If they shall fall away.* Literally, "and having fallen away." "There is no *if* in the Greek in this place—'having fallen away'" (Dr. J. P. Wilson). It is not an affirmation that any *had* actually fallen away, or that in fact they *would* do it; but the statement is, that *on the supposition that they had fallen away,* it would be impossible to renew them again. It is the same as supposing a case which in fact might never occur:—as if we should say, "had a man fallen down a precipice it would be impossible to save him," or "had the child fallen into the stream he would certainly have been drowned." But though this literally means, "having fallen away," yet the sense, in the connection in which it stands, is not impro-

perly expressed by our common translation. The Syriac has given a version which is remarkable, not as a correct translation, but as showing what was the prevailing belief in the time in which it was made (probably the first or second century) in regard to the doctrine of the perseverance of the saints. "For it is impossible that they who have been baptized, and who have tasted the gift which is from heaven, and have received the spirit of holiness, and have tasted the good word of God, and the power of the coming age, should again sin, so that they should be renewed again to repentance, and again crucify the Son of God and put him to ignominy." The word rendered "fall away" means, properly, "to fall near by anyone;" "to fall in with or meet;" and then to fall aside from, to swerve or deviate from; and here means undoubtedly to *apostatize from,* and implies an entire renunciation of Christianity, or a going back to a state of Judaism, heathenism, or sin. The Greek word occurs nowhere else in the New Testament. It is material to remark here that the apostle does not say that any true Christian ever had fallen away. He makes a statement of what would occur on the supposition that such a thing should happen;— but a statement may be made of what *would* occur on the supposition that a certain thing should take place, and yet it be morally certain that the event never would happen. It is easy to suppose what would occur if the ocean should overflow a continent, or if the sun should cease to rise, and still there be entire certainty that such an event would never take place. ¶ *To renew them again.* Implying that they had been before renewed, or had been true Christians. The word "*again*"—πάλιν—supposes this; and this passage, therefore, confirms the considerations suggested above, showing that they were true Christians who were referred to. They had once repented, but it would be impossible to bring them to this state *again.* This declaration is to be read in connection with the first clause of verse 4, "It is impossible to renew

again to repentance those who once were true Christians, should they fall away." I know of no declaration more unambiguous than this. It is not that it would be very difficult to do it; or that it would be impossible for *man* to do it, though it might be done by God; it is an unequivocal and absolute declaration that it would be utterly impracticable that it should be done by anyone, or by any means; and this, I have no doubt, is the meaning of the apostle. Should a Christian fall from grace, he *must perish.* He never could be saved. The *reason* of this the apostle immediately adds. ¶ *Seeing.* This word is not in the Greek, though the sense is expressed. The Greek literally is, "having again crucified to themselves the Son of God." The *reason* here given is, that the crime would be so great, and they would so effectually exclude themselves from the only plan of salvation, that they could not be saved. There is but one way of salvation. Having tried that, and then renounced it, how could they then be saved? The case is like that of a drowning man. If there was but one plank by which he could be saved, and he should get on that, and then push it away and plunge into the deep, he must die. Or if there was but one rope by which the shore could be reached from a wreck, and he should cut that and cast it off, he must die. Or if a man were sick, and there was but one kind of medicine that could possibly restore him, and he should deliberately dash that away, he must die. So in religion. There is *but one* way of salvation. If a man deliberately rejects that, he must perish. ¶ *They crucify to themselves the Son of God afresh.* Our translators have rendered this as if the Greek were ἀνασταυροῦντες πάλιν—*crucify again;* and so it is rendered by Chrysostom, Tindal, Coverdale, Beza, Luther, and others. But this is not properly the meaning of the Greek. The word ἀνασταυρόω is an *intensive* word, and is employed instead of the usual word "to crucify" only to denote *emphasis.* It means that such an act of apostasy would be equivalent to crucifying

him in an aggravated manner. Of course this is to be taken *figuratively.* It could not be literally true that they would thus crucify the Redeemer. The meaning is, that their conduct would be *as if* they had crucified him; it would bear a strong resemblance to the act by which the Lord Jesus was publicly rejected and condemned to die. The act of crucifying the Son of God was the great crime which outpeers every other deed of human guilt. Yet the apostle says that should they who had been true Christians fall away and reject him, they would be guilty of a similar crime. It would be a public and solemn act of rejecting him. It would show that if they had been there, they would have joined in the cry, "Crucify him, crucify him!" The *intensity* and *aggravation* of such a crime, perhaps, the apostle meant to indicate by the intensive or emphatic ἀνά in the word ἀνασταυροῦντες. Such an act would render their salvation impossible, because, (1) the crime would be aggravated beyond that of those who rejected him and put him to death—for they knew not what they did; and, (2) because it would be a rejection of the only possible plan of salvation after they had had experience of its power and known its efficacy. The phrase "to themselves," Tindal renders "as concerning themselves." Others, "as far as in them lies," or as far as they have ability to do. Others, "to their own heart." Probably Grotius has suggested the true sense: "They do it *for themselves.* They make the act their own. It is as if they did it themselves; and they are to be regarded as having done the deed." So we make the act of another our own when we authorize it beforehand, or approve of it after it is done. ¶ *And put him to an open shame.* Make him a public example; or hold him up as worthy of death on the cross. See the same word explained in the Notes on Mat. i. 19, in the phrase "make her a public example." The word occurs nowhere else in the New Testament. Their apostasy and rejection of the Saviour would be like holding him up publicly as deserving the infamy and ignominy of the cross. A great part of the crime attending the crucifixion of the Lord Jesus consisted in exhibiting him to the passing multitude as deserving the death of a malefactor. Of that sin they would partake who should reject him, for they would thus show that they regarded his religion as an imposture, and would in a public manner hold him up as worthy only of rejection and contempt. Such, it seems to me, is the fair meaning of this much-disputed passage—a passage which would never have given so much perplexity if it had not been supposed that the obvious interpretation would interfere with some prevalent articles of theology. The passage *proves* that if true Christians should apostatize, it would be impossible to renew and save them. If, then, it should be asked whether I believe that any true Christian ever did, or ever will fall from grace, and wholly lose his religion, I would answer unhesitatingly, *No.* Comp. Notes on Jn. x. 27, 28; Rom. viii. 38, 39; Gal. v. 4. If, then, it be asked what was the *use* of a warning like this, I answer, (1) It would show the great *sin* of apostasy from God if it were to occur. It is proper to state the greatness of an act of sin, though it might never occur, in order to show how it would be regarded by God. (2) Such a statement might be one of the most effectual means of preserving from apostasy. To state that a fall from a precipice would cause certain death would be one of the most certain means of preserving one from falling; to affirm that arsenic, if taken, would be certainly fatal, would be one of the most effectual means of preventing its being taken; to know that fire certainly destroys, is one of the most sure checks from the danger. Thousands have been preserved from going over the Falls of Niagara by knowing that if it should occur there would be no possibility of escape from death; and so effectual has been this knowledge, that it has preserved all from such a catastrophe, except the very few who have gone over by accident. So in re-

ligion. The knowledge that apostasy would be fatal, and that there could be no hope of being saved should it once occur, would be a more effectual preventive of the danger than all the other means that could be used. If a man believed that it would be an easy matter to be restored again should he apostatize, he would feel little solicitude in regard to it; and it has occurred, in fact, that they who suppose that this may occur, have manifested little of the care to walk in the paths of strict religion which should have been evinced. (3) It may be added, that the means used by God to preserve his people from apostasy have been entirely effectual. There is no evidence that one has ever fallen away who was a true Christian (comp. Jn. x. 27, 28, and 1 Jn. ii. 19); and to the end of the world it will be true, that the means which he uses to keep his people from apostasy will not in a single instance fail.

[This view seems not opposed to the doctrine of the saint's perseverance. It professes, indeed, to meet the objection usually raised from the passage, if not in a new mode, yet in a mode different from that commonly adopted by orthodox expositors. Admitting that *true* Christians are intended, it is asserted only, that if they *should* fall their recovery would be impossible. It is not said that they ever *have* fallen or *will* fall. "The apostle in thus giving judgment on the case, if it should happen, does not declare that it actually does." And as to the use of supposing a case which never can occur, it is argued that *means* are constantly used to bring about that which the decree or determination of God had before rendered certain. These exhortations are the means by which perseverance is secured.

Yet it may be doubted whether there be anything in the passage to convince us that the apostle has introduced an *impossible* case. He seems rather to speak of that which *might* happen, of which there was *danger*. If the reader incline to this view he will apply the description to professors, and learn from it how far these may go, and yet fall short of the mark. But how would this suit the apostle's design? Well. If *professors* may go *so far*, how much is this that fitted to arouse ALL to vigilance and inquiry! We, notwithstanding our gifts and *apparent* graces, may not be *true* Christians, may, therefore, not be *secure*, may fall away and sink under the doom of him whom it is impossible to renew. And he must be a very exalted Christian indeed who does not occa-

sionally find need of inquiry and examination of evidences. Certainly the whole passage may be explained in perfect consistency with this application of it. Men may be enlightened, *i.e.* well acquainted with the doctrines and duties of the Christian faith; may have tasted of the heavenly gift, and been made partakers of the Holy Ghost in his miraculous influences, which many in primitive times enjoyed, without any sanctifying virtue; may have tasted the good word of God, or experienced impressions of affection and joy under it, as in the case of the stony ground hearers; may have tasted the powers of the world to come, or been influenced by the doctrine of a future state, with its accompanying rewards and punishments, and yet not be *true* Christians. "All these things, except miraculous gifts, often take place in the hearts and consciences of men in these days who yet continue unregenerate. They have knowledge, convictions, fears, hope, joys, and seasons of apparent earnestness and deep concern about eternal things; and they are endued with such gifts as often make them acceptable and useful to others: but they are not truly *humbled;* they are not *spiritually minded;* religion is not their element and delight" (Scott).

It should be observed, moreover, that while there are many *infallible* marks of the true Christian, none of these are mentioned in this place. The persons described are not said to have been elected, to have been regenerated, to have believed, or to have been sanctified. The apostle writes very differently when describing the character and privileges of the saints, Rom. viii. 27, 30. The succeeding context, too, is supposed to favour this opinion. "They (the characters in question) are in the following verses compared to the ground on which the rain often falls and beareth nothing but thorns and briars. But this is not so with true believers, for faith itself is an herb peculiar to the inclosed garden of Christ. And the apostle afterwards, discoursing of true believers, doth in many particulars distinguish them from such as may be apostates, which is supposed of the persons here intended. He ascribeth to them, in general, better things, and such as accompany salvation. He ascribes a work and labour of love, asserts their preservation, &c." (Owen). Our author, however, fortifies himself against the objection in the first part of this quotation by repeating and applying at ver. 7 his *principle* of exposition. "The design," says he, "is to show that if Christians should become like the barren earth they would be cast away and lost." Yet the attentive reader of this very ingenious exposition will observe that the author has difficulty in carrying out his principles, and finds it necessary to introduce the *mere professor* ere he has done with the passage.

7 For the earth which drinketh in the rain that cometh oft upon it, and bringeth forth herbs meet for them ²by whom it is dressed, receiveth ᵏblessing from God:

2 or, *for*.　　　　k Ps.65.10.

"It is not supposed," says he, commenting on the 8th verse, "that a true Christian will fall away and be lost, but we may remark that there are many *professed* Christians who seem to be in danger of such ruin. Corrupt desires are as certainly seen in their lives as thorns on a bad soil. Such are nigh unto cursing. *Unsanctified*, &c., there is nothing else which can be done for them, and they must be lost. What a thought!" Yet that the case of the professor in danger cannot very consistently be introduced by him appears from the fact that such ruin as is here described is suspended on a condition which never occurs. It happens *only if* the *Christian* should fall. According to the author, it is not *here* denounced *on any other supposition*. As then true Christians cannot fall, the ruin never can occur *in any case whatever*. From these premises we *dare not* draw the conclusion that any class of professors will be given over to final impenitence.

As to what may be alleged concerning the *apparent* sense of the passage, or the sense which would strike "the mass of readers," everyone will judge according to the sense which himself thinks most obvious. Few, perhaps, would imagine that the apostle was introducing an impossible case. Nor does the "connection" stand much in the way of the application to professors. In addition to what has already been stated let it be farther observed, that although the appropriate exhortation to awakened yet unconverted persons would be "to become converted, not to warn them of the danger of falling away," yet the apostle is writing to the Hebrews at large, is addressing a body of professing Christians concerning whom he could have no infallible assurance that *all of them* were true Christians. Therefore it was right that they should be warned in the way the apostle has adopted. The objection leaves out of sight the important fact that *the exhortations and warnings addressed to the saints in Scripture are addressed to mixed societies, in which there may be hypocrites as well as believers*. Those who profess the faith and associate with the church are addressed without any decision regarding *state*. But the very existence of the warnings implies a fear that there may be some whose state is not safe. And *all*, therefore, have need to inquire whether this be their condition. How appropriate then such warnings! This consideration, too, will furnish an answer to what has been alleged by another celebrated Transatlantic writer, viz. "that whatever may be true in the divine purposes as to the final salvation of all those who are once truly regenerated—and this doctrine I feel constrained to admit—yet nothing can be plainer than that the sacred writers have everywhere addressed saints in the same manner as they would address those whom they considered as constantly exposed to fall away and to perish for ever." Lastly, the phraseology of the passage does not appear to remove it out of all possible application to *mere* professors. It has already been briefly explained in consistency with such application. There is a difficulty, indeed, connected with the phrase παλιν ανακαινιζειν εις μετανοιαν, *again* to renew to repentance, implying, as is said, that they to whom reference is made had been renewed *before*. But what should hinder this being understood of *reinstating in former condition* or in possession of former privilege? Bloomfield supposes there may be an allusion to the non-reiteration of baptism, and Owen explains the phrase of bringing them again into a state of profession by a second renovation and a second baptism as a pledge thereof. The renewing he understands here *externally* of a solemn confession of faith and repentance, followed by baptism. This, says he, was their ανακαινισμος, their renovation. It would seem, then, that there is nothing in the phrase to prevent its interpretation on the same principle that above has been applied to the passage generally.]

7. *For the earth.* The design of the apostle by this comparison is apparent. It is to show the consequences of not making a proper use of the privileges which Christians have, and the effect which would follow should those privileges fail to be improved. He says it is like the earth. If that absorbs the rain, and produces an abundant harvest, it receives the divine blessing. If not, it is cursed, or is worthless. The design is to show that *if* Christians should become like the barren earth, they would be cast away and lost. ¶ *Which drinketh in the rain.* A comparison of the earth *as if* it were "thirsty"—a comparison that is common in all languages. ¶ *That cometh oft upon it.* The frequent showers that fall. The object is to describe fertile land which is often watered with the rains of heaven. The comparison of "drinking

8 But that which *beareth thorns and briers *is* rejected, and *is* nigh

l Is.5.6.

unto cursing; whose end *is* to be burned.

---

in" the rain is designed to distinguish a mellow soil which receives the rain, from hard or rocky land where it runs off. ¶ *And bringeth forth herbs.* The word *herbs* we now limit, in common discourse, to the small vegetables which die every year, and which are used as articles of food, or to such in general as have not ligneous or hard woody stems. The word here means anything which is cultivated in the earth as an article of food, and includes all kinds of grains. ¶ *Meet for them.* Useful or appropriate to them. ¶ *By whom it is dressed.* Margin, "*for* whom." The meaning is, on account of whom it is cultivated. The word "dressed" here means *cultivated.* Comp. Gen. ii. 15. ¶ *Receiveth blessing from God.* Receives the divine approbation. It is in accordance with his wishes and plans, and he smiles upon it and blesses it. He does not curse it as he does the desolate and barren soil. The language is figurative, and must be used to denote that which is an object of the divine favour. God delights in the harvests which the earth brings forth; in the effects of dews and rains and suns in causing beauty and abundance; and on such fields of beauty and plenty he looks down with pleasure. This does not mean, as I suppose, that he renders it *more* fertile and abundant, for (1) it cannot be shown that it is true that God thus *rewards* the earth for its fertility; and (2) such an interpretation would not accord well with the scope of the passage. The design is to show that a Christian who makes proper use of the means of growing in grace which God bestows upon him, and who does not apostatize, meets with the divine favour and approbation. His course accords with the divine intention and wishes, and he is a man on whom God will smile—as he seems to on the fertile earth.

8. *But that which beareth thorns and briers is rejected.* That is, by the farmer or owner. It is abandoned as

worthless. The force of the comparison here is, that God would thus deal with those who professed to be renewed if they should be like such a worthless field. ¶ *And is nigh unto cursing.* Is given over to execration, or is abandoned as useless. The word *cursing* means devoting to destruction. The sense is not that the owner would curse it *in words,* or imprecate a curse on it, as a man does who uses profane language, but the language is taken here from the more common use of the word curse — as meaning to devote to destruction. So the land would be regarded by the farmer. It would be valueless and would be given up to be overrun with fire. ¶ *Whose end is to be burned.* Referring to the land. The allusion here is to the common practice among the Oriental and Roman agriculturists of burning bad and barren lands. An illustration of this is afforded by Pliny: "There are some who burn the stubble on the field, chiefly upon the authority of Virgil; the principal reason for which is, that they may burn the seeds of weeds" (*Nat. Hist.* xviii. 30). The authority of Virgil, to which Pliny refers, may be found in *Georg.* i. 84, 85 :

" Sæpe etiam steriles incendere profuit agros,
    Atque levem stipulam crepitantibus urere flammis."

" It is often useful to set fire to barren lands, and burn the light stubble in crackling flames." The *object* of burning land in this way was to render it available for useful purposes; or to destroy noxious weeds, thorns, and underbrush. But the object of the apostle requires him to refer merely to the *fact* of the burning, and to make use of it as an illustration of an act of punishment. So, Paul says, it would be in the dealings of God with his people. If, after all attempts to secure holy living, and to keep them in the paths of salvation, they should evince none of the spirit of piety, all that could be done would be to abandon them to destruction as such a field is

9 But, beloved, we are persuaded better things of you, and things that accompany salvation, though we thus speak.

10 For *m* God *is* not unrighteous to forget your work and labour of love, which ye have showed to-

m Mat. 25. 40.

---

overrun with fire. It is not supposed that a true Christian will fall away and be lost, but we may remark, (1) That there are many professed Christians who *seem* to be in danger of such ruin. They resist all attempts to produce in them the fruits of good living as really as some pieces of ground do to secure a harvest. Corrupt desires, pride, envy, uncharitableness, covetousness, and vanity, are as certainly seen in their lives as thorns and briers are on a bad soil. Such briers and thorns you may cut down again and again; you may strike the plough deep and seem to tear away all their roots; you may sow the ground with the choicest grain, but soon the briers and the thorns will again appear and be as troublesome as ever. No pains will subdue them or secure a harvest. So with many a professed Christian. He may be taught, admonished, rebuked, and afflicted, but all will not do. There is essential and unsubdued perverseness in his soul, and despite all the attempts to make him a holy man, the same bad passions are continually breaking out anew. (2) Such professing Christians are "nigh unto cursing." They are about to be abandoned for ever. Unsanctified and wicked in their hearts, there is nothing else which can be done for them, and they must be lost! What a thought! A professing Christian *"nigh unto cursing !"* A man, all efforts for whose salvation are about to cease for ever, and who is to be given over as incorrigible and hopeless ! For such a man—in the church or out of it—we should have compassion. We have some compassion for an ox which is so stubborn that he will not work, and which is to be put to death; for a horse which is so fractious that he cannot be broken, and which is to be killed; for cattle which are so unruly that they cannot be restrained, and which are only to be fattened for the slaughter; and even for a field which is desolate and

barren, and which is given up to be overrun with briers and thorns; but how much more should we pity a man all the efforts for whose salvation fail, and who is soon to be abandoned to everlasting destruction !

9. *But, beloved, we are persuaded better things.* We confidently hope for better things respecting you. We trust that you are true Christians; that you will produce the proper fruits of holiness; that you will be saved. ¶ *Things that accompany salvation.* Things that pertain to salvation. The Greek phrase here means "near to salvation," or things that are conjoined with salvation. So Coverdale renders it, "and that salvation is nigher." The form of expression seems to refer to what was said in ver. 8. The land overrun with briers was *nigh* to cursing; the things which Paul saw in them were *nigh* to salvation. From this verse it is evident (1) that the apostle regarded them as sincere Christians, and (2) that he believed they would not fall away. Though he had stated what must be the inevitable consequence if Christians *should* apostatize, yet he says that in their case he had a firm conviction that it would not occur. There is no inconsistency in this. We may be certain that if a man should take arsenic it would kill him, and yet we may have the fullest conviction that he will *not* do it. Is not this verse a clear proof that Paul believed that true Christians would never fall away and be lost? If he supposed that they might how could he be persuaded that it would not happen to them? Why not to them as well as to others? Learn hence, that while we assure men that *if* they should fall away they would certainly perish, we may nevertheless address them with the full persuasion that they will be saved.

10. *For God is not unrighteous.* God will do no wrong. He will not forget or fail to reward the endeavours of his people to promote his glory and to do

ward his name, in that ye have ministered to the saints, and do minister.

11 And we desire that every one

of you do show the same diligence to ⁿthe full assurance of hope unto the end:

n ch.3.6,14.

---

good. The meaning here is, that by their kindness in ministering to the wants of the saints they had given full evidence of true piety. If God should forget that it would be "unrighteous," (1) because there was a propriety that it should be remembered, and (2) because it is expressly promised that such acts shall not fail of reward, Mat. x. 42. ¶ *Your work.* Particularly in ministering to the wants of the saints. ¶ *Labour of love.* Deeds of benevolence when there was no hope of recompense, or when love was the motive in doing it. ¶ *Which ye have showed toward his name.* Toward him, for the word *name* is often used to denote the person himself. They had showed that they loved God by their kindness to his people, Mat. xxv. 40, "Inasmuch as ye have done it unto one of the least of these my brethren, ye have done it unto me." ¶ *In that ye have ministered to the saints.* You have supplied their wants. This may refer either to the fact that they contributed to supply the wants of the poor members of the church (comp. Notes on Gal. ii. 10), or it may refer to some special acts of kindness which they had shown to suffering and persecuted Christians. It is not possible now to know to what particular acts the apostle refers. We may learn, (1) That to show kindness to Christians because they are Christians is an important evidence of piety. (2) That this will in no case be unrewarded. God is not "unjust;" and he will remember an act of kindness shown to his people, even though it be nothing but giving a cup of cold water.

11. *And we desire that every one of you.* We wish that every member of the church would exhibit the same endeavour to do good until they attain to the full assurance of hope. It is implied here that the full assurance of hope is to be obtained by a persevering effort to lead a holy life. ¶ *The same diligence.* The same strenuous endeavour; the same ardour and zeal. ¶ *To the full as-*

surance of hope. In order to obtain the full assurance of hope. The word rendered "full assurance" means firm persuasion, and refers to a state of mind where there is the fullest conviction, or where there is no doubt. See Col. ii. 2; 1 Thes. i. 5; Heb. x. 22; Luke i. 1; Rom. iv. 21; xiv. 5; 2 Tim. iv. 5, 17, where the same word in different forms occurs. Hope is a compound emotion (see Notes on Eph. ii. 12), made up of an earnest *desire* for an object and a corresponding *expectation* of obtaining it. The hope of heaven is made up of an earnest *wish* to reach heaven and a corresponding *expectation* of it or *reason to believe* that it will be ours. The *full assurance* of that hope exists where there is the highest desire of heaven and such corresponding evidence of personal piety as to leave no doubt that it will be ours. ¶ *To the end.* To the end of life. The apostle wished that they would persevere in such acts of piety to the end of their course as to have their hope of heaven fully established and to leave no doubt on the mind that they were sincere Christians. Learn hence, (1) That full assurance of hope is to be obtained only by holy living. (2) It is only when a holy life is persevered in that it can be obtained. (3) It is not by visions and raptures, by dreams and revelations, that it can now be acquired, for God imparts no such direct revelation now. (4) It is usually only as the result of a life of consistent piety that such an assurance is to be obtained. No man can have it who does not persevere in holy living, and they who do obtain it usually secure it only near the end of a life of eminent devotedness to God. God *could* impart it at once, and in every case, when the soul is converted; but such is the tendency of man to indolence and sloth, that even good men would then relax their efforts, and sit down contented, feeling that they had now the undoubted prospect of heaven. As

12 That ye *o* be not slothful, but followers of them who through faith and patience inherit the promises.

13 For when God made promise to Abraham, because he could swear by no greater, he sware by himself,

o Pr.15.19; 2 Pe.1.10.

14 Saying, *p* Surely blessing I will bless thee, and multiplying I will multiply thee.

15 And so, after he had patiently endured, he obtained the promise.

p Ge.22.16,17.

it is, it is held out as a prize to be won—as that whose acquisition is to cheer us in our old age, when the warfare is over, and when amidst the infirmities of years, and in the near prospect of death, we need special consolation. Comp. 2 Tim. iv. 6, 7.

12. *That ye be not slothful.* Indolent; inactive. This was what he was especially desirous of guarding them against. By diligent and strenuous effort only could they preserve themselves from the danger of apostasy. ¶ *But followers.* Imitators. That you may live as they lived. ¶ *Of them who through faith and patience.* By faith or confidence in God, and by patience in suffering—referring to those who in times of trial had remained faithful to God, and had been admitted to heaven. In chap. xi. the apostle has given a long list of such persevering and faithful friends of God. See Notes on that chapter. ¶ *The promise.* The promise of heaven.

13. *For when God made promise to Abraham.* That he would bless him, and multiply his seed as the stars of heaven, Gen. xxii. 16, 17. The object of introducing this case here is, to encourage those to whom the apostle was writing to persevere in the Christian life. This he does by showing that God had given the highest possible assurance of his purpose to bless his people, by an oath. Reference is made to Abraham in this argument, probably, for two reasons: (1) To show the nature of the evidence which Christians have that they will be saved, or the ground of encouragement—being the same as that made to Abraham, and depending, as in his case, on the promise of God; and (2) because the example of Abraham was just in point. He had persevered. He had relied firmly and solely on the promise of God. He

did this when appearances were much against the fulfilment of the promise, and he thus showed the advantage of perseverance and fidelity in the cause of God. ¶ *Because he could swear by no greater.* There is no being greater than God. In taking an oath among men it is always implied that the appeal is to one of superior power, who is able to punish if the oath is violated. But this could not occur in the case of God himself. There was no greater being than himself, and the oath, therefore, was by himself—by his own existence. ¶ *He sware by himself.* Gen. xxii. 16, "By myself have I sworn." Comp. Isa. xlv. 23. In an oath of this kind God pledges his veracity; declares that the event shall be as certain as his existence; and secures it by all the perfections of his nature. The usual form of the oath is, "As I live, saith the Lord." See Num. xiv. 21, 28; Ezek. xxxiii. 11.

14. *Saying, Surely blessing I will bless thee.* That is, I will certainly bless thee. The phrase is a Hebrew mode of expression, to denote emphasis or certainty—indicated by the repetition of a word. Comp. Gen. xiv. 10; Ex. viii. 10; Joel iv. 14; Judg. v. 30; xv. 16. ¶ *Multiplying I will multiply thee.* I will greatly increase thee—I will grant thee an exceedingly numerous posterity.

15. *And so, after he had patiently endured.* After he had waited for a long time. He did not faint or grow weary, but he persevered in a confident expectation of the fulfilment of what God had so solemnly promised. ¶ *He obtained the promise.* Evidently the promise referred to in the oath, that he would have a numerous posterity. The apostle intimates that he had waited for that a long time; that his faith did not waver; and that in due season the object of his wishes was granted. To see the force of this, we

16 For men verily swear by the greater: and an ^{q}oath for confirmation *is* to them an end of all strife.

17 Wherein God, willing more

^{q} Ex.22.11.

abundantly to show unto ^{r} the heirs of promise the ^{s}immutability of his counsel, ^{3}confirmed *it* by an oath:

^{r} Ro.8.17; ch.11.9.
^{s} Ro.11.29.　　^{3} *interposed himself.*

---

are to remember, (1) That when he was called by God from Haran, and when the promise of a numerous posterity was made to him, he was seventy-five years old, Gen. xii. 1–5. (2) Twenty-four years elapsed after this, during which he was a sojourner in a strange land, before the manner in which this promise would be fulfilled was made known to him, Gen. xvii. 1–16. (3) It was only when he was an hundred years old, and when he had persevered in the belief of the truth of the promise against all the natural improbabilities of its accomplishment, that he received the pledge of its fulfilment in the birth of his soon Isaac, Gen. xxi. 1–5. (4) The birth of that son was a pledge that the other blessings implied in the promise would be granted, and, in that pledge, Abraham may be said to have "received the promise." He did not actually *see* the numerous posterity of which he was to be the honoured ancestor, nor the Messiah who was to descend from him, nor the happy influences which would result to mankind from the fulfilment of the promise. But he saw the certainty that all this would occur; he saw by faith the Messiah in the distance (Jn. viii. 56), and the numerous blessings which would result from his coming. It was a remarkable instance of faith, and one well fitted to the purpose of the apostle. It would furnish ample encouragement to the Christians to whom he wrote, to persevere in their course, and to avoid the dangers of apostasy. If Abraham persevered when *appearances* were so much against the fulfilment of what had been promised, then Christians should persevere under the clearer light and with the more distinct promises of the gospel.

16. *For men verily swear by the greater.* That is, they appeal to God. They never swear by one who is inferior to

themselves. The object of the apostle in this declaration is to show that, as far as this could be done, it had been done by God. He could not, indeed, swear by one greater than himself, but he could make his promise as certain as an oath taken by men was when they solemnly appealed to Him. He could appeal to his own existence and veracity, which was at any time the most solemn form of an oath, and thus put the mind to rest in regard to the hope of heaven. ¶ *And an oath for confirmation.* An oath taken to confirm or establish anything. ¶ *Is to them an end of all strife.* That is, when two parties are at variance, or have a cause at issue, an oath binds them to adhere to the terms of agreement concluded on, or contracting parties bind themselves by a solemn oath to adhere to the conditions of an agreement, and this puts an end to all strife. They rest satisfied when a solemn oath has been taken, and they feel assured that the agreement will be complied with. Or this may refer to cases where a man was accused of wrong before a court, and where he took a solemn oath that the thing had not been done, and his oath was admitted to be sufficient to put an end to the controversy. The general meaning is clear, that, in disputes between man and man, an appeal is made to an oath, and that is allowed to settle it. The connection here is, that, as far as the case would admit of, the same thing was done by God. His oath by himself made his promise firm.

17. *Wherein God.* On account of which; or since an oath had this effect, God was willing to appeal to it in order to assure his people of salvation. ¶ *Willing more abundantly.* In the most abundant manner, or to make the case as sure as possible. It does not mean more abundantly than in the case of Abraham, but that he

18 That by two immutable things, in which *it was* ᵗimpossible for God to lie, we might have a strong con-

t Tit.1.2.

solation, who have fled for refuge to ᵘlay hold upon the hope set before us:

u 1 Ti.6.12.

was willing to give the most ample assurance possible. Coverdale renders it correctly, "very abundantly." ¶ *The heirs of promise.* Those to whom the promise of life pertained; that is, to all who were interested in the promises made to Abraham — thus embracing the heirs of salvation now. ¶ *The immutability of his counsel.* His fixed purpose. He meant to show, in the most solemn manner, that his purpose would not change. The plans of God never change; and all the hope which we can have of heaven is founded on the fact that his purposes are immutable. If he changed his plans; if he was controlled by caprice; if he willed one thing to-day and another thing to-morrow, who could confide in him, or who would have any hope of salvation? No one would know what to expect; and no one could put confidence in him. The farmer ploughs and sows because he believes that the laws of nature are settled and fixed; the mariner ventures into unknown seas because the needle points in one direction; we plant an apple-tree because we believe it will produce apples, a peach because it will produce peaches, a pear because it will produce pears. But suppose there were no settled laws—that all was governed by caprice — who would know what to plant? Who then would plant anything? So in religion. If there were nothing fixed and settled, who would know what to do? If God should change his plans by caprice, and save one man by faith to-day and condemn another for the same faith to-morrow; or if he should pardon a man to-day and withdraw the pardon to-morrow, what security could we have of salvation? How grateful, therefore, should we be that God has an *immutable counsel,* and that this is confirmed by a solemn oath! No one could honour a God that had *not* such an immutability of purpose; and all the hope which man *can* have

of heaven is in the fact that He is unchanging. ¶ *Confirmed* it *by an oath.* Margin, *interposed himself.* Tindal and Coverdale, "added an oath." The Greek is, "interposed with an oath"— ἐμεσίτευσεν ὅρκῳ. The word here used —μεσιτεύω—means to mediate or intercede for one; and then to intervene or interpose. The meaning here is, that *he interposed an oath* between himself and the other party by way of a confirmation or pledge.

18. *That by two immutable things.* What the "two immutable things" here referred to are, has been made a matter of question among commentators. Most expositors, as Doddridge, Whitby, Rosenmüller, Koppe, and Calvin, suppose that the reference is to the *promise* and the *oath* of God, each of which would be a firm ground of the assurance of salvation, and in each of which it would be impossible for God to lie. Professor Stuart supposes that the reference is to *two oaths* —the oath made to Abraham, and that by which the Messiah was made High-priest according to the order of Melchisedec, Ps. cx. 4; Heb. v. 6, 10. He supposes that thus the salvation of believers would be amply secured, by the promise that Abraham should have a Son, the Messiah, in whom all the families of the earth would be blessed, and in the oath that this Son should be High-priest for ever. But to this interpretation it may be objected that the apostle seems to refer to two things distinct from each other in their nature, and not to two acts of the same kind. There are two kinds of security referred to, whereas the security furnished according to this interpretation would be the same—that arising from an oath. However numerous the oaths might be, still it would be security of the same kind, and if one of them were broken no certainty could be derived from the other. On the supposition, however, that he refers to the *promise* and the

19 Which *hope* we have as an anchor of the soul, both sure and stedfast, and which entereth into that *ᵛ*within the vail;

v Le. 16. 15.

20 Whither*ʷ* the forerunner is for us entered, *even* Jesus, made an high priest for ever after *ˣ*the order of Melchisedec.

w ch. 4. 14.   *x* ch. 7. 17.

---

oath, there would be two kinds of assurance of different kinds. On the supposition that the *promise* was disregarded—if such a supposition may be made—still there would be the security of the *oath*—and thus the assurance of salvation was twofold. It seems to me, therefore, that the apostle refers to the *promise* and to the *oath* of God, as constituting the two grounds of security for the salvation of his people. Those things were both unchangeable, and when his word and oath are once passed, what he promises is secure. ¶ *In which* it was *impossible for God to lie*. That is, it would be contrary to his nature; it is not for a moment to be supposed. Comp. Tit. i. 2, "God, that cannot lie." The impossibility is a *moral* impossibility, and the use of the word here explains the sense in which the words *impossible, cannot,* &c., are often used in the Scriptures. The meaning here is, that such was the love of God for truth, such his holiness of character, that he *could* not speak falsely. ¶ *We might have a strong consolation*. The strongest of which the mind can conceive. The consolation of a Christian is not in his own strength; his hope of heaven is not in any reliance on his own powers. His comfort is, that God has *promised* eternal life to his people, and that He cannot prove false to his word, Tit. i. 2. ¶ *Who have fled for refuge*. Referring to the fact that one charged with murder fled to the city of refuge, or laid hold on an altar for security, Num. xxxv. 9, seq. So we, guilty and deserving of death, have fled to the hopes of the gospel in the Redeemer. ¶ *To lay hold upon*. To seize and hold fast—as one does an altar when he is pursued by the avenger of blood. ¶ *The hope set before us*. The hope of eternal life offered in the gospel. This is set before us as our refuge, and to this we flee when we feel that we are

in danger of death. On the nature of *hope*, see Notes on Eph. ii. 12.

19. *Which* hope *we have as an anchor of the soul.* Hope accomplishes for the soul the same thing which an anchor does for a ship. It makes it fast and secure. An anchor preserves a ship when the waves beat and the wind blows, and as long as the anchor holds, so long the ship is safe and the mariner apprehends no danger. So with the soul of the Christian. In the tempests and trials of life, his mind is calm as long as his hope of heaven is firm. If that gives way, he feels that all is lost. Among the heaven writers, *hope* is often compared with an anchor. So Socrates said, "To ground hope on a false supposition, is like trusting to a weak anchor." Again: "A ship ought not to trust to one anchor, nor life to one hope." ¶ *Both sure and stedfast.* Firm and secure. This refers to the *anchor*. That is fixed in the sand, and the vessel is secure. ¶ *And which entereth into that within the veil.* The allusion to the *anchor* here is dropped, and the apostle speaks simply of *hope*. The "*veil*" here refers to that which, in the temple, divided the holy from the most holy place. See Notes on Mat. xxi. 12. The place "within the veil"—the most holy place—was regarded as God's peculiar abode, where he dwelt by the visible symbol of his presence. That holy place was emblematic of heaven; and the idea here is, that the hope of the Christian enters into heaven itself; takes hold on the throne of God; is made firm by being fastened there. It is not the hope of future riches, honours, or pleasures in this life—for such a hope would not keep the soul steady; it is the hope of immortal blessedness and purity in the world beyond.

20. *Whither.* To which most holy place—heaven. ¶ *The forerunner.* The word here used occurs nowhere

else in the New Testament. A *fore-runner*—πρόδρομος—is one who goes before others to prepare the way. The word is applied to light troops sent forward as scouts (Diod. Sic. 17. 17). Compare Wisdom of Solomon (Apoc.) xii. 8, "Thou didst send wasps, fore-runners of thy host, to destroy them by little and little." The meaning here is, that Jesus went *first* into the heavenly sanctuary. He led the way. He has gone there on our account, to prepare a place for us, Jn. xiv. 3. Having such a friend and advocate there, we should be firm in the hope of eternal life, and, amidst the storms and tempests around us, we should be calm. ¶ *Made an high priest for ever.* See Notes on chap. v. 6, 10. To illustrate this fact was the object for which this discussion was introduced, and which had been interrupted by the remarks occurring in this chapter on the danger of apostasy. Having warned them of this danger, and exhorted them to go on to make the highest attainments possible in the divine life, the apostle resumes the discussion respecting Melchisedec, and makes the observations which he intended to make respecting this remarkable man. See chap. v. 11.

REMARKS.

(1) We should *aim* at perfection in order that we may have evidence of piety, ver. 1. No man can be a Christian who does *not* do this, or who does not desire to be perfect as God is perfect. No one can be a Christian who is *satisfied* or *contented* to remain in sin; or who would not *prefer* to be made at once as holy as an angel—as the Lord Jesus—as God.

(2) We should aim at perfection in order to make great attainments, ver. 1. No man makes any great advance in anything who does not set his standard high. Men usually accomplish about what they expect to accomplish. If a man expects to be a quack physician, he becomes such; if he is satisfied to be a fourth-rate lawyer, he becomes such; if he is willing to be an indifferent mechanic, he advances no higher; if he has no in-

tention or expectation of being a first-rate farmer, he will never become one. If he sincerely aims, however, to excel, he usually accomplishes his object. And it is so in religion. If a man does not intend to be an eminent Christian, he may be certain that he never will be. Religion is not produced by chance, any more than fine fruit is, or than a good harvest is. One of the principal reasons why President Edwards became so eminent a Christian was, that in early life he adopted the following resolution, to which he appears always to have adhered, that "on the supposition that there never was to be but one individual in the world, at any one time, who was properly a complete Christian, in all respects of a right stamp, having Christianity always shining in its true lustre, and appearing excellent and lovely, from whatever part, and under whatever character viewed: *Resolved*, To act just as I would do if I strove with all my might to be that one, who should live in my time" (*Life*, by S. E. Dwight, D.D., p. 72).

(3) We should aim to acquire as much *knowledge* of religious truth as we possibly can, ver. 1, 2. True piety is *principle.* It is not fancy, or dreaming, or visions, or enthusiasm. It is based on knowledge, and does not go *beyond* that. No man has any more religion than he has *knowledge* of the way of salvation. He cannot force his religion to overstep the bounds of his knowledge; for *ignorance* contributes nothing to devotion. There may be knowledge where there is no piety; but there can be no true religion where there is no knowledge. If, therefore, a Christian wishes to make advances in the divine life, he must gain a knowledge of the truth. He must understand the great doctrines of his religion. And, in like manner, if we wish the next generation to be intelligent and solid Christians, we must train them up to *understand* the Bible.

(4) The consequences of the judgment will be eternal, ver. 3. No truth is more solemn than this. It is this which makes the prospect of the judgment so fearful. If the conse-

quences of the sentence were to continue for a few years, or ages, or centuries only, it would be of much less importance. But who can abide the thought of "*eternal judgment?*"—of an *eternal sentence?* Here the most fearful and solemn sentence of the term is for a short period. The sentence consigning one to a prison will soon expire; or it is mitigated by the hope of a change. Pain, too, on earth is brief. Disgrace, and sorrow, and heaviness of heart, and all the woes that man can inflict here, soon come to an end. There is an outer limit of suffering, for no severity of a sentence, no ingenuity of man, can prolong it far. The man disgraced, and whose life is a burden, will soon die. On the cheeks of the solitary prisoner, doomed to the dungeon for life, a "mortal paleness" will soon settle down, and the comforts of an approaching release by death may soothe the anguish of his sad heart. The rack cheats itself of its own purpose, and the exhausted sufferer is released. "The excess [of grief] makes it soon mortal." But in the world of future woe the sentence will never expire; and death will never come to relieve the sufferer. I may ask, then, of my reader, Are you prepared for the "eternal" sentence? Are you ready to hear a doom pronounced which can never be changed? Would you be willing to have God judge you just as you are, and pronounce such a sentence as ought to be pronounced now, and have the assurance that it will be eternal? You seek worldly honour. Would you be willing to be doomed *always* to seek that? You aspire after wealth. Would you be willing to be doomed to aspire after that *always?* You seek pleasure—in the gay and giddy world. Would you be willing to be doomed always to seek after that? You have no religion; perhaps desire to have none. Would you be willing to be doomed to be *always* without religion? You are a stranger to the God that made you. Would you be willing to be sentenced to be *always* a stranger to God? You indulge in passion, pride, envy, sensuality. Would you be will-

ing to be sentenced *always* to the raging of these passions and lusts? You dread pain for a few hours or a few moments. Would you be *willing* that a sentence should be passed on you that in this respect should be *eternal?* How few are they who would be willing to have an *eternal* sentence passed on them, even to be doomed to pursue their present employments, or to cherish their present opinions, for ever! How few who would *dare* to meet a sentence which should be in strict accordance with what was *just*, and which was never to change! How awful the condition where one should be sentenced to *eternal pain!*

(5) With the righteous it should be matter of rejoicing that the judgment is to be eternal, ver. 3. They can desire no change of the sentence which will assign them to heaven; and it will be no small part of the joy of the heavenly world that the results of the judgment will be everlasting. There will be no further trial; no reversing of the sentence; no withdrawing of the crown of glory. The righteous are the only ones who have not reason to dread an "eternal sentence;" and *they* will rejoice when the time shall come which will fix their doom for ever.

(6) We should dread apostasy from the true religion, ver. 4. We should habitually feel that if we should deny our Lord, and reject his religion, there would be no hope. The die would be cast; and we must then perish for ever. By this solemn consideration God intends to preserve his people, and it is a consideration which has been so effectual that there is not the least reason to suppose that anyone who has ever had any true religion has fallen away and perished. Many have been *almost* Christians, and have then turned back to perdition (Mat. vii. 22, 23; Acts xxvi. 28), but there is no reason to suppose that any who have been true Christians have thus apostatized and been lost. Yet Christians are not kept without watchfulness; they cannot be kept without the most sincere and constant endeavours to preserve themselves from falling.

(7) If the sin of apostasy is so great,

then every approach to it is dangerous, and then every sin should be
avoided. He that habitually indulges
in sin *cannot* be a Christian; and every
sin which a sincere Christian commits should be measured by the guilt
which *would* be incurred should it become final, and should he wholly fall
away. No man can indulge in sin and
be safe; and no professed Christian
who finds himself *disposed* to indulge
in sin should cherish the expectation
of reaching heaven, ver. 4–6.

(8) It is a matter of devout gratitude that God *has* kept all his true
people from apostasy, ver. 4–6. If it
is true that no one who has been regenerated has ever fallen away; if the
means which God has used have been
effectual in a world so full of temptations, and where we have hearts so
prone to evil; and if it is the intention of God to keep all to eternal salvation who are truly converted, then
this should be to us a subject of devout thankfulness and of encouragement. In view of this, we should admire the wisdom of the plan which
thus secures salvation; we should look
to him with the firm assurance that he
will keep what we have committed to
him to the final day.

(9) We should improve the privileges which we enjoy so as to receive
a blessing from God, ver. 7, 8. It is
desirable that a farm should be well
cultivated, so as not to be overrun
with briers and thorns; desirable that
it should produce an abundant harvest, and not exhibit mere barrenness
and desolation. Yet, alas! there are
many professing Christians who resemble such a field of thorns, and
such a scene of desolation. They produce no fruits of righteousness; they
do nothing to extend the kingdom of
the Redeemer! What can such expect but the "curse" of God? What
can the end of such be but to be
"burned?"

(10) God will not fail to reward his
faithful people, ver. 10. What we
have done in his service, and with a
sincere desire to promote his glory,
unworthy of his notice as it may seem
to us to be, he will not fail to reward.
It may be unobserved or forgotten by

the world; nay, it may pass out of
our own recollection, but it will never
fail from the mind of God. Whether
it be "two mites" contributed to his
cause, or a "cup of cold water given
to a disciple," or a life consecrated to
his service, it will be alike remembered. What encouragement there
is, therefore, to labour in the promotion of his glory, and to do all that
we can for the advancement of his
kingdom!

(11) Let us follow those who have
inherited the promises, ver. 12. They
are worthy examples. When from
their lofty seats in heaven they look
back on the journey of life, though to
them attended with many trials, they
never regret the "faith and patience"
by which they were enabled to persevere. We have most illustrious examples to imitate. They are numerous as the drops of dew, and bright as
the stars. It is an honour to tread in
the footsteps of the holy men who
have inherited the promises—an honour to feel that we are walking in the
same path, and are reaching out the
hand to the same crown.

(12) It is the privilege of those who
are truly the children of God to enjoy
strong consolation, ver. 13–18. Their
hope is based on that which cannot
fail. God cannot lie. And when we
have evidence that he has promised *us*
eternal life, we may open our hearts
to the full influence of Christian consolation. It may be asked, perhaps,
how we may have that evidence?
Will God speak to us from heaven,
and assure us that we are his children? Will he reveal our names as
written in his book? Will he come
to us in the night-watches and address
us by name as his? I answer, No.
None of these things are we to expect.
But if we have evidence that we have
true repentance, and sincere faith in
the Redeemer; if we love holiness,
and desire to lead a pure life; if we
delight in the Bible and in the people
of God; then we may regard him as
addressing us in the promises and
oaths of his word, and assuring us of
salvation. These promises belong to
us, and we may apply them to ourselves. And if we have evidence that

God *promises* us eternal life, why should we feel that we are unworthy; our consciences may reproach us for the errors and follies of our past lives; but on the unchanging word and oath of God we may rely, and there we may feel secure.

(13) How invaluable is the Christian hope! ver. 19. To us it is like the anchor to a vessel in a storm. We are sailing along the voyage of life. We are exposed to breakers and tempests. Our bark is liable to be tossed about, or to be shipwrecked. In the agitations and troubles of life, how much we need some anchor of the soul—something that shall make us calm and serene! Such an anchor is found in the hope of the gospel. While that hope is firm we need fear nothing. All is then safe, and we may look calmly forward, assured that we shall ride out the storm, and come at last safely into the haven of peace. Happy they who have fled for refuge to the faith of the gospel; whose hope, like a steady anchor, has entered into heaven, and binds the soul to the throne of God; whose confidence in the Redeemer is unshaken in all the storms of life, and who have the assurance that, when the tempest shall have beaten upon them a little longer, they will be admitted to a haven of rest where storms and tempests are for ever unknown. With such a hope we may well bear the trials of this life for the few days appointed to us on earth; for what are the longest trials here compared with that eternal rest which remains in a brighter world for all who love God?

CHAPTER VII.

ANALYSIS OF THE CHAPTER.

In chap. v. 10, 11, the apostle had introduced the name of Melchisedec, and said that Christ was made an high-priest after the same order as he. He added that he had much to say of him, but that they were not in a state of mind then to receive or understand it. He then (chap. v. 12–14) rebukes them for the little progress which they had made in Christian knowledge; exhorts them to go on and make higher attainments (chap. vi. 1–3); warns them against the danger of apostasy (chap. vi. 4–8); and encourages them to hold fast their faith and hope to the end, in view of the covenant faithfulness of God, chap. vi. 9–20. He now returns to the subject under discussion — *the high-priesthood of Christ.* His object is to show that he was superior to the Jewish high-priest, and for this purpose he institutes these comparisons between him and Melchisedec. The *argument* is the following:—

I. That which is drawn from the exalted rank of Melchisedec, and the fact that the ancestor of the whole Jewish priesthood and community—Abraham—acknowledged him as his superior, and rendered tribute to him. But Christ was of the order of Melchisedec, and the apostle, therefore, infers his superiority to the Jewish priesthood, ver. 1–10. In the prosecution of this argument, the apostle dwells on the import of the name *Melchisedec* (ver. 1, 2); states the fact that he was without any known ancestry or descent, or that he stood alone on the pages of the sacred record, and was, therefore, worthy to be compared with the Son of God, who had a similar pre-eminence (ver. 3); urges the consideration that even Abraham, the ancestor of the whole Jewish community and priesthood, paid tithes to him, and thus confessed his inferiority (ver. 4); shows that he of whom a blessing was received must be superior to the one who receives it (ver. 6, 7), and that even Levi, the ancestor of the whole Levitical priesthood, might be said to have paid tithes in Abraham, and thus to have acknowledged his inferiority to Melchisedec, and consequently to the Son of God, who was of his "order," ver. 9, 10.

II. The apostle shows that "*perfection*" could not arise out of the Levitical priesthood, and that a priesthood that introduced a perfect state must be superior, ver. 11–19. In the prosecution of this argument, he states that perfection could not be arrived at under the Hebrew economy, and that there was need that a priesthood of another order should be formed

CHAPTER VII.

F OR this ^aMelchisedec, king of Salem, priest of the most

a Ge.14.18, &c.

(ver. 11); that a change of the priesthood involved of necessity a change in the law or administration (ver. 12); that the necessity of a change of the law also followed from the fact that the great high-priest was now of another tribe than that of Levi (ver. 13, 14); that the Christian High-priest was constituted not after a commandment pertaining to the flesh and liable to change, but "after the power of an endless life"—adapted to a life that was never to change or to end (ver. 15–17); that consequently there was a disannulling of the commandment going before, because it was weak and unprofitable (ver. 18), and that the old law made *nothing* perfect, but that by the new arrangement a system of entire and eternal perfection was introduced, ver. 19.

III. The apostle shows the superiority of the priesthood of Christ to that of the Jewish system, from the fact that the great High-priest of the Christian system was constituted with the solemnity of an oath; the Jewish priesthood was not, ver. 20–22. His priesthood, therefore, was as much more important and solemn as an oath is superior to a command; and his suretyship became as much more certain as an oath is superior to a simple promise, ver. 22.

IV. The superiority of the priesthood of Christ is further shown from the fact that under the former dispensation there were *many* priests; but here there was but *one*. There they lived but a brief period, and then gave way to their successors; but here there was no removal by death, there was no succession, there was an unchangeable priesthood, ver. 23, 24. He infers, therefore (ver. 25), that the Christian High-priest is able to save to the uttermost all that come to the Father by him, since he ever lives to make intercession.

V. The last argument is, that under the Levitical priesthood it was neces-

high God, who met Abraham returning from the slaughter of the kings, and blessed him;

sary for the priest to offer sacrifice for his own sins as well as for those of the people. No such necessity, however, existed in regard to the High-priest of the Christian system. He was holy, harmless, and undefiled; he had no need to offer sacrifices for his own sins; and in this respect there was a vast superiority of the Christian priesthood over the Jewish, ver. 26–28. The force of these several arguments we shall be able to estimate as we advance in the exposition.

1. *For this Melchisedec.* Comp. Notes on chap. v. 6. The name Melchisedec, from which the apostle derives a portion of his argument here, is Hebrew, מַלְכִּי־צֶדֶק, *malki-tzedek*, and is correctly explained as meaning *king of righteousness*—being compounded of two words—*king* and *righteousness*. *Why* this name was given to this man is unknown. Names, however, were frequently given on account of some quality or characteristic of the man. See Notes on Isa. viii. 18. This name may have been given on account of his eminent integrity. The apostle calls attention to the fact (ver. 2), as a circumstance worthy of notice, that his name and the name of the city where he reigned were so appropriate to one who, as a priest, was the predecessor of the Messiah. The account of Melchisedec, which is very brief, occurs in Gen. xiv. 18–20. The name is found in the Bible only in Gen. xiv., Psa. cx. 4, and in this epistle. Nothing else is certainly known of him. Grotius supposes that he is the same man who in the history of Sanchoniathon is called Συδύκ —*Sydyc.* It has indeed been made a question by some whether such a person ever actually existed, and consequently whether this be a proper name. But the account in Genesis is as simple a historical record as any other in the Bible. In that account there is no difficulty whatever. It is said simply that when Abraham was returning from a successful military

expedition, this man, who it seems was well known, and who was respected as a priest of God, came out to express his approbation of what he had done, and to refresh him with bread and wine. As a tribute of gratitude to him, and as a thank-offering to God, Abraham gave him a tenth part of the spoils which he had taken. Such an occurrence was by no means improbable, nor would it have been attended with any special difficulty if it had not been for the use which the apostle makes of it in this epistle. Yet on no subject has there been a greater variety of opinions than in regard to this man. The bare recital of the opinions which have been entertained of him would fill a volume. But in a case which *seems* to be plain from the Scripture narrative, it is not necessary even to enumerate these opinions. They only serve to show how easy it is for men to mystify a clear statement of history, and how fond they are of finding what is mysterious and marvellous in the plainest narrative of facts. That he was Shem, as the Jews suppose, or that he was the Son of God himself, as many Christian expositors have maintained, there is not the slightest evidence. That the latter opinion is false is perfectly clear—for if he were the Son of God, with what propriety could the apostle say that he "was made *like* the Son of God" (ver. 3); that is, like himself; or that Christ was constituted a priest "*after the order* of Melchisedec"—that is, that he was a type of himself? The most simple and probable opinion is that given by Josephus, that he was a pious Canaanitish prince; a personage eminently endowed by God, who acted as the priest of his people. That he combined in himself the offices of priest and king, furnished to the apostle a beautiful illustration of the offices sustained by the Redeemer, as he was, in this respect, perhaps the only one whose history is recorded in the Old Testament who would furnish such an illustration. That his genealogy was not recorded, while that of every other priest mentioned was so carefully traced and preserved, furnished

another striking illustration. In this respect, like the Son of God, he stood alone. He was not in *a line* of priests; he was preceded by no one in the sacerdotal office; nor was he followed by any. That he was superior to Abraham, and consequently to all who descended from Abraham; that a tribute was rendered to him by the great ancestor of all the fraternity of Jewish priests, was also an illustration which suited the purpose of Paul. His name, therefore, the place where he reigned, his solitariness, his lone conspicuity in all the past, his dignity, and perhaps the air of mystery thrown over him in the brief history in Genesis, furnished a beautiful and striking illustration of the solitary grandeur, and the inapproachable eminence, of the priesthood of the Son of God. There is no evidence that Melchisedec was *designed* to be a type of the Messiah, or that Abraham so understood it. Nothing of this kind is affirmed; and how shall *we* affirm it when the sacred oracles are silent?

[Doubtless great care and sobriety are requisite in the interpretation of types, and we admire the caution that in every instance demands the authority of Scripture, expressed or distinctly implied. From want of this caution the greatest extravagancies have been committed, the most fanciful analogies established where none were intended, and every minute circumstance in the Old Testament exalted into a type of something in the New. The very boards and nails of the tabernacle of Moses have been thus exalted.

Yet in our just aversion to one extreme it is possible we may run into another. Of the typical character of Melchisedec we had thought no doubt could be entertained. The canon of typical interpretation, indeed, demands, that in order to constitute the relation between type and antitype, there be, in addition to mere resemblance, *previous design* and *preordained connection*. And the commentary affirms that "there is no evidence that Melchisedec was *designed* to be a type of the Messiah, or that Abraham so understood it." Let it be observed in reply, that in the 110th Psalm the typical character of Melchisedec *seems* expressly acknowledged. It may be alleged that the prophet simply states resemblance without affirming that such resemblance was designed or intended. But that a prophet should be commissioned to declare that Christ's priesthood should be *after such an order*, and yet that in the insti-

tution of that exalted order there should have been no designed reference to Christ, is improbable. The prediction seems to involve the original design. And this order of priesthood, too, is far superior to that of Aaron, the typical character of which is admitted. Moreover, the last clause of ver. 3 in this chapter, according to our English translation, asserts a designed connection. Melchisedec was "*made like unto the Son of God.*" The translation is accurate. Αφομοιωμενος, according to Parkhurst, is "*made very like.*" So also Scott: "The composition is probably intended to add energy; *made very like.*" And Bloomfield adopts, "*being made by the divine decree* a type of that great High Priest, who, &c.;" see Notes in Greek Testament. Lastly, on any other principle than that of *designed* typical relation it is difficult, if not impossible, to give any just account of the remarkable omissions, the apparently studied silence, in the history of Melchisedec in regard to those things that are commonly related in notices of lives, however brief. He is introduced to us with an air of impenetrable mystery. He appears on the stage as priest of the Most High God, and then disappears, leaving us in complete darkness concerning his birth, parentage, and death. "In all these respects," says Mr. Scott, "the silence of the Scripture is *intentional*, and refers to the great Antitype." Melchisedec, therefore, we may remark, seems not only to have been designed as a type, but *special care* has been taken that the record of him should be in all things suited to that design. That the apostle lighted on a happy coincidence deserving of a passing thought is not probable, whether this remark be meant to apply to the name or to other particulars in this remarkable story. Indeed, divest it of its designed typical character and the grandeur of the passage vanishes. A simple resemblance has been discovered between Christ and a certain character in the Old Testament. This is all the apostle means to affirm! And for this too he introduces Melchisedec with such wondrous caution in chap. v. 11: "Of whom we have many things to say, and hard to be uttered, but ye are dull of hearing." What was hard to be uttered or difficult to be comprehended about a mere "illustration" or "resemblance?"

The following remarks of Owen are pertinent and beautiful. "The true cause of all these omissions was the same with that of the institution of his (Melchisedec's) priesthood and the introduction of his person into the story. And this was that he might be the more express and signal representative of the Lord Christ in his priesthood. And we may herein consider the sovereign wisdom of the Holy Ghost in bringing forth truth unto light

according as the state and condition of the church doth require. And first he prophesieth only a naked story of a person that was a type of Christ. Something the men of the age wherein he lived might learn by his ministrations, but not much. For that which was principally instructive in him, for the use of the church, was not of force till all his circumstances were forgotten. Yea, the contrivance of any tradition concerning his parents, birth, and death had been contrary to the mind of God and what instruction he intended the church by him. Afterwards, when, it may be, all thoughts of any use or design in this story were lost, and the church was fully satisfied in a priesthood quite of another nature, the Holy Ghost in one word of prophecy instructs her, not only that the things spoken concerning Melchisedec were not so recorded for his own sake or on his own account, but with respect to another priest, which was afterwards to arise, by him represented. This gave a new consideration to the whole story, but, moreover, gave the church to know that the priesthood which it then had was not always to continue, but that one of another nature was to be introduced, as was signified long before the institution of that priesthood which they enjoyed, Ps. cx. 4. Yet the church was left greatly in the dark, and at the coming of our Saviour had utterly lost all knowledge of the mystery of the type and the promise renewed in the Psalm. Wherefore our apostle, entering on the unfolding of this mystery, doth not only preface it with an assertion of its difficulty, but also by a long previous discourse variously prepareth their minds to a most diligent attention." The excellence of this quotation will, in the reader's estimation, excuse the length of it. On the whole, he who reflects how all things in the ancient economy were ordered of God, and how great a part of that economy was meant to adumbrate the realities of the gospel, while he will be cautious in admitting typical analogies of a doubtful kind, will be slow to believe that the resemblance between Christ's priesthood and that of the *most* exalted order previously instituted is casual or undesigned—slow to believe that the apostle would make so large use of *such* accidental analogy and found on it an argument so great.]

¶ *King of Salem.* Such is the record in Gen. xiv. 18. The word *Salem*—שָׁלֵם—means *peace;* and from this fact the apostle derives his illustration in ver. 2. He regards it as a point worth remarking on, that the *name* of the place over which he ruled, expressed so strikingly the nature of the kingdom over which the Messiah was placed. In

regard to the *place* here denoted by the name *Salem*, the almost uniform opinion has been that it was that which was afterwards known as Jerusalem. The reasons for this opinion are, (1) That it is a part of the name Jerusalem itself—the name *Jerus*, altered from *Jebus*, having been afterward added, because it was the residence of the *Jebusites*. (2) The name *Salem* is itself given to Jerusalem, Ps. lxxvi. 2, "In *Salem* also is his tabernacle, and his dwelling-place in Zion." (3) Jerusalem would be in the direction through which Abraham would naturally pass on his return from the slaughter of the kings. He had pursued them unto Dan (Gen. xiv. 14), and he was returning to Mamre, that is, Hebron, Gen. xiv. 13. On his return, therefore, he would pass in the vicinity of Jerusalem. Rosenmüller, however, supposes that by the name here Jerusalem is not intended, but the whole region occupied by the Jebusites and Hittites, or the royal seat of this region, situated not far from the cities of the plain—the vale of Siddim, where Sodom and Gomorrah were. But I see no reason for doubting that the common opinion that Jerusalem is intended, is correct. That place was favourably situated for a capital of a nation or tribe; was easily fortified; and would be likely to be early selected as a royal residence. ¶ *Priest of the most high God.* This is the account which is given of him in Gen. xiv. 18. The leading office of *priest* was to offer sacrifice. This duty was probably first performed by the father of the family (compare Notes on Job i. 5; see also Gen. viii. 20; xxii. 2), and when he was dead it devolved on the eldest son. It would seem also that in the early ages, among all nations whose records have reached us, the office of priest and king were united in the same person. It was long before it was found that the interests of religion would be promoted by having the office of priest pertain to an order of men set apart for this special work. That Melchisedec, who was a king, should also be a priest, was not, therefore, remarkable. The only thing remarkable is, that he should have been a priest *of the true God.* In what way he became acquainted with Him, is wholly unknown. It may have been by tradition preserved from the times of Noah; or it is possible that the arrival of Abraham in that land may have been in some way the means of acquainting him with the existence and character of JEHOVAH. The *fact* shows at least that the knowledge of the true God was not extinct in the world. ¶ *Who met Abraham.* He came out to meet him, and brought with him bread and wine. *Why* he did this, is not mentioned. It was probably as an expression of gratitude to Abraham for having freed the country from oppressive and troublesome invaders, and in order to furnish refreshments to the party which Abraham headed, which had become weary and exhausted with the pursuit. There is not the slightest evidence that the bread and wine which he brought forth was designed to typify the sacrament of the Lord's supper, as has been sometimes supposed. Compare Bush on Gen. xiv. 18. What did he know of this ordinance? And why should we resort to such a supposition, when the whole case may be met by a simple reference to the ancient rites of hospitality, and by the fact that the deliverance of the country by Abraham from a grievous invasion made some expression of gratitude on the part of this pious king in the highest degree proper? ¶ *Returning from the slaughter of the kings.* "Amraphel king of Shinar, Arioch king of Ellasar, Chedorlaomer king of Elam, and Tidal king of nations," who had invaded the valley where Sodom and Gomorrah were, and had departed with a great amount of booty. Those kings Abraham had pursued beyond Dan, and to the neighbourhood of Damascus, and had smitten them, and recovered the spoil. ¶ *And blessed him.* For the important service which he had rendered in taking vengeance on these invaders; in freeing the land from the apprehension of being invaded again; and in recovering the valuable booty which they had taken away. From ver. 6, 7, it ap-

2 To whom also Abraham gave a tenth part of all; first being by interpretation King of righteousness, and after that also King of Salem, which is, King of peace;

pears that this act of *blessing* was regarded as that of one who was superior to Abraham. That is, he blessed him as a priest and a king. As such he was superior in rank to Abraham, who never claimed the title of *king*, and who is not spoken of as a *priest*.

2. *To whom also Abraham gave a tenth part of all*. That is, a tenth part of all the spoils which he had taken (Gen. xiv. 20), thus acknowledging that in dignity of office Melchisedec was greatly his superior, ver. 4, 6, 8. This does not appear to have been on the part of Abraham so much designed as a present to Melchisedec personally, as an act of pious thankfulness to God. He doubtless recognized in Melchisedec one who was a minister of God, and to him, as such, he devoted the tenth of all which he had taken, as a proper acknowledgment of the goodness of God and of his claims. From this it is evident that the propriety of devoting a tenth part of what was possessed to God, was regarded as a duty before the appointment of the Levitical law. *Some* expression of this kind is obviously demanded, and piety seems early to have fixed on the *tenth* part as being no more than a proper proportion to consecrate to the service of religion. For the propriety of the use which the apostle makes of this fact, see Notes on ver. 4, 6, 8. ¶ *First being.* The *first* idea in the interpretation of his name and office, &c. First being mentioned as king of righteousness, and then as king of peace. ¶ *King of righteousness.* The literal translation of the name Melchisedec. See Notes on ver. 1. The *argument* implied in this by the remarks of the apostle is, that he bore a name which made him a proper emblem of the Messiah. There was a propriety that one in whose "order" the Messiah was to be found, should have such a name. It would be exactly descriptive of him, and it was *worthy of observation* that he of whose "order" it was said

the Messiah would be, should have had such a name. Paul does not say that this name was given to him with any such reference, or that it was designed to be symbolical of what the Messiah would be, but that there was a *remarkable coincidence;* that it was a fact which was worth at least a *passing thought.* This is a kind of remark which it might occur to anyone to make, and the slight use which Paul makes of it would not be improper anywhere, but it cannot be denied that to one accustomed to the Jewish mode of reasoning—accustomed to dwell much on hidden meanings, and to trace out concealed analogies—it would be much more obvious and striking than it is with us. We are to place ourselves in the situation of those to whom Paul wrote—trained up with Jewish feelings, and Jewish modes of thought—and to ask how this would strike *their* minds. And this is no more unreasonable than it would be in interpreting a Greek classic, or a work of a Hindoo philosopher, that we should endeavour to place ourselves in the situation of the writer and of those for whom he wrote, and ascertain what ideas would be conveyed to them by certain expressions. It is not meant by these observations that there was really no intrinsic force in what Paul here said respecting the import of the *name.* There was force; and all the use which he makes of it is proper. His meaning appears to be merely that it was a fact worthy of remark, that the *name* had a meaning which corresponded so entirely with the character of him who was to be a high-priest of the same "order." ¶ *And after that.* He is mentioned after that with another appellation equally significant. ¶ *King of peace.* A literal translation of the appellation "king of Salem," ver. 1. The idea of Paul is, that it was *worthy of remark* that the appellation which he bore was appropriate to one whose ministry it was said the priesthood of the Messiah would resemble.

3 Without father, without mother, without ¹ descent, having neither beginning of days, nor end of life; but made like unto the Son of God, abideth a priest continually.

¹ *pedigree.*

[Admit the typical character of Melchisedec and the difficulty disappears, and apology of course becomes needless. The apostle does not found an argument on any fanciful analogy, but *seems* to intimate that the very name as well as the other circumstances stated concerning Melchisedec was typical. And why should this surprise us? In the Old Testament we find that names were frequently given to children by the spirit of prophecy, while on other occasions a change of name was made by command of God. In both these cases there was always something significant. Melchisedec, doubtless, had his name under the divine direction. In what way, whether at his birth or by change of name afterwards, it is needless to inquire and impossible to determine. See for further remarks Owen, M'Lean, and the Supplementary Note on chap. i. 5; also ii. 6.]

3. *Without father.* The phrase *without father*—ἀπάτωρ—means literally one who has no father, or who is an orphan. It is applied to one who has lost his father; or to one who has been disowned by his father (Plato, *Legg.* 929, *a.*); then to one whose father is unknown—*spurious* (Passow). The word occurs often in these senses in the classic writers, for numerous examples of which the reader may consult Wetstein, *in loco.* It is morally certain, however, that the apostle did not use the word here in either of these senses, for there is no evidence that Melchisedec was *fatherless* in any of these respects. It was very important in the estimation of the Jews that the line of their priesthood should be carefully kept; that their genealogies should be accurately marked and preserved; and that their direct descent from Aaron should be susceptible of easy and certain proof. But the apostle says that there was no such genealogical table in regard to Melchisedec. There was no *record* made of the name either of his father, his mother, or any of his posterity. *He stood alone.* It is simply said that such a man came out to meet Abraham:—and that is the first and the last which we hear of him and of his family. Now, says the apostle, it is distinctly said (Ps. cx. 4), that the Messiah was to be a priest *according to his order;* and in this respect there is a remarkable resemblance, *so far as the point of his being a priest*—which was the point under discussion—*was concerned.* The Messiah thus, *as a priest,* STOOD ALONE. His name does not appear in the line of priests. He pertained to another tribe, ver. 14. No one of his ancestors is mentioned as a priest; and as a priest he has no descendants, and no followers. He has a lonely conspicuity similar to that of Melchisedec; a standing unlike that of any other priest. This should not, therefore, be construed as meaning that the genealogy of Christ could not be traced out—which is not true, for Matthew (chap. i.) and Luke (chap. iii.) have carefully preserved it; but that he had no genealogical record *as a priest.* As the reasoning of the apostle pertains to this point only, it would be unfair to construe it as implying that the Messiah was to stand unconnected with any ancestor, or that his genealogy would be unknown. The meaning of the word rendered "without father" here is, therefore, *one the name of whose father is not recorded in the Hebrew genealogies.* ¶ *Without mother.* The name of whose mother is unknown, or is not recorded in the Hebrew genealogical tables. Philo calls Sarah ἀμήτορα, *without mother,* probably because her mother is not mentioned in the sacred records. The Syriac has given the correct view of the meaning of the apostle. In that version it is, "Of whom neither the father nor mother are recorded in the genealogies." The meaning here is not that Melchisedec was of low and obscure origin, as the terms "without father and without mother" often signify in the classic writers, and in Arabic (compare Wetstein); for there is no reason to doubt that Melchisedec had an ancestry as honourable as other kings and priests of his time.

The simple thought is, that the name of his ancestry does not appear in any record of those in the priestly office. ¶ *Without descent.* Margin, *pedigree.* The Greek word— ἀγενεαλόγητος —means *without genealogy; whose descent is unknown.* He is merely mentioned himself, and nothing is said of his family or of his posterity. ¶ *Having neither beginning of days, nor end of life.* This is a much more difficult expression than any of the others respecting Melchisedec. The obvious meaning of the phrase is, that *in the records of Moses* neither the beginning nor the close of his life is mentioned. It is not said when he was born, or when he died; nor is it said that he *was* born, or that he died. The apostle adverts to this particularly, because it was so unusual in the records of Moses, who is in general so careful to mention the birth and death of the individuals whose lives he mentions. Under the Mosaic dispensation everything respecting the duration of the sacerdotal office was determined accurately by the law. In the time of Moses, and by his arrangement, the Levites were required to serve from the age of thirty to fifty, Num. iv. 3, 23, 35, 43, 47; viii. 24, 25. After the age of fifty, they were released from the more arduous and severe duties of their office. In later periods of the Jewish history they commenced their duties at the age of twenty, 1 Chr. xxiii. 24, 27. The priests, also, and the high-priest entered on their office at thirty years of age, though it is not supposed that they retired from it at any specified period of life. The idea of the apostle here is, that nothing of this kind occurs in regard to Melchisedec. No period is mentioned when he entered on his office; none when he retired from it. From anything that *appears* in the sacred record it might be perpetual—though Paul evidently did not mean to be understood as saying that it *was* so. It *cannot* be that he meant to say that Melchisedec had *no beginning of days* literally—that is, that he was from eternity; or that he had *no end of life* literally—that is, that he would exist for ever; for this would be to make

him equal with God. The expression used must be interpreted *according to the matter under discussion,* and that was the office of Melchisedec *as a priest.* Of that no beginning is mentioned, and no end. That this is the meaning of Paul there can be no doubt; but there is a much more difficult question about the force and pertinency of this reasoning; about the *use* which he means to make of this fact, and the strength of the argument which he here designs to employ. This inquiry cannot be easily settled. It may be admitted, undoubtedly, that it would strike a Jew with much more force than it would any other person, and to see its pertinency we ought to be able to place ourselves in their condition, and to transfer to ourselves as far as possible their state of feeling. It was mentioned in Ps. cx. 4, that the Messiah was to be a "priest after the order of Melchisedec." It was natural then to turn to the only record which existed of him —the very brief narrative in Gen. xiv. There the account is simple and plain — that he was a pious Canaanitish king, who officiated as a priest. In what point, then, it would be asked, was the Messiah to resemble him? Was it in his personal character; his office; his rank; or in what he did? It would be natural, then, to run out the parallel, and seize upon the points in which Melchisedec *differed from the Jewish priests,* which would be suggested on reading that account, for it was undoubtedly in those points that the resemblance between Christ and Melchisedec was to consist. In doing this the *record* was to be the only guide, and the points in which he differed from the Jewish priesthood, *according to the record,* were such as these : (1) There is no account of his ancestry as a priest—neither father nor mother being mentioned, as was indispensable in the records of the Levitical priesthood. (2) There is no account of any descendants in his office, and no reason to believe that he had any, and that he thus stood alone. (3) There is no account of the commencement or close of his office as a priest, but *so far as the record*

goes, it is just as *it would have been* if his priesthood had neither beginning nor end. It was inevitable, therefore, that those who read the Psalm, and compared it with the account in Gen. xiv., should come to the conclusion that the Messiah was to resemble Melchisedec *in some such points as these* —for these are the points in which he differed from the Levitical priesthood; and to run out these points of comparison is all that the apostle has done here. It is just what would be done by any Jew, or indeed by any other man, and the reasoning grew directly out of the two accounts in the Old Testament. It is not, then, quibble or quirk—it is sound reasoning, based on these two points: (1) that it was said in the Old Testament that the Messiah would be a priest after the order of Melchisedec, and (2) that the only points, *according to the record*, in which there was anything *peculiar* about the priesthood of Melchisedec, or in which he differed from the Levitical priesthood, were such as those which Paul specifies. He reasons *from the record;* and though there is, as was natural, something of a Jewish cast about it, yet it was the *only kind of reasoning that was possible in the case.* ¶ *But made like.* The word here used means to be made like; to be made to resemble; and then *to be* like, to be compared with. Our translation seems to imply that there was a divine agency or intention by which Melchisedec was *made to resemble* the Son of God, but this does not seem to be the idea of the apostle. In the Psalm it is said that the Messiah would resemble Melchisedec in his priestly office, and this is doubtless the idea here. Paul is seeking to illustrate the nature and perpetuity of the office of the Messiah by comparing it with that of Melchisedec. Hence he pursues the idea of this resemblance, and the true sense of the word used here is, "He was like, or he resembled the Son of God." So Tindal and Coverdale render it, "is likened unto the Son of God." The points of resemblance are those which have been already suggested: (1) In the *name*—*king of righteousness*, and

king of peace; (2) in the fact that he had no ancestors or successors in the priestly office; (3) in the fact that he was, according to the record, a perpetual priest—there being no account of his death; and perhaps (4) in the fact that he united in himself the office of king and priest. It may be added, that the expression here, "was made *like unto* the Son of God," proves that he was not *himself* the Son of God, as many have supposed. How could he be "made like" himself? How could a comparison be formally made *between Christ and himself?* ¶ *Abideth a priest continually.* That is, *as far as the record in Genesis goes*—for it was according to this record that Paul was reasoning. This clause is connected with ver. 1; and the intermediate statements are of the nature of a parenthesis, containing important suggestions respecting the character of Melchisedec, which would be useful in preparing the readers for the argument which the apostle proposed to draw from his rank and character. The meaning is, that there is no account of his death, or of his ceasing to exercise the priestly office, and in this respect he may be compared with the Lord Jesus. All other priests cease to exercise their office by death (ver. 23); but of the death of Melchisedec there is no mention. It must have been true that the priesthood of Melchisedec terminated at his death; and it will be also true that that of Christ will cease when his church shall have been redeemed, and when he shall have given up the mediatorial kingdom to the Father, 1 Cor. xv. 25–28. The expression, "abideth a priest *continually*," therefore, is equivalent to saying that he had a *perpetual priesthood*, in contradistinction from those whose office terminated at a definite period, or whose office passed over into the hands of others. See Notes on ver. 24.

4. *Now consider how great this man* was. The object of the apostle was to exalt the rank and dignity of Melchisedec. The Jews had a profound veneration for Abraham, and if it could be shown that Melchisedec was superior to Abraham, then it would be

4 Now consider how great this man *was*, unto whom even the patriarch Abraham gave the tenth of the spoils.

5 And verily they that are of [b] the sons of Levi, who receive the office of the priesthood, have a command-

[b] Nu. 18. 21–26.

ment to take tithes of the people according to the law, that is, of their brethren, though they come out of the loins of Abraham:

6 But he whose [2] descent is not counted from them [c] received tithes of Abraham, and blessed [d] him that had the promises.

[2] pedigree.   [c] Ge. 14. 20.   [d] Ro. 9. 4.

easy to demonstrate the superiority of Christ as a priest to all who descended from Abraham. Accordingly the apostle argues that he to whom even the patriarch Abraham showed so much respect must have had an exalted rank. Abraham, according to the views of the East, the illustrious ancestor of the Jewish nation, was regarded as superior to any of his posterity, and of course was to be considered as of higher rank and dignity than the Levitical priests who were descended from him. ¶ *Even the patriarch Abraham.* One so great as he is acknowledged to have been. On the word *patriarch,* see Notes on Acts ii. 29. It occurs only in Acts ii. 29; vii. 8, 9; and in this place. ¶ *Gave the tenth of the spoils.* See Notes on ver. 2. The *argument* here is, that Abraham acknowledged the superiority of Melchisedec by thus devoting to God through him as a priest the tenth part of the spoils of war. Instead of making a direct consecration by himself, he brought them to him as a minister of religion, and recognized in him one who had a higher official standing in the matter of religion than himself. The Greek word here rendered *spoils*—ἀκροθίνιον—means literally, the *top of the heap,* from ἄκρον, *top,* and θίν, *heap.* The Greeks were accustomed, after a battle, to collect the spoils together, and throw them into a pile, and then, before they were distributed, to take off a portion from the top, and devote it to the gods (Xen. *Cyro.* 7. 5, 35; Herod. i. 86, 90; viii. 121, 122; Dion. Hal. ii.). In like manner it was customary to place the harvest in a heap, and, as the first thing, to take off a portion from the top to consecrate as a thank-offering to God. The word then came

to denote the *first-fruits* which were offered to God, and then the best of the spoils of battle. It has that sense here, and denotes the spoils or plunder which Abraham had taken of the discomfited kings.

5. *And verily they that are of the sons of Levi.* The meaning of this verse is, that the Levitical priests had a right to receive tithes of their brethren, but still that they were inferior to Melchisedec. The apostle admits that their superiority to the rest of the people was shown by the fact that they had a right to require of them the tenth part of the productions of the land for their maintenance, and for the support of religion. But still he says, that their inferiority to Melchisedec, and consequently to Christ as a priest, was shown by the fact that the illustrious ancestor of all the Jewish people, including the priests as well as others, had confessed *his* inferiority to Melchisedec by paying him tithes. ¶ *Who receive the office of the priesthood.* Not all the descendants of Levi were priests. The apostle, therefore, specifies particularly those who "received this office," as being those whom he specially designed, and as those whose inferiority to Christ as a priest it was his object to show. ¶ *Have a commandment to take tithes.* Have by the law a commission, or a right to exact tithes of the people, Deut. xiv. 22, 27–29.

6. *But he whose descent is not counted from them.* Melchisedec. The word *descent* is in the margin *pedigree.* The meaning is, that he was not *in the same genealogy*—μὴ γενεαλογούμενος—he was not of the order of Levitical priests. That Melchisedec is meant there can be no doubt; at the same

7 And without all contradiction the less is blessed of the better.

8 And here men that die receive tithes; but there he *receiveth them,* of whom *e* it is witnessed that he liveth.

e ch.5.6; Re.1.18.

time, also, the thought is presented with prominence on which Paul so much insists, that he was of a different order from the Levitical priesthood. ¶ *And blessed him.* Blessed him as a priest of God; blessed him in such a manner as to imply acknowledged superiority. See ver. 1. ¶ *That had the promises.* The promise that he should have a numerous posterity; that in him all the nations of the earth should be blessed. See chap. vi. 12–16.

7. *And without all contradiction.* It is an admitted principle, a point about which there can be no dispute. ¶ *The less is blessed of the better.* The act of pronouncing a blessing is understood to imply superiority of rank, age, or station. So when a father lays his hand on his children and blesses them, it is understood to be the act of one superior in age, venerableness, and authority; when a prophet pronounced a blessing on the people, the same thing was understood; and the same is true also when a minister of religion pronounces a blessing on a congregation. It is the act of one who is understood to sustain an office above the people on whom the blessing is pronounced. This was understood of the Saviour when parents brought their children to him to lay his hands on them and bless them (Mat. xix. 13); and the same was true of Jacob when, dying, he blessed the sons of Joseph, Heb. xi. 21; Gen. xlviii. 5–20. The word *less* here means the one of inferior rank; who is *less* in office, honour, or age. It does not imply inferiority of moral or religious character, for this is not the point under consideration. The word *better* means one who is of superior office or rank, not one who has necessarily a purer or holier character. That Melchisedec was thus superior to Abraham, Paul says, is implied by the very declaration that he "blessed him." It is also seen to be true by the whole comparison. Abraham was a petty prince; an *emir*—the head of

a company of nomads, or migratory shepherds, having, it is true, a large number of dependants, but still not having the rank here given to Melchisedec. Though called *a prophet* (Gen. xx. 7), yet he is nowhere called either *a priest* or *a king.* In these respects, it was undoubted that he was inferior to Melchisedec.

8. *And here men that die receive tithes.* Another point showing the inferiority of the Levitical priesthood. They who thus received tithes, though by the right to do this they asserted a superiority over their brethren, were mortal. Like others, they would soon die; and in regard to the most essential things they were on a level with their brethren. They had no exemption from sickness or bereavement, and death came to them with just as much certainty as he approached other men. The design of this statement here is to show the inferiority of their office by this fact. Its obvious and natural signification, in the apprehension of the great mass of readers, would not be, as the meaning has been supposed to be, that it refers "to the *brief* and *mutable* condition of the Levitical priesthood." See Stuart, *in loco.* Such an interpretation would not occur to anyone if it were not to avoid the difficulty existing in the correlative member of the verse, where it is said of Melchisedec that "he liveth." But is the difficulty avoided then? Is it not as difficult to understand what is meant by his having an *immutable* and *perpetual* priesthood, as it is to know what is meant by his not dying literally? Is the one any more true than the other? Whatever difficulties, therefore, there may be, we are bound to adhere to the obvious sense of the expression here; a sense which furnishes also a just and forcible ground of comparison. It seems to me, therefore, that the simple meaning of this passage is, that, under the Levitical economy,

those who received tithes were *mortal*, and were thus placed in strong contrast with him of whom it was said "he liveth." Thus they were inferior to him—as a mortal is inferior to one who does not die; and thus also they must be inferior to him who was made a priest after the "order" of him who thus "*lived.*" ¶ *But there.* In contrast with "here" in the same verse. The reference here is to the account of Melchisedec. "*Here,*" in the Levitical economy, men received tithes who are mortal; "*there,*" in the account of Melchisedec, the case is different. ¶ *He* receiveth them. Melchisedec—for so the connection evidently demands. ¶ *Of whom it is witnessed.* Of whom the record is. There is not in Genesis, indeed, any direct record that he *lives*, but there is the absence of a record that he *died*, and this seems to have been regarded as in fact a record of permanency in the office; or of his having an office which did not pass over to successors by the death of the then incumbent. ¶ *That he liveth.* This is an exceedingly difficult expression, and one which has always greatly perplexed commentators. The fair and obvious meaning is, that all the record that we have of Melchisedec is, that *he was* "*alive;*" or, as Grotius says, the record is *merely* that he lived. We have no mention of his death. From anything in the *record*, it might appear that he continued to live on, and did not die. *Arguing from the record*, therefore, there is a strong contrast between him and the Levitical priests, all of whom we know are mortal, ver. 23. The apostle is desirous of making out a contrast between them and the priesthood of Christ, *on this point* among others, and, in doing this, he appeals to the *record* in the Old Testament, and says that this was a case which furnished an intimation that the priestly office of the Messiah was not to pass over from him to others by death. The case was, that he was expressly compared (Ps. cx. 4) with Melchisedec, and that in the account of Melchisedec there is no record of his death. As to the *force* of this argument, it

must be admitted that it would strike a Jew more impressively than it does most readers now; and it may not be improbable that the apostle was reasoning from some interpretation of the passages in Gen. xiv. and Ps. cx. which was then prevalent, and which would then be conceded on all hands to be correct. If this was the admitted interpretation, and if there is no equivocation, or mere *trick* in the reasoning—as there cannot be shown to be—why should we not allow to the Jew a peculiarity of reasoning as we do to all other people? There are modes of reasoning and illustration in all nations, in all societies, and in all professions, which do not strike others as very forcible. The ancient philosophers had methods of reasoning which now seem weak to us; the lawyer often argues in a way which appears to be a mere quirk or quibble; and so the lecturer in science sometimes reasons. The cause of this may not be always that there is *real* quibble or *quirk* in the mode of argumentation, but that he who reasons in this manner has in his view certain points which he regards as undisputed which do not appear so to us; or that he argues from what is admitted in the profession, or in the school where he is taught, which are not understood by those whom he addresses. To this should be added also the consideration, that Paul had a constant reference to the Messiah, and that it is possible that in his mind there was here a transition from the type to the antitype, and that the language which he uses may be stronger than if he had been speaking of the *mere* record of Melchisedec if he had found it standing by itself. Still his reasoning turns mainly on the fact that in the case of Melchisedec there was no one who had preceded him in that office, and that he had no successor, and that, *in regard to the matter in hand*, it was all the same as if he had been a perpetual priest, or *had continued still alive.*

[The reasoning in the whole passage is founded on the Scripture account of Melchisedec. He is not to be regarded *absolutely*, but *typically*. View him just as he appears

9 And as I may so say, Levi also, who receiveth tithes, paid tithes in Abraham.

10 For he was yet in the loins of his father, when Melchisedec met him.

in the record in Genesis and the difficulty will be greatly lessened, if it do not altogether disappear. *There* he is presented to us in his typical character as *living*. All notice of his death is studiously omitted, with the express design, that, appearing *only* as a living priest, he might the better typify our immortal Redeemer. In this view, which indeed is so well brought out in the commentary above, "the apostle's argument unto the dignity and preeminence of Melchisedec above the Levitical priests in this instance is of an *unquestionable evidence*. For, consider Melchisedec, not in his natural being and existence, which belongs not unto this mystery, but in his Scripture being and existence, and he is immortal, always living, wherein he is more excellent than those who were always obnoxious to death in the exercise of their office" (Owen). M'Knight, observing that the Greek verb ζῇ here is not in the present, but the imperfect of the indicative, translates *lived*—a PRIEST ALL HIS LIFE, in contradistinction from those who ceased to be priests at a certain age. But whatever view may be taken of the passage, whatever solution of the difficulty may be adopted, apology for the mode of reasoning may well be spared. An inspired writer needs it not. All his reasoning has, doubtless, a solid basis in truth. It is impossible he should proceed on any peculiarities or modes of reasoning but such as are strictly true, the accuracy of which might anywhere and at any time be admitted by those who had the means and patience for a right understanding of them.]

9. *And as I may so say.* So to speak —ὡς ἔπος εἰπεῖν. For numerous examples in the classic writers of this expression, see Wetstein, *in loco.* It is used precisely as it is with us when we say "so to speak," or "if I may be allowed the expression." It is employed when what is said is not strictly and literally true, but when it amounts to the same thing, or when about the same idea is conveyed. "It is a *softening down* of an expression which a writer supposes his readers may deem too strong, or which may have the appearance of excess or severity. It amounts to an indirect apology for employing an unusual or unexpected assertion or phrase" (Prof. Stuart). Here Paul could not mean that Levi had actually paid tithes

in Abraham—for he had not then an existence; or that Abraham was his representative—for there had been no appointment of Abraham to act in that capacity by Levi; or that the act of Abraham was imputed or reckoned to Levi — for that was not true, and would not have been pertinent to the case if it were so. But it means that, in the circumstances of the case, the same thing occurred in regard to the superiority of Melchisedec, and the inferiority of the Levitical priesthood, which would have occurred *if* Levi had been present with Abraham, and had himself actually paid tithes on that occasion. This was so because Abraham was the distinguished ancestor of Levi, and when an ancestor has done an act implying inferiority of rank to another, we feel as if the whole family, or all the descendants, by that act recognized the inferiority, unless something occurs to change the relative rank of the persons. Here nothing indicating any such change had occurred. Melchisedec had no descendants of which mention is made, and the act of Abraham, as the head of the Hebrew race, stood therefore as if it were the act of all who descended from him. ¶ *Levi.* The ancestor of the whole Levitical priesthood, and from whom they received their name. He was the third son of Jacob and Leah, and was born in Mesopotamia. On account of the conduct of Simeon and Levi toward Shechem, for the manner in which he had treated their sister Dinah (Gen. xxxiv. 25), and which Jacob characterized as "cruelty" (Gen. xlix. 5, 6), Jacob said that they should be "scattered in Israel," Gen. xlix. 7. Afterward the whole tribe of Levi was chosen by God to execute the various functions of the priesthood, and was "scattered" over the land, having no inheritance of its own, but deriving its subsistence from the offerings of the people, Num. iii. 6, seq. Levi is here spoken of as the ancestor of the

tribe, or collectively to denote the entire Jewish priesthood. ¶ *Who receiveth tithes.* That is, his descendants, the priests and Levites, receive tithes. ¶ *Paid tithes in Abraham.* It is the same as if he had paid tithes in or by Abraham.

10. *For he was yet in the loins of his father.* Abraham is here called the *father* of Levi, by a common use of the word, referring to a more remote ancestor than the literal father. The meaning of the apostle is, that he was *even then,* in a certain sense, in the loins of Abraham, when Melchisedec met him; or it was all the same as if he were there, and had then an existence. The relation which subsisted between him and Abraham, in the circumstances of the case, implied the same thing *as if* he had then been born, and had acted for himself by paying tithes. Instances of this occur constantly. A father sells a farm, to which his son would be heir, and it is the same as if the son had sold it. He has no more control over it than if he had been present and disposed of it himself. A father acknowledges fealty to a government for a certain title or property which is to descend to his heirs, and it is all one as if the heir had himself done it; and it is not improper to say that it is the same as if he had been there and acted for himself. For some valuable remarks on the nature of the reasoning here employed, see Stuart on the Hebrews, Excursus xiv. The reasoning here is, indeed, especially such as would be fitted to impress a Jewish mind, and perhaps more forcibly than it does ours. The Jews valued themselves on the dignity and honour of the Levitical priesthood, and it was important to show them, on their own principles, and according to their own sacred writings, that the great ancestor of all the Levitical community had himself acknowledged his inferiority to one who was declared also in their own writings (Ps. cx.) to be like the Messiah, or who was of the same "order." At the same time, the reasoning concedes nothing false, and conveys no wrong impression. It is not mere fancy or accommodation, nor is

it framed on allegorical or cabalistic principles. It is founded in truth, and is such as might be used in any case where regard was shown to pedigree, or where respect was claimed on account of the illustrious deeds of an ancestor. It would be regarded as sound reasoning in a country like England, where titles and ranks are recognized, and where various orders of nobility exist. The fact that a remote ancestor had done homage or fealty to the ancestor of another class of titled birth, would be regarded as proof of acknowledged inferiority in the family, and might be used with force and propriety in an argument. Paul has done no more than this.

[Several excellent and evangelical commentators explain the passage on the principle of *representation*, the admission of which relieves it from many difficulties. If we allow that Abraham was the representative of his seed, and of the sons of Levi among the number, then they unquestionably may be said to have paid tithes in him in a most obvious and intelligible sense. That Abraham is to be here regarded as not only the natural but covenant head of Israel, is argued from what is said in ver. 6 of his having "had the promises," which promises manifestly did not belong to him alone, but to him and to his seed, Gen. xvii. 4–9. The land of Canaan never *was* actually given to Abraham. He obtained the promise or grant of it as the representative of his posterity, who came to its enjoyment when four hundred years had expired. By those who adopt this view the passage is supposed to contain an illustration of the manner in which Adam and Christ represent those who respectively belong to them. And here let it be noticed, that the objection against Abraham's representative character, grounded by our author on the fact "that there had been no appointment of Abraham to act in that capacity by Levi," might with equal force be urged against the representation of Adam and Christ, which the reader will find established in the Supplementary Notes on Rom. v. As to the force of the argument on this principle there can be no doubt. If the representative, the covenant as well as the natural head, of the sons of Levi, paid tithes and acknowledged inferiority to Melchisedec, their inferiority follows as a matter of course. They are supposed to be comprehended in their head. "This," says Mr. Scott, "*incontestably proved* the inferiority of the Levitical priesthood to that of the Messiah, nay, its absolute dependence on him and subserviency to him," and,

11 If therefore perfection were
by the Levitical priesthood, (for
under it the people received the
law,) what further need *was there*
that another priest should rise after

f Ga.2.21; ver.18,19; ch.8.7.

---

the order of Melchisedec, and not be
called after the order of Aaron?

12 For the priesthood being
changed, there is made of necessity a change also of the law.

[we may add, is sound reasoning, alike in every
country—in Palestine and in ours, in England
or America. On the whole we cannot but think
that, whatever difficulties some may have in
admitting the principle of representation here,
far greater difficulties lie on the other side.
Even Prof. Stuart, in his celebrated 14th Excursus (which for ingenuity deserves, perhaps,
all the praise awarded by Bloomfield, Barnes,
and others), resolves the apostle's reasoning
into a mere *argumentum ad hominem*, although
in the passage there is no *evidence* of any such
thing. He has indeed instanced two cases of
argumentum ad hominem, or rather two passages, in both of which the same example occurs, Mat. xii. 27; Luke xi. 19. But if the
reader consult these passages he will find that
mistake is impossible. The plainest indication is given that the argument proceeds on
the principle of an adversary. It would require no small ingenuity, however, to press this
passage into the same rank with those now
quoted. It clearly belongs to a different class,
and the apostle proceeds with his argument,
without the slightest indication that it was
grounded rather on what was admitted than
on what was strictly true.]

11. *If therefore perfection were by the
Levitical priesthood.* As the Jews supposed. They were accustomed to regard the system as perfect. It was an
appointment of God, and they were
tenacious of the opinion that it was
to be permanent, and that it needed
no change. But Paul says that this
could not be. Even from their own
Scriptures it was apparent that a
priest was to arise of another order,
and of a more permanent character,
and this he says was full proof that
there was *defect* of some kind in the
previous arrangement. What this defect was he does not here specify, but
the subsequent reasoning shows that
it was in such points as these: that
it was not permanent; that it could
not make the worshippers perfect;
that the blood which they offered in
sacrifice could not take away sin, and
could not render those who offered
it holy. Comp. ver. 19, 23, 24; chap.

x. 1–4. ¶ *For under it the people received the law.* This assertion seems
necessary in order to establish the
point maintained in ver. 12, that if
the priesthood is changed there must
be also a change of the law. In order
to this, it was necessary to admit that
the law was *received* under that economy, and that *it was a part of it*, so
that the change of one involved also
the change of the other. It was not
strictly true that the whole law was
given *after* the various orders of Levitical priests were established—for
the law on Sinai, and several other
laws, were given before that distinct
arrangement was made; but it was
true (1) that a considerable part of
the laws of Moses were given under
that arrangement; and (2) that *all*
the ceremonial observances were connected with that. They were parts
of one system, and were mutually dependent on each other. This is all
that the argument demands. ¶ *What
further need* was there, &c. "If that
system would lead to perfection; if it
was sufficient to make the conscience
pure, and to remove sin, then there
was no necessity of any other. Yet
the Scriptures have declared that there
would be another of a different order,
implying that there was some defect
in the former." This reasoning is
founded on the fact that there was
an express prediction of the coming
of a priest of a different "order"
(Ps. cx. 4), and that this fact implied
that there was some deficiency in the
former arrangement. To this reasoning it is impossible to conceive that
there can be any objection.

12. *For the priesthood being changed.*
According to the prediction in Ps.
cx., that it would be. When that occurs, the consequence specified must
also follow. ¶ *There is made of necessity a change also of the law.* The law
so far as it grew out of that, or was
dependent on it. The connection re-

13 For he of whom these things are spoken pertaineth to another tribe, of which no man gave attendance at the altar.

14 For *it is* evident that *g*our Lord sprang out of Juda; of which

tribe Moses spake nothing concerning priesthood.

15 And it is yet far more evident: for that after the similitude of Melchisedec there ariseth another priest,

g Is.11.1; Mat.1.3; Re.5.5.

quires us to understand it *only* of the law *so far as it was connected with the Levitical priesthood.* This could not apply to the ten commandments—for they were given *before* the institution of the priesthood; nor could it apply to any other part of the moral law — for that was not dependent on the appointment of the Levitical priests. But the meaning is, that since a large number of laws—constituting a code of considerable extent and importance—was given for the regulation of the priesthood, and in reference to the rites of religion, which they were to observe or superintend, it followed that when they were superseded in their office *by one of a wholly different order,* the law which had regulated *them* vanished also, or ceased to be binding. This was a very important point in the introduction of Christianity, and hence it is that it is so often insisted on in the writings of Paul. The *argument* to show that there had been a change or transfer of the priestly office, he proceeds to establish in the sequel.

13. *For he of whom these things are spoken.* The Lord Jesus, the Messiah, to whom they had reference. The *things* here spoken of pertain to his office as priest; to his being of the order of Melchisedec. The apostle here *assumes* it as a point concerning which there could be no dispute, that these things referred to the Lord Jesus. Those whom he addressed would not be disposed to call this in question, and his argument had conducted him to this conclusion. ¶ *Pertaineth to another tribe.* To the tribe of Judah, ver. 14. ¶ *Of which no man gave attendance at the altar.* The priestly office pertained only to the tribe of Levi. No one of the tribe of Judah had any part in the performance of

the duties of that office. This was settled by the Jewish law.

14. *For* it is *evident that our Lord sprang out of Juda.* It is well known; it cannot be a matter of dispute. About the fact that the Lord Jesus was of the tribe of Judah there could be no doubt. Comp. Mat. i. 3. But probably the apostle means here to refer to more than that simple fact. It was a doctrine of the Old Testament, and was admitted by the Jews, that the Messiah was to be of that tribe. See Gen. xlix. 10; Isa. xi. 1; Mic. v. 2; Mat. ii. 6. This was an additional consideration to show that there was to be a change of some kind in the office of the priesthood, since it was declared (Ps. cx.) that the Messiah was to be a *priest.* The fact that the Messiah is to be of the tribe of Judah is still admitted by the Jews. As their distinction of tribes now, however, is broken up, and as it is impossible for them to tell who belongs to the tribe of Judah, it is held by them that when he comes this will be made known *by miracle.* ¶ *Of which tribe Moses spake nothing concerning priesthood.* That is, in the Mosaic laws respecting the office of priest, this tribe is not mentioned. All the arrangements pertain to the tribe of Levi.

15. *And it is yet far more evident.* Not that our Lord would spring out of Judah, but the point which he was endeavouring to establish, that there must be a change of the priesthood, was rendered still more evident from another consideration. A strong proof of the necessity of such a change of the priesthood was furnished by the fact that the Messiah was to be of the tribe of Judah; but a much stronger because *as a priest* he was to be of the order of Melchisedec; that is, he was of the same rank with one who did not even belong to that tribe. ¶ *Af-*

16 Who is made, not after the law of a carnal commandment, but after the power of an endless life.

17 For he testifieth, *h* Thou *art* a priest for ever after the order of Melchisedec.

18 For there is verily a disan-

h Ps.110.4.

nulling of the commandment going before for the *i* weakness and unprofitableness thereof.

19 For *k* the law made nothing perfect, [3] but the bringing in of a better hope *did; l* by the which we draw nigh unto God.

i Ac.13.39.   *k* Ro.3.20.   [3] or, *but it* was.   *l* Ro.5.2.

ter the similitude. Resembling; that is, he was to be of the order of Melchisedec.

16. *Who is made.* That is, the other priest is made—to wit, the Messiah. He was made a priest by a peculiar law. ¶ *Not after the law of a carnal commandment.* Not according to the law of a commandment pertaining to the flesh. The word *carnal* means *fleshly;* and the idea is, that the law under which the priests of the old dispensation were made was external, rather than spiritual; it related more to outward observances than to the keeping of the heart. That this was the nature of the Mosaic ritual, in the main, it was impossible to doubt, and the apostle proceeds to argue from this undeniable truth. ¶ *But after the power of an endless life.* By an authority of endless duration. That is, it was not concerned mainly with outward observances, and did not pass over from one to another by death, but was unchanging in its character, and spiritual in its nature. It was enduring and perpetual as a priesthood, and was thus exalted far above the service performed by the priests under the former dispensation.

17. *For he testifieth.* "That this is the true account of it, is proved by the testimony of God himself that he was to be a priest *for ever.*" See Notes on chap. v. 6.

18. *For there is verily a disannulling.* A setting aside. The law which existed before in regard to the priesthood becomes now abrogated in consequence of the change which has been made in the priesthood. See Notes on ver. 12. ¶ *Of the commandment.* Relating to the office of priest, or to the ceremonial rites in general. This does not refer to the *moral* law, as if that was abrogated, for (1) the

reasoning of the apostle does not pertain to that; and (2) that law cannot be abrogated. It grows out of the nature of things, and must be perpetual and universal. ¶ *Going before.* Going before the Christian dispensation, and introducing it. ¶ *For the weakness and unprofitableness thereof.* That is, it was not adapted to save man; it had not power to accomplish what was necessary to be done in human salvation. It answered the end for which it was designed—that of introducing a more perfect plan, and then vanished as a matter of course. It did not expiate guilt; it did not give peace to the conscience; it did not produce perfection (ver. 11), and therefore it gave place to a better system.

19. *For the law made nothing perfect.* The Levitical, ceremonial law. It did not produce a perfect state; it did not do what was desirable to be done for a sinner. See Notes on ver. 11. That law, as such, did not reconcile man to God; it did not make an atonement; it did not put away guilt; in one word, *it did not restore things to the condition in which they were before the law was broken and man became a sinner.* If men were saved under that system—as many undoubtedly were —it was not in virtue of any intrinsic efficacy which it possessed, but in virtue of that great sacrifice which it typified. ¶ *But the bringing in of a better hope* did. Margin, "*but* it was." The correct rendering is, probably, "but there is the bringing in of a better hope, by which we have access to God." The law could not effect this. It left the conscience guilty, and sin unexpiated. But there is now the introduction of a better system by which we can approach a reconciled God. The "better hope" here refers

20 And inasmuch as not without an oath *he was made priest:*

21 (For those priests were made without [4]an oath; but this with an oath by him that said unto him,

[4] or, *swearing of an oath.*

*m*The Lord sware and will not repent, Thou *art* a priest for ever after the order of Melchisedec:)

22 By so much was Jesus made a surety of a [n]better testament.

m Ps.110.4. *n* ch.8.6.

---

to the more sure and certain expectation of heaven introduced by the gospel. There is a better foundation for hope; a more certain way of obtaining the divine favour, than the law could furnish. ¶ *By the which.* By which better hope; that is, by means of the ground of hope furnished by the gospel—to wit, that God is now reconciled, and that we can approach him with the assurance that he is ready to save us. ¶ *We draw nigh unto God.* We have access to him. See Notes on Rom. v. 1, 2.

20. *And inasmuch as not without an oath.* In addition to every other consideration showing the superiority of Christ as a priest, there was the solemnity of the oath by which he was set apart to the office. The appointment of one to the office of priest by an oath, such as occurred in the case of Jesus, was much more solemn and important than where the office was received merely by descent.

21. *For those priests were made without an oath.* The Levitical priests were set apart and consecrated without their office being confirmed to them by an oath on the part of God. They received it by regular descent, and when they arrived at a suitable age they entered on it of course. Jesus received *his* office by special appointment, and it was secured to him by an oath. The word rendered "*oath*" is in the margin *swearing of an oath.* This is the proper meaning of the Greek word, but the sense is not materially varied. ¶ *But this with an oath.* This priest, the Lord Jesus, became a priest in virtue of an oath. ¶ *The Lord sware.* See Notes on chap. vi. 13. The reference here is to Ps. cx. 4, "The Lord hath sworn." ¶ *And will not repent.* That is, *will not regret,* or *will not alter his mind through regret*—for this is the meaning of the Greek word.

22. *By so much.* Inasmuch as an oath is more solemn than a mere appointment. The meaning is, that there is the additional security in the suretyship of Jesus which arises from the solemnity of an oath. It is not implied that God would not be true to a mere promise, but the argument here is derived from the custom of speaking among men. An oath is regarded as much more sacred and binding than a mere promise, and the fact that God has *sworn* in a given case furnishes the highest security that what he has promised will be performed. ¶ *Was Jesus made a surety.* The word *surety*—ἔγγυος—occurs nowhere else in the New Testament, nor is it found in the Septuagint. It properly means, a bondsman; one who pledges his name, his property, or his influence, that a certain thing shall be done. When a contract is made, a debt contracted, or a note given, a friend often becomes the *security* in the case, and is himself responsible if the terms of the contract are not complied with. In the case of the new covenant between God and man, Jesus is the "security" or the bondsman. But of what, and to whom, is he the surety? It cannot be that he is a bondsman *for God* that he will maintain the covenant, and be true to the promise which he makes, as Crellius supposes, for we need no such "security" of the divine faithfulness and veracity. It cannot be that he becomes responsible for the divine conduct in any way, for no such responsibility is needed or possible. But it must mean that he is the security or bondsman in relation to man. He is the pledge that we shall be saved. He becomes responsible, so to speak, to law and justice, that no injury shall be done by our salvation, though we are sinners. He has not pledged himself, or become our "security" that

we shall be saved *at anyrate*, without holiness, repentance, faith, or true religion—for he never could enter into a suretyship of that kind; but his suretyship extends to this point, that the law shall be honoured; that all its demands shall be met; that we may be saved though we have violated it; and that its terrific penalty shall not fall upon us. The case is this:—A sinner becomes a true penitent and enters heaven. It might be said that he does this over a broken law; that God treats the good and bad alike; and that no respect has been paid to the law, or to its penalty, in his salvation. Here the Great Surety comes in, and says that it is not so. *He* has become responsible for this; he himself is the surety, the pledge, that all proper honour shall be paid to justice, and that the same good effects shall ensue as if the penalty of the law had been fully borne by the sinner himself. He has died to honour the law, and to open a way by which its penalty may be remitted consistently with justice, and he becomes *the everlasting pledge* or *security* to law, to justice, to the universe, that no injury shall result from the pardon and salvation of the sinner. According to this view, no man can rely on the suretyship of Jesus but he who expects salvation on the terms which he has prescribed in his gospel. The suretyship is not that he shall be saved in his sins, or that he shall enter heaven, no matter what life he leads; it is only that *if* he believes, repents, and enters heaven, no injury shall be done to the universe, no dishonour to the law. For this the Lord Jesus became responsible. ¶ *Of a better testament.* Rather, " of a better *covenant.*" The former covenant was that which God made with his people under the Mosaic dispensation; the new covenant is that made by means of Christ. This is *better*, because (1) the terms are more simple and easy; (2) the observances and rites are less onerous and hard; (3) it relates to all men, not being confined to the Jewish people; (4) it is sure; (5) the former was administered through the instrumentality of the Levitical priesthood, this

by the Son of God; (6) that was transitory and changing, this is permanent and eternal.

[The word rendered " surety " is εγγυος. It occurs, indeed, here only in the New Testament, nor is it found in the Septuagint, *i.e.* the *very word* is not. Yet its derivatives occur there, and bear the sense that is ordinarily and everywhere expressed by suretyship, Prov. xvii. 18; xxii. 26, and other places. The word itself, too, is found in the Apocrypha, Ecclus. xxix. 15; 2 Mac. x. 28, on which last passage a recent and distinguished writer observes: " We find the word (here) conveying the idea of a covenant engagement, and that, too, on the part of the Most High. When the Jews joined battle with Timotheus they are said to have had the Great God for their εγγυος, assuring them of victory. They had prostrated themselves before the altar; they had spread ashes upon their heads and covered themselves with sackcloth; they had poured out their hearts in prayer, pleading with the Most High, and putting him in mind of his promise—the promise in which he had said that he would be an enemy to their enemies—then, seizing their arms and advancing to meet Timotheus, they rushed into the fight, we are told, εγγυον εχοντες ευημεριας και νικης." Indeed, about the meaning of the word and the accuracy of our English translation there can be no doubt. Critics who are very far from admitting the doctrine of Christ's suretyship in the covenant of redemption have freely admitted this. See Peirce on the place.

What then is the sense of the word here? Applied to Christ will it bear its ordinary sense or not? Is he a surety in a sense analogous to that in which men are sureties? Hesitating to answer these questions in the affirmative, a host of commentators, following the Greeks, have observed that εγγυος is substituted for and equivalent to μεσιτης, occurring at chap. viii. 6; ix. 15; xii. 24. But because Christ is called in these places the μεσιτης or mediator of the covenant, it does not follow that εγγυος here has *precisely* the same sense. Or if so, how shall we account for the introduction of this singular word at all? Why was not μεσιτης employed here as in other places in the epistle? This has, indeed, been accounted for by observing, that as the apostle in the 19th verse had used the word εγγιζομεν, we draw near, he employed εγγυος in the 22d for the sake of the *paronomasia*, to which figure he is alleged to have been much attached. But in whatever way the apostle may have been led to the use of the word (and the above account is probable enough), he never would have used it in a sense altogether different from that which ordinarily is attached to it out of fondness for any figure whatever. " A surety has to pay that which they owe for whom he is en-

23 And they truly were many priests, because they were not suffered to continue by reason of death:

gaged; to do what is to be done by them which they cannot perform. *And if this be not the notion of a surety in this place, the apostle makes use of a word, nowhere else used in the whole Scripture, to teach us that which it doth never signify among men, which is improbable and absurd.* For the sole reason why he did make use of it was, that from the nature and notion of it among men, in other cases, we may understand the signification of it, and what, under that name, he ascribes unto the Lord Jesus" (Owen).

Having thus proved that ἔγγυος is properly translated "surety," and that Christ is so styled, in a sense not widely different from that which is usually attached to the word, let us next inquire how Christ discharges this suretyship, or what he does in his capacity of surety. *Is he surety to us for God?* This last question, by orthodox writers, is for the most part answered in the negative, on the ground that there can be no need of security for God, his *promise* and his *oath* being sufficient guarantee that he will fulfil his engagement, on the ground also that a surety must be someone greater than the party for whom he engages, which, in the case of God, renders the thing impossible, since there is none greater than He. Thus Dr. Owen has argued at great length, and is followed by Guyse, Boston, and many others. Yet there are not wanting writers of great reputation for learning and orthodoxy who scruple not to say that Christ is surety *for God.* (See Mr. Scott on this place.) He undertook, on the part of the Father, that all the promises should be made good to the seed. He acts in the behalf of God towards us, and assures us of the divine favour. "If it be asked, What need was there of a mediator to assure us of the fulfilment of the promises made by the God of truth, who cannot lie or deceive us? I answer, The same objection might be made against God's adding his oath to his promise, whereby he intended to give us the greater security of accomplishment" (Peirce). The exclusion of this idea from the suretyship of Christ on the part of so many divines doubtless arose from the improper use made of it by Socinians, who, unwilling to admit that Christ had become bound for our debt of suffering and obedience, and in this sense was surety *for us,* resolved the suretyship into a mere engagement *in behalf of God.* They could not allow more without allowing the atonement. While, however, we see no necessity for discarding this idea because it has been used for bad purposes, we maintain that this is neither all nor even the principal part of the suretyship of Christ. Revert to the original notion of a surety. He is one who engages in behalf of another to pay a debt or discharge a duty which that other may fail to pay or discharge. Christ engaged to stand in that relation toward us, and therefore he is the *surety for us to God* that our debt shall be discharged. God the Father, on his part, engages that Christ shall see his seed, that they shall be saved; and the Son of God, on his part, becomes bound for the debt of penalty and obedience. This is the covenant of redemption, "the counsel of peace" between the Father and the Son before all worlds, Zec. vi. 13; Isa. liii. 10, 12. It is unnecessary farther to observe that Christ, in his capacity of surety, has nobly redeemed his pledge, endured the penalty, and honoured the precept of the broken law, and thereby secured for his people the blessings of the covenant.

Before concluding this Note we may remark that some difference of opinion exists among those who hold the suretyship of Christ in reference to another question, viz. whether he became surety for the faith, repentance, and evangelical obedience of his people. "I answer," says Thomas Boston, "though the elect's believing, repenting, and sincere obedience are infallibly secured in the covenant, yet I judge that Christ did not become surety in the covenant, in way of caution to his Father, that the elect should perform these deeds or any other. These belong rather to the promissory part of the covenant. *They are benefits promised in the covenant* BY GOD UNTO CHRIST, the surety, as a reward of his fulfilling the condition of the covenant. And so they are, by the unchangeable truth of God and his exact justice, ensured beyond all possibility of failure, Ps. xxii. 27, 30, 31; cx. 3; Isa. liii. 10, with ver. 1; Ezek. xxxiv. 26, 27, 31; Heb. viii. 10, 11" (Boston *On the Covenant of Grace;* see also Dr. Dick's admirable lectures on the same subject).

It will be seen from this review of the suretyship of Christ that the sentiments of our author on the subject are not materially different from those of evangelical divines in Scotland. He may not use the same phraseology, but "security to the law, to justice, to the universe, that no injury shall result from the pardon of the sinner," is much the same with "surety to God for us," that our debt shall be discharged, *i.e.* that none of these interests shall suffer.]

23. *And they truly.* Under the Jewish dispensation. The object of this verse and the following is, to state one more reason of the excellence of

24 But this *man*, because he continueth ever, hath [5]an [o]unchangeable priesthood.

25 Wherefore he is [p]able also to save them [6]to the uttermost that come unto God by him, seeing he ever liveth [q]to make intercession for them.

26 For such an high priest be-

[5] or, *which passeth not from one to another*.
o 1 Sa.2.35. p Jude 24.

[6] or, *evermore*. q Ro.8.34; 1 Jn.2.1.

the priesthood of Christ. It is, that owing to the frailty of human nature, and the shortness of life, the office of priest there was continually changing. But here there was no such change. Christ, being exalted to the heavens to live for ever there, has now an unchangeable priesthood, and everything in regard to his office is permanent.

24. *But this* man. Greek, "But he"—referring to Christ. ¶ *Because he continueth ever.* Greek, "because he remains for ever." The idea is, because he does not die, but ever lives, he has an unchanging priesthood. There is no necessity that he should yield it to others, as was the case with the Jewish priests because they were mortal. The reason, in their case, why it passed to others, was not that they did not perform the office well, but that they were *mortal*, and could not continue to hold it. But this reason could not operate in the case of the Lord Jesus, and therefore his priesthood would be permanent. ¶ *Hath an unchangeable priesthood.* Margin, "or, *which passeth not from one to another*." The margin expresses the sense of the passage. The idea is not strictly that it was *unchangeable*, but that *it did not pass over into other hands.* The Levitical priesthood passed from one to another as successive generations came on the stage of action. This reasoning is not designed to prove that the priesthood of Christ will be literally *eternal*—for its necessity may cease when all the redeemed are in heaven—but that it is permanent, and does not pass from hand to hand.

25. *Wherefore he is able also.* As he ever lives, and ever intercedes, he has power to save. He does not begin the work of salvation, and then relinquish it by reason of death, but he lives on as long as it is necessary that anything should be done for the salvation of his people. We need a Saviour who has *power*, and Christ has shown that he has all the power which is necessary to rescue man from eternal death. ¶ *To the uttermost.* This does not mean simply *for ever*—but that he has power to save them so that their salvation will be *complete*—εἰς τὸ παντελὲς. He does not abandon the work midway; he does not begin a work which he is unable to finish. He will aid us *as long* as we need anything done for our salvation; he will save *all* who will intrust their salvation to his hands. Comp. Phil. i. 6. ¶ *That come unto God by him.* In his name; or depending on him. To come to God is to approach him for pardon and salvation. ¶ *Seeing he ever liveth.* He does not die as the Jewish priests did. ¶ *To make intercession for them.* See Notes on Rom. viii. 34. He constantly presents the merits of his death as a reason why *we* should be saved. The precise mode, however, in which he makes intercession in heaven for his people is not revealed. The *general* meaning is, that he undertakes their cause, and assists them in overcoming their foes, and in their endeavours to live a holy life. Comp. 1 Jn. ii. 1. He does in heaven whatever is necessary to obtain for us grace and strength; he secures the aid which we need against our foes; and he is the *pledge* or *security* for us that the law shall be honoured, and the justice and truth of God maintained, though we are saved. It is reasonable to presume that this is somehow by the presentation of the merits of his great sacrifice, and that *that* is the ground on which all this grace is obtained. As that is infinite, we need not fear that it will ever be exhausted.

26. *For such an high priest became us.* Was fitted to our condition. That is, there was that in our character and

came us, *who is* ^rholy, harmless, undefiled, separate from sinners, and made higher than the heavens; 27 Who needeth not daily, as

r ch.4.15; 1 Pe.2.22.

those high priests, to offer up sacrifice, *^sfirst for his own sins, and then for the people's: for this he did once, when he offered up himself.

s Le.9.7.

---

circumstances which required that a high-priest for us should be personally holy. It was not necessary merely that he should have great power; or that he should be of a rank superior to that of the Jewish priesthood; but there was a special propriety that he should surpass all others in *moral* purity. Other priests were mere mortal men, and it was necessary that their office should pass to other hands; they were *sinful* men also, and it was necessary that sacrifices should be made for themselves as well as others. We need, however, a different priest. We need not only one who ever lives, but one who is perfectly holy, and who has no need to bring an offering for himself — one, therefore, all the merit of whose sacrifice may be ours. Such an high-priest we have in the person of the Lord Jesus; and there is no truth more interesting, and no proposition more susceptible of proof, than that HE IS EXACTLY FITTED TO MAN. In his moral character, and in the great work which he has accomplished, he is just such a Saviour as is adapted to the wants of ignorant, fallen, wretched, sinful man. He is benevolent, and pities our woes; wise, and is able to enlighten our ignorance; compassionate, and ready to forgive our faults. He has made such a sacrifice as was necessary to put away our guilt, and he offers such intercession as we need to have offered for us in order that we may be preserved from falling. ¶ *Who is holy.* Not merely *outwardly* righteous, but pure in heart. ¶ *Harmless.* Not injuring anyone. To no one did he do wrong. Neither to their name, person, or property did he ever do injury; nor will he ever. He is the only one who has lived on earth of whom it could be said that he never, in any way, did wrong to another. ¶ *Undefiled.* By sin; by any improper desire or passion. He was unstained by crime;

"unspotted from the world." Sin always defiles the soul; but from every such pollution the Lord Jesus was free. ¶ *Separate from sinners.* That is, he did not associate with them *as such.* He did not partake of their feelings, their plans, their pleasures. Though he mingled with them, yet it was merely to do them good, and in all his life there was an entire separation from the feelings, the principles, and the views of a sinful world. ¶ *And made higher than the heavens.* Exalted above the visible heavens; that is, at the right hand of God. See Notes on Eph. i. 21; Phil. ii. 9. We need a high-priest who is thus exalted, that he may manage our cause before the throne of God.

27. *Who needeth not daily, as those high priests.* As the Jewish high-priests. This is an additional circumstance introduced to show the superior excellency of the High-priest of the Christian profession, and to show also how he was fitted to our wants. The Jewish high-priest was a sinful man. He had the same fallen and corrupt nature as others. He needed an expiatory sacrifice for his own sins as really as they did for theirs. When he approached God to offer sacrifice, it was needful to make an atonement for himself, and when all was done it was still a sacrifice offered by a sinful man. But it was not so in the case of Jesus. He was so holy that he needed no sacrifice for himself, and *all* that he did was in behalf of others. Besides, it was necessary that the sacrifices in the Jewish service should be constantly repeated. They were imperfect. They were mere types and shadows. They who offered them were frail, sinful men. It became indispensable, therefore, to repeat them every day to keep up the proper sense of their transgressions, and to furnish a suitable acknowledgment of the tendency to

28 For the law maketh men high priests which have infirmity; but the word of the oath, which was

since the law, *maketh* the Son, who is ⁷consecrated for evermore.

7 or, *perfected.*

sin alike among the people and the priests. Neither in the nature of the offering, nor in the character of those who made it, was there any sufficient reason why it should *cease* to be offered, and it was therefore repeated day by day. But it was not so with the Lord Jesus. The offering which he made, though presented but *once,* was so ample and perfect that it had sufficient merit for all the sins of the world, and needed never to be repeated. It is not probable that the Jewish high-priest himself *personally* officiated at the offering of sacrifice every day; but the meaning here is, that it was *done* daily, and that there was *need* of a daily sacrifice in his behalf. As one of the Jewish people, the sacrifice was offered on his account as well as on the account of others—for he partook of the common infirmities and sinfulness of the nation. ¶ *For this he did once.* That is, once for all— ἐφάπαξ. He made such an atonement that it was not needful that it should be repeated. Thus he put an end to sacrifice, for when he made the great atonement it was complete, and there was no need that any more blood should be shed for human guilt.

28. *For the law.* The ceremonial law. ¶ *Which have infirmity.* Who are weak, frail, sinful, dying. Such were all who were appointed to the office of priest under the Jewish law. ¶ *But the word of the oath.* By which one was appointed after the order of Melchisedec. See Notes on ver. 21. ¶ *Maketh the Son.* The Son of God. That appointment has resulted in his being set apart to this work. ¶ *Who is consecrated for evermore.* Margin, *perfected.* See Notes on chap. ii. 10. The idea is, that the appointment is *complete* and *permanent.* It does not pass from one to the other. It is now perfect in all the arrangements; it will remain so for ever.

REMARKS.

The subject of this chapter is the exalted high-priesthood of the Re-

deemer. This is a subject which pertains to all Christians, and to all men. All religions contain the idea of a priestly office; all suppose sacrifice of some kind. In regard to the priestly office of Christ as illustrated in this chapter, we may observe,

(1) He stands alone. In that office he had no predecessor, and has no one to succeed him. In this respect he was without father, mother, or descent— and he stands in lonely majesty as the only one who sustains the office, ver. 3.

(2) He is superior to Abraham. Abraham never laid claim to the office of priest, but he recognized his inferiority to one whom the Messiah was to resemble, ver. 2, 4.

(3) He is superior to all the Jewish priesthood — sustaining a rank, and performing an office, above them all. The great ancestor of all the Levitical priests recognized his inferiority to one of the rank or "order" of which the Messiah was to be, and received from him a blessing. In our contemplation of Christ, therefore, as priest, we have the privilege of regarding him as superior to the Jewish high-priest—exalted as was his office, and important as were the functions of his office; as more grand, more pure, more worthy of confidence and love.

(4) The great High-priest of the Christian profession is the only perfect priest, ver. 11, 19. The Jewish priests were all imperfect and sinful men. The sacrifices which they offered were imperfect, and could not give peace to the conscience. There was need of some better system, and they all looked forward to it. But in the Lord Jesus, and in his work, there is absolute perfection. What he did was complete, and his office needs no change.

(5) The office now is permanent. It does not change from hand to hand, ver. 23, 24. He who sustains this office does not die, and we may ever apply to him, and cast our cares on him. Men die; one generation suc-

ceeds another; but our High-priest is the same. We may trust in him in whom our fathers found peace and salvation, and then we may teach our children to confide in the same High-priest — and so send the invaluable lesson down to the latest generations.

(6) His work is firm and sure, ver. 20–22. His office is founded on an oath, and he has become the *security* for all who will commit their cause to him. Can great interests like those of the soul be intrusted to better hands? Are they not safer in *his* keeping than in our own?

(7) He is able to save to the uttermost, ver. 25. That power he showed when he was on earth; that power he is constantly evincing. No one has sought aid of him and found him unable to render it; no one has been suffered to sink down to hell because his arm was weak. What he has done for a few he can do for "all;" and they who will intrust themselves to him will find him as a Saviour faithful and sure. Why will not men, then, be persuaded to commit themselves to him? Can they save themselves? Where is there one who has shown that he was able to do it? Do they not need a Saviour? Let the history of the world answer. Can man conduct his own cause before God? How weak, ignorant, and blind is he! how little qualified for such an office! Has anyone suffered wrong by committing himself to the Redeemer? If there *is* such an one, where is he? Who has ever made this complaint that has tried it? Who ever will make it? In countless millions of instances the trial has been made whether Christ was "able to save." Men have gone with a troubled spirit, with a guilty conscience, and with awful apprehensions of the wrath to come, and have asked him to save them. Not one of those who have done this has found reason to doubt his ability; not one has regretted that he has committed the deathless interest of the soul into his hands.

(8) Christ saves to the *uttermost*, ver. 25. He makes the salvation *complete*. So the Bible assures us; and so we see it *in fact*, as far as we can

trace the soul. When a Christian friend dies, we stand at his bedside, and accompany him as far as we can into the valley of the shadow of death. We ask him whether he feels that Christ is able to save? He replies, "*Yes.*" When he has lost the power of speaking above a whisper, we ask him the same question, and receive in a gentle whisper the same reply. When he gives us the parting hand, and we, still anxious to know whether all is well, ask the same question, a sign, a smile, a lighting up of the dying eye, declares that all is well. As far as we can trace the departing soul when it goes into the dark valley, we receive the same assurance; and why should we doubt that the same grace is bestowed further onward, and that he saves "to the uttermost?" But what else thus saves? Friends give the parting hand at the gloomy entrance to that valley, and the gay and the worldly coolly turn away. The delusions of infidelity there forsake the soul, and minister no comfort then. Flatterers turn away from the dying scene — for who flatters the dying with the praise of beauty or accomplishments? Taste, skill, learning, talent, do not help then, for how can *they* save a dying soul? None but Jesus saves to the "uttermost;" no other friend but he goes with us *entirely through* the valley of death. Is it not better to have such a friend than to go alone through that dark, gloomy path? Any other gloomy and dangerous way may be more safely trod without a friend than the vale of death.

(9) The Christian religion is fitted to our condition, ver. 26, 27. It has just such a High-priest as we need—holy, harmless, undefiled. Just such an atonement has been made as is necessary, ample, rich, full, and not needing to be made again. It reveals just such truths as we want—those pertaining to the immortality of the soul, and the glorious state of the redeemed beyond the grave. It imparts just such consolation as is fitted to our condition —pure, rich, unfailing, elevating. It reconciles us to God just as it should be done—in such a way that God can

CHAPTER VIII.

NOW of the things which we have spoken *this is* the sum: We have such an high priest,

who is set on the right hand of the throne of the Majesty in the heavens;

a Ep.1.20.

---

be honoured, and the purity and dignity of his law maintained. No other system so much consults the true dignity of our nature and the honour of God; no one diffuses such consolations through the life that is, or fills the soul with such hopes in regard to the life to come.

(10) Since, then, we have now such a great High-priest; since the promises of the gospel are settled on so firm a foundation; and since the gospel in its provisions of mercy is all that we can desire it to be, let us yield our hearts entirely to the Saviour, and make this salvation wholly ours. We have the privilege, if we will, of drawing near to God with boldness. We may come near his throne. Though we are poor, and sinful, and deserve neither notice nor mercy, yet we may come and ask for all that we need. We may go to God, and supplicate his favour, with the assurance that all is ready. We may go feeling that the great atonement has been made for our sins, and that no other offering is now needed; that the last bloody offering which God required has been presented, and that all that he now asks is the sacrifice of a contrite and a grateful heart. All that was needful to be done on the part of God to provide a way of salvation has been done; all that remains is for man to forsake his sins, and to come back to a God who waits to be gracious.

CHAPTER VIII.

ANALYSIS OF THE CHAPTER.

This chapter is a continuation of the argument which has been prosecuted in the previous chapters respecting the priesthood of Christ. The apostle had demonstrated that he was to be a priest, and that he was to be, not of the Levitical order, but of the order of Melchisedec. As a consequence, he had proved that this involved a change of the law appointing

the priesthood, and that in respect to permanency, and happy moral influence, the priesthood of Christ far surpassed the Jewish. This thought he pursues in this chapter, showing particularly that it involved a change in the nature of the covenant between God and his people. In the prosecution of this, he (1) states the sum or principal point of the whole matter under discussion—that the priesthood of Christ was real and permanent, while that of the Hebrew economy was typical, and was destined in its own nature to be temporary, ver. 1–3. (2) There was a fitness and propriety in his being removed to heaven to perform the functions of his office there—since, if he had remained on earth, he could not have officiated as priest, that duty being by the law of Moses intrusted to others pertaining to another tribe, ver. 4, 5. (3) Christ had obtained a more exalted ministry than that of the Jewish priests, because he was the Mediator in a better covenant—a covenant that related rather to the heart than to external observances, ver. 6–13. That new covenant excelled the old in the following respects:—(*a*) It was established on better promises, ver. 6. (*b*) It was not a covenant mainly requiring external observances, but it pertained to the soul, and the law of that covenant was written there, ver. 7–10. (*c*) It was connected with the diffusion of the knowledge of the Lord among all classes from the highest to the lowest, ver. 11. (*d*) Under that the evidence of forgiveness might be made more clear than it was under the old dispensation, and the way in which sins are pardoned be much better understood, ver. 12. These considerations involved the consequence, also, which is stated in ver. 13, that the old covenant was of necessity about to vanish away.

1. *Now of the things which we have spoken.* Or, "of the things of which

2 A minister of [1] the [b] sanctuary,   and of the true tabernacle, which
1 or, *holy things.*   b ch.9.8,12,24.   the Lord pitched, and not man.

---

we are speaking" (Stuart) ; or, as we should say, *of what is said.* The Greek does not necessarily mean things that *had been* spoken, but may refer to all that he was saying, taking the whole subject into consideration. ¶ This is *the sum.* Or this is the principal thing; referring to what he was *about* to say, not what he *had* said. Our translators seem to have understood this as referring to a *summing up,* or recapitulation of what he had said, and there can be no doubt that the Greek would bear this interpretation. But another exposition has been proposed, adopted by Bloomfield, Stuart, Michaelis, and Storr, among the moderns, and found also in Suidas, Theodoret, Theophylact, and others, among the ancients. It is that which regards the word rendered *sum—κεφάλαιον—*as meaning the *principal thing;* the chief matter; the most important point. The reason for this interpretation is, that the apostle, in fact, goes into no *recapitulation* of what he had said, but enters on a new topic relating to the priesthood of Christ. Instead of *going over* what he *had* demonstrated, he enters on a more important point, that the priesthood of Christ is performed in heaven, and that he has entered into the true tabernacle there. All which went before was type and shadow; this was that which the former economy had adumbrated. In the previous chapters the apostle had shown that he who sustained this office was superior in rank to the Jewish priests; that they were frail and dying, and that the office in their hands was changing from one to another, but that that of Christ was permanent and abiding. He now comes to consider the *real nature* of the office itself; the sacrifice which was offered ; the substance of which all in the former dispensation was the type. This was the *principal thing—κεφάλαιον—the head,* the most important matter ; and the consideration of this is pursued through the eighth, ninth, and tenth chapters. ¶ *We have such an* high priest. That is settled; proved; indisputable. The Christian system is not destitute of that which was regarded as so essential to the old dispensation—the office of a high-priest. ¶ *Who is set on the right hand of the throne,* &c. He is exalted to honour and glory before God. The right hand was regarded as the place of principal honour, and when it is said that Christ is at the right hand of God, the meaning is, that he is exalted to the highest honour in the universe. See Notes on Mark xvi. 19. Of course the language is figurative—as God has no hands literally—but the language conveys an important meaning, that he is near to God; that he is high in his affection and love, and is raised to the most elevated situation in heaven. See Phil. ii. 9; Eph. i. 21, 22.

2. *A minister of the sanctuary.* Margin, or, *holy things.* Greek, τῶν ἁγίων. The Greek may either mean *the sanctuary*—denoting the holy of holies; or *holy things.* The word *sanctuary—*קֹדֶשׁ *kodesh—*was given to the tabernacle or temple as *a holy place;* and the plural form, which is here used—τὰ ἅγια—was given to the most holy place by way of eminence; the full form of the name being קֹדֶשׁ קֳדָשִׁים—*kodesh kodâshim,* or ἅγια ἁγίων—*hagia hagiōn* (Jahn's *Arche.,* § 328), or, as it is here used, simply as τὰ ἅγια. The connection seems to require us to understand it of the *most holy place,* and not of holy things. The idea is, that the Lord Jesus, the great High-priest, has entered into the holy of holies in heaven, of which that in the tabernacle was an emblem. For a description of the most holy place in the temple, see Notes on Mat. xxi. 12. ¶ *And of the true tabernacle.* The *real* tabernacle in heaven, of which that among the Hebrews was but the type. The word *tabernacle—σκηνὴ—*means properly a *booth, hut,* or *tent,* and was applied to the *tent* which Moses was directed to build as the place for the worship of God. That tabernacle, as

3 For every high priest is ordained to offer gifts and sacrifices:
wherefore *it is* of necessity *c* that this
man have somewhat also to offer.

c Ep.5.2; ch.9.14.

4 For if he were on earth, he
should not be a priest, seeing that
[2]there are priests that offer gifts
according to the law:

[2] or, *they.*

the temple was afterward, was regarded as the peculiar abode of God
on earth. Here the reference is to
heaven, as the dwelling-place of God,
of which that tabernacle was the emblem or symbol. It is called the "*true
tabernacle*," as it is the *real* dwelling of God, of which the one made
by Moses was but the *emblem.* It is
not movable and perishable like that
made by man, but is unchanging and
eternal. ¶ *Which the Lord pitched,
and not man.* The word *pitched* is
adapted to express the setting up of a
tent. When it is said that "the Lord
pitched the true tabernacle"—that is,
the permanent dwelling in heaven—
the meaning is, that heaven has been
fitted up by God himself, and that
whatever is necessary to constitute
that an appropriate abode for the divine majesty has been done by him.
To that glorious dwelling the Redeemer has been received, and there
he performs the office of high-priest
in behalf of man. In what way he
does this, the apostle specifies in the
remainder of this chapter, and in chap.
ix., x.

3. *For every high priest is ordained
to offer gifts and sacrifices.* This is a
general statement about the functions
of the high-priest. It was the peculiarity of the office; it constituted its
essence, that some gift or sacrifice
was to be presented. This was indisputable in regard to the Jewish high-
priest, and this is involved in the nature of the priestly office everywhere.
A *priest* is one who offers sacrifice,
mainly in behalf of others. The *principles* involved in the office are, (1)
that there is need that some offering
or atonement should be made for sin;
and (2) that there is a fitness or propriety that someone should be designated to do it. If this idea that a
priest must offer sacrifice be correct,
then it follows that the name *priest*
should not be given to anyone who

is not appointed to offer sacrifice. It
should not, therefore, be given to the
ministers of the gospel, for it is no
part of their work to offer sacrifice—
the great sacrifice for sin having been
once offered by the Lord Jesus, and
not to be repeated. Accordingly, the
writers in the New Testament are
perfectly uniform and consistent on
this point. The name *priest* is never
once given to the ministers of the
gospel there. They are called ministers, ambassadors, pastors, bishops,
overseers, &c., but never *priests.* Nor
should they be so called in the Christian church. The name *priest*, as applied to Christian ministers, has been
derived from the *papists.* They hold
that the priest *does* offer as a sacrifice
the real body and blood of Christ in
the mass, and, holding this, the name
priest is given to the minister who
does it *consistently.* It is not, indeed,
right or *scriptural*—for the whole doctrine on which it is based is absurd
and false—but while that doctrine is
held the *name* is consistent. But with
what show of consistency or propriety
can the name be given to a Protestant
minister of the gospel? ¶ *Wherefore* it
is *of necessity that this man have somewhat also to offer.* That the Lord Jesus
should made an offering. That is,
since he is declared to be a *priest*,
and since it is essential to the office
that a priest should make an offering,
it is indispensable that he should bring
a sacrifice to God. He could not be
a priest, on the acknowledged principles on which that office is held, unless he did it. What the offering was
which the Lord Jesus made, the apostle specifies more fully in chap. ix.
11–14, 25, 26.

4. *For if he were on earth, he should
not be a priest.* He could not perform
that office. The design of this is, to
show a reason why he was removed
to heaven. The reason was, that on
earth there were those who were set

5 Who serve unto the example and ^dshadow of heavenly things, as Moses was admonished of God when he was about to make the

d Col.2.17; ch.10.1.

tabernacle: for, ^eSee, saith he, *that* thou make all things according to the pattern showed to thee in the mount.

e Ex.25.40; 26.30.

apart to that office, and that he, not being of the same tribe with them, could not officiate as priest. There was an order of men here on earth consecrated already to that office, and hence it was necessary that the Lord Jesus, in performing the functions of the office, should be removed to another sphere.

5. *Who serve unto the example.* Who perform their service by the mere example and shadow of the heavenly things; or, in a sanctuary, and in a mode, that is the mere emblem of the reality which exists in heaven. The reference is to the tabernacle, which was a mere *example* or *copy* of heaven. The word here rendered *example*—ὑποδείγμα—means a *copy*, a *likeness*, an *imitation*. The tabernacle was made after a *pattern* which was shown to Moses; it was so made as to have some faint *resemblance* to the reality in heaven, and *in* that "copy," or "example," they were appointed to officiate. Their service, therefore, had some *resemblance* to that in heaven. ¶ *And shadow.* That is, in the service of the tabernacle where they officiated, there was a mere shadow of that which was real and substantial. Compared with what is in heaven, it was what the shadow is as compared with the substance. A shadow—as of a man, a house, a tree—will indicate the form, the outline, the size of the object; but it has no substance, or reality. So it was with the rites of the Jewish religion. They were designed merely as an outline of the substantial realities of the true religion, or to present dim and shadowy representations of what is true and real in heaven. Comp. Notes on Col. ii. 17; Heb. x. 1. The word *shadow* here—σκιὰ—is used in distinction from the body or reality —σῶμα (comp. Col. ii. 17), and also from εἰκών, a perfect image or resemblance. See Heb. x. 1. ¶ *Of heavenly things.* Of the heavenly sanctuary;

of what is real and substantial in heaven. That is, there exists in heaven a reality of which the service in the Jewish sanctuary was but the outline. The reference is, undoubtedly, to the service which the Lord Jesus performs there as the great High-priest of his people. ¶ *As Moses was admonished of God.* As he was divinely instructed. The word here used — χρηματίζω — means properly to give oracular responses; to make communications to men in a supernatural way—by dreams, by direct revelations, &c. See Mat. ii. 12, 22; Luke ii. 26; Acts x. 22; Heb. xi. 7. ¶ *For, See, saith he.* Ex. xxv. 9, 40; xxvi. 30. In Ex. xl. it is also repeatedly said that Moses executed all the work of the tabernacle as he had been commanded. Great care was taken that an exact copy should be exhibited to him of all which he was to make, and that the work should be exactly like the pattern. The reason doubtless was, that as the Jewish service was to be typical, none but God could judge of the form in which the tabernacle should be made. It was not to be an edifice of architectural beauty, skill, or taste, but was designed to adumbrate important realities which were known only to God. Hence it was needful that an exact model should be given to Moses, and that that model should be scrupulously followed. ¶ That *thou make all things.* Not only the tabernacle itself, but the altars, the ark, the candlestick, &c. The form and materials for each were specified, and the exact pattern shown to Moses in the mount. ¶ *According to the pattern.* Greek τύπον, type; that is, figure, form. The word τύπος, *type,* means, properly, anything produced by the agency or means of *blows* (from τύπτω, *to strike*); hence a mark, stamp, print, impression — as that made by driving nails in the hands (John xx. 25); then a figure or form, as of an image or statue (Acts vii. 43); then

6 But now hath he obtained *a more excellent ministry, by how much also he is the mediator of a

*2 Co.3.6-9; ch.7.22.

the form of a doctrine or opinion (Rom. vi. 17); then an example to be imitated or followed (1 Cor. x. 6, 7; Phil. iii. 17; 1 Thes. i. 7; 2 Thes. iii. 9); and hence a *pattern*, or model after which anything is to be made, Acts vii. 44. This is the meaning here. The allusion is to a pattern such as an architect or sculptor uses; a drawing, or a figure made in wood or clay, after which the work is to be modelled. The idea is, that some such drawing or model was exhibited to Moses by God on Mount Sinai, so that he might have an exact idea of the tabernacle which was to be made. A similar drawing or model of the temple was given by David to Solomon, 1 Chr. xxviii. 11, 12. We are not, indeed, to suppose that there was, in the case of the pattern shown to Moses, any miniature model of wood or stone actually created and exhibited, but that the form of the tabernacle was exhibited to Moses in vision (see Notes on Isa. i. 1), or was so vividly impressed on his mind that he would have a distinct view of the edifice which was to be reared. ¶ *In the mount*. In Mount Sinai; for it was while Moses was there in the presence of God that these communications were made.

6. *But now hath he obtained*. That is, Christ. ¶ *A more excellent ministry*. A service of a higher order, or of a more exalted nature. It was the real and substantial service of which the other was but the emblem; it pertained to things in heaven, while that was concerned with the earthly tabernacle; it was enduring, while that was to vanish away. See Notes on 2 Cor. iii. 6–9. ¶ *By how much*. By as much as the new covenant is more important than the old, by so much does his ministry exceed in dignity that under the ancient dispensation. ¶ *He is the mediator*. See Notes on Gal. iii. 19, 20, where the word *mediator* is explained. It means here that Christ officiates

better ³covenant, which was established upon better promises.

³ or, *testament*.

between God and man according to the arrangements of the new covenant. ¶ *Of a better covenant*. Margin, or *testament*. Greek διαϑήκη—*diathēkē*. This word properly denotes a *disposition*, *arrangement*, or *ordering* of things; and then a *testament*, a *will*. This is its usual meaning in Greek writers. In the Scriptures it is employed to describe the arrangement which God has made to secure the maintenance of his worship on earth, and the salvation of men. It is *uniformly* used in the Septuagint and in the New Testament to denote the *covenant* which God makes with men. The word which *properly* denotes a *covenant* or *compact* — συνϑήκη, *synthēkē*—is never used. The writers of the New Testament evidently derived their use of the word from the Septuagint, but why the authors of that version employed a word denoting a *will*, rather than the proper one denoting a *compact*, is unknown. It has been supposed by some, and the conjecture is not wholly improbable, that it was because they were unwilling to represent God as making a *compact* or *agreement* with men, but chose rather to represent him as making a mere *arrangement* or *ordering* of things. Comp. Notes on ver. 8, and chap. ix. 16, 17.

[See Supplementary Note, chap. ix. 16, for the *evidence* of the covenant of grace.]

This is a *better* covenant than the old, inasmuch as it relates mainly to the heart; to the pardon of sin; to a spiritual and holy religion. See ver. 10. The former related more to external rites and observances, and was destined to vanish away. See ver. 13. ¶ *Which was established upon better promises*. The promises in the first covenant pertained mainly to the present life. They were promises of length of days; of increase of numbers; of seed-time and harvest; of national privileges; and of extraordinary peace, abundance, and prosperity. That there was also the promise of eternal life, it would be wrong to doubt; but this

7 For*g* if that first *covenant* had

g ch.7.11.

been faultless, then should no place have been sought for the second.

---

was not the main thing. In the new covenant, however, the promise of spiritual blessings, and of eternal life, becomes the principal thing. The mind is directed to heaven; the heart is cheered with the hopes of unending happiness; the favour of God and the anticipation of heaven are secured in the most ample and solemn manner.

7. *For if that first* covenant *had been faultless.* See Notes on chap. vii. 11. It is implied here that God had *said* that that covenant was not perfect or faultless. The meaning is not that that first covenant made under Moses had any real *faults*, or inculcated that which was wrong, but that it did not contain the ample provision for the pardon of sin and the salvation of the soul which was desirable. It was merely *preparatory* to the gospel. ¶ *Then should no place have been sought for the second.* There *could* not have been—inasmuch as in that case it would have been impossible to have improved it, and any change would have been only for the worse.

8. *For finding fault with them.* Or rather, "finding fault, he says to them." The difference is only in the punctuation, and this change is required by the passage itself. This is commonly interpreted as meaning that the fault was not found *with* "*them*"—that is, with the Jewish people, for they had had nothing to do in giving the covenant, but *with the covenant itself.* "Stating its defects, he had said to them that he would give them one more perfect, and of which that was only preparatory." So Grotius, Stuart, Rosenmüller, and Erasmus understand it. Doddridge, Koppe, and many others understand it as it is in our translation, as implying that the fault was found with the people, and they refer to the passage quoted from Jeremiah for proof, where the complaint is of the people. The Greek will bear either construction; but may we not adopt a somewhat different interpretation still? May not this be the meaning? "For using

the language of complaint, or language that implied that there was defect or error, he speaks of another covenant." According to this, the idea would be, not that he found fault specifically either with the covenant or the people, but generally that he used language which implied that there was defect somewhere when he promised another and a better covenant. The word rendered "finding fault" properly means to censure, or to blame. It is rendered in Mark vii. 2, "they found fault," to wit, with those who ate with unwashed hands. So in Rom. ix. 9, "why doth he yet find fault?" It occurs nowhere else in the New Testament. The language is such as is used where wrong has been done; where there is ground of complaint; where it is desirable that there should be a change. In the passage here quoted from Jeremiah, it is not expressly stated that God found fault either with the covenant or with the people, but that he promised that he would give another covenant, and that it should be *different* from that which he gave them when they came out of Egypt—implying that there was defect in that, or that it was not *faultless.* The whole meaning is, that there was a deficiency which the giving of a new covenant would remove. ¶ *He saith.* In Jer. xxxi. 31–34. The apostle has not quoted the passage literally as it is in the Hebrew, but he has retained the substance, and the sense is not essentially varied. The quotation appears to have been made partly from the Septuagint, and partly from memory. This often occurs in the New Testament. ¶ *Behold.* This particle is designed to call attention to what was about to be said as important, or as having some special claim to notice. It is of very frequent occurrence in the Scriptures, being much more freely used by the sacred writers than it is in the classic authors. ¶ *The days come.* The time is coming. This refers doubtless to the times of the Messiah. Phrases such as these, "in

8 For finding fault with them, he saith, *ʰBehold, the days come,* saith the Lord, when I will make a new covenant with the house of Israel and with the house of Judah:

h Je.31.31-34.

the last days," "in after times," and "the time is coming," are often used in the Old Testament to denote the last dispensation of the world—the dispensation when the affairs of the world will be wound up. See the phrase explained in the Notes on chap. i. 2, and Isa. ii. 2. There can be no doubt that, as it is used by Jeremiah, it refers to the terms of the gospel. ¶ *When I will make a new covenant.* A covenant that shall contemplate somewhat different ends; that shall have different conditions; that shall be more effective in restraining from sin. The word *covenant* here refers to the arrangement, plan, or dispensation into which he would enter in his dealings with men. On the meaning of the word, see Notes on Acts vii. 8, and on chap. ix. 16, 17. The word *covenant* with us commonly denotes a compact or agreement between two parties that are equal, and who are free to enter into the agreement or not. In this sense, of course, it cannot be used in relation to the arrangement which God makes with them. There is (1) no equality between them, and (2) man is not at liberty to reject any proposal which God shall make. The word, therefore, is used in the Scriptures in a more general sense, and more in accordance with the original meaning of the Greek word. It has been above remarked (see Notes on ver. 6), that the *proper* word to denote *covenant,* or *compact—συνθήκη, synthēkē*—is never used either in the Septuagint or in the New Testament, another word — *διαθήκη, diathēkē*—being carefully employed. Whether the reason there suggested for the adoption of this word in the Septuagint be the real one or not, the fact is indisputable. I may be allowed to suggest, *as possible,* an additional reason why this word so uniformly occurs in the New Testament. It is, that the writers of the New Testament never meant to represent the transactions between God and man as a *compact* or

covenant, properly so called. They have studiously avoided it, and their uniform practice, in making this nice distinction between the two words, may show the real sense in which the Hebrew word rendered *covenant— בְּרִית berith*—is used in the Old Testament. The word which they employ — *διαθήκη, diathēkē*— never means a compact or agreement as between equals. It remotely and secondarily means a *will,* or *testament*—and hence our word "New *Testament.*" But *this* is not the sense in which it is used in the Bible—for God has never made a *will* in the sense of a testamentary disposition of what belongs to him. In order, therefore, to arrive at the true Scripture view of this whole matter, it is necessary to refer to the original meaning of the word *diathēkē— διαθήκη*—as denoting a *disposition, arrangement, plan;* then that which is *ordered,* a law, precept, promise, &c. Unhappily we have no single word which expresses the idea, and hence a constant error has existed in the church—either keeping up the notion of a *compact*—as if God could make one with men; or the idea of a *will*—equally repugnant to truth. The noun used—*διαθήκη*—is derived from a verb —*διατίθημι*—meaning to place apart, to set in order; and then to appoint, to make over, to make an arrangement with. Hence the word *διαθήκη—diathēkē*—means properly the *arrangement* or *disposition* which God made with men in regard to salvation; the system of statutes, directions, laws, and promises by which they are to become subject to him, and to be saved. The meaning here is, that he would make a *new* arrangement, contemplating as a primary thing that the law should be written in the *heart,* an arrangement which would be peculiarly spiritual in its character, and which would be attended with the diffusion of just views of himself.

[See Supplementary Note on the existence of the covenant of grace, chap. ix. 16.]

9 Not according to the covenant that I made with their fathers, in the day when I took them by the hand to lead them out of the land of Egypt; because they continued not in my covenant, and I regarded them not, saith the Lord.

¶ *With the house of Israel.* The *family,* or *race* of Israel, for so the word *house* is often used in the Scriptures and elsewhere. The word "*Israel*" is used in the Scriptures in the following senses: (1) As a name given to Jacob because he wrestled with the angel of God and prevailed as a prince, Gen. xxxii. 28. (2) As denoting all who were descended from him—called "the children of Israel"—or the Jewish nation. (3) As denoting the kingdom of the ten tribes—the kingdom of Samaria, or Ephraim—that kingdom having taken the name *Israel* in contradistinction from the other kingdom, which was called *Judah*. (4) As denoting the people of God in general —his true and sincere friends—his church. See Notes on Rom. ii. 28, 29; ix. 6. In this place, quoted from Jeremiah, it seems to be used to denote the kingdom of Israel in contradistinction from that of Judah, and *together* they denote *the whole people of God,* or *the whole Hebrew nation.* This arrangement was to be ratified and confirmed by the gift of the Messiah, and by implanting his laws in the heart. It is not necessary to understand this as referring to the entire nation of the Jews, as if the ten tribes were to be restored; but the words *Israel* and *Judah* are used to denote the people of God in general, and the idea is, that with the *true* Israel under the Messiah the laws of God would be written in the heart rather than be mere external observances. ¶ *And with the house of Judah.* The kingdom of Judah. This kingdom consisted of two tribes—Judah and Benjamin. The tribe of Benjamin was, however, small, and the name was lost in that of Judah.

9. *Not according to the covenant,* &c. An arrangement or dispensation relating mainly to outward observances, and to temporal blessings. The meaning is, that the new dispensation would be different from that which was made with them when they came out of Egypt. In what respects it would differ is specified in ver. 10–12. ¶ *Because they continued not in my covenant.* In Jeremiah, in the Hebrew, this is, "which my covenant they brake." That is, they failed to comply with the conditions on which I promised to bestow blessings upon them. In Jeremiah this is stated as a simple fact; in the manner in which the apostle quotes it, it is given as a *reason* why he would make a new arrangement. The apostle has quoted it literally from the Septuagint, and the sense is not materially varied. The word rendered "because"—ὅτι— may mean "since"—"since they did not obey that covenant, and it was ineffectual in keeping them from sin, showing that it was not *perfect* or *complete* in regard to what was needful to be done for man, a new arrangement shall be made that will be without defect." This accords with the reasoning of the apostle; and the idea is, simply, that an arrangement may be made for man adapted to produce important ends in one state of society or one age of the world, which would not be well adapted to him in another, and which would not accomplish *all* which it would be desirable to accomplish for the race. So an arrangement may be made for teaching children which would not answer the purpose of instructing those of mature years, and which at that time of life may be superseded by another. In like manner, a system of measures may be adapted to the infancy of society, or to a comparatively rude period of the world, which would be ill adapted to a more advanced state of society. Such was the Hebrew system. It was well adapted to the Jewish community in their circumstances, and answered the end then in view. It served to keep them separate from other people; to preserve the knowledge and the worship of the true God, and to introduce the gospel dis-

10 For this *is* the covenant that
I will make with the house of Israel
after those days, saith the Lord; I
will [4]put my laws into their mind,

4 give.

and write them [5]in their hearts:
and [i]I will be to them a God, and
they shall be to me a people:

5 or, *upon*.   i Ho.2.23; Zec.8.8.

---

pensation. ¶ *And I regarded them
not.* In Jeremiah this is, "although I
was an husband unto them." The Septuagint is as it is quoted here by Paul.
The Hebrew is, וְאָנֹכִי בָּעַלְתִּי בָם—which
may be rendered, "although I was
their Lord," or, as it is translated by
Gesenius, "and I rejected them."
The word בָּעַל—*Bâăl*—means, (1) to
be lord or master over anything, Isa.
xxvi. 13; (2) to become the husband
of anyone, Deut. xxi. 13; xxiv. 1; (3)
with בְּ to disdain, to reject. So Jer.
iii. 14. It is very probable that this
is the meaning here, for it is not only
adopted by the Septuagint, but by the
Syriac. The Arabic word means *to
reject, to loath, to disdain.* All that is
necessary to observe here is, that it
cannot be demonstrated that the apostle has not given the true sense of
the prophet. The probability is, that
the Septuagint translators would give
the meaning which was commonly
understood to be correct, and there
is still more probability that the Syriac translator would adopt the true
sense, for (1) the Syriac and Hebrew
languages strongly resemble each
other; and (2) the old Syriac version
—the Peshito—is incomparably a better translation than the Septuagint.
If this, therefore, be the correct translation, the meaning is, that since they
did not regard and obey the laws
which he gave them, God would reject them as his people, and give new
laws better adapted to save men. Instead of regarding and treating them
as his friends, he would punish them
for their offences, and visit them with
calamities.

10. *For this* is *the covenant.* This is
the arrangement, or the dispensation
which shall succeed the old one.
¶ *With the house of Israel.* With the
true Israel — that is, with all those
whom he will regard and treat as his
friends. ¶ *After those days.* This

may either mean, "after those days I
will put my laws in their hearts," or,
"I will make this covenant with them
after those days." The difference is
merely in the punctuation, and the
sense is not materially affected. It
seems to me, however, that the meaning of the Hebrew in Jeremiah is, "in
those *after days*" (comp. Notes on
Isa. ii. 1), "I will put my laws into
their mind;" that is, in that subsequent period, called in Scripture "the
after times," "the last days," "the
ages to come," meaning the last dispensation of the world. See Notes
on chap. i. 2. Thus interpreted, the
sense is, that this would be done in
the times of the Messiah. ¶ *I will
put my laws into their mind.* Margin,
give. The word *give* in Hebrew is
often used in the sense of *put.* The
meaning here is, that they would not
be mere external observances, but
would affect the conscience and the
heart. The laws of the Hebrews pertained mainly to external rites and
ceremonies; the laws of the new dispensation would relate particularly to
the inner man, and would be designed
to control the heart. The grand peculiarity of the Christian system is,
that it regulates the conscience and
the principles of the soul rather than
external matters. It prescribes few
outward rites, and those are exceedingly simple, and are merely the proper *expressions* of the pious feelings
supposed to be in the heart; and all
attempts either to increase the *number*
of those rites, or to make them imposing by their gorgeousness, have
done just so much to mar the simplicity of the gospel, and to corrupt
religion. ¶ *And write them in their
hearts.* Margin, *upon.* Not on tables
of stone or brass, but on the soul itself. That is, the obedience rendered
will be internal. The law of the new
system will have living power, and
bind the faculties of the soul to obedience. The commandment there will

11 And they shall not teach every man his neighbour, and every man his brother, saying, Know the Lord:

for *k* all shall know me, from the least to the greatest.

be written in more lasting characters than if engraved on tables of stone. ¶ *And I will be to them a God.* This is quoted literally from the Hebrew. The meaning is, that he would sustain to them the appropriate relation of a God; or, if the expression may be allowed, he would be to them what a God should be, or what it is desirable that men should find in a God. We speak of a father's acting in a manner appropriate to the character of a father; and the meaning here is, that *he* would be to his people all that is properly implied in the name *God.* He would be their Lawgiver, their Counsellor, their Protector, their Redeemer, their Guide. He would provide for their wants, defend them in danger, pardon their sins, comfort them in trials, and save their souls. He would be a faithful friend, and would never leave them nor forsake them. It is one of the inestimable privileges of his people that JEHOVAH is their God. The living and everblessed Being who made the universe sustains to them the relation of a Protector and a Friend, and they may look up to Him feeling that he is all which they could desire in the character of a God. ¶ *And they shall be to me a people.* This is not merely stated as *a fact*, but as *a privilege.* It is an inestimable blessing to be regarded as one of the people of God, and to feel that we belong to him; that we are associated with those whom he loves, and whom he treats as his friends.

11. *And they shall not teach every man his neighbour,* &c. That is, no one shall be under a necessity of imparting instruction to another, or of exhorting him to become acquainted with the Lord. This is designed to set forth another of the advantages which would attend the new dispensation. In the previous verse it had been said that one advantage of that economy would be, that the law would be written on the heart, and that they who were thus blessed would be re-

garded as the people of God. Another advantage over the *old* arrangement or covenant is here stated. It is, that the knowledge of the Lord, and of the true religion, would be deeply engraved on the minds of all, and that there would be no necessity for mutual exhortation and counsel. "They shall have a much more certain and effectual teaching than they can derive from another" (Doddridge). This passage does not refer to the fact that the true religion will be universally diffused, but that among those who are interested in the blessings of the new covenant there would be an accurate and just knowledge of the Lord. In some way they would be so taught respecting his character that they would not need the aid to be derived from others. All under that dispensation, or sustaining to him the relation of "*a people*," would *in fact* have a correct knowledge of the Lord. This could not be said of the old dispensation; for, (1) Their religion consisted much in outward observances. (2) It was not to such an extent as the new system a dispensation of the Holy Spirit. (3) There were not as many means as now for learning the true character of God. (4) The fullest revelations had not been made to them of that character, for that was reserved for the coming of the Saviour, and under him it was intended that there should be communicated the full knowledge of the character of God. Many MSS., and those among the best, here have πολίτην, *citizen, fellow-citizen*, instead of πλησίον, *neighbour*, and this is adopted by Griesbach, Tittmann, Rosenmüller, Knapp, Stuart, and by many of the fathers. It is also in the version of the LXX. in the place quoted from Jeremiah. It is not easy to determine the true reading, but the word *neighbour* better accords with the meaning of the Hebrew—רֵעַ —and there is strong authority from the MSS. and the versions for this reading. ¶ *And every man his brother.*

12 For I will be merciful to their unrighteousness, and their sins and their iniquities will I remember no more.

Another form of expression, meaning that there would be no necessity that one should teach another. ¶ *Saying, Know the Lord.* That is, become acquainted with God; learn his character and his will. The idea is, that the true knowledge of Jehovah would prevail as a characteristic of those times. ¶ *For all shall know me.* That is, all those referred to—all who are interested in the new covenant, and who are partakers of its blessings. It does not mean that all *persons, in all lands,* would then know the Lord—though the time will come when that will be true; but the expression is to be limited by the point under discussion. That point is not that the knowledge of the Lord will fill the whole world, but that all who are interested in the new dispensation will have a much more full and clear acquaintance with God than was possessed under the old. Of the truth of this no one can doubt. Christians have a much more perfect knowledge of God and of his government than could have been learned merely from the revelations of the Old Testament.

12. *For I will be merciful to their unrighteousness,* &c. That is, the blessing of *pardon* will be much more richly enjoyed under the new dispensation than it was under the old. This is the *fourth* circumstance adduced in which the new covenant will surpass the old. That was comparatively severe in its inflictions (see chap. x. 28); it marked every offence with strictness, and employed the language of mercy much less frequently than that of justice. It was a system where *law* and *justice* reigned—not where *mercy* was the crowning and prevalent attribute. It was true that it contemplated pardon, and made arrangements for it; but it is still true that this is much more prominent in the new dispensation than in the old. In the gospel this is the leading idea. It is that which separates it from all other systems. The entire arrangement is one for the pardon of sin in a manner consistent with the claims of law and justice, and it bestows the benefit of forgiveness in the most ample and perfect manner on all who are interested in the plan. In fact, the peculiarity by which the gospel is distinguished from *all other* systems, ancient and modern, philosophic and moral, pagan and deistical, is, that it is a system making provision for the forgiveness of sin, and actually bestowing pardon on the guilty. This is the centre, the crown, the glory of the new dispensation. God is merciful to the unrighteousness of men, and their sins are remembered no more. ¶ *Will I remember no more.* This is evidently spoken after the manner of men, and in accordance with human apprehension. It cannot mean literally that God *forgets* that men are sinners, but it means that he treats them *as if* this were forgotten. Their sins are not charged upon them, and they are themselves no more punished than *if* those sins had passed entirely out of the recollection. God treats them with just as much kindness, and regards them with just as sincere affection, *as if* their sins ceased wholly to be remembered, or, which is the same thing, *as if* they had never sinned.

13. *In that he saith, A new* covenant, *he hath made the first old.* That is, the use of the word *"new"* implies that the one which it was to supersede was *"old."* New and old stand in contradistinction from each other. Thus we speak of a new and old house, a new and old garment, &c. The object of the apostle is to show that by the very fact of the arrangement for a *new* dispensation differing so much from the old, it was implied of necessity that *that* was to be superseded, and would vanish away. This was one of the leading points at which he arrived. ¶ *Now that which decayeth and waxeth old is ready to vanish away.* This is a *general* truth which would be undisputed, and which Paul applies to the case under considera-

13 In that he saith, A ¹new *cove-nant*, he hath made the first old. Now that which decayeth and waxeth old *is* ready to vanish away.

l 2 Co.5.17.

---

tion. An old house, or garment; an ancient tree; an aged man—all have indications that they are soon to disappear. They cannot be expected to remain long. The very fact of their growing *old* is an indication that they will soon be gone. So Paul says it was with the dispensation that was represented as *old*. It had symptoms of decay. It had lost the vigour which it had when it was fresh and new; it had every mark of an antiquated and a declining system; and it had been expressly declared that a new and more perfect dispensation was to be given to the world. Paul concluded, therefore, that the *Jewish* system must soon disappear.

REMARKS.

(1) The fact that we have a high-priest is fitted to impart consolation to the pious mind, ver. 1–5. He ever lives, and is ever the same. He is a minister of the true sanctuary, and is ever before the mercy-seat. He enters there not once a year only, but has entered to abide there for ever. We can *never* approach the throne of mercy without having a high-priest there—for he at all times, day and night, appears before God. The merits of his sacrifice are never exhausted, and God is never wearied with hearing his pleadings in behalf of his people. He is the same that he was when he gave himself on the cross. He has the same love and the same compassion which he had then, and that love which led him to make the atonement will lead him always to regard with tenderness those for whom he died.

(2) It is a privilege to live under the blessings of the Christian system, ver. 6. We have a better covenant than the old one was—one less expensive and less burdensome, and one that is established upon better promises. Now the sacrifice is made, and we do not have to renew it day by day. It was made once for all, and need never be repeated. Having now a high-priest in heaven, who has made the sacrifice, we may approach him in any part of the earth, and at all times, and feel that our offering will be acceptable to him. If there is any blessing for which we ought to be thankful, it is for the Christian religion; for we have only to look at any portion of the heathen world, or even to the condition of the people of God under the comparatively dark and obscure Jewish dispensation, to see abundant reasons for thanksgiving for what we enjoy.

(3) Let us often contemplate the mercies of the new dispensation with which we are favoured—of that religion whose smiles and sunshine we are permitted to enjoy, ver. 10–12. It contains all that we want, and is exactly adapted to our condition. It has that for which every man should be thankful; it contains not one thing which should lead a man to reject it. It furnishes all the security which we could desire for our salvation; it lays upon us no oppressive burdens or charges; it accomplishes all which we ought to desire in our souls. Let us contemplate a moment the arrangements of that "covenant," and see how fitted it is to make man blessed and happy.

First. It writes the laws of God on the mind and the heart, ver. 10. It not only *reveals* them, but it secures their observance. It has made arrangements for *disposing* men to keep the laws—a thing which has not been introduced into any other system. Legislators may enact good laws, but they cannot induce others to obey them; parents may utter good precepts, but they cannot engrave them on the hearts of their children; and sages may express sound maxims and just precepts in morals, but there is no security that they will be regarded. So in all the heathen world there is no power to inscribe good maxims and rules of living on the *heart*. They may be written; recorded on tablets; hung up in temples;

but men will not regard them. They will still give indulgence to evil passions, and lead wicked lives. But it is not so with the arrangement which God has made in the plan of salvation. One of the very first provisions of that plan is, that the laws shall be inscribed *on the heart*, and that there shall be a DISPOSITION to obey. Such a system is what man wants, and such a system he can nowhere else find.

Second. This new arrangement *reveals to us a God* such as we need, ver. 10. It contains the promise that he will be "*our* God." He will be to his people all that can be *desired in God;* all that man could wish. He is just such a God as the human mind, when it is pure, most loves; he has all the attributes which it could be desired there should be in his character; he has done all that we could desire a God to do; he is ready to do all that we could wish a God to perform. *Man wants a God;* a God in whom he can put confidence, and on whom he can rely. The ancient Greek philosopher *wanted a God*—and he would then have made a beautiful and efficient system of morals; the heathen *want a God*—to dwell in their empty temples, and in their corrupt hearts; the atheist *wants a God* to make him calm, contented, and happy in his life —for he has no God now; and man everywhere—wretched, sinful, suffering, dying—WANTS A GOD. Such a God is revealed in the Bible—one whose character we may contemplate with ever-increasing admiration; one who has all the attributes which we can desire; one who will minister to us all the consolation which we need in this world; one who will be to us *the same God for ever and ever.*

Third. The new covenant contemplates the diffusion of *knowledge*, ver. 11. This too was what man needed, for everywhere else he has been ignorant of God and of the way of salvation. The whole heathen world is sunk in ignorance, and indeed all men, except as they are enlightened by the gospel, are in profound darkness on the great questions which most nearly pertain to their welfare. But it is not so with the new arrangement which God has made with his people. It is a fact that they know the Lord, and a dispensation which would produce that is just what man needed. There are two things hinted at in ver. 11 of this chapter which are worthy of more than a passing notice, illustrating the excellency of the Christian religion. The *first* is, that in the new dispensation *all would know the Lord.* The matter of fact is, that the obscurest and most unlettered Christian often has a knowledge of God which sages never had, and which is never obtained except by the teachings of the Holy Spirit. However this may be accounted for, the fact cannot be denied. There is a view of God which elevates the soul; a knowledge of him which exerts a practical influence on the heart, and which transforms the soul; and a correctness of apprehension in regard to what truth is, possessed by the humble Christian, though a peasant, which philosophy never imparted to its votaries. Many a sage would be instructed in the truths of religion if he would sit down and converse with the comparatively unlearned Christian, who has no book but his Bible. The other thing hinted at here is, that all would know the Lord *from the least to the greatest.* Children and youth, as well as age and experience, would have an acquaintance with God. This promise is remarkably verified under the new dispensation. One of the most striking things of the system is, the attention which it pays to the young; one of its most wonderful effects is the knowledge which it is the means of imparting to those early in life. Many a child in the Sabbath-school has a knowledge of God which Grecian sages never had; many a youth in the church has a more consistent acquaintance with God's real plan of governing and saving men than all the teachings which philosophy could ever furnish.

Fourth. The new dispensation contemplates the pardon of sin, and is, therefore, fitted to the condition of man, ver. 12. It is what man needs. The knowledge of some way of pardon is that which human nature has been

sighing for for ages; which has been sought in every system of religion, and by every bloody offering; but which has never elsewhere been found. The philosopher had no assurance that God will forgive sin; and indeed one of the chief aims of the philosopher has been to convince himself that he has no *need* of pardon. The heathen have had no assurance that their offerings have availed to put away the divine anger, and to obtain forgiveness. *The only assurance anywhere furnished that sin may be forgiven, is in the Bible.* This is the great peculiarity of the system recorded there, and this it is which renders it so valuable above all other systems of religion. It furnishes the *assurance* that sins may be pardoned, and shows *how* it may be done. This is what we *must* have, or perish. And why, since Christianity reveals a way of forgiveness—a way honourable to God and not degrading to man—why should any man reject it? Why should not the guilty embrace a system which proclaims pardon to the guilty, and which assures all that, if they will embrace him who is the "Mediator of the new covenant," "God will be merciful to their unrighteousness, and will remember their iniquities no more."

CHAPTER IX.
ANALYSIS OF THE CHAPTER.

The general design of this chapter is the same as the two preceding—to show that Christ as high-priest is superior to the Jewish high-priest. This the apostle had already shown to be true in regard to his rank, and to the dispensation of which he was the "mediator." He proceeds now to show that this was also true in reference to the efficacy of the sacrifice which he made; and in order to this, he gives an account of the ancient Jewish sacrifices, and compares them with that made by the Redeemer. The essential point is, that the former dispensation was mere shadow, type, or figure, and that the latter was real and efficacious. The chapter comprises, in illustration of this general idea, the following points:

(1) A description of the ancient tabernacle, and of the utensils that were in it, ver. 1-5.

(2) A description of the services in it, particularly of that performed by the high-priest once a year, ver. 6, 7.

(3) All this was typical and symbolical, and was a standing demonstration that the way into the most holy place in heaven was not yet fully revealed, ver. 8-10.

(4) Christ was now come — the substance of which that was the shadow; the real sacrifice of which that was the emblem, ver. 11-14. He pertained as a priest to a more perfect tabernacle (ver. 11); he offered not the blood of bulls and goats, but his own blood (ver. 12); with that blood he entered into the most holy place in heaven (ver. 12); and if the blood of bulls and goats was admitted to be efficacious in putting away external uncleanness, it must be admitted that the blood of Christ had an efficacy in cleansing the conscience, ver. 13, 14.

(5) His blood is efficacious not only in remitting present sins, but it extends in its efficacy even to past ages, and removes the sins of those who had worshipped God under the former covenant, ver. 15.

(6) The apostle then proceeds to show that it was necessary that the mediator of the new covenant should shed his own blood, and that the blood thus shed should be applied to purify those for whom the sacrifice was made, ver. 16-23. This he shows by the following considerations, viz.:

(*a*) He argues it from the nature of a covenant or compact, showing that it was ratified only over dead sacrifices, and that of necessity the victim that was set apart to confirm or ratify it must be slain. See Notes on ver. 16, 17.

(*b*) The first covenant was confirmed or ratified by blood, and hence it was necessary that, since the "patterns" of the heavenly things were sprinkled with blood, the heavenly things themselves should be purified with better sacrifices, ver. 18-23.

(7) The offering made by the Redeemer was to be made but once. This arose from the necessity of the

CHAPTER IX.

THEN verily the first *covenant* had also ¹ordinances of divine service, and *ᵃ*a worldly sanctuary.

¹ or, *ceremonies.*　　　　*a* Ex.25.8.

2 For there was *ᵇ*a tabernacle made, the first, wherein *was* the candlestick, and *ᶜ*the table, and *ᵈ*the show-bread; which is called the ²Sanctuary.

b Ex.26.1,35.　*c* Ex.40.4.　*d* Ex.25.30.　2 or, *holy.*

case, since it could not be supposed that the mediator would suffer *often*, as the high-priest went once every year into the most holy place. He had come and died once in the last dispensation of things on earth, and then had entered into heaven and could suffer no more, ver. 24-26.

(8) In the close of the chapter the apostle adverts to the fact that there was a remarkable resemblance, in one respect, between the death of Christ and the death of all men. It was appointed to them to die once, and but once, and so Christ died but once. As a man, it was in accordance with the universal condition of things that he *should* die once; and in accordance with the same condition of things it was proper that he should die *but* once. In like manner there was a resemblance or fitness in regard to what would occur after death. Man was to appear at the judgment. He was not to cease to be, but would stand hereafter at the bar of God. In like manner Christ would again appear. He did not cease to exist when he expired, but would appear again that he might save his people, ver. 27, 28.

1. *Then verily.* Or, moreover. The object is to describe the tabernacle in which the service of God was celebrated under the former dispensation, and to show that it had a reference to what was future, and was only an imperfect representation of the reality. It was important to show this, as the Jews regarded the ordinances of the tabernacle and of the whole Levitical service as of divine appointment, and of perpetual obligation. The object of Paul is to prove that they were to give place to a more perfect system, and hence it was necessary to discuss their real nature. ¶ *The first* covenant. The word "covenant" is not in the Greek, but is not improperly supplied. The meaning is, that the

former arrangement or dispensation had religious rites and services connected with it. ¶ *Had also ordinances.* Margin, *ceremonies.* The Greek word means *laws, precepts, ordinances;* and the idea is, that there were laws regulating the worship of God. The Jewish institutions abounded with such laws. ¶ *And a worldly sanctuary.* The word *sanctuary* means a holy place, and is applied to a house of worship, or a temple. Here it may refer either to the temple or to the tabernacle. As the temple was constructed after the same form as the tabernacle, and had the same furniture, the description of the apostle may be regarded as applicable to either of them, and it is difficult to determine which he had in his eye. The term "worldly," applied to "sanctuary," here means that it pertained to this world; that it was contradistinguished from the heavenly sanctuary not made with hands, where Christ was now gone. Comp. ver. 11, 24. It does not mean that it was *worldly* in the sense in which that word is now used as denoting the opposite of spiritual, serious, religious, but worldly in the sense that it belonged to the earth rather than to heaven; it was made by human hands, not directly by the hands of God.

2. *For there was a tabernacle made.* The word "tabernacle" properly means a tent, a booth, or a hut, and was then given by way of eminence to the tent for public worship made by Moses in the wilderness. For a description of this, see Ex. xxv. The tabernacle, like the temple afterwards, was divided into two parts by the veil (Ex. xxvi. 31, 32), one of which was called the "holy place," and the other "the holy of holies." The exact size of the two rooms in the tabernacle is not specified in the Scriptures, but it is commonly supposed that the tabernacle was divided in the same man-

ner as the temple was afterward; that is, two-thirds of the interior constituted the holy place, and one-third the holy of holies. According to this, the holy place or *"first* tabernacle," was twenty cubits long by ten broad, and the most holy place was ten cubits square. The whole length of the tabernacle was about fifty-five feet, the breadth eighteen, and the height eighteen. In the temple, the two rooms, though of the same relative proportions, were of course much larger. See a description of the temple in the Notes on Mat. xxi. 12. In both cases, the holy place was at the east, and the holy of holies at the west end of the sacred edifice. ¶ *The first.* The first room on entering the sacred edifice, here called the "first tabernacle." The apostle proceeds now to enumerate the various articles of furniture which were in the two rooms of the tabernacle and temple. His object seems to be, not for information, for it could not be supposed that they to whom he was writing were ignorant on this point, but partly to show that it could not be said that he spoke of that of which he had no information, or that he undervalued it; and partly to show the real nature of the institution, and to prove that it was of an imperfect and typical character, and had a designed reference to something that was to come. It is remarkable that though he maintains that the whole institution was a "figure" of what was to come, and though he specifies by name all the furniture of the tabernacle, he does not attempt to explain their particular typical character, nor does he affirm that they *had* such a character. He does not say that the candlestick, the table of show-bread, the ark and the cherubim were intended to adumbrate some particular truth or fact of the future dispensation, or had a designed spiritual meaning. It would have been happy if all expositors had followed the example of Paul, and had been content, as he was, to state *the facts* about the tabernacle, and the general truth that the dispensation was intended to introduce a more perfect economy,

without endeavouring to explain the typical import of every pin and pillar of the ancient place of worship. If those things *had* such a designed typical reference, it is remarkable that Paul did not go into an explanation of that fact in the epistle before us. Never could a better opportunity for doing it occur than was furnished here. Yet it was not done. Paul is silent where many expositors have found occasion for admiration. Where they have seen the profoundest wisdom, he saw none; where they have found spiritual instruction in the various implements of divine service in the sanctuary, he found none. Why should we be more wise than he was? Why attempt to hunt for types and shadows where he found none? And why should we not be limited to the views which he *actually expressed* in regard to the design and import of the ancient dispensation? Following an inspired example, we are on solid ground, and are not in danger. But the moment we leave that, and attempt to spiritualize everything in the ancient economy, we are in an open sea without compass or chart, and no one knows to what fairy lands he may be drifted. As there are frequent allusions in the New Testament to the different parts of the tabernacle furniture here specified, we may offer a few remarks on the most material of them.

[Without attempting to explain the typical import of every pin and pillar of the tabernacle, one may be excused for thinking that such *prominent* parts of its furniture as the ark, the candlestick, and the cherubim were designed as types. Nor can it be wrong to inquire into the spiritual significancy of them, under such guidance as the light of Scripture here or elsewhere affords. This has been done by a host of most sober and learned commentators. It is of no use to allege that the apostle himself has given no particular explanation of these matters, since this would have kept him back too long from his main object, and is therefore expressly declined by him. "Yet," says M'Lean, "his manner of declining it implies that each of these sacred utensils had a mystical signification. They were all constructed according to particular divine directions, Ex. xxv. The apostle terms them 'the example and shadow of heavenly things,' Heb. viii. 5; 'the patterns of things

in the heavens,' ix. 23; and these typical patterns included not only the tabernacle and
its services, but every article of its furniture,
as is plain from the words of Moses, Ex. xxv.
8, 9. There are also other passages which seem
to allude to, and even to explain, some of these
articles, such as the golden candlestick, with
its seven lamps, Rev. i. 12, 13, 20; the golden
censer, viii. 3, 4; the vail, Heb. x. 20; the mercy-
seat, Rom. iii. 25; Heb. iv. 16; and, perhaps,
the angelic cherubim, 1 Pet. i. 12." It must,
however, be acknowledged that too great care
and caution cannot be used in investigating
such subjects.]

¶ *The candlestick.* For an account
of the candlestick, see Ex. xxv.
31-37. It was made of pure gold, and
had seven branches—that is, three on
each side and one in the centre. These
branches had on the extremities seven
golden lamps, which were fed with
pure olive-oil, and which were lighted
"to give light over against it;" that
is, they shed light on the altar of incense, the table of show-bread, and
generally on the furniture of the holy
place. These branches were made
with three "bowls," "knops," and
"flowers" occurring alternately on
each one of the six branches, while
on the centre or upright shaft there
were *four* "bowls," "knops," and
"flowers" of this kind. These ornaments were probably taken from the
almond, and represented the flower
of that tree in various stages. The
"bowls" on the branches of the candlestick probably meant the *calyx*, or
cup of that plant from which the
flower springs. The "knops" probably
referred to some ornament on the candlestick mingled with the "bowls"
and the "flowers," perhaps designed
as an imitation of the nut or fruit of
the almond. The "flowers" were
evidently ornaments resembling the
flowers on the almond-tree, wrought,
as all the rest were, in pure gold.
See Bush's Notes on Exodus xxv.
The candlestick was undoubtedly designed to furnish *light* in the dark
room of the tabernacle and temple;
and, in accordance with the general
plan of those edifices, was ornamented
after the most chaste and pure views
of ornamental architecture of those
times; but there is no evidence that
its branches, and bowls, and knops,

and flowers had each a peculiar typical significance. The sacred writers
are wholly silent as to any such reference, and it is not well to attempt to
be "wise above that which is written."
An expositor of the Scripture cannot
have a safer guide than the sacred
writers themselves. How should any
uninspired man know that these things
had such a peculiar typical signification? * The candlestick was placed
on the south, or left hand side of the
holy place as one entered, the row of
lamps being probably parallel with
the wall. It was at first placed in the
tabernacle, and afterwards removed
into the temple built by Solomon.
Its subsequent history is unknown.
Probably it was destroyed when the
temple was taken by the Chaldeans.
The form of the candlestick in the
second temple, whose figure is preserved on the "Arch of Titus" in
Rome, was of somewhat different construction. But it is to be remembered
that the articles taken away from
the temple by Vespasian were not the
same as those made by Moses, and
Josephus says expressly that the candlestick was altered from its original
form. ¶ *And the table.* That is, the
table on which the show-bread was
placed. This table was made of shittim-wood, overlaid with gold. It was
two cubits long, one cubit broad, and
a cubit and a half high; that is, about
three feet and a half in length, one
foot and nine inches in width, and
two feet and a half in height. It
was furnished with rings or staples,
through which were passed staves, by
which it was carried. These staves,
we are informed by Josephus, were
removed when the table was at rest,
so that they might not be in the way
of the priests as they officiated in the
tabernacle. It stood lengthwise east
and west, on the north side of the
holy place. ¶ *And the show-bread.*
On the table just described. This
bread consisted of twelve loaves,
placed on the table every Sabbath.
The Hebrew writers state that they
were square loaves, having the four
sides covered with leaves of gold.
They were arranged in two piles, of

* See Supplementary Note, p. 185.

3 And after *the second vail, | the tabernacle, which is called the
Holiest of all;

e Ex.26.31,33.

course with six in a pile, Lev. xxiv.
5–9. The number twelve was selected with reference to the twelve tribes
of Israel. They were made without
leaven, and were renewed each Sabbath, when the old loaves were then
taken away to be eaten by the
priests only. The Hebrew phrase rendered "show-bread" means properly
"bread of faces" or "bread of presence." The LXX. render it ἄρτους
ἐνωπίους, *foreplaced loaves*. In the
New Testament it is ἡ πρόθεσις τῶν
ἄρτων, *the placing of bread;* and in
Symmachus, "bread of proposition,"
or placing. Why it was called "bread
of presence" has been a subject on
which expositors have been much divided. Some have held that it was
because it was *before*, or in the presence of, the symbol of the divine presence in the tabernacle, though in another department; some that it was
because it was set there to be seen by
men rather than to be seen by God.
Others that it had an emblematic design, looking forward to the Messiah
as the food or nourishment of the soul,
and was substantially the same as the
table spread with the symbols of the
Saviour's body and blood. See Bush,
in loco. But of this last mentioned
opinion, it may be asked where is the
proof? It is not found in the account
of it in the Old Testament, and there
is not the slightest intimation in the
New Testament that it had any such
design. The *object* for which it was
placed there can be only a matter of
conjecture, as it is not explained in
the Bible, and it is more difficult to
ascertain the use and design of the
show-bread than of almost any other
emblem of the Jewish economy (Calmet). *Perhaps* the true idea, after all
that has been written and conjectured,
is, that the *table* and the *bread* were
for the sake of carrying out the idea
that the tabernacle was the *dwelling-
place* of God, and that there was a
propriety that it should be fitted up
with the usual appurtenances of a
dwelling. Hence there was a candle-

stick and a table, because these were
the common and ordinary furniture
of a room; and the idea was to be
kept up constantly that that was the
dwelling-place of the Most High, by
lighting and trimming the lamps every
day, and by renewing the bread on the
table periodically. The most simple
explanation of the phrase "bread of
faces," or "bread of presence," is,
that it was so called because it was
set before the *face*, or in the *presence*
of God in the tabernacle. The various
forms which it has been supposed
would represent the table of show-
bread may be seen in Calmet's *Large
Dictionary.* The Jews say that they
were separated by plates of gold.
¶ *Which is called the Sanctuary.*
Margin, "or, *holy.*" That is, *the holy
place.* The name *sanctuary* was commonly given to the whole edifice, but
with strict propriety appertained only
to this first room.

3. *And after the second vail.* There
were two *veils* to the tabernacle. The
one which is described in Ex. xxvi.
36, 37, was called "the hanging for
the door of the tent," and was made
of "blue, and purple, and scarlet, and
fine-twined linen," and was suspended
on five pillars of shittim-wood overlaid with gold. This answered for a
door to the whole tabernacle. The
second or inner veil, here referred to,
divided the holy from the most holy
place. This is described in Ex. xxvi.
31–33. It was made of the same materials as the other, though, it would
seem, in a more costly manner, and
with more embroidered work. On
this veil the figures of the cherubim
were curiously wrought. The design
of this veil was to separate the holy
from the most holy place; and in regard to its symbolical meaning we
can be at no loss, for the apostle Paul
has himself explained it in this chapter. See Notes on ver. 8–14. ¶ *The
tabernacle.* That is, the *inner* tabernacle; or that which more properly was
called the tabernacle. The name was
given to either of the two rooms into

4 Which had *f* the golden censer, and *g* the ark of the covenant overlaid round about with gold, wherein

f Le.16.12.   *g* Ex.25.10,&c.

---

which it was divided, or to the whole structure. ¶ *Which is called the Holiest of all.* It was called "the Most Holy place;" "the Holy of Holies;" or "the Holiest of all." It was so called because the symbol of the divine presence—the *shekinah*—dwelt there between the cherubim.

4. *Which had the golden censer.* The censer was a *fire-pan*, made for the purpose of carrying fire, in order to burn incense on it in the place of worship. The forms of the censer were various. Some difficulty has been felt respecting the statement of Paul here that the "golden censer" was in the most holy place, from the fact that no such utensil is mentioned by Moses as pertaining to the tabernacle, nor in the description of Solomon's temple, which was modelled after the tabernacle, is there any account of it given. But the following considerations will probably remove the difficulty: (1) Paul was a Jew, and was familiar with what pertained to the temple, and gave such a description of it as would be in accordance with what actually existed in his time. The fact that Moses does not expressly mention it does not prove that *in fact* no such censer was laid up in the most holy place. (2) Aaron and his successors were expressly commanded to burn incense in a "censer" in the most holy place before the mercy-seat. This was to be done on the great day of atonement, and but once in a year, Lev. xvi. 12, 13. (3) There is every probability that the censer that was used on such an occasion was made of gold. All the implements that were employed in the most holy place were made of gold, or overlaid with gold, and it is in the highest degree improbable that the high-priest would use any other on so solemn an occasion. Comp. 1 Ki. vii. 50. (4) As the golden censer was to be used only once in a year, it would naturally be laid away in some secure

was *h* the golden pot that had manna, and *i* Aaron's rod that budded, and *k* the tables of the covenant;

h Ex.16.33.   *i* Nu.17.10.
k Ex.34.29; 40.20; De.10.2,5.

---

situation, and none would so obviously occur as the most holy place. There it would be perfectly safe. No one was permitted to enter there but the high-priest, and being preserved there, it would be always ready for his use. The statement of Paul, therefore, has the highest probability, and undoubtedly accords with what actually occurred in the tabernacle and the temple. The object of the incense burned in worship was to produce an agreeable fragrance or smell. See Notes on Luke i. 9. ¶ *And the ark of the covenant.* This ark or *chest* was made of shittim-wood, was two cubits and a half long, a cubit and a half broad, and the same in height, Ex. xxv. 10. It was completely covered with gold, and had a *lid*, which was called the "mercy-seat," on which rested the shekinah, the symbol of the divine presence, between the outstretched wings of the cherubim. It was called "the ark of the covenant," because within it were the two tables of the covenant, or the law of God written on tables of stone. It was a simple *chest, coffer,* or *box,* with little ornament, though rich in its materials. A golden crown or moulding ran around the top, and it had rings and staves in its sides by which it might be borne, Ex. xxv. 12–16. This ark was regarded as the most sacred of all the appendages of the tabernacle. Containing the law, and being the place where the symbol of the divine presence was manifested, it was regarded as peculiarly holy, and in the various wars and revolutions in the Hebrew commonwealth it was guarded with peculiar care. After the passage over the Jordan it remained for some time at Gilgal (Josh. iv. 19), whence it was removed to Shiloh, 1 Sam. i. 3. From this place the Israelites took it to their camp, apparently to animate them in battle, but it was captured by the Philistines, 1 Sam. iv. The Philistines, however, op-

pressed by the hand of God, resolved to return it, and sent it to Kirjath-jearim, 1 Sam. vii. 1. In the reign of Saul it was at Nob. David conveyed it to the house of Obed-edom, and thence to his palace on Mount Zion, 2 Sam. vi. At the dedication of the temple it was placed in the holy of holies by Solomon, where it remained for many years. Subsequently, it is said, the wicked kings of Judah, abandoning themselves to idolatry, established idols in the most holy place itself, and the priests removed the ark, and bore it from place to place to secure it from profanation (Calmet). When Josiah ascended the throne he commanded the priests to restore the ark to its place in the sanctuary, and forbade them to carry it about from one place to another as they had before done, 2 Chr. xxxv. 3. The subsequent history of the ark is unknown. It is probable that it was either destroyed when the city of Jerusalem was taken by Nebuchadnezzar, or that it was carried, with other spoils, to Babylon. There is no good reason to suppose that it was ever in the second temple, and it is generally admitted by the Jews that the ark of the covenant was one of the things that were wanting there. Abarbanel says, that the Jews flatter themselves that it will be restored by the Messiah. ¶ *Wherein.* That is, *in the ark*—for so the construction naturally requires. In 1 Kings viii. 9, however, it is said that there was nothing *in* the ark, "save the two tables of stone which Moses put there at Horeb," and it has been supposed by some that the pot of manna and the rod of Aaron were not *in* the ark, but that they were in capsules, or ledges made on its sides for their safe-keeping, and that this should be rendered "*by* the ark." But the apostle uses the same language respecting the pot of manna and the rod of Aaron which he does about the two tables of stone, and as they were certainly *in* the ark, the fair construction here is that the pot of manna and the rod of Aaron were in it also. The account in Ex. xvi. 32–34; Num. xvii. 10, is, that they were laid up in the most holy place, "before the testi-

mony," and there is no improbability whatever in the supposition that they were *in* the ark. Indeed, that would be the most safe place to keep them, as the tabernacle was often taken down and removed from place to place. It is clear, from the passage in 1 Kings viii. 9, that they were not *in* the ark in the temple, but there is no improbability in the supposition that before the temple was built they might have been removed from the ark and lost. When the ark was carried from place to place, or during its captivity by the Philistines, it is probable that they were lost, as we never hear of them afterward. ¶ *The golden pot.* In Ex. xvi. 33, it is simply "a pot," without specifying the material. In the Septuagint it is rendered "golden pot," and as the other utensils of the sanctuary were of gold, it may be fairly presumed that this was also. ¶ *That had manna.* A small quantity of manna which was to be preserved as a perpetual remembrancer of the food which they had eaten in their long journey in the wilderness, and of the goodness of God in miraculously supplying their wants. As the manna, also, would not of itself keep (Ex. xvi. 20), the fact that this was to be laid up to be preserved from age to age, was a perpetual miracle in proof of the presence and faithfulness of God. On the subject of the manna, see Bush's Notes on Exodus xvi. 15. ¶ *And Aaron's rod that budded.* That budded and blossomed as a proof that God had chosen him to minister to him. The princes of the tribes were disposed to rebel, and to call in question the authority of Aaron. To settle the matter, each one was required to take a rod or staff of office, and to bring it to Moses with the name of the tribe to which it appertained written on it. These were laid up by Moses in the tabernacle, and it was found on the next day that the rod marked with the name of Levi had budded, and blossomed, and produced almonds. In perpetual remembrance of this miracle, the rod was preserved in the ark, Num. xvii. Its subsequent history is unknown. It was not *in* the ark when the temple was

5 And over it ᶦthe cherubim of glory shadowing the mercy-seat; of

l Ex.25.18,22.

which we cannot now speak particularly.

---

built, nor is there any reason to suppose that it was preserved to that time. ¶ *And the tables of the covenant.* The two tables of stone on which the ten commandments were written. They were expressly called "the words of the covenant" in Ex. xxxiv. 28. On the word *covenant,* see Notes on ver. 16 and 17 of this chapter. These two tables were in the ark at the time the temple was dedicated, 1 Ki. viii. 9. Their subsequent history is unknown. It is probable that they shared the fate of the ark, and were either carried to Babylon, or were destroyed when the city was taken by Nebuchadnezzar.

5. *And over it.* That is, over the ark. ¶ *The cherubim of glory.* A Hebrew mode of expression, meaning *the glorious cherubim.* The word *cherubim* is the Hebrew form of the plural, of which *cherub* is the singular. The word *glory,* used here in connection with " *cherubim,*" refers to the splendour or magnificence of the image, as being carved with great skill, and covered with gold. There were two cherubim on the ark, placed on the lid in such a manner that their faces looked inward toward each other, and downward toward the mercy-seat. They stretched out their wings "on high," and covered the mercy-seat, or the lid of the ark, Ex. xxv. 18–20. Comp. 1 Ki. viii. 6, 7 ; 1 Chr. xxviii. 18. In the temple, the cherubim were made of the olive-tree, and were ten cubits high. They were overlaid with gold, and were so placed that the wing of one touched the wall on one side of the holy of holies, and that of the other the other side, and their wings met together over the ark, 1 Ki. vi. 23–28. It is not probable, however, that this was the form used in the tabernacle, as wings thus expanded would have rendered it inconvenient to carry them from place to place. Of the form and design of the cherubim much has been written, and much that is the mere creation of fancy, and the fruit of wild conjecture.

Their design is not explained in the Bible, and silence in regard to it would have been wisdom. If they were intended to be symbolical, as is certainly possible (comp. Eze. x. 20–22), it is impossible now to determine the object of the symbol. Who is authorized to explain it? Who can give to his speculations anything more than the authority of *pious conjecture?* And of what advantage, therefore, can speculation be, where the volume of inspiration says nothing?* They who wish to examine this subject more fully, with the various opinions that have been formed on it, may consult the following works, viz.: Calmet's *Dictionary,* Fragment No. 152, with the numerous illustrations; Bush's Notes on Ex. xxv. 18; and the *Quarterly Christian Spectator,* vol. viii. pp. 368–388. Drawings resembling the cherubim were not uncommon on ancient sculptures. ¶ *Shadowing.* Stretching out its wings so as to cover the mercy-seat. ¶ *The mercy-seat.* The cover of the ark on which rested the cloud or visible symbol of the divine presence. It was called "mercy-seat," or *propitiatory*—ἱλαστήριον, *hilasterion*—because it was this which was sprinkled over with the blood of atonement or propitiation, and because it was from this place, on which the symbol of the deity rested, that God manifested himself as propitious to sinners. The blood of the atonement was that through or by means of which he declared his mercy to the guilty. Here God was supposed to be seated, and from this place he was supposed to dispense mercy to man when the blood of the atonement was sprinkled there. This was undoubtedly designed to be a symbol of his dispensing mercy to men in virtue of the blood which the Saviour shed as the great sacrifice for guilt. See ver. 13, 14. ¶ *Of which we cannot now speak particularly.* That is, it is not my present design to speak particularly of these things. These

* See the Supplementary Note, ver. 2.

6 Now when these things were thus ordained, *m*the priests went always into the first tabernacle, accomplishing the service *of God.*

7 But into the second *went n*the high priest alone once every year, not without blood, which *o*he offered for himself, and *for* the errors of the people:

8 The Holy Ghost this signifying, that *p*the way into the holiest of all was not yet made manifest, while as the first tabernacle was yet standing:

m Nu.28.3.   *n* Ex.30.10; Le.16.2,&c.   *o* ch.5.3.

p Jn.14.6; ch.10.19,20.

matters were well understood by those to whom he wrote, and his object did not require him to go into a fuller explanation.

6. *When these things were thus ordained.* Thus arranged or appointed. Having shown what the tabernacle *was,* the apostle proceeds to show what was *done in it.* ¶ *The priests went always into the first tabernacle.* The outer tabernacle, called the holy place. They were not permitted to enter the holy of holies, that being entered only once in a year by the high-priest. The holy place was entered every day to make the morning and evening oblation. ¶ *Accomplishing the service of* God. Performing the acts of worship which God had appointed—burning incense, &c., Luke i. 9.

7. *But into the second.* The second apartment or room, called the most holy place, ver. 3. ¶ *Went the high priest alone once every year.* On the great day of atonement, Ex. xxx. 10. On that day he probably entered the holy of holies three or four times, first to burn incense, Lev xvi. 12; then to sprinkle the blood of the bullock on the mercy-seat, Lev. xvi. 14; then he was to kill the goat of the sin-offering, and bring that blood within the veil and sprinkle it also on the mercy-seat; and then, perhaps, he entered again to bring out the golden censer. The Jewish tradition is, that he entered the holy of holies four times on that day. After all, however, the number of times is not certain, nor is it material, the only important point being that he entered it only on one day of the year, while the holy place was entered every day. ¶ *Not without blood.* That is, he bare with him blood to sprinkle on the mercy-seat. This was the blood of the bullock and of the goat—borne in at two different times. ¶ *Which he offered for himself.* The blood of the bullock was offered for himself and for his house or family—thus keeping impressively before his own mind and the mind of the people the fact that the priests, even of the highest order, were sinners, and needed expiation like others, Lev. xvi. 12. ¶ *And for the errors of the people.* The blood of the goat was offered for them, Lev. xvi. 15. The word rendered *errors*—ἀγνόημα—denotes properly *ignorance, involuntary error;* and then error or fault in general—the same as the Hebrew מִשְׁגֶּה—from שָׁגָה, *to err.* The object was to make expiation for *all* the errors and sins of the people, and this occurred *once* in the year. The repetition of these sacrifices was a constant remembrancer of sin, and the design was that neither the priests nor the people should lose sight of the fact that they were violators of the law of God.

8. *The Holy Ghost.* Who appointed all this. The whole arrangement in the service of the tabernacle is represented as having been under the direction of the Holy Ghost, or this was one of his methods of teaching the great truths of religion, and of keeping them before the minds of men. Sometimes that Spirit taught by direct revelation; sometimes by the written word; and sometimes by symbols. The tabernacle, with its different apartments, utensils, and services, was a *permanent* means of keeping important truths before the minds of the ancient people of God. ¶ *This signifying.* That is, showing this truth, or making use of this arrangement to impress the truth on the minds of men that the way into the holiest of all

9 Which *was* a figure for the time then present, in which were offered both gifts and sacrifices, *q* that could

q Ps.40.6,7; Ga.3.21; ch.10.1,11.

was not yet made manifest. ¶ *That the way into the holiest of all.* Into heaven—of which the most holy place in the tabernacle was undoubtedly designed to be an emblem. It was the place where the visible symbol of God —the shekinah—dwelt; where the blood of propitiation was sprinkled; and was, therefore, an appropriate emblem of that holy heaven where God dwells, and whence pardon is obtained by the blood of the atonement. ¶ *Was not yet made manifest.* The way to heaven was not opened or fully understood. It was not known how men could appear before God, or how they could come to him with the hope of pardon. That way has now been opened by the ascension of the Redeemer to heaven, and by the assurance that all who will may come in his name. ¶ *While as the first tabernacle was yet standing.* As long as it stood, and the appointed services were held in it. The idea is, that until that was superseded by a more perfect system, it was *a proof* that the way to heaven was not yet fully and freely opened, and that the Holy Ghost *designed* that it should be such a proof. The apostle does not specify in what the proof consisted, but it may have been in something like the following: (1) That it was a mere *symbol,* and not the *reality*—showing that the true way was not yet fully understood. (2) It was entered but once a year—showing that there was not access at all times. (3) It was entered only by the high-priest— showing that there was not free and full access to all the people. (4) It was accessible only by Jews—showing that the way in which all men might be saved was not then fully revealed. The sense is, that it was a system of types and shadows, in which there were many burdensome rites, and many things to prevent men from coming before the symbol of the divinity, and was, therefore, an *imperfect* system. All these obstructions are

not make him that did the service *r* perfect, as pertaining to the conscience;

r Ps.51.16–19.

now removed; the Saviour—the great High-priest of his people—has entered heaven and "opened it to all true believers," and all of every nation may now have free access to God. See ver. 12. Comp. chap. x. 19–22.

9. *Which* was *a figure for the time then present.* That is, as long as the tabernacle stood. The word rendered *figure* — παραβολὴ, *parabolē*—is not the same as *type*—τύπος, *typos* (Rom. v. 14; Acts vii. 43, 44; Jn. xx. 25; 1 Cor. x. 6, 11; Phil. iii. 17, *et al.*), but is the word commonly rendered *parable,* Mat. xiii. 3, 10, 13, 18, 24, 31, 33–36, 53; xv. 15, *et sæpe,* and means properly *a placing side by side;* then *a comparison,* or *similitude.* Here it is used in the sense of *image,* or *symbol*—something to *represent* other things. The idea is, that the arrangements and services of the tabernacle were a *representation* of important realities, and of things which were more fully to be revealed at a future period. There can be no doubt that Paul meant to say that this service in general was symbolical or typical, though this will not authorize us to attempt to spiritualize every minute arrangement of it. Some of the things in which it was typical are specified by the apostle himself; and wisdom and safety in explaining the arrangements of the tabernacle and its services consist in adhering *very closely* to the explanations furnished by the inspired writers. An interpreter is on an open sea, to be driven he knows not whither, when he takes leave of these safe pilots.* ¶ *Both gifts.* Thank-offerings. ¶ *And sacrifices.* Bloody offerings. The idea is, that all kinds of offerings to God were made there. ¶ *That could not make him that did the service perfect.* That could not take away sin, and remove the stains of guilt on the soul. See Notes on chap. vii. 11. Comp. chap. viii. 7; vii. 27; x. 1, 11. ¶ *As*

* See Supplementary Note, ver. 2.

10 *Which stood* only in *s*meats and drinks, and *t*divers washings, and carnal *3*ordinances,*u* imposed *on them* until the time of reformation.

s Le.11.2,&c.　　　　*t* Nu.19.7,&c.
3 or, *rites*; or, *ceremonies*.　*u* Ep.2.15.

11 But Christ being come *v*an high priest of *w*good things to come, by a *x*greater and more perfect tabernacle, not made with hands, that is to say, not of this building;

v ch.3.1.　　*w* ch.10.1.　　*x* ch.8.2.

pertaining to the conscience. They related mainly to outward and ceremonial rites, and even when offerings were made for *sin*, the conscience was not relieved. They could not expiate guilt; they could not make the conscience pure; they could not of themselves impart peace to the soul by reconciling it to God. They could not fully accomplish what was needed to be done in order to give peace. Nothing will do this but the blood of the Redeemer.

10. Which stood *only in meats and drinks.* The idea is, that the ordinances of the Jews, in connection with the services of religion, consisted much of laws pertaining to what was lawful to eat and drink, &c. A considerable part of those laws related to the distinction between clean and unclean beasts, and to such arrangements as were designed to keep the Jewish people externally distinct from other nations. It is possible also that there may be a reference here to meat and drink offerings. On the grammatical difficulties of this verse, see Stuart on the Hebrews, *in loco.* ¶ *And divers washings.* The various ablutions which were required in the service of the tabernacle and the temple—washing of the hands, of the victim that was to be offered, &c. It was for this purpose that the laver was erected in front of the tabernacle (Ex. xxx. 18; xxxi. 9; xxxv. 16), and that the brazen sea and the lavers were constructed in connection with the temple of Solomon, 2 Chr. iv. 3–5; 1 Ki. vii. 26. The Greek word here is *baptisms.* On its meaning, see Notes on Mat. iii. 6; Mark vii. 4. ¶ *And carnal ordinances.* Margin, " or, *rites* or *ceremonies.*" Greek, "ordinances of the flesh;" that is, which pertained to the flesh, or to external ceremonies. The ob-

ject was rather to keep them *externally* pure than to cleanse the conscience and make them holy in heart. ¶ *Imposed* on them. *Laid on them—ἐπικείμενα.* It does not mean that there was any *oppression* or *injustice* in regard to these ordinances, but that they were appointed for a temporary purpose. ¶ *Until the time of reformation.* The word here rendered *reformation — διόρθωσις —* means properly *emendation, improvement, reform.* It refers to putting a thing in a right condition; making it better; raising up and restoring that which is fallen down (Passow). Here the reference is undoubtedly to the gospel as being a better system — *a putting things where they ought to be.* Comp. Notes on Acts iii. 21. The idea here is, that those ordinances were only temporary in their nature, and were designed to endure till a more perfect system should be introduced. They were of value *to introduce* that better system; they were not adapted to purify the conscience and remove the stains of guilt from the soul.

11. *But Christ being come.* Now that the Messiah has come, a more perfect system is introduced by which the conscience may be made free from guilt. ¶ *An high priest of good things to come.* See chap. x. 1. The apostle having described the tabernacle, and shown wherein it was defective in regard to the real wants of sinners, proceeds now to describe the Christian system, and to show how that meets the real condition of man, and especially how it is adapted to remove sin from the soul. The phrase " high-priest of good things to come," seems to refer to those "good things" which belonged to the dispensation that *was to come;* that is, the dispensation under the Messiah. The Jews anticipated great blessings in his time. They looked forward to better things

12 Neither by the *y* blood of goats and calves, but by *z* his own blood

y ch.10.4.   *z* Ac.20.28; 1 Pe.1.18,19; Re.1.5.

he entered in once into *a* the holy place, having obtained eternal redemption *for us.*

a ch.10.19.

than they enjoyed under the old dispensation. They expected more signal proofs of the divine favour; a clearer knowledge of the way of pardon; and more eminent spiritual enjoyments. Of these, the apostle says that Christ, who had come, was now the high-priest. It was he by whom they were procured; and the time had actually arrived when they might enjoy the long-anticipated good things under the Messiah. ¶ *By a greater and more perfect tabernacle.* The meaning is, that Christ officiated as high-priest in a much more magnificent and perfect temple than either the tabernacle or the temple under the old dispensation. He performed the great functions of his priestly office—the sprinkling of the blood of the atonement—in heaven itself, of which the most holy place in the tabernacle was but the emblem. The Jewish high-priest entered the sanctuary made with hands to minister before God; Christ entered into heaven itself. The word "*by*" here — δià — means probably *through*, and the idea is, that Christ passed *through* a more perfect tabernacle on his way to the mercy-seat in heaven than the Jewish high-priest did when he passed *through* the outer tabernacle (ver. 2), and through the veil into the most holy place. Probably the idea in the mind of the writer was that of the Saviour passing through the *visible heavens* above us, to which the veil, dividing the holy from the most holy place in the temple, bore some resemblance. Many, however, have understood the word "tabernacle" here as denoting the *body* of *Christ* (see Grotius and Bloomfield, *in loco*); and according to this the idea is, that Christ, by means of his own body and blood offered as a sacrifice, entered into the most holy place in heaven. But it seems to me that the whole scope of the passage requires us to understand it of the more perfect temple in heaven where Christ performs his ministry, and of

which the tabernacle of the Hebrews was but the emblem. Christ did not belong to the tribe of Levi; he was not a high-priest of the order of Aaron; he did not enter the holy place on earth, but he entered the heavens, and perfects the work of his ministry there. ¶ *Not made with hands.* A phrase that properly describes heaven as being fitted up by God himself. See Notes on 2 Cor. v. 1. ¶ *Not of this building.* Greek, "of this *creation*"—κτίσεως. The meaning is, that the place where he officiates is not fitted up by human power and art, but is the work of God. The object is to show that his ministry is altogether more perfect than that which could be rendered by a Jewish priest, and performed in a temple which could not have been reared by human skill and power.

12. *Neither by the blood of goats and calves.* The Jewish sacrifice consisted of the shedding of the blood of animals. On the great day of the atonement the high-priest took with him into the most holy place (1) the blood of a young bullock (Lev. xvi. 3, 11), which is here called the blood of a "calf," which he offered for his own sin; and (2) the blood of a goat, as a sin-offering for others, Lev. xvi. 9, 15. It was *by,* or *by means of*—δià—blood thus sprinkled on the mercy-seat, that the high-priest sought the forgiveness of his own sins and the sins of the people. ¶ *But by his own blood.* That is, by his own blood shed for the remission of sins. The meaning is, that it was in virtue of his own blood, or *by means* of that, that he secured the pardon of his people. That blood was not shed for himself—for he had no sin—and consequently there was a material difference between his offering and that of the Jewish high-priest. The difference related to such points as these: (1) The offering which Christ made was wholly for others; that of the Jewish priest for

13 For if the blood of bulls and of goats, and *b* the ashes of an heifer sprinkling the unclean, sanctifieth to the purifying of the flesh;

b Nu.19.2-17.

himself as well as for the people. (2) The blood offered by the Jewish priest was that of animals; that offered by the Saviour was his own. (3) That offered by the Jewish priest was only an emblem or type—for it could not take away sin; that offered by Christ had a real efficacy, and removes transgression from the soul. ¶ *He entered into the holy place.* Heaven. The meaning is, that as the Jewish high-priest bore the blood of the animal that was sacrificed into the holy of holies, and sprinkled it there as the means of expiation, so the offering which Christ has to make in heaven, or the *consideration* on which he pleads for the pardon of his people, is the *blood* which he shed on Calvary. Having made the atonement, he now pleads the merit of it as a *reason* why sinners should be saved. It is not, of course, meant that he literally *bore* his own blood into heaven—as the high-priest did the blood of the bullock and the goat into the most holy place; or that he literally *sprinkled* it on the mercy-seat there, but that that blood, having been shed for sin, is now the ground of his pleading and intercession for the pardon of sin—as the *sprinkled* blood of the Jewish sacrifice was the ground of the pleading of the Jewish high-priest for the pardon of himself and the people. ¶ *Having obtained eternal redemption* for us. That is, by the shedding of his blood. On the meaning of the word *redemption*, see Notes on Gal. iii. 13. The redemption which the Lord Jesus effected for his people is *eternal.* It is not a temporary deliverance leaving the redeemed in danger of falling into sin and ruin, but it makes salvation secure, and in its effects extends through eternity. Who can estimate the extent of that love which purchased for us *such* a redemption? Who can be sufficiently grateful that he is thus redeemed? The *doctrine* in this verse is, that the blood of Christ is the means of redemption, or that

it atones for sin. In the following verses the apostle shows that it not only makes atonement for sin, but that it is the means of sanctifying or purifying the soul.

13. *For if the blood of bulls and of goats.* Referring still to the great day of atonement, when the offering made was the sacrifice of a bullock and a goat. ¶ *And the ashes of an heifer.* For an account of this, see Num. xix. 2-10. In Num. xix. 9, it is said that the ashes of the heifer, after it was burned, should be kept "for a water of separation; it is a purification for sin." That is, the ashes were to be carefully preserved, and, being mixed with water, were sprinkled on those who were from any cause ceremonially impure. The *reason* for this appears to have been that the heifer was considered as a sacrifice whose blood has been offered, and the application of the ashes after she was burned was regarded as an evidence of participation *in* that sacrifice. It was needful, where the laws were so numerous respecting external pollutions, or where the members of the Jewish community were regarded as so frequently "*unclean*" by contact with dead bodies, and in various other ways, that there should be some method in which they could be declared to be cleansed from their "uncleanness." The nature of these institutions also required that this should be in connection with *sacrifice*, and in order to this, it was arranged that there should be this *permanent sacrifice*—the ashes of the heifer that had been sacrificed—of which they could avail themselves at any time, without the expense and delay of making a bloody offering specifically for the occasion. It was, therefore, a provision of convenience, and at the same time was designed to keep up the idea that all purification was somehow connected with the shedding of blood. ¶ *Sprinkling the unclean.* Mingled with water, and sprinkled on the unclean. The word *unclean* here refers to such as had been defiled by contact

14 How much more shall the blood of Christ, *c*who through the eternal Spirit offered himself with-

out [4]spot to God, *d*purge your conscience from dead works *e*to serve the living God?

c 1 Pe.3.18.

[4] or, *fault.*   *d* ch.10.22.   *e* 1 Pe.4.2.

---

with dead bodies, or when one had died in the family, &c. See Num. xix. 11–22. ¶ *Sanctifieth to the purifying of the flesh.* Makes holy so far as the flesh or body is concerned. The uncleanness here referred to related to the body only, and of course the means of cleansing extended only to that. It was not designed to give peace to the conscience, or to expiate moral offences. The offering thus made removed the obstructions to the worship of God so far as to allow him who had been defiled to approach him in a regular manner. Thus much, the apostle allows, was accomplished by the Jewish rites. They *had* an efficacy in removing ceremonial uncleanness, and in rendering it proper that he who had been polluted should be permitted again to approach and worship God. The apostle goes on to argue that if *they* had such an efficacy, it was fair to presume that the blood of Christ would have far greater efficacy, and would reach to the conscience itself, and make that pure.

14. *How much more shall the blood of Christ.* As being infinitely more precious than the blood of an animal could possibly be. If the blood of an animal had any efficacy at all, even in removing ceremonial pollutions, how much more is it reasonable to suppose may be effected by the blood of the Son of God! ¶ *Who through the eternal Spirit.* This expression is very difficult, and has given rise to a great variety of interpretation. Some MSS. instead of *eternal* here, read *holy*, making it refer directly to the Holy Spirit. See Wetstein. These various readings, however, are not regarded as of sufficient authority to lead to a change in the text, and are of importance only as showing that it was an early opinion that the Holy Spirit is here referred to. The principal opinions which have been entertained of the meaning of this phrase are the following: (1) That which regards it as referring to the

Holy Spirit, the third person of the Trinity. This was the opinion of Owen, Doddridge, and Archbishop Tillotson. (2) That which refers it to the *divine nature* of Christ. Among those who have maintained this opinion, are Beza, Ernesti, Wolf, Vitringa, Storr, and the late Dr. J. P. Wilson, *MS. Notes.* (3) Others, as Grotius, Rosenmüller, Koppe, understand it as meaning *endless* or *immortal life*, in contradistinction from the Jewish sacrifices, which were of a perishable nature, and which needed so often to be repeated. (4) Others regard it as referring to the glorified person of the Saviour, meaning that in his exalted or spiritual station in heaven, he presents the efficacy of his blood. (5) Others suppose that it means *divine influence*, and that the idea is, that Christ was actuated and filled with a divine influence when he offered up himself as a sacrifice; an influence which was not of a temporal and fleeting nature, but which was eternal in its efficacy. This is the interpretation preferred by Prof. Stuart. For an examination of these various opinions, see his "Excursus xviii." on this epistle. It is difficult, if not impossible, to decide what is the true meaning of the passage amidst this diversity of opinion; but there are some reasons which seem to me to make it probable that the Holy Spirit is intended, and that the idea is, that Christ made his great sacrifice under *the extraordinary influences of that Eternal Spirit.* The reasons which lead me to this opinion are the following: (1) It is the interpretation which would naturally occur to the readers of the New Testament. It is presumed that the great body of sober, plain, and intelligent Christians, on perusing the passage, suppose that it refers to the Holy Ghost, the third person of the Trinity. There are few better and safer rules for the interpretation of a volume designed, like the Bible, for the mass of mankind, than to abide by the

sense in which they understand it. (2) This interpretation is one which is most naturally conveyed by the language of the original. The phrase *the spirit—τὸ πνέυμα—*has so far a technical and established meaning in the New Testament as to denote the Holy Ghost, unless there is something in the connection which renders such an application improper. In this case there is nothing certainly which *necessarily* forbids such an application. The high names and classical authority of those who have held this opinion are a sufficient guarantee of this. (3) This interpretation accords with the fact that the Lord Jesus is represented as having been eminently endowed with the influences of the Holy Spirit. Comp. Notes on John iii. 34. Though he was divine, yet he was also a man, and as such was under influences similar to those of other pious men. The Holy Spirit is the source and sustainer of all piety in the soul, and it is not improper to suppose that the man Christ Jesus was in a remarkable manner influenced by the Holy Ghost in his readiness to obey God, and to suffer according to his will. (4) If there was *ever* any occasion on which we may suppose he was influenced by the Holy Ghost, that of his sufferings and death here referred to may be supposed eminently to have been such an one. It was expressive of the highest state of piety—the purest love to God and man—which has ever existed in the human bosom; it was the most trying time of his own life; it was the period when there would be the strongest temptations to abandon his work; and as the redemption of the whole world was dependent on that act, it is reasonable to suppose that the richest heavenly grace would be then imparted to him, and that he would then be most eminently under the influence of that Spirit which was granted not "*by measure* unto him." See Notes on John iii. 34. (5) This representation is not inconsistent with the belief that the sufferings and death of the Redeemer were *voluntary*, and that they had all the merit which belongs to a voluntary transaction. Piety in the heart of a Christian now is not less voluntary because it is produced and cherished by the Holy Ghost, nor is there less excellence in true religion because the Holy Ghost imparts strong faith in the time of temptation and trial. It seems to me, therefore, that the meaning of this expression is, that the Lord Jesus was led by the strong influences of the Spirit of God to devote himself as a sacrifice for sin. It was not by any temporary influence; it was not by mere excitement; it was by the influence of the *Eternal* Spirit of God, and the sacrifice thus offered could, therefore, accomplish effects which would be *eternal* in their character. It was not like the offering made by the Jewish high-priest, which was necessarily renewed every year, but it was under the influence of a great agent who was himself *eternal*, and the effects of whose influence might therefore endure for ever. It may be added, that if this is a correct exposition, it follows that the Holy Ghost is *eternal*, and must therefore be divine. ¶ *Offered himself.* That is, as a sacrifice. He did not offer a bullock or a goat, but he offered *himself.* The sacrifice of one's self is the highest offering which he can make; in this case it was the highest which the universe had to make. ¶ *Without spot.* Margin, "or *fault.*" The animal that was offered in the Jewish sacrifices was to be without blemish. See Lev. i. 10; xxii. 19–22. It was not to be lame, or blind, or diseased. The word which is here used and rendered "without spot"—*ἄμωμος*—refers to this fact, that there was no defect or blemish. The idea is, that the Lord Jesus, the great sacrifice, was *perfect.* See chap. vii. 26. ¶ *Purge your conscience.* That is, cleanse, purify, or sanctify your conscience. The idea is, that this offering would take away whatever rendered the conscience defiled or sinful. The offerings of the Jews related in the main to external purification, and were not adapted to give peace to a troubled conscience. They could render the worshipper externally pure, so that he might draw near to God and not be excluded by any ceremonial pollution or defilement; but the mind, the heart, the

15 And for this cause he is the mediator of the new testament, that by means of death, for the redemption of the transgressions *that*

---

conscience, they could not make pure. They could not remove that which troubles a man when he recollects that he has violated a holy law and has offended God, and when he looks forward to an awful judgment bar. The word *conscience* here is not to be understood as a distinct and independent faculty of the soul, but as *the soul* or *mind itself* reflecting and pronouncing on its own acts. The whole expression refers to a mind alarmed by the recollection of *guilt*—for it is guilt only that disturbs a man's conscience. Guilt originates in the soul remorse and despair; guilt makes a man troubled when he thinks of death and the judgment; guilt alarms a man when he thinks of a holy God; guilt, and nothing but guilt, makes the entrance into another world terrible and awful. If a man had no guilt he would never dread his Maker, nor would the presence of his God be ever painful to him (comp. Gen. iii. 6–10); if a man had no guilt he would not fear to die—for what have the innocent to fear anywhere? The universe is under the government of a God of goodness and truth, and, under such a government, how *can* those who have done no wrong have anything to dread? The fear of death, the apprehension of the judgment to come, and *the dread of God*, are strong and irrefragable proofs that every man is a sinner. The only thing, therefore, which ever disturbs the conscience, and makes death dreadful, and God an object of aversion, and eternity awful, is GUILT. If that is removed, man is calm and peaceful; if not, he is the victim of wretchedness and despair. ¶ *From dead works.* From works that are deadly in their nature, or that lead to death. Or it may mean, from works that have no spirituality and no life. By *"works"* here the apostle does not refer to their outward religious acts particularly, but to the conduct of the life—to what men *do;* and the idea is, that their acts are not spiritual and saving, but such as lead to death. See Notes

on chap. vi. 1. ¶ *To serve the living God.* Not in outward form, but in sincerity and in truth; to be his true friends and worshippers. The phrase "the *living* God" is commonly used in the Scriptures to describe the true God as distinguished from idols, which are represented as *dead*, or without life, Ps. cxv. 4–7. The idea in this verse is, that it is only the sacrifice made by Christ which can remove the stain of guilt from the soul. It could not be done by the blood of bulls and of goats—for that did not furnish relief to a guilty conscience, but it could be done by the blood of Christ. The sacrifice which he made for sin was so pure and of such value, that God can consistently pardon the offender and restore him to his favour. That blood, too, can give peace—for Christ poured it out in behalf of the guilty. It is not that he took part with the sinner against God; it is not that he endeavours to convince him who has a troubled conscience that he is needlessly alarmed, or that sin is not as bad as it is represented to be, or that it does not expose the soul to danger. Christ never took the part of the sinner against God; he never taught that sin was a small matter, or that it did not expose to danger. He admitted all that is said of its evil. But he provides for giving peace to the guilty conscience by shedding his own blood that it may be forgiven, and by revealing a God of mercy who is willing to receive the offender into favour, and to treat him as though he had never sinned. Thus the troubled conscience may find peace; and thus, though guilty, man may be delivered from the dread of the wrath to come.

15. *And for this cause.* With this view; that is, to make an effectual atonement for sin, and to provide a way by which the troubled conscience may have peace. ¶ *He is the mediator.* See Notes on Gal. iii. 19, 20. He is the Mediator between God and man in respect to that new covenant which he has made, or that new dispensation

were under the first testament, they which are called might receive the promise of eternal inheritance:

16 For where a testament *is*, there must also of necessity [5] be the death of the testator.

[5] or, *be brought in.*

by which men are to be saved. He stands *between* God and man—the parties at variance—and undertakes the work of mediation and reconciliation. ¶ *Of the new testament.* Not *testament*—for a *testament*, or *will*, needs no mediator; but of the *new covenant*, or the new *arrangement* or *disposition* of things under which he proposes to pardon and save the guilty. See Notes on ver. 16, 17. ¶ *That by means of death.* His own death as a sacrifice for sin. The *old* covenant or arrangement also contemplated *death*—but it was the death of an *animal.* The purposes of this were to be effected by the death of the Mediator himself; or this covenant was to be ratified in his blood. ¶ *For the redemption of the transgressions* that were *under the first testament.* The covenant or arrangement under Moses. The general idea here is, that these were offences for which no expiation could be made by the sacrifices under that dispensation, or from which the blood then shed could not redeem. This general idea may include two particulars: (1) That they who had committed transgressions under that covenant, and who could not be fully pardoned by the imperfect sacrifices then made, would receive a full forgiveness of all their sins in the great day of account through the blood of Christ. Though the blood of bulls and goats could not expiate, yet they offered that blood in faith; they relied on the promised mercy of God; they looked forward to a perfect sacrifice; and now the blood of the great atonement, offered as a *full* expiation for all their sins, would be the ground of their acquittal in the last day. (2) That the blood of Christ would *now* avail for the remission of all those sins which could not be expiated by the sacrifices offered under the law. It not only contemplated the remission of all the offences committed by the truly pious under that law, but would *now* avail to put away sin entirely.

No sacrifice which men could offer would avail, but the blood of Christ would remove all that guilt. ¶ *That they which are called.* Alike under the old covenant and the new. ¶ *Might receive the promise of eternal inheritance.* That is, the fulfilment of the promise; or that they might be made partakers of eternal blessings. That blood is effectual alike to save those under the ancient covenant and the new, so that they will be saved in the same manner, and unite in the same song of redeeming love.

16. *For where a testament* is. This is the same word—διαθήκη, *diathēkē*—which in chap. viii. 6 is rendered *covenant.* For the general signification of the word, see Notes on that verse. There is so much depending, however, on the meaning of the word, not only in the interpretation of this passage, but also of other parts of the Bible, that it may be proper to explain it here more at length. The word—διαθήκη—occurs in the New Testament thirty-three times. It is translated *covenant* in the common version, in Luke i. 72; Acts iii. 25; vii. 8; Rom. ix. 4; xi. 27; Gal. iii. 15, 17; iv. 24; Eph. ii. 12; Heb. viii. 6, 8, 9 *twice,* 10; ix. 4 *twice;* x. 16; xii. 24; xiii. 20. In the remaining places it is rendered *testament,* Mat. xxvi. 28; Mark xiv. 24; Luke xxii. 20; 1 Cor. xi. 25; 2 Cor. iii. 6, 14; Heb. vii. 22; ix. 15–17, 20; Rev. xi. 19. In four of those instances (Mat. xxvi. 28; Mark xiv. 24; Luke xxii. 20, and 1 Cor. xi. 25) it is used with reference to the institution or celebration of the Lord's supper. In the Septuagint it occurs not far from three hundred times, in considerably more than two hundred of which it is the translation of the Hebrew word בְּרִית—*berith.* In one instance (Zec. xi. 14) it is the translation of the word *brotherhood;* once (Deut. ix. 5), of דָּבָר, *word;* once (Jer. xi. 2, 3), of "words of the covenant;" once (Lev. xxvi. 11), of *taber-*

nacle; once (Ex. xxxi. 7), of *testimony.* It occurs once (Ezek. xx. 37), where the reading of the Greek and Hebrew text is doubtful; and it occurs three times (1 Sam. xi. 2; xx. 8; 1 Ki. viii. 9), where there is no corresponding word in the Hebrew text. From this use of the word by the authors of the Septuagint, it is evident that they regarded it as the proper translation of the Hebrew בְּרִית — *berith,* and as conveying the same sense which that word does. It cannot be reasonably doubted that the writers of the New Testament were led to the use of the word, in part, at least, by the fact that they found it occurring so frequently in the version in common use, but it cannot be doubted also that they regarded it as *fairly* conveying the sense of the word בְּרִית — *berith.* On no principle can it be supposed that inspired and honest men would use a word, in referring to transactions in the Old Testament, which did not *fairly* convey the idea which the writers of the Old Testament meant to express. The use being thus regarded as settled, there are some *facts* in reference to it which are of great importance in interpreting the New Testament, and in understanding the nature of the "covenant" which God makes with man. These facts are the following: (1) The word διαϑήκη — *diathēkē* — is not that which properly denotes *compact, agreement,* or *covenant.* That word is συνϑήκη — *synthēkē* — or, in other forms, σύνϑεσις and συνϑεσίας; or, if the word *diathēkē* is used in that signification, it is only remotely, and as a secondary meaning. See Passow; comp. the Septuagint in Is. xxviii. 15; xxx. 1; Dan. xi. 6, and Wisd. i. 16; 1 Mac. x. 26; 2 Mac. xiii. 25; xiv. 26. It is not the word which a *Greek* would have employed to denote a *compact* or *covenant.* He would have employed it to denote a *disposition, ordering,* or *arrangement* of things, whether of religious rites, civil customs, or property; or if used with reference to a *compact,* it would have been with the idea of an *arrangement* or *ordering* of matters, not with the primary

notion of an agreement with another. (2) The word properly expressive of a covenant or compact — συνϑήκη — is *never* used in the New Testament. In all the allusions to the transactions between God and man, this word never occurs. From some cause, the writers and speakers in the New Testament seem to have supposed that that word would leave an impression which they did not wish to leave. Though it might have been supposed that in speaking of the various transactions between God and man they would have selected this word, yet with entire uniformity they have avoided it. No one of them — though the word διαϑήκη — *diathēkē* has been used by no less than six of them — has been betrayed in a single instance into the use of the word συνϑήκη — *synthēkē,* or has differed from the other writers in the language employed. This cannot be supposed to be the result of concert or collusion, but it must have been founded on some reason which operated equally on all their minds. (3) In like manner, and with like remarkable uniformity, the word συνϑήκη — *synthēkē* — is *never* used in the Septuagint with reference to any arrangement or "covenant" between God and man. Once indeed in the Apocrypha, and but once, it is used in that sense. In the only three other instances in which it occurs in the Septuagint, it is with reference to compacts between man and man, Isa. xxviii. 15; xxx. 1; Dan. xi. 6. This remarkable fact, that the authors of that version *never* use the word to denote any transaction between God and man, shows that there must have been some reason for it which acted on *their* minds with entire uniformity. (4) It is no less remarkable that neither in the Septuagint nor the New Testament is the word διαϑήκη — *diathēkē* — *ever* used in the sense of *will* or *testament,* unless it be in the case before us. This is conceded on all hands, and is expressly admitted by Professor Stuart (*Com. on Heb.,* p. 439), though he defends this use of the word in this passage. A very important inquiry presents itself here which has never received a solution generally regarded as satis-

factory. It is, why the word διαϑήκη—*diathēkē*—was selected by the writers of the New Testament to express the nature of the transaction between God and man in the plan of salvation. It might be said, indeed, that they found this word uniformly used in the Septuagint, and that they employed it as expressing the idea which they wished to convey with sufficient accuracy. But this is only removing the difficulty one step further back. Why did the authors of that translation adopt this word? Why did they not rather use the common and appropriate Greek word to express the notion of a covenant? A suggestion on this subject has already been made in the Notes on chap. viii. 6. Comp. *Bib. Repository*, vol. xx. p. 55. Another reason may, however, be suggested for this remarkable fact which is liable to no objection. It is, that in the apprehension of the authors of the Septuagint, and of the writers of the New Testament, the word διαϑήκη—*diathēkē*—in its original and proper signification of an *arrangement*, a *disposition*, an *ordering, fairly* conveyed the sense of the Hebrew word בְּרִית—*berith*, and that the word συνϑήκη—*synthēkē*—or *compact, agreement*, would *not* express that; and *that they never meant to be understood as conveying the idea either that God entered into a* COMPACT *with man, or that he made a* WILL. They meant to represent him as making *an arrangement, a disposition, an ordering* of things, by which his service might be kept up among his people, and by which men might be saved; but they were equally remote from representing him as making either a *compact* or a *will*. In support of this there may be alleged (1) the remarkable uniformity in which the word διαϑήκη—*diathēkē*—is used, showing that there was some *settled principle* from which they never departed; and (2) the meaning of the word itself. Professor Stuart has undoubtedly given the accurate original sense of the word. "The real, genuine, and original meaning of διαϑήκη [*diathēkē*] is, *arrangement, disposition*, or *disposal* of a thing" (p. 440). The word from which

it is derived—διατίϑημι—means to place apart or asunder; and then to set, arrange, dispose in a certain order (Passow). From this original signification is derived the use which the word has with singular uniformity in the Scriptures. It denotes the *arrangement, disposition*, or *ordering* of things which God made in relation to mankind, by which he designed to keep up his worship on earth, and to save the soul. It means neither covenant nor will; neither compact nor legacy; neither agreement nor testament. It is an *arrangement* of an entirely different order from either of them, and the sacred writers, with a uniformity which could have been secured only by the presiding influence of the One Eternal Spirit, have avoided the suggestion that God made with man either a *compact* or a *will*. We have no word which precisely expresses this idea, and hence our conceptions are constantly floating between a *compact* and a *will*, and the views which we have are as unsettled as they are unscriptural. The simple idea is, that God has made an *arrangement* by which his worship may be celebrated and souls saved. Under the Jewish economy this arrangement assumed one form; under the Christian, another. In neither was it a compact or covenant between two parties in such a sense that one party would be at liberty to reject the terms proposed; in neither was it a testament or will, as if God had left a legacy to man, but in both there were some things in regard to the arrangement such as are found *in* a covenant or compact. One of those things, equally appropriate to a compact between man and man, and to this arrangement, the apostle refers to here—that it implied in all cases the death of the victim. If these remarks are well-founded, they should be allowed materially to shape our views in the interpretation of the Bible. Whole treatises of divinity have been written on a mistaken view of the meaning of this word—understood as meaning *covenant*. Volumes of angry controversy have been published on the nature of the "covenant" with Adam, and on its influence on

his posterity. The only *literal* "covenant" which can be supposed in the plan of redemption is that between the Father and the Son—though even the existence of such a covenant is rather the result of devout and learned imagining than of any distinct statement in the volume of inspiration. The simple statement there is, that God has made an arrangement for salvation, the execution of which he has intrusted to his Son, and has proposed it to man to be accepted as the only arrangement by which man can be saved, and which he is not at liberty to disregard.

[Whatever merit may attach to these observations on the meaning of διαθηκη and its corresponding term בְּרִית—and the author displays no small measure of critical research—the doctrine of covenants is not in any way affected by them. The advocates of that doctrine deny that it rests on a mistaken view, or on any view, of the original term ordinarily rendered covenant. These terms, they most freely allow, occur in various senses, in the sense of simple appointment, promise, command, dispensation, and testament, as well as of stipulation or covenant, Jer. xxxiii. 25; Gen. ix. 11; Heb. viii. 7, &c. "It is not," says an able and accurate modern writer, "from the simple occurrence of the Hebrew or the Greek words that we are to infer a federal transaction between God and man, or between any other parties, but *from the circumstances of the case*, which alone can determine in what sense the terms are employed. We may meet with them when no covenant is implied, and we may find a covenant to have been made where neither of them is used to express it. We should beware," he adds, "of falling into the mistake of some superficial readers of the Scripture, who have occasionally misinterpreted passages in which the word occurs by explaining it of the covenant of works or the covenant of grace when something different is intended." Heb. viii. 7 is alleged as an example of passages in regard to which the mistake is made, whereas the apostle, in that place, is not treating of the covenant of grace absolutely, as opposed to the covenant of works, but of the two great dispensations of religion, the one introduced by Moses and the other by Christ. It may serve to explain many passages in the Epistle to the Hebrews to observe that the covenant of grace, strictly so called, is supposed to pervade both the παλαια and καινη διαθηκη of that epistle, its old and new covenant or dispensation alike; that, in fact, these are but different forms in which the same covenant of grace is administered in dif-

ferent ages. More of this shortly. Meanwhile it appears that no such fabric, no such treatise of divinity, as is alleged, has been built on the slender foundation of erroneous verbal criticism. It is of importance that this should be attended to, for the same statement has been put forth with confidence by certain writers in our own country, who, in their antipathy to the doctrine of covenants, have, after the example of the American brethren, greatly lamented "that so many entire systems of theology and bodies of divinity should have been cast into the mould of a single word, which, after all, is found out to be but a mistranslation." The reader will admire the temerity that can venture such groundless assertions, and think that lamentations, which have no better foundation, may in future be spared or kept in reserve till real cause require them.

What, then, is the evidence of the doctrine of covenants? Our author, under the conviction that his criticisms had undermined that doctrine, first assails the covenant of works, and, in a single sentence, clears the ground of it, lamenting that volumes of angry controversy should have been written about a thing so visionary. That such a transaction, as divines have usually designated by this name, has a real existence, the reader will find asserted and proved in a Supplementary Note on Rom. v. 12. The author is not disposed to deal so summarily with the covenant of redemption or of grace. He seems to allow that something of the kind may possibly exist, though he inclines to believe it has its place only in the "imagination of the devout and learned." But his own countryman, Dr. Dwight, though far from being subject to such pious hallucinations, and little inclined to receive any doctrine because it had long passed current, finds the covenant of grace distinctly set forth in Isa. liii. 10, 12, and again abundantly evinced in the eighty-ninth Psalm! Having explained the first of these passages, and commented on the engagements of the Son and the promises of the Father, he thus sums up:—"All these things are exhibited to us *in the form of a covenant*. To this covenant, as to every other, there are two *parties*—GOD who promises, and his servant who was to justify many. A *condition* is specified, to which is annexed a *promise* of reward. The condition is, that Christ should make his soul an offering for sin, and make intercession for the transgressors, or, in other words, execute the whole office of a priest for mankind. The reward is, that he should receive the many for his portion, and that they should prolong their days or endure for ever" (Sermon xliii.). Indeed, no one can read the fifty-third of Isaiah without finding in it the *essentials* of a covenant transaction, unless he

be predetermined not to find such transaction there or anywhere else. According to Lowth's translation the tenth verse runs thus, "IF his soul shall make a propitiatory sacrifice, he SHALL see a seed, which shall prolong their days, and the gracious purpose of Jehovah shall prosper in his hands." That the same transaction is introduced in the eighty-ninth Psalm is obvious enough. None will doubt the application of this Psalm to Christ, concerning whom Jehovah says, "I have made a covenant with my chosen, I have sworn unto David my servant, thy seed will I establish for ever, and build up thy throne to all generations." The *promise* is the very same as in Isaiah. The only difference between the passages is, that the condition is *expressed* in Isaiah and *understood* in the Psalm, in consequence of which the covenant there appears rather in the form of a promissory oath. The covenant itself, however, is *expressly named*. "I have made (stricken) a covenant." It is not possible, in the compass of a brief note, to produce all the evidence which the Scripture contains on this subject. For the present we must content ourselves with a simple statement of the chief heads of evidence. Those theologians, then, who receive the doctrine, suppose that it is necessarily implied, in the surety and representative character of Christ, in the title of the "second Adam" which an apostle gives him, and which is believed to be destitute of meaning, unless, though dissimilar in other respects, he be like the first Adam in this, that he is a covenant head. Many men intervened between Adam and Christ, yet to Christ only is the title applied, and unless the fact now stated be the reason of that application, it must be difficult, if not impossible, to assign any; see Supplementary Note on Rom. v. 12. Further, Christ's repeated declarations that he came to do the will of the Father imply that certain services had been prescribed to him. "Indeed," says an author already quoted, "*the whole scheme of redemption* involves the idea of a covenant; while one divine person prescribes certain services to the other, the other performs them; and the result is not only his own personal exaltation, but the eternal happiness of millions, whose cause he had espoused" (Dick).

The reader must have observed that the parties in this covenant are the Father and the Son, and will naturally be anxious to have that *class* of passages explained in which the parties are God and the saints or the people of Christ, or in which the covenant is supposed to be made WITH THEM, Isa. lv. 3; Heb. viii. 10; 2 Sam. xxiii. 5. From the existence of such passages a double covenant, connected with the salvation of sinners, has been supposed and advocated by certain divines—the one made with Christ in eternity, and the other with his people in time. These have been respectively distinguished as the covenant of redemption and the covenant of grace. By the generality of accurate writers, however, this distinction has been abandoned as untenable, and these two covenants declared to be but *one*, presented *in different aspects*. The covenant made with the saints is but the administration of that made with Christ, the fulfilment, the performance of it. Hence we read of the "blood of the *covenant*" —not "of the *covenants*." For a full discussion of this part of the subject see the admirable treatise of Mr. Bell, once minister in Glasgow, frequently quoted with admiration by Mr. Haldane in his commentary on the Romans. "What some call the covenant of grace," says he, "in distinction from that of redemption, is nothing but the *promulgation* and *performance* of what was transacted with Christ in behalf of the elect. Then the Father promised, that on condition he made his soul an offering for sin he would quicken, justify, sanctify, and save all those sinners whose substitute he was. Now, what is the covenant of grace but the promulgation and performance of these promises? What was originally made to the surety only is now directed to sinners themselves. This, however, can in no propriety of speech be called a different covenant from that made with Christ. It is only the revelation of what before lay hid in the cabinet council of heaven—a making good to the children what was promised to their Father before they had a being."

It would appear, therefore, that from the beginning there have been but two covenants, that of works, and that of grace or redemption—the first made with Adam, and the last with Christ—both being regarded as the covenant heads of the parties that respectively belonged to them. But in consistency with this view how shall we account for the mention of that *other covenant* different from the covenant of works, and with which the new covenant in this epistle is contrasted, chap. viii.–x.? The proper solution of this question lies in the fact already hinted, that but *one* covenant, strictly so called, obtained, *alike under Moses and Christ*, and that the old and the new of the Epistle to the Hebrews point only to *different modes* of its administration. It is certain that the Sinaitic covenant did not supersede the Abrahamic, which was nothing but the covenant of grace, "the covenant that was confirmed before of God in Christ," Gal. iii. 15–17. Nay, the ceremonies and sacrifices of the Mosaic dispensation exhibited, in shadow, the blessings of that very covenant that was ultimately to be administered in a more clear and spiritual form.

Let it be noted, in conclusion, that most of the objections alleged against the doctrine of covenants arise from misconception or misrepresentation. When a covenant is said to be made between God and man, it is allowed on all hands that it differs in many important particulars from a human covenant or covenant between man and man. The parties in the first case are not equal, and there is not liberty, on the part of the inferior, to receive or reject the terms at pleasure. Everything must be set aside, in our conceptions of the subject, that is inconsistent with the majesty and authority of God; see Supplementary Note on Rom. v. 12. And this difference, originating in the unequal character of the parties, may, perhaps, furnish an answer to the question, which the author so frequently puts, concerning the use of διαθηκη in preference to συνθηκη, and as frequently answers, by resolving the covenant between God and man, it is of that nature as cannot properly be termed συνθηκη, which is a covenant or compact upon equal terms of distributive justice between distinct parties." The length of this Note will be excused on the ground of the very frequent recurrence of the subject of it in the present volume, and the expediency of treating it fully in some place, to which simple reference might in other places be made, for the economizing of labour.]

There has been much difference of opinion in reference to the meaning of the passage here, and to the design of the illustration introduced. If the word used—διαθήκη—means *testament*, in the sense of a *will*, then the sense of that passage is that "a will is of force only when he who made it dies, for it relates to a disposition of his property after his death." The force of the remark of the apostle then would be, that the fact that the Lord Jesus made or expressed his *will* to mankind, implied that he would die to confirm it; or that since, in the ordinary mode of making a will, it was of force only when he who made it was dead, therefore it was necessary that the Redeemer should die, in order to confirm and ratify that which he made. But the objections to this, which appears to have

been the view of our translators, seem to me to be insuperable. They are these: (1) The word διαθήκη—*diathēkē*—is not used in this sense in the New Testament elsewhere. See the remarks above. (2) The Lord Jesus made no such *will*. As a man he *had* no property, and the commandments and instructions which he gave to his disciples were not of the nature of a *will* or testament. (3) Such an illustration would not be pertinent to the design of the apostle, or in keeping with his argument. He is comparing the Jewish and Christian dispensations with each other, and the point of comparison in this chapter relates to the question about the efficacy of sacrifice in the two arrangements. He showed that the arrangement for blood-shedding by sacrifice entered into both; that the high-priest of both offered blood as an expiation; that the holy place was entered with blood, and that consequently there was *death* in both the arrangements or dispensations. The former arrangement or dispensation was ratified with blood, and it was equally proper that the new arrangement should be also. The point of comparison is not that Moses made a *will* or *testament* which could be of force only when he died, and that the same thing was required in the *new* dispensation, but it is that the former covenant was *ratified by blood*, or *by the death of a victim*, and that it might be expected that the new dispensation would be confirmed, and that it was in fact confirmed in the same manner. In this view of the argument, what pertinency would there be in introducing an illustration respecting *a will*, and the manner in which it became efficient? Comp. Notes on ver. 18. It seems clear, therefore, to me that the word rendered *testament* here is to be taken in the sense in which it is ordinarily used in the New Testament. The opinion that the word here means such a divine arrangement as is commonly denoted a "*covenant*," and not testament, is sanctioned by not a few names of eminence in criticism, such as Pierce, Doddridge, Michaelis, Steudel, and the late Dr. J. P. Wilson. Bloomfield

says that the connection here demands this. The principal objections to this view are, (1) That it is not proved that no covenants or compacts were valid except such as were made by the intervention of sacrifices. (2) That the word rendered *testator*—διαθέμενος —cannot refer to the death of an animal slain for the purpose of ratifying a covenant, but must mean either a *testator* or a *contractor*—that is, one of two contracting parties. (3) That the word rendered *dead* (ver. 17)— νεκροῖς—means only *dead men*, and never is applied to the dead bodies of animals. See Stuart on the Heb., p. 442. These objections to the supposition that the passage refers to a covenant or compact, Professor Stuart says are, in his view, insuperable, and they are certainly entitled to grave consideration. Whether the view above presented is one which can be sustained, we may be better able to determine after an examination of the words and phrases which the apostle uses. Those objections which depend wholly on the *philological* argument derived from the words used, will be considered of course in such an examination. It is to be remembered at the outset (1) that the word διαθήκη —*diathēkē*—is *never* used in the New Testament in the sense of *testament*, or *will*, unless in this place; (2) that it is *never* used in this sense in the Septuagint; and (3) that the Hebrew word בְּרִית—*berith*—*never* has this signification. This is admitted. See Stuart on the Heb., pp. 439, 440. It must require very strong reasons to prove that it has this meaning here, and that Paul has employed the word in a sense differing from its uniform signification elsewhere in the Bible. Comp., however, the remarks of Professor Stuart in *Bib. Repos.*, vol. xx. p. 364. ¶ *There must also of necessity be*—ἀνάγκη. That is, it is necessary that the thing here specified should be done in order to confirm the covenant, or it would not be binding in cases where this did not occur. The *necessity* in the case is simply to make it valid or obligatory. So we say now there must "necessarily" be a *seal*, or a

deed would not be valid. The fair interpretation of this is, that this was the common and established custom in making a "covenant" with God, or confirming the arrangement with him in regard to salvation. To this it is objected (see the first objection above), that "it is yet to be made out that *no* covenants were valid except those by the intervention of sacrifices." In reply to this, we may observe, (1) That the point to be made out is *not* that this was a custom in compacts between *man and man*, but between *man and his Maker*. There is no evidence, as it seems to me, that the apostle alludes to a compact between man and man. The mistake on this subject has arisen partly from the use of the word "*testament*" by our translators, in the sense of *will*—supposing that it *must* refer to some transaction relating to man only; and partly from the insertion of the word "*men*" in ver. 17, in the translation of the phrase —ἐπὶ νεκροῖς—"upon the dead," or "over the dead." But it is not necessary to suppose that there is a reference here to any transaction between man and man at all, as the whole force of the illustration introduced by the apostle will be retained if we suppose him speaking *only* of a transaction between man and God. Then his assertion will be simply that, in the arrangement between God and man, there was a *necessity* of the death of something, or of the shedding of blood, in order to ratify it. This view will save the necessity of proof that the custom of ratifying compacts between man and man by sacrifice prevailed. Whether that can be made out or not, the assertion of the apostle may be true, that, in the arrangement which God makes with man, sacrifice was necessary in order to confirm or ratify it. (2) The point to be made out is, not that such a custom is or was universal among all nations, but that it was the known and regular opinion among the Hebrews, that a sacrifice was necessary in a "covenant" with God; in the same way as, if an author should say that a deed is not valid without a seal, it would not be necessary to show this in regard to *all*

nations, but only that it was the law or the custom in the nation where the writer lived, and at the time when he lived. Other nations may have very different modes of confirming or ratifying a deed, and the same nation may have different methods at various times. The *fact* or *custom* to which I suppose there is allusion here, is that of sacrificing an animal to ratify the arrangement between man and his Maker, commonly called a "covenant." In regard to the existence of such a custom, particularly among the Hebrews, we may make the following observations : It was the common mode of ratifying the "covenant" between God and man. That was done over a sacrifice, or by the shedding of blood. So the covenant with Abraham was ratified by slaying a heifer, a she-goat, a ram, a turtle-dove, and a young pigeon. The animals were divided and a burning lamp passed between them, Gen. xv. 9, 18. So the covenant made with the Hebrews in the wilderness was ratified in the same manner, Ex. xxiv. 6, seq. Thus also in Jer. xxxiv. 18, God speaks of the "men that had transgressed his covenant which they had made before him, when *they cut the calf in twain, and passed between the parts thereof.*" See also Zec. ix. 11. Indeed all the Jewish sacrifices were regarded as a ratification of the covenant or arrangement for salvation between God and man. It was never supposed that it was ratified or confirmed in a proper manner without such a sacrifice. Instances occur, indeed, in which there was *no* sacrifice offered when a covenant was made between man and man (see Gen. xxiii. 16; xxiv. 9; Deut. xxv. 7, 9; Ruth iv. 7), but these cases do not establish the point that the custom did not prevail of ratifying a covenant with God by the blood of sacrifice. Further, the *terms* used in the Hebrew in regard to making a covenant with God, prove that it was understood to be ratified by sacrifice, or that the death of a victim was necessary (כָּרַת בְּרִית *kârăth berith*)—"to cut a covenant"—the word כָּרַת—*kârăth*—meaning to cut; to cut off; to cut down, and

the allusion being to the victims offered in sacrifice, and *cut in pieces* on occasion of entering into a covenant. See Gen. xv. 10; Jer. xxxiv. 18, 19. The same idea is expressed in the Greek phrases ὅρκια τέμνειν, τέμνειν σπονδάς, and in the Latin *icere fœdus.* Comp. Virgil, *Æn.,* viii. 641 :

> Et cæsâ jungebant fœdera porcâ.

These considerations show that it was the common sentiment, alike among the Hebrews and the heathen, that a covenant with God was to be ratified or sanctioned by sacrifice; and the statement of Paul here is, that the death of a sacrificial victim was needful to confirm or ratify such a covenant with God. It was not secure, or confirmed, until blood was thus shed. This was well understood among the Hebrews, that all their covenant transactions with God were to be ratified by a sacrifice; and Paul says that the same principle must apply to *any* arrangement between God and men. Hence he goes on to show that it was *necessary* that a sacrificial victim should die in the new covenant which God established by man through the Mediator. See ver. 23. This I understand to be the sum of the argument here. It is not that every contract made between man and man was to be ratified or confirmed by a sacrifice—for the apostle is not discussing that point; but it is that every similar transaction with God must be based on such a sacrifice, and that no covenant with him could be complete without such a sacrifice. This was provided for in the ancient dispensation by the sacrifices which were constantly offered in their worship; in the new, by the one great Sacrifice offered on the cross. Hence all our approaches to God are based on the supposition of such a sacrifice, and are, as it were, ratified over it. *We* ratify or confirm such a covenant or arrangement, not by offering the sacrifice anew, but by recalling it in a proper manner when we celebrate the death of Christ, and when in view of his cross we solemnly pledge ourselves to be the Lord's. ¶ *The death of the testator.* According to our common

version, *the death of him who makes a will.* But if the views above expressed are correct, this should be rendered the *covenanter,* or "the victim set apart to be slain." The Greek will admit of the translation of the word διαθέμενος—*diathemenos*—by the word *covenanter,* if the word διαθήκη—*diathēkē*—is rendered *covenant.* To such a translation here as would make the word refer *to a victim slain in order to ratify a covenant,* it is objected that "the word has no such meaning anywhere else. It must either mean a *testator* or a *contractor*—that is, one of two covenanting parties. But where is the death of a person covenanting made necessary in order to confirm the covenant?" (Prof. Stuart, *in loco*). To this objection I reply respectfully, (1) That the word is *never* used in the sense of *testator* either in the New Testament or the Old, unless it be here. It is admitted of the word διαθήκη—*diathēkē*—by Prof. Stuart himself, that it never means *will,* or *testament,* unless it be here, and it is equally true of the word used here that it never means one *who makes a will.* If, therefore, it is necessary that a meaning quite uncommon, or wholly unknown in the usage of the Scriptures, should be assigned to the use of the word here, why should it be *assumed* that that unusual meaning should be that of *making a will,* and *not* that of confirming a covenant? (2) If the apostle used the word διαθήκη—*diathēkē*—in the sense of *a covenant* in this passage, nothing is more natural than that he should use the corresponding word—διαθέμενος—*diathemenos*—in the sense of that by which a covenant was ratified. He wished to express the idea that the covenant was always ratified by the death of a victim—a sacrifice of an animal under the law, and the sacrifice of the Redeemer under the gospel — and no word would so naturally convey that idea as the one from which the word *covenant* was derived. It is to be remembered also that there *was* no word which would properly express that thought. Neither the Hebrew nor the Greek furnished such a word; nor have *we* now any word to express it,

but are obliged to use circumlocution to convey the idea. The word *covenanter* would not do it; nor the words *victim,* or *sacrifice.* We can express the idea only by some phrase like this—"the victim set apart to be slain to ratify the covenant." But it was not an unusual thing for the apostle Paul to make use of a word in a sense quite peculiar to himself. Comp. 2 Cor. iv. 17. (3) The word διατίθημι—*diatithēmi*—properly means, *to place apart, to set in order, to arrange.* It is rendered *appoint* in Luke xxii. 29; *made,* and *make,* with reference to a covenant, Acts iii. 25; Heb. viii. 10; x. 16. It occurs nowhere else in the New Testament, except in the passage before us. The idea of *placing, laying, disposing, arranging,* &c., enters into the word—as to place wares or merchandise for sale, to arrange a contract, &c. See Passow. The fair meaning of the word here may be, whatever is employed to arrange, dispose, or settle the covenant, or to make the covenant secure and firm. If the reference be to a compact, it cannot relate to one of the contracting parties, because the death of neither is necessary to confirm it. But it may refer to that which was well known as an established opinion, that a covenant with God was ratified only by a sacrifice. Still, it must be admitted that this use of the word is not elsewhere found, and the only material question is, whether it is to be presumed that the apostle would employ a word in a single instance in a peculiar signification, where the connection would not render it difficult to be understood. That he might do this *must* be admitted, whichever view is taken of the meaning of this passage, for on the supposition that he refers here to a *will,* it is conceded that he uses the word in a sense which does not once occur elsewhere either in the Old Testament or the New. It seems to me, therefore, that the word here may, without impropriety, be regarded as referring to *the victim that was slain in order to ratify a covenant with God,* and that the meaning is, that such a covenant was not regarded as confirmed until the victim was

17 For a testament *is* of force after men are dead: otherwise it is of no strength at all while the testator liveth.

slain. It may be added that the authority of Michaelis, Macknight, Doddridge, Bloomfield, and Dr. J. P. Wilson is a proof that such an interpretation cannot be a very serious departure from the proper use of a Greek word.

17. *For a testament.* Such an arrangement as God enters into with man. See the remarks on ver. 16. ¶ *Is of force.* Is ratified, or confirmed —in the same way as a deed or compact is confirmed by affixing a seal. ¶ *After men are dead—ἐπὶ νεκροῖς.* "Over the dead;" that is, in accordance with the view given above, after the animal is dead; or over the body of the animal slain for sacrifice, and to confirm the covenant. "For a covenant is completed or confirmed over dead sacrifices, seeing it is never of force as long as the victim set apart for its ratification is still living" (*MS. Notes* of Dr. J. P. Wilson). To this interpretation it is objected, that "νεκροῖς—*nekrois*—means only *dead men;* but *men* surely were not sacrificed by the Jews, as a mediating sacrifice in order to confirm a covenant" (Prof. Stuart, *in loco*). In regard to this objection, and to the proper meaning of the passage, we may remark, (1) That the word "*men*" is not in the Greek, nor is it necessarily implied, unless it be in the use of the Greek word rendered *dead.* The proper translation is, "*upon,* or *over the dead.*" The use of the word "men" here by our translators would seem to limit it to the making of a will. (2) It is to be presumed, unless there is positive proof to the contrary, that the Greeks and Hebrews used the word *dead* as it is used by other people, and that it *might* refer to deceased animals, or vegetables, as well as to *men.* A sacrifice that had been offered was dead; a tree that had fallen was dead; an animal that had been torn by other wild animals was dead. It is *possible* that a people might have one word to refer to *dead men,* another to *dead animals,* and another to *dead vegetables;*

but what is the evidence that the Hebrews or the Greeks had such words? (3) What is the meaning of this word νεκρός—*nekros*—in chap. vi. 1; ix. 14 of this very epistle when it is applied to *works*—"dead works"—if it never refers to anything but *men?* Comp. Jam. ii. 17, 20, 26; Eph. ii. 1, 5; Rev. iii. 1. In Eccl. ix. 4, it is applied to a dead lion. I suppose, therefore, that the Greek phrase here will admit of the interpretation which the "exigency of the place" seems to demand, and that the idea is, that a covenant with God was ratified over the animal slain in sacrifice, and was not considered as confirmed until the sacrifice was killed. ¶ *Otherwise.* Since—ἐπεί. That is, unless this takes place it will be of no force. ¶ *It is of no strength.* It is not *strong*—ἰσχύει—it is not confirmed or ratified. ¶ *While the testator liveth.* Or while the animal selected to confirm the covenant is alive. It can be confirmed only by its being slain. A full examination of the meaning of this passage (Heb. ix. 16, 17) may be found in an article in the *Biblical Repository,* vol. xx. pp. 51–71, and in Prof. Stuart's reply to that article (*Bib. Repos.* xx. pp. 356–381).

[The reader must admire the critical skill which the author has brought to bear on this intricate and long-contested question. The design of the following Note is by no means to enter into the controversy and adjudicate between contending parties—a task as difficult as presumptuous—where, on both sides, are found many of the most eminent names in the history of sacred criticism, where such men as Pierce, Doddridge, Macknight, and Barnes stand opposed to Calvin, Newcome, Kuinoel, and Stuart. A very brief digest of the argument by which the common translation is defended is alone intended in this place.

1. As to the word διαθήκη, it is allowed that neither in the New Testament nor in the LXX. has it anywhere the sense of "*will*" or testamentary deed, unless this place be held an exception, to which many, with Bloomfield, are disposed to add Gal. iii. 15. Yet the classical use of δ., as is alleged on the one hand and admitted on the other, is altogether in favour of "testament." It need not therefore excite

surprise that the apostle, in a few instances, should employ it in that sense.

2. As to the sense of διαθεμενος, it is contended, in opposition to Macknight, who renders it "appointed sacrifice," that διατιθημι is never used in the sense of "ordain," "appoint." That author quotes but one passage, Luke xxii. 29, in which, however, the word obviously has the sense of "grant." Διαθεμενος, besides, being the participle of the 2 aor. middle voice, demands, for the most part, an active signification, and, if the word "appoint" be used at all, should be here translated "appointer." Accordingly Pierce gives the active sense, and adopts the term "pacifier." Others render "mediating sacrifice;" but the word cannot have such meaning, and must signify either testator or contractor. And Scholefield himself, the author of this conjecture, admits that it is quite unsupported by the *usus loquendi*. Indeed, the same may be affirmed of all or most of the emendations that have yet been proposed. The philological argument is against them, and their authors justify them, for the most part, on the ground that they are necessary to the just course of the apostle's reasoning. Those who, with Macknight, render "victim set apart," or "appointed sacrifice," may be reminded of the difficulty which that author has experienced in reconciling the masculine gender of ο διαθεμενος with the various substantives he has found it necessary to supply in his paraphrase. Had the word referred to a sacrifice or victim we should have expected the neuter gender το διαθεμενον. "The Greek scholar," says Donald Fraser, in an elaborate Note on this question appended to his translation of Witsius on the creed, and which contains the ablest digest of argument in favour of the old rendering of "testament" or "will" that the writer of this Note has anywhere found within the same limited compass—"the Greek scholar is requested to observe, that, according to Macknight, θυματος, a sacrifice, or ζωον, an animal, should be supplied to agree with του διαθεμενου, ver. 16, while he supplies a different word, μοσχος, τραγος, or ταυρος, a calf, goat, or bull, to agree with ο διαθεμενος, ver. 17. The truth is, that ο διαθεμενος is necessarily masculine, and του διαθεμενου may be either masculine or neuter, as the structure of the sentence requires. In this passage both these expressions unquestionably refer to the *very same person or else the very same thing*. Why, then, does the doctor entertain the unnatural supposition of a diversity of genders? The reason is manifest. The lexicons could not readily furnish him with a Greek word in the masculine gender that signifies an animal, victim, or sacrifice, and it might have thrown discredit on his version had he alleged that του διαθεμενου, ver. 16, must denote distinctly a calf, goat, or bull. It was equally impossible, on the other side, to compel ο διαθ., ver. 17, to agree with θυμα or ζωον, and thus to signify in general a sacrifice or animal; and, in consequence, he sagaciously alleges that a calf, or bull must be supplied, while, in order to make his version the more plausible, he takes the liberty to repeat the general term '*sacrifice.*' The result of the whole is that the *neuter gender* is requisite to the new rendering, but *no manuscript sanctions* το διαθεμενον."

3. It is important, in connection with this controversy, to ascertain the just sense of νεκροις. Our author has reasoned with ingenuity on this word. The reader, however, must bear in mind that the question is not whether νεκ. be not sometimes applied to designate dead works, animals, or vegetables— not whether it be a word of equally universal application with its corresponding English adjective, but whether, *when occurring without a substantive*, it have, in the New Testament, any such extensive application. In such cases it is affirmed that there is not a *single example of the application to dead animals or sacrifices*. The author has not produced an example of this kind.

4. As to the alleged fact on the reality of which the new translation is founded, what the author asserts carries great weight with it, and, in the estimation of many, will be regarded as conclusive in regard to one part of the question. The allegation is that covenants are ratified only by the death of a victim, which Mr. Barnes has above explained of covenants of a special kind, *i.e.* such as are made between God and men. On the other side it is affirmed that "the proposition is too general here (οπου διαθηκη) to admit of limitation merely to covenants of a special nature."

Finally. According to the old translation of διαθηκη by "*testament*" the connection of the passage is not, in the view of those who adopt it, in the least injured. They suppose that the apostle having, in the 15th verse, introduced the "promise of the eternal *inheritance*," most naturally falls into the idea of testament or will by which inheritances are usually conveyed. They contend that this idea in connection with the death of Christ is exceedingly beautiful. Nor should the circumstance of its frequent abuse on the part of interpreters more ingenious than solid lead to its rejection.]

18. *Whereupon.* Οθεν, *whence.* Or since this is a settled principle, or an indisputable fact, it occurred in accordance with this principle, that the first covenant was confirmed by the shedding of blood. The admitted principle which the apostle had stated, that the death of the victim was ne-

18 Whereupon neither the first *testament* was [6]dedicated without blood.

         6 or *purified*.

19 For[f] when Moses had spoken every precept to all the people according to the law, he took the

         f Ex.24.6,&c.; Le.xiv.xvi.

cessary to confirm the covenant, was the *reason* why the first covenant was ratified with blood. If there were any doubt about the correctness of the interpretation given above, that ver. 16, 17, refer to an arrangement or disposition of things, and not a *will*, this verse would seem to be enough to remove it. For how could the fact that *a will* is ,not binding until he who makes it is dead, be a reason why *a covenant* should be confirmed by blood? What bearing would such a fact have on the question whether it ought or ought not to be confirmed in this manner? Or how could that fact, though it is universal, be given as *a reason* to account for the fact that the covenant made by the instrumentality of Moses was ratified with blood? No possible connection can be seen in such reasoning. But admit that Paul had stated in ver. 16,17, a general principle that in all covenant transactions with God the death of a victim was necessary, and everything is plain. We then see why he offered the sacrifice and sprinkled the blood. It was not on the basis of such reasoning as this: "The death of a man who makes a will is indispensable before the will is of binding force, THEREFORE it was that Moses confirmed the covenant made with our fathers by the blood of a sacrifice;" but by such reasoning as this: "It is a great principle that in order to ratify a covenant between God and his people a victim should be slain, *therefore* it was that Moses ratified the old covenant in this manner, and *therefore* it was also that the death of a victim was necessary under the new dispensation." Here the reasoning of Paul is clear and explicit; but who could see the force of the former? Prof. Stuart, indeed, connects this verse with ver. 15, and says that the course of thought is, "The new covenant of redemption from sin was sanctioned by the death of Jesus; consequently, or wherefore (ὅϑεν) the

old covenant, which is a type of the new, was sanctioned by the blood of victims." But is this the reasoning of Paul? Does he say that *because* the blood of a Mediator was to be shed under the new dispensation, and *because* the old was a type of this, that THEREFORE the old was confirmed by blood? Is he not rather accounting for the shedding of blood at all, and showing that it was *necessary* that the blood of the Mediator should be shed, rather than *assuming* that, and from that arguing that a typical shedding of blood was needful? Besides, on this supposition, why is the statement in ver. 16, 17 introduced? What bearing have these verses on the train of thought? What are they but an inexplicable obstruction? ¶ *The first* testament. Or rather covenant—the word testament being supplied by the translators. ¶ *Was dedicated.* Margin, *purified.* The word which is commonly used to *ratify*, to *confirm*, to *consecrate*, to *sanction.* Literally, to *renew.* ¶ *Without blood.* It was ratified by the blood of the animals that were slain in sacrifice. The blood was then sprinkled on the principal objects that were regarded as holy under that dispensation.

19. *For when Moses had spoken every precept to all the people.* When he had recited all the law, and had given all the commandments intrusted him to deliver, Ex. xxiv. 3. ¶ *He took the blood of calves and of goats.* This passage has given great perplexity to commentators, from the fact that Moses, in his account of the transactions connected with the ratification of the covenant with the people (Ex. xxiv.), mentions only a part of the circumstances here referred to. He says nothing of the blood of calves and of goats; nothing of water, and scarlet wool, and hyssop; nothing of sprinkling the book, the tabernacle, and the vessels of the ministry. It has been made a question, therefore, whence

blood of calves and of goats, with water, and [7] scarlet wool, and hyssop,

[7] or, *purple.*

and sprinkled both the book and all the people,

Paul obtained a knowledge of these circumstances. Since the account is not contained in the Old Testament, it must have been either by tradition, or by direct inspiration. The latter supposition is hardly probable, for (1) the information here can hardly be regarded as of sufficient importance to have required an original revelation; for the illustration would have had sufficient force to sustain his conclusion if the literal account in Exodus only had been given, that Moses sprinkled the people; but (2) such an original act of inspiration here would not have been consistent with the object of the apostle. In the argument which he was pursuing, it was essential that he should state only the facts about the ancient dispensation which were admitted by the Hebrews themselves. Any statement of his own about things which they did not concede to be true, or which was not well understood as a custom, might have been called in question, and would have done much to invalidate the entire force of the argument. It is to be presumed, therefore, that the facts here referred to had been preserved by tradition; and in regard to this, and the authority due to such a tradition, we may remark, (1) that it is well known that the Jews had a great number of traditions which they carefully preserved; (2) that there is no improbability in the supposition that many events in their history would be transmitted in this manner, since in the small compass of a volume like the Old Testament it cannot be presumed that *all* the events of their nation had been recorded; (3) that although they had many traditions of a trifling nature, and many which were false (comp. Notes on Mat. xv. 2), yet they doubtless had many that were true; (4) that in referring to those traditions, there is no impropriety in supposing that Paul may have been guided by the Spirit of inspiration in selecting only those which were true;

and (5) that nothing is more *probable* than what is here stated. If Moses sprinkled "the people;" if he read "the book of the law" on that occasion (Ex. xxiv. 7), and if this was regarded as a solemn act of ratifying a covenant with God, nothing would be more natural than that he should sprinkle the book of the covenant, and even the tabernacle and its various sacred utensils. We are to remember, also, that it was common among the Hebrews to sprinkle blood for the purpose of consecrating, or as an emblem of purifying. Thus Aaron and his sons and their garments were sprinkled with blood when they were consecrated to the office of priests, Ex. xxix. 19–21; the blood of sacrifices was sprinkled on the altar, Lev. i. 5, 11; iii. 2, 13; and blood was sprinkled before the veil of the sanctuary, Lev. iv. 16, 17; comp. Lev. vi. 27; vii. 14. So Josephus speaks of the garments of Aaron and of his sons as having been sprinkled with "the blood of the slain beasts, and with spring water." "Having consecrated them and their garments," he says, "for seven days together, he did the same to the tabernacle, and the vessels thereto belonging, both with oil and with the blood of bulls and of rams" (*Antiq.,* bk. iii. chap. viii. § 6). These circumstances show the strong *probability* of the truth of what is here affirmed by Paul, while it is impossible to prove that Moses did *not* sprinkle the book and the tabernacle in the manner stated. That Moses did not state this does not demonstrate that it was not done. On the phrase "the blood of calves and of goats," see Notes on ver. 12. ¶ *With water.* Agreeably to the declaration of Josephus that "spring water" was used. In Lev. xiv. 49–51, it is expressly mentioned that the blood of the bird that was killed to cleanse a house from the plague of leprosy should be shed over running water, and that the blood and the water should be sprinkled on the walls. It has been suggested also (see

20 Saying, *This *is* the blood of
g Mat.26.28.

the testament which God hath enjoined unto you.

Bloomfield) that the use of water was necessary in order to prevent the blood from coagulating, or so as to make it *possible* to sprinkle it. ¶ *And scarlet wool.* Margin, *purple.* The word here used denotes crimson, or deep scarlet. The colour was obtained from a small insect which was found adhering to the shoots of a species of oak in Spain and in Western Asia, of about the size of a pea. It was regarded as the most valuable of the colours for dyeing, and was very expensive. Comp. Notes on Isa. i. 18. Why the wool used by Moses was of this colour is not known, unless it be because it was the most expensive of colours, and thus accorded with everything employed in the construction of the tabernacle and its utensils. *Wool* appears to have been used in order to *absorb* and *retain* the blood. ¶ *And hyssop.* That is, a bunch of hyssop intermingled with the wool, or so connected with it as to constitute a convenient instrument for sprinkling. Comp. Lev. xiv. 51. Hyssop is a low shrub, regarded as one of the smallest of the plants, and is hence put in contrast with the cedar of Lebanon. It sprang out of the rocks or walls (1 Ki. iv. 33), and was used for purposes of purification. The term seems to have comprised not only the common hyssop, but also lavender and other aromatic plants. Its *fragrance,* as well as its size, may have suggested the idea of using it in the sacred services of the tabernacle. ¶ *And sprinkled both the book.* This circumstance is not mentioned by Moses, but it has been shown above not to be improbable. Some expositors, however, in order to avoid the difficulty in the passage, have taken this in connection with the word λαβὼν— rendered *"he took"*—meaning, "taking the blood, and the book itself;" but the more natural and proper construction is, that the book was sprinkled with the blood. ¶ *And all the people.* Moses says, "and sprinkled it on the people," Ex. xxiv. 8. We are not to suppose that either Moses or Paul

designs to say that the blood was actually sprinkled on each one of the three millions of people in the wilderness, but the meaning doubtless is, that the blood was sprinkled over the people, though, in fact, it might have fallen on a few. So a man now standing on an elevated place, and surrounded by a large assembly, if he should sprinkle water over them from the place where he stood, might be said to sprinkle it *on the people,* though, in fact, but few might have been touched by it. The act would be equally significant whether the emblem fell on few or many.

20. *Saying, This is the blood of the testament.* Of the covenant. See Notes on ver. 16, 17. That is, this is the blood by which the covenant is ratified. It was the means used to confirm it; the sacred and solemn form by which it was made sure. When this was done, the covenant between God and the people was confirmed—as a covenant between man and man is when it is sealed. ¶ *Which God hath enjoined unto you.* In Ex. xxiv. 8, "which God hath made with you." The language used by Paul, "which God hath *enjoined*"—ἐνετεί-λατο, *commanded*—shows that he did not regard this as strictly of the nature of a *covenant,* or *compact.* When a compact is made between parties, one does not *enjoin* or *command* the other, but it is a mutual *agreement.* In the transactions between God and man, though called בְּרִית *berith,* or διαθήκη, *diathēkē,* the idea of a *covenant* or *compact* is so far excluded that God never loses his right to *command* or *enjoin.* It is not a transaction between equals, or a mutual *agreement;* it is a solemn *arrangement* on the part of God which he proposes to men, and which he enjoins them to embrace; which they are not, indeed, at liberty to disregard, but which, when embraced, is appropriately ratified by some solemn act on their part. Comp. Notes on chap. viii. 6.

[See also Supplementary Note on chap. ix. 16; and on Rom. v. 12.]

21 Moreover[h] he sprinkled likewise with blood both the tabernacle, and all the vessels of the ministry.

22 And almost all things are by

the law purged with blood; and [i]without shedding of blood is no remission.

23 *It was* therefore necessary that the patterns of things in the heavens

h Ex.29.12,36.

i Le.17.11.

---

21. *He sprinkled—both the tabernacle.* This circumstance is not stated by Moses. On the probability that this was done, see Notes on ver. 19. The account of setting up the tabernacle occurs in Ex. xl. In that account it is said that Moses *anointed* the tabernacle with the holy anointing oil, ver. 9–11. Josephus (*Antiq.*, bk. iii. chap. viii. § 6) says that he consecrated it and the vessels thereto belonging with the blood of bulls and of rams. This was undoubtedly the tradition in the time of Paul, and no one can *prove* that it is not correct. ¶ *And all the vessels of the ministry.* Employed in the service of God. The altar, the laver (Ex. xl. 10, 11), the censers, dishes, bowls, &c., which were used in the tabernacle.

22. *And almost all things.* It is a general custom to purify everything by blood. This rule was not universal, for some things were purified by fire and water (Num. xxxi. 22, 23), and some by water only, Num. xxxi. 24; Lev. xvi. 26, 28. But the exceptions to the general rule were few. Almost everything in the tabernacle and temple service was consecrated or purified by blood. ¶ *And without shedding of blood is no remission.* Remission or forgiveness of sins. That is, though some things were purified by fire and water, yet when the matter pertained to the forgiveness of sins, it was *universally* true that no sins were pardoned except by the shedding of blood. *Some* impurities might be removed by water and fire, but the stain of *sin* could be removed only by blood. This declaration referred, in its primary meaning, to the Jewish rites, and the sense is, that, under that dispensation, it was universally true that in order to the forgiveness of sin blood must be shed. But it contains a truth of higher order and importance still. *It is univer-*

sally true that sin never has been, and never will be forgiven, except in connection with and in virtue of the shedding of blood. It is on this principle that the plan of salvation by the atonement is based, and on this that God in fact bestows pardon on men. There is not the slightest evidence that any man has ever been pardoned except through the blood shed for the remission of sins. The infidel who rejects the atonement has no evidence that his sins are pardoned; the man who lives in the neglect of the gospel, though he has abundant evidence that he is a sinner, furnishes none that his sins are forgiven; and the Mussulman and the heathen can point to no proof that their sins are blotted out. It remains to be demonstrated that one single member of the human family has ever had the slightest evidence of pardoned sin, except through the blood of expiation. In the divine arrangement there is no principle better established than this, that all sin which is forgiven is remitted through the blood of the atonement; a principle which has never been departed from hitherto, and which never will be. It follows, therefore, (1) that no sinner can hope for forgiveness except through the blood of Christ; (2) that if men are ever saved they must be willing to rely on the merits of that blood; (3) that all men are on a level in regard to salvation, since all are to be saved in the same way; and (4) that there will be one and the same song in heaven—the song of redeeming love.

23. *The patterns of things in the heavens.* The tabernacle and its various utensils. See Notes on chap. viii. 5. ¶ *Be purified with these.* With water and blood, and by these ceremonies. ¶ *But the heavenly things themselves.* The heavenly tabernacle or sanctuary into which Christ has entered, and

should be purified with these; but the heavenly things themselves with better sacrifices than these.

24 For Christ is not entered into the holy places made with hands, *which are* the figures of the true; but into heaven itself, now [k] to

k Ro. 8. 34.

where he performs the functions of his ministry. The use of the word *purified*, here applied to heaven, does not imply that heaven was before *unholy*, but it denotes that it is now made accessible to sinners; or that they may come and worship there in an acceptable manner. The ancient tabernacle was purified or consecrated by the blood of the victims slain, so that men might approach with acceptance and worship; the heavens by purer blood are rendered accessible to the guilty. The necessity for "better sacrifices" in regard to the system in the gospel was, that it was designed to make the conscience pure, and because the service in heaven is more holy than any rendered on earth. ¶ *With better sacrifices than these.* To wit, the sacrifice made by the offering of the Lord Jesus on the cross. This infinitely surpassed in value all that had been offered under the Jewish dispensation.

24. *For Christ is not entered into the holy places made with hands.* Into the temple or tabernacle. The Jewish high-priest alone entered into the most holy place, and the other priests into the holy place. Jesus, being of the tribe of Judah, and not of Levi, never entered the temple proper. He had access only to the courts of the temple, in the same way as any other Jew had. See Notes on Mat. xxi. 12. He has now entered into the true temple—heaven—of which the earthly tabernacle was the type. ¶ *Which are the figures of the true.* Literally, *the antitypes—ἀντίτυπα.* This word properly means that which is formed after a model, pattern, or type; and then that which corresponds to something, or answers to it. The idea here is, that the *type* or *fashion*—the *true* figure or form—was shown to

appear in the presence of God for us:

25 Nor yet that he should offer himself often, as the high priest entereth into the holy place every year with blood of others;

26 For then must he often have suffered since the foundation of

Moses in the mount, and then the tabernacle was made after that model, or corresponded to it. The *true original* figure is heaven itself; the tabernacle was an *antitype* of that—or was so formed as in some sense to resemble it. That is, it resembled it in regard to the matters under consideration—the most holy place denoted heaven; the mercy-seat and the shekinah were symbols of the presence of God, and of the fact that he shows mercy in heaven; the entrance of the high-priest was emblematical of the entrance of the Redeemer into heaven; the sprinkling of the blood on the mercy-seat was a type of what the Redeemer would do in heaven. ¶ *Now to appear in the presence of God for us.* As the Jewish high-priest appeared before the shekinah, the symbol of the divine presence in the tabernacle, so Christ appears before God himself in our behalf in heaven. He has gone to plead for our salvation; to present the merits of his blood as a permanent reason why we should be saved. See Notes on Rom. viii. 34; Heb. vii. 25.

25. *Nor yet that he should offer himself often.* The Jewish high-priest entered the most holy place with blood once every year. In this respect the offering made by Christ, and the work which he performed, differed from that of the Jewish high-priest. It was not needful that he should enter the holy place more than once. Having made the atonement once for all, and having entered there, he permanently remains there. ¶ *With the blood of others.* That is, with the blood of calves and goats. This is a second point in which the work of Christ differs from that of the Jewish high-priest. Christ entered there with his own blood. See Notes on ver. 12.

26. *For then must he often have suf-*

the world: but now once in the end of the world hath he appeared to put away sin by the sacrifice of himself.

27 And as *l*it is appointed unto men once to die, *m*but after this the judgment;

l Ge.3.19.   *m* Ec.12.14.

fered. That is, if his blood had no more efficacy than that which the Jewish high-priest offered, and which was so often repeated, it would have been necessary that Christ should have often died. ¶ *But now once.* Once for all; once in the sense that it is not to be repeated again—ἅπαξ. ¶ *In the end of the world.* In the last dispensation or economy; that under which the affairs of the world will be wound up. See the phrase fully explained in the Notes on chap. i. 2; Acts ii. 17; 1 Cor. x. 11; and Isa. ii. 2. ¶ *Hath he appeared.* He has been manifested in human form. ¶ *To put away sin.* (1) To remove the punishment due to sin, or to provide a way of pardon; and (2) to remove the stain of sin from the soul. See Notes on ver. 14. ¶ *By the sacrifice of himself.* See Notes on chap. i. 3; ii. 14; vii. 27.

27. *And as it is appointed unto men once to die.* Or, "since it is appointed unto men to die once *only.*" The object of this is to illustrate the fact that Christ died but *once* for sin, and this is done by showing that the most important events pertaining to man occur but once. Thus it is with *death.* That does not, and cannot occur many times. It is the great law of our being that men die *but once,* and hence the same thing was to be expected to occur in regard to him who made the atonement. It could not be supposed that this great law pertaining to man would be departed from in the case of him who died to make the atonement, and that he would repeatedly undergo the pains of death. The same thing was true in regard to the *judgment.* Man is to be judged once, and but once. The decision is to be final, and is not to be repeated. In like manner there was a fitness that the great Redeemer should die *but once,* and that his death should, without being repeated, determine the destiny of man. There is a remarkable *oneness* in the great events which most

affect men; and neither death, the judgment, nor the atonement can be repeated. In regard to the declaration here that "it is appointed unto men once to die," we may observe, (1) That death is the result of *appointment,* Gen. iii. 19. It is not the effect of chance, or hap-hazard. It is not a "debt of nature." It is not the condition to which man was subject by the laws of his creation. It is not to be accounted for by the mere principles of physiology. God could as well have made the heart to beat for ever as for fifty years. Death is no more the regular result of physical laws than the guillotine and the gallows are. It is in all cases the result of *intelligent appointment,* and is appointed for *an adequate cause.* (2) That cause, or the reason of that appointment, is sin. See Notes on Rom. vi. 23. This is the adequate cause; this explains the whole of it. Holy beings do not die. There is not the slightest proof that an angel in heaven has died, or that any perfectly holy being has ever died, except the Lord Jesus. In every death, then, we have a demonstration that the race is guilty; in each case of mortality we have an affecting memento that we are individually transgressors. (3) Death occurs but *once* in this world. It cannot be repeated. Whatever truths or facts then pertain to death; whatever lessons it is calculated to convey, pertain to it as an event which is not to occur again. That which is to occur but *once,* in an eternity of existence, acquires, from that very fact, if there were no other circumstances, an immense importance. What is to be done but once, we should wish to be done well. We should make all proper preparation for it; we should regard it with singular interest. If preparation is to be made for it, we must make *all* which we expect *ever* to make. A man who is to cross the ocean *but once,* to go away

from his home never to return, should make the right kind of preparation. He cannot come back to take that which he has forgotten; to arrange that which he has neglected; to give counsel which he has failed to do; to ask forgiveness for offences for which he has neglected to seek pardon. And so of death. A man who dies, dies but once. He cannot come back again to make preparation if he has neglected it; to repair the evils which he has caused by a wicked life; or to implore pardon for sins for which he had failed to ask forgiveness. Whatever is *to be done* with reference to death, is to be done *once for all* before he dies. (4) Death occurs to all. "It is appointed unto men"—to the race. It is not an appointment for one, but for all. No one is appointed by name to die; and not an individual is designated as one who shall escape. No exception is made in favour of youth, beauty, or blood; no rank or station is exempt; no merit, no virtue, no patriotism, no talent, no accomplishment can purchase freedom from it. In every other sentence which goes out against men there may be *some* hope of reprieve. Here there is none. We cannot meet an individual who is not *under sentence of death.* It is not only the poor wretch in the dungeon doomed to the gallows who is to die, it is the rich man in his palace, the gay trifler in the assembly room, the friend that we embrace and love, and she whom we meet in the crowded saloon of fashion with all the graces of accomplishment and adorning. Each one of these is just as much under sentence of death as the poor wretch in the cell, and the execution on any one of them may occur before his. It is, too, for substantially the same cause, and is as really deserved. It is for *sin* that all are doomed to death, and the *fact* that we must die should be a constant remembrancer of our guilt. (5) As death is to occur to us but once, there is a cheering interest in the reflection that when it is passed it is passed *for ever.* The dying pang, the chill, the cold sweat, are not to be repeated. Death is not to approach us often—he is to be allowed to come

to us but once. When we have once passed through the dark valley, we shall have the assurance that we shall never tread its gloomy way again. Once, then, let us be willing to die—since we can die *but* once; and let us rejoice in the assurance which the gospel furnishes, that they who die in the Lord leave the world to go where death in any form is unknown. ¶ *But after this the judgment.* The apostle does not say *how long* after death this will be, nor is it possible for us to know, Acts i. 7. Comp. Mat. xxiv. 36. We may suppose, however, that there will be two periods in which there will be an act of judgment passed on those who die. (1) Immediately after death, when they pass into the eternal world, when their destiny will be made known to them. This seems to be necessarily implied in the supposition that they will continue to live, and to be happy or miserable after death. This act of judgment may not be formal and public, but it will be such as to show them what must be the issues of the final day; and as the result of that interview with God, they will be made happy or miserable until the final doom shall be pronounced. (2) The more public and formal act of judgment, when the whole world will be assembled at the bar of Christ, Mat. xxv. The decision of that day will not change or reverse the former; but the trial will be of such a nature as to bring out all the deeds done on earth, and the sentence which will be pronounced will be in view of the universe, and will fix the everlasting doom. Then the body will be raised, the affairs of the world will be wound up, the elect will all be gathered in, and the state of retribution will commence, to continue for ever. The main thought of the apostle here may be, that after death will commence a state of *retribution* which can never change. Hence there was a propriety that Christ should die but once. In that future world he would not die to make atonement, for there all will be fixed and final. If men, therefore, neglect to avail themselves of the benefits of the atonement here, the

28 So *n*Christ was once offered
to *o*bear the sins of many; and

n 1 Pe.2.24; 3.18; 1 Jn.3.5. *o* Is.53.12; Mat.26.28.

unto *p*them that look for him *q*shall
he appear the second time without
sin *r*unto salvation.

p Tit.2.13; 2 Pe.3.12. *q* Ac.1.11; Re.1.7. *r* Is.25.9.

opportunity will be lost for ever. In
that changeless state which constitutes
the eternal judgment, no sacrifice will
be again offered for sin; there will be no
opportunity to embrace that Saviour
who was rejected here on earth.

28. *So Christ was once offered.* As
men are to die but once, and as all
beyond the grave is fixed by the judgment, so that his death there would
make no change in the destiny, there
was a propriety that he should die but
once for sin. The argument is, there
is *one* probation only, and therefore
there was need of but one sacrifice, or
of his dying but once. If death were
to occur frequently in the existence of
each individual, and if each intermediate period were a state of probation, then there might be a propriety that an atonement should be
made with reference to each state.
Or if beyond the grave there were a
state of probation still, then also there
might be a propriety that an atoning
sacrifice should be offered there. But
since neither of these things is true,
there was a fitness that the great
victim should die but once.

[Rather, perhaps, as in the original sentence,
"once dying" was the penalty denounced on
the sinner, so the substitute in enduring it is
in like manner under necessity of dying but
once. By this he fully answers the requirement of the law. Or there may be in the passage a simple intimation that in this respect,
as in others, Christ is like us, viz. in being but
once subject to death. It would be inconsistent
with the nature which he sustains to suppose
him a second time subject to death.]

¶ *To bear the sins of many.* To suffer
and die on account of their sins. See
Notes on Is. liii. 6, 11; Gal. iii. 13.
The phrase does not mean (1) that
Christ was *a sinner*—for that was in
no sense true. See chap. vii. 26. Nor
(2) that he literally bore the *penalty*
due to transgression—for that is equally
untrue. The penalty of the law for
sin is *all* which the law when executed
inflicts on the offender for his transgression, and includes, *in fact*, remorse

of conscience, overwhelming despair,
and eternal punishment. But Christ
did not suffer for ever, nor did he experience remorse of conscience, nor
did he endure utter despair. Nor (3)
does it mean that he was literally
punished for our sins. Punishment
pertains only to the guilty. An innocent being may *suffer* for what
another does, but there is no propriety
in saying that he is *punished* for it.
A father suffers much from the mis-
conduct of a son, but we do not say
that he is *punished* for it; a child
suffers much from the intemperance
of a parent, but no one would say that
it is a *punishment* on the child. Men
always connect the idea of criminality
with punishment, and when we say
that a man is *punished*, we suppose at
once that there is *guilt*. The phrase
here means simply, that Christ endured
sufferings in his own person which, if
they had been inflicted on us, would
have been the proper punishment of
sin. He who was innocent interposed,
and received on himself what was
descending to meet us, and consented
to be treated *as he would have deserved
if he had been a sinner.* Thus he bore
what was due to us; and this in Scripture phrase is what is meant by *bearing our iniquities.* See Notes on
Is. liii. 4.

[It is indeed true that Christ did not endure
the *very* penalty which we had incurred, and,
but for his interference, should have endured.
His sufferings must be regarded in the light
of an *equivalent* to the law's original claim of
a *satisfaction* to its injured honour which the
Lawgiver has been pleased to accept. It is,
however, equally true that the sufferings of
Christ were strictly *penal.* They were the
punishment of sin. The true meaning of the
important phrase in this verse, "to bear sin,"
establishes this point. It can have no other
meaning than bearing the punishment of sin.
See Stuart's xix. Excursus. That punishment
supposes guilt is not denied. What then? Not
certainly that Christ was personally guilty,
but that our guilt has been *imputed* to him—
that he has taken the place of the guilty and

become answerable for their transgressions. See Supplementary Note, 2 Cor. v. 21.]

¶ *And unto them that look for him.* To his people. It is one of the characteristics of Christians that they *look for* the return of their Lord, Titus ii. 13; 2 Pet. iii. 12. Comp. Notes on 1 Thes. i. 10. They fully *believe* that he will come. They earnestly *desire* that he should come, 2 Tim. iv. 8; Rev. xxii. 20. They are *waiting* for his appearing, 1 Thes. i. 10. He left the world and ascended to heaven, but he will again return to the earth, and his people are looking for that time as the period when they shall be raised up from their graves; when they shall be publicly acknowledged as his, and when they shall be admitted to heaven. See Notes on John xiv. 3. ¶ *Shall he appear the second time.* He first appeared as the man of sorrows to make atonement for sin. His second appearance will be as the Lord of his people, and the Judge of the quick and the dead, Mat. xxv. 31. See Notes on Acts i. 11. The apostle does not say *when* this will be, nor is any intimation given in the Scriptures when it will occur. It is, on the contrary, everywhere declared that this is concealed from men (Acts i. 7; Mat. xxiv. 36), and all that is known respecting the time is, that it will be suddenly, and at an unexpected moment, Mat. xxiv. 42, 44, 50. ¶ *Without sin.* That is, when he comes again he will not make himself a sin-offering; or will not come in order to make atonement for sin. It is not implied that when he came the first time he was in any sense *a sinner*, but that he came then with reference to sin, or that the main object of his incarnation was to "put away sin by the sacrifice of himself." When he comes the second time, it will be with reference to another object. ¶ *Unto salvation.* That is, to receive his friends and followers to eternal salvation. He will come to save them from their sins and temptations; to raise them from their graves; to place them at his right hand in glory, and to confirm them in the everlasting inheritance which he has promised to

all who truly love him, and who wait for his appearing.

In view of this anticipated return of the Redeemer, we may remark—

(1) There is a propriety that he should thus return. He came once to be humbled, despised, and put to death; and there is a fitness that he should come to be honoured in his own world.

(2) Every person on earth is interested in the fact that he will return, for "every eye shall see him," Rev. i. 7. All who are now in their graves; all who now live, and all who will hereafter live, will behold the Redeemer in his glory.

(3) It will not be merely to gaze upon him, and to admire his magnificence that they will see him. It will be for greater and more momentous purposes—with reference to an eternal doom.

(4) The great mass of men are not prepared to meet him. They do not believe that he will return; they do not desire that he should appear; they are not ready for the solemn interview which they will have with him. His appearing now would overwhelm them with surprise and horror. There is nothing in the future which they less expect and desire than the second coming of the Son of God, and in the present state of the world his appearance would produce almost universal consternation and despair. It would be like the coming of the flood of waters on the old world; like the sheets of flame on Sodom and Gomorrah; or as *death* now comes to the great mass of those who die.

(5) Christians *are* prepared for his coming. They believe in it; they expect it; they desire it. In this they are distinguished from all the world besides, and they would be ready to hail his coming as that of a friend, and to rejoice in his appearance as *their* Saviour.

(6) Let us then live in habitual preparation for his advent. To each one of us he will come soon; to all he will come suddenly. Whether he come to remove us by death, or whether in the clouds of heaven to judge the

world, the period is not far distant when *we* shall see him. Yes, our eyes shall behold the Son of God in his glory! That which we have long desired—a sight of *our* Saviour who died for us—will soon, very soon be granted unto us. No Christian begins a week or a day in which there is not a possibility that before its close he may have seen the Son of God in his glory; none lies down upon his bed at night who may not, when the morning dawns upon this world, be gazing with infinite delight on the glories of the Great Redeemer in the heavens.

CHAPTER X.
ANALYSIS OF THE CHAPTER.

The general subject of this chapter is the sacrifice which Christ has made for sin, and the consequences which flow from the fact that he has made a sufficient atonement. In chap. ix. the apostle had shown that the Jewish rites were designed to be temporary and typical, and that the offerings which were made under that dispensation could never remove sin. In this chapter he shows that the true sacrifice had been made by which sin can be pardoned, and that certain very important consequences follow from that fact. The subject of *sacrifice* was the most important part of the Jewish economy, and was also the essential thing in the Christian dispensation, and hence it is that the apostle dwells upon it at so great length. The chapter embraces the following topics:

I. The apostle repeats what he had said before about the inefficacy of the sacrifices made under the law, ver. 1-4. The law was a mere shadow of good things to come, and the sacrifices which were made under it could never render those who offered them perfect. This was conclusively proved by the fact that they continued constantly to be offered.

II. Since this was the fact in regard to those sacrifices, a better offering had been provided in the gospel by the Redeemer, ver. 5-10. A body had been prepared him for this work; and when God had said that he had no pleasure in the offerings under the

law, Christ had come and offered *his* body once for all in order that an effectual atonement might be made for sin.

III. This sentiment the apostle further illustrates by showing how this one great offering was connected with the forgiveness of sins, ver. 11-18. Under the Jewish dispensation sacrifices were repeated every day; but under the Christian economy, when the sacrifice was once made, he who had offered it sat down for ever on the right hand of God, for his great work was done. Having done this, he looked forward to the time when his work would have full effect, and when his enemies would be made his footstool. That this was to be the effect of the offering made by the Messiah, the apostle then shows from the Scriptures themselves, where it is said (Jer. xxxi. 33, 34), that under the gospel the laws of God would be written on the heart, and that sin would be remembered no more. There must then be, the apostle inferred, some way by which this was to be secured, and this was by the great sacrifice on the cross, which had the effect of perfecting for ever those who were sanctified.

IV. Since it was a fact that such an atonement had been made; that one great offering for sin had been presented to God which was never to be repeated, there were certain consequences which followed from that, which the apostle proceeds to state, ver. 19-25. They were these: (*a*) the privilege of drawing near to God with full assurance of faith (ver. 22); (*b*) the duty of holding fast the profession of faith without wavering (ver. 23); (*c*) the duty of exhorting one another to fidelity and to good works (ver. 24); (*d*) the duty of assembling for public worship, since they had a High-priest in heaven, and might now draw near to God, ver. 25.

V. As a *reason* for fidelity in the divine life, and for embracing the offer of mercy now made through the one sacrifice on the cross, the apostle urges the consequence which *must* follow from the rejection of that atonement, and especially after having been made acquainted with the

CHAPTER X.

FOR the law, having a *a*shadow of good things to come, *and* not the very image of the things,

a Col.2.17.

can never with those sacrifices, which they offered year by year continually, make the comers thereunto perfect.

---

truth, ver. 26–31. The result, says he, *must* be certain destruction. If that was rejected, there could remain nothing but a fearful looking for of judgment, for there was no other way of salvation. In support of this, he refers to what was the effect of disobedience under the law of Moses, and says that under the greater light of the gospel much more fearful results must follow.

VI. The chapter closes (ver. 32–39) with an exhortation to fidelity and perseverance. The apostle reminds those to whom he wrote of what they had already endured; he encourages them by the commendation of what they had already done, and especially by the kindness which they had shown to him; he says that they had need only of patience, and that the time of their deliverance from all trial was not far off, for that he who was to come would come; and he then adds that it was their duty to live by faith, but that if anyone drew back, God could have no pleasure in him. Having thus, in the close of the chapter, alluded to the subject of faith, he proceeds in the following chapter to illustrate its value at length. The object of the whole is to encourage Christians to make strenuous efforts for salvation; to guard them against the danger of apostasy; and to exhort them to bear their trials with patience and with submission to the will of God.

1. *For the law, having a shadow.* That is, the whole of the Mosaic economy was a shadow; for so the word *law* is often used. The word *shadow* here refers to a rough outline of anything, a mere sketch, such as a carpenter draws with a piece of chalk, or such as an artist delineates when he is about to make a picture. He sketches an outline of the object which he designs to draw, which has *some* resemblance to it, but is not the

"very image;" for it is not yet complete. The words rendered "the very image" refer to a painting or statue which is finished, where every part is an exact copy of the original. The "good things to come" here refer to the future blessings which would be conferred on man by the gospel. The idea is, that under the ancient sacrifices there was an imperfect representation; a dim outline of the blessings which the gospel would impart to men. They were a typical representation; they were not such that it could be pretended that they would answer the purpose of the things themselves which they were to represent, and that they would make those who offered them perfect. Such a rude outline, such a mere sketch, or imperfect delineation, could no more answer the purpose of saving the soul, than the rough sketch which an architect makes would answer the purpose of a house, or than the first outline which a painter draws would answer the purpose of a perfect and finished portrait. All that could be done by either would be to convey some distant and obscure idea of what the house or the picture might be, and this was all that was done by the law of Moses. ¶ *Can never with those sacrifices, which they offered year by year continually.* The sacrifices here particularly referred to were those which were offered on the great day of atonement. These were regarded as the most sacred and efficacious of all, and yet the apostle says that the very fact that they were offered every year showed that there must be some deficiency about them, or they would have ceased to be offered. ¶ *Make the comers thereunto perfect.* They could not free them from the stains of guilt; they could not give peace to a troubled conscience; there was in them no efficacy by which sin could be put away. Comp. Notes on chap. vii. 11; ix. 9.

2 For then [1] would they not have ceased to be offered? because that the worshippers once purged should

have had no more conscience of sins.

3 But in those *sacrifices there is* a

---

2. *For then would they not have ceased to be offered?* Margin, " or *they would have.*" The sense is the same. The idea is, that the very fact that they were repeated showed that there was some deficiency in them as to the matter of cleansing the soul from sin. If they had answered all the purposes of a sacrifice in putting away guilt, there would have been no need of repeating them in this manner. They were in this respect like medicine. If that which is given to a patient heals him, there is no need of repeating it; but if it is repeated often it shows that there was some deficiency in it; and if taken periodically through a man's life, and the disease should still remain, it would show that it was not sufficient to effect his cure. So it was with the offerings made by the Jews. They were offered every year, and indeed every day, and still the disease of sin remained. The conscience was not satisfied; and the guilty felt that it was necessary that the sacrifice should be repeated again and again. ¶ *Because that the worshippers once purged should have had no more conscience of sins.* That is, if these sacrifices had so availed as to remove past sins, and to procure forgiveness, they who offered them would have had no more trouble of conscience on account of their sins. They would not have felt that it was necessary to make these sacrifices over and over again in order to find peace. When a man has full evidence that an atonement has been made which will meet all the demands of the law, and which secures the remission of sin, he feels that it is enough. It is all that the case demands, and his conscience may have peace. But when he does *not* feel this, or has not evidence that his sins are forgiven, those sins will rise to remembrance, and he will be alarmed. He may be punished for them after all. Thence it follows that if a man obtains peace he must have good

evidence that his sins are forgiven through the blood of the atonement. No temporary expedient; no attempt to cover them up; no effort to forget them will answer the purpose. They *must be blotted out* if he will have peace —and that can be only through a perfect sacrifice. By the use of the word rendered "conscience" here, it is not meant that he who was pardoned would have no *consciousness* that he was a sinner, or that he would forget it, but that he would have no trouble of conscience; he would have no apprehension of future wrath. The pardon of sin does not make it cease to be remembered. He who is forgiven may have a deeper conviction of its evil than he had ever had before. But he will not be troubled or distressed by it as if it were to expose him to the wrath of God. The remembrance of it will humble him; it will serve to exalt his conceptions of the mercy of God and the glory of the atonement, but it will no longer overwhelm the mind with the dread of hell. This effect, the apostle says, was not produced on the minds of those who offered sacrifices every year. The very fact that they did it, showed that the conscience was not at peace.

3. *But in those* sacrifices there is *a remembrance again* made *of sins every year.* The reference here is to the sacrifice made on the great day of atonement. This occurred once in a year. Of course, as often as a sacrifice was offered, it was an acknowledgment of guilt on the part of those for whom it was made. As these sacrifices continued to be offered every year, they who made the offering were therefore constantly reminded of their guilt and their desert of punishment. All the efficacy which could be pretended to belong to those sacrifices, was that they made expiation for the past year. Their efficacy did not extend into the future, nor did it embrace any but those who were engaged in offering them. These sacrifices,

remembrance again *made* of sins every[b] year.

4 For [c]*it is* not possible that the blood of bulls and of goats should take away sins.

b Le.16.34.　　　c Mi.6.6-8.

5 Wherefore, when he cometh into the world, he saith, [d]Sacrifice and offering thou wouldest not, but a body [2]hast thou prepared me:

d Ps.40.6-8.　　2 or, *thou hast fitted.*

therefore, could not make the atonement which man needed. They could not make the conscience easy; they could not be regarded as so bearing on the future, that the sinner at any time could plead the offering which was already made as a ground of pardon; and, as they pertained only to those who offered them, could not meet the wants of all men in all lands and at all times. These things are to be found only in that great sacrifice made by the Redeemer on the cross.

4. *For it is not possible that the blood of bulls and of goats should take away sins.* The reference here is to the sacrifices which were made on the great day of the atonement, for on that day the blood of bulls and of goats alone was offered. See Notes on chap. ix. 7. Paul here means to say, doubtless, that it was not possible that the blood of these animals should make a complete expiation so as to purify the conscience, and so as to save the sinner from deserved wrath. According to the divine arrangement, expiation was made by those sacrifices for offences of various kinds against the ritual law of Moses, and pardon for such offences was thus obtained. But the meaning here is, that there was no efficacy in the blood of a mere animal to wash away a *moral* offence. It could not repair the law; it could not do anything to maintain the justice of God; it had no efficacy to make the heart pure. The mere shedding of the blood of an animal never *could* make the soul pure. This the apostle states as a truth which must be admitted at once as indisputable, and yet it is probable that many of the Jews had imbibed the opinion that there was such efficacy in blood shed according to the divine direction as to remove all stains of guilt from the soul. See Notes on chap. ix. 9, 10.

5. *Wherefore.* This word shows that the apostle means to sustain what he had said by a reference to the Old Testament itself. Nothing could be more opposite to the prevailing Jewish opinions about the efficacy of sacrifice than what he had just said. It was, therefore, of the highest importance to defend the position which he had laid down by authority which they would not presume to call in question, and he therefore makes his appeal to their own Scriptures. ¶ *When he cometh into the world.* When the Messiah came, for the passage evidently referred to him. The Greek is: "Wherefore coming into the world, he saith." It has been made a question *when* this is to be understood as spoken—whether when he was born, or when he entered on the work of his ministry. Grotius understands it of the latter. But it is not material, in order to a proper understanding of the passage, to determine this. The simple idea is, that since it was impossible that the blood of bulls and goats should take away sin, Christ coming into the world made arrangements for a better sacrifice. ¶ *He saith.* That is, this is the language denoted by his great undertaking; this is what his coming to make an atonement implies. We are not to suppose that Christ formally used these words on any occasion—for we have no record that he did—but this language is that which appropriately expresses the nature of his work. Perhaps, also, the apostle means to say that it was originally employed in the Psalm from which it is quoted in reference to him, or was indited by him with reference to his future advent. ¶ *Sacrifice and offering thou wouldest not.* This is quoted from Ps. xl. 6–8. There has been much perplexity felt by expositors in reference to this quotation, and after all which has been written, the difficulty is not entirely removed. The difficulty relates to

these points: (1) To the question whether the Psalm originally had reference to the Messiah. It *appears* to have pertained merely to David, and it would probably occur to no one on reading it to suppose that it referred to the Messiah, unless it had been so applied by the apostle in this place. (2) There are many parts of the Psalm, it has been said, which cannot, without a very forced interpretation, be applied to Christ. See ver. 2, 12, 14, 15, 16. (3) The argument of the apostle in the expression, "a body hast thou prepared me," *seems* to be based on a false translation of the Septuagint which he has adopted, and it is difficult to see on what principles he has done it. It is not the design of these Notes to go into an extended examination of questions of this nature. Such an examination must be sought in more extended commentaries, and in treatises expressly relating to points of this kind. On the design of Ps. xl., and its applicability to the Messiah, the reader may consult Prof. Stuart on the Hebrews, Excursus xx. and Kuinoel, *in loco.* After the most attentive examination which I can give of the Psalm, it seems to me probable that it is one of the Psalms which had an original and exclusive reference to the Messiah, and that the apostle has quoted it just as it was meant to be understood by the Holy Spirit, as applicable to him. The reasons for this opinion are briefly these: (1) There *are* such Psalms, as is admitted by all. The Messiah was the hope of the Jewish people; he was made the subject of their most sublime prophecies, and nothing was more natural than that he should be the subject of the songs of their sacred bards. Under the influence, and by the teaching of the Holy Spirit, they saw him in the distant future in the various circumstances in which he would be placed, and they dwelt with delight upon the vision. Comp. Intro. to Isaiah, § 7, iii. (2) The fact that this Psalm is here applied to the Messiah, is a strong circumstance to demonstrate that it had an original applicability to him. This proof is of two kinds. *First,* that it is so applied by an inspired apostle,

which, with all who admit his inspiration, seems decisive of the question. *Second,* the fact that he so applied it shows that this was an ancient and admitted interpretation. He was writing to those who had been Jews, and whom he was desirous to convince of the truth of what he was alleging in regard to the nature of the Hebrew sacrifices. For this purpose it was necessary to appeal to the Scriptures of the Old Testament, but it cannot be supposed that he would adduce a passage for proof whose relevancy would not be admitted. The presumption is, that the passage was in fact commonly applied to the Messiah. (3) The whole of the Psalm may be referred to the Messiah without anything forced or unnatural. The Psalm throughout seems to be made up of expressions used by a suffering person, who had indeed been delivered from some evils, but who was expecting many more. The principal difficulties in the way of such an interpretation relate to the following points: (*a*) In ver. 2 the speaker in the Psalm says: "He brought me up out of a horrible pit, out of the miry clay, and set my feet upon a rock," and on the ground of this he gives thanks to God. But there is no real difficulty in supposing that this may refer to the Messiah. His enemies often plotted against his life; they laid snares for him, and endeavoured to destroy him, and it may be that he refers to some deliverance from such machinations. If it is objected to this that it is spoken of as having been uttered "when he came into the world," it may be replied, that that phrase does not necessarily refer to the time of his birth, but that he uttered this sentiment sometime *during* the period of his incarnation. "He coming into the world for the purpose of redemption made use of this language." In a similar manner we would say of Lafayette, that "he, coming to the United States to aid in the cause of liberty, suffered a wound in battle." That is, during the period in which he was engaged in this cause, he suffered in this manner. (*b*) The next objection or difficulty relates to the application of ver. 12 to the Mes-

siah — "Mine iniquities have taken hold upon me, so that I am not able to look up; they are more than the hairs of my head; therefore my heart faileth me." To meet this, some have suggested that he refers to the sins of men which he took upon himself, and which he here speaks of as *his own*. But it is not true that the Lord Jesus so took upon himself the sins of others that they could be called *his*. They were *not* his, for he was in every sense "holy, harmless, and undefiled."

[See second Supplementary Note, chap. ix. 28.]

The true solution of this difficulty probably is, that the word rendered *iniquity*— עָוֹן *avon*—means *calamity, misfortune, trouble.* See Ps. xxxi. 10; 1 Sam. xxviii. 10; 2 Ki. vii. 9; Ps. xxxviii. 6; comp. Ps. xlix. 5. The proper idea in the word is that of *turning away, curving, making crooked;* and it is thus applied to anything which is *perverted* or turned from the right way; as when one is turned from the path of rectitude, or commits sin; when one is turned from the way of prosperity or happiness, or is exposed to calamity. This seems to be the idea demanded by the scope of the Psalm, for it is not a penitential Psalm, in which the speaker is recounting his *sins*, but one in which he is enumerating his *sorrows;* praising God in the first part of the Psalm for some deliverance already experienced, and supplicating his interposition in view of calamities that he saw to be coming upon him. This interpretation also seems to be demanded in ver. 12 of the Psalm by the *parallelism.* In the former part of the verse the word to which "iniquity" corresponds, is not *sin*, but *evil*—that is, calamity.

" For innumerable *evils* have compassed me about; Mine *iniquities* [calamities] have taken hold upon me."

If the word, therefore, is used here as it often is, and as the scope of the Psalm and the connection seem to demand, there is no solid objection to the application of this verse to the Messiah. (*c*) A third objection to this application of the Psalm to the

Messiah is, that it cannot be supposed that he would utter such imprecations on his enemies as are found in ver. 14, 15, " Let them be ashamed and confounded; let them be driven backward; let them be desolate." To this it may be replied, that such imprecations are as proper in the mouth of the Messiah as of David; but particularly, it may be said also, that they are *not* improper in the mouth of either. Both David and the Messiah *did*, in fact, utter denunciations against the enemies of piety and of God. God does the same thing in his word and by his providence. There is no evidence of any *malignant* feeling in this; nor is it inconsistent with the highest benevolence. The lawgiver who says that the murderer shall die, may have a heart full of benevolence; the judge who sentences him to death, may do it with eyes filled with tears. The objections, then, are not of such a nature that it is improper to regard this Psalm as wholly applicable to the Messiah. (4) The Psalm cannot be applied with propriety to David, nor do we know of anyone to whom it can be applied but to the Messiah. When was it true of David that he said that he "had come to do the will of God in view of the fact that God did not require sacrifice and offerings?" In what "volume of a book" was it written of him before his birth, that he "delighted to do the will of God?" When was it true that he had "preached righteousness in the great congregation?" These expressions are such as can be applied properly only to the Messiah, as Paul does here; and taking all these circumstances together, it will probably be regarded as the most proper interpretation to refer the whole Psalm at once to the Redeemer, and to suppose that Paul has used it in strict accordance with its original design. The other difficulties referred to will be considered in the exposition of the passage.—The difference between *sacrifice* and *offering* is, that the former refers to *bloody* sacrifices; the latter to *any* oblation made to God—as a thank-offering; an offering of flour, oil, &c. See Notes

on Isa. i. 11. When it is said "sacrifice and offering *thou wouldest not*," the meaning is not that such oblations were *in no sense* acceptable to God — for as his appointment, and when offered with a sincere heart, they doubtless were; but that they were not *as* acceptable to him as obedience, and especially, as the expression is used here, that they could not avail to secure the forgiveness of sins. They were not such as was demanded to make an expiation for sin, and hence a body was prepared for the Messiah by which a more perfect sacrifice could be made. The sentiment here expressed occurs more than once in the Old Testament. Thus, 1 Sam. xv. 22, "Behold, to obey is better than sacrifice, and to hearken than the fat of rams;" Hos. vi. 6, "For I desired mercy and not sacrifice; and the knowledge of God more than burnt-offerings;" Ps. li. 16, 17, "For thou desirest not sacrifice, else would I give it; thou delightest not in burnt-offering. The sacrifices of God are a broken spirit." This was an indisputable principle of the Old Testament, though it was much obscured and forgotten in the common estimation among the Jews. In accordance with this principle, the Messiah came to render obedience of the highest order, even to such an extent that he was willing to lay down his own life. ¶ *But a body hast thou prepared me.* This is one of the passages which has caused a difficulty in understanding this quotation from the Psalm. The difficulty is, that it differs from the Hebrew, and *that the apostle builds an argument upon it, though it thus differs.* It is not unusual, indeed, in the New Testament to make use of the language of the Septuagint even where it varies somewhat from the Hebrew; and where no *argument* is based on such a passage, there can be no difficulty in such a usage, since it is not uncommon to make use of the language of others to express our own thoughts. But the apostle does not appear to have made such a use of the passage here, but to have applied it in the way of *argument*. The argument,

indeed, does not rest *wholly*, perhaps not *principally*, on the fact that a "body had been prepared" for the Messiah; but still, that a body had been thus prepared, was evidently in the view of the apostle an important consideration, and this is the passage on which the proof of this is based. The Hebrew (Ps. xl. 6) is, "Mine ears hast thou opened," or, as it is in the margin, *digged*. The idea there is, that the ear had been, as it were, excavated, or dug out, so as to be made to hear distinctly; that is, certain truths had been clearly revealed to the speaker; or perhaps it may mean that he had been made "readily and attentively obedient" (Stuart). Comp. Isa. l. 5, "The Lord God hath opened mine ear, and I was not rebellious." In the Psalm, the proper connection would seem to be, that the speaker had been made obedient, or had been so led that he was disposed to do the will of God. This was expressed by the fact that the ear had been opened so as to be quick to hear, since an indisposition to obey is often expressed by the fact that the ears are *stopped*. There is manifestly no allusion here, as has been sometimes supposed, to the custom of boring through the ear of a servant with an awl as a sign that he was willing to remain and serve his master, Ex. xxi. 6; Deut. xv. 17. In that case, the outer circle, or rim of the ear, was bored through with an awl; here the idea is that of hollowing out, digging, or excavating—a process to make the passage clear, not to pierce the outward ear. The Hebrew in the Psalm the Septuagint translates, "A body hast thou prepared me," and this rendering has been adopted by the apostle. Various ways have been resorted to of explaining the fact that the translators of the Septuagint rendered it in this manner, none of which are entirely free from difficulty. Some critics, as Cappell, Ernesti, and others, have endeavoured to show that it is probable that the Septuagint reading in Ps. xl. 6, was ὠτίον κατηρτίσω μοι—"My ear thou hast prepared;" that is, for obedience. But of this there is no proof, and

6 In burnt-offerings and *sacrifices* for sin thou hast had no pleasure:

7 Then said I, Lo, I come (in the volume of the book it is written of me) to do thy will, O God.

---

indeed it is evident that the apostle quoted it as if it were σῶμα, *body*. See ver. 10. It is probably altogether impossible now to explain the reason why the translators of the Septuagint rendered the phrase as they did; and this remark may be extended to many other places of their version. It is to be admitted here, beyond all doubt, whatever consequences may follow, (1) that their version does not accord with the Hebrew; (2) that the apostle has quoted their version as it stood, without attempting to correct it; (3) that his use of the passage is designed, to some extent at least, as *proof* of what he was demonstrating. The leading idea, the important and essential point in the argument, is, indeed, not that *a body was prepared*, but that *he came to do the will of God;* but still it is clear that the apostle meant to lay some stress on the fact that a body had been prepared for the Redeemer. Sacrifice and offering, by the bodies of lambs and goats, were not what was required; but, instead of that, the Messiah came to do the will of God by offering a more perfect sacrifice, and in accomplishing that it was necessary that he should be endowed with a body. But on what principle the apostle has quoted a passage to prove this which differs from the Hebrew, I confess I cannot see, nor do any of the explanations offered commend themselves as satisfactory. The only circumstances which seem to furnish any relief to the difficulty are these two : (1) that the *main point* in the argument of the apostle was not that "a body had been prepared," but that the Messiah came to do the "will of God," and that the preparation of a body for that was rather an incidental circumstance; and (2) that the translation by the Septuagint was not a material departure from the *scope* of the whole Hebrew passage. The *main* thought—that of doing the will of God in the place of offering sacri-

fice—was still retained; the opening of the ears—that is, rendering the person attentive and disposed to obey—and the preparation of a body in order to obedience, were not circumstances *so* unlike as to make it necessary for the apostle to re-translate the whole passage in order to the main end which he had in view. Still, I admit, that these considerations do not seem to be wholly satisfactory. Those who are disposed to examine the various opinions which have been entertained of this passage may find them in Kuinoel, *in loco;* Rosenmüller; Stuart on the Hebrews, Excursus xx., and Kennicott on Ps. xl. 7. Kennicott supposes that there has been a change in the Hebrew text, and that instead of the present reading—אָזְנַיִם—*oznaim, ears,* the reading was אָז גּוּף—*oz guph, then a body;* and that these words became united by the error of transcribers, and by a slight change then became as the present copies of the Hebrew text stands. This conjecture is ingenious, and if it were ever allowable to follow a *mere* conjecture, I should be disposed to do it here. But there is no authority from MSS. for any change, nor do any of the old versions justify it, or agree with this, except the Arabic.

6. *In burnt-offerings and* sacrifices *for sin thou hast had no pleasure.* This is not quoted literally from the Psalm, but the sense is retained. The reading there is, "burnt-offering and sin-offering hast thou not required." The quotation by the apostle is taken from the Septuagint, with the change of a single word, which does not materially affect the sense—the word οὐκ ἐνδόκησας— *ouk eudokēsas*—"thou hast no pleasure," instead of οὐκ ἠθέλησας — *ouk ēthelēsas*—"thou dost not will." The idea is, that God had no pleasure in them as compared with obedience. He preferred the latter, and they could not be made to come in the place of it, or to answer the same purpose. When they were performed

with a pure heart, he was doubtless pleased with the offering. As used here in reference to the Messiah, the meaning is, that they would not be what was required of *him.* Such offerings would not answer the end for which he was sent into the world, for that end was to be accomplished only by his being "obedient unto death."

7. *Then said I.* I, the Messiah. Paul applies this directly to Christ, showing that he regarded the passage in the Psalm as referring to him as the speaker. ¶ *Lo, I come.* Come into the world, ver. 5. It is not easy to see how this *could* be applied to David in any circumstance of his life. There was no situation in which he could say that, since sacrifices and offerings were not what was demanded, he *came* to do the will of God in the place or stead of them. The *time* here referred to by the word *"then"* was that when it was manifest that sacrifices and offerings for sin would not answer all the purposes desirable, or when in view of that fact the purpose of the Redeemer is represented as formed to enter upon a work which *would* effect what they could not. ¶ *In the volume of the book it is written of me.* The word here rendered "volume"—κεφαλίς—means properly *a little head;* and then *a knob,* and here refers doubtless to the *head* or *knob* of the rod on which the Hebrew manuscripts were rolled. Books were usually so written as to be rolled up, and when they were read they were unrolled at one end of the manuscript, and rolled up at the other as fast as they were read. See Notes on Luke iv. 17. The rods on which they were rolled had small heads, either for the purpose of holding them or for ornament, and hence the name *head* came metaphorically be given to the roll or volume. But what volume is here intended? And where is that written which is here referred to? If David was the author of the Psalm from which this is quoted (Ps. xl.), then the book or volume which was then in existence must have been principally, if not entirely, the five books of Moses, and perhaps the books of Job, Joshua, and Judges, with probably a few of the Psalms. It is most natural to understand this of the Pentateuch, or the five books of Moses, as the word "volume" at that time would undoubtedly have most naturally suggested that. But plainly, this could not refer to *David himself,* for in what part of the law of Moses, or in any of the volumes then extant, can a reference of this kind be found to David? There is no promise, no intimation that *he* would come to "do the will of God" with a view to effect that which could not be done by the sacrifices prescribed by the Jewish law. The reference of the language, therefore, must be to the Messiah— to some place where it is represented that he would come to effect by his obedience what could not be done by the sacrifices and offerings under the law. But still, in the books of Moses, this language is not *literally* found, and the meaning must be, that this was the language which was there *implied* respecting the Messiah; or that this was the substance of the description given of him, that he would come to take the place of those sacrifices, and by his obedience unto death would accomplish what they could not do. They had a reference to him; and it was contemplated in their appointment that their inefficiency would be such that there should be felt a necessity for a higher sacrifice, and that when he should come they would all pass away. The whole language of the institution of sacrifices, and of the Mosaic economy, was, that a Saviour would hereafter come to do the will of God in making an atonement for the sin of the world. That there are places in the books of Moses which refer to the Saviour, is expressly affirmed by Christ himself (Jn. v. 46), and by the apostles (comp. Acts xxii. 23), and that the general spirit of the institutions of Moses had reference to him is abundantly demonstrated in this epistle. The meaning here is, "I come to do thy will in making an atonement, for no other offering would expiate sin. That I would do this is the language of the Scriptures which predict my coming, and of the whole spirit and design of the ancient dispensation."

8 Above when he said, Sacrifice and offering and burnt-offerings and *offering* for sin thou wouldest not, neither hadst pleasure *therein;* which are offered by the law;

9 Then said he, Lo, I come to do thy will, O God. He taketh away the first, that he may establish the second.

10 By*e* the which will we are sanctified *f*through the offering of the body of Jesus Christ once *for all.*

e Jn.17.19.   *f* ch.9.12.

¶ *To do thy will, O God.* This expresses the amount of all that the Redeemer came to do. He came to do the will of God (1) by perfect obedience to his law; and (2) by making an atonement for sin—becoming "obedient unto death," Phil. ii. 8. The latter is the principal thought here, for the apostle is showing that such sacrifices and offerings as were made under the law would not put away sin, and that Christ came in contradistinction from them to make a sacrifice that would be efficacious. Everywhere in the Scriptures it is declared to be the "will of God" that such an atonement should be made. There was salvation in no other way, nor was it possible that the race should be saved unless the Redeemer drank that cup of bitter sorrows. See Mat. xxvi. 39. We are not to suppose, however, that it was by mere *will* that those sufferings were demanded. There were good *reasons* for all that the Saviour was to endure, though those reasons are not all made known to us.

8. *Above when he said.* That is, the Messiah. The word "above" refers here to the former part of the quotation. That is, "having in the former part of what was quoted said that God did not require sacrifices, in the latter part he says that he came to do the will of God in the place of them." ¶ *Sacrifice and offering and burnt-offerings,* &c. These words are not all used in the Psalm from which the apostle quotes, but the idea is, that the specification there included all kinds of offerings. The apostle dwells upon it because it was important to show that the same remark applied to all the sacrifices which could be offered by man. In the observation which the Redeemer is represented as making about the inefficacy of sacri-

fices, it is meant that there were none of them which would be sufficient to take away sin.

9. *Then said he.* In another part of the passage quoted. When he had said that no offering which man could make would avail, *then* he said that he would come himself. ¶ *He taketh away the first.* The word "*first*" here refers to sacrifices and offerings. He takes *them* away—that is, he shows that they are of no value in removing sin. He states their inefficacy, and declares his purpose to abolish them. ¶ *That he may establish the second.* To wit, the doing of the will of God. The two stand in contrast with each other, and he shows the inefficacy of the former in order that the necessity for his coming to do the will of God may be fully seen. If *they* had been efficacious, there would have been no need of his coming to make an atonement.

10. *By the which will.* That is, by his obeying God in the manner specified. It is in virtue of his obedience that we are sanctified. The apostle immediately states what he means, and furnishes the key to his whole argument, when he says that it was *through the offering of the body of Jesus Christ.* It was not merely his doing the will of God *in general,* but the specific thing was the offering of his body in the place of the Jewish sacrifices. Comp. Phil. ii. 8. Whatever effect his personal *obedience* had in our salvation, yet the particular thing here mentioned is, that it was his doing the will of God by offering himself as a sacrifice for sin that was the means of our sanctification. ¶ *We are sanctified.* We are made holy. The word here is not confined to the specific work which is commonly called *sanctification*—or the process of making the soul holy *after* it is renewed, but

11 And *g*every priest standeth daily ministering and offering oftentimes the same sacrifices, *h*which can never take away sins :

12 But this man, after he had

g Nu. 28. 3.   *h* Ps. 50. 8-13; Is. 1. 11.

offered one sacrifice for sins for ever, *i*sat down on the right hand of God ;

13 From henceforth expecting till *k*his enemies be made his footstool.

i Col. 3. 1.   *k* Ps. 110. 1.

---

it includes *everything* by which we are made holy in the sight of God. It embraces, therefore, justification and regeneration as well as what is commonly known as sanctification. The idea is, that whatever there is in our hearts or lives which is holy, or whatever influences are brought to bear upon us to make us holy, all are to be traced to the fact that the Redeemer became obedient unto death, and was willing to offer his body as a sacrifice for sin. ¶ *Through the offering of the body.* As a sacrifice. A body just adapted to such a purpose had been prepared for him, ver. 5. It was perfectly holy; it was so organized as to be keenly sensitive to suffering; it was the dwelling-place of the incarnate Deity. ¶ *Once* for all. In the sense that it is not to be offered again. See Notes on chap. ix. 28. This idea is repeated here because it was very important to be clearly understood, in order to show the contrast between the offering made by Christ and the offerings made under the law. The object of the apostle is to exalt the sacrifice made by him above those made by the Jewish high-priests. This he does by showing that such was the efficacy of the atonement made by him that it did not need to be repeated; the sacrifices made by them, however, were to be renewed every year.

11. *And every priest standeth daily ministering.* That is, this is done every day. It does not mean literally that *every* priest was daily concerned in offering sacrifices, for they took their turns according to their courses (see Notes on Luke i. 5), but that this was done each day, and that every priest was to take his regular place in doing it, Num. xxviii. 3. The object of the apostle is to prove that under the Jewish economy sacrifices were *repeated* constantly, showing

their imperfection, but that under the Christian economy the great sacrifice had been offered once, which was sufficient for all. ¶ *And offering oftentimes the same sacrifices.* The same sacrifices were offered morning and evening every day. ¶ *Which can never take away sins.* See Notes on chap. ix. 9 ; x. 1.

12. *But this man.* The Lord Jesus. The word *man* is not in the original. The Greek is literally " but this;" to wit, this priest. The apostle does not state here whether he was a *man*, or a being of a higher order. He merely mentions him as *a priest*, in contradistinction from the Jewish priests. ¶ *After he had offered one sacrifice for sins.* By dying on the cross. This he did but once; this *could* not be repeated; this *need* not be repeated, for it was sufficient for the sins of the world. ¶ *For ever sat down.* That is, he sat down there to return no more to our world for the purpose of offering sacrifice for sin. He will no more submit himself to scenes of suffering and death to expiate human guilt. ¶ *On the right hand of God.* See Notes on Mark xvi. 19. Comp. Notes on Eph. i. 20–22.

13. *From henceforth expecting.* Or *waiting.* He *waits* there until this shall be accomplished, according to the promise made to him that all things shall be subdued under him. See Notes on 1 Cor. xv. 25–27. ¶ *Till his enemies.* There is an allusion here to Ps. cx. 1, where it is said, " The Lord said unto my Lord, Sit thou at my right hand, until I make thine enemies thy footstool." The enemies of the Redeemer are Satan, the wicked of the earth, and the evil passions of the heart. The idea is, that all things are yet to be made subject to his will—either by a cheerful and cordial submission to his authority, or by being crushed beneath his power.

14 For by one offering he *hath

l ver.1.

perfected for ever them that are sanctified.

The Redeemer, having performed his great work of redemption by giving himself as a sacrifice on the cross, is represented now as calmly waiting until this glorious triumph is achieved, and this promise is fulfilled. We are not to suppose that he is *inactive*, or that he takes no part in the agency by which this is to be done, but the meaning is, that he looks to the certain fulfilment of the promise. ¶ *His footstool.* That is, they will be thoroughly and completely subdued. The same idea is expressed in 1 Cor. xv. 25, by saying that all his enemies shall be put under his feet. The language had its origin in the custom of conquerors in putting their feet on the necks of their enemies, as a symbol of subjection. See Josh. x. 24. Comp. Notes on Isa. xxvi. 5, 6.

14. *For by one offering.* By offering himself once on the cross. The Jewish priest offered his sacrifices often, and still they did not avail to put away sin; the Saviour made one sacrifice, and it was sufficient for the sins of the world. ¶ *He hath perfected for ever.* He hath laid the foundation of the eternal perfection of his people. The offering is of such a character that it will secure their entire freedom from sin, and will make them holy for ever. It cannot mean that those for whom he died are made at once perfectly holy, for that is not true; but the idea is, that the offering was complete, and did not need to be repeated; and that it was of such a nature as entirely to remove the penalty due to sin, and to lay the foundation for their final and eternal holiness. The offerings made under the Jewish law were so defective that there was a necessity for repeating them every day; the offering made by the Saviour was so perfect that it needed not to be repeated, and secured the complete and final salvation of those who availed themselves of it. ¶ *Them that are sanctified.* Those who are made holy by that offering. It does not mean that they are as yet *wholly* sanc-

tified, but that they have been brought under the influence of that gospel which sanctifies and saves. See chap. ii. 11; ix. 14. The doctrine taught in this verse is, that all those who are in any measure sanctified *will* be perfected for ever. It is not a temporary work which has been begun in their souls, but one which is designed to be carried forward to perfection. In the atonement made by the Redeemer there is a foundation laid for their eternal perfection, and it was with reference to that that it was offered. Respecting this work, and the consequences of it, we may remark, that there is (1) perfection in its nature, it being of such a character that it needs not to be repeated; (2) there is perfection in regard to the pardon of sin—*all* past sins being forgiven to those who embrace it, and being *for ever* forgiven; and (3) there *is to be* absolute perfection for them for ever. They *will be* made perfect at some future period, and when that shall take place it will be a perfection which is to continue for ever and ever.

[The perfection in this place is not to be understood of the perfection of grace or of glory. It is perfection in regard to the matter in hand, in regard to that which was the chief design of sacrifices, namely, expiation, and consequent pardon and acceptance of God. And this indeed is the τελειωσις of the Epistle to the Hebrews generally, vii. 11; ix. 9; x. 1. Perfect moral purity and consummate happiness will doubtless follow as consequences of the sacrifice of Christ, but the completeness of his expiation, and its power to bring pardon and peace to the guilty and trembling sinner, to *justify* him unto eternal life, is here, at all events, *principally* intended. The parties thus perfected or completely justified are τους ἁγιαζομενους, the "sanctified." Ἁγιαζω, however, besides the general sense of "sanctify," has in this epistle, like τελειοω, its *sacrificial* sense of cleansing from *guilt*—"whether ceremonially, as under the Levitical dispensation, Heb.ix.13; comp. Lev.xvi.19; or really and truly, by the offering of the body of Christ, Heb. x. 10, 14, 29; comp. ver. 2 and chap. ii. 11; ix. 14" (Parkhurst's *Greek Lexicon*). The meaning, then, may be, that they who are purged or cleansed by *this* sacrifice—in other words, those to whom *its* virtue is applied—are per-

15 *Whereof* the Holy Ghost also is a witness to us: for after that he had said before,

16 This*ᵐ is* the covenant that I will make with them after those days, saith the Lord; I will put my

m Je.31.33,34.

laws into their hearts, and in their minds will I write them.

17 And³ their sins and iniquities will I remember no more.

18 Now where remission of these *is, there is* no more offering for sin.

³ Some copies have, *Then he said, And their.*

---

fectly justified. Wherever this divine remedy is used it will effectually save. By one offering Christ hath for ever *justified* such as are purged or cleansed by *it.* This could not be said of those sanctified or purged by the legal sacrifices. Mr. Scott gives the *sacrificial* sense of the word, but combines with it the sense of sanctifying morally in the following excellent paraphrase:—"By his one oblation he hath provided effectually for the perfect justification unto eternal life of all those who should ever receive his atonement, by faith springing from regeneration and evidenced 'by the sanctification of the Spirit unto obedience,' and who were thus set apart and consecrated to the service of God."]

15–17. Whereof *the Holy Ghost is a witness to us.* That is, the Holy Ghost has given proof of the truth of the position here laid down — that the one atonement made by the Redeemer lays the foundation for the eternal perfection of all who are sanctified. The witness of the Holy Ghost here referred to, is that which is furnished in the Scriptures, and not any witness in ourselves. Paul immediately makes his appeal to a passage of the Old Testament, and he thus shows his firm conviction that the Scriptures were inspired by the Holy Ghost. ¶ *For after that he had said before.* The apostle here appeals to a passage which he had before quoted from Jer. xxxi. 33, 34. See it explained in the Notes on chap. viii. 8–12. The object of the quotation in both cases is, to show that the new covenant contemplated the formation of a *holy* character, or a holy people. It was not to set apart a people who would be externally holy only, or be distinguished for conformity to external rites and ceremonies, but a people who would be holy in heart and in life. There has been some difficulty felt by expositors in ascertaining what corresponds to the expression "after that he had said before," and some have

supposed that the phrase "then he saith" should be understood before ver. 17. But probably the apostle means to refer to two distinct parts of the quotation from Jeremiah, the former of which expresses the fact that God meant to make a new covenant with his people, and the latter expresses the nature of that covenant, and it is particularly to the latter that he refers. This is seen more distinctly in the passage in Jeremiah than it is in our translation of the quotation in this epistle. The meaning is this: "The Holy Ghost first said, This is the covenant that I will make with them;" and, having said this, he then added, "After those days, I will put my laws into their hearts, and in their minds will I write them, and their sins and their iniquities will I remember no more." The first part expresses the purpose to form such a covenant; the latter states what that covenant would be. The quotation is not, indeed, literally made, but the sense is retained. Comp. Notes on chap. viii. 8–12. Still, it may be asked how this quotation *proves* the point for which it is adduced—that the design of the atonement of Christ was "to perfect for ever them that are sanctified?" In regard to this, we may observe, (1) that it was declared that those who were interested in it would be *holy,* for the law would be in their *hearts* and written on their *minds;* and (2) that this would be *entire* and *perpetual.* Their sins would be *wholly* forgiven; they would *never* be remembered again, and thus they would be "perfected for ever."

18. *Now where remission of these* is. Remission or forgiveness of sins; that is, of the sins mentioned in the previous verse. ¶ There is *no more offering for sin.* If those sins are wholly blotted out, there is no more need of

19 Having therefore, brethren, boldness[4] to enter [n]into the holiest by the blood of Jesus,

4 or, *liberty*.   n ch.9.8,12.

20 By a new and [o]living way, which he hath [5]consecrated for us, through the vail, that is to say, his flesh;

o Jn.14.6.   5 or, *new-made*.

sacrifice to atone for them, any more than there is need to pay a debt again which has been once paid. The idea of Paul is, that in the Jewish dispensation there was a constant repeating of the remembrance of sins by the sacrifices which were offered, but that in reference to the dispensation under the Messiah sin would be entirely cancelled. There would be one great and all-sufficient sacrifice, and when there was faith in that offering, sin would be absolutely forgiven. If that was the case, there would be no occasion for any further sacrifice for it, and the offering need not be repeated. This circumstance, on which the apostle insists so much, made a very important difference between the new covenant and the old. In the one, sacrifices were offered every day; in the other, the sacrifice once made was final and complete: in the one case, there was no *such* forgiveness but that the offender was constantly reminded of his sins by the necessity of the repetition of sacrifice; in the other, the pardon was so complete that all dread of wrath was taken away, and the sinner might look up to God as calmly and joyfully as if he had never been guilty of transgression.

19. *Having therefore, brethren.* The apostle, in this verse, enters on the hortatory part of his epistle, which continues to the end of it. He had gone into an extensive examination of the Jewish and Christian systems, he had compared the founders of the two—Moses and the Son of God—and had shown how far superior the latter was to the former; he had compared the Christian great High-priest with the Jewish high-priest, and had shown his superiority; he had compared the sacrifices under the two dispensations, and had shown that in all respects the Christian sacrifice was superior to the Jewish—that it was an offering that cleansed from sin, and that it was sufficient when once offered,

without being repeated, while the Jewish offerings were only typical, and could not put away sin; he had shown that the great High-priest of the Christian profession had opened a way to the mercy-seat in heaven, and was himself now seated there; and having shown this, he now exhorts Christians to avail themselves fully of their advantages, and to enjoy to the widest extent the privileges now conferred on them. One of the first of these benefits was, that they had now free access to the mercy-seat. ¶ *Boldness to enter into the holiest.* Margin, *liberty*. The word rendered *boldness* — παρρησίαν — properly means *boldness of speech*, or freedom where one speaks all that he thinks (see Notes on Acts iv. 13); and then it means boldness in general, license, authority, pardon. Here the idea is, that before Christ died and entered into heaven, there was no such access to the throne of grace as man needed. Man had no offering which he could bring that would make him acceptable to God. But now the way was open. Access was free for all, and all might come with the most perfect liberty. The word *holiest* here is taken from the holy of holies in the temple (see Notes on chap. ix. 3), and is then applied to heaven, of which that was the emblem. The entrance into the most holy place was forbidden to all but the high-priest; but now access to the *real* "holy of holies" was granted to all in the name of the great High-priest of the Christian profession. ¶ *By the blood of Jesus.* The blood of Jesus is the *means* by which this access to heaven is procured. The Jewish high-priest entered the holy of holies with the blood of bullocks and of rams (see Notes on chap. ix. 7); but the Saviour offered his own blood, and that became the means by which we have access to God.

20. *By a new and living way.* By

a new *method* or *manner*. It was a mode of access that was till then unknown. No doubt many were saved before the Redeemer came, but the method by which they approached God was imperfect and difficult. The word which is here rendered *new*— πρόσφατον—occurs nowhere else in the New Testament. It properly means *slain, or killed thereto;* that is, *newly killed, just dead;* and then *fresh, recent* (Passow). It does not so much convey the idea that it is *new* in the sense that it had never existed before, as new in the sense that it is *recent,* or *fresh.* It was a way which was *recently* disclosed, and which had all the freshness of novelty. It is called a "*living* way," because it is a method that *imparts* life, or because it leads to life and happiness. Doddridge renders it "*ever-living way,*" and supposes, in accordance with the opinion of Dr. Owen, that the allusion is to the fact that under the old dispensation the blood was to be offered as soon as it was shed, and that it could not be offered when it was cold and coagulated. The way by Christ was, however, *always* open. His blood was, as it were, always *warm* and *fresh,* and as if it had been recently shed. This interpretation seems to derive some support from the word which is rendered "*new.*" See above. The word *living,* also, has often the sense of perennial, or perpetual, as when applied to a fountain always running, in opposition to a pool that dries up (see Notes on Jn. iv. 10), and the new way to heaven may be called *living* in all these respects. (*a*) It is a way that conducts *to* life. (*b*) It is *ever-living*—as if the blood which was shed always retained the freshness of that which is flowing from the vein. (*c*) It is *perpetual* and *constant*—like a fountain that always flows—for it is by a sacrifice whose power is perpetual and unchanging. ¶ *Which he hath consecrated for us.* Margin, "or *new-made.*" The word here used means properly *to renew,* and then to initiate, to consecrate, to sanction. The idea is, that he has dedicated this way for our use; as if a temple or house were set apart for our service. It is a path consecrated by him for the service and salvation of man; a way of access to the eternal sanctuary for the sinner which has been set apart by the Redeemer for this service alone. ¶ *Through the vail, that is to say, his flesh.* The Jewish high-priest entered into the most holy place through the vail that divided the holy from the most holy place. That entrance was made by his drawing the vail aside, and thus the interior sanctuary was laid open. But there has been much difficulty felt in regard to the sense of the expression here used. The general meaning, indeed, is plain, that the way to heaven was opened by means, or through the medium of the flesh of Jesus; that is, of his body sacrificed for sin, as the most holy place in the temple was entered by means or through the medium of the veil. We are not to suppose, however, that the apostle meant to say that there was *in all respects* a resemblance between the veil and the flesh of Jesus, nor that the veil was typical of his body, but there was a resemblance *in the respect under consideration*—to wit, in the fact that the holy place was rendered accessible by withdrawing the veil, and that heaven was rendered accessible through the slain body of Jesus. The idea is, that both by the veil of the temple and the body of Jesus there is *a medium of access to God.* God dwelt in the most holy place in the temple, behind the veil, by visible symbols, and was to be approached by removing the veil; and God dwells in heaven, in the most holy place there, and is to be approached only through the offering of the body of Christ. Prof. Stuart supposes that the point of the comparison may be, that the veil of the temple operated as a screen to hide the visible symbol of the presence of God from human view, and that in like manner the body of Jesus might be regarded as a "kind of temporary tabernacle, or *vail* of the divine nature which dwelt within him," and that "as the vail of the tabernacle concealed the glory of Jehovah, in the holy of holies, from the view of men, so Christ's flesh or

21 And *having* ᵖan high priest
over the house of God;

22 Let us draw near with a true
heart, ᑫin full assurance of faith,

p ch.4.14–16.　　　*q* Ep.3.12.

body screened or concealed the higher
nature from our view, which dwelt
within this vail, as God did of old
within the vail of the temple." See
this and other views explained at
length in the larger commentaries.
It does not seem to me to be necessary to attempt to carry out the point
of the comparison in all respects.
The simple idea which seems to have
been in the mind of the apostle was,
that the veil of the temple and the
body of Jesus were alike *in this respect*, that they were *the medium of access to God*. It is by the offering of
the body of Jesus; by the fact that
he was clothed with flesh; that in
his body he made an atonement for
sin, and that with his body raised up
from the dead he ascended to heaven,
that we have access now to the throne
of mercy.

21. *And* having *an high priest over
the house of God.* Over the spiritual
house of God; that is, the church.
Comp. Notes on chap. iii. 1–6. Under
the Jewish dispensation there was a
great high-priest, and the same is
true under the Christian dispensation.
This the apostle had shown at length
in the previous part of the epistle.
The idea here is, that as under the
former dispensation it was regarded
as a privilege that the people of God
might have access to the mercy-seat
by means of the high-priest, so it is
true in a much higher sense that we
may now have access to God through
our greater and more glorious High-
priest.

22. *Let us draw near with a true
heart.* In prayer and praise; in every
act of confidence and of worship. A
sincere heart was required under the
ancient dispensation; it is always
demanded of men when they draw
near to God to worship him. See
Jn. iv. 23, 24. Every form of religion which God has revealed requires
the worshippers to come with pure

having our hearts ʳsprinkled from
an evil conscience, and our bodies
washed with pure water.

r Eze.36.25.

and holy hearts. ¶ *In full assurance of faith.* See the word here
used explained in the Notes on chap.
vi. 11. The "full assurance of faith"
means *unwavering confidence;* a fulness of faith in God which leaves no
room for doubt. Christians are permitted to come thus because God
has revealed himself through the Redeemer as in every way deserving
their fullest confidence. No one approaches God in an acceptable manner who does not come to him in
this manner. What parent would
feel that a child came with any right
feelings to ask a favour of him who
had not *the fullest confidence* in him?

["This πληϱοφοϱια, or full assurance of faith,
is not, as many imagine, absolute certainty of
a man's own particular salvation, for that is
termed *the full assurance of hope,* chap. vi. 11,
and arises from faith and its fruits. But the
full assurance of faith is the assurance of that
truth which is testified and proposed in the
gospel to all the hearers of it in common to
be believed by them unto their salvation, and
is also termed *the full assurance of understanding,* Col. ii. 2. Though all that the
gospel reveals claims the full assurance of
faith, yet here it seems more particularly to
respect the efficacy and all-sufficiency of
Christ's offering for procuring pardon and
acceptance" (M'Lean).]

¶ *Having our hearts sprinkled from
an evil conscience.* By the blood of
Jesus. This was fitted to make the
conscience pure. The Jewish cleansing or sprinkling with blood related
only to that which was external, and
could not make the conscience perfect (chap. ix. 9), but the sacrifice offered by the Saviour was designed to
give peace to the troubled mind, and
to make it pure and holy. An "evil
conscience" is a consciousness of evil,
or a conscience oppressed with sin;
that is, a conscience that accuses of
guilt. We are made free from such
a conscience through the atonement
of Jesus, not because we become convinced that we have not committed
sin, and not because we are led to

suppose that our sins are less than we had otherwise supposed—for the reverse of both these is true—but because our sins are forgiven, and since they are freely pardoned they no longer produce remorse and the fear of future wrath. A child that has been forgiven may feel that he has done very wrong, but still he will not be then overpowered with distress in view of his guilt, or with the apprehension of punishment. ¶ *And our bodies washed with pure water.* It was common for the Jews to wash themselves, or to perform various ablutions in their services. See Ex. xxix. 4; xxx. 19–21; xl. 12; Lev. vi. 27; xiii. 54, 58; xiv. 8, 9; xv. 16; xvi. 4, 24; xxii. 6. Comp. Notes on Mark vii. 3. The same thing was also true among the heathen. There was usually, at the entrance of their temples, a vessel placed with consecrated water, in which, as Pliny says (*Hist. Nat.*, lib. xv. c. 30), there was a branch of laurel placed with which the priests sprinkled all who approached for worship. It was necessary that this water should be pure, and it was drawn fresh from wells or fountains for the purpose. Water from pools and ponds was regarded as unsuitable, as was also even the purest water of the fountain, if it had stood long. Æneas sprinkled himself in this manner, as he was about to enter the invisible world, with fresh water (*Æn.* vi. 635). Porphyry says that the Essenes were accustomed to cleanse themselves with the purest water. Thus Ezekiel also says, "Then will I sprinkle clean water upon you, and ye shall be clean." Sea-water was usually regarded as best adapted to this purpose, as the salt was supposed to have a cleansing property. The Jews who dwelt near the sea were thence accustomed, as Aristides says, to wash their hands every morning on this account in the sea-water (Potter's *Gr. Archæ.*, i. 222; Rosenmüller, *Alte und Neue Morgenland, in loco*). It was from the heathen custom of placing a vessel with consecrated water at the entrance of their temples, that the Roman Catholic custom is derived of placing "holy water" near the door in their churches, that those who worship there may "cross themselves." In accordance with the Jewish custom, the apostle says that it was proper that, under the Christian dispensation, we should approach God having performed an act emblematic of purity by the application of water to the body. That there is an allusion to baptism is clear. The apostle is comparing the two dispensations, and his aim is to show that in the Christian dispensation there is everything which was regarded as valuable and important in the old. So he had shown it to be in regard to the fact that there is a Lawgiver; that there is a great High-priest; and that there are sacrifices and ordinances of religion in the Christian dispensation as well as the Jewish. In regard to each of these, he had shown that they exist in the Christian religion in a much more valuable and important sense than under the ancient dispensation. In like manner, it is true that, as the Jews were required to come to the service of God, having performed various ablutions to keep the body pure, so it is with Christians. Water was applied to the Jews as emblematic of purity, and Christians come, having had it applied to them also in baptism, as a symbol of holiness. It is not necessary, in order to see the force of this, to suppose that water had been applied to the *whole* of the body, or that they had been completely *immersed*, for all the force of the reasoning is retained by the supposition that it is a mere *symbol* or *emblem* of purification. The stress of the argument here turns, not on the fact that *the body had been washed all over*, but that the worshipper had been qualified for the *spiritual* service of the Most High in connection with an appropriate emblematic ceremony. The *quantity* of water used for this is not a material point, any more than the *quantity* of oil was in the ceremony of inaugurating kings and priests. This was not done in the Christian dispensation by washing the body *frequently*, as in the ancient system, nor even necessarily by washing the *whole*

23 Let us hold fast the profession of *our* faith without wavering; (for he[s] *is* faithful that promised;)

s 1 Th.5.24.

24 And let us consider one another to provoke unto love and to good works:

body—which would no more contribute to the purity of *the heart* than by application of water to any part of the body—but by the fact that water had been used as emblematic of the purifying of the soul. The passage before us proves, undoubtedly, (1) that *water* should be applied under the new dispensation as an ordinance of religion; and (2) that *pure* water should be used—for that only is a proper emblem of the purity of the heart.

23. *Let us hold fast the profession of our faith without wavering.* To secure this was one of the leading designs of this epistle, and hence the apostle adverts to it so frequently. It is evident that those to whom he wrote were suffering persecution (chap. xii.), and that there was great danger that they would apostatize. As these persecutions came probably from the Jews, and as the aim was to induce them to return to their former opinions, the object of the apostle is to show that there is in the Christian scheme every advantage of which the Jews could boast—everything pertaining to the dignity of the Founder of the system, to the character of the High-priest, and to the nature and value of the sacrifices offered, and that all this was possessed far more abundantly in the permanent Christian system than in that which was typical in its character, and which was designed soon to vanish away. In view of all this, therefore, the apostle adds, that they should hold fast the profession of their faith without being shaken by their trials, or by the threats or arguments of their enemies. *We* have the same inducement to hold fast the profession of our faith—for it is the same religion still; *we* have the same Saviour, and there is held out to *us* still the same prospect of heaven. ¶ *For he* is *faithful that promised.* To induce them to hold fast their profession the apostle adds this addi-

tional consideration. God, who had promised eternal life to them, was faithful to all that he had said. The argument here is, (1) That since *God* is so faithful to us, we ought to be faithful to him. (2) The fact that *he* is faithful is an *encouragement* to us. We are dependent on him for grace to hold fast our profession. If he were to prove unfaithful, we should have no strength to do it. But this he never does; and we may be assured that all that he has promised he will perform. To the service of *such* a God, therefore, we should adhere without wavering. Comp. Notes on 1 Cor. x. 13.

24. *And let us consider one another.* Let us so regard the welfare of others as to endeavour to excite them to persevere in the Christian life. The idea is, that much might be done in securing perseverance and fidelity by manifesting an interest in the welfare of each other, and by mutual exhortation. They were not to be selfish; they were not to regard their own interests only (see Notes on Phil. ii. 4); they were to have a kind sympathy in the concerns of each other. They had, as Christians have now, the same duties to perform, and the same trials to meet, and they should strengthen each other in their trials, and encourage each other in their work. ¶ *To provoke unto love.* We use the word *provoke* now in a somewhat different sense, as meaning to offend, to irritate, to incense; but its original meaning is *to arouse, to excite, to call into action,* and it is used in this sense here. The Greek is, literally, "unto a *paroxysm* of love"—εἰς παροξυσμὸν; —the word *paroxysm* meaning *excitement* or *impulse,* and the idea is, that they were to endeavour to *arouse* or *excite* each other to the manifestation of love. The word used is that which properly expresses *excitement,* and means that Christians should endeavour to *excite* each other. Men are sometimes afraid of excitement in

25 Not forsaking the assembling of ourselves together, as the manner of some *is;* but exhorting *one an-* | *other:* and so much the more, as *[t]* ye see the day approaching.

[t] Ro.13.11.

religion. But there is no danger that Christians will ever be *excited* to love each other too much, or to perform too many *good works.*

25. *Not forsaking the assembling of ourselves together.* That is, for purposes of public worship. Some expositors have understood the word here rendered *assembling*—ἐπισυναγω-γὴν—as meaning *the society of Christians,* or the church; and they have supposed that the object of the apostle here is, to exhort them not to *apostatize* from the church. The arguments for this opinion may be seen at length in Kuinoel, *in loco.* But the more obvious interpretation is that which is commonly adopted, that it refers to public worship. The Greek word (the noun) is used nowhere else in the New Testament, except in 2 Thes. ii. 1, where it is rendered *gathering together.* The *verb* is used in Mat. xxiii. 37; xxiv. 31; Mark i. 33; xiii. 27; Luke xii. 1; xiii. 34; in all which places it is rendered *gathered together.* It properly means *an act of assembling,* or a *gathering together,* and is nowhere used in the New Testament in the sense of *an assembly,* or *the church.* The command, then, here is, to *meet together* for the worship of God, and it is enjoined on Christians as an important duty to do it. It is *implied,* also, that there is blame or fault where this is "neglected." ¶ *As the manner of some* is. *Why* those here referred to neglected public worship, is not specified. It may have been from such causes as the following: (1) Some may have been deterred by the fear of persecution, as those who were thus assembled would be more exposed to danger than others. (2) Some may have neglected the duty because they felt no interest in it—as professing Christians now sometimes do. (3) It is possible that some may have had doubts about the necessity and propriety of this duty, and on that account may have neglected it. Or (4) it may perhaps have been,

though we can hardly suppose that such reasons existed to any considerable extent, that some may have neglected it from a cause which now sometimes operates—from dissatisfaction with a preacher, or with some member or members of the church, or with some measure in the church. Whatever were the reasons, the apostle says that they should not be allowed to operate, but that Christians should regard it as a sacred duty to meet together for the worship of God. None of the causes above suggested should deter men from this duty. With all who bear the Christian name, with all who expect to make advances in piety and religious knowledge, it should be regarded as a sacred duty to assemble together for public worship. Religion is social; and our graces are to be strengthened and invigorated by waiting together on the Lord. There is an obvious propriety that men should assemble together for the worship of the Most High, and no Christian can hope that his graces will grow, or that he can perform his duty to his Maker, without uniting thus with those who love the service of God. ¶ *But exhorting* one another. That is, in your assembling together—a direction which proves that it is proper for Christians to exhort one another when they are gathered together for public worship. Indeed there is reason to believe that the preaching in the early Christian assemblies partook much of the character of mutual exhortation. ¶ *And so much the more as ye see the day approaching.* The term "day" here refers to some event which was certainly anticipated, and which was so well understood by them that no particular explanation was necessary. It was also some event that was expected soon to occur, and in relation to which there were indications then of its speedily arriving. If it had not been something which was expected soon to happen, the apostle would have

gone into a more full explanation of it, and would have stated at length what these indications were. There has been some diversity of opinion about what is here referred to, many commentators supposing that the reference is to the anticipated second coming of the Lord Jesus to set up a visible kingdom on the earth; and others to the fact that the period was approaching when Jerusalem was to be destroyed, and when the services of the temple were to cease. So far as the *language* is concerned, the reference might be to either event, for the word "day" is applied to both in the New Testament. The language would properly be understood as referring to an expected period when something *remarkable* was to happen which ought to have an important influence on their character and conduct. In support of the opinion that it refers to the approaching destruction of Jerusalem, and not to the coming of the Lord Jesus to set up a visible kingdom, we may adduce the following considerations: (1) The term used—"day"—will as properly refer to that event as to any other. It is a word which would be *likely* to suggest the idea of distress, calamity, or judgment of some kind, for so it is often used in the Scriptures: Ps. xxvii. 13; 1 Sam. xxvi. 10; Jer. xxx. 7; Ezek. xxi. 5. Comp. Notes on Isa. ii. 12. (2) Such a period was distinctly predicted by the Saviour, and the indications which would precede it were clearly pointed out, Mat. xxiv. That event was then so near that the Saviour said that "that generation would not pass" until the prediction had been fulfilled, Mat. xxiv. 34. (3) The destruction of Jerusalem was an event of great importance to the Hebrews, and to the Hebrew Christians to whom this epistle was directed, and it might be reasonable to suppose that the apostle Paul would refer to it. (4) It is not improbable that, at the time of writing this epistle, there *were* indications that that day was approaching. Those indications were of so marked a character that when the time approached they could not well be mistaken

(Mat. xxiv. 6–12, 24, 26), and it is probable that they had already begun to appear. (5) There were no such indications that the Lord Jesus was about to appear to set up a visible kingdom. It was not *a fact* that that was about to occur, as the result has shown; nor is there any positive proof that the mass of Christians were expecting it, and there is *no* reason to believe that the apostle Paul had any such expectation. See Notes on 2 Thes. ii. 1–5. (6) The expectation that the destruction of Jerusalem was about to occur was just that which might be expected to produce the effect on the minds of the Hebrew Christians which the apostle here refers to. It was to be a solemn and fearful event. It would be a remarkable manifestation of God. It would break up the civil and ecclesiastical polity of the nation, and would scatter the people abroad. It would require all the exercise of their patience and faith in passing through these scenes. It might be expected to be a time when many would be tempted to apostatize, and it was proper, therefore, to exhort them to meet together, and to strengthen and encourage each other as they saw that that event was drawing near. The argument then would be this:—The danger against which the apostle desired to guard those to whom he was writing was, that of apostasy from Christianity to Judaism. To preserve them from this, he urges the fact that the downfall of Judaism was near, and that every indication which they saw of its approach ought to be allowed to influence them, and to guard them from that danger. It is for reasons such as these that I suppose that the reference here is not to the "second advent" of the Redeemer, but to the approaching destruction of Jerusalem. At the same time, it would not be improper to use this passage as an exhortation to Christians to fidelity when they shall see that the end of the world draws nigh, and when they shall perceive indications that the Lord Jesus is about to come. And so of death. We should be the more diligent and watchful when we see

26 For "if we sin wilfully after that we have received the know-

u Nu.15.30; ch.6.4,&c.

ledge of the truth, there remaineth no more sacrifice for sins,

indications that the great messenger is about to come to summon us into the presence of our final Judge. And who does not know that he *is* approaching with silent and steady footsteps, and that even now he may be very near to any one of us? Who can fail to see in himself indications that the time approaches when he must lie down and die? Every pang that we suffer should remind us of this; and when the hair changes its hue, and time makes furrows in the cheek, and the limbs become feeble, we should regard them as premonitions that the messenger of death is drawing near, and should be more diligent as we see him in his steady and certain approaches.

26. *For if we sin wilfully after that we have received the knowledge of the truth.* If after we are converted, and have become true Christians, we should apostatize, it would be impossible to be recovered again, for there would be no other sacrifice for sin; no way by which we could be saved. This passage, however, like chap. vi. 4–6, has given rise to much difference of opinion. But that the above is the correct interpretation, seems evident to me from the following considerations: (1) It is the natural and obvious interpretation, such as would occur probably to ninety-nine readers in a hundred, if there were no theory to support, and no fear that it would conflict with some other doctrine. (2) It accords with the scope of the epistle, which is, to keep those whom the apostle addressed from returning again to the Jewish religion, under the trials to which they were subjected. (3) It is in accordance with the fair meaning of the language—the words "after that we have received the knowledge of the truth," referring more naturally to true conversion than to any other state of mind. (4) The sentiment would not be correct if it referred to any but real Christians. It would not be true that one who had

been somewhat enlightened, and who then sinned "wilfully," *must* look on fearfully to the judgment without a possibility of being saved. There are multitudes of cases where such persons *are* saved. They *wilfully* resist the Holy Spirit; they strive against him; they for a long time refuse to yield, but they are brought again to reflection, and are led to give their hearts to God. (5) It is true, and always will be true, that *if* a sincere Christian should apostatize, he could *never* be converted again. See Notes on chap. vi. 4–6. The reasons are obvious. He would have tried the *only* plan of salvation, and it would have failed. He would have embraced the Saviour, and there would not have been efficacy enough in *his* blood to keep him, and there would be no Saviour more powerful, and no blood of atonement more efficacious. He would have renounced the Holy Spirit, and would have shown that *his* influences were not effectual to keep him, and there would be no other agent of greater power to renew and save him after he had apostatized. For these reasons it seems clear to me that this passage refers to true Christians, and that the doctrine here taught is, that if such an one should apostatize, he must look forward only to the terrors of the judgment, and to final condemnation. Whether this, *in fact*, ever occurs, is quite another question. In regard to that inquiry, see Notes on chap. vi. 4–6. If this view be correct, we may add, that the passage should not be regarded as applying to what is commonly known as the "sin against the Holy Ghost," or "the unpardonable sin." The word rendered "wilfully"—ἑκουσίως—occurs nowhere else in the New Testament, except in 1 Pet. v. 2, where it is rendered *willingly*—"taking the oversight thereof [of the church] not by constraint, but *willingly*." It properly means *willingly, voluntarily, of our own accord*, and applies to cases where no constraint is used. It is not to

27 But a certain fearful looking for of judgment and *fiery indignation, which shall devour the adversaries.

v Zep.1.18; 3.8.

28 He *w* that despised Moses' law died without mercy under two or three witnesses:

w De.17.2-13.

be construed here *strictly*, or *metaphysically*, for *all* sin is voluntary, or is committed *willingly*, but must refer to *a deliberate act*, where a man MEANS to abandon his religion, and to turn away from God. If it were to be taken with metaphysical exactness, it would demonstrate that every Christian who ever does *anything* wrong, no matter how small, would be lost. But this cannot, from the nature of the case, be the meaning. The apostle well knew that Christians *do* commit such sins (see Notes on Rom. vii.), and his object here is not to set forth the danger of *such* sins, but to guard Christians against entire apostasy from their religion. In the Jewish law, as is indeed the case everywhere, a distinction is made between sins of *oversight*, *inadvertence*, or *ignorance* (Lev. iv. 2, 13, 22, 27; v. 15; Num. xv. 24, 27, 28, 29; comp. Acts iii. 17; xvii. 30), and sins of *presumption;* sins that are *deliberately* and *intentionally* committed. See Ex. xxi. 14; Num. xv. 30; Deut. xvii. 12; Ps. xix. 13. The apostle here has reference, evidently, to such a distinction, and means to speak of a decided and deliberate purpose to break away from the restraints and obligations of the Christian religion. ¶ *There remaineth no more sacrifice for sins.* Should a man do this, there is no sacrifice for sins which could save him. He would have rejected deliberately the only atonement made for sin, and there will be no other made. It is as if a man should reject the only medicine that could heal him, or push away the only boat that could save him when shipwrecked. See Notes on chap. vi. 6. The sacrifice made for sin by the Redeemer is never to be repeated, and if that is deliberately rejected, the soul must be lost.

27. *But a certain fearful looking for of judgment.* The word "*certain*" here does not mean *fixed, sure, inevitable*, as our translation would seem

to imply. The Greek is the same as "*a* (τις) fearful expectation," &c. So it is rendered by Tindall. The idea is, that if there should be voluntary apostasy after having embraced the Christian religion, there *could be* nothing but an expectation of the judgment to come. Man can have no other hope but that which is offered through the gospel, and as this would have been renounced, it would follow that the soul must perish. The "fearful apprehension" or expectation here does not refer so much to what would be *in the mind itself*, or what would be experienced, as to what *must follow*. It might be that the person referred to would have no realizing sense of all this, and still his situation be that of one who had nothing to expect but the terrors of the judgment to come. ¶ *And fiery indignation.* Fire is often used in the Scriptures as an emblem of fierce punishment. The idea is, that the person referred to could expect nothing but the wrath of God. ¶ *Which shall devour the adversaries.* All who become the adversaries or enemies of the Lord. Fire is often said to *devour*, or *consume*, and the meaning here is, that any who should thus become the enemies of the Lord must perish.

28. *He that despised Moses' law.* That is, the apostate from the religion of Moses. It does not mean that *in all cases* the offender against the law of Moses died without mercy, but only where offences were punishable with death, and probably had in his eye particularly the case of apostasy from the Jewish religion. The subject of apostasy from the Christian religion is particularly under discussion here, and it was natural to illustrate this by a reference to a similar case under the law of Moses. The law in regard to apostates from the Jewish religion was positive. There was no reprieve, Deut. xiii. 6-10. ¶ *Died without mercy.*

29 Of[x] how much sorer punishment, suppose ye, shall he be thought worthy, who hath trodden under foot the Son of God, and hath

counted the blood of the covenant, wherewith he was sanctified, an unholy thing, and hath [y] done despite unto the Spirit of grace?

x ch. 2. 3.

y Mat. 12. 31, 32.

That is, there was no provision for pardon. ¶ *Under two or three witnesses.* It was a settled law among the Hebrews that in all cases involving capital punishment, two or three witnesses were necessary. That is, no one was to be executed unless two persons bore testimony, and it was regarded as important, if possible, that *three* witnesses should concur in the statement. The object was the security of the accused person, if innocent. The *principle* in the law was, that it was to be presumed that two or three persons would be much less likely to conspire to render a false testimony than one would be, and that two or three would not be likely to be deceived in regard to a fact which they had observed.

29. *Of how much sorer punishment, suppose ye, shall he be thought worthy.* That is, he who renounces Christianity *ought* to be regarded as deserving a much severer punishment than the apostate from the Jewish religion; and if he *ought* to be so regarded he will be—for God will treat every man as he *ought* to be treated. This must refer to future punishment, for the severest punishment was inflicted on the apostate from the Jewish religion which *can be* in this world—*death;* and yet the apostle here says that a severer punishment than that would be deserved by him who should apostatize from the Christian faith. The *reasons* why a punishment so much more severe would be deserved are such as these:—the Author of the Christian system was far more exalted than Moses, the founder of the Jewish system; he had revealed more important truths; he had increased and confirmed the motives to holiness; he had furnished more means for leading a holy life; he had given himself as a sacrifice to redeem the soul from death; and he had revealed with far greater clearness the truth that there

is a heaven of glory and of holiness. He who should apostatize from the Christian faith, the apostle goes on to say, would also be guilty of the most aggravated crime of which man could be guilty—the crime of trampling under foot the Son of God, of showing contempt for his holy blood, and of despising the Spirit of grace. ¶ *Who hath trodden under foot the Son of God.* This language is taken either from the custom of ancient conquerors, who were accustomed to tread on the necks of their enemies in token of their being subdued, or from the fact that men tread on that which they despise and condemn. The idea is, that he who should apostatize from the Christian faith would act *as if* he should indignantly and contemptuously trample on God's only Son. What crime could be more aggravated than this? ¶ *And hath counted the blood of the covenant.* The blood of Jesus, by which the new covenant between God and man was ratified. See Notes on chap. ix. 16–20. Comp. Notes on Mat. xxvi. 28. ¶ *Wherewith he was sanctified.* Made holy, or set apart to the service of God. The word *sanctify* is used in both these senses. Prof. Stuart renders it, "by which expiation is made;" and many others, in accordance with this view, have supposed that it refers to the Lord Jesus. But it seems to me that it refers to the person who is here supposed to renounce the Christian religion, or to apostatize from it. The reasons for this are such as these: (1) It is the natural and proper meaning of the word here rendered *sanctified.* This word is commonly applied to Christians in the sense that they are made holy. See Acts xx. 32; xxvi. 18; 1 Cor. i. 2; Jude 1. Comp. Jn. x. 36; xvii. 17. (2) It is unusual to apply this word to the Saviour. It is true, indeed, that he says (Jn. xvii. 19), "for their sakes

I sanctify myself," but there is no instance in which he says that he was *sanctified by his own blood.* And where is there an instance in which the word is used as meaning "to make expiation?" (3) The supposition that it refers to one who is here spoken of as in danger of apostasy, and not of the Lord Jesus, agrees with the scope of the argument. The apostle is showing the great guilt, and the certain destruction, of one who should apostatize from the Christian religion. In doing this, it was natural to speak of the dishonour which would thus be done to the means which had been used for his sanctification—the blood of the Redeemer. It would be treating it as if it were a common thing, or as if it might be disregarded like anything else which was of no value. ¶ *An unholy thing.* Greek, *common;* often used in the sense of *unholy.* The word is so used because that which was holy was separated from a common to a sacred use. What was *not* thus consecrated was free to all, or was for common use, and hence also the word is used to denote that which is unholy. ¶ *And hath done despite unto the Spirit of grace.* The Holy Spirit, called "the Spirit of grace," because he confers favour or grace on men. The meaning of the phrase "done despite unto"—ἐνυβρίσας—is, having reproached, or treated with malignity, or with contempt. The idea is, that if they were thus to apostatize, they would by such an act treat the Spirit of God with disdain and contempt. It was by that Spirit that they had been renewed; that they had been brought to embrace the Saviour and to love God; that they had any holy feelings or pure desires; and if they now apostatized from religion, such an act would be, in fact, treating the Holy Spirit with the highest indignity. It would be saying that all his influences were valueless, and that they needed no help from him. From such considerations the apostle shows that *if* a true Christian were to apostatize nothing would remain for him but the terrific prospect of eternal condemnation. He would

have rejected the only Saviour; he would have, in fact, treated him with the highest indignity; he would have shown that he considered his sacred blood, shed to sanctify men, as a common thing, and would have manifested the highest disregard for the only agent who can save the soul—the Spirit of God. How could such an one afterward be saved? The apostle does not, indeed, say that anyone ever *would* thus apostatize from the true religion, nor is there any reason to believe that such a case ever *has* occurred; but if it *should* occur the doom would be inevitable. How dangerous, then, is every step which would lead to such a precipice! And how strange and unscriptural the opinion held by so many that sincere Christians *may* "fall away" and be renewed again and again!

[See the Supplementary Note on chap. vi. 6, where certain principles are laid down for the interpretation of this and similar passages in consistency with the doctrine of the saints' perseverance. If that doctrine be maintained, and our author's view of the passage at the same time be correct, then plainly it contains an *impossible* case. It is descriptive of real Christians, yet *they* never can fall away. The utility of the warning in this case may indeed successfully be vindicated on the ground that it is the *means* of preventing apostasy in the saints, the means by which the decree of God in reference to their stability is effected. Most, however, will incline to the view which regards this case as something more than imaginary—as *possible,* as *real.* The warning is addressed to *professors* generally, without any attempt of distinguishing or separating into *true* or *false.* Doubtless there might be *some* even of the latter class in the churches whose members the apostles, presuming on their professed character, addressed as "saints," "elect," and "faithful," without distinction. Of course, in consistency with the doctrine of perseverance, only the "*false,*" in whom the "root of the matter" had never existed, could apostatize; yet at the same time, when no distinction was made, when the apostle made none, but addressed all in the language of charity, when Christians themselves might find it difficult at all times to affirm decidedly on their own case, *universal vigilance* was secured, or at all events designed. But is not the party whose apostasy is here supposed, described by two attributes which belong to none but genuine Christians, viz the "reception of the knowledge of the truth,"

30 For we know him that hath said, *z* Vengeance *belongeth* unto me, I will recompense, saith the Lord.

z De. 32. 35, 36.

And again, *a* The Lord shall judge his people.

31 *It is* a fearful thing to fall into the hands of the living God.

a Ps. 135. 14.

and "sanctification through the blood of the covenant?" The answer which has been given to this question is generally, that neither of these things necessarily involves more than *external* dedication to God. The first is parallel to the "once enlightened" of Heb. vi. 4, and of course admits of the same explanation; see Supplementary Note there. The second thing, viz. the sanctification of the party, "is not real or internal sanctification, and all the disputes concerning the total and final apostasy from the faith of them who have been really and internally sanctified from this place are altogether vain. As at the giving of the law, the people, being sprinkled with blood, were *sanctified* or dedicated to God in a peculiar manner, so those who, by baptism and confession of faith, in the church of Christ, were separated from all others, were peculiarly dedicated to God thereby" (Owen). Yet this eminent writer is rather disposed to adopt the opinion of those who construe ἐν ᾧ ἡγιασθη with the immediate antecedent τον Ἱιον του Θεου, thus referring the sanctification to Christ and not to the apostate; see Jn. xvii. 19. Whichever of these views we receive, the great doctrine of perseverance is of course unaffected. In reference to an objection which the author has urged, that "the sentiment (in the 26th and 27th verses) would not be correct if it referred to any but true Christians," let it be noticed that while many may be saved who have long resisted the Spirit, yet the assertion must appear hazardous in the extreme that *any* can be saved who do ALL that the apostate in this passage is alleged to do. The sin described seems to be that of a determined, insulting, final rejection of the *only* remedy for sin.]

30. *For we know him that hath said.* We know who has said this—God. They knew this because it was recorded in their own sacred books. ¶ *Vengeance* belongeth *unto me*, &c. This is found in Deut. xxxii. 35. See it explained in the Notes on Rom. xii. 19. It is there quoted to show that *we* should not avenge ourselves; it is here quoted to show that God will *certainly* inflict punishment on those who deserve it. If any should apostatize in the manner here referred to by the apostle, they would, says he, be guilty of great and unparalleled

wickedness, and would have the certainty that they *must* meet the wrath of God. ¶ *And again, The Lord shall judge his people.* This is quoted from Deut. xxxii. 36. That is, he will judge them if they deserve it, and punish them if they ought to be punished. The mere fact that they *are* his people will not save them from punishment if they deserve it, any more than the fact that one is a beloved child will save him from correction when he does wrong. This truth was abundantly illustrated in the history of the Israelites; and the same great principle would be applied should any sincere Christian apostatize from religion. He would have before him the certainty of the most fearful and severe of all punishments.

31. It is *a fearful thing to fall into the hands of the living God.* There may be an allusion here to the request of David to "fall into the hands of the Lord and not into the hands of men," when, on account of his sin in numbering the people, the question was submitted to him whether he would choose seven years of famine, or flee three months before his enemies, or have three days of pestilence, 2 Sam. xxiv. He preferred "to fall into the hands of the Lord," and God smote seventy thousand men by the pestilence. The idea here is, that to fall into the hands of the Lord, after having despised his mercy and rejected his salvation, would be terrific; and the fear of this should deter from the commission of the dreadful crime. The phrase "living God" is used in the Scripture in opposition to *idols*. God always lives; his power is capable of being always exerted. He is not like the idols of wood or stone which have no life, and which are not to be dreaded, but he always lives. It is the more fearful to fall into his hands, because he will live *for ever.* A man who inflicts punishment will die, and the

32 But call to remembrance the former days, in which, after ye were illuminated, ye endured a great fight of afflictions;

33 Partly, whilst ye were made a gazing-stock, both by reproaches and afflictions; and partly, whilst *b* ye became companions of them that were so used.

b 1 Th. 2. 14.

punishment will come to an end, but God will never cease to exist, and the punishment which he is capable of inflicting to-day he will be capable of inflicting for ever and ever. To fall into his hands, therefore, *for the purpose of punishment*—which is the idea here—is fearful, (1) because he has all power, and can inflict just what punishment he pleases; (2) because he is strictly just, and will inflict the punishment which ought to be inflicted; (3) because he lives for ever, and can carry on his purpose of punishment to eternal ages; and (4) because the actual inflictions of punishment which have occurred show what is to be dreaded. So it was on the old world; on the cities of the plain; on Babylon, Idumea, Capernaum, and Jerusalem; and so it is in the world of woe—the eternal abodes of despair, where the worm never dies. All men *must*, in one sense, fall into his hands. They *must* appear before him. They *must* be brought to his bar when they die. How unspeakably important is it then to embrace his offers of salvation that we may not fall into his hands as a righteous, avenging judge, and sink beneath his uplifted arm for ever!

32. *But call to remembrance the former days.* It would seem from this that at the time when the apostle wrote this epistle they were suffering some severe trials, in which they were in great danger of apostatizing from their religion. It is also manifest that they had on some former occasion endured a similar trial, and had been enabled to bear it with a Christian spirit and with true resignation. The object of the apostle now is to remind them that they were sustained under those trials, and he would encourage them now to similar patience by the recollection of the grace then conferred on them. What was the nature of their former trials or of that which they were then experiencing is not certainly known.

It would seem probable, however, that the reference in both instances is to some form of persecution by their own countrymen. The meaning is, *that when we have been enabled to pass through trials once we are to make the remembrance of the grace then bestowed on us a means of supporting and encouraging us in future trials.* ¶ *After ye were illuminated.* After you became Christians, or were enlightened to see the truth. This phrase, referring here undoubtedly to the fact that they were Christians, may serve to explain the disputed phrase in chap. vi. 4. See Notes on that passage. ¶ *A great fight of afflictions.* The *language* here seems to be taken from the Grecian games. The word "fight" means properly *contention, combat,* such as occurred in the public games. Here the idea is, that in the trials referred to they had a great *struggle*—that is, a struggle to maintain their faith without wavering, or against those who would have led them to apostatize from their religion. Some of the circumstances attending this conflict are alluded to in the following verses.

33. *Partly.* That is, your affliction consisted partly in this. The Greek is "this"—specifying one kind of affliction that they were called to endure. ¶ *Whilst ye were made a gazing-stock.* Greek, θεατριζόμενοι—you were made a public spectacle, as if in a theatre; you were held up to public view or exposed to public scorn. When this was done or in precisely what manner we are not told. It was not an uncommon thing, however, for the early Christians to be held up to reproach and scorn, and probably this refers to some time when it was done by rulers or magistrates. It was a common custom among the Greeks and Romans to lead criminals, before they were put to death, through the theatre, and thus to expose them to the insults and reproaches of the multitude. See

34 For ye had compassion of me in my bonds, and took joyfully the spoiling of your goods, knowing [6] in

6 or, *that ye have in yourselves; or, for yourselves.*

yourselves that [c] ye have in heaven a better and an enduring substance.

c Lu.12.33.

the proofs of this adduced by Kuinoel on this passage. The *language* here seems to have been taken from this custom, though there is no certain evidence that the Christians to whom Paul refers had been treated in this manner. ¶ *By reproaches.* Reproached as being the followers of Jesus of Nazareth; probably as weak and fanatical. ¶ *And afflictions.* Various *sufferings* inflicted on them. They were not merely reviled *in words*, but they were made to endure positive sufferings of various kinds. ¶ *And partly, while ye became companions of them that were so used.* That is, even when they had not themselves been subjected to these trials, they had sympathized with those who were. They doubtless imparted to them of their property; sent to them relief; identified themselves with them. It is not known to what particular occasion the apostle here refers. In the next verse he mentions *one* instance in which they had done this, in aiding *him* when he was a prisoner.

34. *For ye had compassion of me in my bonds.* You sympathized with me when a prisoner, and sent to my relief. It is not known to what particular instance of imprisonment the apostle here refers. It is probable, however, that it was on some occasion when he was a prisoner in Judea, for the persons to whom this epistle was sent most probably resided there. Paul was at one time a prisoner more than two years at Cesarea (Acts xxiv. 27), and during this time he was kept in the charge of a centurion, and his friends had free access to him, Acts xxiv. 23. It would seem not improbable that this was the occasion to which he here refers. It should be added here, however, that many of the best manuscripts here, instead of δεσμοῖς μου, *my bonds*, read τοῖς δεσμίοις, *to the prisoners*—as if referring to some act of kindness to those who were in prison. ¶ *And took joyfully the spoiling of your goods.* The *plunder* of your property.

It was not an uncommon thing for the early Christians to be plundered. This was doubtless a part of the "afflictions" to which the apostle refers in this case. The meaning is, that they yielded their property not only without resistance, but with joy. They, in common with all the early Christians, counted it a privilege and honour to suffer in the cause of their Master. See Notes on Phil. iii. 10. Comp. Phil. iv. 13. Men *may* be brought to such a state of mind as to part with their property *with joy*. It is not usually the case; but religion will enable a man to do it. ¶ *Knowing in yourselves.* Margin, "or, *that ye have in yourselves; or, for yourselves.*" The true rendering is, "knowing that ye have for yourselves." It does not refer to any *internal* knowledge which they had of this, but to the fact that they were assured that they had laid up for themselves a better inheritance in heaven. ¶ *That ye have in heaven a better and an enduring substance.* Better than any earthly possession, and more permanent. It is (1) *better;* it is worth more; it gives more comfort; it makes a man really *richer*. The treasure laid up in heaven is *worth more* to a man than all the wealth of Crœsus. It will give him more solid peace and comfort, will better serve his turn in the various situations in which he may be placed in life, and will do more, on the whole, to make him happy. It is not said here that property is worth *nothing* to a man—which is not true if he uses it well—but that the treasures of heaven are worth *more*. (2) It is more *enduring*. Property here soon vanishes. Riches take to themselves wings and fly away, or at anyrate all that we possess must soon be left. But in heaven all is permanent and secure. No calamity of war, pestilence, or famine; no change of times; no commercial embarrassments; no failure of a crop or a bank; no fraud of sharpers and swindlers, and no act of a pickpocket or highwayman, can

35 Cast not away therefore your confidence, ^dwhich hath great recompense of reward.

36 For^e ye have need of patience,

d Mat.5.12.   e Lu.21.19.

that, after ye have done the will of God, ye might receive the promise.

37 For^f yet a little while, and he that shall come will come, and will not tarry.

f Hab.2.3,4.

---

take it away; nor does death ever come there to remove the inhabitants of heaven from their "mansions." With this hope, therefore, Christians may cheerfully see their earthly wealth vanish, for they can look forward to their enduring and their better inheritance.

35. *Cast not away therefore your confidence.* Greek, "your boldness," referring to their confident hope in God. They were not to cast this away and to become timid, disheartened, and discouraged. They were to bear up manfully under all their trials, and to maintain a steadfast adherence to God and to his cause. The command is not to "cast this away." Nothing could take it from them if they trusted in God, and it could be lost only by their own neglect or imprudence. Rosenmüller supposes (*Alte und Neue Morgenland, in loco*) that there may be an allusion here to the disgrace which was attached to the act of a warrior if he cast away his shield. Among the Greeks this was a crime which was punishable with death (Alexander ab Alexand. *Gen. Dies.* l. ii. c. 13). Among the ancient Germans, Tacitus says, that to lose the shield in battle was regarded as the deepest dishonour, and that those who were guilty of it were not allowed to be present at the sacrifices or in the assembly of the people. Many, says he, who had suffered this calamity closed their own lives with the halter under the loss of honour (Tac. *Germ.* c. 6). A similar disgrace would attend the Christian soldier if he should cast away his shield of faith. Comp. Notes on Eph. vi. 16. ¶ *Which hath great recompense of reward.* It will furnish a reward by the peace of mind which it gives here, and it will be connected with the rewards of heaven.

36. *For ye have need of patience.* They were then suffering, and in all trials we have need of patience. We have need of it because there is in us

so much disposition to murmur and repine, because our nature is liable to sink under sufferings, and because our trials are often protracted. All that Christians can do in such cases is to be *patient*—to lie calmly in the hands of God and submit to his will day by day and year by year. See Jam. i. 3, 4. Comp. Notes on Rom. v. 4. ¶ *That after ye have done the will of God.* That is, in bearing trials, for the reference here is particularly to afflictions. ¶ *Ye might receive the promise.* The promised inheritance or reward—in heaven. It is implied here that this promise will not be received unless we are patient in our trials, and the prospect of this reward should encourage us to endure them.

37. *For yet a little while.* There seems to be an allusion here to what the Saviour himself said: "A little while, and ye shall not see me; and again a little while, and ye shall see me," Jn. xvi. 16. Or more probably it may be to Hab. ii. 3, "For the vision is yet for an appointed time, but at the end it shall speak, and not lie: though it tarry, wait for it; because it will surely come, it will not tarry." The idea which the apostle means to convey evidently is, that the time of their deliverance from their trials was not far remote. ¶ *And he that shall come will come.* The reference here is, doubtless, to the Messiah. But what "*coming*" of his is referred to is more uncertain. Most probably the idea is, that the Messiah who was coming to destroy Jerusalem, and to overthrow the Jewish power (Mat. xxiv.), would soon do this. In this way he would put a period to their persecutions and trials, as the power of the Jewish people to afflict them would be at an end. A similar idea occurs in Luke xxi. 28, "And when these things begin to come to pass, then look up, and lift up your heads; *for your redemption draweth*

38 Now the just shall live by faith: but if *any man* draw back,

my soul shall have no pleasure in him.

---

nigh." See Notes on that passage. The Christians in Palestine were oppressed, reviled, and persecuted by the Jews. The destruction of the city and the temple would put an end to that power, and would be, in fact, the time of deliverance for those who had been thus persecuted. In the passage before us Paul intimates that that period was not far distant. Perhaps there were already "signs" of his coming, or indications that Jerusalem was about to be destroyed, and he therefore urges them patiently to persevere in their fidelity to him during the little time of trial that remained. The same encouragement and consolation may be employed still. To all the afflicted it may be said that "he that shall come will come" soon. The time of affliction is not long. Soon the Redeemer will appear to deliver his afflicted people from all their sorrows; to remove them from a world of pain and tears; to raise their bodies from the dust, and to receive them to mansions where trials are for ever unknown. See Notes on Jn. xiv. 3; 1 Thes. iv. 13-18.

38. *Now the just shall live by faith.* This is a part of the quotation from Habakkuk (ii. 3, 4), which was commenced in the previous verse. See the passage fully explained in the Notes on Rom. i. 17. The meaning in the connection in which it stands here, in accordance with the sense in which it was used by Habakkuk, is, that the righteous should live by *continued confidence* in God. They should pass their lives, not in doubt, and fear, and trembling apprehension, but in the exercise of a calm trust in God. In this sense it accords with the scope of what the apostle is here saying. He is exhorting the Christians whom he addressed to perseverance in their religion even in the midst of many persecutions. To encourage this he says, that it was a great principle that the just—that is, all the pious—ought to live in the constant exercise of *faith in God.* They should not confide in their own merits, works, or strength.

They should exercise unwavering reliance on their Maker, and he would keep them even unto eternal life. The sense is, that a persevering confidence or belief in the Lord will preserve us amidst all the trials and calamities to which we are exposed. ¶ *But if* any man *draw back, my soul shall have no pleasure in him.* This also is a quotation from Hab. ii. 4, but from the Septuagint, not from the Hebrew. *Why* the authors of the Septuagint thus translated the passage, it is impossible now to say. The Hebrew is rendered in the common version, "Behold, his soul which is lifted up is not upright in him." More literally, it would be rendered, "Behold the scornful; his mind shall not be happy" (Stuart); or, as Gesenius renders it, "See, he whose soul is unbelieving shall, on this account, be unhappy." The sentiment there is, that the scorner or unbeliever in that day would be unhappy, or would not prosper—לֹא יָשְׁרָה. The apostle has retained the general sense of the passage, and the idea which *he* expresses is, that the unbeliever, or he who renounces his religion, will incur the divine displeasure. He will be a man exposed to the divine wrath; a man on whom God cannot look but with disapprobation. By this solemn consideration, therefore, the apostle urges on them the importance of perseverance, and the guilt and danger of apostasy from the Christian faith. *If* such a case should occur, no matter what might have been the former condition, and no matter what love or zeal might have been evinced, yet such an apostasy would expose the individual to the certain wrath of God. His former love could not save him, any more than the former obedience of the angels saved them from the horrors of eternal chains and darkness, or than the holiness in which Adam was created saved him and his posterity from the calamities which his apostasy incurred.

39. *But we are not of them,* &c. We

39 But we are not of *g*them who
draw back unto perdition; but of

g ver.26.

them that believe to the saving of
the soul.

who are true Christians do not belong
to such a class. In this the apostle
expresses the fullest conviction that
none of those to whom he wrote
would apostatize. The case which he
had been describing was only a sup-
posable case, not one which he believed would occur. He had been
merely stating what *must* happen if a
sincere Christian should apostatize.
But he did not mean to say that this
would occur in regard to them, or in
any case. He made a statement of a
general principle under the divine administration, and he designed that this
should be a means of keeping them
in the path to life. What could be
a more effectual means of doing this
than the assurance that *if* a Christian
should apostatize *he must inevitably
perish for ever?* See the sentiment in
this verse illustrated at length in the
Notes on chap. vi. 4–10.

REMARKS.

(1) It is a subject of rejoicing that
we are brought under a more perfect
system than the ancient people of
God were. We have not merely a
rude outline—a dim and shadowy
sketch of religion, as they had. We
are not now required to go before a
bloody altar every day, and lead up a
victim to be slain. We may come to
the altar of God feeling that the great
sacrifice has been made, and that the
last drop of blood necessary to make
an atonement for sin has been shed.
A pure, glorious, holy body was prepared for the great Victim, and in
that body he did the will of God and
died for our transgressions, ver. 1–10.
(2) Like that great Redeemer, let
us do the will of God. It may lead
us through sufferings, and we may be
called to meet trials strongly resembling his. But the will of God is to
be done alike in bearing trials, and in
prayer and praise. *Obedience* is the
great thing which he demands, and
which he has always sought. When
his ancient people led up, in faith, a

lamb to the altar, still he preferred
obedience to sacrifice; and when his
Son came into the world to teach us
how to live and how to die, still the
great thing was obedience. He came
to illustrate the nature of perfect conformity to the will of God, and he did
that by a most holy life, and by the
most patient submission to all the
trials appointed him in his purpose to
make an atonement for the sins of the
world. Our model, alike in holy living and holy dying, is to be the Saviour; and, like him, we are required
to exercise simple submission to the
will of God, ver. 1–10.
(3) The Redeemer now looks calmly
forward to the time when all his foes
will be brought in submission to his
feet, ver. 11, 12. He is at the right
hand of God. His great work on
earth is done. He is to suffer no
more. He is exalted beyond the possibility of pain and sorrow, and he is
seated now on high looking to the
period when all his foes shall be subdued, and he will be acknowledged as
universal Lord.
(4) The Christian has exalted advantages. He has access to the mercy-
seat of God. He may enter by faith
into the "holiest"—the very heavens where God dwells. Christ, his
great High-priest, has entered there;
he has sprinkled over the mercy-seat
with his blood, and ever lives there
to plead his cause. There is no privilege granted to men like that of a
near and constant access to the mercy-
seat. This is the privilege not now
of a few; and not to be enjoyed but
once in a year, or at distant intervals,
but which the most humble Christian
possesses, and which may be enjoyed
at all times, by all people, and in all
places. There is not a Christian so
obscure, so poor, so ignorant that he
may not come and speak to God; and
there is not a situation of poverty,
want, or woe, where he may not make
his wants known with the assurance
that his prayers will be heard through
faith in the great Redeemer, ver. 19, 20.

(5) When we come before God, let our hearts be pure, ver. 22. The body has been washed with pure water in baptism, emblematic of the purifying influences of the Holy Spirit. Let the conscience be also pure. Let us lay aside every unholy thought. Our worship will not be acceptable, our prayers will not be heard, if it is not so. "If we regard iniquity in our hearts the Lord will not hear us." No matter though there be a great High-priest; no matter though he have offered a perfect sacrifice for sin; and no matter though the throne of God be accessible to men; yet if there is in the heart the love of sin, if the conscience is not pure, our prayers will not be heard. Is this not one great reason why our worship is so barren and unprofitable?

(6) It is the duty of Christians to exhort one another to mutual fidelity, ver. 24. We should so far regard the interests of each other as to strive to promote our mutual advance in piety. The church is one. All true Christians are brethren. Each one has an interest in the spiritual welfare of every one who loves the Lord Jesus, and should strive to increase his spiritual joy and usefulness. A Christian brother often goes astray and needs kind admonition to reclaim him; or he becomes disheartened and needs encouragement to cheer him on his Christian way.

(7) Christians should not neglect the assembling of themselves together for the worship of God, ver. 25. It is a duty which they owe to God to acknowledge him publicly, and their own growth in piety is essentially connected with public worship. It is impossible for a man to secure the advancement of religion in his soul who habitually neglects public worship, and religion will not flourish in any community where this duty is not performed. There are great benefits growing out of the worship of God, which can be secured in no other way. God has made us social beings, and he intends that the social principle shall be called into exercise in religion, as well as in other things. We have common wants, and it is proper to present them together before the mercy-seat. We have received common blessings in our creation, in the providence of God, and in redemption, and it is proper that we should assemble together and render united praise to our Maker for his goodness. Besides, in any community, the public worship of God does more to promote intelligence, order, peace, harmony, friendship, neatness of apparel, and purity and propriety of intercourse between neighbours, than anything else can, and for which nothing else can be a compensation. Every Christian, and every other man, therefore, is bound to lend his influence in thus keeping up the worship of God, and should always be in his place in the sanctuary. The particular thing in the exhortation of the apostle is, that this should be done *even in the face of persecution*. The early Christians felt so much the importance of this, that we are told they were accustomed to assemble at night. Forbidden to meet in public houses of worship, they met in caves, and even when threatened with death they continued to maintain the worship of God. It may be added, that so important is this, that it should be continued, even when the preaching of the gospel is not enjoyed. Let Christians assemble together. Let them pray and offer praise. Let them read the Word of God, and an appropriate sermon. Even *this* will exert an influence on them and on the community of incalculable importance, and will serve to keep the flame of piety burning on the altar of their own hearts, and in the community around them.

(8) We may see the danger of indulging in any sin, ver. 26, 27. None can tell to what it may lead. No matter how small and unimportant it may appear at the time, yet, if indulged in, it will prove that there is no true religion, and will lead on to those greater offences which make shipwreck of the Christian name, and ruin the soul. He that "wilfully" and deliberately sins "after he professes to have received the knowledge of the truth," shows that his religion is but

a name, and that he has never known anything of its power.

(9) We should guard with sacred vigilance against everything which might lead to apostasy, ver. 26–29. If a sincere Christian *should* apostatize from God, he could never be renewed and saved. There would remain no more sacrifice for sins; there is no other Saviour to be provided; there is no other Holy Spirit to be sent down to recover the apostate. Since, therefore, so fearful a punishment *would* follow apostasy from the true religion, we may see the guilt of everything which has a *tendency* to it. That guilt is to be measured by the fearful consequences which would ensue if it were followed out; and the Christian should, therefore, tremble when he is on the verge of committing any sin whose legitimate tendency would be such a result.

(10) We may learn from the views presented in this chapter (ver. 26–29), the error of those who suppose that a true Christian may fall away and be renewed again and saved. If there is any principle clearly settled in the New Testament, it is, that *if* a sincere Christian should apostatize, *he must perish.* There would be no possibility of renewing him. He would have tried the only religion which saves men, and it would in his case have failed; he would have applied to the only blood which purifies the soul, and it would have been found inefficacious; he would have been brought under the only influence which renews the soul, and that would not have been sufficient to save him. What hope *could* there be? What would then save him if these would not? To what would he apply—to what Saviour, to what blood of atonement, to what renewing and sanctifying agent, if the gospel, and the Redeemer, and the Holy Spirit had all been tried in vain? There are few errors in the community more directly at variance with the express teachings of the Bible than the belief that a Christian may fall away and be again renewed.

(11) Christians, in their conflicts, their trials, and their temptations, should be strengthened by what is past, ver. 32–35. They should remember the days when they were afflicted, and God sustained them; when they were persecuted, and he brought them relief. It is proper also to remember, for their own encouragement now, the spirit of patience and submission which they were enabled to manifest in those times of trial, and the sacrifices which they were enabled to make. They may see in such things evidence that they are the children of God; and they should find in their past experience proof that he who has borne them through past trials is able to keep them unto his everlasting kingdom.

(12) We need patience—but it is only for a little time, ver. 36–39. Soon all our conflicts will be over. "He that shall come will come and will not tarry." He will come to deliver his suffering people from their trials. He will come to rescue the persecuted from the persecutor; the oppressed from the oppressor; the down-trodden from the tyrant; the sorrowful and the sad from their woes. The coming of the Saviour to each one of the afflicted is the signal of release from sorrow, and his advent at the end of the world will be proof that all the trials of the bleeding and persecuted church are at an end. The time, too, is short before he will appear. In each individual case it is to be but a brief period before he will come to relieve the sufferer from his woes, and in the case of the church at large the time is not far remote when the great Deliverer shall appear to receive "the bride," the church redeemed, to the "mansions" which he has gone to prepare.

CHAPTER XI.

ANALYSIS OF THE CHAPTER.

In the close of the previous chapter the apostle had incidentally made mention of faith (ver. 38, 39), and said that the just should live by faith. The object of the whole argument in this epistle was to keep those to whom it was addressed from apostatizing from the Christian religion, and especially from relapsing again into Judaism. They were in the midst of trials, and

CHAPTER XI.

NOW faith is the [1]substance of things hoped for, the evidence of [a]things not seen.

1 or, *ground;* or, *confidence.*　　a Rom.8.24,25.

2 For by it the elders obtained a good report.

3 Through faith we understand

---

were evidently suffering some form of persecution, the tendency of which was to expose them to the danger of relapsing. The indispensable means of securing them from apostasy was *faith,* and with a view to show its efficacy in this respect, the apostle goes into an extended account of its nature and effects, occupying this entire chapter. As the persons whom he addressed had been Hebrews, and as the Old Testament contained an account of numerous instances of persons in substantially the same circumstances in which they were, the reference is made to the illustrious examples of the efficacy of faith in the Jewish history. The object is, to show that *faith,* or confidence in the divine promises, has been in all ages the means of perseverance in the true religion, and consequently of salvation. In this chapter, therefore, the apostle first describes or defines the nature of faith (ver. 1), and then illustrates its efficacy and power by reference to numerous instances, ver. 2–40. In these illustrations he refers to the steady belief which we have that God made the worlds, and then to the examples of Abel, Enoch, Noah, Abraham, Sarah, Isaac, Jacob, Joseph, Moses, and Rahab in particular, and then to numerous other examples without mentioning their names. The object is to show that there is power in faith to keep the mind and heart in the midst of trials, and, that having these examples before them, those whom he addressed should continue to adhere steadfastly to the profession of the true religion.

1. *Now faith is the substance of things hoped for.* On the general nature of faith, see Notes on Mark xvi. 16. The margin here is, "*ground,* or *confidence.*" There is scarcely any verse of the New Testament more important than this, for it states what is the nature of all true faith, and is the only definition

of it which is attempted in the Scriptures. Eternal life depends on the existence and exercise of faith (Mark xvi. 16), and hence the importance of an accurate understanding of its nature. The word rendered *substance—ὑπόστασις—*occurs in the New Testament only in the following places: in 2 Cor. ix. 4; xi. 17; Heb. iii. 14, where it is rendered *confident* and *confidence;* in Heb. i. 3, where it is rendered *person;* and in the passage before us. Comp. Notes on chap. i. 3. Prof. Stuart renders it here *confidence;* Chrysostom, "Faith gives reality or substance to things hoped for." The word properly means *that which is placed under* (German, *Unterstellen*); then *ground, basis, foundation, support.* Then it means also *reality, substance, existence,* in contradistinction from that which is unreal, imaginary or deceptive (*täuschung*) (Passow). It seems to me, therefore, that the word here has reference to something which imparts reality in the view of the mind to those things which are not seen, and which serves to distinguish them from those things which are unreal and illusive. It is that which enables us to feel and act *as if* they were real, or which causes them to exert an influence over us *as if* we saw them. Faith does this on other subjects as well as religion. A belief that there is such a place as London or Calcutta leads us to act *as if* this were so, if we have occasion to go to either; a belief that money may be made in a certain undertaking leads men to act *as if* this were so; a belief in the veracity of another leads us to act *as if* this were so. As long as the faith continues, whether it be well-founded or not, it gives all the force of reality to that which is believed. We feel and act *just as if* it were so, or *as if* we saw the object before our eyes. This, I think, is the clear meaning here. We do not *see* the things of eternity. We do not see God, or heaven, or the angels, or the redeemed in glory, or the crowns of victory, or the harps of praise; but we

that *b*the worlds were framed by the word of God, so that things

b Ge.1.1; Ps.33.6.

have faith in them, and this leads us to act *as if* we saw them. And this is, undoubtedly, the fact in regard to all who live by faith and who are fairly under its influence. ¶ *Of things hoped for.* In heaven. Faith gives them reality in the view of the mind. The Christian hopes to be admitted into heaven, to be raised up in the last day from the slumbers of the tomb, to be made perfectly free from sin, to be everlastingly happy. Under the influence of faith he allows these things to control his mind *as if* they were a most affecting reality. ¶ *The evidence of things not seen.* Of the existence of God, of heaven, of angels, of the glories of the world prepared for the redeemed. The word rendered *evidence—*ἔλεγχος*—*occurs in the New Testament only in this place and in 2 Tim. iii. 16, where it is rendered *reproof.* It means properly proof, or means of proving, to wit, evidence; then proof which convinces another of error or guilt; then vindication or defence; then summary or contents. See Passow. The idea of *evidence* which goes to demonstrate the thing under consideration, or which is adapted to produce *conviction* in the mind, seems to be the elementary idea in the word. So when a proposition is demonstrated, when a man is arraigned and proof is furnished of his guilt, or when one by argument refutes his adversaries, the idea of *convincing argument* enters into the use of the word in each case. This, I think, is clearly the meaning of the word here. " Faith in the divine declarations answers all the purposes of a convincing argument, or is itself a convincing argument to the mind of the real existence of those things which are not seen." But is it a good argument? Is it rational to rely on such a means of being convinced? Is mere *faith* a consideration which should ever convince a rational mind? The infidel says *no;* and we know there may be a faith which *is* no argument of the truth of what is believed. But when a man who has

which are seen were not made of things which do appear.

never seen it believes that there is such a place as London, his belief in the numerous testimonies respecting it which he has heard and read is to his mind a good and rational proof of its existence, and he would act on that belief without hesitation. When a son credits the declaration or the promise of a father who has never deceived him, and acts *as though* that declaration and promise were true, his faith is to him a ground of conviction and of action, and he will act as if these things were so. In like manner the Christian believes what God says. He has never seen heaven, he has never seen an angel, he has never seen the Redeemer, he has never seen a body raised from the grave. *But he has evidence which is satisfactory to his mind that God had spoken on these subjects,* and his very nature prompts him to confide in the declarations of his Creator. Those declarations are to his mind more convincing proof than anything else would be. They are more conclusive evidence than would be the deductions of his own reason; far better and more rational than all the reasonings and declarations of the infidel to the contrary. He feels and acts, therefore, *as if* these things were so, for his faith in the declarations of God has convinced him that they *are* so. The object of the apostle in this chapter is not to illustrate the nature of what is called *saving faith,* but to show the power of *unwavering confidence in God* in sustaining the soul, especially in times of trial, and particularly in leading us to act in view of promises and of things not seen *as if* they were so. "Saving faith" is the same kind of confidence directed to the Messiah— the Lord Jesus—as the Saviour of the soul.

2. *For by it.* That is, by that faith which gives reality to things hoped for and a certain persuasion to the mind of the existence of those things which are not seen. ¶ *The elders.* The ancients; the Hebrew patriarchs and fathers.

¶ *Obtained a good report.* Literally, " were witnessed of "—that is, an honourable testimony was borne to them in consequence of their faith. The idea is, that their acting under the influence of faith in the circumstances in which they were was the ground of the honourable testimony which was borne to them in the Old Testament. See this use of the word in chap. vii. 8 and in ver. 4 of this chapter; also Luke iv. 22; Acts xv. 8. In the cases which the apostle proceeds to enumerate in the subsequent part of the chapter he mentions those whose piety is particularly commended in the Old Testament, and who showed in trying circumstances that they had unwavering confidence in God.

3. *Through faith we understand that the worlds were framed.* The first instance of the strength of faith which the apostle refers to is that by which we give credence to the declarations in the Scriptures about the work of creation, Gen. i. 1. This is selected first evidently because it is the first thing that occurs in the Bible or is the first thing there narrated in relation to which there is the exercise of faith. He points to no particular instance in which this faith was exercised—for none is especially mentioned in the Old Testament— but refers to it as an illustration of the nature of faith which everyone might observe in himself. The *faith* here exercised is confidence in the truth of the divine declarations in regard to the creation of the universe. The meaning is, that our knowledge on this subject is a mere matter of faith in the divine testimony. It is not that we could *reason* this out and demonstrate that the worlds were thus made; it is not that profane history goes back to that period and informs us of it; it is simply that God has told us so in his word. The *strength* of the faith in this case is measured (1) by the fact that it is *mere faith*— that there is nothing else on which to rely in the case; and (2) by the greatness of the truth believed. After all the acts of faith which have ever been exercised in this world, perhaps there is none which is really more strong or

which requires higher confidence in God than the declaration that this vast universe has been brought into existence by a word! ¶ *We understand.* We attain to the apprehension of; we receive and comprehend the idea. Our knowledge of this fact is derived only from faith, and not from our own reasoning. ¶ *That the worlds.* In Gen. i. 1 it is "the heaven and the earth." The phrase which the apostle uses denotes a plurality of worlds, and is proof that he supposed there were other worlds besides our earth. How far his knowledge extended on this point we have no means of ascertaining, but there is no reason to doubt that he regarded the stars as "worlds" in some respects like our own. On the meaning of the Greek word used here see Notes on chap. i. 2. The plural form is used there also, and in both cases, it seems to me, not without design. ¶ *Were framed.* It is observable that the apostle does not here use the word *make* or *create.* That which he does use—καταρτίζω—means to put in order, to arrange, to complete, and may be applied to that which before had an existence, and which is to be put in order, or refitted, Mat. iv. 24; Mark i. 19; Mat. xxi. 6; Heb. x. 5. The meaning here is, that they *were set in order* by the word of God. This implies the act of creation, but the specific idea is that of *arranging* them in the beautiful order in which they are now. Doddridge renders it "*adjusted.*" Kuinoel, however, supposes that the word is used here in the sense of *form* or *make.* It has probably about the meaning which we attach to the phrase "*fitting up anything,*" as, for example, a dwelling, and includes all the previous arrangements, though the thing which is particularly denoted is not the *making*, but the *arrangement.* So in the work here referred to. The meaning is, "We arrive at the conviction that the universe was *fitted up* or *arranged* in the present manner by the word of God." ¶ *By the word of God.* This does not mean here, by the *Logos*, or the second person of the Trinity, for Paul does not use that term here

4 By faith ^cAbel offered unto God a more excellent sacrifice than Cain, by which he obtained witness

c Ge. 4. 4, 5.

that he was righteous, God testifying of his gifts: and by it he being dead ²yet speaketh.

2 or, *is yet spoken of.*

---

or elsewhere. The word which he employs is ῥῆμα — *rēma* — meaning properly a word spoken, and in this place *command*. Comp. Gen. i. 3, 6, 9, 11, 14, 20. See also Ps. xxxiii. 6, "By the word of the Lord were the heavens made; and all the host of them by the breath of his mouth." In regard to the agency of the Son of God in the work of the creation, see Notes on chap. i. 2. Comp. Notes on Jn. i. 3. ¶ *So that things which are seen.* The point of the remark here is, that the visible creation was not moulded out of pre-existing materials, but was made where before there was nothing. In reference to the grammatical construction of the passage, see Stuart, *Comm. in loco.* The doctrine taught is, that matter was not eternal; that the materials of the universe, as well as the arrangement, were formed by God, and that all this was done by a simple command. The *argument* here, so far as it is adapted to the purpose of the apostle, seems to be, that there was nothing which *appeared*, or which was to be *seen*, that could lay the foundation of a belief that God made the worlds; and in like manner our faith now is not to be based on what "*appears*," by which we could infer or *reason out* what would be, but that we must exercise strong confidence in Him who had power to create the universe by a word. If this vast system of worlds has been called into existence by the mere *word* of God, there is nothing which we may not believe he has ample power to perform.

4. *By faith Abel offered.* See Gen. iv. 4, 5. In the account in Genesis of the offering made by Abel, there is no mention of *faith*—as is true also indeed of most of the instances referred to by the apostle. The account in Genesis is, simply, that Abel "brought of the firstlings of his flock, and of the fat thereof, and that the Lord had respect unto Abel, and to his offering."

Men have speculated much as to the reason why the offering of Abel was accepted and that of Cain rejected; but such speculation rests on no certain basis, and the solution of the apostle should be regarded as decisive and satisfactory, that in the one case there was faith, in the other not. It could not have been because an offering of the fruits of the ground was not pleasing to God, for such an offering was commanded under the Jewish law, and was not in itself improper. Both the brothers selected that which was to them most obvious; which they had reared with their own hands; which they regarded as most valuable. Cain had cultivated the earth, and he naturally brought what had grown under his care; Abel kept a flock, and *he* as naturally brought what he had raised; and had the temper of mind in both been the same, there is no reason to doubt that the offering of each would have been accepted. To this conclusion we are led by the nature of the case, and the apostle advances substantially the same sentiment, for he says that the particular state of mind on which the whole turned was, that the one had faith and the other not. *How* the apostle himself was informed of the fact that it was *faith* which made the difference, he has not informed us. The belief that he was inspired will, however, relieve the subject of this difficulty, for according to such a belief, all his statements here, whether recorded in the Old Testament or not, are founded in truth. It is equally impossible to tell with certainty *what* was the nature of the faith of Abel. It has been commonly asserted that it was faith in Christ—looking forward to his coming, and depending on his sacrifice when offering that which was to be a type of him. But of this there is no positive evidence, though, from Heb. xii. 24, it seems to be not improbable. Sacrifice, as a type of the Redeemer's great

offering, was instituted early in the history of the world. There can be no reason assigned for the offering of *blood* as an atonement for sin, except that it had originally a reference to the great atonement which was to be made by blood; and as the salvation of man depended on this entirely, it is probable that this would be one of the truths which would be first communicated to man after the fall. The bloody offering of Abel is the first of the kind which is definitely mentioned in the Scriptures (though it is not improbable that such sacrifices were offered by Adam, comp. Gen. iii. 21), and consequently Abel may be regarded as *the recorded head of the whole typical system, of which Christ was the antitype and the fulfilment.* Comp. Notes on chap. xii. 24. ¶ *A more excellent sacrifice.* Πλείονα θυσίαν—as rendered by Tindall, "more plenteous sacrifice;" or, as Wickliffe renders it more literally, "a much more sacrifice"—that is, a more full or complete sacrifice; a better sacrifice. The meaning is, that it had in it much more to render it acceptable to God. In the estimate of its value, the views of him who offered it would be more to be regarded than the nature of the offering itself.

[" By offering victims of the choice of his flock Abel not only showed a more decided attachment to God, but there is great reason to suppose (as Abp. Magee on Atonement, p. 52, shows) that his faith was especially superior, as being not only directed to God alone (recognizing his existence, authority, and providence), but also to the great Redeemer, promised immediately after the fall (Gen. iii. 15), whose expiatory death was typified by animal sacrifice, by offering which Abel had evinced his faith in the great sacrifice of the Redeemer prefigured by it: and then he obtained that acceptance from God and witnessing of his offering which was refused to Cain. See more in Macknight and Scott" (Bloomfield).]

¶ *By which.* By which sacrifice so offered. The way in which he obtained the testimony of divine approbation was by the sacrifice offered in this manner. It was not *merely* by faith, it was by the offering of a sacrifice in connection with and under the influence of faith. ¶ *He obtained witness that he was righteous.* That is, from

God. His offering made in faith was the means of his obtaining the divine testimonial that he was a righteous man. Comp. Notes on ver. 2. This is implied in what is said in Gen. iv. 4: "And the Lord had respect unto Abel, and to his offering;" that is, he regarded it as the offering of a righteous man. ¶ *God testifying of his gifts.* In what way this was done is not mentioned either here or in Genesis. Commentators have usually supposed that it was by fire descending from heaven to consume the sacrifice. But there is no evidence of this, for there is no intimation of it in the Bible. It is true that this frequently occurred when an offering was made to God (see Gen. xv. 17; Lev. ix. 24; Judg. vi. 21; 1 Ki. xviii. 38); but the sacred writers give us no hint that this happened in the case of the sacrifice made by Abel, and since it is expressly mentioned in other cases and not here, the presumption rather is that no such miracle occurred on the occasion. So remarkable a fact—the first one in all history if it were so—could hardly have failed to be noticed by the sacred writer. It seems to me, therefore, that there was some method by which God "testified" his approbation of the offering of Abel which is unknown to us; but in regard to what it was, conjecture is vain. ¶ *And by it he being dead yet speaketh.* Margin, *is yet spoken of.* This difference of translation arises from a difference of reading in the MSS. That from which the translation in the text is derived, is λαλεῖ, *he speaketh.* That from which the rendering in the margin is derived, is λαλεῖται, *is spoken of;* that is, *is praised* or *commended.* The latter is the common reading in the Greek text, and is found in Walton, Wetstein, Matthæi, Tittmann, and Mill; the former is adopted by Griesbach, Koppe, Knapp, Grotius, Hammond, Storr, Rosenmüller, Professor Stuart, Bloomfield, and Hahn, and is found in the Syriac and Coptic, and is that which is favoured by most of the Fathers. See Wetstein. The authority of MSS. is in favour of the reading λαλεῖται, *is spoken of.* It is impossible in this variety of opinion to determine which is

17

the true reading, and this is one of the cases where the original text must probably be for ever undecided. Happily no important doctrine or duty is depending on it. Either of the modes of reading will give a good sense. The apostle is saying that it is by faith that the "elders have obtained a good report" (ver. 2); he had said (ver. 4), that it was by faith that Abel obtained the testimony of God in his favour, and if the reading "is spoken of" be adopted, the apostle means that, in consequence of that offering thus made, Abel continued even to his time to receive an honourable mention. This act was commended still; and the "good report" of which it had been the occasion, had been transmitted from age to age. A sentiment thus of great beauty and value *may* be derived from the passage—that true piety is the occasion of transmitting a good report, or an honourable reputation, even down to the latest generation. It is that which will embalm the memory in the grateful recollection of mankind; that on which they will reflect with pleasure, and which they will love to transmit to future ages. But after all, it seems to me to be probable that the true sentiment in this passage is that which is expressed in the common version, "He yet speaketh." The reasons are briefly these: (1) The authority of MSS., versions, editions, and critics, is so nearly equal, that it is impossible from this source to determine the true reading, and we must therefore form our judgment from the connection. (2) The apostle had twice in this verse expressed substantially the idea that he was honourably testified of by his faith, and it is hardly probable that he would again repeat it so soon. (3) There seems to be an allusion here to the *language* used respecting Abel (Gen. iv. 10), "The voice of thy brother's blood *crieth* unto me from the ground;" or utters a distinct voice, and the apostle seems to design to represent Abel as still speaking. (4) In Heb. xii. 24, he represents both Abel and Christ as still *speaking*—as if Abel continued to utter a voice of admonition. The reference there is

to the fact that he continued to proclaim from age to age, even to the time of the apostle, the great truth that salvation was only *by blood*. He had proclaimed this at first by his faith when he offered the sacrifice of the lamb; he continued to utter this from generation to generation, and to show that it was one of the earliest principles of religion that there could be redemption from sin in no other way. (5) The expression "yet *speaketh*" accords better with the connection. The other interpretation is cold compared with this, and less fits the case before us. Of the faith of Noah, Abraham, and Moses, it might be said with equal propriety that it is still commended or celebrated as well as that of Abel, but the apostle evidently means to say that there was a voice in that of Abel which was peculiar; there was something in *his* life and character which continued to speak from age to age. His sacrifice, his faith, his death, his blood, *all* continued to lift up the voice, and to proclaim the excellence and value of confidence in God, and to admonish the world how to live. (6) This accords with usage in classic writers, where it is common to say of the dead that they continue to speak. Comp. Virg. *Æn.* vi. 618.

Et magnâ testatur voce per umbras:
Discite justitiam moniti, et non temnere Divos.

If this be the true meaning, then the sense is, that there is an influence from the piety of Abel which continues to admonish all coming ages of the value of religion, and especially of the great doctrine of the necessity of an atonement by blood. His faith and his sacrifice proclaimed from age to age that this was one of the first great truths made known to fallen man; and on this he continues to address the world *as if* he were still living. Thus all who are pious continue to exert an influence in favour of religion long after the soul is removed to heaven, and the body consigned to the grave. This is true in the following respects: (1) They speak by their *example*. The example of a pious father, mother, neighbour, will be remembered. It will often have an effect

after their death in influencing those over whom it had little control while living. (2) They continue to speak by their *precepts*. The precepts of a father may be remembered, with profit, when he is in his grave, though they were heard with indifference when he lived; the counsels of a minister may be recollected with benefit, though they were heard with scorn. (3) They continue to speak from the fact that the good are remembered with increasing respect and honour as long as they are remembered at all. The character of Abel, Noah, and Abraham, is brighter now than it was when they lived, and will continue to grow brighter to the end of time. "The name of the wicked will rot," and the influence which they had when living will grow feebler and feebler till it wholly dies away. Howard will be remembered, and will proclaim from age to age the excellence of a life of benevolence; the character of Nero, Caligula, and Richard III., has long since ceased to exert *any* influence whatever in favour of evil, but rather shows the world, by contrast, the excellence of virtue;—and the same will yet be true of Paine, and Voltaire, and Byron, and Gibbon, and Hume. The time will come when they will cease to exert any influence in favour of infidelity and sin, and when the world will be so satisfied of the error of their sentiments, and the abuse of their talents, and the corruption of their hearts, that their names, by contrast, will be made to promote the cause of piety and virtue. If a man wishes to exert any permanent influence after he is dead, he must be a good man.—The *strength* of the faith of Abel here commended will be seen by a reference to a few circumstances: (1) It was manifested shortly after the apostasy, and not long after the fearful sentence had been pronounced in view of the sin of man. The serpent had been cursed; the earth had been cursed; woe had been denounced on the mother of mankind; and the father of the apostate race, and all his posterity, had been doomed to toil and death. The thunder of this curse had scarcely died away; man had been

ejected from Paradise and sent out to enter on his career of woes, and the earth was trembling under the malediction, and yet Abel maintained his confidence in God. (2) There was then but little truth revealed, and there was only the slightest intimation of mercy. The promise in Gen. iii. 15, that the seed of the woman should bruise the head of the serpent, is so enigmatical and obscure that it is not easy even now to see its exact meaning, and it cannot be supposed that Abel could have had a full understanding of what was denoted by it. Yet this appears to have been *all* the truth respecting the salvation of man then revealed, and on this Abel maintained his faith steadfast in God. (3) Abel had an elder brother, undoubtedly an infidel, a scoffer, a mocker of religion. He was evidently endowed with a talent for sarcasm (Gen. iv. 9), and there is no reason to doubt that, like other infidels and scoffers, he would be disposed to use that talent when occasion offered, to hold up religion to contempt. The power with which he used this, and the talent with which he did this, may be seen illustrated probably with melancholy fidelity in Lord Byron's "Cain." No man ever lived who could more forcibly express the feelings that passed through the mind of Cain—for there is too much reason to think that his extraordinary talents were employed on this occasion to give vent to the feelings of his own heart in the sentiments put into the mouth of Cain. Yet, notwithstanding the infidelity of his elder brother, Abel adhered to God and his cause. Whatever influence that infidel brother might have sought to use over him—and there can be no reason to doubt that such an influence *would be* attempted —yet he never swerved, but maintained with steadfastness his belief in religion, and his faith in God.

5. *By faith Enoch was translated.* The account of Enoch is found in Gen. v. 21–24. It is very brief, and is this, that "Enoch walked with God, and was not, for God took him." There is no particular mention of his *faith*, and the apostle attributes this

5 By faith *d* Enoch was translated that he should not see death; and was not found, because God had

d Ge.5.22,24.

translated him: for before his translation he had this testimony, that he pleased God.

---

to him, as in the case of Abel, either because it was involved in the very nature of piety, or because the fact was communicated to him by direct revelation. In the account in Genesis, there is nothing inconsistent with the belief that Enoch was characterized by eminent faith, but it is rather implied in the expression, "he walked with God." Comp. 2 Cor. v. 7. It may also be implied in what is said by the apostle Jude (ver. 14, 15), that "he prophesied, saying, Behold the Lord cometh, with ten thousand of his saints," &c. From this it would appear that he was a preacher, that he predicted the coming of the Lord to judgment, and that he lived in the firm *belief* of what was to occur in future times. Moses does not say expressly that Enoch was translated. He says "he was not, for God took him." The expression "he was not" means he was no more among men, or he was removed from the earth. *This* language would be applicable to any method by which he was removed, whether by dying or by being translated. A similar expression respecting Romulus occurs in Livy (i. 16), Nec deinde in terris Romulus fuit. The translation of the Septuagint on this part of the verse in Genesis is, οὐχ εὑρίσκετο, "was not found"—that is, he disappeared. The authority for what the apostle says here, that he "was translated," is found in the other phrase in Genesis, "God took him." The reasons which led to the statement that he was translated without seeing death, or that show that this is a fair conclusion from the words in Genesis, are such as these: (1) There is no mention made of his death, and in this respect the account of Enoch stands by itself. It is, except in this case, the uniform custom of Moses to mention the age and the death of the individuals whose biography he records, and in many cases this is about all that is said of them. But in regard to Enoch there is this remarkable exception, that no record

is made of his death, showing that there was something unusual in the manner of his removal from the world. (2) The Hebrew word used by Moses found in such a connection is one which would rather suggest the idea that he had been taken in some extraordinary manner from the world. That word, לָקַח —*lakahh*—means *to take*, with the idea of taking *to one's self*. Thus Gen. viii. 20, "Noah *took* of all beasts and offered a burnt-offering." Thus it is often used in the sense of *taking a wife*—that is, to one's self (Gen. iv. 19; vi. 2; xii. 19; xix. 14); and then it is used in the sense of *taking away*, Gen. xiv. 12; xxvii. 35; Job i. 21; xii. 20; Ps. xxxi. 13; Jer. xv. 15. The word, therefore, would naturally suggest the idea that he had been taken by God to himself, or had been removed in an extraordinary manner from the earth. This is confirmed by the fact that the word is not used anywhere in the Scriptures to denote a removal *by death*, and that in the only other instance in which it is used in relation to a removal from this world it occurs in the statement respecting the translation of Elijah: "And the sons of the prophets that were at Beth-el came forth to Elisha, and said unto him, Knowest thou that the Lord *will take away* (לָקֵחַ— *lokaiahh*) thy master from thy head to-day?" 2 Ki. ii. 3, 5; comp. ver. 11. This transaction, where there could be no doubt about the *manner* of the removal, shows in what sense the word is used in Genesis. (3) It was so understood by the translators of the Septuagint. The apostle has used the same word in this place which is employed in that translation in Gen. v. 24—μετατίθημι. This word means to transpose, to put in another place; and then to transport, transfer, translate, Acts vii. 16; Heb. vii. 12. It properly expresses a removal to another place, and is the very word which would be used on the supposition that one was taken to heaven without dying. (4) This interpretation of the passage in Genesis by Paul is in

accordance with the uniform interpretation of the Jews. In the Targum of Onkelos it is evidently supposed that Enoch was translated without dying. In that Targum the passage in Gen. v. 24 is rendered, "And Enoch walked in the fear of the Lord, and was not, for the Lord did not put him to death" —לֹא אֲמִית יָתֵיהּ. So also in Ecclesiasticus, or the Son of Sirach (xlix. 14), "But upon the earth was no man created like Enoch; for he was taken from the earth." These opinions of the Jews and of the early translators are of value only as showing that the interpretation which Paul has put upon Gen. v. 24 is the natural interpretation. It is such as occurs to separate writers, without collusion, and this shows that this is the meaning most naturally suggested by the passage. ¶ *That he should not see death.* That is, that he should not *experience* death, or be made personally acquainted with it. The word *taste* often occurs in the same sense, Heb. ii. 9, "That he should taste death for every man." Comp. Mat. xvi. 28; Mark ix. 1; Luke ix. 27. ¶ *And was not found.* Gen. v. 24, "And he was not." That is, he was not in the land of the living. Paul retains the word used in the Septuagint. ¶ *He had this testimony, that he pleased God.* Implied in the declaration in Gen. v. 22, that he "walked with God." This denotes a state of friendship between God and him, and of course implies that his conduct was pleasing to God. The apostle appeals here to the *sense* of the account in Genesis, but does not retain the very *words*. The meaning here is, not that the testimony respecting Enoch was actually *given* before his translation, but that the testimony relates to his having *pleased God* before he was removed (Stuart). In regard to this instructive fragment of history, and to the reasons why Enoch was thus removed, we may make the following remarks: (1) The age in which he lived was undoubtedly one of great wickedness. Enoch is selected as the only one of that age signalized by eminent piety, and he appears to have spent his life in publicly reproving a sinful generation and in warning them of the approaching judg-

ment, Jude 14, 15. The wickedness which ultimately led to the universal deluge seems already to have commenced in the earth, and Enoch, like Noah, his great-grandson, was raised up as a preacher of righteousness to reprove a wicked world. (2) It is not improbable that the great truths of religion in that age were extensively denied—probably, among other things, the future state, the resurrection, the belief that man would exist in another world, and that it was maintained that death is the end of being—is an eternal sleep. If so, nothing could be better adapted to correct the prevailing evils than the removal of an eminent man, without dying, from the world. His departure would thus confirm the instructions of his life, and his removal, like the death of saints now, would serve to make an impression which his living instructions would not. (3) His removal is, in itself, a very important and instructive fact in history. It has occurred in no other instance except that of Elijah, nor has any other living man been translated to heaven except the Lord Jesus. That fact was instructive in a great many respects. (a) It showed that there is a future state—another world. (b) It showed that the *body* may exist in that future state, though, doubtless, so changed as to adapt it to the condition of things there. (c) It prepared the world to credit the account of the ascension of the Redeemer. If Enoch and Elijah were removed thus without dying there was no intrinsic improbability that the Lord Jesus would be removed after having died and risen again. (d) It furnishes a demonstration of the doctrine that the saints will exist hereafter—a demonstration which meets all the arguments of the sceptic and the infidel. One single *fact* overturns all the mere *speculations* of philosophy, and renders nugatory all the objections of the sceptic. The infidel argues against the truth of the resurrection and of the future state from the *difficulties* attending the doctrine. A single *case* of one who has been raised up from the dead, or who has been removed to heaven, annihilates all such arguments, for how can supposed difficulties destroy a well-

6 But *e* without faith *it is* impossible to please *him:* for he that

e Ps.106.21-24.

cometh to God must believe that
he is, and *that* he is a rewarder of
them that diligently seek him.

authenticated *fact?* (*e*) It is an encouragement to piety. It shows that
God regards his friends, that their fidelity and holy living please him, and
that, *in the midst of eminent wickedness and a scoffing world, it is possible
so to live as to please God.* The conduct of this holy man, therefore, is an
encouragement to us to do our duty
though we stand alone, and to defend
the truth though all who live with us
upon the earth deny and deride it. (4)
The removal of Enoch shows that the
same thing would be *possible* in the
case of every saint. God could do it in
other cases, as well as in his, with equal
ease. That his friends, therefore, are
suffered to remain on the earth, that
they linger on in enfeebled health, or
are crushed by calamity, or are stricken
down by the pestilence as others are, is
not because God *could* not remove them
as Enoch was without dying, but because there are important *reasons* why
they should remain, and linger, and
suffer, and die. Among those reasons
may be such as the following: (*a*) The
regular operation of the laws of nature,
as now constituted, require it. Vegetables die; the inhabitants of the deep
die; the fowls that fly in the air, and the
beasts that roam over hills and plains,
die; and man, by his sins, is brought
under the operation of this great universal law. It would be *possible*, indeed,
for God to save his people from this law,
but it would require the interposition of
continued *miracles,* and it is better to
have the laws of nature regularly oper-
ating than to have them constantly
set aside by divine interposition. (*b*)
The power of religion is now better
illustrated in the way in which the
saints are actually removed from the
earth, than it would be if they were
all translated. Its power is now seen
in its enabling us to overcome the
dread of death, and in its supporting
us in the pains and sorrows of the departing hour. It is a good thing to
discipline the soul so that it will not
fear to die; it shows how superior re-

ligion is to all the forms of philosophy, that it enables the believer to
look calmly forward to his own certain approaching death. It is an important matter to keep this up from
age to age, and to show to each generation that religion can overcome the
natural apprehension of the most fearful calamity which befalls a creature
—death; and can make man calm in
the prospect of lying beneath the
clods of the valley, cold, dark, alone,
to moulder back to his native dust.
(*c*) The death of the Christian does
good. It preaches to the living. The
calm resignation, the peace, the triumph of the dying believer, is a constant admonition to a thoughtless and
wicked world. The death-bed of the
Christian proclaims the mercy of God
from generation to generation, and
there is not a dying saint who may
not, and who probably *does* not, do
great good in the closing hours of his
earthly being. (*d*) It may be added
that the present arrangement falls in
with the general laws of religion, that
we are to be influenced by *faith,* not
by *sight.* If all Christians were removed like Enoch, it would be an argument for the truth of religion addressed constantly to the senses. But
this is not the way in which the evidence of the truth of religion is proposed to man. It is submitted to
his understanding, his conscience, his
heart; and in this there is, of design,
a broad distinction between religion
and other things. Men act in other
matters under the influence of the
senses; it is intended that in religion
they shall act under the influence of
higher and nobler considerations, and
that they shall be influenced not solely
by a reference to what is passing before their eyes, but to the things which
are not seen.

6. *But without faith* it is *impossible
to please* him. Without *confidence* in
God—in his fidelity, his truth, his
wisdom, his promises. And this is
as true in other things as in religion.

7 By faith*f* Noah, being warned of God of things not seen as yet, moved[3] with fear, prepared an ark

f Ge.6.14-22.   [3] or, *being wary.*

to the saving of his house; by the which he condemned the world, and became heir of the righteousness which is by faith.

It is impossible for a child to please his father unless he has confidence in him. It is impossible for a wife to please her husband, or a husband a wife, unless they have confidence in each other. If there is distrust and jealousy on either part, there is discord and misery. We cannot be pleased with a professed friend unless he has such confidence in us as to believe our declarations and promises. The same thing is true of God. He cannot be pleased with the man who has no confidence in him; who doubts the truth of his declarations and promises; who does not believe that his ways are right, or that he is qualified for universal empire. The requirement of faith or confidence in God is not arbitrary; it is just what we require of our children, our partners in business, our friends, as the indispensable condition of *our* being pleased with them. ¶ *For he that cometh to God.* In any way—as a worshipper. This is alike required in public worship, in the family, and in secret devotion. ¶ *Must believe that he is.* That God exists. This is the first thing required in worship. Evidently we cannot come to him in an acceptable manner if we doubt his existence. We do not see him, but we must believe that he is; we cannot form in our mind a correct image of God, but this should not prevent a conviction that there *is* such a Being. But the declaration here implies more than that there should be a general persuasion of the truth that there is a God. It is necessary that we have this belief in lively exercise in the act of drawing near to him, and that we should realize that we are actually in the presence of the all-seeing JEHOVAH. ¶ *And that he is a rewarder of them that diligently seek him.* This is as really necessary as the belief that he exists. If we could not believe that God would hear and answer our prayers, there could be no encouragement to call upon

him. It is not meant here that the desire of the reward is to be the *motive* for seeking God — for the apostle makes no affirmation on that point; but that it is impossible to make an acceptable approach to him unless we have this belief.

7. *By faith Noah.* It is less difficult to see that Noah must have been influenced *by faith* than that Abel and Enoch were. Everything which Noah did in reference to the threatened deluge was done in virtue of simple faith or belief of what God said. It was not because he could show from the course of events that things were tending to such a catastrophe; or because such an event had occurred before, rendering it probable that it would be likely to occur again; or because this was the common belief of men, and it was easy to fall into this himself. It was simply because God had informed him of it, and he put unwavering reliance on the truth of the divine declaration. ¶ *Being warned of God.* Gen. vi. 13. The Greek word here used means *divinely admonished.* Comp. chap. viii. 5. ¶ *Of things not seen as yet.* Of the flood which was yet future. The meaning is, that there were no visible signs of it; there was nothing which could be a basis of calculation that it would occur. This admonition was given a hundred and twenty years before the deluge, and of course long before there could have been any natural indications that it would take place. ¶ *Moved with fear.* Margin, *being wary.* The Greek word—εὐλα-βηθείς—occurs only here and in Acts xxiii. 10, "The chief captain *fearing* lest Paul," &c. The *noun* occurs in Heb. v. 7, "And was heard in that he *feared*" (see Notes on that place); and in Heb. xii. 28, "With reverence and *godly fear.*" The verb properly means, *to act with caution, to be circumspect,* and then *to fear, to be afraid.* So far as the *word* is concerned, it might mean here that Noah was influenced

by the dread of what was coming, or it may mean that he was influenced by proper caution and reverence for God. The latter meaning agrees better with the scope of the remarks of Paul, and is probably the true sense. His reverence and respect for God induced him to act under the belief that what he had said was true, and that the calamity which he had predicted would certainly come upon the world. ¶ *Prepared an ark to the saving of his house.* In order that his family might be saved, Gen. vi. 14–22. The *salvation* here referred to was preservation from the flood. ¶ *By the which.* By which faith. ¶ *He condemned the world.* That is, the wicked world around him. The meaning is, that by his confidence in God, and his preparation for the flood, he showed the wisdom of his own course and the folly of theirs. We have the same phrase now in common use where one who sets a good example is said to "condemn others." He shows the guilt and folly of their lives by the contrast between his conduct and theirs. The wickedness of the sinner is condemned not only by preaching, and by the admonitions and threatenings of the law of God, but by the conduct of every good man. The language of such a life is as plain a rebuke of the sinner as the most fearful denunciations of divine wrath. ¶ *And became heir of the righteousness which is by faith.* The phrase "heir of righteousness" here means properly that he acquired, gained, or became possessed of that righteousness. It does not refer so much to the *mode* by which it was done, as if it were by inheritance, as to the *fact* that he obtained it. The word *heir* is used in this general sense in Rom. iv. 13, 14; Tit. iii. 7; Heb. i. 2; vi. 17. Noah was not the *heir* to that righteousness by *inheriting* it from his ancestors, but in virtue of it he was regarded as among the heirs or sons of God, and as being a possessor of that righteousness which is connected with faith. The phrase "righteousness which is by faith" refers to the fact that he was regarded and treated as a righteous man. See Notes on Rom. i. 17. It is observable here that it is

not said that Noah had specific faith in Christ, or that his being made heir of the righteousness of faith depended on that, but it was in connection with his believing what God said respecting the deluge. It was *faith* or *confidence* in God which was the ground of his justification, in accordance with the general doctrine of the Scriptures that it is only by faith that man can be saved, though the specific mode of faith was not that which is required now under the gospel. In the early ages of the world, when few truths were revealed, a cordial belief of *any* of those truths showed that there was real confidence in God, or that the *principle* of faith was in the heart; in the fuller revelation which *we* enjoy, we are not only to believe those truths, but specifically to believe in him who has made the great atonement for sin, and by whose merits all have been saved who have entered heaven. The same faith or confidence in God which led Noah to believe what God said about the deluge, would have led him to believe what he has said about the Redeemer; and the same confidence in God which led him to commit himself to his safe-keeping in an ark on the world of waters, would have led him to commit his soul to the safe-keeping of the Redeemer, the true ark of safety. As the *principle* of faith, therefore, existed in the heart of Noah, it was proper that he should become, with others, an "heir of the righteousness by faith."

[If this righteousness which is by faith be the same with that in Rom. i. 17; iii. 21—and of this there can be no doubt; if it be the same with that which forms the ground of the sinner's justification in every age, namely, the glorious righteousness which Christ has wrought out in his active and passive obedience—then clearly there is no way of getting possession of this but by faith in Jesus. And, without doubt, by *this* faith Noah was saved. It is absurd to suppose that the doctrine of salvation by the Redeemer was unknown to him. Was not the ark itself a type and pledge of this salvation? 1 Pet. iii. 21. Was Noah ignorant of the promise concerning the Messiah? Dr. Owen can scarce speak with patience of the view that excludes Christ as the specific object of Noah's faith: "That in this faith of the patriarchs no respect was had unto

Christ and his righteousness, is such a putid figment, is so destructive of the first promises and of all true faith in the church of old, is so inconsistent with and contrary to the design of the apostle, and is so utterly destructive of the whole force of his argument, that it deserves no consideration." The idea, indeed, *seems* to derogate from the glory of Christ as the *alone* object of faith and salvation in every age. See also Scott, Bloomfield, M'Lean.]

In regard to the circumstances which show the strength of his faith, we may make the following remarks : (1) It pertained to a very distant future event; to that which was to happen after a lapse of a hundred and twenty years. This was known to Noah (Gen. vi. 3), and at this long period before it occurred he was to begin to build an ark to save himself and family; to act as though this would be undoubtedly true. This is a much longer period than man *now* is required to exercise faith before that is realized which is the object of belief. Rare is it that three-score years intervene between the time when a man first believes in God, and when he enters into heaven; much more frequently it is but a few months or days; not an instance now occurs in which the period is lengthened out to a hundred and twenty years. (2) There was no outward *evidence* that what Noah believed would occur. There were no appearances in nature which indicated that there would be such a flood of waters after more than a century had passed away. There were no breakings-up of the fountains of the deep; no marks of the far-distant storm gathering on the sky which could be the basis of the calculation. The *word of God* was the only ground of evidence; the only thing to which he could refer gainsayers and revilers. It is so now. There are no visible signs of the coming of the Saviour to judge the world. Yet the true believer feels and acts *as if* it were so—resting on the sure word of God. (3) The course of things was much against the truth of what Noah believed. No such event had ever occurred. There is no evidence that there had ever been a storm of rain half sufficient to drown the world; or that there had ever been the breaking

up of the deep; or that there had been a universal deluge. For sixteen hundred years the course of nature had been uniform, and all the force of this uniformity would be felt and urged when it should be alleged that this was to be disturbed, and to give place to an entire new order of events. Comp. 2 Pet. iii. 4. The same thing is now felt in regard to the objects of the Christian faith. The course of events is uniform. The laws of nature are regular and steady. The dead do not leave their graves. Seasons succeed each other in regular succession ; men are born, live, and die as in former times ; fire does not wrap the earth in flames; the elements do not melt with fervent heat; seed-time and harvest, cold and heat, summer and winter follow each other, and " all things continue as they were from the beginning of the creation." How many probabilities are there now, therefore, as there were in the time of Noah, against that which is the object of faith! (4) It is not improbable that when Noah proclaimed the approaching destruction of the world by a deluge, the *possibility* of such an event was strongly denied by the philosophers of that age. The fact that such an event could have occurred has been denied by infidel philosophers in our own times, and attempts have been gravely made to show that the earth did not contain water enough to cover its surface to the height mentioned in the Scriptures, and that no condensation of the vapour in the atmosphere could produce such an effect. It is not improbable that some such arguments may have been used in the time of Noah, and *it is morally certain that he could not meet those arguments by any philosophy of his own.* There is no reason to think that he was endowed with such a knowledge of chemistry as to be able to show that such a thing was possible, or that he had such an acquaintance with the structure of the earth as to demonstrate that it contained within itself the elements of its own destruction. All that he could oppose to such speculations was the simple declaration of God; and the same thing is also true

now in regard to the cavils and philosophical arguments of infidelity. Objections drawn from philosophy are often made against the doctrine of the resurrection of the body; the destruction of the earth by the agency of fire; and even the existence of the soul after death. These difficulties may be obviated partly by science; but the proof that these events will occur does not depend on science. It is a matter of simple faith; and all that we can, in fact, oppose to these objections is the declaration of God. The result showed that Noah was not a fool or a fanatic in trusting to the word of God against the philosophy of his age; and the result will show the same of the Christian in his confiding in the truth of the divine declarations against the philosophy of *his* age. (5) It is beyond all question that Noah would be subjected to much ridicule and scorn. He would be regarded as a dreamer; a fanatic; an alarmist; a wild projector. The purpose of making preparation for such an event as a universal flood, to occur after the lapse of a hundred and twenty years, and when there were no indications of it, and all appearances were against it, would be regarded as in the highest degree wild and visionary. The design of building a vessel which would outride the storm, and which would live in such an open sea, and which would contain all sorts of animals with the food for them for an indefinite period, could not but have been regarded as eminently ridiculous. When the ark was preparing, nothing could have been a more happy subject for scoffing and gibes. In such an age, therefore, and in such circumstances, we may suppose that all the means possible would have been resorted to, to pour contempt on such an undertaking. They who had wit, would find here an ample subject for its exercise; if ballads were made then, no more fertile theme for a profane song could be desired than this; and in the haunts of revelry, intemperance, and pollution, nothing would furnish a finer topic to give point to a jest, than the credulity and folly of the old man who was building

the ark. It would require strong faith to contend thus with the wit, the sarcasm, the contempt, the raillery, and the low jesting, as well as with the wisdom and philosophy of a whole world. Yet it is a fair illustration of what occurs often now, and of the strength of that faith in the Christian heart which meets meekly and calmly the scoffs and jeers of a wicked generation. (6) All this would be heightened by delay. The time was distant. What now completes four generations would have passed away before the event predicted would occur. Youth grew up to manhood, and manhood passed on to old age, and still there were no signs of the coming storm. That was no feeble faith which could hold on in this manner for a hundred and twenty years, believing unwaveringly that all which God had said would be accomplished. But it is an illustration of faith in the Christian church now. The church maintains the same confidence in God from age to age—and, regardless of all the reproaches of scoffers, and all the arguments of philosophy, still adheres to the truths which God has revealed. So with individual Christians. They look for the promise. They are expecting heaven. They doubt not that the time will come when they will be received to glory; when their bodies will be raised up glorified and immortal, and when sin and sorrow will be no more. In the conflicts and trials of life the time of their deliverance may seem to be long delayed. The world may reproach them, and Satan may tempt them to doubt whether all their hopes of heaven are not delusion. But their faith fails not, and though hope seems delayed, and the heart is sick, yet they keep the eye on heaven. So it is in regard to the final triumphs of the gospel. The Christian looks forward to the time when the earth shall be full of the knowledge of God as the waters cover the sea. Yet that time may seem to be long delayed. Wickedness triumphs. A large part of the earth is still filled with the habitations of cruelty. The progress of the gospel is slow. The church comes up reluctantly to the work.

8 By faith *g* Abraham, when he was called to go out into a place which he should after receive for an inheritance, obeyed; and he went out, not knowing whither he went.

9 By faith he sojourned in the

g Ge.12.1,4,&c.

The enemies of the cause exult and rejoice, and ask, with scoffing triumph, Where is the evidence that the nations will be converted to God? They suggest difficulties; they refer to the numbers, and to the opposition of the enemies of the true religion, to the might of kingdoms, and to the power of fixed opinion, and to the hold which idolatry has on mankind; and they sneeringly inquire, At what period will the world be converted to Christ? Yet in the face of all difficulties, and arguments, and sneers, *faith* confides in the promise of the Father to the Son, that the "heathen shall be given to him for an inheritance, and the uttermost parts of the earth for a possession," Ps. ii. 8. The faith of the true Christian is as strong in the fulfilment of this promise, as that of Noah was in the assurance that the guilty world would be destroyed by a flood of waters.

8. *By faith Abraham.* There is no difficulty in determining that Abraham was influenced by faith in God. The case is even stronger than that of Noah, for it is expressly declared, Gen. xv. 6, "And he believed in the LORD; and he counted it to him for righteousness." Comp. Notes on Rom. iv. 1–5. In the illustrations of the power of faith in this chapter, the apostle appeals to two instances in which it was exhibited by Abraham, "the father of the faithful." Each of these required confidence in God of extraordinary strength, and each of them demanded a special and honourable mention. The first was that when he left his own country to go to a distant land of strangers (ver. 8–10); the other when he showed his readiness to sacrifice his own son in obedience to the will of God, ver. 17–19. ¶ *When he was called.* Gen. xii. 1, "Now the LORD had said unto Abram, get thee out of thy country, and from thy kindred, and from thy father's house, unto a land that I will

show thee." ¶ *Into a place which he should after receive for an inheritance, obeyed.* To Palestine, or the land of Canaan, though that was not indicated at the time. ¶ *And he went out, not knowing whither he went.* Gen. xii. 4. Abraham at that time took with him Sarai, and Lot the son of his brother, and "the souls that they had gotten in Haran." Terah, the father of Abraham, started on the journey with them, but died in Haran, Gen. xi. 31, 32. The original call was made to Abraham (Gen. xii. 1; Acts vii. 2, 3), but he appears to have induced his father and his nephew to accompany him. At this time he had no children (Gen. xi. 30), though it seems probable that Lot had, Gen. xii. 5. Some, however, understand the expression in Gen. xii. 5, "and the souls they had gotten in Haran," as referring to the servants or domestics that they had in various ways procured, and to the fact that Abraham and Lot gradually drew around them a train of dependants and followers who were disposed to unite with them, and accompany them wherever they went. The Chaldee Paraphrast understands it of the *proselytes* which Abraham had made there—"All the souls which he had subdued unto the law." When it is said that Abraham "went out, not knowing whither he went," it must be understood as meaning that he was ignorant to what country he would in fact be led. If it be supposed that he had some general intimation of the nature of that country, and of the direction in which it was situated, yet it must be remembered that the knowledge of geography was then exceedingly imperfect, that this was a distant country, that it lay beyond a pathless desert, and that probably no traveller had ever come from that land to apprise him what it was. All this serves to show what was the strength of the faith of Abraham.

9. *By faith he sojourned in the land*

land of promise, as *in* a strange country, *ʰ*dwelling in tabernacles with Isaac and Jacob, the heirs with him of the same promise:

10 For*ⁱ* he looked for a city which hath foundations, *ᵏ*whose builder and maker *is* God.

h Ge.13.3,18; 18.1,9.

i ch.12.22; 13.14.   *k* Re.21.2,10.

of promise, as in *a strange country.* The land of Canaan that had been promised to him and his posterity. He resided there *as if* he were a stranger and sojourner. He had no possessions there which he did not procure by honest purchase; he owned no land in fee-simple except the small piece which he bought for a burial-place. See Gen. xxiii. 7–20. In all respects he lived there as if he had no peculiar right in the soil, as if he never expected to own it, as if he were in a country wholly owned by others. He exercised no privileges which might not have been exercised by any foreigner, and which was not regarded as a right of common— that of feeding his cattle in any unoccupied part of the land; and he would have had no power of ejecting any other persons excepting that which anyone might have enjoyed by the preoccupancy of the pasture-grounds. To all intents and purposes he was a stranger. Yet he seems to have lived in the confident and quiet expectation that that land would at some period come into the possession of his posterity. It was a strong instance of *faith* that he should cherish this belief for so long a time when he was a stranger there, when he gained no right in the soil except in the small piece that was purchased as a burial-place for his wife, and when he saw old age coming on and still the whole land in the possession of others. ¶ *Dwelling in tabernacles.* In tents— the common mode of living in countries where the principal occupation is that of keeping flocks and herds. His dwelling thus in movable tents looked little like its being his permanent possession. ¶ *With Isaac and Jacob, the heirs with him of the same promise.* That is, the same thing occurred in regard to them which had to Abraham. *They* also lived in tents. They acquired no fixed property, and no title to the land except to the small portion purchased as a burial-place.

Yet they were heirs of the same promise as Abraham, that the land would be theirs. Though it was still owned by others, and filled with its native inhabitants, yet they adhered to the belief that it would come into the possession of their families. In their movable habitations—in their migrations from place to place—they seem never to have doubted that the fixed habitation of their posterity was to be there, and that all that had been promised would be certainly fulfilled.

10. *For he looked for a city which hath foundations.* It has been doubted to what the apostle here refers. Grotius and some others suppose that he refers to Jerusalem as a permanent dwelling for his posterity, in contradistinction from the unsettled mode of life which Abraham, Isaac, and Jacob led. But there is no evidence that Abraham looked forward to the building of such a city, for no promise was made to him of this kind; and this interpretation falls evidently below the whole drift of the passage. Comp. ver. 14–16; chap. xii. 22; xiii. 14. Phrases like that of "the city of God," "a city with foundations," "the new Jerusalem," and "the heavenly Jerusalem," appear to have acquired a kind of technical signification in the time of the apostles. They referred to *heaven,* of which Jerusalem, the seat of the worship of God, seems to have been regarded as the emblem. Thus in chap. xii. 22, the apostle speaks of the "heavenly Jerusalem;" and in chap. xiii. 14 he says, "here have we no continuing city, but we seek one to come." In Rev. xxi. 2, John says that he "saw the holy city, new Jerusalem, coming down from God, out of heaven," and proceeds in that chapter and the following to give a most beautiful description of it. Even so early as the time of Abraham, it would seem that the future blessedness of the righteous was foretold under the image of

a splendid city reared on permanent foundations. It is remarkable that Moses does not mention this as an object of the faith of Abraham, and it is impossible to ascertain the degree of distinctness which this had in his view. It is probable that the apostle in speaking of his faith in this particular did not rely on any distinct record, or even any tradition, but spoke of his piety in the language which he would use to characterize religion of any age, or in any individual. He was accustomed, in common with others of his time, to contemplate the future blessedness of the righteous under the image of a beautiful city; a place where the worship of God would be celebrated for ever—a city of which Jerusalem was the most striking representation to the mind of a Jew. It was natural for him to speak of strong piety in this manner wherever it existed, and especially in such a case as that of Abraham, who left his own habitation to wander in a distant land. This fact showed that he regarded himself as a stranger and sojourner, and yet he had a strong expectation of a fixed habitation, and a permanent inheritance. He must, therefore, have looked on to the permanent abodes of the righteous—the heavenly city; and though he had an undoubted confidence that the promised land would be given to his posterity, yet as he did not possess it himself, he must have looked for his own permanent abode to the fixed residence of the just in heaven. This passage seems to me to prove that Abraham had an expectation of future happiness after death. There is not the slightest evidence that he supposed that there would be a magnificent and glorious capital where the Messiah would personally reign, and where the righteous dead, raised from their graves, would dwell in the second advent of the Redeemer. All that the passage fairly implies is, that while Abraham expected the possession of the promised land for his posterity, yet his faith looked beyond this for a permanent home in a future world. ¶ *Whose builder and maker* is *God.* Which would not be reared by the agency

of man, but of which God was the immediate and direct architect. This shows conclusively, I think, that the reference in this allusion to the "city" is not to Jerusalem, as Grotius supposes; but the language is just such as will appropriately describe heaven, represented as a city reared without human hands or art, and founded and fashioned by the skill and power of the Deity. Comp. Notes on 2 Cor. v. 1. The language here applied to God as the "architect" or framer of the universe, is often used in the classic writers. See Kuinoel and Wetstein. The apostle here commends the faith of Abraham as eminently strong. The following *hints* will furnish topics of reflection to those who are disposed to inquire more fully into its strength: (1) The journey which he undertook was then a long and dangerous one. The distance from Haran to Palestine by a direct route was not less than four hundred miles, and this journey lay across a vast desert—a part of Arabia Deserta. That journey has always been tedious and perilous; but to see its real difficulty, we must put ourselves into the position in which the world was four thousand years ago. There was no knowledge of the way; no frequented path; no facility for travelling; no turnpike or railway; and such a journey then must have appeared incomparably more perilous than almost any which could now be undertaken. (2) He was going among strangers. Who they were he knew not; but the impression could not but have been made on his mind that they were strangers to religion, and that a residence among them would be anything but desirable. (3) He was leaving country, and home, and friends, the place of his birth and the graves of his fathers, with the moral certainty that he would see them no more. (4) He had no right to the country which he went to receive. He could urge no claim on the ground of discovery, or inheritance, or conquest at any former period; but though he went in a peaceful manner, and with no power to take it, and could urge no claim to it whatever, yet he went

11 Through faith also [l]Sarah herself received strength to conceive seed, and was delivered of a child when she was past age, because she judged [m]him faithful who had promised.

l Ge.21.1,2.   *m* ch.10.23.

12 Therefore sprang there even of one, and him as good as dead, [n]*so many* as the stars of the sky in multitude, and as the sand which is by the sea shore innumerable.

n Ge.22.17; Ro.4.17.

with the utmost confidence that it would be his. He did not even expect to buy it—for he had no means to do this, and it seems never to have entered his mind to bargain for it in any way, except for the small portion that he needed for a burying-ground. (5) He had no means of obtaining possession. He not only had no wealth to purchase it, but no armies to conquer it, and no title to it which could be enforced before the tribunals of the land. The prospect of obtaining it must have been distant, and probably he saw no means by which it was to be done. In such a case, his only hope could be in God. (6) It is not impossible that the enterprise in that age might have been treated by the friends of the patriarch as perfectly wild and visionary. The prevailing religion evidently was idolatry, and the claim which Abraham set up to a special call from the Most High might have been deemed entirely fanatical. To start off on a journey through a pathless desert; to leave his country and home, and all that he held dear, when he himself knew not whither he went; to go with no means of conquest, but with the expectation that the distant and unknown land would be given him, could not but have been regarded as a singular instance of visionary hope. The whole transaction, therefore, was in the highest degree an act of simple confidence in God, where there was no human basis of calculation, and where all the principles on which men commonly act would have led him to pursue just the contrary course. It is, therefore, not without reason that the faith of Abraham is so commended.

11. *Through faith also Sarah herself received strength to conceive seed.* The word "herself" here—*αὐτὴ*—implies that there was something remarkable

in the fact that *she* should manifest this faith. Perhaps there may be reference here to the incredulity with which she at first received the announcement that she should have a child, Gen. xviii. 11, 13. Even though everything seemed to render what was announced impossible, and though she was so much disposed to laugh at the very suggestion at first, yet her unbelief was overcome, and she ultimately credited the divine promise. The apostle does not state the authority for his assertion that the strength of Sarah was derived from her faith, nor *when* particularly it was exercised. The argument seems to be, that here was a case where all human probabilities were against what was predicted, and where, therefore, there must have been simple trust in God. Nothing else *but* faith could have led her to believe that in her old age she would bear a son. ¶ *When she was past age.* She was at this time more than ninety years of age, Gen. xvii. 17. Comp. Gen. xviii. 11. ¶ *Because she judged him faithful who had promised.* She had no other ground of confidence or expectation. All human probability was against the supposition that at her time of life she would be a mother.

12. *Therefore sprang there even of one.* From a single individual. What is observed here by the apostle as worthy of remark is, that the whole Jewish people sprang from one man, and that as the reward of his strong faith he was made the father and founder of a nation. ¶ *And him as good as dead.* So far as the subject under discussion is concerned. To human appearance there was no more probability that he would have a son at that period of life than that the dead would have. ¶ So many *as the stars of the sky,* &c. An innumerable multitude.

13 These all died ⁴in faith, not having received the promises, but having seen them afar off, and

⁴ *according to.*

were persuaded of *them*, and embraced *them*, and ᵒconfessed that they were strangers and pilgrims on the earth.

ᵒ 1 Ch.29.15; 1 Pe.2.11.

This was agreeable to the promise, Gen. xv. 5; xxii. 17. The phrases here used are often employed to denote a vast multitude, as nothing appears more numerous than the stars of heaven, or than the sands that lie on the shores of the ocean. The strength of faith in this case was, that there was simple confidence in God in the fulfilment of a promise where all human probabilities were against it. This is, therefore, an illustration of the nature of faith. It does not depend on human reasoning; on analogy; on philosophical probabilities; on the foreseen operation of natural laws; but on the mere assurance of God— no matter what may be the difficulties to human view, or the improbabilities against it.

13. *These all died in faith.* That is, those who had been just mentioned— Abraham, Isaac, Jacob, and Sarah. It was true of Abel and Noah also, that they died in faith, but they are not included in *this* declaration, for the "promises" were not particularly intrusted to them, and if the word "these" be made to include them it must include Enoch also, who did not die at all. The phrase here used, "these all died *in faith*," does not mean that they died in the exercise or possession of religion, but more strictly that they died not having possessed what was the object of their faith. They had been looking for something future which they did not obtain during their lifetime, and died believing that it would yet be theirs. ¶ *Not having received the promises.* That is, not having received the *fulfilment* of the promises; or *the promised blessings.* The promises themselves they *had* received. Comp. Luke xxiv. 49; Acts i. 4; ii. 33; Gal. iii. 14, and ver. 33, 39 of this chapter. In all these places the word *promise* is used by metonymy *for the thing promised.* ¶ *But having seen them afar off.* Having seen that they would be fulfilled

in future times. Comp. Jn. viii. 56. It is probable that the apostle here means that they saw *the entire fulfilment* of all the promises in the future; that is, the bestowment of the land of Canaan, the certainty of a numerous posterity, and of the entrance into the heavenly Canaan—the world of fixed and permanent rest. According to the reasoning of the apostle here the "promises" to which they trusted included all these things. ¶ *And were persuaded of* them. Had no doubt of their reality. ¶ *And embraced* them. This word implies more than our word *embrace* frequently does; that is, *to receive as true.* It means properly *to draw to one's self;* and then to embrace as one does a friend from whom he has been separated. It then means to greet, salute, welcome, and here means a joyful greeting of those promises; or a pressing them to the heart, as we do a friend. It was not a cold and formal reception of them, but a warm and hearty welcome. Such is the nature of true faith when it embraces the promises of salvation. No act of pressing a friend to the bosom is ever more warm and cordial. ¶ *And confessed that they were strangers.* Thus Abraham said (Gen. xxiii. 4), "I am a stranger and a sojourner with you." That is, he regarded himself as a foreigner; as having no home and no possessions there. It was on this ground that he proposed to *buy* a burial-place of the sons of Heth. ¶ *And pilgrims.* This is the word— παρεπίδημος—which is used by Abraham, as rendered by the LXX. in Gen. xxiii. 4, and which is there translated "sojourner" in the common English version. The word *pilgrim* means properly *a wanderer, a traveller,* and particularly one who leaves his own country to visit a holy place. This sense does not *quite* suit the meaning here, or in Gen. xxiii. 4. The Hebrew

14 For they that say such things declare plainly that they seek a country.

15 And truly, if they had been mindful of that *country* from whence they came out, they might have had opportunity to have returned.

word תּוֹשָׁב—*toshab*—means properly one who *dwells in a place*, and particularly one who is a *mere* resident without the rights of a citizen. The Greek word means a *by-resident;* one who lives *by* another; or among a people not his own. This is the idea here. It is not that they confessed themselves to be wanderers, or that they had left their home to visit a holy place, but that they *resided* as mere sojourners in a country that was not theirs. What might be their ultimate destination, or their purpose, is not implied in the meaning of the word. They were such as reside awhile among another people, but have no permanent home there. ¶ *On the earth.* The phrase here used—ἐπὶ τῆς γῆς—might mean merely on the land of Canaan, but the apostle evidently uses it in a larger sense as denoting the earth in general. There can be no doubt that this accords with the views which the patriarchs had—regarding themselves not only as strangers in the land of Canaan, but feeling that the same thing was true in reference to their whole residence upon the earth—that it was not their permanent *home.*

14. *For they that say such things,* &c. That speak of themselves as having come into a land of strangers; that negotiate for a small piece of land, not to cultivate, but to bury their dead. So we should think of any strange people coming among us now—who lived in tents; who frequently changed their residence; who became the purchasers of no land except to bury their dead; and who never spake of becoming permanent residents. We should think that they were in search of some place as their home, and that they had not yet found it. Such people were the Hebrew patriarchs. They lived and acted just *as if* they had not yet found a permanent habitation, but were travelling in search of one.

15. *And truly if they had been mind-*

ful of that country, &c. If they had remembered it with sufficient interest and affection to have made them desirous to return. ¶ *They might have had opportunity to have returned.* The journey was not so long or perilous that they could not have retraced their steps. It would have been no more difficult or dangerous for them to return than it was to make the journey at first. This shows that their remaining as strangers and sojourners in the land of Canaan was voluntary. They preferred it, with all its inconveniences and hardships, to a return to their native land. The same thing is true of all the people of God now. If they choose to return to the world, and to engage again in all its vain pursuits, there is nothing to hinder them. There are "opportunities" enough. There are abundant inducements held out. There are numerous gay and worldly friends who would regard it as a matter of joy and triumph to have them return to vanity and folly again. They would welcome them to their society; rejoice to have them participate in their pleasures; and be willing that they should share in their honours and their wealth. And they might do it. There are multitudes of Christians who could grace, as they once did, the ball-room; who could charm the social party by song and wit; who could rise to the highest posts of office, or compete successfully with others in the race for the acquisition of wealth or fame. They have seen and tasted enough of the pursuits of the world to satisfy them with their vanity; they are convinced of the sinfulness of making these things the great objects of living; their affections are now fixed on higher and nobler objects, and they *choose* not to return to those pursuits again, but to live as strangers and sojourners on the earth—for there is nothing more *voluntary* than religion.

16. *But now they desire a better coun-*

16 But now they desire a better *country,* that is, an heavenly: wherefore *p*God is not ashamed to be

p Ex.3.6,15.

called their God: *q*for he hath prepared for them a city.

q ver.10.

try, *that is, an heavenly.* That is, at the time referred to, when they confessed that they were strangers and sojourners, they showed that they sought a better country than the one which they had left. They lived as if they had no expectation of a permanent residence on earth, and were looking to another world. The argument of the apostle here appears to be based on what is apparent from the whole history, that they had a confident belief that the land of Canaan would be given to *their posterity,* but as for *themselves* they had no expectation of permanently dwelling there, but looked to a home in the heavenly country. Hence they formed no plans for conquest; they laid claim to no title in the soil; they made no purchases of farms for cultivation; they lived and died without owning any land except enough to bury their dead. All this appears as if *they* looked for a final home in a "better country, even a heavenly." ¶ *Wherefore God is not ashamed to be called their God.* Since they had such an elevated aim, he was willing to speak of himself as their God and Friend. They acted as became his friends, and he was not ashamed of the relation which he sustained to them. The language to which the apostle evidently refers here is that which is found in Ex. iii. 6, "I am the God of Abraham, the God of Isaac, and the God of Jacob." We are not to suppose that God is ever *ashamed* of anything that he does. The meaning here is, that they had acted in such a manner that it was fit that he should show toward them the character of a Benefactor, Protector, and Friend. ¶ *For he hath prepared for them a city.* Such as they had expected—a heavenly residence, ver. 10. There is evidently here a reference to heaven, represented as a city —the New Jerusalem—prepared for his people by God himself. Comp.

Notes on Mat. xxv. 34. Thus they obtained what they had looked for by faith. The wandering and unsettled patriarchs to whom the promise was made, and who showed all their lives that they regarded themselves as strangers and pilgrims, were admitted to the home of permanent rest; and their posterity was ultimately admitted to the possession of the promised land. Nothing could more certainly demonstrate that the patriarchs believed in a future state than this passage. They did not expect a permanent home on earth. They made no efforts to enter into the possession of the promised land themselves. They quietly and calmly waited for the time when God would give it to their posterity, and in the meantime for themselves they looked forward to their permanent home in the heavens. Even in this early period . the world, therefore, there was the confident expectation of the future state. Comp. Notes on Mat. xxii. 31, 32. We may remark that the life of the patriarchs was, in all essential respects, such as we should lead. They looked forward to heaven; they sought no permanent possession here; they regarded themselves as strangers and pilgrims on the earth. So should we be. In our more fixed and settled habits of life, in our quiet homes, in our residence in the land in which we were born, and in the society of old and tried friends, we should yet regard ourselves as "strangers and sojourners." We have here no fixed abode. The houses in which we dwell will soon be occupied by others; the paths in which we go will soon be trod by the feet of others; the fields which we cultivate will soon be ploughed and sown and reaped by others. Others will read the books which we read; sit down at the tables where we sit; lie on the beds where we repose; occupy the chambers where we shall die, and from whence we shall be removed to our graves. If

17 By faith *r* Abraham, when he was tried, offered up Isaac: and he that had received the promises offered up his only begotten *son,*

r Ge.22.1,&c.; Ja.2.21.

18 Of [5] whom it was said, *s* That in Isaac shall thy seed be called:

19 Accounting that God *was* able to raise *him* up, even from the dead; from whence also he received him in a figure.

[5] or, *To.*   *s* Ge.21.12.

we *have* any permanent home, it is in heaven; and that we have, the faithful lives of the patriarchs teach us and the unerring word of God everywhere assures us.

17. *By faith Abraham.* The apostle had stated one strong instance of the faith of Abraham, and he now refers to one still more remarkable—the strongest illustration of faith, undoubtedly, which has ever been evinced in our world. ¶ *When he was tried.* The word here used is rendered *tempted* in Mat. iv. 1, 3; xvi. 1; xix. 3; xxii. 18, 35, and in twenty-two other places in the New Testament; *prove,* in Jn. vi. 6; *hath gone about,* in Acts xxiv. 6; *examine,* 2 Cor. xiii. 5; and *tried,* in Rev. ii. 2, 10; iii. 10. It does not mean here, as it often does, to place inducements before one to lead him to do wrong, but to subject faith to a *trial* in order to test its genuineness and strength. The meaning here is, that Abraham was placed in circumstances which showed what was the real strength of his confidence in God. ¶ *Offered up Isaac.* That is, he showed that he was ready and willing to make the sacrifice, and would have done it if he had not been restrained by the voice of the angel, Gen. xxii. 11, 12. So far as the intention of Abraham was concerned the deed was done, for he had made every preparation for the offering, and was actually about to take the life of his son. ¶ *And he that had received the promises offered up his only begotten* son. The promises particularly of a numerous posterity. The fulfilment of those promises depended on him whom he was now about to offer as a sacrifice. If Abraham had been surrounded with children, or if no special promise of a numerous posterity had been made to him, this act would not have been so remarkable. It would in any case have been a strong act of faith; it was *peculiarly* strong in his case from

the fact that he had only one son, and that the fulfilment of the promise depended on his life.

18. *Of whom it was said, That in Isaac shall thy seed be called.* Gen. xxi. 12. A numerous posterity had been promised to him. It was said expressly that this promise was not to be fulfilled through the son of Abraham by the bond-woman Hagar, but through Isaac. Of course it was implied that Isaac was to reach manhood; and yet notwithstanding this, and notwithstanding Abraham fully believed it, he prepared deliberately, in obedience to the divine command, to put him to death. The phrase "thy seed be called," means that his posterity was to be named after Isaac, or was to descend only from him. The word *"called"* in the Scriptures is often equivalent to the verb *to be.* See Isa. lvi. 7. To *name* or *call* a thing was the same as to say that it was, or that it existed. It does not mean here that his *spiritual* children were to be called or selected from among the posterity of Isaac, but that the posterity promised to Abraham would descend neither from Ishmael nor the sons of Keturah, but in the line of Isaac. This is a strong circumstance insisted on by the apostle to show the strength of Abraham's faith. It was evinced not only by his willingness to offer up the child of his old age—his only son by his beloved wife—but by his readiness, at the command of God, to sacrifice even him on whom the fulfilment of the promises depended.

19. *Accounting that God* was *able to raise* him *up, even from the dead.* And that he *would* do it; for so Abraham evidently believed, and this idea is plainly implied in the whole narrative. There was no other way in which the promise could be fulfilled; and Abraham reasoned correctly in

the case. He had received the promise of a numerous posterity. He had been told expressly that it was to be through this favourite child. He was now commanded to put him to death as a sacrifice, and he prepared to do it. To fulfil these promises, therefore, there was no other way possible but for him to be raised up from the dead, and Abraham fully believed that this would be done. The child had been given to him at first in a supernatural manner, and he was prepared, therefore, to believe that he would be restored to him again by miracle. He did not doubt that He who had given him to him at first in a manner so contrary to all human probability could restore him again in a method as extraordinary. He therefore anticipated that God would raise him up immediately from the dead. That this was the expectation of Abraham is apparent from the narrative in Gen. xxii. 5, "And Abraham said unto his young men, Abide ye here with the ass; and I and the lad will go yonder and worship, *and come again to you;*" in the plural—וְנָשׁוּבָה אֲלֵיכֶם —"and we will return;" that is, I and Isaac will return, for no other persons went with them, ver. 6. As Abraham went with the full expectation of sacrificing Isaac, and as he expected Isaac to return with him, it follows that he believed that God would raise him up immediately from the dead. ¶ *From whence also he received him in a figure.* There has been great difference of opinion as to the sense of this passage, but it seems to me to be plain. The obvious interpretation is, that he then received him by his being raised up from the altar *as if* from the dead. He was to Abraham dead. He had given him up. He had prepared to offer him as a sacrifice. He lay there before him as one who was dead. From that altar he was raised up by direct divine interposition *as if* he was raised from the grave, and this was to Abraham a *figure* or a representation of the resurrection. Other interpretations may be seen in Stuart, *in loco.*—The following circumstances will illustrate the strength of

Abraham's faith in this remarkable transaction: (1) The strong persuasion on his mind that God had commanded this. In a case of this nature —where such a sacrifice was required —how natural would it have been for a more feeble faith to have doubted whether the command could come from God. It might have been suggested to such a mind that this *must* be a delusion, or a temptation of Satan; that God *could not* require such a thing; and that whatever might be the *appearance* of a divine command in the case, there *must be* some deception about it. Yet Abraham does not appear to have reasoned about it at all, or to have allowed the strong feelings of a father to come in to modify his conviction that God had commanded him to give up his son. What an example is this to us! And how ready should *we* be to yield up a son— an only son—when God comes himself and removes him from us. (2) The strength of his faith was seen in the fact that, in obedience to the simple command of God, all the strong feelings of a father were overcome. On the one hand there were his warm affections for an only son; and on the other there was the simple command of God. They came in collision —but Abraham did not hesitate. The strong paternal feeling was sacrificed at once. What an example this too for us! When the command of God and our own attachments come into collision, we should not hesitate a moment. God is to be obeyed. His command and arrangements are to be yielded to, though most tender ties are rent asunder, and though the heart bleeds. (3) The strength of his faith was seen in the fact that, in obedience to the command of God, he resolved to do what in the eyes of the world would be regarded as a most awful crime. There is no crime of a higher grade than the murder of a son by the hand of a father. So it is now estimated by the world, and so it would have been in the time of Abraham. All the laws of God and of society appeared to be against the act which Abraham was about to commit, and he went forth not ignorant of the esti-

20 By faith *Isaac blessed Jacob
t Ge.27.27-40.

and Esau concerning things to come.

mate which the world would put on this deed if it were known. How natural in such circumstances would it have been to argue that God *could not* possibly give such a command; that it was against all the laws of heaven and earth; that there was required in this what God and man alike must and would pronounce to be wrong and abominable! Yet Abraham did not hesitate. The command of God in the case was to his mind a sufficient proof that this was right; and it should teach *us* that whatever our Maker commands us should be done —no matter what may be the estimate affixed to it by human laws, and no matter how it may be regarded by the world. (4) The strength of his faith was seen in the fact that there was a positive promise of God to himself which would *seem* to be frustrated by what he was about to do. God had expressly promised to him a numerous posterity, and had said that it was to be through this son. How could this be if he was put to death as a sacrifice? And how *could* God command such a thing when his promise was thus positive? Yet Abraham did not hesitate. It was not for him to *reconcile* these things; it was his to *obey.* He did not doubt that *somehow* all that God had said would prove to be true; and as he saw but *one way* in which it could be done—by his being immediately restored to life— he concluded that *that* was to be the way. So when God utters his will to us, it is ours simply to obey. It is not to inquire in what way his commands or revealed truth can be reconciled with other things. He will himself take care of that. It is ours at once to yield to what he commands, and to believe that *somehow* all that he has required and said will be consistent with everything else which he has uttered. (5) The strength of the faith of Abraham was seen in his belief that God would raise his son from the dead. Of that he had no doubt. But what evidence had he of

that? It had not been promised. No case of the kind had ever occurred; and the subject was attended with all the difficulties which attend it now. But Abraham believed it; for, *first,* there was no other way in which the promise of God could be fulfilled; and *second,* such a thing would be no more remarkable than what had already occurred. It was as easy for God to raise him from the dead as it was to give him at first contrary to all the probabilities of the case, and he did not, therefore, doubt that it would be so. Is it less easy for *us* to believe the doctrine of the resurrection than it was for Abraham? Is the subject attended with more difficulties now than it was then? The faith of Abraham in this remarkable instance shows us that the doctrine of the resurrection of the dead, notwithstanding the limited revelations then enjoyed, and all the obvious difficulties of the case, was early believed in the world; and as those difficulties are no greater now, and as new light has been shed upon it by subsequent revelations, and especially as in more than one instance the dead have been actually raised, those difficulties should not be allowed to make us doubt it now.

20. *By faith Isaac blessed Jacob and Esau concerning things to come.* See Gen. xxvii. 26-40. The meaning is, that he pronounced a blessing on them in respect to their future condition. This was by faith in God who had communicated it to him, and in full confidence that he would accomplish all that was here predicted. The act of faith here was simply that which believes that all that God says is true. There were no human probabilities at the time when these prophetic announcements were made, which could have been the basis of his calculation, but all that he said must have rested merely on the belief that God had revealed it to him. A blessing was pronounced on each, of a very different nature, but Isaac had no doubt that both would be fulfilled.

21 By faith Jacob, when he was a dying, *u*blessed both the sons of Joseph; *v*and worshipped, *leaning* upon the top of his staff.

u Ge.48.5-20.   v Ge.47.31.

21. *By faith Jacob, when he was a dying.* Gen. xlvii. 31; xlviii. 1–20. That is, when he was about to die. He saw his death near when he pronounced this blessing on Ephraim and Manasseh, the sons of Joseph. ¶ *And worshipped,* leaning *upon the top of his staff.* This is an exact quotation from the Septuagint in Gen. xlvii. 31. The English version of that place is, "And Israel bowed himself upon the bed's head," which is a proper translation, in the main, of the word מִטָּה—*mittĕh.* That word, however, with different points— מַטֶּה—*măttĕh,* means a branch, a bough, a rod, a staff, and the translators of the Septuagint have so rendered it. The Masoretic points are of no authority, and either translation, therefore, would be proper. The word rendered "head" in Gen. xlvii. 31—"bed's *head*"—רֹאשׁ—*rōsh,* means properly *head,* but may there mean the *top* of anything, and there is no impropriety in applying it to the *head* or *top* of a staff. The word rendered in Gen. xlvii. 31, *bowed*—וַיִּשְׁתַּחוּ—implies properly the idea of *worshipping.* It is *bowing,* or *prostration,* for the purpose of worship or homage. Though the Septuagint and the apostle here have, therefore, given a somewhat different version from that commonly given of the Hebrew, and sustained by the Masoretic pointing, yet it cannot be demonstrated that the version is unauthorized, or that it is not a fair translation of the Hebrew. It has also the probabilities of the case in its favour. Jacob was tenderly affected in view of the goodness of God, and of the assurance that he would be conveyed from Egypt when he died, and buried in the land of his fathers. Deeply impressed with this, nothing was more natural than that the old man should lean reverently forward and incline his head upon the top of

22 By faith *w*Joseph, when he died, [6]made mention of the departing of the children of Israel; and gave commandment concerning his bones.

w Ge.50.24,25.   6 or, *remembered.*

his staff, and adore the covenant faithfulness of his God. Such an image is much more natural and probable than that he should "bow upon his bed's head"—a phrase which at best is not very intelligible. If this be the true account, then the apostle does not refer here to what was done when he "blessed the sons of Joseph," but to an act expressive of strong faith in God which had occurred just before. The meaning then is, "By faith, when about to die, he blessed the sons of Joseph; and by faith also he reverently bowed before God in the belief that when he died his remains would be conveyed to the promised land, and expressed his gratitude in an act of worship, leaning reverently on the top of his staff." The order in which these things are mentioned is of no consequence, and thus the whole difficulty in the case vanishes. *Both* the acts here referred to were expressive of strong confidence in God.

22. *By faith Joseph, when he died.* When about to die. See Gen. l. 24, 25. ¶ *Made mention of the departing of the children of Israel.* Margin, "*remembered.*" The meaning is, that he called this to their mind; he spake of it. "And Joseph said unto his brethren, I die; and God will surely visit you, and bring you out of this land unto the land which he sware to Abraham, to Isaac, and to Jacob." This prediction of Joseph *could* have rested only on faith in the promise of God. There were no events then occurring which would be likely to lead to this, and nothing which could be a basis of calculation that it would be so except what God had spoken. The faith of Joseph, then, was simple confidence in God; and its *strength* was seen in his firm conviction that what had been promised would be fulfilled, even when there were no appearances that to human view jus-

23 By faith Moses, when he was born, ˣwas hid three months of his parents, because they saw *he was* a

x Ex.2.2.

proper child; and they were ʸnot afraid of the king's commandment.

24 By faith ᶻMoses, when he was

y Ex.1.16,22.   z Ex.2.10,11.

tified it. ¶ *And gave commandment concerning his bones.* Gen. l. 25, "And Joseph took an oath of the children of Israel, saying, God will surely visit you, and ye shall carry up my bones from hence." He had such a firm belief that they would possess the land of promise that he exacted an oath of them that they would remove his remains with them that he might be buried in the land of his fathers. He could not have exacted this oath, nor could they have taken it, unless both he and they had a sure confidence that what God had spoken would be performed.

23. *By faith Moses, when he was born.* That is, by the faith of his parents. The faith of Moses himself is commended in the following verses. The statement of the apostle here is, that his parents were led to preserve his life by *their* confidence in God. They *believed* that he was destined to some great purpose, and that he would be spared, notwithstanding all the probabilities against it and all the difficulties in the case. ¶ *Was hid three months of his parents.* By his parents. In Ex. ii. 2 it is said that it was done *by his mother.* The truth, doubtless, was, that the mother was the agent in doing it, since the concealment, probably, could be better effected by one than where two were employed; but that the father also concurred in it is morally certain. The concealment was, at first, probably in their own house. The command seems to have been (Ex. i. 22) that the child should be cast into the river as soon as born. This child was concealed in the hope that some way might be found out by which his life might be spared. ¶ *Because they saw he was a proper child.* A fair or beautiful child—ἀστεῖον. The word properly means *pertaining to a city* (from ἄστυ, *a city*); then urbane, polished, elegant; then fair, beautiful. In Acts vii. 20 it is said that he was

"*fair to God*" (margin); that is, exceedingly fair, or very handsome. His extraordinary beauty seems to have been the reason which particularly influenced his parents to attempt to preserve him. It is not impossible that they supposed that his uncommon beauty indicated that he was destined to some important service in life, and that they were on that account the more anxious to save him. ¶ *And they were not afraid of the king's commandment.* Requiring that *all* male children should be given up to be thrown into the Nile. That is, they were not *so* alarmed, or did not *so* dread the king, as to be induced to comply with the command. The strength of the faith of the parents of Moses appears, (1) Because the command of Pharaoh to destroy all the male children was positive, but they had so much confidence in God as to disregard it. (2) Because there was a strong improbability that their child could be saved. They themselves found it impossible to conceal him longer than three months, and when it was discovered, there was every probability that the law would be enforced and that the child would be put to death. Perhaps there was reason also to apprehend that the parents would be punished for disregarding the authority of the king. (3) Because they probably believed that their child was destined to some important work. They thus committed him to God instead of complying with the command of an earthly monarch, and, against strong probabilities in the case, they *believed* that it was possible that in some way he might be preserved alive. The remarkable result showed that their faith was not unfounded.

24. *By faith Moses.* He had confidence in God when he called him to be the leader of his people. He believed that he was able to deliver them, and he so trusted in him that

come to years, refused to be called
the son of Pharaoh's daughter;

25 Choosing *a* rather to suffer afflic-

a Ps. 84. 10.

tion with the people of God, than
to enjoy the pleasures of sin for a
season;

he was willing at his command to
forego the splendid prospects which
opened before him in Egypt. ¶ *When
he was come to years.* Greek, "being
great;" that is, when he was grown
up to manhood. He was at that time
forty years of age. See Notes on Acts
vii. 23. He took this step, therefore,
in the full maturity of his judgment,
and when there was no danger of
being influenced by the ardent passions of youth. ¶ *Refused to be called
the son of Pharaoh's daughter.* When
saved from the ark in which he was
placed on the Nile he was brought up
for the daughter of Pharaoh, Ex. ii. 9.
He seems to have been *adopted* by her
and trained up as her own son. What
prospects this opened before him cannot now be certainly known. There
is no probability that he would be the
heir to the crown of Egypt, as is often
affirmed, for there is no proof that the
crown descended in the line of daughters; nor, if it did, is there any probability that it would descend on an
adopted son of a daughter. But his
situation could not but be regarded as
highly honourable, and as attended
with great advantages. It gave him
the opportunity of receiving the best
education which the times and country
afforded—an opportunity of which he
seems to have availed himself to the
utmost. See Notes on Acts vii. 22.
It would doubtless be connected with
important offices in the state. It furnished the opportunity of a life of
ease and pleasure such as they commonly delight in who reside at courts.
And it doubtless opened before him
the prospect of wealth, for there is no
improbability in supposing that he
would be the *heir* of the daughter of
a rich monarch. Yet all this, it is
said, he "*refused.*" There is, indeed,
no express mention made of his *formally* and *openly* refusing it, but his
leaving the court and identifying himself with his oppressed countrymen
was *in fact* a refusal of these high

honours and of these brilliant prospects. It is not impossible that, when
he became acquainted with his real
history, there was some open and decided refusal on his part to be regarded as the son of the daughter of
this heathen monarch.

25. *Choosing rather to suffer affliction
with the people of God.* With those
whom God had chosen to be his people
—the Israelites. They were then oppressed and down-trodden; but they
were the descendants of Abraham,
and were those whom God had chosen
to be his peculiar people. Moses saw
that if he cast in his lot with them he
must expect trials. They were poor,
and crushed, and despised—a nation
of slaves. If he identified himself
with them, his condition would be like
theirs—one of great trial; if he sought
to elevate and deliver them, such an
undertaking could not but be one of
great peril and hardship. Trial and
danger, want and care, would follow
from any course which he could adopt,
and he knew that an effort to rescue
them from bondage must be attended
with the sacrifice of all the comforts
and honours which he enjoyed at court.
Yet he "*chose*" this. He on the whole
preferred it. He left the court, not
because he was driven away; not because there was nothing there to gratify
ambition, or to be a stimulus to avarice;
and not on account of harsh treatment
—for there is no intimation that he was
not treated with all the respect and
honour due to his station, his talents,
and his learning—but because he deliberately *preferred* to share the trials
and sorrows of the friends of God. So
everyone who becomes a friend of
God, and casts in his lot with his people, though he may anticipate that
it will be attended with persecution,
with poverty, and with scorn, *prefers*
this to all the pleasures of a life of
gaiety and sin, and to the most brilliant prospects of wealth and fame
which this world can offer. ¶ *Than
to enjoy the pleasures of sin for a season.*

26 Esteeming the *b*reproach [7]of Christ greater riches than the trea-

b ch.13.13.　　　　[7] or, *for*.

sures in Egypt: for he had respect unto *c*the recompense of the reward.

c ch.10.35.

We are not to suppose that Moses, even at the court of Pharaoh, was leading a life of vicious indulgence. The idea is, that sins were practised there such as those in which pleasure is sought, and that if he had remained there it must have been because he loved the pleasures of a sinful court, and a sinful life, rather than the favour of God. We may learn from this, (1) That there *is* a degree of *pleasure* in sin. It does not deserve to be called *happiness*, and the apostle does not call it so. It is "*pleasure*," excitement, hilarity, merriment, amusement. *Happiness* is more solid and enduring than "*pleasure;*" and solid happiness is not found in the ways of sin. But it cannot be denied that there is a degree of *pleasure* which may be found in amusement; in the excitement of the ball-room; in feasting and revelry; in sensual enjoyments. All which wealth and splendour, music and dancing, sensual gratifications, and the more refined pursuits in the circles of fashion, can furnish, may be found in a life of irreligion; and if disappointment, and envy, and sickness, and mortified pride, and bereavements do not occur, the children of vanity and sin can find no inconsiderable enjoyment in these things. They *say* they do; and there is no reason to doubt the truth of their own testimony in the case. They *call* it a "life of pleasure;" and it is not proper to withhold from it the appellation which they choose to give it. It is not the most pure or elevated kind of enjoyment, but it would be unjust to deny that there is *any* enjoyment in such a course. (2) It is only "for a season." It will all soon pass away. Had Moses lived at the court of Pharaoh all his days, it would have been only for a little "season." These pleasures soon vanish; for, (*a*) life itself is short at best, and if a career of "pleasure" is pursued through the whole of the ordinary period allotted to man, it is *very* brief. (*b*) Those who live for

pleasure often abridge their own lives. Indulgence brings disease in its train, and the votaries of sensuality usually die young. The art has never been yet discovered of combining intemperance and sensuality with length of days. If a man wishes a reasonable prospect of long life, he must be temperate and virtuous. Indulgence in vice wears out the nervous and muscular system, and destroys the powers of life—just as a machine without balance-wheel or governor would soon tear itself to pieces. (*c*) Calamity, disappointment, envy, and rivalship mar such a life of pleasure; and he who enters on it, from causes which he cannot control, finds it *very short*. And, (*d*) compared with eternity, O how brief is the longest life spent in the ways of sin! Soon it *must* be over, and then the unpardoned sinner enters on an immortal career where *pleasure* is for ever unknown! (3) In view of all the "pleasures" which sin *can* furnish, and in view of the most brilliant prospects which this world *can* hold out, religion enables man to pursue a different path. They who become the friends of God are willing to give up all those fair and glittering anticipations, and to submit to whatever trials may be incident to a life of self-denying piety. Religion, with all its privations and sacrifices, is *preferred*, nor is there ever occasion to regret the choice. Moses deliberately made that choice:—nor in all the trials which succeeded it— in all the cares incident to his great office in conducting the children of Israel to the promised land—in all their ingratitude and rebellion—is there the least evidence that he ever once wished himself back again that he might enjoy "the pleasures of sin" in Egypt.

26. *Esteeming the reproach of Christ.* Margin, "*for;*" that is, on account of Christ. This means either that he was willing to bear the reproaches incident to his belief that the Messiah

27 By faith he forsook Egypt, [d] not fearing the wrath of the king: for

d Ex.10.28,29; 12.31.

he endured, as seeing [e] him who is invisible.

e 1 Ti.1.17.

would come, and that he gave up his fair prospects in Egypt with that expectation; or that he endured such reproaches as Christ suffered; or the apostle uses the expression as a sort of *technical* phrase, well understood in his time, to denote sufferings endured in the cause of religion. Christians at that time would naturally describe all sufferings on account of religion as endured *in the cause of Christ;* and Paul, therefore, may have used this phrase to denote sufferings in the cause of religion—meaning that Moses suffered what, when the apostle wrote, would be called "the reproaches of Christ." It is not easy, or perhaps possible, to determine which of these interpretations is the correct one. The most respectable *names* may be adduced in favour of each, and every reader must be left to adopt his own view of that which is correct. The original will admit of either of them. The general idea is, that he would be reproached for the course which he pursued. He could not expect to leave the splendours of a court and undertake what he did, without subjecting himself to trials. He would be *blamed* by the Egyptians for his interference in freeing their "slaves," and in bringing so many calamities upon their country, and he would be exposed to ridicule for his folly in leaving his brilliant prospects at court to become identified with an oppressed and despised people. It is rare that men are zealous in doing good without exposing themselves both to blame and to ridicule. ¶ *Greater riches.* Worth more; of greater value. Reproach *itself* is not desirable; but reproach, when a man receives it in an effort to do good to others, is worth more to him than gold, 1 Pet. iv. 13, 14. The scars which an old soldier has received in the service of his country are more valued by him than his pension; and the reproach which a good man receives in endeavouring to save others is a subject of

greater joy to him than would be all the wealth which could be gained in a life of sin. ¶ *Than the treasures in Egypt.* It is implied here that Moses had a prospect of inheriting large treasures in Egypt, and that he voluntarily gave them up to be the means of delivering his nation from bondage. Egypt abounded in wealth; and the adopted son of the daughter of the king would naturally be heir to a great estate. ¶ *For he had respect unto the recompense of the reward.* The "recompense of the reward" here must mean the blessedness of heaven—for he had no earthly reward to look to. He had no prospect of pleasure, or wealth, or honour, in his undertaking. If he had sought these, so far as human sagacity could foresee, he would have remained at the court of Pharaoh. The declaration here proves that it is right to have respect to the rewards of heaven in serving God. It does not prove that this was the *only* or the *main* motive which induced Moses to abandon his prospects at court; nor does it prove that this should be *our* main or only motive in leading a life of piety. If it were, our religion would be mere selfishness. But it is right that we should desire the rewards and joys of heaven, and that we should allow the prospect of those rewards and joys to influence us as *a* motive to do our duty to God, and to sustain us in our trials. Comp. Phil. iii. 8–11, 13, 14.

27. *By faith he forsook Egypt.* Some have understood this of the first time in which Moses forsook Egypt, when he fled into Midian, as recorded in Ex. ii.; the majority of expositors, however, have supposed that it refers to the time when he left Egypt to conduct the Israelites to the promised land. That the latter is the time referred to is evident from the fact that it is said that he did "not fear the wrath of the king." When Moses first fled to the land of Midian it is expressly said that he went because

28 Through faith he *kept the passover, and the sprinkling of

f Ex. 12. 21, &c.

blood, lest he that destroyed the first-born should touch them.

---

he *did* fear the anger of Pharaoh for his having killed an Egyptian, Ex. ii. 14, 15. He was at that time in fear of his life; but when he left Egypt at the head of the Hebrew people, he had no such apprehensions. God conducted him out with " an high hand," and throughout all the events connected with that remarkable deliverance he manifested no dread of Pharaoh and had no apprehension from what he could do. He went forth, indeed, at the head of his people when all the power of the king was exerted to destroy them, but he went confiding in God; and this is the faith referred to here. ¶ *For he endured.* He persevered amidst all the trials and difficulties connected with his leading forth the people from bondage. ¶ *As seeing him who is invisible. As if* he saw God. He had no more doubt that God had called him to this work and that he would sustain him than if he saw him with his bodily eyes. This is a most accurate account of the nature of faith. Comp. Notes on ver. 1.

28. *Through faith he kept the passover.* Greek, "he *made*—πεποίηκε—the passover," which means more than that he merely *kept* or *celebrated* it. It implies that he *instituted* this rite and *made* the arrangements for its observance. There is reference to the special agency and the special faith which he had in its institution. The faith in the case was *confidence* that this would be the means of preserving the first-born of the Israelites when the angel should destroy the first-born of the Egyptians, and also that it would be celebrated as a perpetual memorial of this great deliverance. On the Passover, see Notes on Mat. xxvi. 2. ¶ *And the sprinkling of blood.* The blood of the paschal lamb sprinkled on the lintels and door-posts of the houses, Ex. xii. 22. ¶ *Lest he that destroyed the first-born should touch them.* The first-born of the Egyptians, Ex. xii. 23. The apostle has

thus enumerated some of the things which illustrated the faith of Moses. The *strength* of his faith may be seen by a reference to the circumstances which characterized it. (1) It was such confidence in God as to lead him to forsake the most flattering prospects of worldly enjoyment. I see no evidence, indeed, that he was the heir to the throne: but he was evidently heir to great wealth; he was encompassed with all the means of worldly pleasure; he had every opportunity for a life of literary and scientific pursuits; he was eligible to high and important trusts; he had a rank and station which would be regarded as one of the most honoured and enviable on earth. None of those who are mentioned before in this chapter were required to make just such sacrifices as this. Neither Abel, nor Noah, nor Enoch were called to forsake so brilliant worldly prospects; and though Abraham was called to a higher act of faith when commanded to give up his only son, yet there were some circumstances of trial in the case of Moses illustrating the nature of faith which did not exist in the case of Abraham. Moses, in the maturity of life, and with everything around him that is usually regarded by men as objects of ambition, was ready to forego it all. So, *wherever* true faith exists, there is a readiness to abandon the hope of gain and brilliant prospects of distinction and fascinating pleasures in obedience to the command of God. (2) Moses entered on an undertaking wholly beyond the power of man to accomplish and against every human probability of success. It was no less than that of restoring to freedom two millions of downtrodden, oppressed, and dispirited *slaves,* and conducting aged and feeble men, tender females, helpless children, with numerous flocks and herds, across barren wastes to a distant land. He undertook this against the power of probably the most mighty monarch of his time, and when the whole

29 By faith they *g* passed through the Red Sea as by dry *land:* which

g Ex.14.22,29.

the Egyptians assaying to do, were drowned.

nation would be kindled into rage at *the loss of so many slaves,* and when he might expect that all the power of their wrath would descend on him and his undisciplined and feeble hosts. He did this when he had no wealth that he could employ to furnish provisions or the means of defence, no armies at his command to encircle his people on their march, and even no influence among the people himself, and with every probability that they would disregard him. Comp. Ex. iii. 11; iv. 1. He did this when the whole Hebrew people were to be aroused to a *willingness* to enter on the great undertaking, when there was every probability that they would meet with formidable enemies in the way, and when there was nothing human whatever on which the mind could fix as a basis of calculation of success. If there ever was any undertaking commenced opposed to every human probability of success, it was that of delivering the Hebrew people and conducting them to the promised land. In all the difficulties and discouragements of the undertaking of Moses, therefore, his only hope of success must have arisen from his confidence in God. (3) It was an undertaking where there were many certain trials before him. The people whom he sought to deliver were poor and oppressed. An attempt to rescue them would bring down the wrath of the mighty monarch under whom they were. They were a people unaccustomed to self-government, and, as the result proved, prone to ingratitude and rebellion. The journey before him lay through a dreary wilderness, where there was every prospect that there would be a want of food and water, and where he might expect to meet with formidable enemies. In all these things his only hope must have been in God. It was he only who could deliver them from the grasp of the tyrant, who could conduct them through the wilderness,

who could provide for their wants in the desert, and who could defend a vast multitude of women and children from the enemies which they would be likely to encounter. (4) There was nothing in this to gratify ambition or to promise an earthly reward. All these prospects he gave up when he left the court of Pharaoh. To be the leader of a company of emancipated slaves through a pathless desert to a distant land had nothing in itself that could gratify the ambition of one who had been bred at the most magnificent court on earth, and who had enjoyed every advantage which the age afforded to qualify him to fill any exalted office. The result showed that Moses never designed to be himself the king of the people whom he led forth, and that he had no intention of aggrandizing his own family in the case.

29. *By faith they passed through the Red Sea, as by dry* land. Ex. xiv. 22–29. That is, it was only by confidence in God that they were able to do this. It was not by power which they had to remove the waters and to make a passage for themselves; and it was not by the operation of any natural causes. It is not to be supposed, indeed, that *all* who passed through the Red Sea had saving faith. The assertion of the apostle is, that the passage was made in virtue of strong confidence in God, and that if it had not been for this confidence the passage could not have been made at all. Of this no one can entertain a doubt who reads the history of that remarkable transaction. ¶ *Which the Egyptians assaying to do, were drowned.* Ex. xiv. 27, 28. The fact is referred to here as showing the effects of *not* having faith in God, and of what must inevitably have befallen the Israelites if they had had no faith. The destruction of the Egyptians by the return of the waters, in accordance with natural laws, showed that the Israelites would have been destroyed in the passage if a divine

30 By faith *h* the walls of Jericho fell down, after they were compassed about seven days.

31 By faith the harlot *i* Rahab

h Jos.6.12-20.　　*i* Jos.6.23; Ja.2.25.

perished not with them that [8] believed not, when she had *k* received the spies with peace.

[8] or, *were disobedient.*　　*k* Jos.2.4,&c.

---

energy had not been employed to prevent it. On the passage through the Red Sea, see Robinson's *Biblical Researches*, vol. i. pp. 81–86.

30. *By faith the walls of Jericho fell down*, &c. Josh. vi. 12–20. That is, it was not by any natural causes, or by any means that were in themselves adapted to secure such a result. It was not because they fell of themselves, nor because they were assailed by the hosts of the Israelites, nor because there was any natural tendency in the blowing of horns to cause them to fall. None of these things were true; and it was only by confidence in God that means so little adapted to such a purpose could have been employed at all; and it was only by continued faith in him that they could have been persevered in day by day when no impression whatever was made. The *strength* of the faith evinced on this occasion appears from such circumstances as these: that there was no natural tendency in the means used to produce the effect; that there was great apparent improbability that the effect would follow; that they might be exposed to much ridicule from those within the city for attempting to demolish their strong walls in this manner; and from the fact that the city was encircled day after day without producing any result. This may teach us the propriety and necessity of faith in similar circumstances. Ministers of the gospel often preach where there seems to be as little prospect of beating down the opposition in the human heart by the message which they deliver, as there was of demolishing the walls of Jericho by the blowing of rams' horns. They blow the gospel trumpet from week to week, and month to month, and there seems to be no tendency in the strong citadel of the heart to yield. Perhaps the only apparent result is to excite ridicule and scorn. Yet let

them not despair. Let them blow on. Let them still lift up their voice with faith in God, and in due time the walls of the citadel will totter and fall. God has power over the human heart as he had over Jericho; and in our darkest day of discouragement let us remember that we are never in circumstances indicating *less* probability of success, from any apparent tendency in the means used to accomplish the result, than those were who encompassed this heathen city. With similar confidence in God we may hope for similar success.

31. *By faith the harlot Rahab.* She resided in Jericho, Josh. ii. 1. When Joshua crossed the Jordan, he sent two men as spies to her house, and she saved them by concealment from the enemies that would have destroyed their lives. For this act of hospitality and kindness they assured her of safety when the city should be destroyed, and directed her to give an indication of her place of abode to the invading Israelites, that her house might be spared, Josh. ii. 18, 19. In the destruction of the city she was accordingly preserved, Josh. vi. The apostle seems to have selected this case as illustrating the nature of faith, partly because it occurred at Jericho, of which he had just made mention, and partly to show that strong faith had been exercised not only by the patriarchs, and by those who were confessed to be great and good, but by those in humble life, and whose earlier conduct had been far from the ways of virtue (Calvin). Much perplexity has been felt in reference to this case, and many attempts have been made to remove the difficulty. The main difficulty has arisen from the fact that a woman of this character is enumerated among those who were eminent for piety, and many expositors have endeavoured to show that the word rendered *harlot* does not necessarily denote a woman of abandoned

character, but may be used to denote *a hostess*. This definition is given by Schleusner, who says that the word may mean one who prepares and sells food, and who receives strangers to entertain them. Others have supposed that the word means an *idolatress*, because those devoted to idolatry were frequently of abandoned character. But there are no clear instances in which the Greek word and the corresponding Hebrew word—זוֹנָה—is used in this sense. The usual and the fair meaning of the word is that which is given in our translation, and there is no good reason why that signification should not be retained here. It is not implied by the use of the word here, however, that Rahab was a harlot at the time to which the apostle refers; but the meaning is, that this *had been* her character, so that it was proper to designate her by this appellation. In regard to this case, therefore, and in explanation of the difficulties which have been felt in reference to it, we may remark, (1) That the obvious meaning of this word here, and of the corresponding place in Josh. ii. vi., is, that she had been a woman of abandoned character, and that she was known as such. That she might have been *also* a hostess, or one who kept a house of entertainment for strangers, is at the same time by no means improbable, since it not unfrequently happened, in ancient as well as modern times, that females of this character kept such houses. It might have been the fact that her house was *known* merely as a house of entertainment which led the spies who went to Jericho to seek a lodging there. It would be natural that strangers coming into a place should act in this respect as all other travellers did, and should apply for entertainment at what was known as a public house. (2) There is no improbability in supposing that her course of life had been changed either before their arrival, or in consequence of it. They were doubtless .wise and holy men. Men would not be selected for an enterprise like this in whom the leader of the Hebrew army could not put entire confidence. It is not unfair, then, to suppose that they were men of eminent piety as well as sagacity. Nor is there any improbability in supposing that they would acquaint this female with the history of their people; with their remarkable deliverance from Egypt; and with the design for which they were about to invade the land of Canaan. There is evidence that some such representations made a deep impression on her mind, and led to a change in her views and feelings, for she not only received them with the usual proofs of hospitality, but jeoparded her own life in their defence, when she might easily have betrayed them. This fact showed that she had a firm belief that they were what they professed to be—the people of God, and that she was willing to identify her interests with theirs. (3) This case—supposing that she had been a woman of bad character but now was truly converted—does not stand alone. Other females of a similar character have been converted, and have subsequently led lives of piety; and though the number is not comparatively great, yet the truth of God has shown its power in renewing and sanctifying some at least of this, the most abandoned and degraded class of human beings. "Publicans and *harlots*," said the Saviour, "go into the kingdom of God," Mat. xxi. 31. Rahab seems to have been one of them; and her case shows that such instances of depravity are not hopeless. This record, therefore, is one of encouragement for the most abandoned sinners, and one too which shows that strangers, even in a public house, may do good to those who have wandered far from God and virtue, and that we should never despair of saving the most degraded of our race. (4) There is no need of supposing that the apostle in commending this woman approved of *all* that she did. That she was not perfect is true. That she did some things which cannot be vindicated, is true also—and who does not? But admitting all that may be said about any imperfection in her character (comp. Josh. ii. 4), it was still true that she had *strong faith*—and that is *all* that

32 And what shall I more say? for the time would fail me to tell of [l]Gedeon, and *of* [m]Barak, and *of* [n]Samson, and *of* [o]Jephthae; *of* [p]David also, and [q]Samuel, and *of* the prophets:

l Ju.vi.vii. m Ju.4.6, &c. n Ju.xv.xvi. o Ju.11.32,&c. p 1 Sa.17.45,&c. q 1 Sa.7.9,&c.

the apostle commends. We are under no more necessity of vindicating *all* that she did, than we are all that David or Peter did—or all that is now done by those who have the highest claims to virtue. (5) She had strong faith. It was only a strong belief that Jehovah was the true God, and that the children of Israel were his people, which would have led her to screen these strangers at the peril of her own life; and when the city was encompassed, and the walls fell, and the tumult of battle raged, she showed her steady confidence in their fidelity, and in God, by using the simple means on which she was told the safety of herself and her family depended, Josh. vi. 22, 23. ¶ *With them that believed not.* The inhabitants of the idolatrous city of Jericho. The margin is, "*were disobedient.*" The more correct rendering, however, is, as in the text, *believed not.* They evinced no such faith as Rahab had, and they were therefore destroyed. ¶ *Received the spies with peace.* With friendliness and kindness, Josh. ii. 1, seq.

32. *And what shall I more say?* "There are numerous other instances showing the strength of faith which there is not time to mention." ¶ *For the time would fail me to tell.* To recount all that they did; all the illustrations of the strength and power of faith evinced in their lives. ¶ *Of Gedeon.* The history of Gideon is detailed at length in Judg. vi. vii., and there can be no doubt that in his wars he was sustained and animated by strong confidence in God. ¶ *And* of *Barak.* Judg. iv. Barak, at the command of Deborah the prophetess, who summoned him to war in the name of the Lord, encountered and overthrew the hosts of Sisera. His yielding to her summons, and his valour in battle against the enemies of the Lord, showed that he was animated by faith. ¶ *And* of *Samson.* See the history of Samson in Judg. xiv.–xvi. It is not by any means necessary to suppose that in making mention of Samson the apostle approved of *all* that he did. All that he commends is his *faith;* and though he was a very imperfect man, and there were many things in his life which neither sound morality nor religion can approve, yet it was still true that he evinced on some occasions remarkable confidence in God, by relying on the strength which he gave him. This was particularly true in the instance where he made a great slaughter of the enemies of the Lord and of his country. See Judg. xv. 14; xvi. 28. ¶ *And* of *Jephthae.* The story of Jephthah is recorded in Judg. xi. The mention of his name among those who were distinguished for *faith* has given occasion to much perplexity among expositors. That a man of so harsh and severe a character—a man who sacrificed his own daughter in consequence of a rash vow—should be numbered among those who were eminent for piety, as if he were one distinguished for piety also, has seemed to be wholly inconsistent and improper. The same remark, however, may be made respecting Jephthah which has been made of Samson and others. The apostle does not commend *all* which they did. He does not deny that they were very imperfect men, nor that they did many things which cannot be approved or vindicated. He commends only *one thing—their faith;* and in these instances he particularly alludes, doubtless, to their remarkable valour and success in delivering their country from their foes and from the foes of God. In this it is implied that they regarded themselves as called to this work by the Lord and as engaged in his service, and that they went forth to battle depending on *his* protection and nerved by confidence in *him* as the God of their country. Their views of God himself might be very erroneous;

33 Who through faith subdued kingdoms, wrought righteousness,

r obtained promises, *s* stopped the mouths of lions,

r Ga.3.16.   s Da.6.22.

their notions of religion—as was the case with Jephthah—very imperfect and obscure; many things in their lives might be wholly inconsistent with what *we* should now regard as demanded by religion; and still it might be true that, in their efforts to deliver their country, they relied on the aid of God, and were animated to put forth extraordinary efforts, and were favoured with extraordinary success from their confidence in him. In the case of Jephthah all that it is necessary to suppose in order to see the force of the illustration of the apostle is, that he had strong confidence in God—the God of his nation; and that, under the influence of this, he made extraordinary efforts in repelling his foes. And this is not unnatural or improbable, even on the supposition that he was not a pious man. How many a Greek, a Roman, a Goth, and a Mohammedan has been animated to extraordinary courage in battle by confidence in the gods which they worshipped! That Jephthah had this no one can doubt. See Judg. xi. 29–32.

[It is not likely that Jephthah's faith would have found a record *here* had it been of no higher kind than this. Peirce admits his unnatural crime, but supposes him to have repented. "It must be owned," says he, "that if Jephthah had not repented of this very heinous wickedness he could not have been entitled to salvation. The apostle, therefore, who has assured us of his salvation, must undoubtedly have gone upon the supposition that Jephthah actually repented of it before he died. That he had *time* to repent is beyond dispute, because he lived near *six* years after this, for it is expressly said *he judged Israel six years,* Judg. xii. 7, and it is as certain he made this vow in the beginning of his government. What evidence the apostle had of Jephthah's repentance I cannot say. He might know it by the help of old Jewish histories or by inspiration."]

Even in the great and improper sacrifice of his only daughter, which the obvious interpretation of the record respecting him in Judg. xi. 39 leads us to suppose he made, he did it as an offering to the Lord; and, under these mistaken views of duty, he showed by the greatest sacrifice which a man *could* make—that of an only child— that he was disposed to do what he believed was required by religion. A full examination of the case of Jephthah, and of the question whether he really sacrificed his daughter, may be found in Warburton's *Divine Legation of Moses,* book ix., Notes; in Bush's Notes on Judg. xi.; and in the *Biblical Repository* for January, 1843. It is not necessary to go into the much-litigated inquiry here whether he really put his daughter to death, for whether he did or not, it is equally true that he evinced strong confidence in God. If he *did* do it, in obedience, as he supposed, to duty and to the divine command, no higher instance of faith in God as having a right to dispose of all that he had could be furnished; if he did *not,* his eminent valour and success in battle show that he relied for strength and victory on the arm of Jehovah. The single reason why the piety of Jephthah has ever been called in question has been the fact that he sacrificed his own daughter. If he did *not* do that, no one will doubt his claims to an honoured rank among those who have evinced faith in God. ¶ Of *David also.* Commended justly as an eminent example of a man who had faith in God, though it cannot be supposed that *all* that he did was approved. ¶ *And Samuel.* In early youth distinguished for his piety, and manifesting it through his life. See 1 Sam. ¶ *And of the prophets.* They were men who had strong confidence in the truth of what God directed them to foretell, and who were ever ready, depending on him, to make known the most unwelcome truths to their fellowmen, even at the peril of their lives.

33. *Who through faith subdued kingdoms.* That is, those specified in previous verses and others like them. The meaning is, that some of them

34 Quenched *the violence of fire, escaped *u* the edge of the sword, out of weakness were made strong, waxed valiant in fight, turned to flight the armies of the aliens.

t Da.3.25. *u* 1 Ki.19.3; 2 Ki.6.16.

35 Women *v* received their dead raised to life again: and others were tortured, *w* not accepting deliverance; that they might obtain a better resurrection:

v 1 Ki.17.22; 2 Ki.4.35,36. *w* Ac.4.19.

subdued kingdoms, others obtained promises, &c. Thus, Joshua subdued the nations of Canaan; Gideon the Midianites; Jephthah the Ammonites; David the Philistines, Amalekites, Jebusites, Edomites, &c. ¶ *Wrought righteousness.* Carried the laws of justice into execution, particularly on guilty nations. They executed the great purposes of God in punishing the wicked and in cutting off his foes. ¶ *Obtained promises.* Or obtained *promised blessings* (Bloomfield, Stuart); that is, they obtained, as a result of their faith, promises of blessings on their posterity in future times. ¶ *Stopped the mouths of lions.* As Samson, Judg. xiv. 6; David, 1 Sam. xvii. 34, seq.; and particularly Daniel, Dan. vi. 7, seq. To be able to subdue and render harmless the king of the forest—the animal most dreaded in early times—was regarded as an eminent achievement.

34. *Quenched the violence of fire.* As Shadrach, Meshach, and Abednego did, Dan. iii. 15–26. ¶ *Escaped the edge of the sword.* As Elijah did when he fled from Ahab, 1 Ki. xix. 3; as Elijah did when he was delivered from the king of Syria, 2 Ki. vi. 16; and as David did when he fled from Saul. ¶ *Out of weakness were made strong.* Enabled to perform exploits beyond their natural strength, or raised up from a state of bodily infirmity and invigorated for conflict. Such a case as that of Samson may be referred to, Judg. xv. 15; xvi. 26–30; or as that of Hezekiah, 2 Ki. xx., who was restored from dangerous sickness by the immediate interposition of God. See Notes on Isa. xxxviii. ¶ *Waxed valiant in fight.* Became valiant. Like Joshua, Barak, David, &c. The books of Joshua, Judges, Samuel, and Kings supply instances of this in abundance. ¶ *Turned to flight the armies of the aliens.* The foreigners,

as the invading Philistines, Ammonites, Moabites, Assyrians, &c.

35. *Women received their dead raised to life again.* As in the case of the woman of Zarephath, whose child was restored to life by Elijah, 1 Ki. xvii. 19–24; and of the son of the Shunammite woman, whose child was restored to life by Elisha, 2 Ki. iv. 18–37. ¶ *And others were tortured.* The word which is here used—τυμπανίζω, *to tympanize*—refers to a form of severe *torture* which was sometimes practised. It is derived from τύμπανον —*tympanum*—a drum, tabret, timbrel; and the instrument was probably so called from resembling the drum or the timbrel. This instrument consisted in the East of a thin wooden rim covered over with skin, as a tambourine is with us. See it described in the Notes on Isa. v. 12. The engine of torture here referred to probably resembled the drum in form, on which the body of a criminal was *bent* so as to give greater severity to the wounds which were inflicted by scourging. The lash would cut deeper when the body was so extended, and the open gashes exposed to the air would increase the torture. See 2 Mac. vi. 19–29. The punishment here referred to seems to have consisted of two things—the stretching upon the instrument, and the scourging. See Robinson's *Lex.*, and Stuart, *in loco.* Bloomfield, however, supposes that the mode of the torture can be best learned from the original meaning of the word τύμπανον—*tympanum* —as meaning (1) a beating-stick, and (2) a beating-post, which was in the form of a T, thus suggesting the posture of the sufferer. This beating, says he, was sometimes administered with sticks or rods; and sometimes with leather thongs inclosing pieces of lead. The former account, however, better agrees with the usual meaning

36 And others had trial of *cruel* mockings and scourgings, yea, moreover, of [x]bonds and [y]imprisonment.

37 They were [z]stoned, they were

sawn asunder, were tempted, were slain with the sword : they wandered about in sheep-skins and goat-skins; being destitute, afflicted, tormented :

x Ge.39.20.　　*y* Je.20.2.　　*z* Ac.7.59.

of the word. ¶ *Not accepting deliverance.* When it was offered them, that is, on condition that they would renounce their opinions, or do what was required of them. This is the very nature of the spirit of martyrdom. ¶ *That they might obtain a better resurrection.* That is, when they were subjected to this kind of torture they were looked upon as certainly *dead.* To have accepted deliverance *then* would have been a kind of restoration to life, or a species of *resurrection.* But they refused this, and looked forward to a more honourable and glorious restoration to life—a resurrection, therefore, which would be better than this. It would be in itself more noble and honourable, and would be permanent, and therefore better. No particular instance of this kind is mentioned in the Old Testament; but amidst the multitude of cases of persecution to which good men were subjected, there is no improbability in supposing that this may have occurred. The case of Eleazer, recorded in 2 Mac. vi., so strongly resembles what the apostle says here, that it is very possible he may have had it in his eye. The passage before us *proves* that the doctrine of the resurrection was understood and believed before the coming of the Saviour, and that it was one of the doctrines which sustained and animated those who were called to suffer on account of their religion. In the prospect of death under the infliction of torture on account of religion, or under the pain produced by disease, nothing will better enable us to bear up under the suffering than the expectation that the body will be restored to immortal vigour, and raised to a mode of life where it will be no longer susceptible of pain. To be raised up to *that* life is a "better resurrection" than to be saved from death when persecuted, or to be raised up from a bed of pain.

36. *And others had trial of* cruel *mockings.* Referring to the scorn and derision which the ancient victims of persecution experienced. This has been often experienced by martyrs, and doubtless it was the case with those who suffered on account of their religion before the advent of the Saviour as well as afterward. Some instances of this kind are mentioned in the Old Testament (2 Ki. ii. 23; 1 Ki. xxii. 24); and it was frequent in the time of the Maccabees. ¶ *And scourging.* Whipping. This was a common mode of punishment, and was usually inflicted before a martyr was put to death. See Notes on Mat. x. 17; xxvii. 26. For instances of this, see Jer. xx. 2; 2 Mac. vii. 1; v. 17. ¶ *Of bonds.* Chains, Gen. xxxix. 20. ¶ *And imprisonment.* See 1 Ki. xxii. 27; Jer. xx. 2.

37. *They were stoned.* A common method of punishment among the Jews. See Notes on Mat. xxi. 35, 44. Thus Zechariah, the son of Jehoiada the priest, was stoned. See 2 Chr. xxiv. 21; comp. 1 Ki. xxi. 1–14. It is not improbable that this was often resorted to in times of popular tumult, as in the case of Stephen, Acts vii. 59. Comp. Jn. x. 31; Acts xiv. 5. In the time of the terrible persecutions under Antiochus Epiphanes, and under Manasseh, such instances also probably occurred. ¶ *They were sawn asunder.* It is commonly supposed that Isaiah was put to death in this manner. For the evidence of this, see Introduction to Isaiah, § 2. It is known that this mode of punishment, though not common, did exist in ancient times. Among the Romans, the laws of the twelve tables affixed this as the punishment of certain crimes; but this mode of execution was very rare, since Aulius Gellius says that in his time no one remembered to have seen it practised. It appears, however, from Suetonius that

38 (Of whom the world was not worthy:) they wandered in deserts, and *in* mountains, and *in* dens and caves of the earth.

---

the emperor Caligula often condemned persons of rank to be sawn through the middle. Calmet, writing above a hundred years ago, says, "I am assured that the punishment of the saw is still in use among the Switzers, and that they put it in practice not many years ago upon one of their countrymen, guilty of a great crime, in the plain of Grenelles, near Paris. They put him into a kind of coffin, and sawed him lengthwise, beginning at the head, as a piece of wood is sawn" (*Pict. Bib.*). It was not an unusual mode of punishment to *cut* a person asunder, and to suspend the different parts of the body to walls and towers as a warning to the living. See 1 Sam. xxxi. 10, and Morier's *Second Journey to Persia*, p. 96. ¶ *Were tempted.* On this expression, which has given much perplexity to critics, see the Notes of Prof. Stuart, Bloomfield, and Kuinoel. There is a great variety of reading in the MSS. and editions of the New Testament, and many have regarded it as an interpolation. The difficulty which has been felt in reference to it has been, that it is a much *milder* word than those just used, and that it is hardly probable that the apostle would enumerate this among those which he had just specified, as if *to be tempted* deserved to be mentioned among sufferings of so severe a nature. But it seems to me there need be no real difficulty in the case. The apostle here, among other sufferings which they were called to endure, may have referred to the *temptations* which were presented to the martyrs, when about to die, to abandon their religion and live. It is very possible that this might have been among the highest aggravations of their sufferings. We know that in later times it was a common practice to offer life to those who were doomed to a horrid death on condition that they would throw incense on the altars of a heathen god, and we may easily suppose that a temptation of that kind, artfully presented in the midst of keen tortures, would greatly aggravate their sufferings. Or suppose, when a father was about to be put to death for his religion, his wife and children were placed before him, and should plead with him to save his life by abandoning his religion, we can easily imagine that no pain of the rack would cause so keen torture to the soul as their cries and tears would. Amidst the sorrows of martyrs, therefore, it was not improper to say that they were *tempted*, and to place this among their most aggravated woes. For instances of this nature, see 2 Mac. vi. 21, 22; vii. 17, 24. ¶ *Were slain with the sword.* As in the case of the eighty-five priests slain by Doeg (1 Sam. xxii. 18); and the prophets, of whose slaughter by the sword Elijah complains, 1 Ki. xix. 10. ¶ *They wandered about in sheep-skins and goat-skins.* Driven away from their homes, and compelled to clothe themselves in this rude and uncomfortable manner. A dress of this kind, or a dress made of hair, was not uncommon with the prophets, and seems indeed to have been regarded as an appropriate badge of their office. See 2 Ki. i. 8; Zec. xiii. 4. ¶ *Being destitute, afflicted, tormented.* The word *tormented* here means *tortured.* The apostle expresses here in general what in the previous verses he had specified in detail.

38. *Of whom the world was not worthy.* The world was so wicked that it had no claim that such holy men should live in it. These poor, despised, and persecuted men, living as outcasts and wanderers, were of a character far elevated above the world. This is a most beautiful expression. It is at once a statement of *their* eminent holiness, and of the wickedness of the rest of mankind. ¶ *They wandered in deserts,* &c. On the Scripture meaning of the word *desert* or *wilderness*, see Notes on Mat. iii. 1. This is a description of persons driven away from their homes, and wandering about from place to place to procure a scanty subsistence. Comp. 1 Mac. i. 53; 2 Mac. v. 27;

39 And these all, having obtained a good report through faith, received not the promise:

40 God having [9]provided some better thing for us, that they [a] without us should not be made perfect.

[9] or, *foreseen.* [a] Re.6.11.

vi. 7. The instances mentioned in the Books of Maccabees are so much in point, that there is no impropriety in supposing that Paul referred to some such cases, if not these very cases. As there is no doubt about their historic truth, there was no impropriety in referring to them, though they are not mentioned in the canonical books of Scripture. One of those cases may be referred to as strikingly illustrating what is here said: " But Judas Maccabeus with nine others, or thereabout, withdrew himself into the wilderness, and lived in the mountains after the manner of beasts, with his company, who fed on herbs continually, lest they should be partakers of the pollution," 2 Mac. v. 27.

39. *And these all, having obtained a good report through faith.* They were all commended and approved on account of their confidence in God. See Notes on ver. 2. ¶ *Received not the promise.* That is, did not receive the fulfilment of the promise, or did not receive *all* that was promised. They still looked forward to some future blessings. See Notes on ver. 13.

40. *God having provided some better thing for us.* Margin, *foreseen.* That is, "God having provided, or determined on giving some better thing than any of them realized, and which we are now permitted to enjoy." That is, God gave them promises; but they were not allowed to see their fulfilment. *We* are permitted now to see what those promises referred to, and in part, at least, to witness their completion; and thus, though the *promise* was made to them, the *fulfilment* more particularly pertains to us. ¶ *That they without us should not be made perfect.* That is, *complete.* The entire system of revelation was not finished at once, or in one generation. It required successive ages to make it complete, so that it might be said that it was *finished,* or *perfect.* Our existence, therefore, and the developments in our times,

were as necessary to the perfection of the system as the promise made to the patriarchs. And as the system would not have been complete if the blessings had been simply conferred on us without the previous arrangements, and the long series of introductory measures, so it would not have been complete if the promises had been merely given to them without the corresponding fulfilment in our times. They are like the two parts of a *tally.* The fathers had one part *in the promises,* and we the other *in the fulfilment,* and neither would have been complete without the other. The "better things" then referred to here, as possessed by Christians, are the privilege of seeing those promises fulfilled in the Messiah; the blessings resulting from the atonement; the more expanded views which we have under the gospel; the brighter hopes of heaven itself, and the clearer apprehension of what heaven will be, which we are permitted to enjoy. This, therefore, accords entirely with the argument which the apostle is pursuing—which is, to show that the Christians whom he addressed should not apostatize from their religion. The argument is, that in numerous instances, as specified, the saints of ancient times, even under fiery trials, were sustained by faith in God, and that too when they had not seen the fulfilment of the promises, and when they had much more obscure views than we are permitted to enjoy. If they, under the influence of the mere *promise* of future blessings, were enabled thus to persevere, how much more reason is there for us to persevere, who have been permitted, by the coming of the Messiah, to witness the perfection of the system!

There is no part of the New Testament of more value than this chapter; none which deserves to be more patiently studied, or which may be more frequently applied to the circum-

stances of Christians. These invaluable records are adapted to sustain us in times of trial, temptation, and persecution; to show us what faith has done in days that are past, and what it may do still in similar circumstances. Nothing can better show the value and the power of faith, or of true religion, than the records in this chapter. Faith has done what nothing else could do. It has enabled men to endure what nothing else would enable them to bear, and it has shown its power in inducing them to give up, at the command of God, what the human heart holds most dear. And among the lessons which we may derive from the study of this portion of divine truth, let us learn, from the example of Abel, to continue to offer to God the sacrifice of true piety which he requires, though we may be taunted or opposed by our nearest kindred; from that of Enoch, to walk with God, though surrounded by a wicked world, and to look to the blessed translation to heaven which awaits all the righteous; from that of Noah, to comply with all the directions of God, and to make all needful preparations for the future events which he has predicted, in which we are to be interested— as death, judgment, and eternity— though the events may seem to be remote, and though there may be no visible indications of their coming, and though the world may deride our faith and our fears; from that of Abraham, to leave country, and home, and kindred, if God calls us to, and to go just where he commands, through deserts and wilds, and among strange men, and like him also to be ready to give up the dearest objects of our earthly affection, even when attended with all that can try or torture our feelings of affection—feeling that God who gave has a right to require their removal in his own way, and that however much we may fix our hopes on a dear child, he can fulfil all his purposes and promises to us though such a child should be removed by death; from that of Abraham, Isaac, and Jacob, to regard ourselves as strangers and pilgrims on earth, having here no permanent home, and

seeking a better country; from that of Moses, to be willing to leave all the pomp and splendour of the world, all our brilliant prospects and hopes, and to welcome poverty, reproach, and suffering, that we may identify ourselves with the people of God; from the example of the host of worthies who met danger, and encountered mighty foes, and vanquished them, to go forth in our spiritual conflicts against the enemies of our souls and of the church, assured of victory; and from the example of those who were driven from the abodes of men, and exposed to the storms of persecution, to bear every trial, and to be ready at any moment to lay down *our* lives in the cause of truth and of God. Of all those holy men who made these sacrifices, which of them ever regretted it when he came calmly to look over his life, and to review it on the borders of the eternal world? None. Not one of them ever expressed regret that he had given up the world; or that he had obeyed the Lord too early, too faithfully, or too long. Not Abraham, who left his country and kindred; not Moses, who abandoned his brilliant prospects in Egypt; not Noah, who subjected himself to ridicule and scorn for a hundred and twenty years; and not one of those who were exposed to lions, to fire, to the edge of the sword, or who were driven away from society as outcasts, to wander in pathless deserts or to take up their abodes in caverns, ever regretted the course which they had chosen. And who of them *now* regrets it? Who, of these worthies, now looks from heaven and feels that he suffered one privation too much, or that he has not had an ample recompense for all the ills he experienced in the cause of religion? So *we* shall feel when from the bed of death we look over the present life, and look out on eternity. Whatever our religion may have cost us, we shall not feel that we began to serve God too early, or served him too faithfully. Whatever pleasure, gain, or splendid prospects we gave up in order to become Christians, we shall feel that it was the way of wisdom, and shall

rejoice that we were able to do it. Whatever sacrifices, trials, persecution, and pain, we may meet with, we shall feel that there has been more than a compensation in the consolations of religion, and in the hope of heaven, and that by every sacrifice we have been the gainers. When we reach heaven, we shall see that we have not endured one pain too much, and that, through whatever trials we may have passed, the result is worth all which it has cost. Strengthened then in our trials by the remembrance of what faith has done in times that are past; recalling the example of those who through faith and patience have inherited the promises, let us go cheerfully on our way. Soon the journey of trials will be ended, and soon what are now objects of faith will become objects of fruition, and in their enjoyment how trifling and brief will seem all the sorrows of our pilgrimage below!

CHAPTER XII.

ANALYSIS OF THE CHAPTER.

The apostle having illustrated the nature and power of faith in the previous chapter, proceeds in this to exhort those to whom he wrote to apply the same principles to their own case, and to urge them to manifest the same steady confidence in God and the same perseverance in their holy walk. For this purpose he adverts to the following arguments or considerations:

I. He represents the ancient worthies who had so faithfully persevered and so gloriously triumphed as witnesses of their strife in the Christian race, and as cheering them on to victory, ver. 1.

II. He appeals to the example of the Saviour, ver. 2–4. This was a more illustrious instance than any of those which had been adverted to, and is not referred to *with* theirs, but is adduced as deserving a separate and a special specification. The circumstances in his case which are an encouragement to perseverance in the Christian conflict are these: (1) He endured the cross, and is now exalted to the right hand of God. (2) He bore the contradiction of sinners against himself, as those were called to do to whom Paul wrote. (3) He went *beyond* them in his trials and temptations—beyond anything which they could have reason to apprehend—for he "resisted unto blood, striving against sin."

III. He encourages them by showing that their trials would result in their own good, and particularly that the hand of a *Father* was in them, ver. 5–13. Particularly he urges—(1) that God addressed those who suffered as his *sons,* and called on them not to receive with improper feeling the chastening of the Lord, ver. 5; (2) that it is a general principle that the Lord chastens those whom he loves, and the fact that we receive chastening is to be regarded as evidence that we are under his paternal care, and that he has not forsaken us, ver. 6–8; (3) that they had been subject to the correction of earthly fathers and had learned to be submissive, and that there was much higher reason for submitting to God, ver. 9, 10; and (4) that however painful chastisement may be at present, yet it will ultimately produce important benefits, ver. 11. By these considerations he encourages them to bear their trials with patience, and to assume new courage in their efforts to live a Christian life, ver. 12, 13.

IV. He exhorts them to perseverance and fidelity by the fact that if they should become remiss, and renounce their confidence in God, it would be impossible to retrieve what was lost, ver. 14–17. In illustrating this he appeals to the case of Esau. For a trifling consideration, when in distress, he parted with an invaluable blessing. When it was gone it was impossible to recover it. No consideration could induce a change, though he sought it earnestly with tears. So it would be with Christians, if, under the power of temptation, they should renounce their religion and go back to their former state.

V. He urges them to perseverance by the nature of the dispensation under which they were, as compared with the one under which they had formerly been—the Jewish, ver. 18–29. Under the former everything was fitted to

CHAPTER XII.

WHEREFORE, seeing we also are compassed about with so great a cloud of witnesses, let us ^alay

_{a 2 Co.7.1.}

aside every weight, and the sin which doth so easily beset *us,* and let us run with patience the race that is set before us,

---

alarm and terrify the soul, ver. 18–21. The new dispensation was of a different character. It was adapted to encourage and to win the heart. The real Mount Zion—the city of the living God—the New Jerusalem—the company of the angels—the church of the first-born— the Judge of all—the great Mediator —to which they had come under the new dispensation, all these were fitted to encourage the fainting heart and to win the affections of the soul, ver. 22–24. Yet, in proportion to the sacredness and tenderness of these considerations, and to the light and privileges which they now enjoyed, would be their guilt if they should renounce their religion, for under this dispensation, as under the old, God is a consuming fire, ver. 25–29.

1. *Wherefore.* In view of what has been said in the previous chapter. ¶ *Seeing we also are compassed about with so great a cloud of witnesses.* The apostle represents those to whom he had referred in the previous chapter as *looking on* to witness the efforts which Christians make and the manner in which they live. There is allusion here, doubtless, to the ancient games. A great multitude of spectators usually occupied the circular seats in the amphitheatre, from which they could easily behold the combatants. See Notes on 1 Cor. ix. 24–27. In like manner the apostle represents Christians as encompassed with the multitude of worthies to whom he had referred in the previous chapter. It cannot be fairly inferred from this that he means to say that all those ancient worthies were *actually* looking at the conduct of Christians and saw their conflicts. It is a figurative representation, such as is common, and means that we ought to act *as if* they were in sight and cheered us on. How far the spirits of the just who are departed from this world are permitted to behold what is done on earth—if at all—is not revealed in the Scriptures. The phrase "a *cloud* of witnesses"

means *many* witnesses, or a number so great that they seem to be a *cloud.* The comparison of a *multitude* of persons to a cloud is common in the classic writers. See Homer, *Iliad,* iv. 274; xxiii. 133; Statius, i. 340, and other instances adduced in Wetstein, *in loco.* Comp. Notes on 1 Thes. iv. 17. ¶ *Let us lay aside every weight.* The word rendered *weight*—ὄγκον—means that which is *crooked* or *hooked,* and thence anything that is attached or suspended by a hook—that is, by its whole weight —and hence means *weight.* See Passow. It does not occur elsewhere in the New Testament. The word is often used in the classic writers in the sense of swelling, tumour, pride. Its usual meaning is that of *weight* or *burden,* and there is allusion here, doubtless, to the runners in the games, who were careful not to encumber themselves with anything that was heavy. Hence their clothes were so made as not to impede their running, and hence they were careful in their training not to overburden themselves with food, and in every way to remove what would be an impediment or hindrance. As applied to the racers, it does not mean that they began to run with anything like a burden and then threw it away —as persons sometimes aid their jumping by taking a stone in their hands to acquire increased *momentum*—but that they were careful *not to allow* anything that would be a weight or an encumbrance. As applied to Christians, it means that they should remove *all* which would obstruct their progress in the Christian course. Thus it is fair to apply it to whatever would be an impediment in our efforts to win the crown of life. This is not the same thing in all persons. In one it may be pride; in another vanity; in another worldliness; in another a violent and almost ungovernable temper; in another a corrupt imagination; in another a heavy, leaden, insensible heart; in another some improper and

unholy attachment. Whatever it may be, we are exhorted to lay it aside, and this general direction may be applied to anything which prevents our making the highest possible attainment in the divine life. Some persons would make much more progress if they would throw away many of their personal ornaments; some if they would disencumber themselves of the heavy *weight* of gold which they are endeavouring to carry with them. So some very light objects, in themselves considered, become material and weighty encumbrances. Even a feather or a ring—such may be the fondness for these toys—may become such a weight that those who wear them will never make much progress toward the prize. ¶ *And the sin which doth so easily beset* us. The word which is here rendered "*easily beset*"—εὐπερίστατον—*euperistaton*—does not elsewhere occur in the New Testament. It properly means "*standing well around,*" and hence denotes that which is near, or at hand, or readily occurring. So Chrysostom explains it. Passow defines it as meaning, "easy to encircle." Tindall renders it "the sin that hangeth on us." Theodoret and others explain the word as if derived from περίστασις —*peristasis*—a word which sometimes means affliction, peril—and hence they regard it as denoting that *which is full of peril,* or the sin which so easily subjects one to calamity. Bloomfield supposes, in accordance with the opinion of Grotius, Crellius, Kype, Kuinoel and others, that it means "the sin which especially winds around us and hinders our course," with allusion to the long Oriental garments. According to this, the meaning would be, that as a runner would be careful not to encumber himself with a garment which would be apt to wind around his legs in running and hinder him, so it should be with the Christian, who especially ought to lay aside everything which resembles this; that is, all sin which *must* impede his course. The former of these interpretations, however, is most commonly adopted, and best agrees with the established sense of the word. It will then mean that we are to lay aside

every encumbrance, *particularly* or *especially*—for so the word καὶ, "*and,*" should be rendered here—the sins to which we are most exposed. Such sins are appropriately called "easily-besetting sins." They are those to which *we* are particularly liable. They are such as the following: (1) Those to which we are particularly exposed by our natural temperament or disposition. In some this is pride, in others indolence, gaiety, levity, avarice, ambition, or sensuality. (2) Those in which we freely indulged before we became Christians. They will be likely to return with power, and we are far more likely, from the laws of association, to fall into them than into any other. Thus a man who has been intemperate, is in special danger from that quarter; a man who has been an infidel, is in special danger of scepticism; a man who has been avaricious, proud, gay, or ambitious, is in special danger, even after conversion, of again committing these sins. (3) Sins to which we are exposed by our profession, by our relations to others, or by our situation in life. They whose condition will entitle them to associate with what are regarded as the more elevated classes of society, are in special danger of indulging in the modes of living and of amusement that are common among them; they who are prospered in the world are in danger of losing the simplicity and spirituality of their religion; they who hold a civil office are in danger of becoming mere politicians, and of losing the very form as well as the substance of piety. (4) Sins to which we are exposed from some peculiar *weakness* in our character. On some points we may be in no danger. We may be constitutionally so firm as not to be especially liable to certain forms of sin. But every man has one or more *weak points* in his character; and it is *there* that he is particularly exposed. A bow may be in the main very strong. All along its length there may be no danger of its giving way—save at one place where it has been made too thin, or where the material was defective— and if it ever breaks, it will of course be at that point. *That* is the point,

2 Looking unto Jesus the [1] author
and finisher of *our* faith; who, for
the [b] joy that was set before him,

[1] or, *beginner*.　　　　[b] Lu. 24. 26.

endured the cross, despising the
shame, and is set down at the right
hand of the throne of God.

---

therefore, which needs to be guarded
and strengthened. So in reference to
character. There is always some weak
point which needs specially to be
guarded, and our principal danger is
there. Self-knowledge, so necessary
in leading a holy life, consists much
in searching out those points of character where we are most exposed; and
our progress in the Christian course
will be determined much by the fidelity with which we guard and strengthen
them. ¶ *And let us run with patience the race that is set before us.*
The word rendered "patience" rather
means in this place *perseverance.* We
are to run the race without allowing
ourselves to be hindered by any obstructions, and without giving out or
fainting in the way. Encouraged by
the example of the multitudes who
have run the same race before us, and
who are now looking out upon us from
heaven where they dwell, we are to
persevere as they did to the end.

2. *Looking unto Jesus.* As a further
inducement to do this, the apostle exhorts us to look to the Saviour. We
are to look to his holy life; to his patience and perseverance in trials; to
what he endured in order to obtain
the crown, and to his final success and
triumph. ¶ *The author and finisher
of* our *faith.* The word "*our*" is not
in the original here, and obscures the
sense. The meaning is, he is the *first*
and the *last* as an example of faith, or
of confidence in God—occupying in
this, as in all other things, the pre-eminence, and being the most complete
model that can be placed before us.
The apostle had not enumerated him
among those who had been distinguished for their faith, but he now
refers to him as above them all—as a
case that deserved to stand by itself.
It is probable that there is a continuance here of the allusion to the Grecian games which the apostle had
commenced in the previous verse.
The word *author*—ἀρχηγὸν (margin,

beginner)—means properly *the source,*
or *cause* of anything; or one who
makes a beginning. It is rendered in
Acts iii. 15; v. 31, *Prince;* in Heb. ii.
10, *captain;* and in the place before
us, *author.* It does not elsewhere
occur in the New Testament. The
phrase "the beginner of faith," or the
leader on of faith, would express the
idea. He is at the head of all those
who have furnished an example of
confidence in God, for he was himself
the most illustrious instance of it.
The expression, then, does not mean
properly that he produces faith *in us,*
or that we believe *because* he causes us
to believe—whatever may be the truth
in respect to that—but that he stands
at the head as the most eminent example that can be referred to on the subject of faith. We are exhorted to look
to him, as if at the Grecian games
there was *one* who stood before the
racer who had previously carried away
every palm of victory; who had always
been triumphant; with whom there
was no one who could be compared.
The word *finisher*—τελειωτὴν—corresponds in meaning with the word *author.* It means that he is the *completer*
as well as the *beginner;* the *last* as well
as the *first.* As there has been no one
hitherto who could be compared with
him, so there will be no one hereafter.
Comp. Rev. i. 8, 11, "I am Alpha
and Omega, the beginning and the
ending, the first and the last." The
word does not mean that he was the
"finisher" of faith in the sense that
he makes *our* faith complete or perfects it—whatever may be true on that
subject—but that he occupies the elevated position of being beyond comparison above all others in this respect.
Alike in the commencement and the
close, in the beginning of faith and in
its ending, *he* stands pre-eminent. To
this illustrious model we should look
—as a racer would on one who had
been always so successful that he surpassed all competitors and rivals. If
this be the meaning, then it is not

properly explained, as it is commonly (see Bloomfield and Stuart, *in loco*), by saying that the word here is synonymous with *rewarder*, and refers to the βραβευτής—*brabeutēs*—or *the distributer of the prize*. Comp. Notes on Col. iii. 15. There is no instance where the word is used in this sense in the New Testament (compare Passow), nor would such an interpretation present so beautiful and appropriate a thought as the one suggested above. ¶ *Who for the joy that was set before him.* That is, who, in view of all the honour which he would have at the right hand of God, and the happiness which he would experience from the consciousness that he had redeemed a world, was willing to bear the sorrows connected with the atonement. ¶ *Endured the cross.* Endured patiently the ignominy and pain connected with the suffering of death on the cross. ¶ *Despising the shame.* Disregarding the ignominy of such a mode of death. It is difficult for us now to realize the force of the expression, "enduring the shame of the cross," as it was understood in the time of the Saviour and the apostles. The views of the world have changed, and it is now difficult to divest the "cross" of the associations of honour and glory which the word suggests, so as to appreciate the ideas which encompassed it then. There is a degree of dishonour which we attach to the guillotine, but the ignominy of the cross was greater than that; there is disgrace attached to the block, but the ignominy of the cross was greater than that; there is a much deeper infamy attached to the gallows, but the ignominy of the cross was greater than that. And that word— *the cross*—which when now proclaimed in the ears of the refined, the intelligent, and even the gay, excites an idea of honour, in the ears of the people of Athens, of Corinth, and of Rome, excited deeper disgust than the word *gallows* does with us—for it was regarded as the appropriate punishment of the most infamous of mankind. We can now scarcely appreciate these feelings, and of course the declaration that Jesus "endured the cross, despising the shame," does not make the impression on our minds in regard to the nature of his sufferings, and the value of his example, which it should do. When we now think of the "cross," it is not of the multitude of slaves, and robbers, and thieves, and rebels, who have died on it, but of the one great Victim whose death has ennobled even this instrument of torture, and encircled it with a halo of glory. We have been accustomed to read of it as an imperial standard in war in the days of Constantine, and as the banner under which armies have marched to conquest; it is intermingled with the sweetest poetry; it is a sacred object in the most magnificent cathedrals; it adorns the altar, and is even worshipped; it is in the most elegant engravings; it is worn by beauty and piety as an ornament near the heart; it is associated with all that is pure in love, great in self-sacrifice, and holy in religion. To see the true force of the expression here, therefore, it is necessary to divest ourselves of these ideas of glory which encircle the "cross," and to place ourselves in those times when the most infamous of mankind were stretched upon it, and when it was regarded as an appropriate mode of punishment for such men. That infamy Jesus was willing to bear; and the strength of his confidence in God, his love for man, and the depth of his humiliation, was shown in the readiness and firmness with which he went forward to such a death. ¶ *And is set down at the right hand of the throne of God.* Exalted to the highest place of dignity and honour in the universe. See Notes on Mark xvi. 19; Eph. i. 20–22. The sentiment here is, "Imitate the example of the great Author of our religion. He, in view of the honour and joy before him, endured the most severe sufferings to which the human frame can be subjected, and the form of death which is regarded as the most shameful. So amidst all the severe trials to which you are exposed on account of religion, patiently endure all—for the glorious rewards, the happiness and the triumphs of heaven, are before you."

3. *For consider him.* Attentively reflect on his example, that you may

3 For consider him that endured such contradiction of sinners against himself, lest ye be wearied and faint in your minds.

4 Ye have not yet resisted unto blood, striving against sin.

5 And ye have forgotten ^cthe exhortation which speaketh unto

c Pr. 3. 11, 12.

be able to bear your trials in a proper manner. ¶ *That endured such contradiction of sinners.* Such opposition. The reference is to the Jews of the time of the Saviour, who opposed his plans, perverted his sayings, and ridiculed his claims. Yet, regardless of their opposition, he persevered in the course which he had marked out, and went patiently forward in the execution of his plans. The idea is, that we are to pursue the path of duty, and to follow the dictates of conscience, let the world say what they will about it. In doing this we cannot find a better example than the Saviour. No opposition of sinners ever turned him from the way which he regarded as right; no ridicule ever caused him to abandon any of his plans; no argument, or expression of scorn, ever caused him for a moment to deviate from his course. ¶ *Lest ye be wearied and faint in your minds.* The meaning is, that there is great danger of being disheartened and wearied out by the opposition which you meet with. But with the bright example of one who was *never* disheartened, and who never became weary in doing the will of God, you may persevere. The best means of leading a faithful Christian life amidst the opposition which we may encounter, is to keep the eye steadily fixed on the Saviour.

4. *Ye have not yet resisted unto blood, striving against sin.* The general sense of this passage is, "You have not yet been called, in your Christian struggles, to the highest kind of sufferings and sacrifices. Great as your trials may seem to have been, yet your faith has not yet been put to the severest test. And since this is so, you ought not to yield in the conflict with evil, but manfully resist it." In the *language* here used there is undoubtedly a continuance of the allusion to the *agonistic* games—the strugglings and wrestlings for mastery there. See

Notes on 1 Cor. ix. 24–26. In those games, the boxers were accustomed to arm themselves for the fight with the cæstus. This at first consisted of strong leathern thongs wound around the hands, and extending only to the wrist, to give greater solidity to the *fist*. Afterward these were made to extend to the elbow, and then to the shoulder, and finally they sewed pieces of lead or iron in them, that they might strike a heavier and more destructive blow. The consequence was, that those who were engaged in the fight were often covered with blood, and that resistance "unto blood" showed a determined courage, and a purpose not to yield. But though the *language* here may be taken from this custom, the *fact* to which the apostle alludes, it seems to me, is the struggling of the Saviour in the garden of Gethsemane, when his conflict was so severe that great drops of blood fell down to the ground. See Notes on Mat. xxvi. 42–44. It is, indeed, commonly understood to mean that they had not yet been called to shed their blood as martyrs in the cause of religion. See Stuart, Bloomfield, Doddridge, Clarke, Whitby, Kuinoel, &c. Indeed, I find in none of the commentators what seems to me to be the true sense of this passage, and what gives an exquisite beauty to it, the allusion to the sufferings of the Saviour in the garden. The reasons which lead me to believe that there *is* such an allusion are briefly these: (1) The connection. The apostle is appealing to the example of the Saviour, and urging Christians to persevere amidst their trials by looking to him. Nothing would be more natural, in this connection, than to refer to that dark night, when, in the severest conflict with temptation which he ever encountered, he so signally showed his own firmness of purpose, and the effects of resistance on his own bleed-

you as unto children, My son, despise not thou the chastening of | the Lord, nor faint when thou art rebuked of him:

---

ing body, and his signal victory, in the garden of Gethsemane. (2) The expression "striving against sin" seems to demand the same interpretation. On the common interpretation, the allusion would be merely to their resisting *persecution;* but here the allusion is to some struggle in their minds against *committing sin.* The apostle exhorts them to strive manfully and perseveringly against *sin* in every form, and especially against the sin of apostasy. To encourage them, he refers to the highest instance on record where there was a "striving against sin"—the struggle of the Redeemer in the garden with the great enemy who there made his most violent assault, and where the resistance of the Redeemer was so great as to force the blood through his pores. What was the exact *form* of the temptation there, we are not informed. It *may* have been to induce him to abandon his work even then, in view of the severe sufferings of his approaching death on the cross. If there ever was a point where temptation would be powerful, it would be there. When a man is about to be put to death, how strong is the inducement to abandon his purpose, his plans, or his principles, if he may save his life! How many, of feeble virtue, have yielded just there! If to this consideration we add the thought that the Redeemer was engaged in a work never before undertaken; that he designed to make an atonement never before made; that he was about to endure sorrows never before endured; and that on the decision of that moment depended the ascendency of sin or holiness on the earth, the triumph or the fall of Satan's kingdom, the success or the defeat of all the plans of the great adversary of God and man; and that, on such an occasion as this, the tempter would use all his power to crush the lonely and unprotected man of sorrows in the garden of Gethsemane, it is easy to imagine what may have been the terror of that fear-

ful conflict, and what virtue it would require in him to resist the concentrated energy of Satan's might to induce him even then to abandon his work. The apostle says of those to whom he wrote, that they had not *yet* reached that point. Comp. Notes on chap. v. 7. (3) This view furnishes a proper *climax* to the argument of the apostle for perseverance. It presents the Redeemer before the mind as *the* great example; directs the mind to him in various scenes of his life— as looking to the joy before him—disregarding the ignominy of his sufferings—enduring the opposition of sinners—and *then* in the garden as engaged in a conflict with his great foe, and so resisting *sin* that, rather than yield, he endured that fearful mental struggle which was attended with such remarkable consequences. This is the highest consideration which *could* be presented to the mind of a believer to keep him from yielding in the conflict with evil; and if we could keep him in the eye, resisting even unto blood rather than yield in the least degree, it would do more than all other things to restrain us from sin. How different his case from ours! How readily we yield to sin! We offer a faint and feeble resistance and then surrender. We think it will be unknown, or that others do it, or that we may repent of it, or that we have no power to resist it, or that it is of little consequence, and our resolution gives way. Not so the Redeemer. Rather than yield in any form to sin, he measured strength with the great adversary when alone with him in the darkness of the night, and gloriously triumphed. And so would *we* always triumph if we had the same settled purpose to resist sin in every form *even unto blood.*

5. *And ye have forgotten the exhortation.* This exhortation is found in Prov. iii. 11, 12. The object of the apostle in introducing it here is to show that afflictions are designed on the part of God to produce some happy effects in the lives of his people, and that they ought,

therefore, to bear them patiently. In the previous verses he directs them to the example of the Saviour. In this verse and the following, for the same object, he directs their attention to the design of trials, showing that they are necessary to our welfare, and that they are, in fact, proof of the paternal care of God. This verse might be rendered as a question, "And have ye forgotten?" &c. This mode of rendering it will agree somewhat better with the design of the apostle. ¶ *Which speaketh unto you.* Which may be regarded as addressed to you, or which involves a principle as applicable to you as to others. He does not mean that when Solomon used the words he had reference to *them* particularly, but that he used them with reference to the children of God, and that they might therefore be applied to them. In this way we may regard the language of the Scriptures as addressed to *us.* ¶ *As unto children.* As if he were addressing children. The language is such as a father uses. ¶ *My son.* It is *possible* that in these words Solomon may have intended to address a son literally, giving him paternal counsel, or he may have spoken as the head of the Jewish people, designing to address all the pious, to whom he sustained, as it were, the relation of a father. Or it is possible also that it may be regarded as the language of God himself addressing his children. Whichever supposition is adopted, the sense is substantially the same. ¶ *Despise not thou the chastening of the Lord.* Literally, "Do not regard it as a small matter or as a trivial thing"—ὀλιγώρει. The Greek word here used does not occur elsewhere in the New Testament. The word here rendered *chastening*—παιδεία—and in ver. 6, 7, 8, and the word also which occurs in ver. 9, and rendered "corrected"—παιδευτὰς—does not refer to affliction in general, but to that kind of affliction which is designed to *correct* us for our faults, or which is of the nature of *discipline.* The verb properly relates to the training up of a child, including instruction, counsel, discipline, and correction (see this use of the verb in Acts vii. 22; 2 Tim. ii. 25; Tit. ii. 12), and then especially disci-

pline or correction for faults—to *correct, chastise, chasten,* 1 Cor. xi. 32; 2 Cor. vi. 9; Rev. iii. 19. This is the meaning here; and the idea is, not that God will *afflict* his people in general, but that if they wander away he will *correct* them for their faults. He will bring calamity upon them as a *punishment* for their offences, and *in order* to bring them back to himself. He will not suffer them to wander away unrebuked and unchecked, but will mercifully reclaim them, though by great sufferings. Afflictions have many objects, and produce many happy effects. That referred to here is, that they are means of reclaiming the wandering and erring children of God, and are proofs of his paternal care and love. Comp. 2 Sam. vii. 14; xii. 13, 14; Ps. lxxxix. 31–34; Prov. iii. 11, 12. Afflictions, which are always sent by God, should not be regarded as small matters, for these reasons: (1) The fact that they *are* sent by God. Whatever he does is of importance, and is worthy of the profound attention of men. (2) They are sent for some important purpose, and they should be regarded, therefore, with attentive concern. Men *despise* them when (1) they treat them with affected or real unconcern; (2) when they fail to receive them as divine admonitions and regard them as without any intelligent design; and (3) when they receive them with *expressions* of contempt, and speak of them and of the government of God with scorn. It should be a matter of deep concern when we are afflicted in any manner not to treat the matter *lightly,* but to derive from our trials all the lessons which they are adapted to produce on the mind. ¶ *Nor faint,* &c. Bear up patiently under them. This is the second duty. We are first to study their character and design, and secondly, we are to bear up under them, however severe they may be and however long they may be continued. "Avoid the extremes of proud insensibility and entire dejection" (Doddridge).

6. *For whom the Lord loveth he chasteneth.* This is also a quotation from Prov. iii. It means that it is a universal rule that God sends trials on

6 For *d*whom the Lord loveth he chasteneth, and scourgeth every son whom he receiveth.

7 If ye endure chastening, God dealeth with you as with sons; for

d Re.3.19.

*e*what son is he whom the father chasteneth not?

8 But if ye be without chastisement, whereof all are partakers, then are ye bastards, and not sons.

e Pr.13.24.

those whom he truly loves. It does not, of course, mean that he sends chastisement which is not deserved, or that he sends it *for the mere purpose* of inflicting pain. That cannot be. But it means that, by his chastisements, he shows that he has a paternal care for us. He does not treat us with neglect and unconcern, as a father often does his illegitimate child. The very fact that he corrects us shows that he has toward us a father's feelings and exercises toward us a paternal care. If he did not, he would let us go on without any attention, and leave us to pursue a course of sin that would involve us in ruin. To restrain and govern a child, to correct him when he errs, shows that there is a parental solicitude for him, and that he is not an outcast. And as there is in the life of every child of God *something* that deserves correction, it happens that it is universally true that "whom the Lord loveth he chasteneth." ¶ *And scourgeth every son whom he receiveth.* Whom he receives or acknowledges as his child. This is not quoted literally from the Hebrew, but from the Septuagint. The Hebrew is, "even as a father the son in whom he delighteth." The general sense of the passage is retained, as is often the case in the quotations from the Old Testament. The meaning is the same as in the former part of the verse, that everyone who becomes a child of God is treated by him with that watchful care which shows that he sustains toward him the paternal relation.

7. *If ye endure chastening.* That is, if you undergo or are called to experience correction. It does not mean here, "if you endure it patiently," or "if you bear up under it," but, "if you *are* chastised or corrected by God." The affirmation does not relate to the manner of *bearing* it, but to the *fact* that we are disciplined. ¶ *God dealeth with you as with sons.* He does not

cast you off and regard you as if you were in no way related to him. ¶ *For what son is he whom the father chasteneth not?* That is, he evinces toward his son the care which shows that he sustains the relation of a father. If he deserves correction he corrects him; and he aims by all proper means to exhibit the appropriate care and character of a father. And as we receive such attention from an earthly parent we ought to expect to receive similar notice from our Father in heaven.

8. *But if ye be without chastisement.* If you never meet with anything that is adapted to correct your faults, to subdue your temper, to chide your wanderings, it would prove that you were in the condition of illegitimate children—cast, off and disregarded by their father. ¶ *Whereof all are partakers.* All who are the true children of God. ¶ *Then are ye bastards, and not sons.* The reference here is to the neglect with which such children are treated, and to the general want of care and discipline over them:

" Lost in the world's wide range; enjoin'd no aim,
Prescrib'd no duty, and assign'd no name."
SAVAGE.

In the English law, a bastard is termed *nullius filius.* Illegitimate children are usually abandoned by their father. The care of them is left to the mother, and the father endeavours to avoid all responsibility, and usually to be concealed and unknown. His own child he does not wish to recognize; he neither provides for him, nor instructs him, nor governs him, nor disciplines him. A *father* who is worthy of the name will do all these things. So Paul says it is with Christians. God has not cast them off. In every way he evinces toward them the character of a father. And if it should be that they pass along through life without any occurrence that would indicate the paternal care and atten-

9 Furthermore, we have had fathers of our flesh which corrected *us*, and we gave *them* reverence:

shall we not much rather be in subjection unto *f* the Father of spirits, and live?

f Nu.16.22; 27.16.

tion designed to correct their faults, it would show that they never had been his children, but were cast off and wholly disregarded. This is a beautiful argument; and we should receive every affliction as full proof that we are not forgotten by the High and Holy One who condescends to sustain to us the character, and to evince toward us, in our wanderings, the watchful care of a father.

9. *Furthermore.* As an additional consideration to induce us to receive chastisement with submission. The argument in this verse is derived from the difference in the spirit and design with which we are corrected by God and by an earthly parent. In God everything is without any intermingling of passion, or any improper feeling. In an earthly parent there is often much that is the result of hasty emotion, of an irascible temper, perhaps of the mere love of power. There is much that is inflicted without due reflection, and that produces only pain in the bosom of the parent himself in the recollection. Yet with all this imperfection of parental government, we were patient and unmurmuring. How much more should we submit to one whose paternal discipline is caused by no excited feeling; by no love of power; by no want of reflection; and which never furnishes occasion for regret! ¶ *Fathers of our flesh.* Earthly fathers; those from whom we have derived our being here. They are contrasted here with God, who is called "the Father of spirits," not because the father does not sustain the paternal relation to the soul as well as the body, but to designate the nature of the dominion over us. The dominion of God is that which pertains to a spiritual kingdom, having more direct reference to the discipline of the soul, and being designed to prepare us for the spiritual world; that of the earthly father pertains primarily to our condition here, and the discipline is designed to subdue our un-

ruly passions, to teach us to restrain our appetites, to impress upon us the maxims of health and prosperity, and to prevent those things which would impede our happiness in the present world. See, however, many curious instances of the manner in which these phrases were used by the Jewish writers, collected by Wetstein. ¶ *We gave* them *reverence.* We submitted to them; honoured them; loved them. Painful at the time as correction may have been, yet when we have fully understood the design of it, we have loved them the more. The effect of such discipline, properly administered, is to produce real veneration for a parent—for he who in a timely and appropriate manner restrains his child is the only one who will secure ultimate reverence and respect. ¶ *Shall we not much rather be in subjection.* Since God's government is so much more perfect; since he has so much better right to control us; and since his administration is free from all the defects which attend parental discipline on earth, there is a much higher reason for bowing with submission and reverence to him. ¶ *The Father of spirits.* Thus in Num. xvi. 22, God is called "the God of the spirits of all flesh." So also Num. xxvii. 16. Comp. Job xxxiii. 4. The idea seems to be that, as the soul is the most important part of man, this name is given to God by way of eminence, or he is eminently and supremely our Father. It was his to create the immortal part, and to that spirit which is never to die he sustains the relation of Father. The earthly father is parent to the man as mortal; God is the Father of man as immortal. God is himself a spirit. Angels and human souls, therefore, may be represented as peculiarly his offspring. It is the highest designation which could be given to God to say that he is at the head of the universe of mind; not implying that he is not also at the head

10 For they verily for a few days chastened *us* [2] after their own pleasure; but he for *our* profit, that

[2] or, *as seemed good*, or, *meet* to them.

we might be partakers of his holiness.

11 Now no chastening for the present seemeth to be joyous, but

---

of the material universe, but designing to bring into view this high prerogative of the Almighty, that all created minds throughout the universe sustain to him the relation of children. To this Great Being we should, therefore, more cheerfully subject ourselves than to an earthly parent. ¶ *And live.* Meaning that his fatherly chastisements are adapted to secure our spiritual life. He corrects us that he may promote our final happiness, and his inflictions are the means of saving us from eternal death.

10. *For they verily for a few days.* That is, with reference to a few days (προς); or it was a chastisement that had reference mainly to this short life. The apostle seems to bring in this circumstance in order to contrast the dealings of earthly parents with those of God. The corrections of earthly parents had a much less important object than those of God, as they were related mainly to this life—a life so brief that it may be said to continue but a "few days." Yet, in order to secure the benefit to be derived for so short a period from fatherly correction, we submitted without murmuring. Much more cheerfully ought we to submit to that discipline from the hand of our heavenly Father which is designed to extend its benefits through eternity. This seems to me to afford a better sense than that adopted by Prof. Stuart and others, that it means "during our childhood, or minority;" or than that which is proposed by Doddridge, that it refers *both* to our earthly parents and to our heavenly Father. ¶ *After their own pleasure.* Margin, "*as seemed good*, or *meet* to them;" meaning that it was sometimes done arbitrarily, or from caprice, or under the influence of passion. This is an additional reason why we should submit to God. We submitted to our earthly parents, though their correction was sometimes passionate, and was designed to

gratify their own pleasure rather than to promote our good. There is much of this kind of punishment in families; but there is none of it under the administration of God. ¶ *But he for our profit.* Never from passion, from caprice, from the love of power, or from mere superiority, but always for our good. The exact benefit which he designs to produce we may not be able always to understand, but we may be assured that no other cause influences him than a desire to promote our real welfare, and as he can never be mistaken in regard to the proper means to secure that, we may be assured that our trials are always *adapted* to that end. ¶ *That* we *might be partakers of his holiness.* Become so holy that it may be said that we are partakers of the very holiness of God. Comp. 2 Pet. i. 4. This is the elevated object at which God aims by our trials. It is not that he delights to produce pain; not that he envies us and would rob us of our little comforts; not that he needs what we prize to increase his own enjoyment, and therefore rudely takes it away; and not that he acts from caprice—now conferring a blessing and then withdrawing it without any reason: it is, that he may make us more pure and holy, and thus promote our own best interest. To be holy as God is holy; to be so holy that it may be said that we "are partakers of *his* holiness," is a richer blessing than health, property, and friends without it; and when by the exchange of the one we acquire the other, we have secured infinitely more than we have lost. To obtain the greater good we should be willing to part with the less; to secure the everlasting friendship and favour of God we should be willing, if necessary, to surrender the last farthing of our property; the last friend that is left us; the last feeble and fluttering pulsation of life in our veins.

11. *Now no chastening for the present seemeth to be joyous, but grievous.* It

grievous: nevertheless, afterward it yieldeth *g* the peaceable fruit of righteousness unto them which are exercised thereby.

g Is.32.17; Ja.3.18.

does not impart pleasure, nor is this its design. All chastisement is *intended* to produce pain, and the Christian is as sensitive to pain as others. His religion does not blunt his sensibilities and make him a stoic, but it rather *increases* his susceptibility to suffering. The Lord Jesus, probably, felt pain, reproach, and contempt, more keenly than any other human being ever did; and the Christian feels the loss of a child, or bodily suffering, as keenly as anyone. But while religion does not render him insensible to suffering, it does two things—(1) it enables him to bear the pain without murmuring; and (2) it turns the affliction into a blessing on his soul. ¶ *Nevertheless, afterward.* In future life. The effect is seen in a pure life, and in a more entire devotedness to God. We are not to look for the proper fruits of affliction *while* we are suffering, but *afterward.* ¶ *It yieldeth the peaceable fruit of righteousness.* It is a tree that bears good fruit, and we do not expect the fruit to form and ripen at once. It may be long maturing, but it will be rich and mellow when it is ripe. It frequently requires a long time before all the results of affliction appear—as it requires months to form and ripen fruit. Like fruit it may appear at first sour, crabbed, and unpalatable; but it will be at last like the ruddy peach or the golden orange. When those fruits *are* ripened, they are (1) fruits "*of righteousness.*" They make us more holy, more dead to sin and the world, and more alive unto God. They are (2) "*peaceable.*" They produce peace, calmness, submission in the soul. They make the heart more tranquil in its confidence in God, and more disposed to promote the religion of peace. The apostle speaks of this as if it were a *universal* truth in regard to Christians who are afflicted. And it is so. There is no Christian who

12 Wherefore *h* lift up the hands which hang down, and the feeble knees;

h Is.35.3.

is not ultimately benefited by trials, and who is not able at some period subsequently to say, "It was good for me that I was afflicted. Before I was afflicted I went astray; but now have I kept thy word." When a Christian comes to die, he does not feel that he has had one trial too many, or one which he did not deserve. He can then look back and see the effect of some early trial, so severe that he once thought he could hardly endure it, spreading a hallowed influence over his future years, and scattering its golden fruit all along the pathway of life. I have never known a Christian who was not benefited by afflictions; I have seen no one who was not able to say that his trials produced some happy effects on his religious character, and on his real happiness in life. If this be so, then no matter how severe our trials, we should submit to them without a murmur. The more severe they are, the more we shall yet be blessed—on earth, or in heaven.

12. *Wherefore.* In view of the facts which have been now stated—that afflictions are sent from God, and that they are evidences of his paternal watchfulness. ¶ *Lift up the hands which hang down.* As if from weariness and exhaustion. Renew your courage; make a new effort to bear them. The hands fall by the side when we are exhausted with toil, or worn down by disease. See Notes on Isa. xxxv. 3, from which place this exhortation is taken. ¶ *And the feeble knees.* The knees also become enfeebled by long effort, and tremble as if their strength were gone. Courage and resolution may do much, however, to make them firm, and it is to this that the apostle exhorts those to whom he wrote. They were to make every effort to bear up under their trials. The hope of victory will do much to strengthen one almost exhausted in battle; the desire to reach

13 And ⁱmake ³straight paths for your feet, lest that which is lame be turned out of the way; but ᵏlet it rather be healed.

i Pr.4.26,27. *3* or, *even.* *k* Ga.6.1.

home invigorates the frame of the weary traveller. So it is with the Christian. In persecution, sickness, and bereavement, he may be ready to sink under his burdens. The hands fall, the knees tremble, and the heart sinks within us. But confidence in God, the hope of heaven, and the assurance that all this is for our good, will reinvigorate the enfeebled frame, and enable us to bear what we once supposed would crush us to the dust. A courageous mind braces a feeble body, and hope makes it fresh for new conflicts.

13. *And make straight paths for your feet.* Margin, *even.* The word here used means properly *straight,* in the sense of *upright, erect,* Acts xiv. 10; but it is here used in the sense of straight *horizontally,* that is, *level, plain, smooth.* The meaning is, that they were to remove all obstacles out of the way, so that they need not stumble and fall. There is probably an allusion here to Prov. iv. 25–27, "Let thine eyes look right on, and let thine eyelids look straight before thee. Ponder the path of thy feet, and let all thy ways be established. Turn not to the right hand nor to the left: remove thy foot from evil." The idea is, that, by every proper means, they were to make the way to heaven as plain and easy as possible. They were to allow no obstruction in the path over which the lame and feeble might fall. ¶ *Lest that which is lame be turned out of the way.* A lame man needs a smooth path to walk in. The idea is here, that everything which would prevent those in the church who were in any danger of falling—the feeble, the unestablished, the weak—from walking in the path to heaven, or which might be an occasion to them of falling, should be removed. Or it may mean, that in a road that was not level, those who were lame would be in danger of

14 Follow ˡ peace with all *men,* and holiness, ᵐwithout which no man shall see the Lord :

l Ps.34.14. *m* Mat.5.8; Ep.5.5.

spraining, distorting, or wrenching a lame limb; and the counsel is, that whatever would have a tendency to this should be removed. Divested of the figure, the passage means, that everything should be removed which would hinder anyone from walking in the path to life. ¶ *But let it rather be healed.* As in the case of lameness pains should be taken to heal it rather than to suffer it to be increased by careless exposure to a new sprain or fracture, so it should be in our religious and moral character. Whatever is defective we should endeavour to restore to soundness, rather than to suffer the defect to be increased. Whatever is feeble in our faith or hope we should endeavour to strengthen and amend, lest it should become worse, and we should entirely fall.

14. *Follow peace with all* men. Do not give indulgence to those passions which lead to litigations, strifes, wars. See Notes on Rom. xiv. 19. The connection here requires us to understand this mainly of persecutors. The apostle is referring to the trials which those whom he addressed were experiencing. Those trials seem to have arisen mainly from persecution, and he exhorts them to manifest a spirit of kindness toward *all*—even though they were engaged in persecuting them. This is the temper of the gospel. We are to make war with *sin,* but not with *men;* with bad passions and corrupt desires, but not with our fellow-worms. ¶ *And holiness.* Instead of yielding to contending passions and to a spirit of war; instead of seeking revenge on your persecutors and foes, make it rather your aim to be holy. Let *that* be the object of your pursuit; the great purpose of your life. Men might in such cases counsel them to seek revenge; the spirit of religion would counsel them to strive to be holy. In such times they were in great danger of giving indulgence to evil passions, and hence

15 Looking[n] diligently lest any man [4]fail of the grace of God; lest

n 2 Pe.1.10. 4 or, *fall from.*

the special propriety of the exhortation to be holy. ¶ *Without which no man shall see the Lord.* That is, shall see him in peace, or shall so see him as to dwell with him. *All* will see him in the day of judgment (Rev. i. 7), but to "*see*" one is often used in the sense of being with one, dwelling with one, enjoying one. See Notes on Mat. v. 8. The principle here stated is one which is never departed from, Rev. xxi. 27; Isa. xxxv. 8; lii. 1; lx. 21; Joel iii. 17; Mat. xiii. 41; 1 Cor. vi. 9, 10. No one *has* ever been admitted to heaven in his sins, nor is it desirable that anyone ever should be. Desirable as it is that lost men should be happy, yet it is *benevolence* which excludes the profane, the impious, and the unbelieving from heaven, just as it is benevolence to a family to exclude profligates and seducers, and as it is benevolence to a community to confine thieves and robbers in prison. This great principle in the divine administration will *always* be adhered to; and hence they who are expecting to be saved without holiness or religion are destined to certain disappointment. Heaven and earth will pass away, but God will not admit one unrepenting and unpardoned sinner to heaven. It was the importance and the certainty of this principle which made the apostle insist on it here with so much earnestness. Amidst all their trials, when exposed to persecution, and when everything might tempt them to the indulgence of feelings which were the opposite of holiness, they were to make it their great object to be like God. For this they were to strive, to labour, to pray. This with *us* in all our trials should also be the great aim of life. How deeply affecting, then, is the inquiry whether *we* have that holiness which is indispensable to salvation! Let us not deceive ourselves. We may have many things else—many things which are in themselves desirable—but without this *one* thing we shall never see the Lord in peace. We may have wealth, genius, learning, beauty, accom-

any [o]root of bitterness springing up trouble *you*, and thereby many be defiled;

o De.29.18.

plishments, houses, lands, books, friends; but without religion they will be all in vain. Never *can* we see God in peace without a holy heart, never can we be admitted into heaven without that religion which will identify us with the angels around the throne.

15. *Looking diligently.* This phrase denotes close attention. It is implied that there are *reasons* why we should take special care lest we should fail of the favour of God. Those reasons are found in the propensities of our hearts to evil, in the temptations of the world, in the allurements to apostasy offered by the great adversary of our souls. ¶ *Lest any man fail.* As every man is in danger, it is his personal duty to see to it that his salvation be secure. ¶ *Fail of the grace of God.* Margin, *fall from.* The Greek is, "Lest any-one *be wanting* or *lacking*"—ὑστερῶν. There is no intimation in the words used here that they already *had* grace and might fall away—whatever might be true about that — but that there was danger that they might be found at last to be *deficient* in that religion which was necessary to save them. Whether this was to be by *losing* the religion which they now had or by the fact that they never *had* any—however near they may have come to it—the apostle does not here intimate, and *this* passage should not be used in the discussion of the question about falling from grace. It is a proper exhortation to be addressed to any man in the church or out of it to inquire diligently whether there is not reason to apprehend that when he comes to appear before God he will be found to be wholly destitute of religion. ¶ *Lest any root of bitterness springing up.* Any bitter root. There is, doubtless, an allusion here to Deut. xxix. 18, "Lest there should be among you man, or woman, or family, or tribe, whose heart turneth away this day from the Lord our God, to go and serve the gods of these nations; lest there should be among

16 Lest there *be* any *p*fornicator, or profane person, as Esau, *q*who for one morsel of meat sold his birthright.

p 1 Co.6.13,18.   *q* Ge.25.33.

you a root that beareth gall and wormwood." The allusion in that passage is to those who were idolaters, and who, instead of bearing the fruits of righteousness and promoting the piety and happiness of the nation, would bear the fruits of idolatry and spread abroad irreligion and sin. The allusion, in both cases, is to a bitter plant springing up among those that were cultivated for ornament or use, or to a tree bearing bitter and poisonous fruit among those that produced good fruit. The reference of the apostle is to some person who might produce a similar effect in the church—to one who should inculcate false doctrines, or who should apostatize, or who should lead an unholy life, and thus be the means of corrupting and destroying others. They were to be at especial pains that no such person should start up from among themselves or be tolerated by them. ¶ *Trouble* you. By his doctrines and example. ¶ *And thereby many be defiled.* Led away from the faith and corrupted. One wicked man, and especially one hypocrite in the church, may be the means of destroying many others.

16. *Lest there* be *any fornicator.* The sin here referred to is one of those which would spread corruption in the church, and against which they ought to be especially on their guard. Allusion is made to Esau as an example, who, himself a corrupt and profane man, for a trifle threw away the highest honour which as a son he could have. Many have regarded the word here used as referring to *idolatry*, or defection from the true religion to a false one—as the word is often used in the Old Testament—but it is more natural to understand it literally. The crime here mentioned was one which abounded everywhere in ancient times, as it does now, and it was important to guard the church against it. See Notes on Acts xv. 20; 1 Cor. vi. 18. ¶ *Or profane person.* The word *profane* here refers to one who by word

or conduct treats religion with contempt, or has no reverence for that which is sacred. This may be shown by words, by the manner, by a sneer, by neglect of religion, or by openly renouncing the privileges which might be connected with our salvation. The allusion here is to one who should openly cast off all the hopes of religion for indulgence in temporary pleasure, as Esau gave up his birthright for a trifling gratification. In a similar manner the young, for temporary gratification, neglect or despise the privileges and hopes resulting from their being born in the bosom of the church, from being baptized and consecrated to God, and from being trained up in the lap of piety. ¶ *As Esau.* It is clearly implied here that Esau sustained the character of a fornicator and a profane person. The former appellation is probably given to him to denote his licentiousness, shown by his marrying many wives, and particularly foreigners, or the daughters of Canaan. See Gen. xxxvi. 2; comp. Gen. xxvi. 34, 35. The Jewish writers abundantly declare that that was his character. See Wetstein, *in loco.* In proof that the latter appellation—that of a profane person—belonged to him, see Gen. xxv. 29–34. It is true that it is rather by inference than by direct assertion that it is known that he sustained this character. The birthright, in his circumstances, was a high honour. The promise respecting the inheritance of the land of Canaan, the coming of the Messiah, and the preservation of the true religion had been given to Abraham and Isaac, and was to be transmitted by them. As the eldest son, all the honour connected with this, and which is now associated with the name *Jacob*, would have properly appertained to Esau. But he undervalued it. He lived a licentious life. He followed his corrupt propensities and gave the reins to indulgence. In a time of temporary distress, also, he showed how little he really valued all this by bartering it away for a single

17 For ye know how that after-ward, *r* when he would have inherited the blessing, he was re-

jected : for he found no [5]place of repentance, though he sought it carefully with tears.

r Ge.27.34-38.

[5] or, *way to change his mind.*

---

meal of victuals. Rather than bear the pain of hunger for a short period, and evidently in a manner implying a great undervaluing of the honour which he held as the first-born son in a pious line, he agreed to surrender all the privileges connected with his birth. It was this which made the appellation appropriate to him; and this will make the appellation appropriate in any similar instance. ¶ *Who for one morsel of meat.* The word *meat* here is used, as it is commonly in the Scriptures, in its primitive sense in English, to denote *food,* Gen. xxv. 34. The phrase here, "morsel of meat," would be better rendered by "a single meal." ¶ *Sold his birthright.* The birthright seems to have implied the first place or rank in the family, the privilege of offering sacrifice and conducting worship in the absence or death of the father, a double share of the inheritance, and, in this instance, the honour of being in the line of the patriarchs and transmitting the promises made to Abraham and Isaac. What Esau parted with we can easily understand by reflecting on the honours which have clustered around the name of Jacob.

17. *For ye know how that afterward,* &c. When he came to his father, and earnestly besought him to reverse the sentence which he had pronounced. See Gen. xxvii. 34-40. The "blessing" here referred to was not that of the birthright, which he knew he could not regain, but that pronounced by his father Isaac on him whom he regarded as his first-born son. This Jacob obtained by fraud, when Isaac really *meant* to bestow it on Esau. Isaac appears to have been ignorant wholly of the bargain which Jacob and Esau had made in regard to the birthright, and Jacob and his mother contrived in this way to have that confirmed which Jacob had obtained of Esau by contract. The sanction of the father, it seems, was

necessary, before it could be made sure, and Rebecca and Jacob understood that the dying blessing of the aged patriarch would establish it all. It was obtained by dishonesty on the part of Jacob; but so far as Esau was concerned, it was an act of righteous retribution for the little regard he had shown for the honour of his birth. ¶ *For he found no place of repentance.* Margin, "*way to change his mind.*" That is, no place for repentance *in the mind of Isaac,* or no way to change *his* mind. It does not mean that Esau earnestly sought to repent and could not, but that when once the blessing had passed the lips of his father he found it impossible to change it. Isaac firmly declared that he *had pronounced* the blessing, and though it had been obtained by fraud, yet, as it was of the nature of a divine prediction, it *could* not now be changed. He had not, indeed, intended that it should be thus. He had pronounced a blessing on another which had been designed for him. But still the benediction had been given. The prophetic words had been pronounced. By divine direction the *truth* had been spoken, and how *could* it be changed? It was impossible now to reverse the divine purposes in the case, and hence the "blessing" must stand as it had been spoken. Isaac did, however, all that *could* be done. He *gave* a benediction to his son Esau, though of far inferior value to that which he had pronounced on the fraudulent Jacob, Gen. xxvii. 39, 40. ¶ *Though he sought it carefully with tears.* Gen. xxvii. 34. He sought to change the purpose of his father, but could not do it. The meaning and bearing of this passage, as used by the apostle, may be easily understood. (1) The decision of God on the human character and destiny will soon be pronounced. That decision will be according to truth, and cannot be changed. (2) If we should despise our privileges as Esau did his

18 For ye are not come unto the* mount that might be touched,

*Ex. 19.12-19.

and that burned with fire, nor unto blackness, and darkness, and tempest,

birthright, and renounce our religion, it would be impossible to recover what we had lost. There would be no possibility of changing the divine decision in the case, for it would be determined for ever. (3) This passage should not be alleged to show that a sinner *cannot* repent, or that he cannot find "place for repentance," or assistance to enable him to repent, or that tears and sorrow for sin would be of no avail, for it teaches none of these things; but it *should* be used to keep us from disregarding our privileges, from turning away from the true religion, from slighting the favours of the gospel, and from neglecting religion till death comes; because when God has once pronounced a sentence excluding us from his favour, no tears, or pleading, or effort, of our own can change *him*. The sentence which *he* pronounces on the scoffer, the impenitent, the hypocrite, and the apostate, is one that will abide for ever without change. This passage, therefore, is in accordance with the doctrine more than once stated before in this epistle, that if a Christian should really apostatize it would be impossible that he should be saved. See Notes on chap. vi. 1–6.

18. *For ye are not come.* To enforce the considerations already urged, the apostle introduces this sublime comparison between the old and new dispensations, ver. 18–24. The object, in accordance with the principal scope of the epistle, is to guard them against apostasy. To do this, he shows that under the new dispensation there was much more to bind them to fidelity, and to make apostasy dangerous, than there was under the old. The main point of the comparison is, that under the Jewish dispensation, everything was adapted to awe the mind, and to restrain by the exhibition of grandeur and of power; but that, under the Christian dispensation, while there was as much that was sublime, there was much more that was adapted to

win and hold the affections. There were revelations of higher truths. There were more affecting motives to lead to obedience. There was that of which the former was but the type and emblem. There was the clear revelation of the glories of heaven, and of the blessed society there, both of them adapted to prompt to the earnest desire that they might be our own. The considerations presented in this passage constitute the climax of the argument so beautifully pursued through this epistle, showing that the Christian system was far superior in every respect to the Jewish. In this closing argument, the apostle first refers to some of the circumstances attending the former dispensation which were designed to keep the people of God from apostasy, and then the considerations of superior weight existing under the Christian economy. ¶ *The mount that might be touched.* Mount Sinai. The meaning here is, that *that* mountain was *palpable, material, touchable*—in contradistinction from the Mount Zion to which the church had now come, which is above the reach of the external senses, ver. 22. The apostle does not mean that it was *permitted* to the Israelites to touch Mount Sinai—for this was strictly forbidden, Ex. xix. 12; but he evidently alludes to that prohibition, and means to say that a command forbidding them to "touch" the mountain, implied that it was a material or palpable object. The sense of the passage is, that all that occurred there was fitted to fill the soul with terror. Everything accompanying the giving of the law, the setting of bounds around the mountain which they might not pass, and the darkness and tempest on the mountain itself, was adapted to overawe the soul. The phrase "the *touchable* mountain"—if such a phrase is proper—would express the meaning of the apostle here. The "Mount Zion" to which the church now has

19 And the sound of a trumpet, and the voice of words; *t* which *voice* they that heard entreated that the word should not be spoken to them any more:

20 (For they could not endure

t Ex.20.18,19.

that which was commanded, *u* And if so much as a beast touch the mountain, it shall be stoned, or thrust through with a dart:

21 And so terrible was the sight, *that* Moses said, I exceedingly fear and quake:)

u Ex.19.13,16.

come, is of a different character. It is not thus visible and palpable. It is not enveloped in smoke and flame, and the thunders of the Almighty do not roll and re-echo among its lofty peaks as at Horeb; yet it presents *stronger* motives to perseverance in the service of God. ¶ *And that burned with fire.* Ex. xix. 18. Comp. Deut. iv. 11; xxxiii. 2. ¶ *Nor unto blackness, and darkness, and tempest.* See Ex. xix. 16.

19. *And the sound of a trumpet.* Ex. xix. 19. The sound of the trumpet amidst the tempest was fitted to increase the terror of the scene. ¶ *And the voice of words.* Spoken by God, Ex. xix. 19. It is easy to conceive what must have been the awe produced by a voice uttered from the midst of the tempest so distinct as to be heard by the hundreds of thousands of Israel, when the speaker was invisible. ¶ *Which* voice *they that heard,* &c. Ex. xx. 18, 19. It was so fearful and overpowering that the people earnestly prayed that if they must be addressed it might be by the familiar voice of Moses, and not by the awful voice of the Deity.

20. *For they could not endure that which was commanded.* They could not sustain the awe produced by the fact that God uttered his commands himself. The meaning is not that the commands themselves were intolerable, but that the *manner* in which they were communicated inspired a terror which they could not bear. They feared that they would die, Ex. xx. 19. ¶ *And if so much as a beast touch the mountain, it shall be stoned.* Ex. xix. 13. The prohibition was, that neither beast nor man should touch it on pain of death. The punishment was to be either by stoning, or being "shot through." ¶ *Or thrust through with a dart.* Ex. xix. 13. This phrase, how-

ever, though it is found in the common editions of the New Testament, is wanting in all the more valuable manuscripts; in all the ancient versions; and it occurs in none of the Greek ecclesiastical writers, with one exception. It is omitted now by almost all editors of the New Testament. It is beyond all doubt an addition of later times, taken from the Septuagint of Ex. xix. 13. Its omission does not injure the sense.

21. *And so terrible was the sight,* that *Moses said,* &c. This is not recorded in the account of the giving of the law in Exodus, and it has been made a question on what authority the apostle made this declaration respecting Moses. In Deut. ix. 19, Moses indeed says, of himself, after he had come down from the mountain, and had broken the two tables of stone that were in his hand, that he was greatly afraid of the anger of the Lord on account of the sin of the people. "I was afraid of the anger and hot displeasure wherewith the Lord was wroth against you to destroy you;" and it has been supposed by many that this is the passage to which the apostle here alludes. But it is very evident that that was spoken on a different occasion from the one which is referred to in the passage before us. That was *after* the law was promulgated, and Moses had descended from the mount; and it was not said in view of the terrors of the scene *when* the law was given, but of the apprehension of the wrath of God against the people for their sin in making the golden calf. I know not how to explain this, except by the supposition that the apostle here refers to some tradition that the scene produced this effect on the mind of Moses. In itself it is not improbable that Moses

22 But ye are come unto mount Sion, and unto *v*the city of the living God, the heavenly Jeru-

v Re.3.12.

salem, and to *w*an innumerable company of angels,

w Ps.68.17.

thus trembled with alarm (compare Ex. xix. 16), nor that the remembrance of it should have been handed down among the numerous traditions which the Jews transmitted from age to age. There must have been many things that occurred in their journey through the wilderness which are not recorded in the Books of Moses. Many of them would be preserved naturally in the memory of the people, and transmitted to their posterity; and though those truths might become intermingled with much that was fabulous, yet it is not irrational to suppose that an inspired writer may have adduced pertinent and true examples from these traditions of what actually occurred. It was one method of preserving *the truth*, thus to select such instances of what actually took place as would be useful in future times, from the mass of traditions which were destined to perish. The circumstance here mentioned was greatly fitted to increase the impression of the sublimity and fearfulness of the scene. Moses was accustomed to commune with God. He had met him at the "bush," and had been addressed by him face to face, and yet so awful were the scenes at Horeb, that even *he* could not bear it with composure. What may we then suppose to have been the alarm of the body of the people, when the mind of the great leader himself was thus overpowered!

22. *But ye are come unto mount Sion.* You who are Christians; all who are under the new dispensation. The design is to *contrast* the Christian dispensation with the Jewish, and to show that its excellencies and advantages were far superior to the religion of their fathers. It had more to win the affections; more to elevate the soul; more to inspire with hope. It had less that was terrific and alarming; it appealed less to the fears and more to the hopes of mankind; but

still apostasy from this religion could not be less terrible in its consequences than apostasy from the religion of Moses. In the passage before us, the apostle evidently contrasts Sinai with Mount Zion, and means to say that there was more about the latter that was adapted to win the heart, and to preserve allegiance, than there was about the former. Mount Zion literally denoted the southern hill in Jerusalem, on which a part of the city was built. That part of the city was made by David and his successors the residence of the court, and soon the name *Zion* was given familiarly to the whole city. Jerusalem was the centre of religion in the land; the place where the temple stood, where the worship of God was celebrated, and where God dwelt by a visible symbol; and it became the type and emblem of the holy abode where He dwells in heaven. It cannot be literally meant here that they had come to the Mount Zion in Jerusalem, for that was as true of the whole Jewish people as of those whom the apostle addressed; but it must mean that they had come to the Mount Zion of which the holy city was an emblem; to the glorious mount which is revealed as the dwelling-place of God, of angels, of saints—that is, they had "come" to this by the revelations and hopes of the gospel. They were not, indeed, literally in heaven, nor was that glorious city literally on earth, but the dispensation to which they had been brought was that which conducted them directly up to the city of the living God, and to the holy mount where he dwelt above. The view was not confined to an earthly mountain enveloped in smoke and flame, but opened at once on the holy place where God abides. By the phrase "ye *are* come," the apostle means that this was the characteristic of the new dispensation, that it conducted them there, and that they were already, in fact, inhabitants of that glorious city. They were citi-

23 To the general assembly and church *x* of the first-born, *y* which are [6] written in heaven, and to God

x Re.14.4.   *y* Lu.10.20.   [6] or, *enrolled*.

zens of the heavenly Jerusalem (comp. Notes on Phil. iii. 20), and were entitled to its privileges. ¶ *And unto the city of the living God.* The city where the living God dwells—the heavenly Jerusalem. Comp. Notes on chap. xi. 10. God dwelt by a visible symbol in the temple at Jerusalem, and to *that* his people came under the old dispensation. In a more literal and glorious sense his abode is in heaven, and to *that* his people have now come. ¶ *The heavenly Jerusalem.* Heaven is not unfrequently represented as a magnificent city where God and angels dwell; and the Christian revelation discloses this to Christians as certainly their final home. They should regard themselves already as dwellers in that city, and live and act *as if* they saw its splendour and partook of its joy. In regard to this representation of heaven as a *city* where God dwells, the following places may be consulted: Heb. xi. 10, 14–16; xii. 28; xiii. 14; Gal. iv. 26; Rev. iii. 12; xxi. 2, 10–27. It is true that Christians have not yet *seen* that city by the bodily eye, but they look to it with the eye of faith. It is revealed to them; they are permitted by anticipation to contemplate its glories, and to feel that it is to be their eternal home. They are permitted to live and act *as if* they saw the glorious God whose dwelling is there, and were already surrounded by the angels and the redeemed. The apostle does not represent them as if they were expecting that it would be visibly set up on the earth, but as being now actually dwellers in that city, and bound to live and act *as if* they were amidst its splendours. Comp. Notes on Phil. iii. 20. ¶ *And to an innumerable company of angels.* The Greek here is, "to myriads [or ten thousands] of angels in an assembly, or joyful convocation." The phrase "tens of thousands" is often used to denote a great and indefinite number.

the *z* Judge of all, and to [a] the spirits of just men made perfect,

z Ge.18.25.   [a] 1 Co.15.49,54.

The word rendered "general assembly" (ver. 22) — πανήγυρις — refers properly to "an assembly or convocation of the whole people in order to celebrate any public festival or solemnity, as the public games or sacrifices" (Rob. *Lex.*). It occurs nowhere else in the New Testament, and refers here to the angels viewed as assembled around the throne of God and celebrating his praises. It should be regarded as connected with the word *angels*, referring to *their* convocation in heaven, and not to the church of the first-born. This construction is demanded by the Greek. Our common translation renders it as if it were to be united with the church— "to the general assembly *and* church of the first-born;" but the Greek will not admit of this construction. The interpretation which unites it with the *angels* is adopted now by almost all critics, and in almost all the editions of the New Testament, meaning "to myriads of angels in full assembly." On the convocation of angels, see Notes on Job i. 6. The writer intends doubtless to contrast that joyful assemblage of the angels in heaven with those who appeared in the giving of the law on Mount Sinai. God is always represented as surrounded by hosts of angels in heaven. See Deut. xxxiii. 2; 1 Ki. xxii. 19; Dan. vii. 10; Ps. lxviii. 17. Comp. Notes on Heb. xii. 1. See also Rev. v. 11; Mat. xxvi. 53; Luke ii. 13. The meaning is, that, under the Christian dispensation, Christians, in their feelings and worship, become united to this vast host of holy angelic beings. It is, of course, not meant that they are *visible*, but they are seen by the eye of faith. The *argument* here is, that as, in virtue of the Christian revelation, we become associated with those pure and happy spirits, we should not apostatize from such a religion, for we should regard it as honourable and glorious to be identified with them.

23. *To the general assembly.* See

24 And to Jesus the *ᵇmediator* of the new ⁷covenant, and to *ᶜthe* blood of sprinkling, that speaketh better things than *ᵈthat of* Abel.

ᵇ ch.8.6.   ⁷ or, testament.   ᶜ Ex.24.8.   *ᵈ Ge.4.10.*

Notes on ver. 22. ¶ *And church of the first-born.* That is, you are united with the church of the first-born. They who were first-born among the Hebrews enjoyed peculiar privileges, and especially pre-eminence of rank. See Notes on Col. i. 15. The reference here is, evidently, to those saints who had been distinguished for their piety, and who may be supposed to be exalted to peculiar honours in heaven— such as the patriarchs, prophets, martyrs. The meaning is, that by becoming Christians, we are in fact identified with that happy and honoured church, and that this is a powerful motive to induce us to persevere. It is a consideration which should make us adhere to our religion amidst all temptations and persecutions, that we are identified with the most eminently holy men who have lived, and that we are to share their honours and their joys. The Christian is united in feeling, in honour, and in destiny, with the excellent of all the earth and of all times. He should feel it, therefore, an honour to be a Christian; he should yield to no temptation which would induce him to part from so goodly a fellowship. ¶ *Which are written in heaven.* Margin, *enrolled.* The word here used was employed by the Greeks to denote that one was enrolled as a citizen, or entitled to the privileges of citizenship. Here it means, that the names of the persons referred to were registered or enrolled among the inhabitants of the heavenly world. See Notes on Luke x. 20. ¶ *And to God the Judge of all.* God, who will pronounce the final sentence on all mankind. The object of the reference here to God as *Judge* does not appear to be to contrast the condition of Christians with that of the Jews, as is the case in some of the circumstances alluded to, but to bring impressively before their minds the fact that they sustained a peculiarly near relation to him from whom all were to receive their final allotment. As the destiny

of all depended on him, they should be careful not to provoke his wrath. The design of the apostle seems to be to give a rapid glance of what there is in heaven, as disclosed by the eye of faith to the Christian, which should operate as a motive to induce him to persevere in his Christian course. The thought that seems to have struck his mind in regard to God was, that he will do right to all. They had, therefore, everything to fear if they revolted from him; they had everything to hope if they bore their trials with patience, and persevered to the end. ¶ *And to the spirits of just men made perfect.* Not only to the more eminent saints—the " church of the first-born "—but to *all* who were made perfect in heaven. They were not only united with the imperfect Christians on earth, but with those who have become completely delivered from sin, and have been admitted to the world of glory. This is a consideration which ought to influence the minds of all believers. They are even now united with *all* the redeemed in heaven. They should, therefore, so live as not to be separated from them in the final day. Most Christians have among the redeemed already not a few of their most tenderly beloved friends. A father may be there; a mother, a sister, a smiling babe. It should be a powerful motive with us so to live as to be prepared to be reunited with them in heaven.

24. *And to Jesus the mediator of the new covenant.* This was the crowning excellence of the new dispensation in contradistinction from the old. They had been made acquainted with the true Messiah; they were united to him by faith; they had been sprinkled with his blood. See Notes on chap. vii. 22, and chap. viii. 6. The highest consideration which can be urged to induce anyone to persevere in a life of piety is the fact that the Son of God has come into the world and died to save sinners. Comp. Notes on ver.

25 See that ye refuse not him that speaketh : for if they escaped not who refused him that spake on

earth, much more *shall not* we *escape*, if we turn away from him that *speaketh* from heaven :

2–4 of this chapter. ¶ *And to the blood of sprinkling.* The blood which Jesus shed, and which is sprinkled upon us to ratify the covenant. See Notes on chap. ix. 18–23. ¶ *That speaketh better things than* that of *Abel.* Greek, "than Abel;" the words "*that of*" being supplied by the translators. In the original there is no reference to the blood of Abel shed by Cain, as our translators seem to have supposed, but the allusion is to the faith of Abel, or to the testimony which he bore to a great and vital truth of religion. The meaning here is, that the blood of Jesus speaks better things than Abel did; that is, that the blood of Jesus is the *reality* of which the offering of Abel was a *type.* Abel proclaimed by the sacrifice which he made the great truth that salvation could be only by a bloody offering—but he did this only in a typical and obscure manner; Jesus proclaimed it in a more distinct and better manner by the reality. The object here is to compare the Redeemer with Abel, not in the sense that the blood shed in either case calls for vengeance, but that salvation by blood is more clearly revealed in the Christian plan than in the ancient history; and hence illustrating, in accordance with the design of this epistle, the superior excellency of the Christian scheme over all which had preceded it. There were *other* points of resemblance between Abel and the Redeemer, but on them the apostle does not insist. Abel was a martyr, and so was Christ; Abel was cruelly murdered, and so was Christ; there was aggravated guilt in the murder of Abel by his brother, and so there was in that of Jesus by his brethren— his own countrymen; the blood of Abel called for vengeance, and was followed by a fearful penalty on Cain, and so was the death of the Redeemer on his murderers—for they said, "his blood be on us and on our children," and they are yet suffering under the fearful malediction then invoked;—

but the point of contrast here is, that the blood of Jesus makes a more full, distinct, and clear proclamation of the truth that salvation is by blood than the offering made by Abel did. The apostle alludes here to what he had said in chap. xi. 4. See Notes on that verse. Such is the contrast between the former and the latter dispensations; and such the motives to perseverance presented by both. In the former, the Jewish, all was imperfect, terrific, alarming. In the latter everything is comparatively mild, winning, alluring, animating. Terror is not the principal element, but heaven is opened to the eye of faith, and the Christian is permitted to survey the Mount Zion; the New Jerusalem; the angels; the redeemed ; the blessed God; the glorious Mediator, and to feel that that blessed abode is to be his home. To that happy world he is tending; and with all these pure and glorious beings he is identified. Having stated and urged this argument, the apostle in the remainder of the chapter warns those whom he addresses in a most solemn manner against a renunciation of their Christian faith.

25. *See that ye refuse not.* That you do not reject or disregard. ¶ *Him that speaketh.* That is, in the gospel. Do not turn away from him who has addressed you in the new dispensation, and called you to obey and serve him. The meaning is, that God had addressed *them* in the gospel as really as he had done the Hebrews on Mount Sinai, and that there is as much to be dreaded in disregarding his voice now as there was then. He does not speak, indeed, amidst lightnings, and thunders, and clouds, but he speaks by every message of mercy; by every invitation; by every tender appeal. He spake by his Son (chap. i. 1); he speaks by the Holy Spirit; he speaks by all his calls and warnings in the gospel. ¶ *For if they escaped not.* If they who heard God under the old dispensation, and who refused to obey

26 Whose voice then shook the earth: but now he hath promised, saying, *Yet once more I shake not the earth only, but also heaven.

27 And this *word*, Yet once

e Hag.2.6.

more, signifieth the removing of those things that [8]are shaken, as of things that are made, that those things which cannot be shaken may remain.

[8] or, *may be.*

---

him, were cut off. See Notes on chap. x. 28. ¶ *Who refused him that spake on earth.* That is, Moses. The contrast here is between Moses and the Son of God—the head of the Jewish and the head of the Christian dispensation. Moses was a mere man, and spake as such, though in the name of God. The Son of God was from above, and spake as an inhabitant of heaven. ¶ *Much more,* &c. See Notes on chap. ii. 2, 3; ix. 29.

26. *Whose voice then shook the earth.* When he spake at Mount Sinai. The meaning is, that the mountain and the region around quaked, Ex. xix. 18. The "voice" here referred to is that of God speaking from the holy mount. ¶ *But now hath he promised, saying.* The words here quoted are taken from Hag. ii. 6, where they refer to the changes which would take place under the Messiah. The meaning is, that there would be great revolutions in his coming, *as if* the universe were shaken to its centre. The apostle evidently applies this passage, as it is done in Haggai, to the first advent of the Redeemer. ¶ *I shake not the earth only.* This is not quoted literally from the Hebrew, but the sense is retained. In Haggai it is, "Yet once, it is a little while, and I will shake the heavens, and the earth, and the sea, and the dry land; and I will shake all nations, and the desire of all nations shall come." The apostle lays emphasis on the fact that not only the *earth* was to be shaken but also *heaven.* The shaking of the earth here evidently refers to the commotions among the nations that would prepare the way for the coming of the Messiah. ¶ *But also heaven.* This may refer either (1) to the extraordinary phenomena in the heavens at the birth, the death, and the ascension of Christ; or (2) to the revolutions in morals and religion which would be caused by the intro-

duction of the gospel, as if everything were to be changed—expressed by " a shaking of the heavens and the earth;" or (3) it may be more literally taken as denoting that there was a remarkable agitation in the heavens—in the bosoms of its inhabitants—arising from a fact so wonderful as that the Son of God should descend to earth, suffer, and die. I see no reason to doubt that the latter idea may have been included here; and the meaning of the whole then is, that while the giving of the law at Mount Sinai, fearful and solemn as it was, was an event that merely shook the earth in the vicinity of the holy mount, the introduction of the gospel agitated the universe. Great changes upon the earth were to precede it; one revolution was to succeed another preparatory to it; and the whole universe would be moved at an event so extraordinary. The meaning is, that the introduction of the gospel was a much more solemn and momentous thing than the giving of the law, and that, therefore, it was much more fearful and dangerous to apostatize from it.

27. *And this* word, Yet once more. That is, this reference to a great agitation or commotion in some future time. This is designed as an explanation of the prophecy in Haggai, and the idea is, that there would be such agitations that everything which was not fixed on a permanent and immovable basis would be thrown down as in an earthquake. Everything which was temporary in human institutions; everything which was wrong in customs and morals; and everything in the ancient system of religion which was merely of a preparatory and typical character, would be removed. What was of permanent value would be retained, and a kingdom would be established which nothing could move. The effect of the gospel would be to

28 Wherefore we receiving a kingdom which cannot be moved,

let us [9]have grace, whereby we

9 or, *hold fast.*

---

overturn all which was of a temporary character in the previous system, and all in morals which was not founded on a solid basis, and to set up in the place of these principles which no revolution and no time could change. The coming of the Saviour, and the influence of his religion on mankind, had this effect in such respects as the following: (1) All that was of a sound and permanent nature in the Jewish economy was retained; all that was typical and temporary was removed. The whole mass of sacrifices and ceremonies that were designed to prefigure the Messiah of course then ceased; all that was of permanent value in the law of God, and in the principles of religion, was incorporated in the new system and perpetuated. (2) The same is true in regard to morals. There was much truth on the earth before the time of the Saviour; but it was intermingled with much that was false. The effect of his coming has been to distinguish what is true and what is false; to give permanency to the one, and to cause the other to vanish. (3) The same is true of religion. There are some views of religion which men have by nature which are correct; there are many which are false. The Christian religion gives permanence and stability to the one, and causes the other to disappear. And in general, it may be remarked, that the effect of Christianity is to give stability to all that is founded on truth, and to drive error from the world. Christ came that he might destroy all the systems of error—that is, all that *could* be shaken on earth, and to confirm all that is true. The result of all will be that he will preside over a *permanent* kingdom, and that his people will inherit "a kingdom which cannot be moved," ver. 28. ¶ *The removing of those things that are shaken.* Margin, more correctly, "*may be.*" The meaning is, that those principles of religion and morals which were not founded on truth would be removed by his coming. ¶ *As of things*

that are made. Much perplexity has been felt by expositors in regard to this phrase, but the meaning seems to be plain. The apostle is contrasting the things which are fixed and stable with those which are temporary in their nature, or which are settled on no firm foundation. The former he speaks of as if they were uncreated and eternal principles of truth and righteousness. The latter he speaks of as if they were *created*, and therefore liable, like all things which are "made," to decay, to change, to dissolution. ¶ *That those things which cannot be shaken may remain.* The eternal principles of truth, of law, and of righteousness. These would enter into the new kingdom which was to be set up, and of course *that* kingdom would be permanent. These are not changed or modified by time, by circumstances, by human opinions or laws. They remain the same from age to age, in every land, and in all worlds. They have been permanent in all the fluctuations of opinion among men; in all the varied forms of government on the earth; in all the revolutions of states and empires. To bring out these is the result of the events of divine Providence, and the object of the coming of the Redeemer; and on these principles that great kingdom is to be reared which is to endure for ever and ever.

28. *Wherefore we receiving a kingdom which cannot be moved.* We who are Christians. We pertain to a kingdom that is permanent and unchanging. The meaning is, that the kingdom of the Redeemer is never to pass away. It is not, like the Jewish dispensation, to give place to another, nor is there any power that can destroy it. See Notes on Mat. xvi. 18. It has *now* endured for eighteen hundred years amidst all the revolutions on earth, and in spite of all the attempts which have been made to destroy it; and it is now as vigorous and stable as it ever was. The past has shown that there is no power of earth or hell that can

may serve God acceptably with reverence and godly fear:

29 For* our God *is* a consuming fire.

f De.4.24.

destroy it, and that in the midst of all revolutions this kingdom still survives. Its great principles and laws will endure on earth to the end of time, and will be made permanent in heaven. This is the *only* kingdom in which we can be certain that there will be no revolution; the only empire which is destined never to fall. ¶ *Let us have grace whereby we may serve God.* Margin, "*let us hold fast.*" The Greek is, literally, *let us have grace;* the meaning is, "let us hold fast the grace or favour which we have received in being admitted to the privileges of that kingdom." The object of the apostle is, to keep them in the reverent fear and service of God. The *argument* which he presents is, that this kingdom is permanent. There is no danger of its being overthrown. It is to continue on earth to the end of time; it is to be established in heaven for ever. If it were temporary, changeable, liable to be overthrown at any moment, there would be much less encouragement to perseverance. But in a kingdom like this there is every encouragement, for there is the assurance (1) that all our interests are safe; (2) that all our exertions will be crowned with ultimate success; (3) that the efforts which we make to do good will have a permanent influence on mankind, and will bless future ages; and (4) that the reward is certain and eternal. A man subject to a government about whose continuance there is the utmost uncertainty, has little encouragement to labour with a view to any permanent interest. In a government where nothing is settled; where all policy is changing, and where there are constantly vacillating plans, there is no inducement to enter on any enterprise demanding time and risk. But where the policy is settled; where the principles and the laws are firm; where there is evidence of permanency, there is the highest encouragement. The highest possible encouragement of this kind is in the permanent and established kingdom of God. All other

governments may be revolutionized; this never will be;—all others may have a changeful policy; _this has none;—all others will be overthrown; this never will. ¶ *With reverence and godly fear.* With true veneration for God, and with pious devotedness.

29. *For our God* is *a consuming fire.* This is a further reason why we should serve God with profound reverence and unwavering fidelity. The quotation is made from Deut. iv. 24, "For the Lord thy God is a consuming fire, even a jealous God." The object of the apostle here seems to be, to show that there is the same reason for fearing the displeasure of God under the new dispensation which there was under the old. It is the same God who is served. There had been no change in his attributes, or in the principles of his government. He is no more the friend of sin now than he was then; and the same perfections of his nature which would then lead him to punish transgression also lead him to do it now. His anger is really as terrible, and as much to be dreaded, as it was at Mount Sinai; and the destruction which he will inflict on his foes will be as terrible now as it was then. The fearfulness with which he will come forth to destroy the wicked may now be compared to a *fire* that consumes all before it. See Notes on Mark ix. 44–46. The image here is a most fearful one, and is in accordance with all the representations of God in the Bible, and with all that we see in the divine dealings with wicked men, that punishment as inflicted by him is awful and overwhelming. So it was on the old world; on the cities of the plain; on the hosts of Sennacherib; and on Jerusalem—and so it has been in the calamities of pestilence, war, flood, and famine with which God has visited guilty men. By all these tender and solemn considerations, therefore, the apostle urges the friends of God to perseverance and fidelity in his service. His goodness and mercy;

CHAPTER XIII.

LET *a* brotherly love continue. 2 Be not forgetful to entertain strangers: for thereby *b*some have entertained angels unawares.

a 1 Pe.1.22; 1 Jn.4.7,20.   *b* Ge.18.3; 19.2.

the gift of a Saviour to redeem us; the revelation of a glorious world; the assurance that all may soon be united in fellowship with the angels and the redeemed; the certainty that the kingdom of the Saviour is established on a permanent basis, and the apprehension of the dreadful wrath of God against the guilty, all should lead us to persevere in the duties of our Christian calling, and to avoid those things which would jeopard the eternal interests of our souls.

CHAPTER XIII.

ANALYSIS OF THE CHAPTER.

The closing chapter of this epistle is made up almost entirely of exhortations to the performance of various practical duties. The exhortations relate to the following points: brotherly love, ver. 1; hospitality, ver. 2; sympathy with those in bonds, ver. 3; fidelity in the marriage relation, ver. 4; contentment, ver. 5, 6; submission to those in authority, ver. 7, 8; stability in the doctrines of religion, ver. 9–15; benevolence, ver. 16; obedience to those intrusted with office, ver. 17; and special prayer for him who wrote this epistle, ver. 18, 19. The epistle then closes with a beautiful and impressive benediction, ver. 20, 21; with an entreaty that they would receive with favour what had been written, ver. 22; with the grateful announcement that Timothy, in whom they doubtless felt a great interest, was set at liberty, ver. 23; and with a salutation to all the saints, ver. 24, 25.

1. *Let brotherly love continue.* Implying that it now existed among them. The apostle had no occasion to reprove them for the want of it, as he had in regard to some to whom he wrote, but he aims merely to impress on them the importance of this virtue, and to caution them against the dan-

3 Remember *c* them that are in bonds, as bound with them; *and* them which suffer adversity, as being yourselves also in the body.

c Mat.25.36.

ger of allowing it ever to be interrupted. See Notes on John xiii. 34.

2. *Be not forgetful to entertain strangers.* On the duty of hospitality, see a full explanation in the Notes on Rom. xii. 13. ¶ *For thereby some have entertained angels unawares.* Without knowing that they were angels. As Abraham (Gen. xviii. 2, seq.) and Lot did, Gen. xix. The *motive* here urged for doing it is, that by entertaining the stranger we may perhaps be honoured with the presence of those whose society will be to us an honour and a blessing. It is not well for us to miss the opportunity of the presence, the conversation, and the prayers of the good. The influence of such guests in a family is worth more than it costs to entertain them. If there is danger that we may sometimes receive those of an opposite character, yet it is not wise on account of such possible danger to lose the opportunity of entertaining those whose presence would be a blessing. Many a parent owes the conversion of a child to the influence of a pious stranger in his family; and the hope that this *may* occur, or that our own souls may be blessed, should make us ready, at all proper times, to welcome the feet of the stranger to our doors. Many a man, if he had been accosted as Abraham was at the door of his tent by strangers, would have turned them rudely away; many a one in the situation of Lot would have sent the unknown guests rudely from his door; but who can estimate what would have been the results of such a course on the destiny of those good men and their families? For a great number of instances in which the heathen were supposed to have entertained the *gods*, though unknown to them, see Wetstein, *in loco.*

3. *Remember them that are in bonds.* All who are *bound;* whether prisoners of war; captives in dungeons; those

4 Marriage[d] *is* honourable in all, and the bed undefiled : but [e]whore-

d Pr.5.15-23.　　　e 1 Co.6.9; Re.22.15.

detained in custody for trial; those who are imprisoned for righteousness' sake; or those held in slavery. The word used here will include *all* instances where *bonds, shackles, chains* were ever used. Perhaps there is an immediate allusion to their fellow-Christians who were suffering imprisonment on account of their religion, of whom there were doubtless many at that time; but the *principle* will apply to every case of those who are imprisoned or oppressed. The word *remember* implies more than that we are merely to *think* of them. Compare Ex. xx. 8; Eccl. xii. 1. It means that we are to remember them *with appropriate sympathy;* or as we should wish others to remember us if we were in their circumstances. That is, we are (1) to feel deep compassion for them; (2) we are to bear them on our hearts in our prayers; (3) we are to remember them, as far as practicable, with aid for their relief. Christianity teaches us to sympathize with all the oppressed, the suffering, and the sad; and there are more of this class than we commonly suppose, and they have stronger claims on our sympathy than we commonly realize. In this land there are many thousands confined in prison—the father separated from his children; the husband from his wife; the brother from his sister; and all cut off from the living world. Their fare is coarse, and their couches hard, and the ties which bound them to the living world are rudely snapped asunder. Many of them are in solitary dungeons; all of them are sad and melancholy men. True, they are there for crime; but they are men— they are our brothers. They have still the feelings of our common humanity, and many of them *feel* their separation from wife and children and home as keenly as we would. That God who has mercifully made our lot different from theirs has commanded us to sympathize with them; and we should sympathize all the more when we re-

mongers and adulterers God will judge.

member that but for *his* restraining grace we should have been in the same condition. ¶ *As bound with them.* There is great force and beauty in this expression. Religion teaches us to identify ourselves with all who are oppressed, and to feel what they suffer as if we endured it ourselves. Infidelity and atheism are cold and distant. They stand aloof from the oppressed and the sad. But Christianity unites all hearts in one; binds us to all the race, and reveals to us, in the case of each one oppressed and injured, a brother. ¶ And *them which suffer adversity.* The word here used refers properly to those who are maltreated, or who are injured by others. It does not refer to those who merely experience calamity. ¶ *As being yourselves also in the body.* As being yourselves exposed to persecution and suffering, and liable to be injured. That is, do to them as you would wish them to do to you if you were the sufferer. When we see an oppressed and injured man, we should remember that it is possible that we may be in the same circumstances, and that then we shall need and desire the sympathy of others.

4. *Marriage* is *honourable in all.* The object here is to state that *honour* is to be shown to the marriage relation. (*a*) It is not to be undervalued by the pretence of the superior purity of a state of celibacy, as if marriage were improper for any class of men or any condition of life; and (*b*) it should not be dishonoured by any violation of the marriage contract. The course of things in the world has shown that there was abundant reason for the apostle to assert with emphasis that "marriage is an honourable condition of life." There has been a constant effort made to show that celibacy is a more holy state; that there is something in marriage that renders it *dishonourable* for those who are in the ministry, and for those of either sex who would be eminently pure. This sentiment has been the cause of more

5 *Let your* conversation *be* without covetousness; *and 'be* content with such things as ye have : for he hath said, *g* I will never leave thee, nor forsake thee.

6 So that we may boldly say,

f Mat.6.25,34. *g* Ge.28.15; De.31.6,8; 1 Ch.28.20.

h The Lord *is* my helper, and I will not fear what man shall do unto me.

7 Remember them which [1] have the rule over you, who have spoken unto you the word of God : *i* whose

h Ps.27.1.   1 or, *are the guides.*   *i* ch.6.12.

corruption in the world than any other single opinion claiming to have a religious sanction. It is one of the supports on which the Papal system rests, and has been one of the principal upholders of all the corruptions in monasteries and nunneries. The apostle asserts, without any restriction or qualification, that marriage is honourable in "*all;* " and this *proves* that it is lawful for the ministers of religion to marry, and that the whole doctrine of the superior purity of a state of celibacy is false.   See this subject examined in the Notes on 1 Cor. vii. ¶ *And the bed undefiled.* Fidelity to the marriage vow. ¶ *But whoremongers and adulterers God will judge.* All licentiousness of life, and all violations of the marriage covenant, will be severely punished by God. See Notes on 1 Cor. vi. 9. The sins here referred to prevailed everywhere, and hence there was the more propriety for the frequent and solemn injunctions to avoid them which we find in the Scriptures.

5. Let your *conversation.* Your *conduct* — for so the word conversation means in the Scriptures. See Notes on Phil. i. 27. ¶ Be *without covetousness.* See Notes on Eph. v. 3; Col. iii. 5. ¶ And be *content with such things as ye have.* See Notes on Phil. iv. 11, 12; Mat. vi. 25–31. The particular *reason* here given for contentment is, that God has promised never to leave his people. Compare with this the beautiful argument of the Saviour in Mat. vi. 25, seq. ¶ *For he hath said.* That is, God has said. ¶ *I will never leave thee, nor forsake thee.* See Deut. xxxi. 6; Josh. i. 5; 1 Chr. xxviii. 20. Substantially the same expression is found in each of those places, and all of them contain the *principle* on which the apostle here relies, that God will not forsake his people.

6. *So that we may boldly say.* Without any hesitation or doubt. In all times of perplexity, and threatening, and want; in all times when we scarcely know whence the supplies for our necessities are to come, we may put our trust in God, and be assured that he will not leave us to suffer. In the facts which occur under the providential dealings, there is a ground for confidence on this subject which is not always exercised even by good men. It remains yet to be shown that they who exercise simple trust in God for the supply of their wants are ever forsaken.   Comp. Ps. xxxvii. 25. ¶ *The Lord* is *my helper.* Substantially this sentiment is found in Ps. xxvii. 1, and Ps. cxviii. 6.   The apostle does not adduce it as a *quotation,* but as language which a true Christian may employ. The sentiment is beautiful, and full of consolation. What can we fear if we have the assurance that the Lord is on our side, and that he will help us? Man can do no more to us than God permits, and of course no more than will be for our own good; and under whatever trials we may be placed, we need be under no painful apprehensions, for God will be our protector and our friend.

7. *Remember them which have the rule over you.* Margin, "*are the guides.*" The word here used means properly *leaders, guides, directors.* It is often applied to military commanders. Here it means *teachers*—appointed to lead or guide them to eternal life. It does not refer to them so much as *rulers* or *governors,* as *teachers* or *guides.* In ver. 17, however, it is used in the former sense. The duty here enjoined is that of *remembering* them—that is, remembering their counsel; their instructions; their example. ¶ *Who have spoken to you the word of God.* Preachers; either apostles or others.   Re-

faith follow, considering the end of *their* conversation:

8 Jesus Christ *k* the same yesterday, and to-day, and for ever.

k Re.1.4.

spect is to be shown to the ministerial office by whomsoever it is borne. ¶ *Whose faith follow.* That is, imitate. See Notes on chap. vi. 12. ¶ *Considering the end of* their *conversation.* Of their conduct; of their manner of life. The word here rendered *"the end"*—ἔκβασις—occurs only here and in 1 Cor. x. 13, where it is rendered *"a way* of escape.*"* It properly means, *a going out, an egress,* and is hence spoken of as a going out from life, or of an exit from the world—*death.* This is probably the meaning here. It does not mean, as our translation would seem to imply, that Jesus Christ, the same yesterday, to-day, and for ever, was the *aim* or *end* for which they lived—for the Greek will not bear that construction; but it means that they were attentively to contemplate the *end* or the *issue* of the conduct of those holy teachers—the close or *going out* of all that they did; to wit, in a peaceful death. Their faith sustained them. They were enabled to persevere in a Christian course, and did not faint or fail. There is allusion, doubtless, to those who had been their religious instructors, and who had died in the faith of the gospel, either by persecution or by an ordinary death, and the apostle points to them as examples of that to which he would exhort those whom he addressed—of perseverance in the faith until death. Thus explained, this verse does not refer to the duty of Christians toward *living* teachers, but toward those who are *dead.* Their duty toward living teachers is enforced in ver. 17. The sentiment here is, that the proper remembrance of those now deceased who were once our spiritual instructors and guides should be allowed to have an important influence in inducing us to lead a holy life. We should remember them with affection and gratitude; we should recall the truths which they taught, and the exhortations which they addressed to us; we should cherish with kind affection the memory of all that they did for our

welfare, and we should not forget the effect of the truths which they taught in sustaining their own souls when they died.

8. *Jesus Christ the same yesterday,* &c. As this stands in our common translation it conveys an idea which is not in the original. It would seem to mean that Jesus Christ, the unchangeable Saviour, was the *end* or *aim* of the conduct of those referred to, or that they lived to imitate and glorify him. But this is by no means the meaning in the original. There it stands as an absolute proposition, that "Jesus Christ *is* the same yesterday, to-day, and for ever;" that is, that he is unchangeable. The evident design of this independent proposition here is, to encourage them to persevere by showing that their Saviour was always the same; that he who had sustained his people in former times was the same still, and would be the same for ever. The *argument* here, therefore, for perseverance is founded on the *immutability* of the Redeemer. If he were fickle, vacillating, changing in his character and plans; if to-day he aids his people and to-morrow will forsake them; if at one time he loves the virtuous and at another equally loves the vicious; if he formed a plan yesterday which he has abandoned to-day; or if he is ever to be a different being from what he is now, there would be no encouragement to effort. Who would know what to depend on? Who would know what to expect? For who could have any certainty that he could ever please a capricious or a vacillating being? Who could know how to shape his conduct if the principles of the divine administration were not always the same? At the same time, also, that this passage furnishes the strongest argument for fidelity and perseverance, it is an irrefragable proof of the divinity of the Saviour. It asserts immutability—sameness in the past, the present, and to all eternity; but of whom can this

9 Be[l] not carried about with divers and strange doctrines: for *it is* a good thing that the heart be established with grace; not with meats, which have not profited

l 1 Jn. 4. 1.

them that have been occupied therein.

10 We have an altar, whereof they have no right to eat which serve the tabernacle.

---

be affirmed but God? It would not be possible to conceive of a declaration which would more strongly assert immutability than this.

9. *Be not carried about with divers and strange doctrines.* That is, they should have settled and fixed points of belief, and not yield to every new opinion which was started. The apostle does not exhort them to adhere to an opinion merely because they *had* before held it, or because it was an *old* opinion, nor does he forbid their following the leadings of truth though they might be required to abandon what they had before held; but he cautions them against that vacillating spirit, and that easy credulity, which would lead them to yield to any novelty, and to embrace an opinion because it was new or strange. Probably the principal reference here is to the judaizing teachers, and to their various doctrines about their ceremonial observances and traditions. But the exhortation is applicable to Christians at all times. A religious opinion, once embraced on what was regarded as good evidence, or in which we have been trained, should not be abandoned for slight causes. Truth, indeed, should always be followed, but it should be only after careful inquiry. ¶ *For it is a good thing that the heart be established with grace.* This is the proper foundation of adherence to the truth. The *heart* should be established with the love of God, with pure religion, and then we shall love the truth, and love it in the right manner. If it is the *head* merely which is convinced, the consequence is bigotry, pride, narrow-mindedness. If the belief of the truth has its seat in the *heart*, it will be accompanied with charity, kindness, good-will to all men. In *such* a belief of the truth it is a good thing to have the heart established. It will produce (1) firm-

ness and stability of character; (2) charity and kindness to others; (3) consolation and support in trials and temptations. When a man is thrown into trials and temptations, he *ought* to have some settled principles on which he can rely; some fixed points of belief that will sustain his soul. ¶ *Not with meats.* The meaning is, that it is better to have the heart established with grace, or with the principles of pure religion, than with the most accurate knowledge of the rules of distinguishing the clean from the unclean among the various articles of food. Many such rules were found in the law of Moses, and many more had been added by the refinements of Jewish rulers and by tradition. To distinguish and remember all these required no small amount of knowledge, and the Jewish teachers, doubtless, prided themselves much on it. Paul says that it would be much better to have the principles of grace in the heart than all this knowledge; to have the mind settled on the great truths of religion, than to be able to make the most accurate and learned distinctions in this matter. The same remark may be made about a great many other points besides the Jewish distinctions respecting meats. The principle is, that it is better to have the *heart* established in the grace of God than to have the most accurate knowledge of the distinctions which are made on useless or unimportant subjects of religion. This observation would extend to many of the shibboleths of party; to many of the metaphysical distinctions in a hair-splitting theology; to many of the points of controversy which divide the Christian world. ¶ *Which have not profited,* &c. Which have been of no real benefit to their souls. See Notes on 1 Cor. viii. 8.

10. *We have an altar.* We who are Christians. The Jews had an altar

11 For the bodies of those beasts, whose blood is brought into the sanctuary by the high priest for sin, are ^mburned without the camp.

m Le.16.27.

12 Wherefore Jesus also, that he might sanctify the people with his own blood, ⁿsuffered without the gate.

n Jn.19.17,18.

on which their sacrifices were offered which was regarded as sacred, and of the benefit of which no others might partake. The design of the apostle is to show that the same thing substantially, so far as *privilege* and *sanctifying influence* were concerned, was enjoyed by Christians. The "altar" to which he here refers is evidently the cross on which the great sacrifice was made. ¶ *Whereof they have no right to eat which serve the tabernacle.* That is, to partake of. A part of the meat offered in sacrifice among the Jews became the property of the priests and Levites, and they had, by the law, a *right* to this as a part of their support. See Lev. vi. 25, 26; Num. xviii. 9, 10. But the apostle says that there is a higher and more valuable sacrifice of which they have no right to partake while they remain in the service of the "tabernacle" or temple; that is, while they remain Jews. The participation in the great Christian sacrifice appertained only to those who were the friends of the Redeemer, and however much they might value themselves on the privilege of partaking of the sacrifices offered under the Jewish law, that of partaking of the great sacrifice made by the Son of God was much greater. ¶ *Which serve the tabernacle.* See Notes on chap. ix. 2, 3. The Jewish priests and Levites.

11. *For the bodies of those beasts,* &c. The word here rendered "*for*"—γὰρ —would be here more properly rendered "*moreover*" (Stuart). The apostle is not urging a reason for what he had said in the previous verse, but is suggesting a *new* consideration to excite those whom he addressed to fidelity and perseverance. In the previous verse the consideration was, that Christians are permitted to partake of the benefits of a higher and more perfect sacrifice than the Jews were, and *therefore* should not relapse into

that religion. In this verse the consideration is, that the bodies of the beasts that were burned were taken without the camp, and that in like manner the Lord Jesus suffered *without* the gate of Jerusalem, and that we should be willing to go out with him to that sacrifice, whatever reproach or shame it might be attended with. ¶ *Whose blood is brought into the sanctuary,* &c. See Notes on chap. ix. 7, 12. ¶ *Are burned without the camp.* Lev. iv. 12, 21; xvi. 27. The reference here is to the time when the Israelites were in the wilderness, and lived in encampments. The same custom was observed after the temple was built, by conveying the body of the animal slain for a sin-offering, on the great day of atonement, beyond the walls of Jerusalem to be consumed there. "Whatever," says Grotius, "was not lawful to be done in the camp, afterward was not lawful to be done in the city."

12. *Wherefore Jesus also, that he might sanctify the people with his own blood.* That there might be a conformity between his death for sin and the sacrifices which typified it. It is implied here that it was *voluntary* on the part of Jesus that he suffered out of the city; that is, it was so ordered by Providence that it should be so. This was secured by his being put to death as the result of a judicial trial, and not by popular tumult. See Notes on Isa. liii. 8. If he had been killed in a tumult, it is possible that it might have been done, as in other cases (compare the case of Zacharias, son of Barachias, Mat. xxiii. 35), even at the altar. As he was subjected, however, to a judicial process, his death was effected with more deliberation, and in the usual form. Hence he was conducted *out* of the city, because no criminal was executed within the walls of Jerusalem. ¶ *Without the gate.* Without the gate of Jerusalem,

13 Let us go forth therefore unto him without the camp, *o* bearing his reproach.

14 For *p* here have we no con-

o Ac.5.41.   *p* Mi.2.10.

tinuing city, but we seek one to come.

15 By *q* him therefore let us offer the sacrifice of praise to God con-

q Ep.5.20.

Jn. xix. 17, 18. The place where he was put to death was called Golgotha, the place of a skull, and hence the Latin word which we commonly use in speaking of it, *Calvary*, Luke xxiii. 33. Comp. Notes on Mat. xxvii. 33. Calvary, as it is now shown, is within the walls of Jerusalem, but there is no reason to believe that this is the place where the Lord Jesus was crucified, for that was outside of the walls of the city. The precise direction from the city is not designated by the sacred writers, nor are there any historical records, nor any traditional marks by which it can now be known where the exact place was. All that we know on the subject from the New Testament is, that the *name* was Golgotha; that the place of the crucifixion and sepulchre were near each other; that they were without the gate and nigh to the city, and that they were in a frequented spot, Jn. xix. 20. "This would favour the conclusion that the place was probably upon a great road leading from one of the gates; and such a spot would only be found upon the western or northern sides of the city, on the roads leading toward Joppa or Damascus." See the question about the place of the crucifixion examined at length in Robinson's *Biblic. Research.*, vol. ii. pp. 69–80, and *Bibliotheca Sacra*, No. 1.

13. *Let us go forth therefore unto him without the camp.* As if we were going forth with him when he was led away to be crucified. He was put to death as a malefactor. He was the object of contempt and scorn. He was held up to derision, and was taunted and reviled on his way to the place of death, and even on the cross. To have been identified with him then; to follow him; to sympathize with him; to be regarded as his friend, would have subjected one to similar shame and reproach. The meaning here is, that we should be willing to regard ourselves

as identified with the Lord Jesus, and to bear the same shame and reproaches which he did. When he was led away amidst scoffing and reviling to be put to death, would *we*, if we had been there, have been willing to be regarded as his followers, and to have gone out with him as his avowed disciples and friends? Alas, how many are there who profess to love him when religion subjects them to no reproach, who would have shrunk from following him to Calvary! ¶ *Bearing his reproach.* Sympathizing with him; or bearing such reproach as he did. See 1 Pet. iv. 13. Comp. Notes on chap. xii. 2; Phil. iii. 10; Col. i. 24.

14. *For here we have no continuing city, &c.* We do not regard this as our final home, or our fixed abode, and we should be willing to bear reproaches during the little time that we are to remain here. Comp. Notes on chap. xi. 10, 13, 14. If, therefore, in consequence of our professed attachment to the Saviour, we should be driven away from our habitations, and compelled to wander, we should be willing to submit to it, for our permanent home is not here, but in heaven. The *object* of the writer seems to be to comfort the Hebrew Christians on the supposition that they would be driven by persecution from the city of Jerusalem, and doomed to wander as exiles. He tells them that their Lord was led from that city to be put to death, and they should be willing to go forth also; that their permanent home was not Jerusalem, but heaven; and that they should be willing, in view of that blessed abode, to be exiled from the city where they dwelt, and made wanderers in the earth.

15. *By him therefore.* The Jews approached God by the blood of the sacrifice, and by the ministry of their high-priest. The exhortation of the apostle here is founded on the general course of argument in the epistle.

tinually, that is, ʳthe fruit of our lips, ²giving thanks to his name.

16 But to do good and ˢto communicate forget not: for ᵗwith such sacrifices God is well pleased.

17 Obeyᵘ them that ³have the

r Ho.14.2.   2 confessing.   s Ro.12.13.
t Phi.4.18.   u 1 Th.5.12,13.   3 or, guide.

rule over you, and submit yourselves: for ᵛthey watch for your souls, as they that must give account; that they may do it with joy, and not with grief: for that is unprofitable for you.

v Eze.3.17.

"In view of all the considerations presented respecting the Christian High-priest—his dignity, purity, and love; his sacrifice and his intercession —let us persevere in offering through him praise to God." That is, let us persevere in adherence to our religion. ¶ *The sacrifice of praise.* For all the mercies of redemption. The Jews, says Rosenmüller (*Alte u. neue Morgenland, in loco*), had a species of offerings which they called *peace-offerings*, or *friendship-offerings*. They were designed not to *produce* peace or friendship with God, but to *preserve* it. Burnt-offerings, sin-offerings, and trespass-offerings, were all on account of transgression, and were designed to remove transgression. But in their peace-offerings, the offerer was regarded as one who stood in the relation of a friend with God, and the oblation was a sign of thankful acknowledgment for favours received; or they were connected with vows in order that further blessings might be obtained; or they were brought voluntarily as a means to continue themselves in the friendship and favour of God, Lev. vii. 11, 12. Comp. Jenning's *Jew. Ant.*, i. 335. ¶ *That is, the fruit of our lips.* The phrase "fruit of the lips," is a Hebraism, meaning what the lips *produce;* that is, words. Comp. Prov. xviii. 20; Hos. xiv. 2. ¶ *Giving thanks to his name.* To God; the *name* of a person being often put for the person himself. *Praise* now is one of the great duties of the redeemed. It will be their employment for ever.

16. *But to do good and to communicate forget not.* To communicate or *impart* to others; that is, to share with them what we have. The Greek word means *having in common* with others. The meaning is, that they were to show *liberality* to those who

were in want, and were to take special pains not to *forget* this duty. We are prone to think constantly of our own interests, and there is great danger of *forgetting* the duty which we owe to the poor and the needy. On the duty here enjoined, see Notes on Gal. vi. 10. ¶ *For with such sacrifices God is well pleased.* He is pleased with the sacrifices of prayer and of praise; with the offerings of a broken and a contrite heart; but he is especially pleased with the religion which leads us to do good to others. This was eminently the religion of his Son, the Lord Jesus; and to this all true religion prompts. The word "sacrifices" here is not taken in a strict sense, as denoting that which is offered as an expiation for sin, or in the sense that we are by doing good to attempt to make atonement for our transgressions, but in the general sense of an *offering* made to God. God is pleased with this, (1) because it shows in us a right state of heart; (2) because it accords with his own nature. *He* does good continually, and he is pleased with all who evince the same spirit.

17. *Obey them that have the rule over you.* Margin, *guide.* See Notes on ver. 7. The reference here is to their religious teachers, and not to civil rulers. They were to show them proper respect, and to submit to their authority in the church, so far as it was administered in accordance with the precepts of the Saviour. The obligation to obedience does not, of course, extend to anything which is wrong in itself, or which would be a violation of conscience. The doctrine is, that subordination is necessary to the welfare of the church, and that there ought to be a disposition to yield all proper obedience to those who are set over us in the Lord. Comp. Notes on 1 Thes. v. 12, 13. ¶ *And submit your-*

18 Pray for us: for we trust we have *w*a good conscience, in all things willing to live honestly.

w Ac.24.16.

19 But I beseech *you* the rather to do this, that I may be restored to you the sooner.

---

selves. That is, to all which they enjoin that is lawful and right. There are in relation to a society, (1) those things which God has positively commanded — which are always to be obeyed; (2) many things which have been *agreed on* by the society as needful for its welfare—and these are to be submitted to unless they violate the rights of conscience; and (3) many things which are, in themselves, a matter of no express divine command, and of no formal enactment by the society. They are matters of convenience; things that tend to the order and harmony of the whole, and to the promotion of the objects of the association, and of the propriety of these, "rulers" in the church and elsewhere should be allowed to judge, and we should submit to them patiently. Hence in the church, we are to submit to all the proper regulations for conducting public worship; for the promotion of religion; for the time of observing the Lord's supper; for meetings for prayer; and for the administration of discipline. ¶ *For they watch for your souls.* They have no selfish aim in this. They do not seek "to lord it over God's heritage." It is for your own good that they do this, and you should therefore submit to these arrangements. And this shows, also, the true principle on which authority should be exercised in a church. It should be in such a way as to promote the salvation of the people; and all the arrangements should be with that end. The measures adopted, therefore, and the obedience enjoined, should not be arbitrary, oppressive, or severe, but should be such as will really promote true religion. ¶ *As they that must give account.* To God. The ministers of religion must give account to God for their fidelity. For all that they teach, and for every measure which they adopt, they must soon be called into judgment. There is, therefore, the best security that, under the

influence of this solemn truth, they will pursue only that course which will be for your good. ¶ *That they may do it with joy, and not with grief.* Greek, μὴ στενάζοντες—not *sighing*, or *groaning;* as they would who had been unsuccessful. The meaning is, that they should *so* obey, that when their teachers came to give up their account, they need not do it with sorrow over their perverseness and disobedience. ¶ *For that is unprofitable for you.* That is, their giving up their account in that manner—as unsuccessful in their efforts to save you —would not be of advantage to you, but would be highly injurious. This is a strong mode of expressing the idea that it *must* be attended with imminent peril to their souls to have their religious teachers give an account *against* them. As they would wish, therefore, to avoid that, they should render to them all proper honour and obedience.

18. *Pray for us.* This is a request which the apostle often makes in his own behalf and in behalf of his fellow-labourers in the gospel. See 1 Thes. v. 25; Eph. vi. 18, 19. ¶ *For we trust we have a good conscience,* &c. See Notes on Acts xxiv. 16. The apostle here appeals to the uprightness of his Christian life as a reason why he might claim their sympathy. He was conscious of having aimed to do good; he sought the welfare of the church; and, having this aim, he felt that he might appeal to the sympathy of all Christians in his behalf. It is only when we aim to do right, and to maintain a good conscience, that we can with propriety ask the prayers of others, or claim their sympathy. And if we are "willing in all things to live honestly," we may expect the sympathy, the prayers, and the affections of all good men.

19. *That I may be restored to you the sooner.* It is here clearly implied that the writer was deterred from visiting them by some adverse circum-

20 Now the *God of peace, that brought* again from the dead our Lord Jesus, that great *Shepherd of the sheep, *through the blood of the everlasting *covenant,

x 1 Th.5.23.   y 1 Pe.1.21.   z Eze.34.23.
a Zec.9.11.   4 or, testament.

21 Make* you perfect in every good work to do his will, *working *in you that which is well pleasing in his sight, through Jesus Christ; to whom *be* glory for ever and ever. Amen.

b 1 Pe.5.10.   5 or, doing.   c Phi.2.13.

stances over which he had no control. This might be either by imprisonment, or sickness, or the want of a convenient opportunity of reaching them. The probability is, judging particularly from the statement in ver. 23, that he was then a prisoner, and that his detention was on that account. See Intro., § 4, (6). The language here is such as Paul would use on the supposition that he was then a prisoner at Rome, and this is a slight circumstance going to show the probability that the epistle was composed by him.

20. *Now the God of peace.* God who is the author, or the source of peace. See Notes on 1 Thes. v. 23. The word *peace* in the New Testament is used to denote every kind of blessing or happiness. It is opposed to all that would disturb or trouble the mind, and may refer, therefore, to reconciliation with God; to a quiet conscience; to the evidence of pardoned sin; to health and prosperity, and to the hope of heaven. See Notes on Jn. xiv. 27. ¶ *That brought again from the dead our Lord Jesus.* See Notes on Acts ii. 32; 1 Cor. xv. 15. It is only by the fact of the resurrection of the Lord Jesus that we have peace, for it is only by him that we have the prospect of an admission into heaven. ¶ *That great Shepherd of the sheep.* See Notes on Jn. x. 1, 14. The idea here is, that it is through the tender care of that great Shepherd that true happiness is bestowed on the people of God. ¶ *Through the blood of the everlasting covenant.* The blood shed to ratify the everlasting covenant that God makes with his people. See Notes on chap. ix. 14 – 23. This phrase, in the original, is not connected, as it is in our translation, with his being raised from the dead, nor should it be so rendered; for what can be the meaning of "raising Christ

from the dead *by the blood of the covenant?"* In the Greek it is: "The God of peace, who brought again from the dead the Shepherd of the sheep, great by the blood of the everlasting covenant, our Lord Jesus," &c. The meaning is, that he was made or constituted the great Shepherd of the sheep—the great Lord and Ruler of his people, by that blood. That which makes him so eminently distinguished; that by which he was made superior to all others who ever ruled over the people of God, was the fact that he offered the blood by which the eternal covenant was ratified. It is called everlasting or eternal, because (1) it was formed in the councils of eternity, or has been an eternal plan in the divine mind; and (2) because it is to continue for ever. Through such a covenant God can bestow permanent and solid "peace" on his people, for it lays the foundation of the assurance of eternal happiness.

21. *Make you perfect.* The apostle here does not affirm that they were then perfect, or that they would be in this life. The word here used—καταρτίζω—means *to make fully ready; to put in full order; to make complete.* The meaning here is, that Paul prayed that God would fully endow them with whatever grace was necessary to do his will and to keep his commandments. See the word explained in the Notes on chap. xi. 3. It is an appropriate prayer to be offered at all times, and by all who love the church, that God would make all his people perfectly qualified to do his will. ¶ *Working in you.* Margin, *doing.* The idea here is, that the only hope that they would do the will of God was, that *he* would, by his own agency, cause them to do what was well-pleasing in his sight. Comp. Notes on Phil. ii. 12. It is not from any ex-

22 And I beseech you, brethren, suffer the word of exhortation : for I have written a letter unto you in few words.

23 Know ye that *our* brother Timothy is set at liberty ; with whom, if he come shortly, I will see you.

---

pectation that man would do it himself. ¶ *Through Jesus Christ.* The idea is, that God does not directly and by his own immediate agency convert and sanctify the heart, but it is through the gospel of Christ, and all good influences on the soul must be expected through the Saviour. ¶ *To whom* be *glory for ever and ever.* That is, to Christ; for so the connection evidently demands. It is not uncommon for the apostle Paul to introduce doxologies in this way in the midst of a letter. See Notes on Rom. ix. 5. It was common among the Jews, as it is now in the writings and conversation of the Mohammedans, when the name of God was mentioned, to accompany it with an expression of praise.

22. *Suffer the word of exhortation.* Referring to the arguments and counsels in this whole epistle, which is in fact a practical exhortation to perseverance in adhering to the Christian religion amidst the temptations which existed to apostasy. ¶ *For I have written a letter unto you in few words.* This does not mean that this epistle is short compared with the others that the author had written, for most of the epistles of Paul are shorter than this. But it means, that it was brief compared with the importance and difficulty of the subjects of which he had treated. The topics introduced would have allowed a much more extended discussion, but in handling them he had made use of as few words as possible. No one can deny this who considers the sententious manner of this epistle. As an illustration of this, perhaps we may remark, that it is easy to *expand* the thoughts of this epistle into ample volumes of exposition, and that in fact it is difficult to give an explanation of it without a commentary that shall greatly surpass in extent the text. None can doubt, also, that the author of this epistle could have himself greatly expanded

the thoughts and the illustrations if he had chosen. It is with reference to such considerations, probably, that he says that the epistle was *brief.*

23. *Know ye that* our *brother Timothy is set at liberty.* Or, *is sent away.* So it is rendered by Prof. Stuart, and others. On the meaning of this, and its importance in determining who was the author of the epistle, see the Intro., § 3, (5), (*a*), and Prof. Stuart's Intro., § 19. This is a strong circumstance showing that Paul was the author of the epistle, for from the first acquaintance of Timothy with Paul he is represented as his constant companion, and spoken of as a brother. 2 Cor. i. 1; Phil. i. 1; Col. i. 1; Phil. i. There is no other one of the apostles who would so naturally have used this term respecting Timothy, and this affectionate allusion is made to him here because he was so dear to the heart of the writer, and because he felt that they to whom he wrote would also feel an interest in his circumstances. As to the meaning of the word rendered "set at liberty"— ἀπολελυμένον—there has been much difference of opinion, whether it means "set at liberty from confinement," or "sent away on some message to some other place." That the latter is the meaning of the expression appears probable from these considerations: (1) The connection seems to demand it. The writer speaks of him as if he were now away, and as if he hoped that he might soon return. "With whom, if he come shortly, I will see you." This is language which would be used rather of one who had been sent on some embassy, than of one who was just released from prison. At all events, he was at this time away, and there was some expectation that he might soon return. But on the supposition that the expression relates to release from imprisonment, there would be an entire incongruity in the language. It is not, as we should then suppose,

24 Salute all them that have the rule over you, and all the saints. They of Italy salute you.

25 Grace *be* with you all. Amen.

Written to the Hebrews from Italy by Timothy.

" our brother Timothy is now released from prison, and *therefore* I will come soon with him and see you;" but "our brother Timothy is now sent away, and if he return soon, I will come with him to you." (2) In Phil. ii. 19, 23, Paul, then a prisoner at Rome, speaks of the hope which he entertained that he would be able to send Timothy to them, as soon as he should know how it would go with him. He designed to retain him until that point was settled, as his presence with him would be important until then, and then to send him to give consolation to the Philippians, and to look into the condition of the church. Now the passage before us agrees well with the supposition that that event had occurred—that Paul had ascertained with sufficient clearness that he would be released, so that he might be permitted yet to visit the Hebrew Christians ; that he had sent Timothy to Philippi, and was waiting for his return ; that as soon as he should return he would be prepared to visit them ; and that in the meantime, while Timothy was absent, he wrote to them this epistle. (3) The supposition agrees well with the meaning of the word here used—ἀπολύω. It denotes properly, to let loose from; to loosen ; to unbind ; to release ; to let go free ; to put away or divorce ; to *dismiss* simply, or let go, or send away. See Mat. xiv. 15, 22, 23 ; xv. 32, 39; Luke ix. 12, *et al.* Comp. Rob. *Lex.* and Stuart's Intro., § 19. The meaning, then, I take to be this, that Timothy was then sent away on some important embassage; that the apostle expected his speedy return ; and that then he trusted that he would be able with him to visit those to whom this epistle was written.

24. *Salute all them.* See Notes on Rom. xvi. 3, seq. It was customary for the apostle Paul to close his epistles with an affectionate salutation. ¶ *That have the rule over you.* See Notes on ver. 7, 17. None are

mentioned by name, as is usual in the epistles of Paul. The cause of this omission is unknown. ¶ *And all the saints.* The common name given to Christians in the Scriptures. See Notes on Rom. i. 7. ¶ *They of Italy salute you.* The saints or Christians in Italy, showing that the writer of the epistle was then in Italy. He was probably in Rome. See the Intro., § 4, (6).

25. *Grace* be *with you all.* See Notes on Rom. xvi. 20.

The subscription at the close of the epistle, "Written to the Hebrews from Italy by Timothy," like the other subscriptions, is of no authority. See Notes at the end of 1 Cor. It is demonstrably erroneous here, for it is expressly said by the author of the epistle that at the time he wrote it Timothy was absent, chap. xiii. 23. In regard to the time and place of writing it, see the Intro., § 4.

At the close of this exposition, it is not improper to refer the reader to the remarks on its design at the end of the Intro., § 6. Having passed through the epistle, we may see more clearly the importance of the views there presented. There is no book of the New Testament more important than this, and of course none whose want would be more perceptible in the canon of the Scriptures. Every reader of the Old Testament *needs* such a guide as this epistle, written by some one who had an intimate acquaintance from childhood with the Jewish system; who had all the advantages of the most able and faithful instruction ; and who was under the influence of inspiration, to make us acquainted with the true nature of those institutions. Nothing was more important than to settle the principles in regard to the nature of the Jewish economy; to show what was typical, and how those institutions were the means of introducing a far more per-

fect system—the system of the Christian religion. If we have right feelings, we shall have sincere gratitude to God that he caused the Christian religion to be prefigured by a system in itself so magnificent and grand as that of the Jewish, and higher gratitude for that sublime system of religion of which the Jewish, with all its splendour, was only the shadow. There was much that was beautiful, cheering, and sublime in the Jewish system. There was much that was grand and awful in the giving of the law, and much that was imposing in its ceremonies. In its palmy and pure days, it was incomparably the purest and noblest system of religion then on earth. It taught the knowledge of the one true God; inculcated a pure system of morals; preserved the record of the truth on the earth, and held up constantly before man the hope of a better system still in days to come. But it was expensive, burdensome, precise in its prescriptions, and wearisome in its ceremonies, Acts xv. 10. It was adapted to one people —a people who occupied a small territory, and who could conveniently assemble at the central place of their worship three times in a year. It was not a system fitted to the whole world; nor was it designed for the whole world. When the Saviour came, therefore, to introduce whom was the design of the Jewish economy, it ceased as a matter of course. The Jewish altars were soon thrown down; the temple was razed to the ground, and the city of their solemnities was destroyed. The religion of the Hebrews passed away to be revived no more in its splendour and power, and it has never lived since, except as an empty form.

This epistle teaches us why it passed away, and why it can never be restored. It is the true key with which to unlock the Old Testament; and with these views, we may remark, in conclusion, that he who would understand the Bible thoroughly should make himself familiar with this epistle; that the canon of Scripture would be incomplete without it; and that, to one who wishes to understand the revelation which God has given, there is no portion of the volume whose loss would be a more irreparable calamity than that of the Epistle to the Hebrews.